The Reign of Thutmose IV

The Reign of Thutmose IV

Betsy M. Bryan

The Johns Hopkins University Press
Baltimore and London

The Johns Hopkins University Press
701 West 40th Street
Baltimore, Maryland 21211
The Johns Hopkins Press Ltd., London

The paper used in this book meets the minimum requirements of American National Standard for Information Sciences—Permanence of Paper for Printed Library Materials, ANSI Z39.48-1984.

Library of Congress Cataloging-in-Publication Data
Bryan, Betsy Morrell.
    The reign of Thutmose IV / Betsy M. Bryan.
        p.   cm.
    Includes bibliographical references and index.
    ISBN 0-8018-4202-6
    1. Thutmose IV, King of Egypt. 2. Egypt—History—Eighteenth dynasty,
ca. 1570–1320 B.C. 3. Pharaohs—Biography. I. Title.
DT87.B78   1991
932′.014′092—dc20   90-27688

Contents

Preface 1

Introduction 2

I. Chronology 4

II. All the Kings' Sons 38

III. King's Wives and Kings' Daughters 93

IV. Royal Monuments of Thutmose IV 141

    Appendix I: Tomb Objects Supplement 208

    Appendix II: Statuary 211

    Appendix III: Varia 214

V. Civil, Religious, and Military Administration 242

    Appendix IV: Officeholders 294

    Appendix V: Theban Tombs 300

VI. Thutmose IV Abroad and at Home 332

    Works Cited 369

    Indices 387

    Plates I–XIX

PREFACE

To acknowledge all the people who have helped me with this project over the years would be quite impossible. I issue a large "thank you",however, to the many colleagues and friends who have generously given of their expertise and time. Dr. Bettina Schmitz deserves a first mention as editor during a period when the book was planned for publication in the Hildesheimer Ägyptologische Beiträge series. Her careful attention, particularly to the references, has improved the manuscript enormously.

To my husband, Charles E. Bryan, I am inexpressibly grateful for his support which has been unfailing. My teacher Kelly Simpson deserves thanks for the topic and the scores of references he sent my way. To Bernard V. Bothmer and to the staff of The Brooklyn Museum's Egyptian, Classical and Middle Eastern Department I owe a special debt, particularly to Richard A. Fazzini, James F. Romano, and Robert S. Bianchi. I thank also the present and past members of the staff of the Egyptian Department at the Metropolitan Museum of Art, particularly Edna R. Russmann, Christine Lilyquist, Cathleen A. Keller, and Peter Dorman who, when they occupied pertinent curatorial roles in that Department, were greatly generous. Likewise the past and present staff of the Boston Museum of Fine Arts have my deep gratitude, especially Edward Brovarski, Timothy Kendall, Peter Lacovara, Peter Der Manuelian, and now Rita Freed. To the Keeper of Egyptian Antiquities of the British Museum, Vivian Davies, and to Morris Bierbrier and Geoffrey Spencer, to the staff of the Department, and to the past Keeper, T.G.H. James,I offer thanks as well. J. DeCenival of the Louvre Museum was kind and generous; Bernadette Letellier of that same institution shared her material from Karnak without hesitation. John Ruffle of the Durham Oriental Museum has been most helpful indeed.

Claude Vandersleyen has helped me over the years, and I wish to thank him here formally. Likewise Alan R. Schulman was always ready to listen and offer valuable advice. Donald B. Redford was both willing to read through the dissertation form of the manuscript and available as inspiration through his many writings. Naturally such a list is not complete without an expression of thanks to Egyptian colleagues, particularly in this case to Dr. Sayed Tawfik, Chairman of the EAO, Dr. Mohammed Saleh, past Director of the Egyptian Museum, Dr. El Sayed Hegazy, Dr. M. Mohsen, Dr. A. Qadry, and the late Sayed abdel Hamid. To the many representatives of the Centre franco-égyptien at Karnak I express deep appreciation for the opportunity to view and study the Thutmose IV material. I particularly thank J.-C Golvin, past director of the Centre, Mssrs. J.-C Goyon and J. Lauffray, and also P. Martinez and L. Gabolde. To my colleagues and friends at Johns Hopkins University, especially to Jerrold Cooper, Hans Goedicke, David Lorton, and Glenn Schwartz, I express deep gratitude. To the many I have omitted for the sake of space, I say again "thanks".You are in my heart, if not here in print.

INTRODUCTION

In the analysis of any topic it is necessary to state the limitations of the data. The evidence brought to bear on the rule of Thutmose IV, king of Egypt in the early 14th century B.C., is largely monumental, often royal, and derives to the greatest extent from temple and tomb contexts. Inscriptions and decoration intended as eternal testament are formal rather than personal, and they contain ideological or religious symbolism rather than individual motives or characteristics. In interpreting these data, therefore, the following monograph has sought to isolate patterns from both the royal and non-royal material and thereby to identify the ideological, religious, and political attributes of Thutmose IV's kingship. The method employed has combined the techniques of historical and art historical analysis in an effort to interpret the types of evidence most fully.

Dr. William Kelly Simpson in his section of <u>The Ancient Near East A History</u> identified a number of topics relating to Egyptian kings' reigns which could be examined with our evidence. This study treats a number of those subjects, and, as such, is a history of the rule of Thutmose IV. The first priority of this work was to provide a catalogue of the monuments from the reign, and although such a compendium will inevitably be outmoded by new discoveries, it can be of use as a starting point for historical discussion. To supplement this primary function, a number of hitherto unpublished monuments are included in the photographic plates, and several appendices provide the results of research which could not be fully accommodated in the text.

Chapter One assesses the length of Thutmose IV's reign by evaluating individually the sorts of data used to construct chronologies. Although the major goal of the discussion is to determine whether the king had a short or long reign, the reliability of astronomical, anatomical and philological evidence pertinent to the chronology of the 18th Dynasty is of great interest and is considered at length.

Chapter Two explores the material bearing on Thutmose's position as heir apparent before his accession. In an effort to test the conventional hypothesis that he usurped the throne from the legitimate heir, the discussion catalogues and evaluates the monuments of contemporary kings' sons as well as those of Thutmose IV himself. A by-product of this exploration is a clearer definition of the social and religious roles played by princes in the mid-18th Dynasty. Chapter Three concerns the female members of the royal family. It compiles the material naming the king's mother, wives and daughters and examines it to determine the ceremonial and cultic roles performed by these royal women.

Chapter Four catalogues the royal monuments by site and attempts to place them in a historical or religious context. These buildings, statues, inscriptions, and miscellaneous fragments contribute to our understanding of the official persona of the king. Thutmose IV appears, for example, as the adherent of Heliopolitan religion, as well as the devotee of Thebes and the favored sites of the Thutmosid rulers. In Chapter Five the people employed in Thutmose's administration are identified and their monuments noted. Their families, titles, and responsibilities provide significant information about the king's approach to rule, while their tombs and funerary objects illustrate the standard of living enjoyed by the nobility of the period.

Chapter Six discusses major historical issues of the reign, acting as both a summary for some topics and a full expression of others. Issues relating to Thutmose IV's internal ruling policies, such as co-regency and the king's role in the development of the later Atenist religion of Akhenaten, are included along with the foreign policy of the period. Thutmose IV's military involvement in Asia and Nubia are discussed, and his diplomatic agreements with the Syrian kingdom of Mitanni are explored as well. An image of the king as the ruler of a powerful nation dealing from strength with its neighbors emerges from the investigation. Thutmose IV is seen to have prepared in a number of ways for the glorification of the sovereign which characterized his son Amenhotep III's long rule.

CHAPTER ONE

CHRONOLOGY

For those most interested in interpretive history, the problem of chronology often delays discussion. For those, however, who recognize the pitfalls and rewards of examining chronological evidence, this introductory chapter will be expected and, I hope, appreciated--if not completely agreed to. How long did Thutmose IV reign? The traditional answer to this question has been about eight years, a figure corresponding both to the attested year dates and the Manethonian king lists. Recently, however, the chronology for the New Kingdom proposed by Wente and Van Siclen used a figure quadrupling the reign.[1] Such a dramatic extension of Thutmose's years as ruler warrants full discussion before it is embraced or rejected. The discussion below, therefore, before passing on to the events, characters, and monuments of the period, will examine the evidence for Thutmose IV's length of rule and weigh the arguments bearing on his reign contained in the new chronology.

We begin by an admission that our evidence is spotty. Regnal dates, our most reliable indicators, are not of themselves decisive in determining the last year of a king. To ignore them, however, is irresponsible, for in a discussion of chronology, speculation, a tool often useful in historical interpretation, has no place. It is by examining the regnal dates along with all other types of evidence bearing on chronological determination that we will best conclude the length of Thutmose IV's (or any other king's) reign. Several sources of information, of varying degrees of reliability, exist. These include: year dates; king lists; the anatomical evidence of the royal mummy; the astronomical evidence as interpreted in various chronologies; the Jubilee monuments; the time spans suggested by the lives of officials who served under several kings; and the evidence of both inscriptions and building activity. Analyzing the relative weight and reliability of these seven sources should tip the balance in favor of either a short or a long reign for Thutmose IV and, as a by-product, provide an insight, based on a single reign, regarding the accuracy of Wente and Van Siclen's method of reconstructing chronology for the mid-18th dynasty.

King Lists

Traditionally the king lists of Manetho's extractors have provided scholars with estimates for reigns. Josephus recorded a Thmosis son of Misphragmuthosis who ruled 9 years, 8 months. Africanus and Eusebius gave a Thmosis with 9 years.[2] This king's placement approximately matches that of Thutmose IV, but the identification is not positive. The list is confused and Thmosis is preceded not by

Amenophis but by Misphragmuthosis. He is succeeded by Amenophis and then Orus. Helck pointed out several scribal mistakes that could have produced the garbling and argued plausibly for a transposition of Thutmose IV and Amenhotep II. Helck's reconstruction also reversed the 31 years of Amenophis and the 26 of Misphragmuthosis. To the latter king he added the 22 years of the female king Amessis and proposed to find the reign of Thutmose III.[3] Redford[4] accepted this reconstitution in his 18th dynasty chronology and has confirmed his faith in both Manetho's accuracy and Helck's method of unraveling technical copying errors. Both scholars have now been joined by Krauss whose lengthy discussion of the king list sources supported Thmosis as Thutmose IV.[5] Nonetheless, identifying Manetho's Thmosis as Thutmose IV yields no conclusive proof of the reign's length, particularly if the figures given for other kings in the dynasty are garbled. We must depend on the more ancient contemporary information.

Year Dates of Thutmose IV

The number of year dates from the reign of Thutmose IV is small but evenly divided over eight years. In Year 1 are dated the Sphinx stela,[6] a monument of the king erected between the paws of the Great Sphinx at Giza, and a newly-discovered stela from the Luxor Temple mentioning offering dedications.[7] The stela was recut by Seti I, who restored both the scene and the text, but there is no reason to believe the inscription and date are not authentic to Thutmose IV. No dates are known from Years 2 and 3, but from Year 4 there exists an inscription at the entrance to a mine at Serabit-el Khadim[8] left, in all probability, by the Mayor of Tjaru, Neby, to commemorate the opening of work in the area. There is a questionable date, "[Year] 5 under the Majesty of this [good] god" from the temple at Serabit-el Khadim.[9] Since the style of inscription follows that of the year 4 date, Weill included his no. 100 with Thutmose IV inscriptions. The year of this inscription is partially broken, however, and it was found in the temple, not at the mine. It cannot be included as an identified year date for the pharaoh. Year 6 is attested from the Theban tomb of Nebamun, Chief of Police in Western Thebes (TT 90 tempus Thutmose IV-Amenhotep III.) This date no longer exists and indeed has been missing since shortly after the visit of Hay.[10] Champollion,[11] however, reported it at the heading of Nebamun's appointment as Police Chief. This text does not name the king referred to as "my Majesty", but the identification of Thutmose IV is nearly certain. The scene of Nebamun hearing the order read to him by the royal scribe Yuny is the left one on the double-scene southwest wall. To the right Nebamun offers praise to Thutmose IV in a kiosk. While it is undoubtedly true that the date of year 6 refers to the left-hand scene only,[12] it is nonetheless visually unlikely that Amenhotep III and not Thutmose IV was intended in the dated inscription, both because of the scene of the latter king on the same wall and because the textual use of "my Majesty" would have been ambiguous.

Year 7 of Thutmose IV is attested twice, at Konosso and at Serabit-el Khadim. These two dates are of double interest, since they both include the royal wife ⟨hieroglyph⟩ , commonly called Iaret (for no stronger reason than convention). She will be discussed in Chapter 3. The Konosso Year 7[13] appears at the beginning of a now destroyed inscription which likely recorded a military action. The scene above showed the king, followed by Iaret, striking an enemy before Dedwen and Ha. Helck has suggested that the year 7 date be emended to year 8 to agree with the other Konosso inscription of this king.[14] Since this stela was positioned differently at Konosso from the Year 8 text, and since the Year 7 with Iaret figuring prominently has an analogue at Sinai, there is no need to emend the date. Surely Thutmose IV could have carried out more than one action in the southern region.

The Sinai Year 7 date exists on a tablet which Birch found at the entrance of a mine two miles southeast of the temple of Serabit-el Khadim. This text has recently been refound.[15] Apparently this is another record of a mine-opening, but there is no scene preserved with this tablet, as in the case of Neby's Year 4 inscription. Below the Year 7, written horizontally, are four vertical lines. The cartouche names of Thutmose IV and that of the King's Daughter Iaret face the name of Hathor Mistress of Turquoise. Giveon's photograph shows clearly seven strokes in the year date.

Year 8 occurs at Konosso,[16] where it commences a description of the king's personal involvement in a military skirmish on the Eastern desert. The scene above depicts Thutmose IV offering wine to Amun and Khnum.

There are two more year dates which should not be included among Thutmose IV's attestations. On a jar label from Deir el Medina, published only in transcription, exists the notation: "Year 19: Wine of the Estate of Menkheprure from the mw n Ptah: from the hand of Hekay".[17] Although one cannot absolutely rule that date out until the hieratic paleography has been judged, the date is almost certainly one of a later New Kingdom ruler. The estate of Thutmose IV is attested in a number of later 18th and 19th dynasty sources; and the jar labels from Deir el Medina naming 18th dynasty kings, if dated by the royal estates named, would contradict the paleography on numerous examples.[18] We may reasonably assume this date does not belong to the reign of Thutmose IV.

Some years ago, the late Dr. Klaus Baer reported discovering a hitherto unnoticed Year 20 of Thutmose IV.[19] He did not publish his find, but the date has since been cited as chronological data.[20] Dr. Baer kindly replied to a query concerning the date and confirmed that it is a rock inscription at Tombos published by Breasted[21] and later by Save-Soderbergh[22] with photo and Breasted's handcopy.

Breasted stated that both Menkheperre and Menkheprure were possible readings for a broken cartouche in the inscription. He opted for the former reading in his publication, and he has been consistently followed in that. Baer found that Breasted had first identified Thutmose IV as the king when he made his field notes. He later changed his mind because of the short reign of Thutmose IV. The cartouche in question is broken on the left end and shows, both in the handcopy and photo, (⬚⬚⬚○) including the upturn of the cartouche enclosure on the left. There is, as a cursory glance reveals, more room between the beetle and the left end of the cartouche than between the sundisk and the right end. This might lead to the conclusion that three plural strokes once existed in the broken section.[23] However, other examples from Nubia--from   Semna-Kumma and Gebel Barkal and elsewhere--show that Thutmose III wrote his prenomen in the fashion described above, both horizontally and vertically.   The horizontal examples are more relevant, although less numerous: a year 21 inscription from   Semna shows the writing (○⬚⬚))[24] with both the n under mn and the spacing seen at Tombos; two other examples from Semna are parallel.[25] From Kumma there is an inscription (⬚⬚⬚ ⬚⬚○)[26] where the names of both kings show unequal spacing on the ends. Most convincing is the writing of the king's prenomen in line 1 of the Barkal stela[27] -- this context, within the body of an incised text, shows the form (⬚⬚○) with 2-3 times more space on the left than the right. A recently-found year 16 of Thutmose III also shows the writing as at Tombos:[28]   (⬚ ⬚ ○) Likewise, a year 18 text from Shelfak-Dudora.[29] These examples demonstrate that the Tombos cartouche can easily represent Thutmose III.

The argument must rest on other grounds, as well, since the prenomen cannot be surely read.   The name of the official is erased in two places, once imperfectly, then completely. There are traces of the first writing that are readable: Breasted read Ani;   Reisner, perhaps without benefit of a photo, restored Nehy for his viceroy lists;[30] Save-Soderbergh read Inebny.[31] Edel, who collated the text in 1963, read Any. He felt Amun-nekhu was not possible, thus casting doubt on the proposition that the Atenists erased the name.[32] Breasted's reading of Any confirms what the photo shows, at least at the beginning of the name: ⬚⬚ is the first group. The reed leaf is clear and compares favorably with the writing in Imn. The writing, though entirely readable, was partly destroyed, but it is unclear, because of the gap above it and to the right, whether it was deliberately tampered with. The seated man's outline is visible, and the traces would not fit any low broad signs ,for the bottom of a tall sign is clear. The following sign is difficult; a horizontal is sure, and nb is possible. The name is too long simply to be Iny.

It is highly unlikely that the name read Nehy. The reed leaf is sure, and the other traces are not suitable. There is likewise no argument for Usersatet for the reasons which apply to Nehy. In addition, supposing Thutmose IV was the king here, Usersatet is not likely still to have been performing a demanding job at this late date. Nehy's tenure in office is now attested only in years 23 and 25 of

Thutmose III; Amun-nekhu is known for year 18.[33]

Finally, the viceroy of Nubia under Thutmose IV, Amenhotep,[34] comes to mind. The names' first elements are identical, but there is no low broad trace, such as for <u>mn</u> in the second position. And this is not the only discouragement for Amenhotep. The monuments identified for that official are consistent in one way: in every mention of Amenhotep's titles he is called Royal scribe; on three monuments he is four times called by the title. He was also the first to be called King's Son of Kush and,therefore, uses that title and variants of it. Amenhotep's inscriptions have been assigned to the reigns of both Thutmose IV (by cartouche) and Amenhotep III (by style); they use Royal Scribe, always, and King's Son of Kush, Overseer of Southern Lands[35] (1 time), King's Son of Kush[36] (1 time), King's Son and Confidant of Kush[37] (1 time). However, the Viceroy who left the Tombos inscription was simply <u>King Son Overseer of Southern Lands</u>,[38] the common viceroy title in the first part of the dynasty. Amenhotep's monuments never employ this early formula. It is thus most unlikely that he was the viceroy named in the Tombos text.

As to Save-Soderbergh's suggestion of Inebny in the inscription , we can cite his statue in the British Museum,[39] which records his service under Hatshepsut and Thutmose III simultaneously.[40]   His titles do not include "Overseer of Southern Countries", but he was a "King's son" and "Troop Commander".[41] Inebny was an important military man of a Viceroy rank; for him to have performed the duties of the King's Son of Nubia would thus not have been unexpected. His name on the statue is written ░░░.[42] The Tombos traces would fit such a spelling. Nor is it outside the realm of possibility that the 3rd Cataract text also once showed two kings' names. The text is well-preserved for five lines beneath three lines which are most fragmentary:

1)[ḥ3]t sp 20 nṯr nfr sḫr pḥ-sw//////// (2) pr ỉt.f di.f ḫt///////// (3) /////////Mn-ḫpr(?)r°//////(4) ḥtp [di nsw] ỉmn nb nswt t3wy psdt ỉmyw T3-Sty di.sn knt rs-tp///.[43] 1) [Year] 20, the Good god who overthrows him who attacked him]/////(2) the house of his father, may he give [every] thing /// (3) /////Menkhep[(?)]re//// (4) An offering which [the king gives] and Amun lord of the thrones of the Two lands and the Ennead within Ta-Sety, may they give valiance and vigilance ///.

It may be that weathering produced all but the name erasure, but it could also be, in view of two offering formulas (lines 1-2 and 4) and the poor and odd preservation of the first three lines, that originally both Hatshepsut and Thutmose III were cited. This suggestion is supported by the removal of the Viceroy's name, a form of <u>damnatio</u> which a number of Hatshepsut's followers suffered; Breasted cited three of her viceroys whose names were expunged.[44] The Atenists were not responsible, as can be seen by the undisturbed name of Amun in line 4. The year date is likewise within a period in which the coregents appeared together, even in Nubia. A number of monuments declare their shared regency from at least year 7.[45] In the same year 20 as the Tombos text, they appeared together in a rock stela from the Sinai.[46] And in Nubia a year 15 rock inscription from Tangur West named both rulers before its defacement.[47] Another monument belonging to the time[48] is a stela in the British Museum on which Hatshepsut's name has been erased, while Menkheperre remains. The dedicant was the "mouth of the Lower Egyptian king in Khent-hennefer, Overseer of the Southern land before the rekhyt, King's son and Overseer of [Southern] countries [/////]". This is likely to be either Amun-nekhu or the man (Inebny?) in the Tombos rock inscription, in view of the presence of both monarchs. The viceroy at Tombos cannot be surely identified, but the text most certainly belongs to Thutmose III's reign, not Thutmose IV's.

To summarize the evidence of contemporary year dates, Thutmose IV is last known by a year 8 inscription at Konosso.

Anatomical Evidence

Anatomical studies of Thutmose IV's mummy have been available since the early years of this century. G. Elliot Smith, who studied the royal mummies for the Cairo Museum, published two different estimates of the king's age at death.[49] In 1903 and 1904 Smith suggested 25 as the most probable age.[50] He described the king as "a young clean-shaved effeminate, and extremely emaciated man, 5 feet 6 inches in height".[51] Through x-ray examination Smith learned that the epiphyses of the tibia were fully joined, indicating to him an age of at least 20 and probably more than 24. Because the epiphyses of the crest of the ilium were not joined, however, he felt the king could not have been more than 25 years.[52] In 1912 Smith published the royal mummies for the Cairo Museum and had by then revised his conclusions. Since he had observed other examples of incompletely joined epiphyses of ilia, he believed it was not uncommon for Egyptians to exhibit a delayed union of epiphysis cristae.[53] The results of a skiagram of the epiphyses of the vertebral border of the scapula showed an apparent separation. This led Smith still to support a low age estimate, though perhaps as high as 28.[54] He concluded that the texture of bones should admit that "Thutmose IV might possibly have been even older than this."[55] It should be added, however, that Smith's assessment of delayed union has not impressed all modern radiologists, however, whose work on providing age at death has been built up from increasingly larger numbers of radiological projects. The comparative "bone-age" material continues to be however, the modern population.

The x-ray evidence left questions, but Smith commented in the introduction to his mummy catalogue that no one test could be expected to provide an unassailable age at death: "Had I been aware of these facts seven years ago, when I wrote my report on Thoutmosis IV, I would still have suggested 25 years as his age, as I support most anatomists would have done; but with my present experience of the variability of the relative dates of epiphyseal unions in ancient Egyptian bones, I would make the reservation that the anatomical evidence, when based upon the penultimate stage of consolidation of a single bone, cannot be regarded as conclusive."[56]   This statement would no doubt win the support of all modern radiologists.

Newer studies have been carried out and, in the case of the royal mummy project, have yielded radiological bone ages and tooth-wear indications sometimes in clear conflict with contemporary year date evidence. The dramatic nature of these discrepancies has created doubts among Egyptologists whether 1) scientific studies can be useful for chronological purposes and 2) the mummies from the cachettes of Egyptian kings are correctly identified.[57]   Here only the method and results of new studies on Thutmose IV's body will be examined for their bearing on his length of rule.

For the x-raying project undertaken to study the Cairo Museum's royal mummies, Krogman and Baer conducted new radiological examinations on Thutmose IV's mummy.[58]   The x-rays themselves are included in microfiche form with the book. The researchers described the bone age indicators as well as the x-rays needed to determine each. They did not, however, discuss each mummy separately, but rather gave only their conclusions as reported on a table. Krogman and Baer concluded that Thutmose IV could have been 30-40 years old at death, but they preferred an age of 35. From a brief look at the authors' chart, the tests conducted on the mummy of Thutmose IV seem to point clearly to a bone age of 30-40, but upon further examination a number of questions arise that are puzzling to the Egyptologist.

The table is arranged head to toe with a cryptically worded radiological finding and an age estimate to accompany it, yet the material is not arranged in this order in the authors' narrative. More important, the relative value of the bones as age indicators is obscured by this presentation. In fact, only two or three types of bones have been shown to indicate bone age with enough precision to suggest absolute ages.[59]   Even Krogman and Baer note this, and describe the other x-ray results as corroborative only.[60]   The radiological findings which have been shown to be most age indicative come from the epiphyses of several regions (these are reliable up to the mid-twenties), from changes exhibited by the pubic symphysis, as outlined by Todd,[61] and from changes in the long bones. J.L. Angel notes concerning the developmental stages of the best indicator up to age 55 or 60--the pubic symphysis--that even here "[t]here is a 5- to 10-year leeway in any of these processes, and the variation increases with age."[62] Of the long bones, Krogman and Baer themselves caution that the results "do not yield themselves, in our present state of knowledge, to an age estimation other than to within a decade."[63] It is, therefore, with some bewilderment that the Egyptologist reads in Krogman and Baer's introductory narrative that "it is likely that age at death can be fixed within a decade, and probably within the first or second half of a decade.... Hence age can often be estimated in lustra of five years."[64]

The researchers concluded that Thutmose IV's epiphyses (contrary to Smith's early study of the ilium) were all united. This sort of contradiction is difficult to evaluate. On the one hand there is surely a major contrast between x-ray quality of 1912 and 1980. On the other the modern researchers were not privileged ,as was Smith, to unwrap and x-ray the mummy out of its coffin. They took their films through the wood in most cases and were likewise limited in possible views.[65] Assuming all epiphyses were united, however, it is the evidence of the pubic symphysis and the long bones that should best indicate how much older than age 25 was the king at death. The king's pubic symphysis is described on the table: "Symphyseal surface shows SL [slight] ossific nodules; white line parallel to surface is MO [moderately] developed. 35.0-40.0". There is nothing in the text to explain the age assigned (nor to acknowledge Angel's caveat quoted above). Indeed, in comparing Krogman and Baer's description to the schematic figure in Angel's article which represented Todd's phases of the pubic symphysis, the reader is likely to conclude that Thutmose IV's symphyseal surface is more like those stages assigned to years 27-30 and 31-35 than to later phases.

The entries for long bones chart the degree to which the fine-meshed outer cortex of bone has become thinner and less dense while the narrow medulla cavity within has become widened. The description given for Thutmose IV's Cortex/Medulla ratio states: "COR/MED ratio good; TR [trabeculation, that is, the fineness of the bone mesh seen in the cortex] tends to open mesh; 35.0".[66] Having already written that this indicator cannot be dated more precisely than to a decade, the researchers without further comment assign an exact age. The reasoning is likewise unexplained. Since no other entry contains the same wording comparison is impossible. The identical complaint may be made about the entry for changes in the humeral head.

The process of ossification in later life was studied by Stewart for the vertebral bones,[67] but Krogman and Baer have not followed his original classification system devised for dating this process called "lipping". Thutmose IV, for example was identified as having lipping of class "+" in the thoracic and lumbar regions. The original Stewart studies rated this score below 30 years. Krogman and Baer, however, assigned an age of 35-<u>40</u>, writing: "In my experience lipping begins on the vertebral bodies <u>before</u> [his emphasis] it begins on the articular ends of the long bones. Therefore I rate long-bone lipping about a decade older than vertebral-body lipping."[68]   The researchers found slight lipping on the knee (a long bone) of Thutmose IV and assigned a "35.0+" to the entry. Did they then enter an older age for the vetebral evidence, in contradiction to Stewart's vertebral classifications, because of their experience with the long bones? Perhaps this is the correct methodology for reporting results, but it is frustrating to the Egyptologist hoping to make use of the data.

All but one chart category contains an age estimate, although the authors, Angel and others warn that the data from skull x-rays and dentition is additive only. If we eliminate the scores which are not age determinant,[69] and the ages that are questionable due to the authors' or other scientists' warnings or due to confusing, contradictory descriptions,[70] the table entries for Thutmose IV provide not a single age estimate that has been well-justified within the five years claimed by Krogman and Baer.

It remains only to comment on the reliability of physical examinations. As Wente pointed out, x-ray results have led the modern investigators to lower the ages of many pharaohs, and he is interested in reconciling the biological discrepancies with the inscriptional evidence.[71] But what degree of precision can an Egyptologist expect from scientific examinations? Are they not subject to the limitations of the tests and the interpretations of the testers?

Interestingly, in sharp contrast to Smith's reading, Krogman and Baer's x-ray of the crest of Thutmose IV's ilium was identified not with an unfused epiphysis but with a slight atrophy in the iliac fossa, a common indicator of adult age progression. An Egyptologist cannot argue with a radiologist's reading of an x-ray, but unanimous agreement about the interpretation of findings and the precision of age-scale indicators is not to be found.[72]   Dr. Owen Lovejoy, Professor of Anthropology and pathologist whose specialty is ageing skeletons through x-ray studies, did not agree that the epiphysis was clearly fused, and saw no atrophy. While the studies to date tend to confirm that the bone development progressions are the same for ancient and modern populations (contradicting Smith's conclusions based on his experience with Egyptian mummies), identical rates of maturation cannot and have not been clearly determined.[73] Indeed, according to some, there may be "a general tendency towards earlier skeletal maturation in ancient Egyptians".[74] This could make common age estimates, including those of Baer and Krogman, too high and would reverse Smith's interpretation. Acsadi and Nemeskeri gave some guidelines for age determination and concluded: "Age can only be determined if several age indicators are studied in a systematic and co-ordinated manner"; this would include reliable control groups of identical ethnic and geographic origin.[75] Until now the royal mummies have not been studied alongside such a control group.

In recent years the work of Dr. Owen Lovejoy with Richard Meindl, Robert Mensforth and others has demonstrated over and over that the only reliable ageing of skeleton relies on multifactorial testing. By comparison, for example, to age determination by wear on the pubic symphyuseal face, Lovejoy found that a five indicator method showed "a marked superiority of the multifactorial method over any single indicator with respect to both bias and accuracy." In conversations with Dr. Lovejoy during and after he reviewed the results of the Krogman and Baer findings along with the x-rays, he repeatedly informed me that the x-rays of the royal mummies were insufficient to allow the type of interpretation attempted.[76] In view of the questions remaining, not to mention the disagreements with contemporary inscriptional evidence for individuals such as Thutmose IV, Amenhotep I, Thutmose III, Ahmose, Ramesses III, and the Elderly Lady,[77] chronological evaluations cannot rely heavily on the present state of anatomical assessments. Of course to refuse to consider anatomical information would be too extreme, but Egyptologists need to understand the uses and limitations of the scientific data offered them.[78]

As has been shown, there is no assurance of Thutmose IV's absolute age at death. It is logical, however, to conclude that the radiographic age estimation, whether accepted as offered by Krogman and Baer, or lowered as suggested by Stewart's studies, by the data mentioned by Isherwood and by Smith's original anatomical examintion, supports a reign of 8+ years more than one of 33.

Astronomical Data

A fourth means of assessing the length of Thutmose IV's reign is through dating of astronomical phenomena. The king's placement within the determined absolute dates for the dynasty may be seen as requiring a short or long reign. It is due to Wente's absolute dating of the 18th Dynasty that he assigned 33+ years to Thutmose IV. Wente's impetus for revision, however, stems most sensibly from recent alterations in Near Eastern chronology. Brinkman's work[79] on the Assyrian and Kassite king lists, indicating that the Cambridge Ancient History dates for Babylonian kings could be lowered by as much as 18 years for the period between Kurigalzu II and the Tikulti Ninurta Interregnum, and 9 years between the Interregnum and Enlil-nadin-ahi, has led several scholars to reexamine the Egyptian dates for the contemporary period. Kitchen [80], for example, moved the end of the Ramesside period from 1085 to 1070/69 and proposed 1279 as the accession date of Ramesses II, citing Parker's possible Sothic and lunar dates. Hornung[81] had earlier made the suggestion regarding the end of the Ramesside period, independently of Brinkman's conclusions. And the lower chronology continues to be favored by Egyptologists, having been championed by Bierbrier early and Krauss in a series of expertly documented articles and monographs.[82]

Although Wente, in pursuing the implications of Brinkman's work for Egypt, agreed with the 1279 accession for Ramesses II,[83] he first fully tackled the accession of Thutmose III[84], rather than that of the later king. The length of the Ramesside period is more fully addressed in his joint article with Van Siclen where the authors proceeded from Wente's conclusion about the accession dates. The heart of the new chronology is therefore in the earlier work.

The discussion below focuses on the inscriptions that provide new moon dates in the reign of Thutmose III. The moon dates have been discussed at length by a number of scholars and seem to be regarded as a settled question by some.[85] In discussion below I do not assume this to be the case; while not insistent that a solution yielding 1479 or even 1504 B.C. for Thutmose III's accession is wrong, I point out the lack of scholarly unanimity regarding the Megiddo campaign lunar date and raise difficulties with both Wente's and Von Beckerath's arguments concerning the Karnak moon date.[86] Short summations of the state of Sothic siting arguments and the choice between the absolute dates provided by the astronomical data conclude the section. The conclusions state that the length of Thutmose IV's reign may not be determined by attempts at absolute dating and that Wente's impetus in assigning a long reign is his faith in the Jubilee as a chronological tool.

Arguing against the older 1490 date for Thutmose III, and rejecting 1479 as well, Wente proposed 1504 B.C. as the king's accession, while still assuming 1279 for Ramesses II. Naturally this produced a period for the Eighteenth dynasty exceeding earlier estimates and greatly contradicted both Manetho and the year dates available; the _heb sed_ texts were then drawn in to support the lengthened reigns.

Addressing himself to two moon dates, Wente began by citing Helck's discussion of the dates given in the Megiddo campaign.[87] There Helck criticized Faulkner's emendation of day 21 to day 20 as unnecessary and explained the missing day 20 by dividing the entry under day 19 (rs m [ᶜnh] m im3m n ᶜnh wd3 snb r dmi n ᶜrn into two parts. He emended r dmi n ᶜrn to yield spr r dmi n ᶜrn, assigning this "arrival" to day 20. Wente characterized Helck's discussion as "convincing"[88], but Spalinger[89] has more recently pointed out that Helck's solution also required a change, one which is syntactically unnecessary. Spalinger attempted his own outline of the facts referred to in the entries for days 16-19.[90] His outline needed no emendation as did Helck's. He also made the point that, whether or not one accepts day 20 as being the actual day of battle, it is clear that the events recorded subsequent to that conflict from the daybook account in Urk. IV 652,15 did at least occur on the day prior to the military conflict.[91] Lello demonstrated how the text as given can be accepted, yielding a new moon on I Shemu day 21[92]. He suggests that the "awakening in life" recorded for Day 19 took place during the late night hours, before the day had changed. Therefore the scribe recorded this as Day 19. Day 20 began soon thereafter but did not need to be so noted. This is an

ingenious solution and one which Krauss embraces.[93]   Parker was more skeptical
whether the Egyptians observed regular night and day hours throughout the year,
given the variability of light and dark from month to month.[94] He believes the
emendation to day 20 is still necessary. The absolute dating yielded by Helck's
elimination of Faulkner's emendation of day 21 to day 20 gives either 1479 or 1504
for Thutmose III's accession. Krauss accepts the former, while Wente chose the
latter.

Wente formulated a new argument for the second lunar date in year 24,[95]
concluding that the date given in a Karnak building inscription referred to the
king's order to prepare for stretching the cord on the day before the new moon
and not to the new moon itself. Wente argued that the planned foundation ceremony
took place early because the god Amun did not return from his feasting to his
sanctuary. This lunar date has recently been republished and discussed by von
Beckerath,[96] who identifies it as the foundation text for the Akh Menu and argues
that the god disregarded Thutmose III's plan for performing the cord-stretching on
III peret 1 and performed it a day early. He concludes that the date is that of the
foundation ceremony, but not of the new moon. Helck extended this argument
saying that we cannot tell how many days passed between the cord-stretching and
the new moon; therefore the date is chronologically useless.[97] Parker[98] strongly felt
that the date was given in the text only as a record of the foundation ceremony and
therefore must be seen as such. He finds no reason to believe new moon day was
a day later.

Since one major confusion concerns the precise event that is actually dated by
this inscription, whether the order for preparing the ceremony, the ceremony itself
or the new moon (or all three), some grammatical notes bearing on Wente's
proposed reading of the text may be or use. A discussion of the sequence of events
then follows.

Citing a discussion by Barns of emphasized time expressions in Wenamun,
Wente's translation of the foundation inscription moved the phrase that begins with
the date to the front of the main verb:
wd hm.i sspd pd šs hr s3wt hrw n psdntyw r pd šs hr mnw pn m h3t sp 24 3bd 2
prt ꜥrky hrw hb mh hrw 10 n ꞽmn m ꞽpt-swt. "It was in year 24, II prt 30, (being)
the day of the tenth day feast of Amon in Karnak, that my Majesty gave the order
to prepare for the stretching of the cord while awaiting the day of the new moon
in order to stretch the cord for this monument."[99] Wente believed wd hm.i was a
narrative infinitive,[100] but nonetheless read the main verb phrase plus adjuncts
emphatically. The emphasizing translation was explained only by stating that it
"serves to indicate a different understanding of the text".[101] Wente then proceeded
directly to discuss why the date might refer to the order to prepare rather than to

the new moon. This interpretation will be discussed below, but already it can be
seen that a reading changing the grammar of the passage should be better
justified.[102] The question here is both whether the time adverbial is a major
emphasized   part, and also to what part of the translated sentence the time
expression should refer.

As a grammatical reference for his discussion, Wente noted Barns' comments
on some Egyptian texts.[103] There Barns referred to Nims' reading of the lines
1,43-46 of Wenamun,[104] and retranslated himself, "Are you the one who every day
has kept coming to me saying: ,Get out of my harbor'?--and tonight do you say
'Stay'so that the ship which I've found will depart? (And then you'll come again
and say 'Go away!')". His point was that adverbial expressions in Late Egyptian
often are placed at the end of the clause but have a force earlier in the phrase.
(He gave the example of "again" (^{c}n).) Barns noted that the harbor master had
come to Wenamun for 29 days saying "get out" and then came that night and said
"stay"; therefore he felt the time expressions were the emphasized elements.[105]

The Wenamun passage, however, does not necessarily concern the timing of
these trips by the harbor master; it may more concern the motive for the harbor
master's change of heart. Wenamun believed it was "in order to let the ship which
[Wenamun] found to depart and to let [the harbor master] come again saying 'move
on'."   But the actual reason was that the entranced boy had called for Wenamun
and his god to be brought to Tjekkerbaal, and so his departure had to be
prevented.[106] The adverbial expressions of time reinforce the contrast in the
harbor master's behavior, but when he came was not as significant as why he came
when he did. It is no doubt true that adverbials at the end of clauses can have
earlier force, but there is no conclusive reason to think these cited time expressions
are the major emphasized elements.

A second difficulty with Barns' comments more directly   affects Wente's
discussion. His article referred to "the postponement of adverbial expressions to
the end of the sentence",[107] but there is no definition of "end of the sentence".
Barns' examples of m mnt and m p3 grh, which he apparently places in that
category, precede other adverbial adjuncts which would be translated as part of a
sentence. This confusion surfaces through Wente's use of Barns' examples.

Although Barns' Wenamun examples do not necessarily demonstrate
emphasized time expressions, there are valid examples of such. In fact there is an
occurrence of an exact date, such as in the building inscription text of Thutmose III,
used after emphasizing sdm n.tw.f[108]. The Rhind Mathematical Papyrus title states:
ỉw ỉst grt sphr.n.tw šfdw pn m h3t-sp 33 3bd 3 3ht//// nsw-bit ^{c}3-wsr-r^c di ^{c}nh m
snt r sšw n ỉswt ỉry m h3w////////^{c}t. "It Was   in Year 33, month 4 of Akhet
[under the Majesty of] the king of Upper and Lower Egypt Aauserre, given life, in
accordance with ancient writings made in the time of ////at, that this book was

transcribed." In this example the time expression <u>precedes</u> the additional adverbials and clearly is meant to date the making of a copy referred to in the main verb. By analogy with the Rhind date, Thutmose III's date is unlikely to refer to the main verb.

Wente used Barns' Wenamun example as analogy to support his emphatic translation and stated that time adverbials should be "positioned relatively late in a sentence, thus avoiding an abrupt interruption in a sequence of thought."[109] In the Thutmose III example the date is the final of three adverbials and is placed after both <u>ḥr</u> + infinitive and <u>r</u> + infinitive. In Wenamun, however, both time expressions precede <u>r</u> + infinitive[110] thus demonstrating that "avoiding an abrupt interruption in a sequence of thought" in no way requires placement after both main verb and subordinate constructions. Here it is clear that Wente's understanding of "sentence" may not be the same as Barns'. The former appears to interpret it as main verb to main verb, while the latter seems to identify it as thought pause to thought pause.

Wente also objected to an "interpretation according to which a formal date is applied to an event that is yet to occur in relation to the main verb".[111] Formal dates are not common within sentences, but other time expressions, as in Barns' examples, can be used to compare the construction. In the annal inscriptions of the Megiddo campaign, Thutmose III's troops were addressed prior to doing battle:[112] "Then one commanded the entire army, saying: 'Furnish yourselves, prepare your weapons, since one will engage (ỉw.f r sdm) to fight with that enemy (defeated) tomorrow'". Now <u>tomorrow</u> (m dw3) can be placed after <u>since</u> (r ntt) earlier in the phrase for translation smoothness, but it cannot be moved ahead of this adverbial clause of purpose. It would senseless to read, with the time expression brought up to the initial verb, "It is tomorrow that one commanded...". That attachment of <u>m dw3</u> to <u>r ntt ỉw.tw r thn</u> is sure because the time reference would otherwise be illogical. This can help explain the placement of the formal date.

The time expression in the lunar date text, if interpreted as "tomorrow," likewise could not refer to "my Majesty commanded," but there are two subordinate constructions which provide logical time reference, "while awaiting" and "in order to stretch the cord". "My Majesty commanded to prepare for stretching the cord tomorrow while awaiting...."; or "My Majesty commanded to prepare for stretching the cord while awaiting the day of the new moon tomorrow in order to...." Both of these are prospective in meaning and are physically closer to the date than is the non-prospective initial verb. This was also the case in the Megiddo example. On the other hand, to translate the date as though it meant "today" should, on analogy with the Wenamun passage, have required the time expression to be near its verb of reference, i.e., before the adverbial phrases. The Rhind papyrus given above also demonstrates this. Since a meaning and a translation tying the date to wd hm.i "My Majesty commanded" violates the examples from Wenamun, the annals, and the general sequence of adverbials, and since a translation of "today" would not fit the time reference of hr s3wt and r pd, the date should refer to a future time.

The translation best supported by the examples would   be: "My Majesty ordered to prepare for stretching-the-cord while awaiting the day of the new moon in order to stretch the cord for this monument in year 24, month 2 of peret 30th day, the day of the 10th day feast of Amun in Karnak."

Discussion as to whether the date refers to the order of preparation, the foundation ceremony or the new moon will continue in the literature. Wente and Von Beckerath discussed the events which followed the order for preparation and related that the king went to fetch the god so that he might perform his oracle. He told the god to celebrate a good feast and that he (the king) would return to perform the ceremony. Wente referred to the lacunae here, stating "that one cannot be absolutely certain that all the events described fell on the same day, though this seems most probable."[113] Von Beckerath interpreted the text to mean that the god Amun carried out the foundation ceremony a day early, thus disregarding the king's order. He does not provide explanation for assuming this occurred on the day of the order.[114] The text indeed has gaps, but only 1/3 of line 10   lacks here.[115]

(6)...wḏ ḥm.i sspd pd šs hr s3wt sw n psḏnt (7) r pd šs hr mnw pn m h3t sp 24 3bd 2 prt ꜥrky hrw hb-mḥ n ꞽmn m ꞽpt Swt ꜥhꜥ n rdi /////// hr hwt-ntr tn ꞽw htp n ntr st.f wrt mht nn wd3 nb r shꜥ it (8) ꞽmn wd3 r nmtt.f ntr ꞽr ꞽrt hb.f pn nfr wn.ꞽn hm.n ntr pn hr bꞽ3wt ꜥš3wt hr nb.ti.hm.f ꞽr.f ///////[ꞽ]n [hmꞽ] n ntr pn ꜥhꜥw/////ꜥhꜥ n rdi n.f. hm.f hr h3t.f ꞽr mnw pn s3 n hm.f wn (9) ꞽn hm n ntr pn hꜥ m mnw pn hr ////////[hm] n ntr pn /////[ꜥhꜥ n dd n hm.f hr hm n ntr pn wḏ3 ꞽr hb.k nfr nb.i k3 ꞽw.i r ꞽrt pd šs hr ntt (10) ///hn/1/3 line// [ꜥhꜥ n rdi n.f hm.f] hr h3t.f bs n.f sw r st bit hb tpy n pd šs ꞽst 3b n hm.n ntr pn šps ꞽrt pd šs ds.f (11) [m] hbw nb nt k3t tn ꜥpr m////

"(6)... My majesty commanded to prepare for stretching the cord while awaiting the day of the new moon (7) in order to stretch the cord for this monument in Year 24 month 2 of peret, 30th day, the day of the Tenth day feast of Amun in Karnak. Then caused...for this temple, while the god rested in his great seat. After this the lord proceeded in order to cause that father (8) Amun appear so that the god might travel on his processions to do this his beautiful feast. Then the Majesty of this god was doing numerous wonders for the Lord, while his Majesty did//// Then the Majesty of this god...[his] stations.///Then he placed his Majesty in front of him at this monument which his Majesty had ordained. Then (9) the Majesty of this god rejoiced at this monument because///////////[Majesty] of this god///[Then his Majesty said to the majesty] of this god: Proceed! Make a good festival, my lord. Then I will return to perform stretching-the-cord since 10 ////// [He placed his Majesty] before him. He presented him at the seat of the lower Egyptian king, the first festival station of stretching the cord. At this time the

Majesty of this noble god desired[116] to perform the stretching-the-cord himself (11) [in][117] all the   festival stations[118] of this construction prepared with ///."
Sethe restored ꜥḥꜥ n rdi n.f ḥm.f because of that specific   reading in line 8. Von Beckerath continues that reading.

Despite lacunae in the inscription, the sequence of events is not lost in a gap. Both Wente and Von Beckerath assume that there is no break in the action after the command to prepare. But line 7 finds the god resting in his sanctuary while other activity was going on in the temple. A time change is then indicated by m ht nn, "After this", and the succeeding clause describes the king's visit to the god to bring him out on procession for the 10th Day of Amun. The god's movements included a visit to the Akh Menu where he positioned Thutmose III before himself and where he showed great approval foreshadowing the miracle of the foundation ceremony itself. The pharaoh then sent the god to continue his feast and said he would return to perform the foundation ceremony.   A ḥr ntt at the end of line 9 indicating a subordinate phrase followed the king's avowal to return.[119] A 1/3 line lacuna follows "since", and then the god placed the king before him and introduced him at the first ceremonial station. (A parallel for this placement of the king by the god at festival stations is attested.)[120] This leaves very little room to relate a change in plans. Instead the sequence shows the matter went as intended until the god interrupted, a point marked by the use of ꜣist + sdm n.f[121] which describes the action contained in the narrative. Therefore, at the point when the king took up the first station for the foundation ceremony, the god's oracle interrupted. No other change in the arrangement is suggested.

The king had stated that the ceremony would take place on new moon day, not before.[122] Beginning with line 7, "After this the Lord proceeded to cause that father Amun appear...", the events surrounding the festival day [i.e., the Tenth Day Feast of Amun] and the foundation ceremony are occurring. There is nothing in the text which suggests the king changed his mind; nor is there evidence that the god did so until the end of line 10. Therefore, since the king had returned to stretch the cord, and had been presented routinely at the first festival place for the foundation rite, the action must refer to new moon day, not to the day of the order. The date in the text refers both to the new moon and to the important date on which the god himself stretched the cord for the Karnak temple. This argument, together with that concerning the syntactical placement of the formal date, makes it most doubtful that the year 24 lunar date took place in 3 peret 1, while, 2 peret 30 remains the most likely observed date of the new moon.[123]

Sothic Siting Locations

Wente's other argument involved the location of Sothic sightings. He chose

Memphis, placing the burden of proof on those who support Thebes. The discussion of Sothic sighting locations resembles the proverbial dog-chasing-tail. In the last decade nearly every scholar interested in chronology has entered the debate with the result that several scholars defend several locations for several time periods.[124] Krauss' recent book Sothis- und Monddaten gives priority to Elephantine as the siting place for the Ebers papyrus year 9 date in the reign of Amenhotep I[125] and argues persuasively for the same siting location, agreeing with Barta in this, during the Middle Kingdom.[126] But others now doubt the Ebers date can be used as reliable data for chronological calculation.[127]

Parker accepted 1490 versus 1504 or 1479 for Thutmose III's accession, thus opting for a Theban observation point.[128] He gave as one reason that the lower range of dates derived from a southern sighting did not require maximum reigns for Amenhotep I, Thutmose I and Thutmose II. Wente rejected a 1479 date from Thebes because it would have required such maximums.[129] But the adoption of 1504, with Ramesses II's accession placed at 1279, required some 30 more years in the 18th dynasty, 6 before and 24 after Thutmose III, than does Parker's chronology. Indeed the new proposal adds 25 years to Thutmose IV's reign alone (33) and 8 years to Amenhotep II's (34). The means of providing the excess years is to be found in Wente's interpretation of Jubilee texts. Thus he gave Amenhotep I 21 years, plus 6 of co-regency, based on prepared Jubilee monuments for the king.[130] More will be said of this; but for now, a summation of the investigation reveals that Wente's 1504/1479 dates are far from certain based on the lunar texts. The Sothic sighting at Memphis is unresolved. The astronomical evidence cannot be considered conclusive enough to support either a long or a short reign for Thutmose IV.

Jubilee Festivals

Wente's chronology assigned thirty-three years to Thutmose IV.[131] This was no accident, and has its source in the pillar inscriptions of the Amada Temple Hall C which Thutmose altered and decorated.[132] On the pillars below the scenes showing the king with various deities were the inscriptions, "first occasion repeating the Jubilee Sed festival, may he perform very greatly" (sp tpy whm hb sd ir.f ꜥꜣ wrt). Until recently the Amada inscriptions were the only known source of jubilee texts for this king. The Third pylon foundation at Karnak temple, however, has yielded from among its spectacular secrets a sandstone chapel of Thutmose IV, the pillars of which bear the inscriptions, "first occasion of the Jubilee" (sp tpy hb sd) together with either "may he perform very greatly" (ir.f ꜥꜣ wrt) or "may he perform 'given life'" (ir.f di ꜥnh). But two pillars use the form "the first occasion of repeating the Jubilee" (sp tpy whm hb sd).[133] One additional piece of evidence is the small alabaster bark sanctuary[134] excavated both from the Third pylon foundation and from the Hypostyle Hall floor.   One   block of this incomplete chapel bears the vague text ".[May you do million]s of Jubilees".[135]

The existence of the "repetition" texts has puzzled scholars for many years. None has suggested that Thutmose ruled for 33 years in order to celebrate a second jubilee[136] but this is clearly the position Wente advocates. Wente and Van Siclen's chronology extended Thutmose IV's reign from 8+ years to 33+ principally because Wente considered jubilee inscriptional formulae to be evidence that a sed festival took place after 30 years of rule. Wente wrote that "all kings with reigns of thirty years or more celebrated their first jubilee according to this principle"[137], and in a note he specified   Thutmose III, Amenhotep III, Ramesses II and Ramesses III.[138] Elsewhere he referred to his investigation of the jubilee concluding "that the celebration of a jubilee by a king can be utilized as a valuable indicator for the length of reign".[139]

There are two problems inherent in using jubilee monuments for chronological or historical purposes: 1) the 30-year principle appears to have been regularly neglected and 2) the proof that festivals took place is difficult to amass for most reigns. Wente himself cautioned about this latter problem.[140] Murnane defended the use of sed festival material for historical purposes, but he is ambivalent about the 30-year principle. He concluded that the jubilee formula "... indicated that he [the named king] had already celebrated a Jubilee. It seems logical, also, that buildings erected for or just prior to the Jubilee rites would be inscribed with the formula before the actual celebration had taken place."[141] This assessment is helpful chronologically only if we can depend on the 30-year principle; nor does it address the objection raised by Haeny long ago that these buildings in which jubilee texts appear can hardly be sed festival-related.[142]

Redford has offered the ingenious suggestion that during the Second Intermediate Period jubilees ceased and that early 18th Dynasty sed festivals were only minor occasions observed whenever monarchs wished.[143] He, too, wishes to retain the thirty-year principle, for the Middle Kingdom at least, and again for Amenhotep III. He believes the hb sd monuments are not useful for chronology at all and regards the jubilee formula as "a pious hope and expectation".[144] To date Redford's explanation is the most sensible, but the existence of the 30-year principle remains unresolved. Since it is this principle that distinguishes the sed festival material as a tool for absolute dating--and more than quadrupled the reign of Thutmose IV in the Wente-Van Siclen chronology--it should be better resolved.

The 30-year jubilee is attested from trilingual inscriptions of the Ptolemaic period where "lord of Jubilees" (nb hbw-sd) is translated by the Greek KURIOU TRIAKONTASTHRIDWN[145] Simpson wrote that a 30-year principle appears to have been observed during the 12th Dynasty,[146] possibly as late as Amenemhet III.[147] But for kings other than Sesostris I and Amenemhet III we cannot

demonstrate that 30/31 years had any special significance. Amenemhet I, who died
in his thirtieth year left a reference to the First occasion of the sed festival on a
statue as well as relief blocks with jubilee scenes used in foundations at his Lisht
pyramid complex. The material is undatable within the reign. Amenemhet II's long
rule has produced no jubilee monuments. Sesostris III, for whom only 19 years are
in evidence, left some reliefs of the "double sed chapel". The Twelfth Dynasty thus
only slightly better upholds the integrity of the 30-year festival than do earlier and
later eras.[148] And as for the Ptolemies, neither Ptolemy IV Philopator nor Ptolemy
V Epiphanes who proclaimed the 30-year periodicity of the festival by translating
their epithets of "lords of Jubilees" reigned as many as three decades. Apparently the
Egyptian rulers never deemed it inappropriate to use the iconography and descriptive
imagery of the jubilee if it suited the context of a monument. In the same way it
was not inappropriate that an Egyptian ruler was shown enacting the rituals of a
temple festival at which he was rarely or never present.

Hornung's analysis of the "Sedfest" called for corroborative evidence to
demonstrate that a jubilee had taken place. He found that corroboration most
convincingly in the materials from Malkata and the announcements of Ramesses
II.[149] He likewise expressed faith in the jubilees of Pepi II, Ramesses III and
Amenemhet III, and with lesser assurance, those of a number of others including
Sesostris I and Hatshepsut. It is the witness of non-monumental evidence which
differentiates Hornung's categories.

Confirmations of jubilee ceremonies result simply from the elaborate festivities
held upon the (in most cases unexpected) achievement of 30 or more years of rule.
This is undeniable for Amenhotep III and Ramesses II who left various types of
materials relating to their jubilees. Pepi I's Hammammat texts include the jubilee
formulae as late as the year after the 18th and 25th counts.[150] Such Jubilee
notations on graffiti would have been senseless twenty years after a sed unless the
magnificence and rarity of the celebration were memorable. But this king also left
a healthy number of small objects referring to the First Occasion of the Jubilee.
These commemorative seals, statuettes and vessels are the true confirmation of the
Hammammat texts since they are not monumental. The existence of dates on
inscriptions, unless they are specifically claimed to be the dates of jubilee festivals
does not necessarily provide a year for the sed.[151]

Our disparate evidence, often bearing dates that may be valueless for the sed
celebration,[152] does not entirely validate a 30-year principle; nor does it directly
contradict it from the Old Kingdom on. In the case of Amenemhet III's notation the
hbw sd was a later addition to a Year 30 inscription. This may well reflect the
celebration of the jubilee during that year. It appears that the ideal of 30 years was
recognized at an early time, certainly by the Middle Kingdom, and perhaps during
the Old Kingdom. Nonetheless, from the beginning of the 12th Dynasty to the reign

of Amenhotep III <u>only two rulers within a six-hundred year period are known to</u> <u>have claimed a connection between thirty years of rule and a jubilee festival</u>. We are likewise forced to admit that rulers regularly dedicated monuments either in expectation of future jubilees or as minor celebrations of their rejuvenation at an early date. <u>The ideal 30-year principle was regularly ignored</u>.

In view of the ambiguity of our jubilee evidence, chronology can benefit but little from its use. Monuments such as the jubilee formula pillars of Thutmose IV, provide no chronological indication at all regardless whether they can be seen to record a <u>sed</u> festival. We might add that the elimination of the 30-year barrier will dispose of the need to contrive explanations for early celebrations of the jubilee.[153]

If from the presence of jubilee formulae we cannot assume the passage of 30 years, then the argument whether Thutmose IV actually held a rejuvenation festival once or twice becomes moot. In sum, the argument for assigning 33+ years to Thutmose IV based on jubilee texts is quite unconvincing, and any employment of these inscriptions for chronological purposes must be rejected.

<u>Careers of Officials serving several reigns.</u>

The evidence of officials who served under more than one king is small for Thutmose IV and should be weighed with skepticism. The average lifespan for ancient Egypt is unknown, and individual variations are great in all populations. We know that the Egyptians held 110 years to be an ideal old age, but it is difficult to believe such long life was other than exceptional. Recent studies have shown that in the Ancient Near East, virtually 100% of the population died before age 60; between 70% and 90% were dead by age 40.[154] Because the exact age of persons at death is unknown, the testimony of tomb biographies, suggestive of lifespans, may be contributory but is in no way conclusive.

Horemhab (Th.tb.78)[155] is the sole representative for this category. He survived Thutmose IV and served Amenhotep III. In his tomb testament before the weighing scene Horemhab said:[156] "I followed[157] the Good God, lord of the Two Lands, Aakheprure, given life, his beloved son, lord of diadems, Menkheprure, given life, his beloved son, lord of the desert (?), Nebmaatre, son of Re, Amenhotep Heka Waset, beloved of Amun". Although this speech mentions only three kings whom he served, the judgment scene facing this testimony portrays four cartouches--written left to right: "the Good God, given life like Re, Nebmaatre, Menkheprure, Aakheprure, Menkheperre".[158] These cartouches, surmounted by plumes and resting on gold signs, occupy the uppermost of three registers. In the middle register sit the four sons of Horus; below them sit three mummiform gods called the "great ennead in (blank)".[159] Since these three registers are preceded by Maat and Horus who face Thoth and the testimony of Horemhab, they should all be included in the   judgment group.   The cartouches are not, as Bouriant suggested,[160] included in the valuable equipment   illustrated above the weighing scene--those articles, like the testimony, face right and are separated by the phrase, facing left, "The Good God...".   These kings, represented by their prenomina, are thus meant to witness the judgment of the deceased along with the sons of Horus and the great ennead. The valuables, including two crowns, have their analogue in the offerings set before the other gods--they are the kings' not Horemhab's. That Thutmose III is included as a witness may indicate that the ruler knew the deceased and his character well enough to judge his truthfulness.[161]

The idea that Horemhab served under Thutmose III was   assumed by Bouriant,[162] and was recently adopted by Hari,[163] but the tombowner never purported to have been in his following. Since beside the weighing scene Horemhab portrayed Thutmose III's ka in a kiosk receiving offerings, he surely felt ties to that king.   The conclusion may be that Horemhab was born during the reign of Thutmose III and knew the pharaoh but   perhaps was not among his entourage.

Horemhab's autobiography may respond to the question, "Does the testimony support a short or long reign for Thutmose IV?". If Horemhab served all 26+ years of Amenhotep II's rule and was 15-20 when Thutmose III   died, then giving Thutmose IV 9 years would have made the official some 41/46+-50/51+ years of age during his floruit as Scribe of recruits. His duties must have been active ones, since he was principally a Royal scribe and Recruits scribe, as well as Overseer of all royal scribes of the army.[164] While not those of a warrior, his duties would have required travel.[165] A very old man would not be the best qualified to carry out such tasks.   On the other hand, if Thutmose IV reigned 33 years and Horemhab served a minimum of 26 years under Amenhotep II, being but 15 when Thutmose   III died, then he would have been at least 73 at the accession of Amenhotep III. This is not impossible, but since his floruit included a period after the death of Thutmose IV, one would not expect such an advanced age. Naturally these estimates must be hypothetical, but Horemhab's biography better supports a 9-year reign than a 33-year one.

Inscriptions and Monuments

A monument of Thutmose IV that might seem to have direct relevance for chronology is the Lateran obelisk,[166] cut and inscribed for Thutmose III who announced on it the "first commencement of erecting a single obelisk in Thebes".[167] The obelisk was never set up, however, but lay at Karnak until Thutmose IV added an inscription and raised it. He spoke of this act for his grandfather saying: "So his Majesty finished the very great single obelisk which his father the king of Upper and Lower Egypt Menkheperre brought, after his Majesty found this obelisk, it having spent thirty-five years lying on its side in the hands of the craftsmen on the southern side of Karnak. My father commanded that I erect it for him since I am his son and his protector."[168] Since the king gave an exact number of years during which the obelisk lay in the craftsmen's quarter, this inscription provides information of a reliable nature. Unfortunately we cannot interpret it because we do not know from what point Thutmose IV reckoned the 35 years. We cannot assume it was from Menkheperre's death; nor especially can we say the 35 represents Amenhotep II's rule; Wente's conclusion to that effect assumed Thutmose IV raised the obelisk in his first year. This is unsubstantiated.[169]

Other inscriptions of Thutmose IV shed little light on the chronology of the reign. For example, there is a reference to the "first campaign of victory".[170] There is extant mention of a second, but there is also no reason to believe a second was necessary.[171] Finally, the numbers of constructions are poor indicators of reign length. Only as a general index can it be noted that Thutmose IV did not construct major buildings, as did his son Amenhotep III. Nor are the numbers of private tombs overwhelming.[172] A total of 12 name the king; 3 include Amenhotep III; 2 Amenhotep II; 2 Thutmose III; and 1 was decorated under Amenhotep II, but the cartouche was changed to Thutmose IV. Seven name only Thutmose IV. (See Chapter 5, Appendix III.)

The chronological evidence for Thutmose IV's reign, taken as a whole, weighs in favor of a short reign. The year dates stop at 8; the anatomical evidence has some margin for error but favors a shorter reign than 33+ years. The astronomical data will be discussed for a long time to come, but Wente's lunar date argument has faults. There is no final settlement for 1490, 1504 or 1479. The heb sed formulae are chronologically valueless and as Kitchen pointed out "do not constitute proof of any historical jubilee in any reign...."[173] Horemhab's testimony supports a short reign over a long one. The Lateran obelisk erected by Thutmose IV is worthless here. So for now there is little reason to quadruple the king's reign, and far more to suppose it short in conformance with Manetho's estimates. A reign of 10-12 years seems to fit the evidence, but absolute dating eludes us still. Nonetheless, Thutmose's family, court circle and major achievements are tangible enough to provide us a long look at the king's decade of rule. We begin with his closest relations -- the princes.

1. E.F. Wente, C. Van Siclen, "A Chronology of the New Kingdom", in <u>SAOC</u> 39 [Festschrift George Hughes], 218. <u>Idem</u>., in <u>An X-ray Atlas of the Royal Mummies</u> (Chicago 1980) 252-54.

2. W.G. Waddell, <u>Manetho</u>, 112-17.

3. W. Helck, <u>Untersuchungen zu Manetho und den Ägyptischen Königslisten</u>, 38-41, 64-69. See now, D.B. Redford, <u>Pharaonic King-Lists, Annals and Day-Books</u>, 242-47.

4. D.B. Redford, <u>Pharaonic King-Lists, Annals and Day-Books</u> (Mississauga, Ontario 1986) 242-47.

5. D. Redford, <u>JNES</u> 25 (1966) 119-20 and <u>Orientalia NS</u> 39 (1970) 4-7; R. Krauss, <u>Das Ende der Amarnazeit</u>, especially 175, 242-43.

6. W. Helck, <u>Urkunden</u> IV, 1539-44. See below, Chapter 4, for full bibliography.

7. El Sayed Higazy, <u>Dossiers d'histoire et d'archéologie</u> 101 (January 1986) 20; El Sayed Higazy and Betsy M. Bryan, "A New Stela of Thutmose IV from the Luxor Temple", <u>Varia Aegyptiaca</u> 2 (1986) 93-100.

8. Urk. IV 1564; A.R. Weill, <u>Recueil</u>, #99.

9. <u>Ibid</u>., #100, 204-05.

10. N. Davies, <u>The Tombs of Two Officials of Tuthmosis IV</u>, 35, pl.XXVI and XXXVII, copy of Hay MSS. with date.

11. J. Champollion, <u>Notices descriptives</u> I, 841-42.

12. C. Aldred, <u>JEA</u> 56 (1970) 113-14.

13. <u>Urk.</u> IV, 1555-56; C.R. Lepsius, <u>Denkmaeler aus Aegypten und Aethiopien</u>, III 69e.

14. W. Helck, <u>Übersetzung</u>, 148.

15. <u>Urk.</u> IV 1564 B; Weill, <u>Recueil</u>, #101; R. Giveon, <u>Tel Aviv</u> 5 (1978) 170-74, pl.44.

16. <u>Urk.</u> 1545. See Chapter 4 for full bibliography. DeMorgan, <u>Cat.</u> 66ff., copied the inscription as a Year 8; Lepsius, <u>Denkmäler Text</u> IV 128, described it as a Year 7. The Year 8 has been adopted here following DeMorgan who recorded the entire inscription. Since the texts are now submerged, we cannot be certain at present.

17. Yvan Koenig, <u>Catalogue des Etiquettes des Jarres hiératiques de Deir el-Médineh"</u> Nos 6242-6497 Fascicle II. #6337.

18. Koenig, op.cit. For comparison with hieratic and royal names, see #'s 6339, 6342 (Horemhab) 6343, 6344, 6353, 6390 (Amenhotep III), 6396 (Horemhab), 6399 (Ay) 6403 (Horemhab) 6405 (Amenhotep III). See also W. Hayes, JNES 10 (1951) fig. 6 #45 "estate of Menkheprure; Year 36: wine", a sealing from Amenhotep III's palace at Malkata; and especially page 97 n.173 for later examples.

19. "Notes on activities" in Report of The Oriental Institute 1976, 50.

20. Called "possible Year 20" in Wente, X-ray Atlas, 253. Kitchen, reviewing Wente's and Van Siclen's chronology, agreed to accept the date apparently without knowing from whence it came. Review in Serapis 4 (1977-78) 69.

21. J.H. Breasted, AJSL 25 (1908) 47-48; Breasted Field Notebook #8, Napata-Soleb 1906-07, 53. I am grateful to Dr. Wente and the Oriental Institute for the opportunity to see Breasted's field notebook. I express my deep thanks to the late Dr. Baer who kindly sent me his ideas about the inscription and generously offered that they be used in whatever way was deemed useful.

22. T. Säve-Söderbergh, Ägypten und Nubien, 207-09, photo on 209.

23. Breasted also makes this point, thus raising the question, AJSL 25, 47-48.

24. LD III 55a.

25. LD III 47a, 49a.

26. D. Dunham, Semna Kumma, pl. 57. Also pl. 56B with Mn-ḫpr-rꜥ only.

27. G. Reisner, ZÄS 69 (1934) 24ff.

28. F. Hintze, Kush 12 (1964) 41, pl. VIIb.

29. F. Hintze, Kush 13 (1965) 14-15 pl. III.

30. Breasted, AJSL 25, 47-48; G. Reisner, JEA 6 (1920) 31.

31. Save-Soderbergh, op. cit., 175, 208.

32. E. Edel, noted in F. Hintze, Kush 13 (1965) 14 n. 12

33. On Nehy see M. Dewachter, Rd'E 28 (1976) 151-53; R. Caminos, The Shrine and Rock Inscriptions of Ibrim, 43.

34. Urk. IV 1635-37. W. Wolf, ZÄS 59 (1924) 157-58.

35. Urk. IV 1637, 6.

36. Urk. IV 1635, 16.

37. Urk. IV 1636, 6 12.

38. Säve-Söderbergh, op. cit., 209, line 5.

39. BM 1131, HTES V, pl. 34.

40. 1) [hieroglyphs]   2) [hieroglyphs]

41. HTES V, pl. 34, line 10.

42. Ibid., line 12.

43. Säve-Söderbergh, op. cit., 209.

44. Breasted, AJSL 25, 105.

45. W.J. Murnane, Ancient Egyptian Coregencies, 32-44, outlines the evidence for the coregency of Hatshepsut and Thutmose III.

46. Cf., Gardiner-Peet, The Inscriptions of Sinai[2], pl. 57, #181, where in year 20 Hatshepsut and Thutmosis III are shown as dual rulers.

47. F. Hintze, Kush 13, (1965) 14-15 notes that RIK [Kumma Rock Inscription] 129 was actually in Tangur West. J. Janssen's publication in Semna Kumma pl. 103f., 169, is by the Oriental Institute photo # 3337. Hintze notes that Breasted's reading of the names as Maatkare and Menkheperre rather than Janssen's 12th dynasty reconstruction is probably correct.

48. BM 1015 HTES V, pl. 35. Two large cartouches, Menkheperre on right and erased name on left. Figures in the scene are erased on both sides, but their legs show they once faced each other. Cartouches and figure are same size.

49. Reported in G.E. Smith, ASAE 4 (1903- 112-15; and G.E. Smith in H. Carter and P.. Newberry, The Tomb of Thoutmosis IV, XLI-XLV. The later report appeared in G.E. Smith, The Royal Mummies, #61073, pls. 29-30, 42=46. The royal mummies have more recently been the subject of a full x-ray study. J.E. Harris, K.R. Weeks, X-raying the Pharaohs, is a cursory look at the findings. Harris and Weeks agreed with Smith's comments on Thutmose IV, but since the latter's discussions are more detailed and have the benefit of being less subject to any effects of exposure, they were utilized for the anatomical description given here. See further below for the fuller discussion in An X-ray Atlas of the Royal Mummies, edited by J.E. Harris and E. F. Wente.

50. Carter and Newberry, op.cit., XLIII.

51. Ibid., XLI.

52. Ibid. XLIII.

53. Smith, The Royal Mummies, 44.

54. Ibid., 45.

55. Ibid.

56. Ibid., VI.

57. For example, E.F. Wente, The Oriental Institute Report 1973/74, 53; idem, "A Chronology", 219; G. Robins, "The Value of the Estimated Ages of the Royal Mummies at Death as Historical Evidence", GM 45 (1981) 63-68.

58. W.M. Krogman and M.J. Baer in J.E. Harris and E.F. Wente, An X-ray Atlas of the Royal Mummies, 188-213, Table with conclusions on 208-09.

59. J.L. Angel, "Physical anthropology: determining sex, age, and individual features", in A. and E. Cockburn, Mummies, Disease, and Ancient Cultures, (Cambridge 1980) 245-248.

60. Krogman and Baer, op.cit., 191ff.

61. T.W. Todd, "Age Changes in the pubic bone. I. The male white pubis.", American Journal of Physical Anthropology 3 (1920) 285-334. idem, "Age changes in the pubic bone; roentgenographic differentiation", American Journal of Physical Anthropology 14 (1930) 255-71. Updated by T.W. McKern and T.D. Stewart, "Skeletal age changes in young American males", Technical report EP-45. Natick, Mass. (1957) Quartermaster Research and Development Command.

62. Angel, op.cit., 247, fig. 14.2.

63. Krogman and Baer, op.cit., 194. On page 196 they note that studies of the humeral head are generally indicative for the 30's, 40's and 50's.

64. Krogman and Baer, op.cit., 189.

65. J.Harris and E. Wente, X-ray Atlas, Foreword, xiii; W. Russell, A. Storey, P. Ponitz, "Radiographic Techniques in the Study of the Mummy", X-ray Atlas, 164-67 with discussion of the problems encountered and the obscurities resulting from the caskets and wrappings.

66. Krogman and Baer, op.cit., 209.

67. T.D. Stewart, "The rate of development of vertebral osteoarthritis in American whites and its significance in skeletal age identification", Leech 28 (1958) 144-51.

68. Ibid., 195; 198, the authors state that they believe vertebral lipping begins in the lumbar region and spreads upward. This should mean that the slight lipping seen on the lumbar and thoracic bodies rated a younger age than for other vertebral regions.

69. I.e., Vault Sutures, Tooth wear, Alveolar Resorption and Tooth Loss, and Clavicle and Sternum. Krogman and Baer, op.cit., 192; Angel, op.cit., 248; T. Todd and D. Lyon, American Journal of Physical Anthropology 7 (1924) 325-84.

70. E.g., pubic symphysis changes, long bone determinations, vertebral age developments and lipping assessments.

71. E.F. Wente in An X-ray Atlas, 234.

72. And see above, n.65, for drawbacks to recent x-ray procedures.

73. Krogman and Baer, X-ray Atlas, 189.

74. I.Isherwood, H. Jarvis and R.A. Fawcitt in Manchester Museum Mummy Project, 36.

75. G. Acsadi, J. Nemeskeri, History of Human Life Span and Mortality, 100-01; the same point is made by Isherwood et als., op.cit., 36.

76. Dr. Lovejoy examined the x-rays on a microfiche reader in August 1989, and despite the lack of original x-rays, strongly asserted that the conditions of the x-ray examinations were simply inadequate to produce the detail needed. The doctor is a pathologist and notes that his own x-rays are prepared with fresh bone, uncontaminated by the effects of mummification, burial, and millennia. In addition, the fact that many mummies were x-rayed in their wooden coffins places a wood fiber overlay pattern within the x-ray which he pointed out countless times on the micro-fiche. For the difficulty of creating a reliable ageing method, even for freshly dead skeletons, see Dr. Owen Lovejoy, et als in several of the following: "Multifactorial Determination of Skeletal Age at Death: A Method and Blind Tests of its Accuracy", American Journal of Physical Anthropology 68 (1985) 1-14; "Chronological Metamorphosis of the Auricular Surface of the Ilium: A New Method for the Determination of Adult Skeletal Age at Death", American Journal of Physical Anthropology 68 (1985) 15-28; "A Revised Method of Age Determination Using the Os Pubis, With a Review and Tests of Accuracy of Other Current Methods of Pubic Symphyseal Aging", American Journal of Physical Anthropology 68 (1985) 28-45; "Dental Wear in the Libben Population: Functional Pattern and Role in the Determination of Adult Skeletal Age at Death", American Journal of Physical Anthropology 68 (1985) 47-56, and four others in the same volume.

77. See E.F. Wente in An X-ray Atlas, 234-85 for the historical materials concerning these people.

78. A similar conclusion appears in Renate Germer, "Problems of Science in Egyptology", in Science in Egyptology, R.A. David, ed.,(Manchester 1986) 525. For another Egyptologist's view of the problems associated with radiographic age estimation, see, Gay Robins, "The Value of the Estimated Ages of the Royal Mummies at Death as Historical Evidence", GM 45 (1981) 63-68.

79. J. Brinkman, BiOr 27 (1970) 305-07; AJA 76 (1972) 271-81.

80. K.A. Kitchen, foreword to M. Bierbrier, <u>The Late New Kingdom</u>; K.A. Kitchen, <u>Serapis</u> 4, 165-80.

81. E. Hornung, <u>Untersuchungen zu Chronologie und Geschichte des Neuen Reiches</u>, 100.

82. Morris Bierbrier, <u>The Late New Kingdom in Egypt</u>. Rolf Krauss, <u>Das Ende der Amarnazeit</u>, and more recently in R. Krauss, <u>Sothis- und Monddaten</u>, 127, where he states quite confidently, "Es gibt derzeit principiell zwei chronologische Ansätze für diese Epoche, die kurze bzw. lange Chronologie genannt seien. In beiden Fällen gilt 1279 v. Chr. als 1. Jahr von R II. Dieser Ansatz ist unseres Erachtens korrekt, weil die Fixierung von 9 Amenhotep I. in 1506 v. Chr. in Kombination mit der relativen Chronologie keine Alternative zu erlauben scheint."

83. Wente, "A Chronology," 223ff.

84. E. Wente, <u>JNES</u> 34 (1975) 265-72.

85. For a recent recapitulation supporting in some ways the conclusions here, see Peter Der Manuelian, <u>Studies in the Reign of Amenophis II</u> Hildesheimer Ägyptologische Beiträge 26 (1987) 1-44, especially 7-16.

86. See Rolf Krauss, "Korrekturen und Ergänzungen zur Chronologie des MR und NR - ein Zwischenbericht", <u>GM</u> 70 (1984) 37-39 for brief recapitulation concerning the moon dates.

87. W. Helck, <u>MDAIK</u> 28 (1972) 101-02. Year 23 new moon date on 3 <u>shemu</u>, day 20 or 21. <u>Urk</u>. IV 652, 13-14 are the day 19 entries emended by Helck.

88. Wente, <u>JNES</u> 34, 265.

89. A. Spalinger, <u>MDAIK</u> 30 (1974) 227-28; see now also A. Spalinger, <u>GM</u> 33 (1979) 47-54 with a reaffirmation of his earlier position.

90. Spalinger, <u>MDAIK</u> 30, 222-26.

91. <u>Ibid</u>., 227.

92. Glen Lello, "Thutmose III's First Lunar Date", <u>JNES</u> 37 (1978) 327-30.

93. Krauss, <u>Sothis- und Monddaten</u>, 121-22.

94. Richard A. Parker, "Some Reflections on the lunar dates of Thutmose III and Ramesses II", in <u>Studies in Ancient Egypt, the Aegean, and the Sudan, Essays in Honor of Dows Dunham</u>, W.K. Simpson and W.M. Davis, eds., (Boston 1981) 146-48.

95. Urk. IV 835, 17-838, 10. This is the final section of the inscription. Wente, JNES 34, 265-72.

96. J. von Beckerath, "Ein Wunder des Amun bei der Tempelgründung in Karnak", MDAIK 37 (1981) 41-49.

97. W. Helck, GM 69 (1983) 37ff.

98. Parker, op.cit., 146-47.

99. Wente, JNES 34, 265-66.

100. Ibid., 266, but n. 12 considers this possibility.

101. Ibid., 266.

102. For the same conclusion see Der Manuelian, op.cit., 15-17.

103. W. Barns, JEA 58 (1972) 159-66.

104. C. Nims, JEA 54, (1968) 162.

105. Barns, op. cit., 64.

106. A. Gardiner, LES, 64-65, 1, 36-46.

107. Barns, op. cit., 164.

108. T.E. Peet, The Rhind Mathematical Papyrus, Pl. A. This example is cited by H. J. Polotsky in "The Emphatic SDM N.F Form," Collected Papers, 45 #4.

109. Ibid.

110. Gardiner, LES 65, 11-14. in mntk p3 nty i.ir.f nw iy n.i m mnt r dd i.rwi3 tw.k t3y.i mr in i.irw.k dd smn.tw m p3 grh r dit wdw t3 b3r i.gm.i.

111. Wente, JNES 34, 266. Some examples of formal dates may be found at: K. Sethe, Lesestücke, 84, 19; 83, 1; 90, 19; 96, 26-97, 1; Urk. IV 367, 3-4. All examples unambiguously refer to near-by verbal constructions. Les. 96, 23-97, 1 is the most relevant here: dd rh.k r ntt hpr prt spdt m 3bd 4 prt sw 16 "saying, "May you know that the going forth of Sothis will occur in the 4th month of peret, day 16'." rh.k should be a substantive prospective sdm.f with the adverbial following clause. The date clearly refers to "will occur" and cannot be brought to the front of "may you know." See the same situation in the Mediggo example discussed in the text.

112. Urk. IV 655, 16-656, 5. rdi in.tw m hr n mš°w r dr.f r [dd] grg.tn sspd h°w.tn r ntt iw.tw r thn r °h3 hn° hrw.pf hsy m dw3. D. Lorton, JARCE 10 (1973) 69 for "defeated."

113. Wente, <u>JNES</u> 34, 266.

114. Von Beckerath, <u>op.cit.</u>, 47.

115. P. Lacau, <u>Stèles du Nouvel Empire</u>, pl. VIII, CG 34012.

116. 'Ist could have begun a separate emphasizing clause. The combination of 'ist + <u>sdm.n.f</u> has been recognized by Polotsky (Egyptian Tenses," 91-93) as a separate particle marker affixed to the emphatic form of <u>sdm.n.f</u>. There is no need to propose any dependence on the foregoing <u>bs.n.f</u>. All three clauses, "then he placed him"; "he introduced him"; and "then the majesty of this noble god desired" function with particles and adjuncts as independent units. This is paralleled at <u>Urk</u>. IV 836, 4-7 where three other constructions are used (see Polotsky, "Les Transpositions," <u>IOS</u> 6, 33; 21 and "Egyptian Tenses" s36). The various constructions used in both passages all achieve a single purpose--relating several independent events in a brief space; and this underscores the fact that 'ist 3b n began such a separate clause.

117. CG 34012 shows space for <u>m</u> at the beginning of line 11.

118. <u>Wb</u> III, 57-61, gives both <u>hb</u> and <u>hbt</u> for this word, though the latter reference is of late date. The confusion of <u>hb</u> and <u>hbyt</u> is also possible. That the genitival adjective is meant, not the relative, follows from the use of <u>n(y)</u> in <u>hb tpy n pd šs</u>.

119. A. Gardiner, <u>Grammar</u>[3], s223.

120. There is a parallel to the god placing the king at ceremonial stations and using the same preposition. <u>Urk</u>. IV 158, 17-159, 1.

121. Polotsky, "Egyptian Tenses", 91-93. See above, n.90 for further references.

122. <u>Urk</u>. IV 835, 17-836, 1. As said before, the text shows an uninterrupted sequence in the lines cited. If there is any question concerning the timing of events it involves not whether the miracle occurred before new moon day but when the day changed in the course of the incidents related. It may be that the space which the god spent celebrating included the passage of a night, or it may be that 836, 6 <u>m ht nn wd3 nb</u>... shows new moon day has arrived. In the latter case, the festival would have taken place on the same day as the ceremony, just as Wente suggested, <u>JNES</u> 34, 266 with note 14. In either case there is no indication in the text that "... the oracle of Amon, carried on the shoulders of lay priests, upset the planned program of Thutmose III by not returning to the holy of holies."

123. R. Parker, <u>JNES</u> 16 (1957) 39-42.

124. J. Von Beckerath, review of M. Bierbrier, <u>BiOr</u> 33 (1976) 177ff. W. Barta, "Die Ägyptischen Sothisdaten und ihre Bezugsorte", <u>JEOL</u> 26 (1979-80) 26-34. J. Von Beckerath, "Noch einmal zu den Bezugspunkten der Sothisdaten", <u>GM</u> 83 (1984) 13-15.

125. Krauss, Sothis- und Monddaten, passim. If we must eliminate the P. Ebers date, then ths question is moot. Krauss' argument for an Upper Egyptian siting location is convincing, however. Thebes provides most of the evidence for the early 18th Dynasty and the end of the Second Intermediate Period even now. For example, the Rhind Papyrus, the Kamose stelae, the royal tomb material. Hornung considered Thebes the working capital in the early part of the dynasty (E. Hornung, Untersuchungen, 20; also J. Von Beckerath, Tanis und Theben, 106.) Stock believed Memphis would have been repugnant to the early kings of the 18th Dynasty (H. Stock, MDOG 94 (1963) 79.) This seems an unlikely notion and one countered by Wente's assertions that a continuity of Memphite priesthood during the Hyksos domination (JNES 34, 269-70) could be proven from the 22nd Dynasty genealogy of high priests at Memphis who named Hyksos rulers immediately prior to Ahmose.(Recent excavations in Memphis apparently bear Wente out in demonstrating the existence of early 18th Dynasty levels.) Wente also considered that Egypt could not have tolerated dual lunar calendars during the Second Intermediate Period. This last suggestion simply cannot be addressed without information. Even the organization of the counry during that period is still uncertain. Helck, Oriens Antiquus 8 (1969) 281-85, suggested that the 17th Dynasty produced its own ranks of organizations based on ancient Upper Egyptian types. The speculations have not brought the question to conclusion.

126. R. Krauss, Sothis-und Monddaten, 44ff.

127. W. Helck, "Haremhab und das Sothisdatum des Pap. Ebers", GM 67 (1983) 47-49; U. Luft, "Noch einmal zum Ebers-Kalender", GM 92 (1986) 69-77. But now, J. Von Beckerath, "Das Kalendarium des Papyrus Ebers und das Sothisdatum vom 9. Jahr Amenophis' I", SAK 14 (1987) 27-33, defends the Ebers date for chronological purposes, but sites it in Thebes giving absolute solutions for such.

128. R. Parker, rev. of Hornung, Untersuchungen, Rd'E 19 (1967) 188.

129. Wente, JNES 34, 268. Actually Wente's proposal uses only six fewer years before Thutmosis III than would a 1479 date.

130. Wente, "A Chronology", 218-21.

131. Ibid., 218.

132. P. Barguet and M. Dewachter, Le Temple d'Amada II & IV; see one text in Urk. IV 1568, 18.

133. See bibliography below in Chapter 4. B. Letellier, Hommages Sauneron, 64. Translated as a wish by Helck, Übersetzung, 156, for example. This ꜣr.f may be a substantive form of sdm.f prospective, (Polotsky, IOS 6, 23-25) or it may have a separate base (Callender, Middle Egyptian, 25-26, 37-38).

134. Further below. For example, PM II^2 71.

135. Chapter 4 section 13 for discussion of the chapel.

136. Generally the assumption has been that the 30-year principle was not inflexible. L. Borchardt and H. Ricke, Ägyptische Tempel, 43 n. 2; and E. Meyer, Geschichte des Altertums II, 1, 149 n. 2. C. Aldred, ZÄS 94 (1967) 2, suggested that the Amada texts referred to Amenhotep II and that Thutmose IV was co-regent at the time.

137. Wente, JNES 34, 271-72.

138. Ibid., 272, n. 51; see also "A Chronology", 219.

139. Wente, The Oriental Institute Report 1973/74, 53.

140. Wente, "A Chronology", 219.

141. William J. Murnane, "The Sed Festival: A Problem in Historical Method", MDAIK 37 (1981) 369-76. Quotation from p. 375.

142. G. Haeny, Beiträge Bfo 9(1970) 16.

143. Redford, Pharaonic King-Lists, 185-86.

144. Ibid., 182.

145. G. Wagner, "Inscriptions Grecques du Temple de Karnak", BIFAO 70 (1971) 10, citing the titularies of Ptolemy Epiphanes V and Ptolemy IV Philopator. It is a trilingual of Ptolemy IV that he cites with a hieroglyphic translation. See also references given by Simpson, "Studies in the Twelfth Egyptian Dynasty: I-II", JARCE 2 (1963) 59 n.31.

146. In fact it is Sesostris I who appears to be the inspiration for many temple constructions at Karnak and for correct kingship in general. The rulers of Dynasty 18, from its early years, imitated the buildings and relief styles of Sesostris I; Redford pointed out that Amenhotep I so emulated the Middle Kingdom ruler that he recreated his chapels and decorated a gate at Karnak "on which the list of festivals is copied from a 12th Dynasty original without even shifting the prt-spdt to its new position in the calendar!" [Redford, Pharaonic King-Lists, 171.] But it might be fair to say that Sesostris I, like his later imitators, was interested in promoting his family's legitimacy. His long reign produced a number of monuments linking him and his father to the Old Kingdom rulers and to the cult of the great god of Heliopolis. His celebration of the sed festival in year 30/31 may well have reactivated a principle abandoned since the Sixth Dynasty.

147. Ibid., 59-63.

148. See E. Hornung, Studien zum Sedfest (1974); Simpson, op.cit., 59-63; Murnane, op.cit., 369-70, for dated inscriptional references to the jubilee from the earliest times onward.

149. Hornung, op.cit., 51-54.

150. For the Year after the 25th count, see Murnane, op.cit., 369 and note 5.

151. The Year 2 of Nebtawyre Mentuhotep is the best example of this. In the Wadi Hammamat is a scene of Pepi I before Min of Coptus with sp tpy hb sd behind the king. The exact date, "year after the 18th time", 3 shemu, day 27" for the first sed appears on a nearby text.[J. Couyat, P. Montet, Hammamat, #63 Pl. XVI; #107 Pl. XXVII, has the date running h orizontally above.] Also in the Wadi Hammamat is the scene of Mentuhotep Nebtawyre before Min of Coptus in a very similar fashion. Here is included the date, running above the scene, year 2, month 2 of akhet day 3, and sp tpy hb sd behind the king. [Hammamat, #110, 77 Pl. XXIX. The scenes differ only in the headdresses of Min and in the kings' hand motions.] The coincidence is difficult to ignore. Hornung suggested Mentuhotep was celebrating the 30th year after Mentuhotep Nebhepetre unified Egypt, but it is more probable that Nebtawyre simply borrowed the scene from his honored predecessor and placed the present date on it. The borrowing would represent a hope by the later king to enjoy what the earlier had. Mueller made a similar conclusion in noting that the date of year 2 referred to Vizier Amenemhet's quarry report below the scene. He stated "the inscription thus attests only the hope Mentuhotep would eventually reach his jubilee, not that he was about to celebrate it".[D. Mueller, rev. of Hornung, Studien zum Sedfest, in BiOr 33 (1976) 172.

152. E.g., Year 2 of Nebtawyre Mentuhotep; Year 22 of Osorkon II; the cattle counts of Pepi I; Year 31 of Sesostris I; and perhaps even Year 16 of Hatshepsut. While these dates might refer to the jubilee ceremonies, in no case is this sure. Sesostris I left monuments linking himself to the sp tpy hb sd as did Osorkon II and Hatshepsut.

153. Hornung, op.cit., 54-55. Wente and Van Siclen, "A Chronology", 226. Removal of the 30-year principle may reveal political or religious motives lurking behind the celebrations of rulers such as Hatshepsut and Amenhotep IV.

154. Acsadi and Nemeskéri, op. cit., 195-98, Table 62, 196.

155. A. and A. Brack, Das Grab des Haremheb. Theben Nr. 78 (Mainz 1980).

156. Brack and Brack, op.cit., pls. 56, 65. U. Bouriant, "Tombeau d'Harmhabi", MMAF V, 413-33, pl. V; Urk. IV 1589-90.

157. Text reads 𓆄𓏤 𓏠𓂝𓈖𓇋𓏏 but must be a mistake for iw šms n.i as in Urk. IV 1004, 2 & 11; 1005, 2 (Tjanni).

158. Bouriant, op. cit., pl. V; Brack and Brack, op. cit., pl. 56, 65.

159. Bouriant says Thebes, op. cit., 432.

160. Ibid., 432.

161. But cf. Brack and Brack, op.cit., 85, who see Thutmose III as a necropolis deity. To their observation of his name in the tombs of Nakht (52) and Khonsu (31), add the representation in the tomb of Amenmose (89), also of Amenhotep III date. They may be correct in their observation, but this would not eliminate Haremhab's affinity to him as the ruler of his childhood.

162. Bouriant, op. cit., 432.

163. R. Hari, Aegyptus 47 (1967) 66.

164. Urk. IV 1595-96.

165. A. Schulman, Military Rank, Title and Organization in the Egyptian New Kingdom, 63-64.

166. Urk. IV 1548-52; O. Marucchi, Gli Obelischi egiziani de Roma, Tav. I, II.

167. Ibid., south side.

168. Urk. IV 1550, 3-9.

169. Wente, "A Chronology", 227.

170. Urk. IV 1554, 17.

171. A treaty was struck between Mitanni and Egypt. Chapter 6.

172. Wente's total of 19 is inaccurate; "A Chronology", 230, citing PM I^{2}1, but without giving any tomb numbers.

173. Kitchen, in Serapis 4, 73.

ALL THE KINGS' SONS

About most Egyptian kings we know little or nothing before their accession, and what we do know is often written retrospectively in the rulers' own reigns. The mid-18th Dynasty, however, is an exception to the rule. Princes are quite visible at this time, both by their numbers and their activity as officials, priests, military officers and dedicants. Since early in the Dynasty the institution of Royal Nurse had functioned for the nurture and tutelage of royal children. The documentation for princes in the middle of the Dynasty is, in part, likely witness to the success of that institution which trained several generations of princes (and princesses) to represent the kingship in official and cultic settings--and someday to take it over. There is a sizeable amount of evidence concerning the brothers of Thutmose IV, for example, and there are more than a handful of young "princes" whose family connections to Thutmose are apparent but unclear. It is against the backdrop of the expansive middle-18th Dynasty royal family that we must consider the succession of Thutmose IV, bearing in mind that our information, largely from monumental inscriptions, is ambiguous as concerns historical questions.

The question of Thutmose IV's Succession

The Sphinx Stela relates an incident about a prince Thutmose who stopped to rest in the shadow of the Sphinx.[1] In a dream the god Horemakhet spoke to him and called him, "my son, Thutmose"; he promised to deliver the kingship of Egypt to him and asked him to clear the sand away from the god's image. The prince then immediately advised his comrades to bring offerings to the god and no doubt set about clearing the sphinx (the text, however, breaks off).

Selim Hassan excavated the area of the Sphinx amphitheatre and temple of Amenhotep II in 1936 and 1937.[2] During that time he discovered mudbrick revetment walls of Thutmose IV which prove the king cleared the sand from the Sphinx as directed on the Stela. During this period Hassan was assisted by Mohsin Bakir, who aided in the excavations, and Miss Dorothy Eady, who was his secretary.[3] Miss Eady is better known to the world at large as "Omm Sety", an Englishwoman whose love for Egypt and things Egyptian led her to a simple existence working on a jigsaw puzzle of fragments from Sety I's Abydos Temple. Omm Sety always felt King Sety had raised a naughty son to become pharaoh. But Sety I's child Ramesses II was not the only prince whom Omm Sety believed had mischievously eliminated an older brother's claim to kingship. Thutmose IV was, in Omm Sety's opinion, every bit as malicious. Miss Eady composed in large part the section for Selim Hassan's Great Sphinx in which Thutmose IV appears as the evil usurper,[4] and the dramatic expression of the argument presented there haunts discussions of the king's accession even today.[5] In conversations held with Omm Sety several years before her death, she proclaimed with the same vehemence the judgment of prince Thutmose that she expressed in her writing. The tone is one that would be difficult to parallel from recent works. It bears quotation at length because of its conclusions and its influence.

[Referring to princes whose names are erased on stelae from Giza] "... If this is true, then the most likely person to have erased their names was Thothmes IV, their younger brother. When we come to consider the inscription on the Granite Stela, we shall see that the Sphinx speaks to Thothmes in a dream, and makes a bargain with him, to the effect that if he, the Prince, will clear away the sand which is encumbering his image, the Sphinx will give him the Crown of Egypt. Clearly then, Thothmes was not the Heir to the Throne... We may suppose, then, that these elder brothers stood in the way of his ambitions, and that Thothmes removed them in some way, either by death or disgrace, and then obliterated their names, in order that their very memories might be forgotten. He may even have fabricated the story of his dream in order to justify his action, and this would account for the promptitude with which he fulfilled his part of the 'bargain'.

...I am afraid that this theory does not present Thothmes IV in a very favourable light, and if he was not actually a wholesale murderer (and there seem to be grounds for supposing that he was), at least he was a cold-hearted egoist. Perhaps he was the cause of the sadness which his mother, Queen Tyaa, complains in the inscription on her statue.

But to return to the unfortunate Prince Amen-em-Apt; he apparently upheld the family tradition of visiting the Sphinx and dedicating stelae, so we may suppose that he was also a hunter in the Valley of Gazelles. Probably he and his brothers used to hunt regularly in this district, and among their number was the sly and secretive youth who was afterwards to become Thothmes IV."[6]

Although the condemnatory tone Omm Sety employed is no longer present in historical discussions, Thutmose IV is still often considered a possible usurper[7] as a result of the dramatic scenario quoted here. None of the facts of the succession are certain, however, and now some scholars are turning away from a grim interpretation of the Sphinx Stela.[8] A recent attempt[9] to sweep away the issue entirely in my opinion may have gone too far, but it emphasized the argument I made with in the unpublished form of this work with respect to the Sphinx Stela, that Thutmose IV should not be considered a usurper on the basis of that text. The Sphinx Stela without the burden of Omm Sety's story contains motifs common to royal inscriptions of the period.

Prince Thutmose of the Sphinx Stela was, of course, King Thutmose IV himself.[10] The story cleverly describes him both as a royal son and a divine one (of Horemakhet, Atum, and Re, as well as the inheritor of Horus). One must assume that Thutmose was therefore content to be termed simply "king's son" and that he did not think it necessary to disguise that rank. Nor need we assume that the Sphinx Stela proves that Thutmose was not the eldest son.[11] The Sphinx Stela of Amenhotep II also calls prince Amenhotep "king's son"[12]; and again the ruler apparently felt that was appropriate. Once within the narrative, however, Thutmose III spoke of "his eldest son"[13], thereby revealing the actual position of the prince. Thus although Amenhotep was "eldest King's son", he did not always use the title. We may conclude that the age distinction was <u>not necessarily</u> the functional one. Thutmose's omission of it, therefore, provides no clear indication of his true rank.

The Sphinx Stela like other 18th Dynasty royal inscriptions emphasizes divine determination and birth for kings.[14] So it is that Hatshepsut, followed by Thutmose III[15] used the same mode of appointment as did Thutmose IV--that is, the divine oracle. The rulers of the 18th Dynasty, without exception, term themselves offspring of gods.[16] Amenhotep II's lengthy prologue to his Sphinx Stela makes him the son of at least six deities, most notably Amun, and Thutmose IV on his Giza monument claims to be the "son of Atum of his body". Visual demonstration of divine kinship appears in temple scenes[17] of the gods themselves engendering, birthing and suckling the pharaoh. Evidence of Thutmose IV's own divine birth from an unprovenanced temple scene will be presented in Chapter 4.

Kings sometimes claimed their succession by both divine and earthly origins in the same text: in the coronation text of Hatshepsut Amun boasts of his daughter before the gods; Thutmose I likewise proclaims her kingship to his people.[18] The same is true in Amenhotep II's Sphinx Stela, where the gods are given ultimate credit for the king's right to rule, but Thutmose III also recognizes his son's destiny to rule.[19]

Since we are satisfied that Amenhotep II was his father's choice[20], we accept the description of his appointment on his Sphinx Stela as historical documentation[21]. However, since we know that Hatshepsut did not actually succeed her father as pharaoh (although her equal status with Thutmose II on Karnak monuments suggest she may have shared power with her husband),[22] we read her Coronation text as a purely legitimating fiction.[23] This interpretation ignores the purpose of these texts which is to illustrate that the divine source of rule has been rightly bestowed on the gods' choice. The motif of divine appointment effectively negated the issue of usurpation, for Hatshepsut was determined as ruler in the same manner as other kings. The texts provide the illustrations that the pharaohs' fitness to rule has been divinely recognized.

Zivie believed the importance of Horemakhet as a royal protector in the 18th

Dynasty and the antiquity of Giza itself were most significant in Thutmose's choice of the Sphinx as divine benefactor.[24] However, by bestowing the rule through a regional form of the sun god Re (Horemakhet was called Re-Horakhty on occasion) Thutmose IV was following custom. Re-Horakhty, together with Amun-Re, appear as officiants at Hatshepsut's coronation.[25] Amenhotep II's Sphinx Stela calls the king both the son of Amun and the offspring of Horakhty, and it states that both Amun and Re ordained the kingship for him.[26] Thutmose IV also received the rule from the sun god and from Amun-Re as a separate monument attests.[27]

The text of a naos, most likely from Upper Egypt, states, "Now his Majesty found this stone in the form of a divine falcon when he was very young (inpu). Then [Amun] decreed [to him] to perform the kingship of the Two Lands as the Horus Strong Bull, Perfect of diadems, lord of diadems, Menkheprure, given life like Re".

The stone, apparently an image of a falcon, had been in the shrine. In any case the oracle proclaiming Thutmose IV's rule by the southern national god confirms that he received his hegemony over the Two Lands from both major gods. Its original location is unknown, but one might surmise by the shrine's average quality that it rested near the stone's find place, perhaps not in a temple at all. (The stone within was probably a nodding falcon of the type known since the Predynastic.)

In summation, Thutmose IV's employment of the "divine happenstance" setting on his Sphinx Stela and the naos was normative in the mid-18th Dynasty. Although we cannot be sure that political events do not lurk behind the king's actions described on the Stela, the text itself is not a useful indicator of the king's legitimacy.

Thutmose's Seniority among Princes

A scene from the tomb of Hekarnehhe at Thebes shows young Thutmose IV seated on the lap of his nurse Hekareshu.[28] The inscription above called the prince "eldest king's son of his body, beloved of him, whom Amun himself magnified to be lord of what the Aten encircles, the lord of the Two Lands, Menkheprure". The nurse's title appears as "Nurse to the eldest king's son of his body, Thutmose kha-khau (appearance of crowns)".[29] This is the only monument which terms Thutmose the "eldest king's son". It is difficult to assess the significance of such a title in this context, since the tomb dates to Thutmose's reign, and he appears twice elsewhere in the chapel as a full-grown ruler.

If the title is to be taken literally, Thutmose was an eldest son at some undetermined point, for the rank probably designates the "eldest surviving son"[30]. Thus Thutmose IV may have acquired the right to such a title no earlier than the date of the tomb's decoration. It is, however, also possible that "king's eldest son" (s3 nsw smsw) was here an honorific title. . Parallel epithets called rulers "eldest son of [X deity]". Thutmose IV, for example, is referred to as "the eldest son beneficial to him whom made him" on the Lateran obelisk.[31] Amenhotep III is titled "eldest son of [Amun] great of [monuments], numerous of miracles" in the Luxor Temple.[32] The seniority of Thutmose IV at his accession, based on the term "eldest king's son" in Hekarnehhe's tomb cannot be supported.

Thutmose's Age at Accession

Brunner, followed by Wente and Van Siclen, suggested that Thutmose IV was a small child when he took the throne.[33] Brunner based his assertion on a reference to Thutmose as an inpu "small child" on a foundation stone from his Theban residence (?)[34]. A plaque is inscribed for "the Good God Menkheprure, beloved of Amun-Re king of the gods: the house of his Majesty when he was/is an inpw". (pr ḥm.f ti sw m inpw.) Brunner argued that inpw applies to small children and that the text proved Thutmose was still such after he became king. The meaning of inpw defended by Brunner, however, must stand. Meeks, in discussing the term, concluded that inpw technically referred to children not yet walking (like Anubis, still on the bed). He pointed out that inpw paralleled the common phraseology of rulers who acted or were ordained "while still in the egg."[35]

Brunner's interpretation of Thutmose IV's plaque is, however, contradicted by the very existence of a statue of Prince Thutmose shown as a man. A look at two other texts confirms the evidence from his statue as prince that the inscriptions do not refer to Thutmose as a small child upon accession.

On the Sphinx Stela, Thutmose's fitness to be king in year 1 is explained by his precocious beauty and strength "when his Majesty was an inpw like Horus in Chemmis". (ist ḥm.f m inpw mi Ḥr m ȝḫ-bit).[36] The use of ist here, introducing several retrospective segments, is the common situational one[37]-i.e., providing necessary information outside the straight narrative.[38] "When his Majesty was an inpw like Horus in Chemmis, his beauty like Harendotes, he was seen [already] like the god himself." Four such passages introduced by ist are employed up to the point where the distinctive time marker wˁ m nn n hrw ḫpr "one of these days it happened that...." appears. The retrospective is not a simple narrative but a series of characterizations about the prince and his activities up to the significant event-- his dream. The purpose is obvious--to explain Thutmose's suitability to the task and to the kingship. In what remains of the text ist does not recur, for its use as a time and situation particle is no longer necessary. One can find the same employment within Amenhotep II's Sphinx Stela where it is used to describe Amenhotep's brilliant youth as a co-regent and earlier. As in the Dream Stela the time is brought forward abruptly by m ḫt nn šˁw ḥm.f m nsw, "after this, his Majesty was caused to appear as king."[39]

Clearly Amenhotep does not appear as an inpw upon his accession. Although

the text does not provide the age at which he became a hwn-nfr, it does tell us that
his feats of prowess occurred at that time of his youth, not earlier. As an ỉnpw he
loved and understood horses already, but as a hwn-nfr he performed his now-famous
equestrian acts. Likewise, although Thutmose's inscription notes that as an ỉnpw his
perfection of goodness (nfrw) and power was already apparent to others, at the
time of his dream Thutmose was old enough to ride alone with companions amidst
the pyramids.

A past time setting also appears in the naos inscription of Thutmose IV referred
to above.[40] ỉst gm n ḥm.f ỉnr pn m shr bỉk ntr[y] ỉw.f ỉnpw ỉst wḏ n [n.f ỉmn] ỉrt
nsyt t3wy m Hr k3 nḫt twt ḥᶜw Mnhprwrᶜ dỉ ᶜnḫ mỉ Rᶜ. "Now his Majesty found
this stone in the form of a divine falcon while he was very young. Then [Amun]
decreed [to him] to perform the kingship of the Two Lands as the Horus Strong
Bull perfect of diadems, lord of diadems, Menkheprure, given life like Re." The use
of two ỉst particles with the sḏm.n.f provides us two completed situations describing
the statue.[41] There is no indication of when in time the events occurred with
respect to each other. The inscription on the naos therefore describes the
significance of this statue in having provided the oracle for Thutmose's kingship, and
the reference to ỉnpw, as Brunner indicated with respect to Hatshepsut, is to "das
unreife Alter des späteren Königs"[42]. In both the Sphinx Stela and the naos,
Thutmose's fitness to be king has been emphasized by notice of his precocity and
divine favor.

The foundation plaque's reference to "the house of his Majesty tỉ sw m ỉnpw
may also be considered. Brunner's interpretation supposes that a house was
dedicated in which the king was to reside only as a toddler. This is difficult to
imagine. More likely, if this is a foundation plaque employed at a ceremony, then
it represented the rebuilding of Thutmose's childhood home and should be translated
"the house of his Majesty when he was very young". Weinstein noted particularly
the commemorative function of foundation deposits and mentioned, as well, deposits
associated with royal secular buildings.[43]

In conclusion, neither text may reasonably be understood to recognize Thutmose
IV as a ruling monarch while he was a small child. The Sphinx Stela portrayed the
pre-accession prince as of age to race chariots and respond to the requests of the
Sphinx. A statue of the prince, made before his throne-taking, depicts a grown
male. The conclusion is inescapable that Thutmose IV was of at least adolescent
years at the death of Amenhotep II.

The Princes and their Monuments
Was Thutmose Crown Prince?

As said earlier, Thutmose IV is himself known from a statue he dedicated while
still a prince. A statue excavated at the Mut temple (CG 923)[44] represents Prince

Thutmose kneeling and holding a Hathor symbol. The statue of fine limestone is of high quality despite its broken condition. The prince is headless and preserved from the mid-torso only. Two pieces, broken through the sistrum pillar, remain. The prince has stylized abdominal folds and wears an ankle-length kilt belted similarly to royal kilts. The form of statue is similar to that of Senmut in the Metropolitan Museum (48.149.7), but it does not have an inscribed backrest.[45] A translation of the stelophore follows; photographs appear here for the first time in figs. 1-4.

Around base:
Facing left: A gift which the King gives to Mut [Mistress of A]sher, lady of Heaven, mistress of the gods, that she may give life, prosperity and health to the Ka of the King's Son, beloved of the Lord of the Two Lands, Thutmose.
Facing right: A gift which the King gives to Mut the Great, the Mistress of Asher, who propitiates the Lord of the gods, that she may give pleasure, joy, the highest of praises and love to the Ka of the King's Son Thutmose.
Sistrum column: [Mut] Mistress of Asher.
Atop the sistrum, before dedicant's [face]: Everything which goes forth from the offering table of the Mistress of the Two Lands to the Ka of the King's Son Thutmose.
Atop base: Right: Nurse of the Royal Children, Hekareshu
Left: True King's Son, beloved of him, Thutmose.

Thutmose is termed either simply "king's son" (s3 nsw) or "king's true son beloved of him" (s3 nsw m3^c mry.f), a title applied to true princes in the New Kingdom. Interesting but not entirely explainable is the mention of Thutmose's nurse Hekareshu on the statuette's socle. His title as "Nurse of the royal children" precedes his name, but all other texts and dedications are for the prince alone. Since there are a number of nurse statues known from the mid-18th Dynasty, this exceptional case of a nurse mentioned by the nursling can only be interpreted as evidence that Thutmose was older than a young child. Hekareshu perhaps accompanied the prince at the presentation of this statuette, but Thutmose's image remained in the Mut temple as adorant and offerer.

Some years ago Frandsen[46] supported the view, also held by Habachi[47], that this prince was the future Thutmose IV and not, as Gauthier[48] followed in the revised edition of Porter and Moss[49] believed, a son of that king. Frandsen's conclusion must be correct, for the association of Hekareshu with young Thutmose IV is proudly displayed on the tomb chapel wall of TT 64. There Hekareshu's nurse title specifically links him to the king. However, Hekareshu's title on the statue is solely royal nurse; he does not bear the title consistently applied to him in Thutmose IV's reign, "God's Father" (it ntr). The "God's Father" rank was used by Frandsen in the same discussion[50] to assert that because Hekareshu lacked the God's Father rank on the prince's statue, Thutmose was not eldest son and crown prince at the time of the statue's making.[51] Since this interpretation of the title assumes a specific meaning for ỉt ntr, further discussion is in order.

Frandsen relied on Brunner's discussion whether the "Erzieher der Kronprinzen" was designated by the title of "God's Father" during the 18th Dynasty. He proposed that Senmut, Hekareshu and Ay fell in that category, although he allowed that the title was held by diverse officials and relatives of the royal family. In noting the combination of mnˁy with ỉt ntr in the titles of Senmut and Hekareshu, Brunner concluded God's father meant Crown Prince Preceptor for those men, and he further concluded that Ay's rank as God's Father indicated that he was Akhenaten's nurse as well, although he did not bear the nurse's title.[52] Frandsen extended Brunner's conclusions to presume a nurse's charge was not crown prince if the guardian was not a God's Father.

The first difficulty with Brunner's study is his failure to mention when (and by whom) the rank of God's Father was awarded; but he did agree with Gardiner that ntr referred to the living king.[53] If Gardiner was correct, then one can suggest when nurses received their God's Fathers titles. The datable examples of ỉt ntr pertaining to Hekareshu belong to the reign of Thutmose IV,[54] and the logical assumption is that the title was awarded by the ruler to honor his childhood educator. With respect to Ay, Brunner himself proposed that Ay's use of the title at Amarna and his prestige there reflected Akhenaten's veneration for his own nurse.[55] As to Senmut we are uncertain, but we can say that he received the title during Hatshepsut's reign. Senmut said: "I raised the eldest princess and God's Wife Nefrure, may she live!, I being given to her as God's Father inasmuch as I was beneficial to the king".[56] This would be of greater aid if we knew that Nefrure was throne heir at the time, and if we knew whether ỉt ntrt referred to Hatshepsut or Nefrure. We can observe that the text honored Senmut's service to Hatshepsut and stated that because of it he was entrusted with Nefrure's care. We must conclude, therefore, that two and perhaps all three of Brunner's examples of God's Father as "Erzieher der Kronprinzen" indicate that meaning only in hindsight.

In fact the title of God's Father is a poor indicator of throne heirs: it does not appear with some nurses who did educate kings-to-be (Min and Hekarnehhe)[57] while it does appear with persons who have no known connection with princes as well as with persons linked to princes of low rank; e.g., the Herald Re in the reign of Thutmose IV was linked to princes Aakheprure and Amenhotep by a graffito at Konosso.[58] The argument for an "Erzieher der Kronprinzen" meaning of God's Father is further weakened by the large numbers of titleholders--six in Thutmose IV's reign alone.[59] Three of those men have some known relationship to a prince, and three have none whatever. Other God's Fathers who served between the reigns of Thutmose III and Amenhotep III lacked ties with princes: they were viziers, Viceroys of Nubia, generals, heralds and priests.[60] No doubt all were close to the court, but their titles did not involve the crown princes in any verifiable way.

A court advisor's role is the most sensible understanding for the function of a God's Father,[61] for the title was given to a variety of officials. The coincidence of two nurses of future kings as God's Fathers is hardly astonishing, since nurses were naturally close to the royal family. And the one thing God's Fathers consistently exhibit is such a closeness. Brunner's speculation that because Ay was God's Father, he must have been Akhenaten's nurse is not consistent with the distribution of the title.[62] Frandsen's conclusion likewise requires proof. If no example of God's Father can be proven to mean "Erzieher der Kronprinzen", one cannot argue that Thutmose IV or any other king was not heir because his nurse was not God's Father. The statue of Prince Thutmose which mentions the nurse Hekareshu is neither proof that the boy was throne heir nor proof that he was not. Its importance is rather in its evidence of the independent participation of the prince in the Theban cult center.

Other Kings' Sons

Thutmose IV was the son of Amenhotep II by the claim of his monuments and once by a private tomb owner. And anatomist Elliot Smith marveled at Thutmose' resemblance to Amenhotep II.[63] Other sons are in evidence, two attested early in Amenhotep's reign perhaps among them. On a Cairo museum statue of one Minmose,[64] a royal scribe and Overseer of works, whose career bridged the rules of Thutmose III and Amenhotep II appear the princes, Nedjem and Webensenu both called "king's son beloved of him". The assumption that Amenhotep was their father is made likely by a find of Webensenu's canopics in KV 35, Amenhotep II's tomb, apparently unrelated to the cache of royal mummies.[65] The prince was there called "king's son of his body, beloved of him",[66] and another fragment named him as "king's son and Overseer of horses".[67] The second son, Nedjem, is attested only on Minmose's statue, but his presence with Webensenu would at least imply their brotherhood. Since Webensenu and Nedjem were probably brothers (less likely uncles) of Thutmose, the question of their age is of some interest, and the career of Minmose appears to be the sole means for inquiry.

Minmose is a well-known person who has left a number of inscribed monuments, including three statues. A block statue of black granite from Medamud[68] bears a long autobiographical inscription and contains several phrases helpful in dating. Minmose said he followed Thutmose III and was present at the defeat of the Nehesy and also kept the accounts of a victory in Retenu.[69] After this he mentioned duty as a royal agent with the army in the Takhsy region.[70] The Nubian produce which would have accrued from a razzia of Nehesy first appeared in the annals with years 31/32, and the Takhsy expedition appears to represent the year 33 campaign.[71] This would point to Minmose's activity at that time. Such a date is supported by the year 33 annal mention of a stela emplacement in Nahrin.[72] Minmose, on an inscription he left later in his career, recalled that he erected such a stela.[73]

The text in the statue inscription followed Minmose's military career by detailing his appointment as director of works in all temples, and a list of the institutions followed.[74] He performed priest services in temples of Horus of Letopolis, Bast of Memphis, and Montu of Thebes and also directed the work there.[75] Minmose finally termed himself "hereditary prince and Mayor, Overseer of Nefrut cattle of Amun and royal scribe" in addition to his major title, Overseer of Works in the temples of Upper and Lower Egyptian Gods.[76] All of these titles may be presumed to have been Minmose's while Thutmose III still lived, since no other ruler was mentioned on the statue. ("Menkheperre" appears on Minmose's shoulder and in the text.)[77] A date in that king's rule is therefore firm.

A black granite statue of Minmose and his parents from Nebesheh,[78] now in the Ashmolean, contains the full titles conferred on Minmose by Thutmose III after his military service. He is called Overseer of Prophets of Montu lord of Thebes, Overseer of major works in the temples of the Gods of Upper and Lower Egypt, Overseer of bulls of Amun, true royal scribe, beloved of him. Minmose's father, the Judge Nay, and his mother, Rennefer, received offerings on the statue along with him.

The Cairo statue mentioned above was dedicated to Osiris lord of Busiris and great god lord of Abydos.[79] It is much weathered and faceless but is of black granite and in a block style similar to the Medamud piece. The heads of the princes are visible on either side of Minmose.[80] The inscription is short and names the "Overseer of works in this Temple and royal scribe". Minmose's parents are also mentioned.[81] The titles, though abbreviated, are his characteristic ones on the Medamud and Nebesheh statues. As Overseer of works in this temple Minmose was specifically linked to the place of his donation; the title was a variant of his fuller rank.

Beyond the titles on the Cairo museum statue, several phrases in the inscription indicate the piece was made late in Minmose's life. The short offering formula asks for two things: offerings from Osiris' table and a fine burial after old age.[82] Minmose's other two statues do not request burial, although his Medamud autobiography indicates he had prepared for a fine tomb in anticipation of the next world.[83] That the request for burial (by no means a rare one) is here substituted for the conventional "thousand of..." which he asked for on his other monuments might reflect his increase in years and a concentration on the afterlife. Such a suggestion concerning Minmose's psychology becomes more plausible in view of his further phraseology on the Cairo statue. He spoke of himself as "one who has reached old age without his misdeed having been found" (ph i3w n gm.tw. wn.f).[84]

He continued, saying: "who did those things which his lord said, building immediately by embellishing his monuments of eternity" (ir ddwt.nb.f hws hr-ꜥ m smnh mnw.f n nhh)[85]. The former phrase, although formulaic, should indicate a stage of life already attained, that is, old age. The phrase n gm.tw wn.f is a negation of a past action as analyzed by Callender[86]; and Polotsky has noted the alternation of n sdm.tw.f with n sdmw.f which is a non-circumstantial form representing action already completed.[87] Indeed here on the Cairo statue, ph, itself not indicative of time determination, follows hs n ntr.f s-ꜥ3 n nsw dr hrdw.f, "one whom his god praised, whom the king magnified since his childhood", where two past relative forms appear. Ph is followed by Polotsky's "participe accompli", ir ddwt ... as quoted above, with a specific description of the statue owner's performance; he was said to have acted immediately, and the "participe accompli" was used to show the particular task ordered by the king was completed.

The inferences from these lines for our discussion are two: first, although the description of Minmose as "one who reached old age, etc." is not unusual, it is grammatically expressed as completed fact; this strengthens the proposal that this monument represents Minmose's late life; second, the reference to Minmose's building efforts and his immediate response indicate he was already serving Amenhotep II. The titles of Overseer of works in the Temples of Upper and Lower Egyptian Gods and Royal scribe were without doubt his ultimate ones; they appear in some form on all three statues and also in his year 4 inscription under Amenhotep II.[88]

On his Medamud statue, Minmose never called himself a builder but always simply a director of temple constructions; hws does not appear, but rather hrp. In the Medamud text Minmose said three times that he "directed the works", hrp k3wt[89], but on the Cairo statue he used the word only in his title.[90] The difference in wording and the characterization of his action as immediate, hr-ꜥ, might be due to the statue's date in Amenhotep II's reign. Since he served that king in his early years of sole rule and a text from Tura shows he quarried limestone for temples in year 4, it is clear that Minmose did set to work quickly building for the new king. In view of the long list of temples in which Minmose oversaw works for Thutmose III (he named twenty-two) it is unlikely that his speed for that monarch's projects was of paramount importance. Amenhotep, on the other hand, might well have praised swift construction of his newly-planned monuments. Therefore, the Cairo statue stems from the reign of Amenhotep II.[91] Further, it is not unreasonable to suggest that Webensenu and Nedjem were the first born of Amenhotep II (or last born of Thutmose III). Given Minmose's length of service under Thutmose III and his assignment to supervisory jobs even in the reign of that king, he probably died rather early in Amenhotep's rule. He never received a promotion from the new pharaoh.

This lengthy discussion strongly suggests that Webensenu and Nedjem were older princes than Thutmose IV. To have died at an age approaching 35 years, the king must have also been born early in Amenhotep II's reign if we accept Amenhotep II ruled but 26 years[92] and Thutmose some 10. A 30 + rule for Amenhotep, as suggested by Wente and Van Siclen, would put his birth even later. We can infer that Webensenu and Nedjem held positions of seniority among royal children (by their appearance with Minmose) and could have been Amenhotep II's first-born. Against any identification of Webensenu as throne heir, however, is his name which, as Cannuyer[93] rightly points out, is not at all suggestive of throne names of the period.[94] The possibility remains that Thutmose was not Amenhotep's first son. It remains to be seen whether this affected his placement in the line of succession.

Prince Amenhotep of P. BM10056.

Redford proposed to see Prince Amenhotep, a <u>sem</u> priest mentioned in P. BM 10056[95], as an elder brother of Thutmose IV, and Der Manuelian supports this view. Three papyri of similar orthography[96] were considered together and redated by Redford to Amenhotep II's reign from Thutmose III's and from the co-regency of the two.[97] Redford identified the prince Amenhotep as a grown son of Amenhotep II who was performing adminstrative duties in year 20 of that king. In addition, Redford considered this prince to be the owner of a defaced stela from Giza and the prince Amenhotep who visited Konosso during Thutmose IV's rule.   The secondary identification will be discussed below; here our concern is the date of the papyrus and whether this Amenhotep was an elder brother of Thutmose.

The argument presented by Redford is cogent, and it is not at all his reasoning that makes the new dating uncertain; rather it is the unsure regnal dates in the papyri and the fact that there is no assurance these three documents were written at about the same time. In Hermitage 1116B, both the prenomen of Amenhotep II and that of Thutmose III appear. The name of the latter was compounded in the name of a building.[98] Redford argued that Amenhotep II was the ruling king in this instance, and this is a sound   conclusion. Many dead kings' names are posthumously referred to by naming their funerary estates. A year 18 appears in Hermitage 1116A[99], but no royal name is present there. An official's name, $^c3$- hpr-r-nhh, was offered by Golenischeff as proof that Amenhotep II was king when 1116A was written, and Redford adopted this interpretation.[100] But this name does not contain the   prenomen of Amenhotep II, and there are other kings who could have inspired such a name--namely, Thutmose I and Thutmose II, as well as Kamose. Hermitage 1116B has no regnal date, and it is tied to 1116A and to BM 10056 only on orthographic grounds.   (1116A and 1116B were originally one papyrus, but that does not   suggest they were written at the same time. Their contents are entirely different.) In fact, Glanville allowed that BM 10056, which Redford has demonstrated by the presence of a regnal year change at iv akhet 1 belongs to Amenhotep II's reign, could have been dated in year 30 or 15, 25, or 35--he would not then have objected on paleographic grounds to separating BM 10056 from Hermitage 1116A by at least 20 years. Must we then assume all three were written between year 18 and 20? It is clear that Hermitage 1116B was written in Amenhotep II's rule; 1116A and BM 10056 might easily be separated from each other by 15-20 years and from 1116B by half of Amenhotep's reign. The fact that these texts mention Peru-nefer does not tie them all to Amenhotep II necessarily, for that king claims to have been a small child in that town, thus ensuring its existence under Thutmose III. And it is notable that the onomasticon of these papyri, two of which (BM 10056 and 1116A) mention Peru-nefer, do not show any repetition.

Since a time gap could exist among the three documents,[101] Redford's year date of 20 may be incorrect. Wente and Van Siclen suggested (a yet-unattested) year 30 of Amenhotep II;[102] they took the reign suggested by Redford and the year most favored by Glanville. In considering whether prince Amenhotep was an elder brother of Thutmose IV, Year 20 would argue that he was, and Year 30 might not. If Year 15 should be considered, then Amenhotep might have been an older sib or an ineligible older prince (or even deceased by Year 30). The unsure age of Thutmose IV at accession--he could have been as old as 25--discourages any result from this discussion. The seniority of Prince Amenhotep of P. BM 10056 remains shadowy until his position at the end of Amenhotep II's rule can be assessed. One thing is clear, however, about this man. He was a functioning adult member of the royal family before Thutmose IV's reign commenced. That much is certainly established by the British Museum papyri.

Prince Amenhotep at Konosso.

A prince Amenhotep is attested twice in graffiti from Konosso.[103] He was accompanied by another prince, Aakheprure (see below) and once by the child of the Nursery, Hekarnehhe, as well. The Herald Re appeared once with the princes, and the God's Father Hekareshu was attested in another instance. The prince has been called a son of Thutmose IV by Newberry, Habachi, and, by inference of argument, by Davies. Redford and Frandsen called him a son of Amenhotep II.[104] Actually neither king can be demonstrated as father, but what we know of this prince Amenhotep will be examined to establish what conclusions are possible.

Contrary to what is often said, the graffiti at Konosso are dated by cartouche and not simply by the names of contemporaries to Thutmose IV.[105] Lepsius' notes clearly describe the Konosso rock face as follows:[106] double cartouches of Thutmose IV appear over the representation of royal princes. The scene was once

larger than now, but Apries erased a portion on the left in order to carve his
own name. Still shown, however, were, in addition to the princes, texts naming the
Herald Re, the princes Aakheprure, Amenhotep, and the child of the Nursery
Hekarnehhe. Immediately to the right was an offering formula for Hekareshu.
Right of this, but on the same rock face, was the name of Psamtik II and below this
the long year 8 inscription of Thutmose IV. Directly beneath the year 8 text was
the second inscription of the princes--this time in association with Hekareshu.

The description given by Lepsius not only confirms that the princes' texts are
of Thutmose IV date, but also strongly suggests that the family inscriptions belong
to year 7/8 as does the long stela. A year 7 for the king also appears at Konosso,
but it is on another rock-face further east. All the above were on the same cliff.
As will be argued below, the king's Konosso stela was less a military text than one
showing divine approvals by Upper Egyptian gods. The "war" was a simple police
action in the Eastern desert.   It is likely that Konosso was the stop in years 7 and
8 for Thutmose's official tours, accompanied by court and family (his wife Iaret
appeared in the year 7 scene). It need hardly be said that the graffiti from Konosso
represent a number of Thutmose IV's well-known officials--Hekareshu, Hekarnehhe,
Re and Horemhab.

The information provided by the Konosso inscriptions shows that prince
Amenhotep was old enough to travel in year 8 of Thutmose IV, but he was
accompanied by nurses and guardians. Can his minority be further confirmed? It
has been suggested that Amenhotep, the sem priest of BM 10056, was identical
with this Amenhotep at Konosso[107] who visited Upper Egypt during Thutmose'
reign.[108] But this proposal must be rejected, for it can be demonstrated that the
princes at Konosso were presented as small children, not adults. The two graffiti
show similar form: in both cases the names of Hekareshu (God's Father) and Re
(First royal herald) are inscribed horizontally, while the princes' names are written
vertically, either following the officer's name or below it.

Re_____			Hekareshu	Amen-	Aa-
Amen-	Aa-	Heka-		hotep	khepru-
hotep	khepru-	r-			re
	re	nehhe			

Such a visual alignment portrays a subordinate status on the part of the princes and
Hekarnehhe, whose title (Child of the Nursery) and name were also written
vertically. The princes were almost certainly still immature--an independent royal
son would surely outrank a commoner and be named before or above him. There
is no example (known to me) which shows an elder official in protective attitude

to a grown prince on a journey or on official business. Commonly a grown prince was shown <u>leading</u> other officials in an activity,--e.g., at Medinet Habu, the prince led viziers before Ramesses III.[109] And the statuette of prince Thutmose described above showed the prince alone; his nurse's name figured there only once and was not prominent. The vast majority of non-funerary documents involving princes represent men working for their fathers. For example, the many sons of Ramesses II were most active and exhibited diverse   titles and functions.[110] Nurses are generally depicted with children, both Amenhotep II and Thutmose IV were shown small on the laps of their nurses, but as enthroned rulers the same kings received the homage and offerings of their tutors.

A second argument concerns the titles exhibited by the princes and officials in the graffiti. Both Re and Hekareshu used their characteristic titles known for them only in the reign of Thutmose IV and later,[111] but if prince Amenhotep, normally called <u>sem</u> in BM 10056, had been an administrator for some years he would surely have outranked Hekareshu and Re. That he would have tolerated the simple title of king's son under guardianship of lesser men is most unlikely. For these reasons, the <u>sem</u> priest Amenhotep who, if Redford's dating is correct, would have been in his thirties at this time, could not have been the prince at Konosso. Given that four kings of the 18th Dynasty ruled under the name of Amenhotep, it is not unlikely that at least one prince of each generation bore the name. It is hardly daring, therefore, to suggest that our documents record more than one Amenhotep.

It is likely that Amenhotep and Aakheprure were immature in year 8 of Thutmose IV. It would be difficult to imagine children much younger than 10 years traveling widely with the court, and probably the princes were some 8-15 years old. If this is correct, then these boys could have been born to either Thutmose IV or Amenhotep II, for Thutmose would have reached puberty and could have married in the latter years of Amenhotep. And the minority of this Prince Amenhotep is consistent with the probable youth of Amenhotep III at accession. It might be pointed out, in addition, that even though Amenhotep and Aakheprurc appeared together at Konosso, they were not necessarily brothers. There is insufficient evidence to identify the fathers of either or both, but it is possible that their parentage was different.[112]

Prince Aakheprure

Prince Aakheprure left his name in the same two graffiti discussed above. For the reasons given there Aakheprure must, like Amenhotep, have been a youth at the time of the visit. The question of this prince's parentage has been raised by Newberry, who called him a son of Thutmose IV, and by Redford, who identified Amenhotep II as his father.[113] Der Manuelian likewise makes of him a son of Amenhotep II.[114] Newberry based his argument on the graffiti naming Hekareshu, and he suggested a link to two princes known from TT 226 whose names bear the elements ^{c}3-hpr-[?]-r^c. Newberry identified all the princes as sons of Thutmose IV and cross-identified at least one with Aakheprure from Konosso. Tomb 226, dated to the reign of Amenhotep III by a scene of that king in a kiosk, gives no support to Newberry's argument but rather provided him with another monument naming these princes. The name Aakheprure does not actually appear in the tomb, and therefore any identification must be demonstrated, not assumed; and the date of the graffiti in Thutmose IV's reign does not automatically make that king the princes' father. The parentage of Aakheprure remains entirely unsettled. It is therefore arguable that one or more of the Konosso princes was a son of Thutmose IV and possibly the future ruler. The estimate given above of 8-15 years of age for the princes at Konosso is compatible with age estimates for Amenhotep III.[115] Since he died after 38 years of reign as a man apparently in late middle age, an accession age of 10-15 is likely. We must keep in mind that this is possible, not that it is demonstrable by the present evidence.

Prince Amenhotep in Theban Tomb 64

A king's son Amenhotep appeared in Theban tomb 64 as the nursling of Hekarnehhe.[116] He was portrayed standing in front of Hekarnehhe and a group of royal children and offering a bouquet to Thutmose IV, who was depicted as on a small scale on the lap of his nurse Hekareshu, fig. 5. Hekareshu and Thutmose are seated on a chair raised slightly above Amenhotep who is himself elevated above his nurse Hekarnehhe and the other children. Amenhotep's pectoral, now lacking, bore the cartouche names of Thutmose. Hekarnehhe held a bouquet and was identified as "[nurse] of the royal children" and also "nurse of the prince Amenhotep". Elsewhere in the tomb Hekarnehhe is termed "Child of the nursery".[117]

The tomb scene does not represent an event in true time but rather a fictitious commemorative event.[118] It is known, for example, that Thutmose IV was not a small boy at the time.[119] The adult ruler was represented twice in kiosk scenes in the same   chapel where he received bouquets from Hekareshu and Hekarnehhe. Nor was Thutmose represented as a small child. Rather he was labelled as king, both in the text above and on the pectorals worn by the princes. He also wore the royal garb, not the sidelock of youth. The representation was thus an   artistic fiction showing the king reduced in size in order to depict Hekareshu's earlier relationship to him. There are parallels from temple scenes where kings, shown smaller than normal but in full regalia, suckle from Hathor or a goddess.[120] This scene never took place as an event and cannot therefore be used to argue that at a certain point Hekareshu was nurse to the child Thutmose and simultaneously Hekarnehhe was nurse to prince Amenhotep. This is a timeless scene, combining elements of time and situation.

The stronger evidence to determine the identity of princes exists in the inscriptions identifying Hekarnehhe and Hekareshu at both Konosso and Thebes. At Konosso Hekareshu was already God's Father, which he cannot be shown to have borne in Amenhotep II's reign. Hekarnehhe was Child of the nursery at Konosso alongside a Prince Amenhotep under the guardianship of the Herald Re (attested only in the reign of Thutmose IV and Amenhotep III).[121]   Since Hekarnehhe was not Royal Nurse at Konosso Frandsen concluded that the Konosso princes were sons of Amenhotep II, while those of tomb 64 were   fathered by Thutmose IV.[122] In a note Frandsen stated that nurses were often combat officers who were promoted after   long service, and he cited Helck's discussion of 18th Dynasty military leaders.   But Helck had said that some Children of the nursery (often termed "pages") were trusted military officers,[123] and that some were court nurses. He also noted that the "pages" became nurses.[124] The training of Children of the Nursery in sports may have been useful for a nurse occupation, but combat experience was by no means the norm.[125]

Indeed, there is no reason to believe Hekarnehhe ever saw   combat. Hekarnehhe did leave funerary cones with the title of "master of horses" on them.[126] This title, however, was not necessarily a military one; Helck pointed out it was often given as an honor--Yuya and Ay held the post, as did several princes. Horemhab of tomb 78 was an army scribe,[127] and Helck felt he and Hekarnehhe both   received the rank because of their nurse or court positions.   Schulman pointed out the indefinite meaning of "master of horses".[128] We can only assume that Hekarnehhe did not serve   as an army officer, but rather it is likely that Hekarnehhe was nearly grown when he visited Konosso in year 7/8. He must have been appointed as a royal nurse soon after this and entrusted with the care of princes who could have been close to him, in age and familiarity, though obviously younger.

One of these children was a prince Amenhotep who may have been the future king. Prince Amenhotep of tomb 64 was clearly the most highly ranked royal son in the tomb. He was specially named in Hekarnehhe's title and was given an elevated   position in the tomb scene. This favored position would support an assertion that the prince was the future Amenhotep III. The prince's yet immature age at the time of tomb decoration is also compatible with this identification.[129] But one might wonder why the cartouches of Amenhotep III did not appear in the tomb of his own nurse.[130] This must   surely have been because Hekarnehhe predeceased his charge (and his father). The tomb was probably designed for Hekareshu (who appears frequently in the wall scenes) and was quickly converted for Hekarnehhe's use first. The jamb texts naming the latter were unfinished; otherwise the monochrome ceiling inscriptions are the only texts without Hekareshu. They could have been added quickly just as the funerary cones which name only Hekarnehhe could have been rapidly produced.   It is quite likely that had

Hekarnehhe lived   he would have received the same honors given his father
Hekareshu by Thutmose IV (notably the title God's Father or   perhaps more
prestigious ranks).

Two major points emerge from this discussion. First, Prince Amenhotep of TT
64 cannot be identified with any man fully   grown before the latter years of
Thutmose IV's reign. This eliminates the prince of BM 10056[131] who would have
been far   too old to be Hekarnehhe's nursling. The question of fatherhood is
open, however, for chronologically this Amenhotep, like the princes from Konosso,
could have been a son   of Amenhotep II or Thutmose IV.[132] Second, Prince
Amenhotep from TT 64 could have been identical by age with Prince Amenhotep
of Konosso, and both could have been the future king Amenhotep III. Although
there is no assurance here, the suggestion does fit the evidence.

Prince Amenemhet

Prince Amenemhet is known from a representation in tomb   64 and from
canopic jars found in the tomb of Thutmose IV. (CG   46037-39 and Boston MFA
03.1129a-b).[133] He was called "king's son of his body" on the objects. Since his
canopics were found in the king's tomb, it is   quite likely that Thutmose was
Amenemhet's father, and it is also possible, though of course not certain, that the
mummy of a young boy found in KV 43 was that of this prince.[134] If this was the
case, then Amenemhet must have died as a child, perhaps soon after tomb 64 was
painted.

Additional Princes in TT 64

Five other princes were shown in tomb 64. Several of their figures are now
lost, and only one shows any trace of a name. That son shown standing behind
Amenemhet was called "king's son beloved of him, [Amun]///".[135] The name was
restored as Amenhotep by some,[136] but other names are just as likely. See, for
example, a Prince Amenemipet known from a Royal Nurse's Sakkara tomb stela.
Although he may have been identical with a son of Amenhotep II, the name is a
common one in the New Kingdom. One may suppose the children in tomb 64 were
all sons of Thutmose IV, but this is not at all sure. Hekarnehhe, their nurse
(called "Nurse to the royal children" may have tended children of more than one
king--nor need they all have been offspring of rulers; the children of other royal
family members could be represented, for they, too, could be termed "King's Son"
(see Prince Si-atum below).

Theban Tomb 226

Theban tomb 226[137] provides four more princes[138] for   consideration as
brothers, sons, or grandsons of Thutmose IV. The children in tomb 226 are all

shown naked, small and with sidelocks.[139]   From the paintings, their age is indeterminate and even their importance as royal children is uncertain, since they appear in the tomb only on a pillar scene rather than on a main wall.[140] The owner of tomb 226 is unknown and has been identified variously by Davies as one Merire,[141] by Newberry as Hekarnehhe[142] and by Habachi[143] and Frandsen[144] as Hekareshu. This problem will be discussed in Chapter 5, but the princes are of interest here. Two of the children shown on the tombowner's knee were named ꜥ3-ḫpr-[?]r ͨ.[145] Davies' description of the scene states that the texts identify "the veritable son of the king whom he loves, 'A-kheper...re',twice repeated, the lost syllable alone differentiating the two names which survive".[146] His note gives his opinion that m3 ͨ after the names "excludes any similar but merely official designation and also the possibility of their being grandsons".[147] Schmitz has adopted the same understanding of this title in her recent study of kings' sons.[148] Thus two true princes were represented in this tomb with the same name elements.

Amenhotep III is pictured in tomb 226 in an exquisite kiosk scene together with his mother Mutemwia.[149] Newberry felt that the king's mother's presence dated the tomb to the first years of Amenhotep's reign, and he noted that no wife was present for the king. Redford later agreed with Newberry and suggested that Amenhotep had not married Tiy yet. Redford felt that the children were Amenhotep II's.[150]   His argument was based on the existence of this prenomen-type name. Redford concluded that "the majority (though by no means all) of the persons bearing such names seem to have been born under the king whose prenomen their name contains".[151] The fact still exists, however, that two princes in tomb 226 had names showing ꜥ3-ḫpr-[?]-r ͨ.[152]   If one was named Aakheprure, what name did the other child have?   We must admit that prenomen-type names are not entirely dependable indicators of fatherhood.

Davies, in contrast to Redford, believed these were Amenhotep III's children in TT 226,[153] but unlike both Redford and Newberry, he did not think that Mutemwia's presence meant Amenhotep III was not yet married.[154] Indeed, the evidence from private tombs does not speak authoritatively to the question. There are eleven private tombs in Thebes that clearly illustrate Amenhotep III.[155] Tiy appears in three tombs (47,120,192), but the king appears alone three times, with the goddess Hathor three times and once with Mut.[156] It would seem, therefore, that Tiy's presence was not normal but occasional. Her absence in the tomb of a royal nurse might suggest she had no attachment to the children in question, while Mutemwia might have had a closer connection to them. Habachi[157] believed a special relationship existed between the tombowner and Mutemwia. While this may have been true, there is no title or text suggesting it in the tomb. The best conclusion, though by no means the most satisfying, is that tomb 226 does not necessarily date to the first years of Amenhotep's rule. Mutemwia's death date is unknown; she of course appears on the colossi of Memnon from the Mortuary temple, and her estate is mentioned at Malkata in Year 27. The exaggeratedly youthful appearance of the king in the tomb's kiosk scene may suggest a time in the king's last decade for the chapel's decoration.[158]

The children in tomb 226 need not have been born late in the reign regardless of the date of its decoration, since their representation probably commemorated a past and no longer relevant function of the tombowner. The nursing scene was shown only on a pillar, while other titles dominate the texts on the walls. The functioning title of the deceased was Royal Scribe sš nsw, but the man was also a Chief Steward, Overseer of works for the King, and a Chief Steward and Doorkeeper for two Theban temples in addition to the Overseer of Royal Nurses rank.[159] The honorific titles this man held, along with the supervisory capacities suggest the inflated titulary of a pensioner. If the scene of royal children recalled the tombowner's past career, then we cannot eliminate Amenhotep II, Thutmose IV or Amenhotep III as the father of these children.

In another attempt to identify the children of tomb 226, Newberry thought to see the Konosso prince Aakheprure there. He suggested Thutmose IV was the father and Hekarnehhe was the tombowner.[160] Redford supposed Aakheprure was present in the tomb but made him a son of Amenhotep II.[161] Davies dismissed the identification and assigned the Konosso prince to Thutmose' children while making the tomb 226 princes into sons of Amenhotep III.[162] Davies'approach is actually the most judicious simply because he did not assume the existence of a prince Aakheprure in the tomb when the name was not present. Davies even suggested that the name Aakheperre may have been present, since it was an unused possibility[163] for a prenomen. Whatever the case may have been, we cannot surely link the children in tomb 226 to Aakheprure at Konosso; rather, the existence of two names exhibiting the elements ꜥ3-ḫpr-[?]-rꜥ makes the possibility of a third one, Aakheprure at Konosso, all the more believable. The information is not now available to us to identify the father of these children.

The Princes of Giza.

The princes of Giza form the next group for consideration. These are the persons pictured on stelae excavated by Selim Hassan in the region of the Great Sphinx. He designated them simply Stelae A,B,C. The three were treated together in the original publication and were identified as belonging to one man, Amenemipet, named on stela C. Hassan believed Amenemipet was the true throne heir whom Thutmose deposed and whose monuments he then defaced. This romantic reconstruction which Hassan and Dorothy Eady published has been mentioned already and will receive further comment at the end of the chapter.[164]

A new publication of the Giza materials appeared not many years ago, collected and translated by Christiane Zivie.[165] It is an excellent and authoritative work, but the introduction reveals Zivie's disappointment in finding, as I did, that the location of these stelae is unknown. Therefore, her handcopies and translations were based on the poor photos published in The Great Sphinx and The Sphinx some forty-odd years ago. The treatment below presents few disagreements with Zivie's readings; only a study of the original monuments could resolve a number of questions.

Hassan did not report where he found the stelae, but they must have come from the debris of the Amenhotep II temple amphitheatre. These are large monuments which would have prominently represented the dedicants in the Sphinx Temple precinct. Stela A[166] measures 91 X 78 cm., but this represents only the top part of the original limestone work. Zivie pointed out that stela B measures 100 cm X 170 cm., including horizontal lines of text below the scene. Stela A would then have been closer to that size originally.[167] Stela A represents a man wearing the sidelock and clothed in a short kilt; he is shown offering a lotus bouquet before the Sphinx who is labelled as Horemakhet. Between the god's paws stands a statue of Amenhotep II (on a pedestal) wearing the blue crown. No other reference to Amenhotep II appears on the monument either in speech by the gods or speech by the offerer.

Six lines of inscription originally existed above the offerer, but three have been erased leaving the rest unblemished. The text offers all produce, etc., to the ka of Horakhty. (Note the sphinx is here not named Horemakhet as on the legend above him.) The carving of the stela is elegant and shows great detail on the Sphinx's regalia-- he wears the atef crown and a broad collar. Even the markings of falcon feathers are clear on the Sphinx's back.[168] The dedicant was surely intentionally disgraced by the careful erasure of all references to him, and his placement before a statue of Amenhotep II would imply a relationship vis-à-vis that ruler. The quality of carving must indicate the donor was a person of means, and the assumption that he was a son of Amenhotep II is a valid one.[169]

Schmitz rejected Hassan's assumption that this man (and the two others) were Amenhotep II's sons; she identified the men on stelae A and B as sem priests of Ptah and redated stela C to the Ramesside period.[170] Schmitz objected on the grounds that "king's son" does not appear on either monument. But such a negative assessment is perhaps unwarranted when the exact positions where the prince's title would have been inscribed are destroyed. Since the activity of princes at Giza is well-documented in the 18th dynasty, and since Stela B's inscription can refer only to a prince, Stela A too is treated here as the donation of one of Amenhotep II's sons.

Stela B[171], found smashed into four pieces, was originally wider even than A. The scene depicts a man wearing a sidelock offering before the Sphinx who resembles the god on Stela A. A statue of Amenhotep II appears again between the Sphinx's paws. Re-Horakhty also appears in the scene standing behind the Sphinx, holding a <u>was</u> scepter in his far hand and an <u>ankh</u> in his near. The legend: "may he give life and dominion like Re" above him may refer to Behdety who apears here and on Stela A, where the phrase occurs in a similar position. It is unclear for whom this phrase is intended, but it may be for Amenhotep II, whose statue was addressed by Re-Horakhty in another text. The address of Re-Horakhty was as follows: "Utterance by Re-Horakhty: 0 beloved son of my body, lord of the Two lands, Aakheprure; I have given all life and dominion and all health to you". The Sphinx is here named both Horemakhet and Horakhty, and the offerer, just as on Stela A, presents a lotus bouquet. The text above him is nearly identical to that on the other monument and promises all produce for the <u>ka</u> of Horakhty, great god lord of love.

The prince's figure on Stela B is finely sculpted; he wears a short kilt, and the <u>shebiu</u> collar in addition to a broad necklace. The offerer's title and name (including a cartouche according to Hassan[172]) have been entirely cut away. Similarly the functional title and name of the offerer are removed from the lengthy inscription below the scene. There can be no question that the owner was intentionally disgraced. The facial representation of this prince is quite similar to that of Thutmose IV on his Sphinx Stela and on other stelae left by the king at the Sphinx amphitheater.[173] On the Sphinx Stela Thutmose IV has a short round face and stumpy chin. His nose is straight and rather small. The prince's image on B, like Thutmose's, is differently sculpted from that of the prince on Stela A; that prince resembled far more the relief images of Amenhotep II (e.g., CG 34170), who is known for his "dishpan profile". The features of Prince B may be favorably compared not only to Thutmose IV's on the Sphinx Stela, but also to his on Hassan figs. 17 and 66 and his pls. 41B, 44A & B, and 47. Although the existence of two or more sculptural styles for this period at Giza does not necessarily indicate a chronological separation of stelae A and B, it does point out that the stelae donors need not have been offered simultaneously, nor by the same man.

The horizontal text below Stela B's scene is extremely difficult to read. This translation differs only in minor respects from Zivie's. The left half is almost entirely destroyed, and the owner's name and most significant titles have been erased in the last line. What can be read is of interest, however, for this inscription provides us with one of the fullest lists known of a prince's titles:

(1) A gift which the king gives to Horakhty [a], great god, variegated of plumage, Horemakhet, who presides at the Setpet, may he give invocation offerings of bread, beer, water, breath, incense and oil for the <u>ka</u> of the courtier [great] of love [b] ...[break on left side begins] ...[who walks about] (2) among the dignitaries, who enters before his father [c] without being announced, who escorts the king of Upper

and Lower Egypt, he who is in the heart of [Horus in his palace [d]]...who goes forth
in front (3) of all the   chiefs [e], whose face and whose respect are in the sights of
the   multitude, for his words are pure (?) the people ($p^c t$) indeed, are made
content; they [his words]   cause peacefulness when [he] makes known...[f] ... the
stablemaster [g], (4) for   the lord of the Two lands, the Chief Master of horses, the
judge, he of the curtain, the one of Nekhen, the prophet of Maat, the mouth who
satisfies in the land to its limits, he who is benevolent, who hears speeches... (5)
the hereditary   prince and count, sem, controller of every kilt, God's Father,
[God's] beloved, who enters before the secrets of the Great   Seat, who moves
unhindered to the august throne steps... (6) [a man of] rectitude, he having trebled
the gifts, pure of arms bearing the censer when he propitiates him who divided
heaven from earth, beautiful of arms to adorn the god on the day of ... (7) ..[h]
[clean] of arms, pure of fingers, he who is over the secrets in the Temple of Ptah
in the [procession] of him who bore the gods, sem in the temple of Sokar... (8)
Horus [i] ///(or Horemakhet ?) ... in this place: May you praise [j] the king, the lord
of eternity, Atum [k] ...[l]... (9)... divine egg who comes forth from him, [whose]
name is proclaimed(?)[m]"...[174]

     The importance of the donor is apparent by a reading of these lines, but the
functional title for the offerer is lost. Many of these titles were held by viziers and
High priests of Ptah, but the man in question was neither, for he lacks the explicit
titles--of vizier, $\underline{t}3t$ mr niwt, and of High priest of Ptah, wr hrp hmwtyw. Schmitz
argued that the owner of stela B was a High Priest of Memphis,[175] but the title is
absent where it might have been expected, making her identification less likely.
Zivie pointed out that if this man had been a High priest, that title should have
appeared in line 5 along with "controller of every kilt".[176] This is the case too for
the vizier's titles which would have been expected in line 4 with "judge" and "he
of the curtain". In addition the High Priest of Ptah title is known to have been
held by princes: both Thutmose, son of Amenhotep III, and Khaemwast, son of
Ramesses II, were Memphite pontiffs so this might have left the identification
ambiguous. We should add that the offerers do not wear the characteristic garb of
the High Priest of Ptah which includes the panther skin as well as elaborate apron
and necklace.
     Another argument raised by Schmitz concerned the title $rp^c t$ which was applied
to this stela owner. Schmitz believed this man could not have been a true prince,
since to her knowledge the title $rp^c t$ does not belong to king's sons in the 18th
dynasty.
     In the Ramesside period, however, Schmitz found many attestations, and she
attributed its use to the fact that Horemheb employed it, thereby legitimating its
meaning as "crown prince".[177] Although Schmitz cited Helck's earlier discussion
of $rp^c t$, Helck did not state that princes were not titled $rp^c t$ in the 18th dynasty.
Rather he said that the rank did not designate a crown prince in that period. His
discussion in no way excluded true princes from holding this honorary title.[178]

It should be recalled that this stela is an exceptional document providing the full titles of a king's son. A second monument, belonging to a prince Ahmose, to be discussed further below, includes rp^{c}t as part of a long titulary. Ahmose's statue and stela can only belong stylistically to the mid-18th Dynasty.[179] The only other example of a rp^{c}t appearing in the titulary of a "true king's son beloved of him" is that of Amenemipet, the owner of Giza stela C. Schmitz redated his monument to the 19th dynasty because of the rp^{c}t title. Clearly then princes carried the same honorific titles as other nobility. It was their "true King's Son" s3 nsw m3^c rank which distinguished them from the upper class as a whole.

That the owner of Stela B was a true prince is verified by phrases from the inscription. In line 2 the offerer is called "he who enters before his father without being announced," and in line 9, the "divine seed who came forth from him". The former epithet must refer to the king, while the latter is similar to the description of Amenhotep II on his Sphinx Stela as "the shining seed of the god's body".[180] Hatshepsut too was termed "the pure seed".[181] The owner of Stela B must therefore have been a true prince, and he was sem priest as well. Redford, who felt the owner of Stela B was the rightful heir, noted nonetheless that the sem office was not related to the succession.[182] This point should be borne in mind.

Amenhotep II must have been the father of this prince (or princes if Stela A's donor was a different man). The king appeared in statue form on both monuments and the Stela B inscription refers indirectly to the king as "father". This could hardly be other than the pharaoh named in the scene above. Clearly the titles attributed to this man show that he was an adult at some point in Amenhotep II's rule, and any prince who reached the age of 20 before Amenhotep's 26th year of reign would have been older than Thutmose. It is possible that this prince was senior to Thutmose given his wealth of titles and functions on Stela B. It remains to us to identify this man, if possible.

There are three known princes who might have been the owner of Stela B (and A). Redford suggested the prince Amenhotep from P. BM 10056;[183] he was termed a sem in the papyrus, and that title appears in the titles of our prince. Clearly Amenhotep, if Redford's dating is correct, would have been an elder brother of Thutmose and was functioning in the north during Amenhotep's reign (at Peru-Nefer). If the document in which he appears can be more securely dated to the reign of Amenhotep II, this Amenhotep would be the likeliest prince to identify as the owner of Stelae A and B.

Two princes held non-religious titles which appear in the titulary of our prince. The priest's rank need not be characteristic of this man's functions, for it would be natural to enumerate cultic ranks on a temple donation stela. It is quite noticeable that the titles and epithets on Stela B are divided into civil and religious designations, and we cannot be sure which were those he most often used (especially since his name and last titles are erased). A man named Khaemwast left two graffiti at Sehel that identified the "king's son and stablemaster, Khaemwast".[184] This prince has usually been considered an official of prince's rank, not one of blood. That he is known only from graffiti limits our assessment of him but it is possible that he could have been a true prince; to exclude him would be premature. Without more information, it is difficult to assess the possibility that Khaemwast was the prince of Stela B.

Webensenu was discussed earlier in this chapter where it was determined that he may have been older than Thutmose, and it was noted that his canopic jars were found in the tomb of Amenhotep II. One of those alabaster fragments called Webensenu the "king's son and Master of horses". The title "Master of horses" was held by numerous kings'sons;[185] among them were the future king Sety I, Pareherwenemef, third son of Ramesses II, Montuherkhepeshef, fifth son of Ramesses II, Amunherkhepeshef, crown prince of Ramesses II, Sethherkhepeshef, fourth son of Ramesses III, and Amunherkhepeshef, also son of Ramesses III.

The office of Master of horses is considered in Chapter 5, but it is useful to observe that the rank was largely honorary. Helck noted this in regard to the 18th Dynasty civil officials who were given the rank (Minnakht, Horemhab, and Hekarnehhe),[186] and the Ramesside princes often compound the title with an epithet of the king, thus stressing its court importance. The royal penchant for equestrianism, particularly Amenhotep II's,[187] suggests that the most active princes were also the most favored. Note Thutmose III's pride in Amenhotep II's horsemanship referred to on Amenhotep's Sphinx stela. Witness, too, Thutmose IV's Sphinx Stela reference to his chariot exercises in the Memphite region. Thus Webensenu's title as Master of Horses might well betray his father's affection for him.

The title of a "Master of horses" appears in Stela B in line 4 of the stela where the prince is termed "stablemaster for the lord of the Two lands, Chief master of horses". "Chief", hry-tp is not a title but rather an honorific addition to the rank. This same combination is attested on two funerary cones in the 18th dynasty for a man who was also titled "overseer of cattle and steward".[188] Schulman concluded that the "chief of mnf3t was an epithet analogous to "every great one of the army".[189] Goedicke identified the hry-tp as "one who is in charge", connoting relative elevation but no authority.[190] Goedicke said that in "combination titles, it appears to specify an otherwise general title, such as sš. It states a specific concern rather than a commanding authority."[191] In this instance, hry-tp mr ssmwt would be translated "master of horses-in-charge". The man in question, according to either Schulman's or Goedicke's understanding, would have held an alternative title to simple "master of horses", but he was not of another rank entirely.[192] Zivie's translation of "celui qui est a la tete des chefs des chevaux" is thus perhaps too ambiguous.[193]

Webensenu was provided some tutelage by an old court favorite, Minmose, who was associated with him and his brother Nedjem. As said above, Minmose's activities in Amenhotep II's early years are attested at Tura near the royal residence at Memphis. The origins of Webensenu in the north are thus not unlikely.

Such a home would have been appropriate both to a priest of Ptah and Sokar and to a horseman. Amenhotep II himself referred to stables there;[194] his mastery of riding skills is legend. In fact, it is possible that young Amenhotep held the offices of "master of horses" and "stablemaster" himself, since he was expressly said to have tended horses from the king's stable in Memphis. The owner of Stela B was "stablemaster for the lord of the Two lands", and that title too might have suited Amenhotep's duties. According to Schulman the phrases added to hry ihw, "for the lord of the Two lands" and "for his Majesty" indicated the royal stables.[195]

The placement of Webensenu's canopic jars in Amenhotep II's tomb demonstrates a close relationship to the king. However, it is not necessarily true that the prince predeceased Amenhotep simply because his funerary goods were in the tomb. His objects were mixed with those of the king, but all the pieces were in a heap. One suggestion is that Webensenu was originally interred elsewhere. Wente and Thomas suggested that Webensenu was originally buried in tomb 42 in the Valley of the Kings and that he was a crown prince (though, they believed, of Thutmose III). Webensenu might have been moved with his grave goods at a later date into his father's tomb so that KV 42 could be re-used.[196] (This would have been early in Thutmose IV's reign if Sentnay occupied KV 42.)[197] There are, however, no indications of Webensenu's occupation of KV 42, and there is no reason to believe that he could not have been laid to rest in Amenhotep II's tomb after the ruler's death. Webensenu's burial in KV 35 certainly suggests his recognized position in the royal family, but to conclude that he was crown prince is perhaps too enthusiastic.

The owner of Stelae A and B cannot be surely identified. Webensenu, however, is at present the only prince surely known to have been 1) as old as or older than Thutmose; 2) the possessor of a title identical to one on Stela B; 3) at least sometimes in the north; and 4) honored among princes by burial with Amenhotep II. No other prince can be shown to have as many claims to identity with Prince B. As said above, if Prince Amenhotep of BM 10056 could be better placed chronologically then he would contend strongly with Webensenu here, since he was known to have held the sem title. As is all too often the case, no certainty exists.

Of course the significance of the erasures and destruction of Stelae A and B has been linked to Thutmose's treachery[198] in killing his brother(s) to seize the throne by usurpation. The Sphinx Stela has been separated from this issue above, and the stelae must be considered alone. It would be naive to ignore the witness of princes' monuments consciously defaced, and therefore we must accept that the mutilator viewed the stelae donor(s) as a threat. Still, the nature of the threat is an entire blank, and treachery, if such existed, need not have been Thutmose's solely. There is as great a likelihood that the prince(s) attempted to seize the throne from Thutmose. The inscription of Stela B certainly emphasizes the prince's relationship with the king and the people. This can be interpreted as his rightful position or as a support for intended usurpation. We simply do not know which. But a summary at the end of this chapter briefly resumes the discussion.

Prince Amenemipet, owner of Stela C

Stela C also came from the Hassan excavations around the Amenhotep II temple, and, like Stelae A and B, it is now misplaced.[199] This monument is in false door form, a type well known from Memphis in the 18th Dynasty. It was broken into large fragments of which four were excavated. The relief is of fine quality, but the state of preservation is poor. Although Hassan and others have dated this piece to Amenhotep II's reign, Schmitz recently redated it to the Ramesside period.[200] Stylistically the work is clearly mid-18th dynasty, and only the simplicity of design is a bit unusual, for the artist appears to have deliberately archaized by using rather stiff and formal stances as well as an uncluttered background. But the same double strand of shebiu beads seen on the prince of Stela B is worn here. The tall bouquets presented to the gods are without curvature just as were those up to the reigns of Thutmose IV and Amenhotep III.[201] Zivie dated the Sphinx's representation and the stela in general to Amenhotep II, "probablement".

There are vertical inscriptions on the jambs of the shrine. The interior is divided into two registers; the upper shows the Sphinx (Horakhty/Horemakhet) receiving lotus bouquets and incense from two men, the first wearing a sidelock. The remains of a king's statue appear between the Sphinx's paws, but without text. The end of a three-column inscription is visible before the prince. The titles of "hereditary prince and count" occur in the third column; there may have been a fourth line or perhaps the text was retrograde.[202] The middle column is largely erased according to Hassan, but an ⊏ is visible at the bottom. A seated man ended the first line, and probably identified the prince. The missing section of the middle column may once have contained (if a retrograde reading is supposed) 2) [s3 nsw 'Imn]m 1) [ipt].

The lower register shows three offerers before Isis seated in a kiosk; the goddess holds a was scepter and an ankh. Zivie pointed out that the ankh was held by goddesses up until the end of the 18th dynasty when it was supplanted by the wadj scepter. The only text identified Isis, the Great, God's mother, Mistress of the Gods, Unique one in heaven without her equal, premier one of Atum" and her supplicant, the "excellent seed who goes forth...[from before   his father", or similar?].[203]

The jamb texts give more titles for this prince.

Left: who follows the king over water and land, who is not   absent from the journeys of the lord of the Two lands, great of praise in the Per-Nesut, possessor of love in   the palace, the king's son beloved of him, Amenemipet."

Right: "... lord of the Two lands[204] who goes forth from his limbs, Amenemipet."

That Amenemipet was a true prince is not in doubt. The argument provided by Schmitz that rp^{c}t did not designate   royal family before the 19th dynasty was rejected above, and   stylistically the monument fits the mid-18th dynasty. This stela, and the prince named on it, must therefore remain in the category in which Hassan placed them. Amenemipet's father was very likely Amenhotep II, and the stela was   probably dedicated at a time not far removed from the   donation of Stelae A and B. As to Amenemipet himself, we should conclude that he likely was not the same man named on Stela B; his titles do not include those religious functions and high court designations described above. Rather the preserved inscriptions stress the prince's intimacy with the ruler rather than assign him ranks. His epithet "one who follows the king" is common in this period but is not otherwise known for a prince in the 18th dynasty. A certain "king's son" of the Second Intermediate period did use this flourish, however,[205] but it is unclear whether that man was a blood prince. Amenemipet must have been another of Thutmose IV's brothers, but it is improbable that he was the owner of either Stela A or B. His name was left untouched in the vicinity of the two defaced monuments. However, all three were found broken in the same area. And the name of Amun was not damaged on Stela C. This would certainly tend to date the destruction of the stelae before the Amarna period and most probably to Thutmose IV's restoration project at the Sphinx amphitheatre.

A stela from Sakkkara hitherto unpublished (fig. 6) provides us the name of a Prince Amenemipet's wet nurse and probably shows the owner of Stela C retrospectively as a small child. It could alternatively commemorate a son of Thutmose IV with the same name. There was at least one prince shown in TT 64 of Hekarnehhe with a name compounded with Amun. JE 20221, discovered in 1862, is a limestone false-door type stela 50 cm ht. by 39 cm. in width. A frieze of hanging lotuses decorates the top of the inner surface. The hanging lotus motif begins in painted kiosk scenes in the reign of Amenhotep II (in TT 93 of Kenamun), but typifies tomb painting decoration only from Thutmose IV's rule. (Generally during this period of artistic development, motifs appeared in relief later than in painting.)

On JE 20221 in the upper register sits a woman suckling a child. She receives food offerings from a woman standing before her. The dedication is to Osiris of Dedu on behalf of the ḥsyt n Mwt nb[t] pt mnᶜt nsw Sntrwiw. The child is identified as s3-nsw Imn-m-ipt. The s3 bird appears to be followed by a t, but the child clearly has male genitalia, and the name Amenemipet is determined by a seated male.

This stela is likely to have come from the nurse's tomb, but the size of the monument is not impressive. The observation may be made, however, that, while the scene and texts appear to have been completed in a reasonably good, though simple style, the remainder of the piece is rough, and the entire inner scene, as well as the torus molding is rimmed with pinpoint chisel marks. Either the stela was left in this unfinished state or perhaps more likely was once decorated by the application of gold leaf, or some other applied material. We are fortunate to have this additional work attesting to prince Amenemipet. The style is quite comfortably suited to the reign of Thutmose IV in facial features, by the style of wig (Amenhotep II or later), the length of the offerer's dress (later than early Amenhotep II, the size of the funerary cone (shorter than normally shown in the reign of Amenhotep III) and by the lotus frieze (Amenhotep II/Thutmose IV or later). If this Prince Amenemipet was identical with the donor of Stela C, then nurse Sentruyu looked after Prince Amenemipet in the Memphite palace well before the Giza stelae were fashioned. But the nurse's tomb stela might well have memorialized her long past relationship with the prince. This same type of commemoration occurs in Merire's tomb where he appeared with prince Si-atum who was certainly grown at the time.

Prince Si-atum

Prince Si-atum was pictured on a stela, now in Vienna (5814)[206], seated on his tutor Merire's lap. There is no cartouche on this piece, but the style must date it to Amenhotep III's reign, probably in the last decade.[207] The monument no doubt comes from the official's tomb at Sakkara[208] by its style and dedication. A corner of the stela still in situ was seen by Gunn early in this century.[209] The gods named are Re-Horakhty and Osiris of Busiris, and the bouquet of Ptah appears as offering. Merire's tomb at Sakkara has recently been found by Alain Zivie.[210]

On the Vienna tomb stela prince Si-atum was simply termed "king's son whom his father loves",[211] and Merire was described as "chief nurse for the Good God". Davies and Brunner felt that the absence of the king's name suggested that "his father" referred to Merire as "foster-father". This is an artificial interpretation, and it is probable that this title was a mere variant on "the king's son truly beloved of him". Si-atum's father could have been Thutmose IV or Amenhotep III, perhaps even an earlier ruler. The date of the stela in the reign of Amenhotep III is unclear, but Si-atum appears to have been born at least early enough to father a princess who died in Amenhotep III's reign.

A Prince Si-atum is named on a mummy label found by Rhind in Thebes.[212] The label is dated in year 27 or 37 of an unnamed pharaoh, but it was found together with mummy tags naming princesses of Thutmose IV and Amenhotep III's households in a tomb said to be dated by the seal of Amenhotep III. (See Chapter 3 further) The label identified "the king's daughter Nebiu, daughter of the king's son Si-atum". The tomb may have been a reburial place for Nebiu, but the association of other women from this location with the court of Thutmose IV strengthens Rhinds's early assertion that Amenhotep III's reign was the time of Nebiu's original entombment. The reign in which Si-atum would thus have been born cannot be more precisely suggested. Since Si-atum's genealogy is so uncertain, we should not include him as either a son or grandson of Thutmose IV but recognize him as part of the royal family.

Prince Ahmose

Another prince attested from the north of Egypt is one Ahmose, a High Priest of Re at Heliopolis. This prince is attested by two monuments, one of which provides extensive titles for the man. Despite earlier publications in which Ahmose is assigned to the 19th Dynasty, the style of his stela in Berlin (14200), the orthography and titles attested on his statue in Cairo (CG 589) and the language of the dedication itself assure a date in the mid-18th Dynasty. Helck recognized this, and his Materialien correctly refers to Ahmose as first half of the 18th Dynasty.[213]

In fact, the features of Ahmose on Berlin 14200, together with those of the minor figures, provide material for stylistic comparison. The best comparative material is from Abydos stelae which conveniently have cartouches. Those of Pa-aa-aku (Louvre C53) and Amenhotep, High Priest of Onuris (BM 902)[214] are the closest parallels and both have the cartouches of Thutmose IV. Details which necessitate a date in this reign include the almond-shaped eye appearing on the figure of Ahmose, the straight nose and the small stub of a chin, which are features of Thutmose IV distinctively.[215] The dated stelae from Thutmose's reign regularly show a heightened interest in wig and jewelry details juxtaposed against broad and relatively unbusy spaces. This contrasts with generally more severe wigs, wardrobe and accessories on stelae from Amenhotep II's reign.[216] The figures in the lower register of Ahmose's stela compare favorably with those of both dated works.

Berlin 14200[217]

The limestone round-topped stela of Ahmose, some 55 cm high by 38 cm wide, depicts the prince censing before a statue of the Mnevis bull atop a standard pole.

The prince appears as <u>s3 nsw wr m3w R</u>^c-ĩtm Ỉ^cḥms, "King's son, Chief of seers of Re-Atum, Ahmose". The prince wears the sidelock, a <u>shebiu</u> collar, upper arm bracelets, and the panther skin over a kilt with decorated apron. Two offerers beneath bring offerings, probably from the Temple of Re.

CG 589[218]

This brown quartzite statue, 54 cm. in height, is preserved only to the waist. Ahmose appears seated on a square seat which is inscribed on both sides and down the backpillar as well. Text runs down the front of Ahmose's kilt in three lines, while a decorated apron, such as may be seen on the Berlin stela, hangs from the priest's waist. Despite the formality of the pose, Ahmose's sensitively modeled legs emerge from between the sharply geometrical seat and kilt and soften the overall image. This was the work of a master craftsman.

The text translation runs as follows:[219]

Left side of seat:

"An offering which the king gives to Horus-Min of Coptos and Isis, the Divine mother who created his beauty, that they may give praises, joy, <u>t3 k3 ḥwt</u> (bearing the bull of palaces?[a]), death (<u>pḥ nn</u>) with a good burial after an enduring old age to the Ka of the hereditary prince and noble, the courtier great of love, unique one of the entire land, the good dignitary who is obeyed, the venerated one, enduring of praises, chosen by the king before the Two lands in order to do everything which he ordained in the Temple of father Atum, it being enclosed by walls as an enduring project; one who supervises the affairs of the serfs and the cattle stalls (<u>shm ḥr ḥrwt dt mdwt</u>); a pleasing tongue in the estates, who fills the granaries approaching the sky, Heliopolis and the Temple of Re being made festive with food and daily offerings. Never has the like occurred since the primeval time (except) by the true king's son, his beloved of the place of his heart, the Greatest of seers, beloved of Re, Ahmose.

Right side of seat:

A gift which the king gives to Min of Coptos son of Isis, sweet of love, that he may give his favors before the king, existence before[b] the land following his ka with the gifts of the king to the Ka of the hereditary prince and noble, God's father, beloved of the God, one over the secrets of every shrine, he to whom is reported the condition of the Two lands, he who repeats the words of the King of Lower Egypt to the dignitaries, to whom is spoken the secrets of the heart concerning that which Horus of the palace (<u>ḥwt</u> ^c3t) presented[c] , he who goes forth carrying the offerings (<u>m</u>^c3t) of the lord of the Two lands, the <u>ankh</u> bouquets in his hand for his [presentation] at the nose of the Horus of Horuses[d] by the true king's son, his beloved, Overseer of the houses of silver, Overseer of the houses of gold, Overseer of all royal works, Overseer of bulls, Overseer of granaries, Overseer of pure fields of Atum lord of Heliopolis who seals[e] documents by his own warrants, Greatest of seers Ahmose.

Front of the kilt:

The hereditary prince and noble, sealbearer of the King of Lower Egypt, unique courtier, whom the king chose when he was a sage youth (<u>ḥwn-nfr rḥw</u>), that he might work the land for him in order to sanctify the temple of Atum, exorcising evils from it, the true king's son, his beloved, the Greatest of seers, excellent in his dignity, Ahmose.

<u>Backpillar:</u>

[True king's son, his beloved], Greatest of seers, beloved of Re, Ahmose, may [protection] be placed behind him while his Ka is before him; he is a pillar (<u>iwny</u>), a vindicated one.

<u>Notes:</u>

a: This was translated by Moursi as "mogen sie geben, in die Jahre zu kommen (hs) (?) dem Jungen von den Stierhäusern(?)". The reading of ršwt is quite clear, however, and does not necessitate making of <u>hs</u> a verb; there is no dative so that <u>t3 k3 hwt</u> may mean "carrying the bull of palaces" referring to the Mnevis bull of Heliopolis.

b: <u>wnn [m] b3h t3 hr šms k3.f</u> . Moursi reads "so dass die Leute des Landes (t3j-t3) seinen Ka loben".

c: <u>dd.tw.n.f imnt nt ib r s^crt n Hr hwt ^c3t</u> Moursi reads: "welcher ihm die Geheimnisse des Herzens sagt, um (sie) aufsteigen zu lassen zum hw.t ^c3.t (Tempel in Heliopolis)". This passage is obscure and probably contains a copyist's error, but I have tried to render the falcon as it is written, since there are both <u>3</u> and <u>tyw</u> vultures elsewhere in the text written differently.

d: Moursi reads: "die seine Opfergabe an die Nase des Horus der Falkengötter sind".

e: <u>mr 3hwt w^cb n 'Itm</u>. The same on a model coffin of Royal Herald Re, tp TIV-AIII. CG 48483.

f: <u>htm</u> is written with a phonetic <u>t</u>, but is probably to be taken as masculine participle.

Ahmose, it may be seen from these two monuments, was a man of considerable influence and power in the north of Egypt. He enjoyed respect in the south, as well, as may be concluded from his statue, undoubtedly from Coptos. (The piece reached the Cairo Museum by way of the Consul in Qena.) Concerning Ahmose himself, we must conclude that he was an effective cleric and administrator; his titles and epithets are largely unrelated to his status as a royal family member; they stress his usefulness to the king as an official, not as a son. The fact that he is referred to as "true king's son, his beloved", however, assures Ahmose's position as a prince. Whether he was a son of Amenhotep II or Thutmose IV is unanswerable, but he functioned during the latter's rule. It should be noted here and will be referred to further in Chapter 4 that Ahmose's inscription gives us a firm description of Thutmose IV's building activity at Heliopolis. He is credited with building an enclosure wall which defined the sacred space for the temple of Atum. Ahmose's text also informs us that Thutmose made significant dedications to the Atum temple, while no mention is made of the Temple of Re.

Prince Amenhotep mer-khepesh

The last male prince in consideration is the boy represented on a black granite statue now in the Musées royaux of Brussels (E6856). The statue was published by Capart and Van de Walle who discussed the child and the man Sobekhotep shown holding the prince.[220] A new discussion will appear in the publication of Sobekhotep's tomb, TT 63.[221] The monument depicts a prince seated on the lap of a noble who appears cross-legged. Sobekhotep holds the child by arms placed around his torso. The statue's upper portion is lacking, but the sidelock of the prince and an inscription reveal that a royal child was present. The prince is named Amenhotep   Thus the name was, at least in its form here, Amenhotep mery-khepesh. That name is not attested, but the epithet mry ḥpš, by no means well-known, describes a king at least once in Papyrus Anastasi II,10,1, where it refers to "the bull strong of arm, who loves strength".[222] The prince's name must therefore have meant "Amenhotep who loves (or desires) strength". The identity of this child is not certain because of the unusual name, but at least the two scholars named above identified him as the future Amenhotep III[223]. That the prince was a son of Thutmose IV can hardly be denied. The official Sobekhotep shown holding him was Thutmose's Treasurer and is not known to have been associated with any other monarch. (On this man see Chapter 5.) It is therefore worth consideration that Amenhotep mery-khepesh was the future Amenhotep III.

Van de Walle identified this prince as the future king for a reason other than his name. The child is placed in front-facing position on the cross-legged lap of Sobekhotep. The impression given by this arrangement is, as Van de Walle points out, magisterial and emphasizes the youth greatly over the noble. To compare this statue of prince and tutor with that of Minmose discussed above (CG 638) or with one of Senmut (CG 42116) shows a difference in rendering that should not be ignored. The princes with Minmose were surely his young wards at the time, since they were shown in the block statue by their heads only, exactly as was Minmose. CG 42116 of Senmut, since it is not a block statue, is more analogous to E 6856. Senmut was shown squatting with his left leg straight from knee to foot; Nefrure was seated at a 90° angle to Senmut's body and used the tutor's left leg as a back rest. This arrangement accentuates her importance, but still the statue does not allow the viewer to look directly into her face. Both Nefrure and Senmut are clothed in cloaks which do not delineate between the bodies of the two figures. This continuous garment underscores the attachment of the princess to Senmut. On the statue of Sobekhotep and Amenhotep mery-khepesh, however, the youth appears nearly in the round. The child's clothing is separately indicated and is different in type from Sobekhotep's. The prince is shown wearing the shendyt style kilt, and this caused Van de Walle to suggest that Amenhotep III had already taken the throne when this piece was sculpted.

While the prince on this statue is clearly shown as an important person, his shendyt does not signify that he was already king. Khaemwast (CG 42147) appeared on a statue wearing this kilt. That prince was neither crown prince nor king. Prince Wadjmose, in a stela from his mortuary temple (CG 34016 dated to year 21 of Thutmose III), wore the shendyt as did Ahmose si-pair (CG 34029) on a votive stela. The High priest of Amun and son of Shabako, Horemakhet, also appeared in this garb (CG 42204). Thus princes could wear the royal kilt on occasion,and further it is true that Amenhotep mery-khepesh did not have a pleated kilt on his statue. The ungoffered version was occasionally worn by private persons, as in the case of the youth Huwebenef (MMA 26.7.1414).[224] Hayes suggested this child wore the kilt as an indication of technical manhood. Perhaps Hayes' comment might also explain Amenhotep mery-khepesh's use of the shendyt kilt on this statue.

Given that the reasoning above is sound, Amenhotep mery-khepesh may have been a boy near puberty when he was portrayed with Sobekhotep. The statue was probably made in the last years of Thutmose' reign. Sobekhotep's titles on his statue were those in his tomb, and yet the boy was not pictured there. There is no chronological barrier to suggesting Amenhotep III is represented by this prince. And of course he might also have been the Amenhotep named on Konosso graffiti and the prince shown in private tomb 64. That last prince Amenhotep was given preferential treatment as was Amenhotep mery-khepesh on the statue. It is reasonable to identify these three princes named Amenhotep as one and the same boy. (And if this is true, we are in possession of an interesting name variation for the future king.)

A final piece of information may be gleaned from Brussels E 6856. The statue is dedicated to Sobek Shedty, Horus in the Midst of Crocodilopolis and Osiris in the midst of Ta She. These titles belong to Fayumic gods and imply an origin from that region. This should not surprise us since Sobekhotep was a native of the Fayum and functioned as Mayor of the Southern She of Sobek before he took his father Min's position as Treasurer. But there may be a further link to the Fayum. Thutmose IV and his mother Tiaa had attachments to the Fayum. Sobekhotep was involved in raising princes and his wife was nurse to Thutmose's daughter Tiaa. It is probable that the Fayum harem was the site of activity by both Sobekhotep and his wife Meryt, and it is therefore likely that Amenhotep mery- khepesh also resided for a time in that institution. If the prince was the future Amenhotep III, then he may have spent some years in the region of Gurob as a child. Perhaps he developed a fondness for the area; it is known that several of his family members spent time late in his rule at the Fayum palace.

The succession of Thutmose IV: Resumed

The most important question remains in the realm of pure speculation. Was the prince (or princes) of Stelae A and B a rival for the throne to which Thutmose acceded? The stelae are lost, and any historical conclusions from them must remain tentative, as Cannuyer has wisely noted.[225] To achieve precision is beyond our present capability; our hope is rather to suggest the milieu from which these stelae stem.

A number of princes can be documented for the reign of Thutmose III and Amenhotep II, disregarding the reign of Thutmose IV altogether: Amenemhet, Siamun, Menkheper, Amenhotep, Thutmose, Khaemwast(?), Prince A/B; Amenemipet, Webensenu, Nedjem. Perhaps Aakheprure was born late in Amenhotep's reign. This plurality of young royal males is in contrast to the earlier part of the dynasty when adult princes appeared to be scarce: perhaps they died on military campaigns, or from childhood illnesses. Ahmose (sa-pair), Wadjmose, Amenmose, and Amenemhet are the few names left us of those who did not reach the throne. Amenhotep I left no heir; Thutmose I left Thutmose II whose age and competence are in some doubt. Thutmose II left the young Thutmose III; we know of no other princes. The scarceness of princes may, of itself, be expected to have inspired rulers to take lesser wives. There is at least some reason to think that Thutmose III did just that.[226] How Amenhotep II produced his numerous offspring, however, remains uncertain.

It was not only his able procreative powers that separates Amenhotep II from his predecessors. For unlike those before him this king had no publicly acknowledged wife. Amenhotep's mother Meryt-re served as his consort as Great Royal Wife for much of his reign, and even appears in his Jubilee kiosk at Karnak.[227] The absence of wives might be considered a conscious rejection of the powerful role played by queens from the establishment of the Dynasty through the reign of Hatshepsut. Her usurpation of the throne may have encouraged Thutmose III's and Amenhotep II's desire both to leave male sons and to prevent queens from becoming independently wealthy and powerful. Perhaps this was the motivation for kings to marry outside the royal family, as did Thutmose III in choosing Sit-Iah and Meryt-re[228]. And perhaps also the office of God's Wife of Amun was intentionally granted to these non-royal king's wives and mothers over whom the kings had effective control.   Whatever princes were born to Thutmose III and Amenhotep II must have been raised with the assurance of the family line in mind. Thus Thutmose III made no premature announcement of the heir to his throne. Meryt-re's appearance on Thutmose III's monuments is probably to be linked with Amenhotep's designation as intended heir. Likewise the Mayor of Thinis and Royal Nurse Min would have claimed the specific title "[Father] and Nurse to the Prince [Amenhotep]"[229] only after the intent of succession had been announced. (The royal announcement of Amenhotep's kingship on his Sphinx Stela may even have been the signal that the dishonoring of Hatshepsut's line was legitimate.) On the statue dedicated by Prince Thutmose in the Mut Temple of Karnak, Hekareshu is termed generally Nurse of the Royal Children, despite the fact that he accompanies but one prince. In tomb 64, however, he is "Nurse to the eldest king's son of his body Thutmose Khakhau". Certainly we cannot then conclude that Thutmose was the designated successor of Amenhotep II from his statue. Nor can we conclude that he was not.

Tiaa, Thutmose's mother, cannot be certainly attested on a monument of Amenhotep II's other than as a later addition, but like Meryt-re, she served as Great Royal Wife and God's Wife of Amun for Thutmose, alongside two more contemporary women. There is no evidence before her son's reign that Tiaa's position influenced the succession. We would then be safe in concluding that Thutmose was raised in a manner common to all the sons of Amenhotep II that we know of--at court by royal nurses and tutors. Despite the fact that Amenhotep II may have hoped to see a particular son succeed him, prudence dictated that all the princes be similarly trained.

The institution to nurture these princes was already in place and was most useful in this period. Royal nurses, together with tutors from the ranks of retired courtiers, nurtured and educated royal children during the 18th Dynasty. The burgeoning documentation for princes at this time is thus probably no accident at all. Offspring of the king received attention and training through the Royal Nurses whose court recognition served to honor both the children and the tutors. The institution likewise allowed the king to oversee the content of the royal children's education.

Competition among the swelling ranks of capable young princes, particularly with the cessation of regular military campaigns in Asia after the first decade of Amenhotep II's reign, is not difficult to imagine. And competition can erupt unexpectedly into struggle among ambitious youths. The defacement of the Giza stelae suggests some sort of damnatio memoriae, but there is presently no way to demonstrate that 1) Thutmose was or was not the heir and that 2) his victory over another prince provoked the defacement of stelae A, B and C. It is equally possible that Prince B attempted to disrupt Thutmose's succession. By virtue of his given name, Thutmose may have been considered a favored prince, while Webensenu may not have been. (This, however, is an unproven argument, since kings could certainly change their names at will.) If his brother had tried to usurp his title to the throne, Thutmose would understandably have wished to remove the evidence. His interest in Giza generally would also be natural if another prince had tried to win support in the region. Despite the speculative character of this discussion, we continue to believe the Giza stelae should not be ignored as evidence of a struggle; but we do not conclude that Thutmose IV was a usurper.

1. Urk. IV 1540-45.

2. Selim Hassan, The Great Sphinx and its Secrets: Excavations at Giza Vol. VIII (Cairo 1953).

3. Ibid., IX, where she is called sic "Miss Edith Dorothy", an understandable error.

4. By her own admission. She is not credited by Selim Hassan, no doubt because of Antiquities Service regulations. She has related this fact, however, to a number of people during her frequent visits to the Epigraphic Expedition of the University of Chicago's Luxor "Chicago House". Indeed, I am indebted to Dr. William Murnane for first informing me of Omm Sety's views.

5. W.K. Simpson in W.W. Hallo and W.K. Simpson, The Ancient Near East: A History (New York 1971); my own dissertation bears the continued mark, The Reign of Tuthmosis IV, Chapter 2.

6. Hassan, The Great Sphinx, 90-91.

7. C. Zivie, Giza au deuxième millénaire, 266, still supporting an overthrow by Thutmose.

8. Redford, Pharaonic King-Lists, 168.

9. C. Cannuyer, "Notules à propos de la stèle du Sphinx", VA 1 (1985) 83-90. Bryan, The Reign of Tuthmosis IV, 46-52.

10. But this position has been taken at least once. W. Budge, Book of the Kings I, 134, called him a son of Thutmose IV.

11. Cf. Maspero in The Tomb of Thoutmôsis IV, XVIII.

12. Urk. IV 1282, 13.

13. Urk. IV 1281, 17.

14. For example, E. Hornung, "Zur geschichtlichen Rolle des Königs in der 18. Dynastie", MDAIK 15 (1957) 120-33. R. Moftah, Studien zum Ägyptischen Königsdogma im Neuen Reich, Deutsches Archaologisches Institut Abteilung Kairo, Sonderschrift 20, hereafter ADAIK, (Mainz 1985) 99-117, especially 105.

15. Urk. IV 157-161; E. Naville, Deir el Bahri VI, 166. See D. Redford, Seven Studies, 74-76.

16. Ahmose, Urk. IV 14; Thutmose I, Urk. IV 86, 96; Thutmose II, Urk. IV 139; Thutmose III, Urk. IV 610-19; Amenhotep II, Urk. IV 1276 ff; Thutmose IV, Urk. IV 1540, 20. E. Hornung, MDAIK 15 (1957), discussed this aspect of the royal role in the 18th dynasty and cited Thutmose IV several times as an example of the "divine seed" (130-31). This emphasis is evident from the 4th dynasty on and shows intensification with the description of Sesostris I on the Berlin Leather Roll, and 18th dynasty hieratic copy. A de Buck, Studia Aegyptiaca I, 48-57, where the king calls himself the son of Horakhty. On this see also W. Helck, Oriens Antiquus 8 (1969) 312-17, who also identified Thutmose IV as part of this trend.

17. Urk. IV 215-34.

18. Urk. IV 243; 255-58.

19. Urk. IV 1281ff.

20. Most scholars believe there was a brief co-regency of Thutmose III and Amenhotep II. Recently, Wente and Van Siclen, "A Chronology", 227.

21. D. Redford, JEA 51 (1965) 117; G. Steindorff, K. Seele, When Egypt Ruled the East, 67.

22. P. Dorman, Monuments of Senenmut, (London 1988).

23. B.J. Kemp, Ancient Egypt Anatomy of a Civilization (London 1989) 200, makes this same point. "To dismiss the sources as propaganda misses the point, particularly if it implied that they differ in purpose from documents from other reigns". However, even recent sources make reference to the legitimating force of Hatshepsut's inscriptions: W. Seipel, "Hatshepsut I", Lexikon der Ägyptologie, hereafter LÄ, II, 1045; J. Ruffle, The Egyptians,(Ithaca, New York 1977) 66.

24. C. Zivie, Giza au Deuxieme Millenaire, 322-24.

25. PM II² 347.

26. Urk. IV, 1276, 13-14. s3 [Imn] shpr n.f. n.f mstyw n Hr3hty.
1276,16. wtt n P3wty-t3wy r itt hk3t itt n.f. "The son of Amun whom he sired by himself, the offspring of Horakhty...he whom the Primeval god of the Two Lands begot in order to take possession of the rule which he has taken." 1283,4. dd.f m ib.f hr hr.f r hpr.t wd n n.f it Rᶜ "It was until that which father Re commanded for him should happen [sdm.t] that he placed his desire in check." [literally, "under his control".

27. Urk. IV 1565.

28. Urk. IV 1572.

29. LD III Text 260.

30. K. Sethe, Untersuchungen, 59 n. 1; F. Gomaa, Chaemwese, 10-11. B. Schmitz, Untersuchungen, 297, suggested, however, that although s3 nsw smsw meant "eldest surviving son" in the 19th dynasty, it meant "first-born" in the 18th. She argued that as a rule every king had one son whom he designated s3 nsw smsw and so it probably means first-born. Schmitz expalined that two sons of Ahmose did not actually have the title, but the princes were one and the same. She also denied that two "king's eldest sons" belonged to Thutmose III's family. She removed the title from Amenhotep II by stating that the Sphinx Stela reference was not to a formal title and therefore was not vaid (he was called "my eldest son" by Thutmose III.) But see D. Redford, JEA 51, 118. She did not explain why Thutmose IV was called "king's eldest son" only after he became king.

31. Urk. IV 1551, 4, Amun being the one who made him.

32. Urk. IV 1689, 20.

33. H. Brunner, Die Geburt, 28. Wente and Van Siclen, "A Chronology", 230; Wente, X-ray Atlas, 252-53.

34. W. Helck, Historisch-biographische Texte, 137; W. F. Petrie, Buttons and Design Scarabs, pl. XXIV, 18.8.15, in University College London. J. Weinstein, Foundation Deposits, 213-14, and 128. He noted that the use of these plaques in the mid-18th dynasty (until Amenhotep IV in fact) is confined to Thebes. Thus the provenance is strengthened.

35. D. Meeks, RdE 28 (1976) 88-89. See also W.J. Murnane, Ancient Egyptian Coregencies, 254-55. He calls the inpw a "puppy".

36. Urk. IV 1540-41. Especially, 1540, 10, where he is described as being prepared for kingship. The retrospective, 1541, 1ff., describes his pre-accession abilities.

37. A.H. Gardiner, Egyptian Grammar[3], Sections 119,2; 212; 231.

38. See, particularly, Gr[3] 119 note 3, from the Eloquent Peasant. A description of the location of Nemty-nakht's house on the river bank where the road narrowed. This information was descriptive but essential to an understanding of what ensued between Nemty-nakht and the peasant.

39. Urk. IV, 1283.

40. Urk. IV 1565.

41. See, especially, Gr[3], Section 414.

42. Brunner, Die Geburt, 28, citing Urk. IV 260, 2-3, which reads m3t.sn m3t.sn rn n hmt.s m nsw sk hmt.s m inpw. "They proclaim and proclaim the name of her Majesty as king while she is [yet] a young child."

43. Weinstein, op. cit., 432-33.

44. Found in Trench A (Benson and Gourlay, <u>The Temple of Mut in Asher</u>, 328-30). <u>PM</u> II² 258-59. See also in L. Borchardt, <u>Statuen</u> III, 156; <u>Urk</u>. IV 1575.

45. W. Hayes, <u>The Scepter of Egypt</u> II, 106, fig. 57. A color photograph in A. Eggebrecht, ed., <u>Ägyptens Aufstieg zur Weltmacht</u> (Mainz 1987) 158-59.

46. J. P. Frandsen, <u>Acta Orientalia</u> 37 (1976) 7.

47. L. Habachi in <u>Festschrift für Siegfried Schott zur seinem 70. Geburtstag</u>, 61-70.

48. H. Gauthier, <u>LdR</u> II, 303.

49. <u>PM</u> II² 260.

50. H. Brunner, <u>ZÄS</u> 86 (1961) 90-100.

51. Frandsen, op. cit., 10.

52. Brunner, <u>ZÄS</u> 86, 93 with n. 2.

53. <u>Ibid</u>., 90.

54. Theban tomb 64 scenes show the king enthroned twice and on the lap of Hekareshu twice. <u>PM</u> 1² 1 128. The four graffiti of Hekareshu from Konosso consistently use God's father as his title and are associated with the cartouches and texts of Thutmose IV. <u>PM</u> V 254-55. For other bibliography see under Royal nurses in Chapter 5.

55. Brunner, <u>ZÄS</u> 86, 94.

56. <u>Ibid</u>., 91.

57. <u>Urk</u>. IV 976-82. This is a more serious objection to Brunner's thesis that the title ỉt designated those who raised princes without throne rights. Min may have borne the title, but he was not God's Father. The original publication shows a gap (see below n. 85). And what of female nurses? Amenemipet, mother of Kenamun, was pictured as nurse to Amenhotep II. She was never given any title paralleling God's Father, but her son Kenamun was a ỉt ntr. He had no known relationship to a son of Amenhotep II. <u>Urk</u>. IV 1389. For Hekarnehhe, see <u>PM</u> I 1 128.

58. As in the case of the Second Prophet of Amun, Amenhotep si-se in the reign of Thutmose IV, <u>Urk</u>. IV 1213, 15. The Herald Re appeared with princes at Konosso, <u>Urk</u>. IV 1575. He may, however, have received the ỉt ntr title from Amenhotep III. The rank is attested on his model coffins.

59. Hekareshu, Th. tb. 64, <u>Urk</u>. IV 1572ff.
    Sobekhotep, Th. tb. 63, <u>Urk</u>. IV 1582ff.
    Tjenuna, Th. tb. 76, <u>Urk</u>. IV 1581.
    Hepu, Th. tb. 66, <u>Urk</u>. IV 1576-77.
    Amenhotep si-se, Th. tb. 75, <u>Urk</u>. IV 1208-16.
    Re, Th. tb. 201, texts unpublished. Title appears on model coffin, CG 48483.
    Meri, High priest of Amun, <u>Urk</u>. IV 1570-71 (reign of Amenhotep II)
    Amenemhet, High priest of Amun, Th. tb. 75, <u>Urk</u>. IV 1408-14.

60. See Kees, <u>ZÄS</u> 86 (1961) 111-25, for the viziers of the 18th dynasty who held the title. Some examples of various holders of the title include: Djehuty, General under Thutmose III, <u>Urk</u>. IV 999; Rekhmire, <u>Urk</u>. IV 1119-71, Vizier under Thutmose III; Iamunedjeh, <u>Urk</u>. IV 958, 16, Judge; Amenemipet, <u>Urk</u>. IV 1438, 11, Vizier under Amenhotep II; Suemniwet, Royal butler, <u>Urk</u>. IV 1452; Usersatet, Viceroy of Nubia, <u>Urk</u>. IV 1488. These are by no means all the officeholders but are representative. Brunner attempted to explain this diversity by suggesting they all shared responsibility for crown princes, <u>ZÄS</u> 86, 93.

61. Kees, <u>ZÄS</u> 86, 117, notes that Sobekhotep, Hekareshu, Tjenuna, among others, received the God's Father rank because of their personal relationship to the king. Senmut and Kenamun, according to Kees, received their titles because of close family ties to the rulers. But Kees believed they exercised sacerdotal duties as God's Fathers, and while this is no doubt true, it is difficult to assess the cultic importance of the office in contrast to its prestige at court for some individuals.

62. Brunner's opinion about Ay is based implicitly on his frequent and major use of the title God's father. Ay cannot be shown to have borne the title before Akhenaten took the throne, but he did choose to use it almost exclusively. Apparently Brunner saw that Hekareshu also used God's father on his shabtis and graffiti and made the conclusion that both men were publicizing their nurse relationships to crown princes. Brunner felt that the frequency with which the title was used by these men indicated how active they were as "Erzieher". But their use of God's father could have been influenced by other factors. Hekareshu had no true functions in titulary beyond "nurse". Ay's other ranks were paramilitary. No doubt the latter wished, as Brunner said, to point up his closeness to the court, and he may have been active in cultic performances as well. And Senmut, major tutor to Nefrure, used the title God's father seldom (see Kees, <u>ZÄS</u> 86, 115). The suggestion that Ay was a God's father because of his marriage to Nefertiti's nurse (Kees, <u>ZÄS</u> 86, 117, e.g.) may have more credibility if it is noted that his position at court would have been enhanced by his attachment and therefore he may have assumed a counselor's relation toward Akhenaten. 'It ntr as a title did not designate him as "father-in-law of the god", however. Gardiner's original interpretation is best. See A. H. Gardiner, <u>Onomasticon</u>, I 51*.

63. Thutmose called Amenhotep II his father on a statue of the latter at Karnak, <u>Urk</u>. IV 1561; Horemhab (tomb 78) called Thutmose a son of Amenhotep, <u>Urk</u>. IV 1589, 11. See Elliot Smith's remarks about the resemblance of father and son, <u>The Royal Mummies</u>, 44-45.

64. Borchardt, Statuen, pl. 117, CG 638, Urk. IV 1447. The statue was said to be from Karnak based on oral communication by Barsanti. It is of black granite, 1.09m. ht. A block type. The face is weathered away and the princes' heads are nearly eroded away. The names are slightly destroyed: 𓍿𓏲𓏏𓀀 and 𓊽𓏤𓈖𓏌𓏲, but identification as Webensenu is sure. Kees, Das Priestertum, Nachträge, 35, supported the notion that this was Minmose's last monument, dating after Year 4 of Amenhotep II's reign. See now Der Manuelian, op.cit., 166; 176 for discussion and agreement that these are sons of Amenhotep II.

65. CG 5031 𓊽𓏤𓈖𓏌𓏲 ;CG 24269-73. The canopics were found in the second hall following the stairs where there was a bed of broken objects--funerary statuettes, pottery with the name of Amenhotep II and some objects of Webensenu. E. Thomas, The Royal Necropoleis of Thebes, 80, refers to "a canopic jar, four probable lids, and five ushebtis" which belonged to the prince. See also Loret, Les tombeaux de Thoutmés III: et d'Amenophis II, 13.

66. CG 24269.

67. CG 5031.

68. E. Drioton, "Rapport...Medamoud", 1926, FIFAO, 52ff; Urk. IV 1441-45.

69. Urk. IV 1441, 15-1442, 15. As royal scribe.

70. Urk. IV 1442, 16-20.

71. Urk. IV 695-96. Year 33, Urk. IV 702-03. W. Helck, Beziehungen, 140-42, 151-52, with note 93.

72.Urk. IV 1232, 11.

73. Urk. IV 1448, 13. A.H. Gardiner, Ancient Egyptian Onomasticon I, 150*-151*. Der Manuelian, op.cit., 53-54.

74. Urk. IV 1443, 1-20.

75. Urk. IV 1444, 11-14. (Also ḥ3ty-ᶜ mr ḥmw-ntr m pr Mntw nb w3st See W. Helck, Verwaltung, 221-23 on this combination of titles.)

76. Urk. IV 1444, 15 and 1441, 14. (Overseer of works in the temples of the gods of Upper and Lower Egypt, royal scribe.)

77. Drioton, op. cit., 52.

78. W. F. Petrie, Nebesheh, pl. X, 5; Urk. IV 1445-46. Found in the small temple at Nebesheh. Three figures are shown seated before two altars. A retrograde inscription runs on the front of the altars.

79. Urk. IV 1447, 5.

80. Borchardt, Statuen, CG 638.

81. Urk. IV 1447, 13-15.

82. Urk. IV 1447, 6-7.

83. Urk. IV 1441, 6, 1445, 18, 1445, 5-6. "I am one who goes forth being happy, who goes down happy, who enters safe at the Per-Nefer, I having provided my place with property and workers." In contrast to himself, Minmose did request "a thousand of" for prince Webensenu, Urk. IV 1447, 20.

84. Urk. IV 1447, 10.

85. Urk. IV 1447, 11-12.

86. Callender, Middle Egyptian, 111, cites from Sinuhe B41: n wf3:tw.i n psg:tw r-hr.i "I was not gossiped about; I was not spit in the face." and page 102-03, n sdmw.f serves as past tense of the passive, substituting for our passage: n gm(y):w wn.i m r3w-prw. "No transgression of mine has been found in the temples", Urk. IV 484. He gives no specific discussion of n sdm.tw.f under Negation and cited Sinuhe under Passivization as a "past" example, 110-11.

87. J. Polotsky, "Les Transpositions", 29. On page 25 in note 46, Polotsky translates an n sdm.tw.f without deciding between present or past, but all his other argument tends to force the conclusion that it must be a completed past action. The best example of how the tense alternates with sdmw.f can be found in the context cited above at Urk. IV 484, 5-10: šms n.f Hr nb ꜥh/mdd n.f rdit n.f m hr.i/ n wny.i hr sp n nb t3wy/ ndr n mtrt n.f hr.i/ n ỉw sp.i m stp-š3/ n srh.tw.i mm šnyt/n gm.wn.i m rw-prw/ nn bš pf sh3w n.(i) r rwty. Here past narrative sdm.n.i is negated by n sdm.f, n sdm.tw.f and n sdm.f. One might argue about the name for sms.n.i but not that it relates to past actions. Polotsky, op. cit., 20, concludes that sdm.n.tw.f is excluded from circumstantial function (as would be n sdm.tw.f). These forms therefore appear to be substantives with following adverbials, i.e., m stp-s3, mm šnyt, etc.

88. Urk. IV 1448, 14.

89. Urk. IV 1443, 1; 1444, 2; 1444, 14.

90. Urk. IV 1447, 13.

91. H. DeMeulenaere, "Le directeur des travaux Minmose", MDAIK 37 (1981) 315-19, taf. 50-51. The assignment of the statuette to this man is questionable since the laconic title wr w3d read by DeMeulenaere on the statuette was given to Minmose by Thutmose III only after the Syrian campaigns (Urk IV, 1441-44) His title as Royal scribe, Overseer of Works in the Temples of Upper and Lower Egypt or Overseer of Priests of Montu Lord of Thebes should therefore be present. Instead

two titles otherwise unattested for him occur: Overseer of the Ges-Per for the God's Wife (Ahmose Humay, father of Mayor of Thebes Sennefer held the same title. See Helck, Verw. 297 n.1) and Processional Leader for Osiris. Stylistically the statuette suits a date in the first half of Thutmose III's reign, probably during the coregency. (Cf., Luxor Museum of Ancient Egyptian Art Catalogue (Cairo 1979), nrs. 55, 58 = J 138, J 151. Also nr. 52. It is not inconceivable that Minmose was already functioning with a son as High Priest of Osiris and a daughter was a royal nurse. It is, however,not at all assured.

92. See discussion of length of Amenhotep II's reign in Der Manuelian, op.cit., 42-44, who suggests caution and rejects the extended reign proposed by Wente and Van Siclen.

93. C. Cannuyer, "Notules à propos de la stèle du Sphinx", Varia Aegyptiaca 1 (1985) 89 n .29.

94. One might note in this instance that the current Prince of Wales carries a name not used by a ruler since the Restoration, despite the fact that all kings of the past two and a half centuries have been named either Edward or George.

95. S.R.K. Glanville, ZÄS 66 (1930) 105-21; ZÄS 68 (1932) 7-41. D. Redford, JEA 51 (1965) 105-22. Der Manuelian, op.cit., 174-76.

96. V. Golenischeff, Les Papyrus hiératiques No. 1115, 1116A, et 1116B de l'Hermitage impérial à St. Petersbourg. Glanville had been the one originally to place the papyri together. He supposed 1116B and BM 10056 to have been written by the same hand, but he also thought they all resembled Louvre 3226 of Thutmose III's reign.

97. Glanville, ZÄS 66, 106, believed the date in Vs. 9, 8 (also ZÄS 66, 120 n. 8) was certainly 30, but he gave other readings. Redford chose 20 (JEA 51, 110), because Amenhotep II was considered to have ruled 26 years.

98. Golenischeff, op. cit., 1116B, Vs. 56, 61, and 66.

99. Ibid., 1116A, Vs. 19.

100. Ibid., 1116A, Vs. 50.

101. Golenischeff did not assert that the Hermitage papyri were of the same date, but Redford seems to have thought so. In fact there is no repetition of onomastica or of matters dealt with. The records of 1116A show details of Palestinian places strongly associated with Thutmose III's campaigns. The name restored by Golenischeff and Redford as ˤ3-ḫpr[rˤ]r-nḥḥ was not broken but never contained "Re" as an element. It may not be a prenomen-type name. (But one of the Horus names of Kamose was ˤ3-ḫprw.)

102. Wente and Van Siclen, "A Chronology", 228.

103. J. DeMorgan, Catalogue I, 69, 5 = LD IV Text 127 = W.F. Petrie, A Season I #32 = Champollion, Notices I 618 #10. Also DeMorgan, Cat. 70, 19 = LD IV Text 128 = Petrie, A Season I #23; J. Newberry, JEA 14 (192d) 85 n. 1-2 gives fuller bibliography. A second graffito of Re with prince Aakheprure is given for Sehel by DeMorgan, Cat. 103, 16 = A. Mariette, Mon. Div. 70, 16.

104. Newberry, JEA 14, 85; Habachi, Schott Festschrift, 66 and 69; Norman Davies, Tombs of Menkheperreseneb, 40; Redford, JEA 51, 113; Frandsen, Acta Orientalia 37, 10.

105. Der Manuelian, op.cit., 174-75, does not accept the date of the nearby stela, Year 7 or 8, for the inscription and perhaps does not accept the graffiti's dating in the reign of Thutmose IV. This, however, is the only acceptable interpretation of Lepsius' description: "Neben den Schildern des Apries stehen rechts etwas höher die Thutmosis'IV, unter diesen waren konigliche Prinzen dargestellt; die Darstellung war ehemals grösser nach links und nach unten als jetzt, Apries hat sie, als er seine Namen aufsetzte, abpolieren lassen. [Jetzt nur] rechts unter den Namen Thutmosis 'IV [noch zu lesen]: [here is the drawn graffito of Re (horizontal) and the two princes and Hekarnehhe beneath (vertically).] Rechts daneben: [here the graffito with a htp di nsw formula for the God's Father Hekareshu]. Noch weiter rechts immer an demselben Felsen stehen, schon von weitem sichtbar, die Schilder Psammetich's II LD III 274 e; darunter eine grösse Stele von Thutmosis IV, die lange Inschrift ist datiert vom 2ten Tage des 3 ten Wintermonats des 7ten Jahres; oben opfert der König Wein dem Amon-Re, der wieder in ganzer Figur ausgekratzt ist, und dem Chnubis. Unter der Stele erscheinen wieder die Prinzen. [Here the graffito, written horizontally of Hekareshu, followed by the princes written vertically.]"

106. Supra n. 101. For Hekareshu, see Habachi, Schott Fest. 68-69; PM I 1 128, 129; LD III 69a, Newberry, JEA 14, pl. XII.

107. Redford, JEA 51, 113.

108. Ibid., 113, also based on the cartouches.

109. PM 112 492; W. Wreszinski, Atlas II, 139; Medinet Habu II, pl. 61, 75, 76, 81-83.

110. For example, in the Luxor Temple reliefs, Ramesses II is shown on Syrian campaigns. Princes follow the king; soldiers and chariots are shown behind. There also the king receives captives from princes. The Ramesseum, princes were present in scenes when the king is given life and heb sed insignia. LD III 168b, PM 112 438. Many of Ramesses' sons had military titles, e.g., mr mš^{c}w, mr ssmwt; Khaemwast had religious functions. See, protocols in Schulman, Military Rank, #349: Merneptah, mr mš^{c}w, mr mš^{c}w wr; Ramessu, mr mš^{c}w; mr mš^{c}w wr; Amenherkhepeshef, mr mš^c wr; Pareherwenemef, mr ssmwt; Montuherkhepeshef, mr ssmwt.

111. Re was termed "first royal herald" and Hekareshu, "God's father," their most widely-cited and, presumably, major ranks.

112. This is of no great historical moment, but Redford did assume that the parallelism of their names indicated a fraternal relationship, JEA 51, 113. This may be, but it cannot be sure.

113. Supra, n. 102.

114. Der Manuelian, op.cit., 180.

115. G. Elliot Smith, The Royal Mummies. 41-42, gives a 40-50 age estimate for Amenhotep III. J. Harris and K. Weeks, op. cit., 142, agreed with this and further opted for 50 years based on the length of his reign.

116. Newberry, JEA 14, pl. XII; LD III 69; Champollion, Not. I 863, gives readings for the pectorals.

117. Both titles appear consistently in the tomb and on the funerary cones. See, for example, Urk. IV 1572-76. The nurse title occurs five time in the tomb and three times on funerary cones.(Based on personal inspection of the tomb). "Child of the Nursery" occurs three times in the tomb and twice on funerary cones. It appears twice alone on tombs texts, but probably only once originally. An unpublished Northwest wall scene of Hekarnehhe before Thutmose IV in a kiosk called him "Child of the Nursery", but the legend above, now lost, also identified him at one time. All but the start of two short columns beginning ⌣⌣⌣ is destroyed. It is probably that the twin to this text appeared on the Southwest wall where Hekareshu was named: mn hswt m stp-s3 ᶜnh wd3 snb t3y hw hr wnmy nsw... "enduring of praises from the palace (life, prosperity, health), fanbearer on the right of the king". In a ceiling text Hekarnehhe was termed mn hswt m stp-s3 ᶜnh wd3 snb mnᶜy n s3 nsw n ht.f mr.f Imn-htp hrd n k3p Hk3rnhh. "enduring of praises from the palace (life, prosperity, health), Nurse of the King's son of his body, beloved of him, Amenhotep, the Child of the Nursery Hekarnehhe".

　　Child of the Nursery does not appear alone on a funerary cone, although Helck, Urk. IV 1576, showed Daressy 39 bis as if only that title were present. Actually the gap and writing of β rather than ∫ demonstrates that Daressy's 39 bis and Berlin Nr. 8750 were identical. That cone was misread by Helck who saw ⚹ "royal butler". The drawing in Berlin Inschriften II, 302, shows rather that ⚹ "Royal Nurse" as in Davies, Corpus #102, is the correct reading. Frandsen recognized that "Royal Butler" was impossible on Berlin 8750, but he thought that cone was identical with Davies #102. Examination of the references will verify the conclusion made here.

　　The nurse's title appears alone twice in tomb 64 for Hekarnehhe, and once on a funerary cone. Hekarnehhe's nurse titles were, from this evidence, more numerous and could be used alone, while "Child of the Nursery" normally accompanied his nursing rank, at least at the time of his tomb's completion.

118. Gaballa, Narrative in Egyptian Art, 5-6, makes it clear that time was portrayed visually in two ways, by specific dating and by implication, that is, by selected elements in the scene. Gaballa had no comment on whether retrospectives such as the scene in tomb 64 could also name persons who were, on the one hand, perhaps grown at the time remembered, e.g., whether the prince Amenhotep might have

been an adult in Thutmose IV's youth, or on the other hand, not yet born at the time remembered, e.g., whether the prince Amenemhet pictured there are Thutmose IV's child buried with him in KV 43.

119. Discussion of this point was given above, since Brunner, followed by Wente and van Siclen, concluded that Thutmose IV took the throne while still a child.

120. See, for example, K. Michalowski, <u>Art of Ancient Egypt</u>, (Abrams New York) 405 fig. 515. Sety I as a small king suckles standing from the greatly larger seated goddess Mut. From the Temple of Abydos.

121. See the discussion of Re as Royal Herald in Chapter 5.

122. Frandsen, <u>op.cit.</u>, 9-10, n. 28.

123. Helck, <u>Einfluss</u>, 34.

124. <u>Ibid.</u>, 35.

125. <u>Ibid.</u>, 36. It might be noted in addition that two of Helck's examples of children of the Nursery who became nurses were incorrect. Neither Hekareshu nor the owner of tomb 226 was a "page". <u>Ibid.</u> 35, n.1 See a discussion in Chapter 5.

126. <u>Urk</u>. IV 1575.

127. Helck, <u>Einfluss</u>, 60-62.

128. Schulman, <u>Military Rank</u>, 46-47.

129. M. Wegner, <u>MDAIK</u> 4, (1933) 120, dated the tomb to the last part of Thutmose' reign.

130. Tomb 64 has been correctly identified by Frandsen as the last resting place of Hekarnehhe, not Hekareshu, as Habachi, <u>Schott Fest.</u>, 70, proposed. <u>Acta Orientalia</u> 37, 9.

131. Redford, <u>JEA</u> 51, 113.

132. The fact that the prince was termed "king's son of his body" does not indicate only Thutmose IV's body. The notion that princes lost their "king's son" title at their father's death is contradicted by the fact that many queens employed their "king's daughter" titles while wife to their father's successor. The term <u>nsw</u> in these ranks does not indicate only the reigning king. Thus a queen could be both "king's daughter" and "king's sister" referring to two different monarchs. That it worked differently for males is hardly believable. See H. DeMeulenaere, "Le Vizir Ramesside Hori", <u>Ann. de l'inst. de Phil. et d'Hist. Orient et Slaves</u> 20 (1968-72) 191-86, esp. 195 n. 1, who argued that the son of Ramesses II, Khaemwast, was named on a statue as Hori's ancestor without being called "king's son" because

Merneptah was reigning when the statue was made. There may have been less motivation to use the title after the fathers died, but there is no evidence that "king's son" was revoked. (See CG 34016 = Urk. IV 108, for posthumous use.)

133. Newberry, JEA 14, pl. XII; Carter and Newberry, The Tomb of Thoutmôsis IV, 6-7. 4 jars, CG 46037-39, one in Boston, MFA, 03.1129, Edward Brovarski, Canopic Jars Corpus Antiquitatum Aegyptiacarum Museum of Fine Arts Boston Fascicle I (Mainz 1978) 1/3 to 3/3. He is termed simply "king's son".

134. Ibid., X and Thomas, op. cit., 81.

135. Newberry, JEA 14, pl. XII.

136. Urk. IV 1573.

137. Davies, Menkheperreseneb, 35-40, pls. XXX, XL-XLV.

138. Ibid., 40. Davies notes that two could be princesses.

139. Ibid., pl. XXX.

140. Compare the tomb of Amenemheb, 85, whose wife Baky, appeared three times holding a prince (Amenhotep II?). Twice this occurred on pillars rather than on wall scenes. Amenemheb was a military officer, but his wife's court connection made her figure strongly in minor scenes from the chapel. The owner of tomb 226 was not mainly "chief nurse" but was termed "Overseer of all works of the king" in the kiosk scene. He was also "hereditary prince and count, royal scribe true and beloved of him, fanbearer on the right of the king". Davies, Menkheperreseneb, pl. XLII.

141. Ibid., 37.

142. Newberry, JEA 14, 82-83, n.4.

143. Habachi, Schott Fest., 70.

144. Frandsen, Acta Orientalia 37, 9.

145. Davies, Menkheperreseneb, pl. XXX, E.

146. Ibid., 39-40.

147. Ibid., 39 n. 7.

148. Schmitz, op. cit., 266.

149. Now restored and on display in the Luxor Museum, #J 134.

150. Redford, <u>JEA</u> 51, 113.

151. Redford, <u>JEA</u> 51, 113 n. 7.

152. Schmitz, <u>op. cit.</u>, 294; Newberry pointedly illustrated the damaged texts in his drawing. Redford did not indicate that the names were damaged, <u>JEA</u> 51, 113.

153. Davies, <u>Menkheperreseneb</u>, 40.

154. Norman Davies, <u>BMM</u> Dec. 1923 II, 42-43.

155. <u>PM</u> 12 1: 47, 48, 57, 58, 89, 91, 120, 192, 201, 226, 253.

156. Alone in 48, 253, 57; with Mut in 201; with Hathor in 58, 89, 91, 192; and with Tiy in 47, 120, 192. (The last two were personally associated with Tiy.) This is not an exhaustive survey and no doubt does not account for all the tombs which represented Amenhotep III. Many scenes have been lost and <u>PM</u> is not necessarily comprehensive. The distribution, however, demonstrates Tiy was not expected in the kiosk scenes. This is nearly opposite the statement made by Habachi that the king was "almost always accompanied by his strong queen Teye", <u>Schott Fest.</u>, 69.

157. <u>Ibid.</u>, 69.

158. Raymond Johnson, "Some Observations on the Relief and Painting Styles of Amenhotep III in Thebes", a lecture in Cleveland, November 1987. Publication by the Cleveland Museum of Art, 1990, L. Berman, editor. For the mural of TT 226, Luxor J 134, see <u>Luxor Museum of Ancient Art Catalogue</u>, Pl. VII (color), pp. 78-79.

159. <u>Urk</u>. IV 1877-79.

160. Newberry, <u>JEA</u> 14, 83, 85.

161. Redford, <u>JEA</u> 51, 113.

162. Davies, <u>Menkheperreseneb</u>, 40, 37. He felt it would have been insulting to show another king's son with Amenhotep III in the tomb.

163. <u>Ibid.</u>, 40.

164. Hassan, <u>The Great Sphinx</u>, 90.

165. Zivie, <u>Giza au Deuxième Millénaire</u>.

166. Hassan, <u>The Great Sphinx</u> fig. 67, page 84; Zivie, <u>op. cit.</u>, 93-96; a line drawing in S. Hassan, <u>The Sphinx</u>, fig. 39.

167. Zivie, op. cit., 93.

168. Ibid., 94.

169. Hassan shows a cartouche above the offerer on his line drawing, The Sphinx, fig. 39. It is not visible on the photograph.

170. Schmitz, op. cit., 302-05.

171. Hassan, The Great Sphinx, 85, fig. 68. Zivie, op. cit., 96-104; Hassan, The Sphinx, 187-90, fig. 40.

172. There is room for a cartouche, and Zivie seems to adopt the proposal as well. Op. cit., 98.

173. Hassan, The Great Sphinx, pls. 42-51, for example.

174. Notes on Stela B. I have addressed points not discussed by Zivie or provided alternative readings. Her discussion is extensive.

a. The hieroglyphs in fact 𓈖𓏤 𓈖𓏤𓏤 which, once carved, would have prompted the following epithet of Horus Behdet. That Horakhty is intended must be assumed, since the god is called by both names in the upper portion of the stela.

b. Zivie omits, but Hassan's drawing shows 𓈖𓏤𓏤𓏤 The two tall signs, show on the photo, and 𓈖 is clear. Thus restore smr ᶜ3 n mrwt rather than smr n mrwt (Urk IV 1578, 7). The line ends with a w and perhaps a 𓈖 or 𓈖 . Perhaps restore 𓈖𓏤𓏤 .

c. Zivie, unlike Hassan, read ḥr ḥm.f rather than ḥr ỉt.f. A close study shows that 𓏤 as clear as the best signs on the stela and easily comparable to the reed leaf in smi in line 3.

d. Only one of many possibilities.

e. The first sign in line three appears to be tp rather than ḥr. I have thus read "all the chiefs" instead of "everybody".

f. Reading twr(?) mdw.f pᶜt grt sndmwt di.sn sgr sr.[f].
Zivie has not attempted a reconstruction of these garbled signs, and she read simply: , "...ses paroles (?); le peuple... le silence et les previsions?". Her notes add the following. "Au debut, trois signs verticaux dont le dernier ressemble un 𓏤 puis le mot 𓈖𓏤 suivi de 𓈖 ; une lacune de deux ou trois signes ou on croit reconnaitre des hieroglyphes verticaux, suive de 𓈖𓏤 ; la ligne se termine par 𓈖𓏤𓏤𓏤𓏤𓏤 .

The first two signs are nearly impossible, but the meaning should refer to the beneficial effects of "his word". The second sign could be a bone, although there is none to match it with. Thus I suggest twr. The vertical taken for mdw bulges at the top, not the bottom but resembles the mdw in line 4. I have taken this phrase as a participle preceded by enclitic grt; sndmwt is clear. I have assumed the pronoun sn was written n.s (a rather common mistake) and that sr was the meaning "make known" with an f restored after it. This last assumption may not be warranted, but since great persons often are credited with inluence through their words, the possibility exists. For rdi sgr as "to cause peacefulness", Wb. IV, 322.

g. ⌐𝍱 Zivie has omitted this reading, but Hassan has no hesitance about it. The hry sign is legible, and the w is clear; tops of the reed leaf and flax signs are visible.

h. The two arms are readable, and the top of a vertical before them. The "clean of arms" is a suggestion.

i. Zivie takes it as an m, but the falcon is definite; the following signs are unreadable, but should indicate Horakhty or Horemakhet.

j. This address, in the plural, hs.tn must speak to persons enumerated in missing sections or to the Horakhty Horemakhet gods at the start of line 9.

k. This phrase was not discussed by Zivie. Is Atum the king and lord of eternity or does his name begin a new phrase?

l. Hassan shows Δ 𝍱 on his line drawing, but the formula makes no sense here. Zivie omitted it.

m. Reading dmw rn while the text shows ⟶𝍱/////// The second half of the line shows 𝍱 clearly. Hassan draws it in also, but Zivie omitted.

175. Schmitz, op. cit., 302-05.

176. Zivie, op. cit., 104.

177. Ibid., 315-16, citing Helck, Einfluss, 79ff.

178. Helck, Einfluss, 78-80; Schmitz, op. cit., 318 and n. 2, with references, even notes that 19th dynasty princes often used extended titularies combining rpᶜt h3ty-ᶜ on their personal monuments, rather than those of their fathers. Additionally, Thutmose IV specifically called himself a successor to a rpᶜt. The sphinx says to Thutmose, "You will wear its crown of Upper Egypt, and its crown of Lower Egypt, upon the seat of Geb, the rpᶜt". Urk. IV 1543, 1.

179. CG 589, L. Borchardt, Statuen II, 144-45, pl. 106. Berlin 14200, A. Erman, Die Religion der Ägypter (1934) 37 Abb. 12. See W. Helck, Materialien I (1961) 125 for the date contra H. Kees, Das Priestertum (1953) 114, and further below.

180. Urk. IV 1276.

181. Urk. IV 361, 14.

182. Redford, JEA 51, 114 n. 4.

183. Ibid., 114.

184. Schmitz, op. cit., 274; (cites one) DeMorgan, Cat., 44, shows two. There is a third text from Sehel with the cartouche of Amenhotep II topped by plumes just as in Khaemwast's graffiti. The broken text mentions "the valiant warrior of defeated Kush". This inscription may also have been Khaemwast's who must have been a major figure in the military administration of the south.

185. See Schulman, Military Rank, 145-46; J. Lopez and J. Yoyotte, review of Schulman, BiOr 26 (1969) 15, #s 376a-378b. Schmitz, op. cit., 317, referring to several sons of Ramesses II and denying the functional military significance of the ranks.

186. Helck, Einfluss, 61.

187. See now Der Manuelian, op.cit., 196-200.

188. Davies, Corpus, #s 114, 115. Nebymes was also an Overseer of horn, hoof, feather, and scale.

189. Schulman, Military Rank, 57.

190. H. Goedicke, rev. of Eva Martin-Pardey, Untersuchungen zur Ägyptischen Provinzialverwaltung bis zum Ende des Alten Reiches, JARCE 14 (1977) 121-23, especially 122.

191. Ibid., 122.

192. The 20th dynasty princes used "great master of horses" as a title; perhaps this was a later variant for "chief master of horses".

193. Zivie, op. cit., 101.

194. Urk. IV 1275-77.

195. Schulman, Military Rank, 52 and n. 1.

196. Thomas, op. cit., citing Wente as authority, 80, and 239. Wente felt that the child's mummy found in KV 35 was not Webensenu.

197. Ibid., PM I^2 2, 586. Vases of Sennefer and canopics of Sentnay found in debris of KV 42. The royal nurse may have been awarded burial here.

198. Hassan, op.cit., 83-91.

199. Hassan, <u>The Great Sphinx</u>, 87-89, fig. 69; drawing in <u>The Sphinx</u>, fig. 41; Zivie, <u>op. cit.</u>, 104-10.

200. See note 175. Badawi, <u>Memphis</u>, 105, also placed it under Sety I believing this person was a viceroy of Nubia. He clearly was not. Zivie, <u>op. cit.</u>, 265-66, makes him a third son of Amenhotep II.

201. A. Kozloff, <u>NARCE</u> abstract 95 (1976) 8.

202. Zivie, <u>op. cit.</u>, 108 n. (a).

203. <u>Ibid.</u>, 109 n. (a).

204. Not seen by Zivie, but clear on the photo. No doubt it read "king's son of the lord of the Two lands" just as on CG 923 for the young Thutmose IV.

205. Schmitz, <u>op. cit.</u>, 262.

206. <u>Rec. Trav.</u> 9, 47. Photo in Brunner, <u>ZÄS</u> 86, pl. III.

207. B. Bryan, "Private Tomb Relief Sculpture outside Thebes and its Relationship to Theban Relief Sculpture", Proceedings of Symposium on the Art of Amenhotep III, Cleveland Museum of Art, (1990) 65-80, pls. 18-19.

208. <u>Ibid.</u>, 95 n. 4.

209. David Berg, "The Vienna Stela of Meryre", <u>JEA</u> 73 (1987) 213-16.

210. A.-P. Zivie, "Trois Saisons à Saqqarah: Les Tombeaux du Bubasteion", <u>BSFE</u> 98 (1983) 51, pls. 1-2.

211. <u>Ibid.</u>, 96 n.2.

212. S. Birch and H. Rhind, <u>Facsimiles of Two Papyri</u>, pl. XII. A duplicate inscription in Berlin <u>Inschriften</u> II, 204, where the year was transcribed as 37 rather than 27. These labels have been republished and discussed by A. Dodson and J. J. Janssen, "A Theban Tomb and its Tenants", <u>JEA</u> 75 (1989) 125-38. That concerning Si-atum is discussed on 136-37. The labels are now paleographically dated to the 21st Dynasty, and the year 27 is assigned to Psusennes I.

213. Helck, <u>Materialien</u>, I (1961) 125. <u>contra</u> H. Kees, <u>Das Priestertum</u> (1952) 114 and S. Morenz, <u>Aegyptologische Studien</u> (1955) (Festschrift Grapow) 240-43.

214. C53 P. Pierret, <u>Recueil</u> II, 14-15. BM 902, I.E.S., Edwards, <u>HTES</u> VIII (1939) 8-9, pl. 9.

215. B. Bryan, "Portrait Sculpture of Thutmose IV", JARCE 24 (1987) 3-20. Observe the royal relief of Amenhotep II and Amenhotep III compared to that of Thutmose IV in K. Mysliwiec, Le portrait royal dans le bas-relief du nouvel empire (Varsovie 1976).

216. The best foil may be the relief from the tomb of Sennefer, mayor of Thebes for Amenhotep II, TT96. Florenz, Museo Archeologico 7637. Here the plainness of ornamentation is clear, the stiffness of the lotuses is apparent, despite the richness of the offerings placed before Osiris. And most prominent is the profile of Sennefer which betrays the characteristic "dishpan" face of Amenhotep II lacking almost entirely a bridge at the base of the forehead. The eye of the offerer is nearly almond-shaped, but, as described by Bryan, JARCE 24, characteristically falls short of the shape seen for Ahmose and Thutmose IV. Color photos of this relief in A. Eggebrecht, ed., Ägyptens Aufstieg zur Weltmacht, #256, 302-303. A. Minto, Il Regio Museo Archeologico di Firenze (Rome 1931) 24.

217. A. Erman, Die Religion der Ägypter (1934) 37 ill. 12.; M. Moursi, Die Hohenpriester des Sonnengottes von der Frühzeit Agyptens bis zum Ende des Neuen Reiches, #32; M. Moursi, SAK 14 (1987).

218. L. Borchardt, Statuen und Statuetten II (Cairo 1925) 144-45, pl. 106. See also S. Morenz, Festschrift Grapow, 240-43. Moursi, Hohenpriester, #32.

219. Another translation may be found in Moursi, Hohenpriester, #32.

220. J. Capart, "Une Statue de Sebekhotep, Precepteur Royal", Bulletin des Musées Royaux d'Art et d'Histoire (1938) No. 4, 83-86, figs. 8 and 9; B. van de Walle, "Precisions Nouvelles sur Sobek-hotep Fils de Min", RdE 15 (1963) 77-85.

221. B. Bryan, "The Career of Sobekhotep" in E. Dziobek's publication of TT 63, forthcoming in the AV series.

222. I thank Mr. Vivian Davies of the British Museum for this reference, and also Dr. H. DeMeulenaere who kindly collated the writing of the epithet on Brussels E6856. He felt that mry hpš was unsure but did not suggest another certain reading.

223. Supra, n.205.

224. Hayes, Scepter II, fig. 30; See also a 17th dynasty statue, MMA 16.10.369, for a pleated version. Compare the naked and, probably younger, brother of Huwebenef, MMA 26.7.1413.

225. Cannuyer, op.cit., citing The Reign of Tuthmosis IV, Dissertation Yale University, 91-93.

226. <u>PM</u> I^2 1, 591-92, H. Winlock, <u>The Treasure of Three Egyptian Princesses</u>, with objects naming three women as King's Wife. (This tomb's funerary objects, largely now located in the Metropolitan Museum of Art are being republished by Dr. Christine Lilyquist.) Also a King's Wife Nebtta known from KV 34, the tomb of Thutmose III, along with his major wives Meryt-re and Sitiah. <u>PM</u> I^2 553 Pillar A. For all these see Lana Troy, <u>Patterns of Queenship in ancient Egyptian myth and history</u>, (Uppsala 1986) 164-65.

227. C. Van Siclen, <u>VA</u> 3 (1987) 63, fig. 8.

228. Very likely the daughter of one Huy of BM 1280; see C. Van Siclen, <u>The Alabaster Shrine of Amenhotep II</u>, 2 n.12.

229. <u>Urk.</u> IV 976-82.

CHAPTER 3

KING'S WIVES AND KINGS' DAUGHTERS

Throughout the 18th Dynasty kings' wives, sisters and daughters are better attested than princes. Only in the middle of the Dynasty are male family members perhaps as visible. A difference remains, however, for the women of the royal family appear on the kings' monuments throughout the period, while the men are largely attested on their own or on those of their tutors. Queens and princesses accompany the ruler on temple walls,[1] monumental statuary,[2] on scarabs and, in the case of Thutmose III, even on his tomb wall.[3] Independent of the king, some royal women are known from the monuments of officials who served them as administrators or tutors.[4] A few queens and princesses who also held the cultic title of God's Wife of Amun required the services of administrators to oversee the institution's holdings.[5] The monuments of those officials stress their connection to the royal women as God's Wives.

The visibility of the royal women on royal monuments as mentioned above may appear to suggest that females of the royal family lent legitimacy to the kingship, but this view may not be the correct one. In fact, the roles ascribed to queens and princesses are largely cultic ones associated with particular divinities in temple rituals. For example, queens and queen-mothers are the appropriate counterparts for the king in Thebes, who both worships before Amun and his consort Mut and embodies that god on earth. The same is true of the king as Horus or Horakhty accompanied by royal women as Hathor or Isis.[6] In the funerary context it is perhaps the resuscitative power of Isis' fertility that is linked to royal women in Thutmose III's tomb. We see, however, that it is the divinities' roles which are inherently powerful. The women who were most fit to fill those roles were naturally the king's wives, sisters, daughters, and most importantly, mothers. In the royal ideology of the period, the king was divinely borne of the god Amun through his earthly mother. Through this union the king's share of divinity was assured, and his mother was sanctified. Her role as King's Mother was thus of enormous significance, both in Thebes as Mut and elsewhere as Isis, Hathor, Nekhbet or another goddess. The discussion begins here, then, with Thutmose IV's mother, who was extremely visible during her son's reign.

Tiaa, the King's Mother

By far the largest number of monuments dated to Thutmose IV's reign and naming a female family member belong to his mother, Tiaa.[7] She is attested from four principal locations: Giza, the Fayum, Karnak and Thebes, but there is no monument which assures us that Tiaa was queen before her son took the throne. Nor is it then possible to assess her role in Amenhotep's court; and of course the titles granted Tiaa by her son cannot be employed in a discussion concerning Thutmose's throne rights. Many now doubt that the Egyptian throne succession was dependent on female royal family members;[8] it certainly was not in the second half of the 18th dynasty. Only the kings' mothers maintained an elevated position and were honored by ancient, but not necessarily hereditary, titles. Tiaa's monuments illustrate this trend.

Tiaa at Giza

The objects of Tiaa from Giza[9] are probably the least well-known but are actually the most informative, since they give us full titles for her. Two fragments of limestone statues were excavated by Hassan in the temple of Amenhotep II. The first fragment is the base of a standing statue with only the feet preserved. The technique was good, and the inscription of nine lines, running both vertically and horizontally on the pedestal, was also well-cut. Hassan believed his second fragment was a plinth of the same statue. It measures 48 by 25.5 cm. The dimensions of the base are not available. Although this monument, like so many found by Hassan at Giza, has disappeared, a handcopy by Grdseloff, probably done at the time of the excavations, resides in the Griffith Institute, Oxford. The handcopy along with an excellent commentary, was published by Christiane Zivie and by Gitton in his work on God's wives in the 18th Dynasty.[10] A transliteration and translation follow here. It would be difficult to add anything to the textual references provided by Zivie. Notes will be confined to variances with other readings and any areas not dealt with elsewhere.

Socle: vertical lines, right to left
1)prrt nbt m b3h Itm Hr3hty 2) n rp°tt wrt hswt wrt im3t bnrt mrwt hnwt t3wy tm 3) -w m3t Hr St mwt-nsw Ti°3 4) mht h3 m sty idt.s mwt-nsw Ti°3

Socle: horizontal lines, right to left
5) ddt ht nbt ir.tw n.s hmt-nsw Ti°3 °nh-ti 6) ht-Hr hm-ntr B3-pf hmt-ntr Ti°3 7) sdti P hwnt Dp Ti°3 8) s3t Gb hrpt ssmwt sndt hmt-nsw-bit hmt-ntr Ti°3 9) hmt-mwt-nsw hmt-ntr Ti°3 drt-ntr w°bt °wy Ti°3.

(1) Everything which goes forth before Atum-Horakhty shall belong (2) to the hereditary princess, great of favors, great of charm, sweet of love, the mistress of the Two lands and all (3) people, she who sees Horus and Seth, King's Mother Tiaa. (4) She who fills the hall with the scent of her fragrance, the King's Mother Tiaa. (6) She for whom is done everything which is said, King's wife Tiaa, may she live. The follower of Horus, the priestess of Bapef, the God's wife Tiaa (7) the child of Pe, the youth of Dep, Tiaa (8) the daughter of Geb,[a] the Directress of the processions of the

Acacia house, Wife of the King of Upper and Lower Egypt,[b] God's wife, Tiaa; (9) Wife and Mother of the King, God's wife, Tiaa, the God's hand, pure of hands, Tiaa.

Plinth: (read retrograde 6) vertical lines written right to left.

(1) [nsw-bit Mn-ḫprw-rᶜ s3 Rᶜ Dhw]ty-ms [ḫᶜ] ḫᶜw di ᶜnh hmt-ntr nfrt nmtt m pr Ỉmn mwt-nsw Tỉᶜ3 (2) [prrt nbt m b3h Ḥr-m-]3ht hnt stpt n k3 n rpᶜtt m pr wr ḥnwt ḥmwt (3)nbt ḥmt-nsw mwt-nsw ḥmt-ntr Tỉᶜ3 ntr-niwty.ỉ h3.ỉ k3.f hft-hr.ỉ shry.f (4) šnwt hr.ỉ hsr.f dwt.ỉ

> (1) [The King of Upper and Lower Egypt Menkheprure, the son of Re Th]utmose [kha] khau, given life, the God's wife, beautiful of steps in the temple of Amun, King's Mother Tiaa (2) [everything which goes forth before Horem]akhet, foremost of the Setpet, for the Ka of the hereditary princess in the Per-Wer, mistress of [all] women, the King's Wife, King's Mother, God's wife, Ti]aa. May my city god be behind me, his ka being before me.[c] May he remove ills from me; may he drive off my evils.

a) s3t Gb appears on the handcopy to have two t's, but one should belong to hrpt. Zivie noted that there are occurrences of this title, sometimes associated with rpᶜtt.[11] She noted, with respect to the title sdtt P that the queen might be associated with Wadjet or Isis.[12] The title "daughter of Geb" is an even clearer assimilation of Tiaa to Isis who was already a goddess of Giza. This same connection to the Heliopolitan deities appears in Thtumose's Sphinx Stela where the king is termed the son of Atum, the son of Nut, the heir of Khepri, and is said to be "upon the throne of Geb" and "in the office of Atum".[13] This association for Tiaa should therefore be seen in the light of Thutmose's desire to stress his divine parentage, here specifically from the solar deities and their colleagues in Heliopolis.

b. hmt-nsw-bit. This title is difficult to parallel, but Ahmose, mother of Hatshepsut is termed mwt-nsw-bit in the midst of titles designating her suitability as consort to Amun. The titles include s3t Gb.[14]

c. The Saite formula, well-noted by Zivie,[15] appears on the statue of Prince Ahmose discussed in Chapter 2. As with Tiaa, the formula appears on the backpillar. The notion that this formula is not suitable to royal family members is perhaps not warranted since Tiaa's inscription is not unique.

The text may be read in forward direction also, but it makes the restorations less obvious. Zivie also recognized that the text was retrograde, but chose not to so render it in her book on Giza monuments. The republication, however, contains a retrograde translation.[16]

Hassan's interpretation of the statue inscription, especially that of the plinth, led him to believe the queen was an unhappy woman praying for relief,[17] and he identified the cause of grief in the erased stelae discussed in the preceding chapter.

To Hassan and Dorothy Eady (Omm Sety) Thutmose IV was "if not a wholesale murderer, at least a cold-hearted egoist", and they believed he may have been "the cause of the sadness which his mother, Queen Tyaa" complained of.[18] The inscription, as noted above contains the well-known "Saite" formula to safe-guard against troubles [19] and does not require extraordinary explanations.

The historical importance of the two fragments is rather their wealth of titles for the Queen mother. Many are known for other Kings' mothers,[20] including Mutemwia and Ahmose, others are known for God's wives, some are titles borrowed from the Fourth Dynasty queens buried at Giza, and a few are unparalleled.[21] Note that Tiaa is hmt nsw and hmt nsw-bit, but never Great king's wife. We will come back to this in discussing her queen's monuments generally. Without doubt, the statue was placed in Amenhotep's temple without doubt by Thutmose, whose name appears on one fragment. Because of Giza's significance for the king, it is not surprising to see him place his mother's statue there, especially as Tiaa's association to Amenhotep II within the sun temple of the Sphinx dramatized Thutmose IV's claims to divine generation. Tiaa's titles describe her relationships to the gods as much as to kings; she is daughter of Geb and associated with Isis and Wadjet; she is priestess of Bapef and God's wife of Amun who served the cult with a highly prized ritual purity. (Finally, can the reference to "my city god" mean that Tiaa resided in the region, at least at some point?)

We may suggest that Tiaa through her statue in the Sphinx Temple, like Isis in "The Contendings of Horus and Seth", stood before the sun god to claim the rights of family relationship. The role suggested by the titles as an aggregate is that of "god's mother", and the implicit father is the sun god in the form of Amenhotep II. We will return to this idea in Chapter 4.

<u>Tiaa at Karnak: The Puzzle of Amenhotep II.</u>

Karnak has yielded several objects with Tiaa's name. The most puzzling found in the Cachette is a stela, fig. 7,[22] of which only the upper part is preserved. Helck included the piece in the <u>Urkunden IV</u> as part of Tiaa's monuments, but it may not be entirely reliable to evaluate the queen's historical position. The stela has a double-winged sun disc at the top. The remains of a scene show Amun's plumes on the right and opposite him the pharaoh's double crown. On the left is the head of the queen wearing the modius with double feathers. The inscription names Amun-Re King of the gods, lord [of the thrones of the Two Lands]. The king is called "The Good God, lord of the Two lands, lord of making offerings", and his cartouches are cut below the wings without any further titles and without any epithet, such as the frequent ntr hk3 w3st. The queen is titled [hmt] nsw wrt nb[t] t3wy (sic). The land sign is written as ⟶ . Naturally the spelling of the name of the king is mistaken, the artisan having cut ⟿ for ⟝ .   The queen's name is also incorrect, written ⟨ 𓂝 𓏤 𓏥 ⟩ . It is true that names with several half consonants often show great variation,[23] but this writing is most unusual as it omits the second guttural. Tiaa's name does not show such a variation in its writings[24]: Ti^{c}3 is found for her in each case but this one, and the sign is consistently used for the spelling. All examples demonstrate there were two consonants after the Ti. The double or group writing for Ti is less disturbing, although it too is otherwise unknown for the queen.

Incorrect names, however, are not the only problem with this stela. Everything beneath the winged sun disk has been recarved, one supposes, to reproduce the original scene. The recutting apparently was unfinished; the surface is pocked all around the cut figures, and the queen's ear has not been carved. Her face is certainly mid-18th dynasty in style, as is the form of her crown-- the modius and plumes, without the sundisk and horns. Finally, the right side of the stela shows more damage than the left, and it is probable that Amun and his inscription were completely obliterated by Atenists, forcing the restorer to invent an inscription for the god. Therefore, the label "Amun-re King of the Gods" is carved differently from the remainder of the stela inscription. In summary, the stela cannot be judged for the date of its original manufacture; nor can one rely on the inscriptions as accurate 18th Dynasty texts. If the king and queen do represent Amenhotep II and Tiaa, then the stela was certainly recarved at a later date and contains errors resulting from the sculptor's inability to detect the original signs correctly.[25] Perhaps the sculptor's mistakes were noticed and the work abandoned, accounting for its unfinished appearance. (But this might not explain its appearance in the Cachette.)

No other inscription naming Tiaa can be strictly dated to Amenhotep II's reign; but that does not mean the queen does not appear with Amenhotep II on monuments. Thutmose included his mother in works of his father, erasing the queens originally present. Unless another piece surfaces which depicts Amenhotep II and Tiaa without evidence of retouching, it is safer to assume her importance emerged only at Thutmose' accession.

Tiaa appeared on a colossal statue of Amenhotep II[26] placed before the south face of the Eight pylon. That seated statue is destroyed except for part of the throne and the queen's statuette. A block forming a section of the throne bore an inscription: Mn-ḫprw-r^c 'in ḥm.f snfr mnw pn n 'it.f ^{c}3-ḫprw-r^c and to the left of this: [ḥmt]-nsw wr[t] ḥnw[t] t3wy mwt-nsw "Menkheprure: It was his Majesty who embellished this monument for his father Aakheprure; Great King's [wife], Mistress of the Two Lands, King's mother". The name Tiaa and additional text is provided by unpublished Lacau manuscripts.[27] The statue was thus inscribed for Amenhotep II by Thutmose IV, and it is possible that the statue was without text before such time. Mariette reported that the prenomen of Thutmose III appeared on the king's belt, but Habachi stated that he could not find any trace of inscription there. A confusion of statues seems to have occurred. It is possible that the queen's statue had originally been identified as Meryt-re, for the titles of Amenhotep II's mother would suit well here.

Queen Tiaa appears on block fragments reused within the walls of the Amenhotep II festival building between the 9th and 10th pylons.[28] Van Siclen, in publishing the fragments, noted that the name of Meryt-re was replaced by that of Tiaa, although only the arm sign of the ayyin is visible. A portion of the final t of Meryt-re remains. The remaining inscriptions identify [rp]ᶜt[t] wr[t] hsw[t] [//] nbw mwt-nsw [////] hmt-ntr [Ti]ᶜ[3]. The queen holds an elaborate sistrum decorated with atef-crowned falcons and topped by a figure of the king in a blue crown offering nu pots; he is surrounded by a falcon with wings spread. The queen's other hand holds a mace and menat. Probably the role of God's wife is emphasized here through the sequencing of titles (God's wife last) and the presence of the ritual objects. Tiaa's Giza statue referred to her pure arms and beautiful steps in the temple of Amun. Meryt-re and Tiaa were presented as active cult participants holding emblems of position. See further below concerning the mace.

Tiaa is known from a monument of Amenhotep II at North Karnak.[29] In the forecourt of the Montu Temple parts of a sandstone doorway of Amenhotep II were reused. The lintel scene shows the king followed by Tiaa, both offering to Amun. The left jamb, nearly complete, is inscribed with two lines of titles and epithets for the king and one for the queen. The right is preserved by only six small fragments, but it can be seen to have been similar. The lintel scene calls her: hmt-nsw mwt-nsw wrt hnwt t3wy, while the jambs provide some of the titles of Queen mother seen on the Giza statue: left jamb: rpᶜtt wrt hswt bnrt [mrwt] hmt-nsw [//////] Tiᶜ3. right jamb shows: hmt-nsw hnwt t3wy hnmt nf[r] hdt.[30]

Tiaa's presence in the door of Amenhotep must have been the work of Thutmose IV. She is already called King's Mother on the lintel, but more significantly, as on the fragments from Amenhotep II's Karnak pavilion, her name is carved over that of Amenhotep's mother Meryt-re. If Amenhotep had wished to replace his wife for his mother, it seems logical to assume he would have removed King's Mother from the lintel inscription. The left jamb shows hmt-nsw cut over curved traces which could be the mwt vulture; this is not sure, however. If "king's mother" was removed, however, it may have been done simply to repeat the sequence in the lintel, hmt-nsw mwt-nsw wrt. Traces above the cartouche appear to be bird's legs, which would support this reconstruction. The reading remains unsure. The recutting was covered by a plaster surface over all the door elements. Tiaa's name is not the only evidence of Thutmose IV in the North Karnak precinct. Level C, in which this door was found also produced the reused forecourt door element of Thutmose IV,[31] as well as fragments of relief with his name. (See Chapter 4.)

Although it is entirely likely that Thutmose IV's removal of Meryt-re's name from Amenhotep II's two Karnak monuments and the subsequent replacement of Tiaa's name venerated the latter queen without dishonoring the former, we should perhaps entertain the notion that Thutmose wished to excise Meryt-re's name from Amenhotep's monuments. In addition to the Karnak reliefs, Tiaa probably replaced Amenhotep's mother on his Memphis stela recording the Asiatic campaigns completed in Year 9.[32] Indeed no scene remains of Amenhotep II with Meryt-re as his mother, but her appearances as queen with Thutmose III have not been usurped.[33]

In Chapter 2 it was noted that Wente and Thomas considered KV 42 a possible early resting place for prince Webensenu. (There are no objects of his from the tomb, however.) The foundation deposit of Meryt-re suggests that that tomb had been intended for her, but the only objects naming her come from the tombs of Thutmose III and Amenhotep II.[34] It may be that re-use of KV 42 during the reign of Thutmose IV (for the nurse Sentnay) followed the removal of Meryt-re's and Webensenu's tomb goods to Amenhotep II's burial place. The brick stamped with the name of Meryt-re Hatshepsut and found in the funerary temple of Thutmose IV[35] has no title. It could have derived from an earlier building of that queen removed by Thutmose's builders. This is, however, the most speculative of suggestions and is mentioned only in an attempt to present a coherent explanation of the scanty evidence. Recognizing the paucity of material available for interpretation, might we tentatively suggest a family relationship between Meryt-re and Webensenu and that both were considered out of favor during Thutmose IV's reign. Meryt-re was, however, threatening only as mother of Amenhotep II--and advocate of Webensenu? We can only speculate at this time how to interpret the evidence, but it remains a fact that Meryt-re was replaced by Tiaa during Thutmose IV's reign whenever she appeared with Amenhotep II. The alternative to this daring explanation is simply to see Thutmose IV's usurpation of Meryt-re's monuments as a convenient means of identifying his mother with Amenhotep II without having to add the title "King's Mother".

Tiaa and Thutmose IV.

Perhaps the best known statue of the reign of Thutmose IV includes his mother Tiaa. The seated double statue of the king and Queen mother, fig. 8,[36] was apparently hidden during a temple-cleaning at the same time as the major cachette but not in the same place [37]. This statue and one of Mentuemhat were placed below the floor of the South court to the granite sanctuary of Hatshepsut and Thutmose III. No doubt because of the protection afforded the piece, its preservation is surpassed by few statues from pharaonic Egypt. The king is shown wearing the round wig and has his left arm around his mother. Tiaa in turn has her right arm around her son. She wears a tripartite wig tightly curled and covered by a vulture headdress. Her ankle-length gown is decorated by a broad collar and rosettes on the breasts. The inscription on the seat beside her left leg runs vertically: "the Great Royal Wife, beloved of him, King's Mother, Tiaa, vindicated". The king is termed: "the Good God, Menkheprure, beloved of Amun-Re lord of the thrones of the Two lands, given life".

Tefnin[38] has recently suggested that this famous statue, like the monuments discussed above, was usurped from Amenhotep II. He based this on the condition of the inscription by the king's right leg.[39] He suggested that ntr nfr Mn-ḫprw-rꜥ 𓏏𓊃𓊖𓏏𓂝 had been cut on a damaged surface, and footnoted Legrain as having said likewise. But a look at the statue will demonstrate that this is not the case. The seat was never cut completely square (or level, as any glance frontally will reveal) and the stone against which the legs rest is not strictly perpendicular but inclines a bit out toward the feet. This is even more prominent on the inscription to the proper left of Tiaa's leg. While it is true that "Good God Menkheprure" is fainter than the rest of the text, it is clearly not recut and the surface is in no way deeper than that outside the vertical and horizontal lines bordering the inscription. Since both ntr nfr and the royal prenomen are scratched, the damage probably occurred during the burial of the statue. Legrain's comment which Tefnin cited regarding the inscription refers to the god's name and epithet and not to the king's.[40] Legrain mentioned that there may have been retouching, not that there had been erasure and new inscription. Tefnin's argument rested only with the inscription, and it is unsatisfying. Tiaa's text[41] and that of her son must have been done simultaneously and thus the statue belongs to them. Any possibility that the style belongs to Amenhotep II[42] must rest on the assertion that the statue was uninscribed when Thutmose found it, for the king's name is not recut. Further comments on the statue and its place in the style of the reign will be made in the next chapter.

There is one more record of Tiaa from Karnak. Thutmose IV built a sandstone court which abutted the Fourth pylon; his mother appears in at least one scene from the building.[43] A block shows Thutmose stretching the cord for his chapel with Sefkhet-abu. Tiaa stands behind the king wearing the vulture headdress and modius with high plumes. She holds a flywhisk in her right hand and a mace in her left. No title is preserved for the Queen, only the cartouche bearing her name "Tiaa". The text on the block explains: "stretching the cord in the Temple of Amun". There is no sure means of ascertaining Tiaa's function in the ritual, for there are no parallel scenes from Karnak, nor indeed from any Theban temple[44], showing a queen or God's wife assisting a king at the foundation ceremony. The God's wife Shepenwepet appears in Amenirdis' Medinet Habu Chapel, however, stretching the cord with Sefkhet-abu--without a king[45], and 18th Dynasty queens do appear in other capacities in temple scenes.[46] Queens carrying maces are not common, and there is a possibility that the mace is an indicator of the God's wife's political power. Meryt-re and Tiaa appeared on the fragments from the pavillion of Amenhotep II holding maces. Other examples are cited in the section dealing with Iaret below.[47]

The relative importance of this Queen mother may be preserved to us in a 20th dynasty papyrus. The Wilbour Papyrus lists various institutional land holdings in the region of Middle Egypt and the Fayum. The great Temple of Amun in Karnak is a major landowner and is represented by numerous entries. In addition to the vast general domains, several separate chapels within the temple are listed together with their holdings, and among them is the entry for the ⌐ (𝘩𝘪𝘦𝘳𝘰𝘨𝘭𝘺𝘱𝘩𝘴) "the House/estate of Tiaa in the Temple of Amun".[48] Gardiner's commentary referred to the chapel as a hitherto unknown temple of Amenhotep II's consort.[49] In two other sections of the Wilbour Papyrus the temple of Amenhotep II in Karnak is listed as a land-holding entity.[50]

If there was a chapel of Queen Tiaa in Karnak,[51] then either it has not been found as Gardiner asserted; or it is represented in the building of Thutmose.[52] That Tiaa was shown as part of the foundation ceremony would at least suggest that she shared in the dedication--this is especially noteworthy since no other examples of stretching-the-cord scenes included queens. Amenhotep III did not destroy the whole building when he built the IIIrd pylon; parts of it were reinscribed as late as in Ramesses VI's reign.[53] Letellier noted that the Third Pylon remains of Thutmose's court belong to the western end of the structure only; the eastern wall of the court as well as parts of the northern and southern walls may have stood through the Ramesside period. Nothing is known of the eastern wall and little remains of the north and south decoration.[54] It would thus have been possible for the Queen to have received part of the landholdings for the chapel. This is only speculation, naturally, but would explain her presence in the scene as well as the papyrus entry.

Luxor

Tiaa is also attested at the Luxor Temple. It is now apparent that more building activity took place at the site than was earlier believed, and Thutmose IV has left at least three large memorials from the approach area of the temple.[55] Found in the southeast section of the Avenue of Sphinxes, before the east wing of the pylon, was a portion of a large black granite stela.[56] Only the top half is preserved, but its measurements are 70cm.Ht. X 110 W. X 25 D. The full stela must have been twice this height. The double winged disk is in the lunette and Horus of Behdet is named. Below this Amun appears twice; he is shown in the center in both cases facing the king and a queen. Between the figures of the god runs a vertical restoration text of Seti I. The photo in publication is so poor as to be nearly useless, and the epithets of Amun-Re are unreadable. On the left the king pours a libation; he is named by both cartouches and epithets including "lord of the khepesh". Behind him is mwt-nsw Ti^{c}3, "King's Mother Tiaa"; she wears a tripartite wig with the modius and holds a fly whisk. On the right the figures of the king and queen are completely missing but for the top of the pharaoh's head. He is again named by both cartouches but is not followed by Tiaa in this instance.

This stela from the Luxor Temple is the last of Tiaa's East Thebes monuments that can be identified. But it, like those described above, shows the Queen mother in an active role, helping her son perform religious duties. Her titles, almost without doubt, reflect her position as Thutmose' mother, not as Amenhotep's wife. One need only look for comparison's sake at the titles and flourishes of Ahmose, mother of Hatshepsut,and Mutemwia, mother of Amenhotep III, from the divine birth scenes. The number of appearances of Tiaa in the Amun temples may simply show the closeness of sons to mothers seen with earlier 18th Dynasty rulers. Amenhotep II left perhaps the best such precedent. But one might at least wonder whether the quantity of Tiaa's monuments is related to her function as God's wife of Amun.   As noted before,Tiaa's Giza statue referred to her as "beautiful of steps in the Temple of Amun", a phrase specifically recording her presence in the temple. The sacerdotal duties that the God's wife performed required her involvement,[57] and although Gitton and Graefe believe the royal God's wife was represented by a substitute,[58] that was not necessarily always the case.

Gitton argued that because, with the exception of Ahmose-Nofretari, the God's wives are depicted anonymously, a queen could not have performed the actual rituals. That seems a hasty conclusion when, in fact, the God's wives of the 18th dynasty are more prominent in Karnak ,Luxor and other Amun temples in Thebes than are queens who are not God's wives.[59] This is true for Ahmose-Nofretari (25 times), Ahhotep (once), Sitamun (once or twice), Ahmose-Merytamun (once), Hatshepsut as queen (numerous occurrences on her monuments with Thutmose II), Nefrure (6 times), Sitiah (twice), Merytamun (2 times), Merytre-Hatshepsut (5 times), and Tiaa (6 times). Only one god's wife, Ahmose-Sit-Kamose, a daughter of Kamose or Ahmose,[60] is not attested. The queens and princesses who do appear but who are not known to have been God's wife[61] include Ahmose[62] (mother of Hatshepsut, once), Mutnefert (mother of Thutmose II, once), Esi (mother of Thutmose III, once), Nefertiry (once), Mutemwia (3 times), Nefertiti (numerous scenes from Karnak talatat), Ankhesenamun (three times), Mutnodjmet (four times). (One need hardly point out that the queens of the latest kings of the Dynasty are better attested, and in that period there are no God's wives of Amun--Tiaa was the last until the Nineteenth Dynasty.) Although these God's wives are not necessarily labelled as such in all their appearances, their presence in far greater numbers and frequency than ladies who were not God's wives indicates their personal involvement with the Amun temples. Among those queens (not necessarily Great Royal Wife) of the 18th Dynasty not found at any Amun temple in Thebes are Iaret, Tiy (wife of Amenhotep III, Sitamun, Nebetnehet, Kiya, Meritaton, and Teye (wife of Ay).

It is quite possible that the God's wives in the 18th dynasty did perform their functions personally, and that the monuments preserved in Luxor and Karnak are records in some fashion. If not, it is difficult to comprehend Tiy's absence from the temples in which her husband was so active. It is well-known that Tiy never bore the title God's wife and that the office languished from Amenhotep's reign until that of Ramesses I.[63] Thus Tiaa's visibility in the Theban temples was at least partially a function of her position as the highest priestess of Amun; she assumed the role held by Meryt-re in this. We should stress, however, that Tiaa's influence as queen and king's mother was also significant; it is only her frequent appearance in Theban temples which we link to her sacerdotal role.

Fayum

Unfortunately none of Tiaa's objects have left us any clues regarding her liaison with Amenhotep II or her family ties. Her rise to importance may well have elevated her allies, however, and it may be that her origins were in the Fayum. A nearly-life-size black granite statue of fine quality from that region is preserved from the waist down.[64] It is in the Cairo Museum (CG 1167,see fig. 9). Tiaa was originally represented seated with her son (presumably) on a throne decorated with the traditional Upper and Lower Egyptian plant motif. Only the legs and left side of the seat remain, with two short columns of text vertically written on opposing sides of the queen's legs. The text to the proper left of the queen's legs reads as follows: mwt-nsw hmt-nsw wrt Ti°3 °nh.ti; on the right is hmt-nsw wrt mrt.f mrt Sbk šdty. "King's Mother, Great Royal Wife, Tiaa, may she live. Great Royal Wife, beloved of him, beloved of Sobek Shedty". When Borchardt published the Cairo Museum statues, the provenance of the piece was recorded as unknown. But Brugsch had mentioned the piece in his discussion of Lake Moeris as early as 1893.[65] He said he had found it in the ruins of the city of Crocodilopolis, but it had gone into the hands of private dealers. There is no doubt it is the same statue, since he provided the full two-line text in his discussion. Naturally a dedication to Sobek Shedty would have suggested a Fayumic origin, but through Brugsch the statue's position in the major temple of Crocodilopolis can be postulated with confidence. Of course Tiaa's statue in the Fayum does not of itself prove that she originated from the region, but there are other indications.

The reigns of Amenhotep II and Thutmose IV can be documented in the Fayum, in strong contrast to the early 18th dynasty. Thutmose III founded a royal residence at Medinet Gurob,[66] but none of his queens or administrators is yet attested there. Two regional governors, however, both of the name Sobekhotep,[67] are known for the reigns of Amenhotep II and Thutmose IV. The monuments of one of these men is useful in linking Tiaa to the Fayum. The earlier man is dated by stylistic analysis of his statues; the later Sobekhotep was Thutmose's Treasurer and son to a Treasurer named Min who served Thutmose III.[68]   Min's family is unknown, but he himself is not known to have borne any of the Fayumic civil titles. That fact, together with the information that the other Sobekhotep (under Amenhotep II) was son to one Kapu, who did bear the Fayum governor's rank, suggests that Treasurer Sobekhotep married into the Fayum's leading family and assumed its civil leadership through his wife.

The following chart shows the probable family ties which produced Treasurer Sobekhotep. Further discussion in Chapter 5 will elaborate on Sobekhotep son of Min, but this new genealogy removes certain chronological problems normally associated with the two Sobekhoteps.   Some years ago Charles constructed a genealogy which dated Sobekhotep son of Kapu to the reign of Amenhotep III.[69] Stylistically this is impossible: the facial features of his two statues are not compatible with such a late date; more importantly, the block statue (Marseille 208) holds a lotus in one hand, and this is a trait characteristic of the reign of Amenhotep II, but not later.[70] In addition Charles' reconstruction required brother-sister marriage and produced two governors of the Fayum functioning simultaneously. Even more dissatisfying, both were sandwiched between Thutmose IV and Amenhotep III.[71] In fact, it can be demonstrated that one Itunema,[72] father of an Amenemhet buried in Sedment late in Amenhotep III's reign, held the Mayor's office in this time period. Paser, son of Mayor and then Treasurer Sobekhotep, held the Mayor's office at least from late in Thutmose IV's rule until the third decade of Amenhotep III's rule.[73] This would hardly leave time for Sobekhotep son of Kapu's mayoralty.

New Genealogy

```
Kapu* m. Meryt              Min+ m. ?
  Sobekhotep* m. ?             |
    |                          |
  Meryt II  m.   Sobekhotep+*
      Djehuty  Paser*
```


Charles' Model

```
        Min+
  Sobekhotep+* m.   Meryt
Djehuty  Paser*  Kapu* m. Meryt II
        Sobekhotep II*
```

* Indicates ḥ3ty-ᶜ of Fayum   + Indicates mr ḥtm Treasurer

The new genealogy provides a logical union of the offices of Treasurer and Fayum Mayor and does not require brother-sister marriage. The time frame is looser and does not place Paser and Kapu together as Fayum mayors.

The persons involved having been sorted out, their relation to Tiaa can now be postulated. The Fayum suddenly became important at this time, without doubt because of the newly built palace of Thutmose III. Given her later interest in the Fayum, it is quite possible that Tiaa was a resident of that palace during Amenhotep II's reign. There she would have had occasion to know the governing family. It is well-known that the <u>Mayor of the Southern She (Fayum) (ḥȝty-ᶜ Š rsy)</u> and later also the Mayor of Miwer (ḥȝty-ᶜ Mi-wr) was responsible for some lands of the Medinet Gurob residence (pr ḥnr). He also alloted provisions for the institution on occasion.[74] Gardiner even suggested the Mayor of the Southern She may have resided at Gurob.[75] Such responsibilities toward the palace must have drawn the royal inhabitants into acquaintance with the mayors, so Tiaa would have met Sobekhotep the Mayor and Treasurer.

In his Theban tomb Sobekhotep (Th.tb.63) was represented on the north wall of the back hall with his wife Meryt[76] receiving offerings from their sons Paser and Djehuty. There is little doubt the scene was intended as a "Fayum memorial", for Sobekhotep and his wife appear there with their regional titles, Mayor of the Fayum, Overseer of Priests of Sobek Shedty and Greatest of Entertainers of Sobek Shedty. Elsewhere on the tomb walls Sobekhotep is called Treasurer and Meryt is termed Royal Ornament.[77] In addition, Paser the eldest son pictured in this scene was already Mayor of the Fayum (š sbk) by title. This office was not known to have been shared, but rather confirms that the painting memorializes his father's earlier rank as Mayor.[78]

The scene thus pertains to the Fayumic origins of this family but also includes a princess on the lap of Meryt. The child is called King's Daughter Tiaa, and Meryt is called Nurse of the King's Daughter Tiaa and also Greatest of the Entertainers (wrt ḥnrt) of Sobek Shedty. The appearance of princess Tiaa in this particular scene was surely not accidental. Meryt's nursing title pertained to a princess from the Fayum palace and her religious one to a temple in the same region. (The interconnection of temple women's groups with the royal nursing institution is attested already in P. Boulaq XVIII, where the harem of Montu was attached to the Royal house of nurses (pr mnᶜt).[79]

Princess Tiaa will be discussed further below. She was a daughter of Thutmose IV, named for her grandmother. Her youth apparently passed in the Fayum, as did some of Amenhotep III's, and her guardians must have had close attachments to the

Gurob palace. Sobekhotep's liaison with Queen Tiaa's namesake was surely then more than coincidence. The conclusion that Thutmose's mother, Tiaa, lived some time in the Fayum as Amenhotep II's wife, is reasonable in view of this circumstantial evidence. No single monument demands the conclusion, but taken together the evidence suggests that a common link must have brought the Fayum out of obscurity. The royal residence[80] there was the vehicle through which the local line of mayors emerged and became quite prominent, and it was doubtless the reason for Tiaa's notable presence there well after her son took the throne.

Thebes

   The last site from which objects bearing the name of Queen Tiaa have been recovered is the West bank of Thebes. These few funerary pieces have not, however, all been assigned to Thutmose's mother.[81] A faience shabti from Medinet Habu,[82] very crude in manufacture and some five inches in length, bears a shabti spell on behalf of the "Great Royal Wife Tiaa". It is now in the Metropolitan Museum, as is a portion of a shabti coffin in blue and yellow faience.[83] The coffin fragments are decorated by figures of Anubis and the four sons of Horus; they preserve three columns of text dedicated to the "Osiris Tiaa, God's wife and King's Mother".   The fragments were found near KV 47 (Siptah), together with a vase of Seti I, a limestone splinter with a Ramesside cartouche, and numerous ostraca. This information is provided by Carter manuscripts. The Brooklyn Museum has a high quality blue glazed shabti basket[84] inscribed for the "Great Royal Wife Tiaa"; it has no provenance. The Lord Amherst of Hackney's collection contained a vase fragment of blue glaze with the identical text.[85] It too has no provenance.   A miniature corded vase of blue-green glaze identifying the Great Royal Wife Tiaa was published by Petrie in Buttons and Design Scarabs.[86] No provenance is given, but it was likely a funerary object. Its present location is unknown to me.

   The difficulty with these objects is suggested by the coffin fragments found near Siptah's tomb. Inside that royal tomb were found numerous parts of an alabaster canopic box decorated and inscribed for the "[Great] royal wife Tiaa"[87]-- they were found in water-washed rubbish thrown aside in the first corridor by grave robbers. Beneath the rubbish in a room below two corridors was found a fragment of a wooden adze showing "King's Mother Ti[aa]".[88] The alabaster fragments came to the Metropolitan Museum where attempts to unite them have failed. The adze is now in the Cairo Museum. Other objects of Sety II were found in association with it, including part of a fine alabaster female shabti as well--of better quality than Siptah's.[89] The confusion is now apparent.

   The Museum, following Aldred's publication of the KV 47 material as proof Siptah's mother was named Tiaa, re-dated both its coffin fragments and its faience shabti. But the shabti may now need to return to the 18th dynasty, because of an unusual phrase on its Chapter VI spell: m prt s r hrt.f, a variant which appears on four shabtis of Amenhotep II (CG 24251-53).[90] The Brooklyn Museum's basket will remain dated to the 18th Dynasty when shabti baskets were commonplace, and the vase fragment's current location is not known to me.

The second Tiaa is nowhere else attested, and the objects from KV 47 are not reassuringly late 19th dynasty.[91] Aldred relied for dating on the long slim female figures incised on the alabaster fragments; but 18th dynasty boxes show the same slim lines.[92] The fragments of an alabaster canopic box from the tomb of Thutmose IV are of a very similar stone and style[93], although the Tiaa fragments show an incised rather than relief goddess figure. The box from Amenhotep II's tomb compares favorably as well.[94] A second alabaster box from the KV 47 bears the cartouche of Merneptah Ba-en-Re Mer-Amun, but the alabaster is quite different (of poorer quality and yellowish) from Tiaa's. The inscription is painted in yellow rather than in blue as on the Queen's. The adze, by the excavation notes, was found under the rubbish level, but it tells nothing of its own about a date. A similar wooden adze was found in the tomb of Amenhotep II.

The facts are so ambiguous as to argue neither case. It is preferable to identify only one Tiaa with the titles of Great Royal Wife King's Mother and God's Wife, particularly since she is attested only <u>outside</u> KV 47. In this case, however, the mother of Siptah does not exist beyond the funerary objects in question making the case for two Tiaas even less strong. But it clearly is not impossible--the God's wife title was held by queens of the 19th dynasty. If the objects must be divided between two Tiaas, then objects found within KV 47 should be assigned to the later queen. The coffin fragments resemble a sarcophagus of 18th Dynasty, not 20th Dynasty type.[95] The faience shabti has textual affinities to the mid-18th dynasty and resembles crude pieces from Thutmose IV's tomb; the shabti basket has a close parallel in CG 24176 from Amenhotep II's tomb[96]; the vase fragment is impossible to judge.

The argument for two Tiaas is weak in my view, but it has some wider interest because the mummy of Thutmose's mother has never been found. The find of the shabti at the south end of Thebes, as well as the mix of objects in the King's Valley, suggests the familiar story of late reburials effected by a temporary station at Medinet Habu. Siptah was re-interred in Amenhotep II's tomb; could a switch have been enacted, placing the 18th dynasty queen in KV 47? Human bones were found in the king's sarcophagus, but they are not Siptah.[97] Possibly more data will come to light to guide the discussion further.

Thebes

Private tomb. A painting of a statuette of The Great Royal Wife Tiaa appeared alongside one of Thutmose IV in the tomb of the steward Tjenuna (TT 76).[98]

Summary of Queen Tiaa's monuments

Thutmose IV's mother cannot be said to have functioned as a Great Royal Wife to Amenhotep II during his lifetime. Her elevation to that rank and to that of God's Wife, and of course King's Mother, occurred in the reign of her son. A few observations may be made here which have not been given before. First, "King's Mother" is the expected designation for Tiaa on all public royal monuments; it appears on all such documents excepting the ineptly restored stela from Karnak. "Great Royal Wife" is the commonest title Tiaa bears, occurring on eleven monuments. It appears with "King's Mother" or by itself. Both of these titles could singly label Tiaa. The queen's influence derived from her role as mother of a pharaoh and therefore of a god; but the functioning title for a queen was "Great Royal Wife". When Tiaa is referred to as God's wife, however, she is never also "Great Royal Wife", but she is "King's Mother". The functioning title in these cases is therefore that of the priestess. We can add to this observation the fact that whenever another queen of Thutmose IV's appears on the same or complementary monuments with Tiaa, the King's Mother or God's wife rank is applied, while the other queen is designated Great Royal Wife. This happens at Giza, where Nefertiry appears on a series of stelae with Thutmose IV, and at Luxor.

We are at a loss to state when Tiaa died, but her tomb goods certainly would not suggest a date late in the reign of Amenhotep III. If any clue exists it is in the sudden promotion of Princess Iaret in year 7 to the rank of Great Royal Wife. This is, of course, uncertain. There is no uncertainty, however, that Tiaa was an extremely influential woman who supported Thutmose IV through much of his reign as his principal consort.

Before other queens of Thutmose IV are discussed, it should be pointed out that the princess Tiaa, included below, was clearly not identical with the king's mother. Some scholars have incorrectly assumed such an identity, but the daughter remained simply King's Daughter (s3t-nsw) even on funerary objects. Any discussion of succession that makes Thutmose the son of a true king's daughter is inaccurate.[99]

Nefertiry

This queen of Thutmose IV was largely ignored until recently; and ironically, it was an attempt to negate her existence that gave her some notoriety. Harris[100] suggested that the Great Royal Wife shown on a stela from Giza together with Thutmose IV was actually Ahmose-Nofretari. Harris compared the dedicatory object with Abydene votive stelae showing Ahmose, (Ahmose)Nofretari and Amenhotep I together with private individuals. He concluded that since the deified queen could be represented by shorthand spellings of her name, and since Thutmose IV already had two consorts in his short reign, then the most sensible conclusion was that the Giza stela depicted Ahmose-Nofretari. Her presence was meant to underline

Thutmose IV's links with the past.

Nefertiry at Giza

Harris' discussion does not include all the monuments for Nefertiry. Presently I know of ten. Gitton[101] responded to Harris by pointing out eight of these works in a concise and conclusive fashion. Gitton's argument noted the following: 1) there is no evidence to support an assumption that only one Great Royal Wife existed at a time (indeed the facts indicate the opposite--the wives of Ramesses II, for example); 2) even so the wives could have succeeded each other; 3) Harris was unaware of a scarab with the cartouches of Menkheprure and Nefertiry; 4) there are seven [actually eight], not one, stelae from Giza depicting Thutmose IV and Queen Nefertiry before deities. [These were in addition to nine showing the king only before the gods]; 5) such a large number of Ahmose-Nofretari appearances in a region where no cult existed for her is unlikely; 6) the Giza queen is always called Great Royal Wife, but never God's wife--Ahmose-Nofretari's most common title. Gitton's article was convincing, and since all but three of Thutmose' Giza stelae had been published in photographic form, Harris had little room for rebuttal.

Seven of the eight examples of Thutmose and Nefertiry at Giza have been republished in text copy and translation by Zivie.[102] She included one stela omitted from Hassan's publication. Her work need not be repeated here, but a list of her new numbers, matched to Hassan's plates, may be useful:

Zivie's NE 15 = Hassan's pl.XLI, Thutmose IV and Nefertiry before Thoth
NE 17 = pl. XLII, Thutmose and Nefertiry
before Horus lord of Sakhbu
NE 18 = pl. XLIIIa, Thutmose and Nefertiry
before Sokar lord of Shetyt
NE 19 = pl. XLIIIb, Thutmose and Nefertiry
before Amun-Re
NE 26 = Zivie's pl.9 (JE 59461), Thutmose
and Nefertiry before Ptah (see below, pl. 4).
NE 28 = pl. XLIX (JE 59462), Thutmose and
Nefertiry before an unknown goddess
NE 30 = Hölscher, Chephren. fig.161 (Leipzig
2429), Thutmose and Nefertiry before Mut.
NE 31 = unpublished and incorrectly described
until now, PM III^2 38; Cairo, Temp. 19.4.47.1,
Thutmose and Nefertiry before Atum lord of   Heliopolis

Zivie's discussion of all seventeen Giza stelae demonstrated   that the gods chosen were of national, regional and local importance.[103] The same distribution exists for those including Nefertiry, and one might conclude that Nefertiry's role as consort was thereby recognized before the entire country. The date, style and

importance of the Giza stelae generally will be treated in Chapter 4. We have
already noted, however, that Nefertiry's appearance at Giza in proximity to the
statue of Tiaa as God's wife and King's Mother (not Great Royal Wife) is as
Thutmose IV's consort, who accompanies him but does not participate in the cult
act. Temple scenes depicting queens from the pre-Amarna 18th Dynasty attribute
passive roles to Great royal wives but sometimes active ones to God's wives. In the
Amarna period and later queens regularly perform roles associated with priestesses,
since the God's wife was superceded for a time. In secular settings the Great royal
wives could be more active throughout the Dynasty.

Gurob

The scarab[104] mentioned above was originally published by Loat. Petrie
included it in his Scarabs and Cylinders, and it is now in the London University
College. It was excavated at Gurob, but the exact location was not reported.   The
material is obsidian, and the only decoration of the piece is two cartouches.
Without titles, ⊙𓃭𓊖 is written to the left of 𓇋𓏏𓆑𓂋 . This spelling for Nefertiry
does not appear on the Giza stelae which instead employed the 𓃭 sign. The Gurob
writing is an expected variation, however.

Luxor

The spelling of Nefertiry's name, as it appears on the scarab, does have another
attestation, hitherto unnoticed. In the discussion of Tiaa a stela from the Luxor
Temple was mentioned,[105] and it was noted there that a wife of Thutmose IV was
represented on the right side. The cartouche naming that queen identifies Nefertiry
with the spelling ⌊𓏏𓆑𓂋 .[106] The granite stela is preserved in a magazine in
Luxor[107], and this spelling has been verified by sight inspection and a close-up
photograph kindly taken by Alain Bellod of the Centre Franco-Egyptien for El-Sayed
Higazy, Director of Karnak and Luxor Temples. The writing is thus similar to that
of the scarab, confirming that more than one spelling existed. The location of the
stela at Luxor may be of more significance, for it verifies Nefertiry's recognition as
Thutmose's queen in Upper Egypt as well as in the north; this would not necessarily
have been the case if she had appeared only at Giza and Gurob, near the northern
royal residences. But her appearance in the religious capital of the south is
important, and it would not be surprising to discover more objects bearing the name
of this queen. (Naturally her burial place would be of interest.)

Iaret

The name of this wife of Thutmose IV is unsure at best. It is written 𓆓 on her
three known monuments, and it is due to custom alone that she is called Iaret.
Fortunately this queen has been made known to us on two dated inscriptions, both

of year 7.

Sinai

In year 7 Iaret is documented at Serabit el Khadim at the turquoise mine some two miles southeast of the Hathor temple.[108] The inscription, which has recently been relocated, was a mine-opening commemoration. There was no scene, and the king, as well as Iaret, was represented by name only. She was called King's Daughter, a title which of course does not designate the king's wife. This is a notable distinction, for Nefertiry never bears this title; nor does Tiaa or Mutemwia. Iaret, however, bears it on all three of her inscriptions, making it a reliable indicator of her rank. Giveon's rediscovery of the inscription has provided additional text identifying "the Royal messenger and Troop commander of Tjeku, Amenemhet. The Overseer of stone-masons for the Temple of Ptah, Amenemhet". This inscription informs us that Iaret (Giveon calls her Wadjet) had her own messenger accompanying her, just as did Thutmose IV in year 4 when Neby left an inscription at the Sinai in his capacity as "Royal messenger in every foreign country, Overseer of the House for the apartment of the Queen, Mayor of Sile and child of the Nursery".[109] Giveon believed the title was "messenger of the princess Wadjet", but this reading is unlikely from the photo. It would also be unique, although it is true that princes could have their own representatives.[110]

Konosso

From Year 7 Iaret is also known at Konosso on a rock stela scene above a now-lost inscription.[111] Thutmose IV appeared in the scene smiting foreigners on the head before the gods Dedwen and Ha. Iaret stood behind the king wearing a long wig and the modius crown with tall plumes. In her right hand she held a mace and <u>ankh</u> and in in her left, a now-erased object. The inscription called her King's Daughter, King's Sister, Great Royal Wife (s3t-nsw snt-nsw ḥmt-nsw wrt), providing the fullest titles of her queenship. There can be no question that she acted as consort for Thutmose, and she must have traveled with him in year 7 when he made a visit south, and perhaps north too.

Iaret's appearance in the scene with a mace in her hand is interesting, for this unusual attribute for female royalty appears (to my knowledge) only a handful of times in the 18th Dynasty. It has been mentioned that Meryt-re and Tiaa held a mace along with a menat and sistrum in Amenhotep II's festival chapel at Karnak. Tiaa held a mace in the Karnak court scene[112] where she accompanied Thutmose IV in the foundation ceremony. The other examples 18th dynasty date apparently represent a relatively short span of time: Hatshepsut[113] as queen appeared with Senmut on an Aswan rock inscription. She there held a mace in her right hand and rested it on her shoulder; the same pose appeared for Ahmose-Nofretari[114] in the

Tuthmoside temple of Medinet Habu. In two scenes at Deir el Bahri, Nefrure[115] was pictured in the same pose as that of Iaret and Tiaa. She held the mace (with an _ankh_ or sistrum) horizontally at her side in one hand and a baton on her shoulder in the other. In both scenes Nefrure stood behind the kneeling king(s). Finally Sitiah's statue is shown in relief in a corridor north of Thutmose III's Festival hall near scenes of other royal statues.[116]

The significance of the mace is difficult to assess from these scenes, but it is tempting to attribute some political significance to it. This is especially so because the persons pictured are known to have been influential, and the female royalty of the 18th dynasty acquired increasingly more power through time.[117] The representations of Iaret, Tiaa and Nefrure, especially, evoke an impression of support for the ruler and have an element of protectiveness about them as well. In this regard, scenes showing Waset carrying a mace and bow and standing protectively behind pharaoh are relevant (e.g., CG 34010).

Another point must be made here, however. Although the mace attribute is not common in 18th Dynasty queens' representations, it does appear as one of the elements held by the God's wives of Amun in the 25th and 26th Dynasties.[118] It is perhaps no coincidence that all the 18th Dynasty royal women shown holding a mace--except Iaret--are known to have been God's wives. The temporal power of that office has been much discussed[119], but the nature of its political influence in the 18th Dynasty remains cloudy. The iconography of the mace suggests that the God's wives both wielded their power and used it to support the kings with whom they appear. In view of the association of the mace with the God's wives, and of Iaret's sudden appearance in year 7 with a full queen's titulary, I tentatively suggest that Tiaa died at this point in the reign and that Iaret perhaps assumed the post of God's wife as well as that of Great Royal Wife. We have seen already that during the 18th Dynasty God's wives often appeared without the title of Amun's priestess.

Unprovenanced

The third object naming Iaret is a scarab now in Basle[120] which calls her _s3t-nsw wrt_, "Great king's daughter". The title was discussed by Schmitz[121] who felt that it was revived for Iaret because God's wife had been lost to true king's daughters; this might be an alternative for the suggestion given above. For Schmitz this title therefore designated the female destined to marry the future king. She relied on the titularies of Ahhotep and a princess Ahmose for her argument. Only the former is known to have become a king's wife. Sitamun, daughter to Amenhotep III and Tiye also bore the title, and although she did not marry her brother, she functioned as consort to her father. It may be that Schmitz's interpretation is correct, but insufficient data exists at present to conclude from it anything other than a recognition of this princess' preferred status.

Iaret herself remains enigmatic. Her mother and father are unknown, but it would be safe to assume that she came of age during Thutmose's reign, perhaps in Year 7 when she was "introduced" on official visits in the south and north. That "King's Daughter" was more common for her than was "King's Great Wife" supports this conclusion; and so does her sudden appearance in year 7. Schmitz has opted to call Iaret a daughter of Amenhotep II, no doubt born at the end of his reign. This is reasonable, if the title King's Sister (snt-nsw) must be taken literally. There is, however, the possibility of Thutmose' own fatherhood.[122]

That royal female family members were increasingly required to participate in the cults seems evident from temple illustrations, such as in the Deir el Bahri Hathor chapel of Thutmose III and Amenhotep II, as well as in Amarna and Ramesside scenes showing princesses.[123] And Helck's suggestion, followed by Harris, that kings married young daughters or sisters, as they reached puberty (?), for ceremonial and sacerdotal purposes is a sensible assumption.[124] Thus one need not, for example, assume a sculptor's error in making Sitamun "Great Royal Wife" while Tiye yet lived.[125] In the context of Helck's discussion, this has helpful repercussions for the Amarna period, and with Thutmose IV it applies equally well. Iaret, either his sister or daughter, reached the culturally acceptable age and took on ritual duties as the highest ranking female royal family member. If Nefertiry was still alive, she may have then retired. But again, as Gitton noted, there is no clear evidence that kings had only one Great Royal Wife; they do not seem to appear together, however, a fact which may reflect functional differences.

Nefertiry and Iaret are the two major wives of Thutmose, and as has just been seen, Iaret was probably wife only in the ritual sense. Thus Nefertiry emerges as the king's chosen mate. It has been suggested that she was the daughter represented in the tomb of Thutmose III, called King's Daughter Nefertiry.[126] This would certainly have made her older than Thutmose IV, though not necessarily too old to provide him children. But Queen Nefertiry never called herself King's Daughter; and since one cannot be sure when Thutmose III's tomb was decorated, it would be too speculative to make this identification. If the tomb was painted even five years before Thutmose III's death, Nefertiry could have been a minimum of fifteen years older than Thutmose IV. It is more acceptable to identify two women of the same name. The major point to be made here is that Thutmose IV did not have the great number of consorts attributed to him. Nefertiry was clearly his chosen wife, and Iaret, due to her family rank, replaced Tiaa. They, together with Tiaa, are the only Great royal wives known during Thutmose's reign.[127] Tiaa (as King's Mother) and Nefertiry were simultaneously officiating with Thutmose IV, while Iaret appeared briefly towards the end of the king's life.

Mutemwia.[128]

Amenhotep III's mother is known from monuments datable only to her son's rule and so cannot be included as Great Royal Wife for Thutmose IV. Such titles have no authority for the earlier period,[129] and as has been seen, the king himself recognized two women by the consort's rank. Years ago it was felt necessary to argue Amenhotep III's parentage and to prove him a son of Thutmose IV or Amenhotep II or some other person. Mutemwia was eventually recognized as Thutmose's wife, but it was some years before the king was credited with fathering Amenhotep.[130]

Mutemwia herself has been identifed as a Mitanni princess [131] (see below 3.5), as the enigmatic Iaret [132], as the daughter of Amenhotep II [133], and more recently, as a commoner from the family of Yuya and Tuya.[134] The last suggestion is attractive, but it has nothing to support it other than Tiye's appearance early in the reign when Mutemwia may have been regent. This will be discussed a bit further on, but it should be underlined that the only established fact is that Mutemwia and Thutmose IV produced a son (perhaps even during the reign of Amenhotep II) who later became Amenhotep III. One should reasonably surmise that Mutemwia was a wife to the king, but her status can only have been minor. This follows from her absence from any contemporary monuments, at a time when her son was himself visible and quite likely the expected heir.[135] Note that an identical situation obtained regarding Thutmose IV who left a pre-accession monument naming himself and the Royal Nurse Hekareshu--but not his mother. She is unknown until his reign.

It has been recognized that Mutemwia's monuments belong to her son's reign, but it must still be pointed out that her titles in her son's reign do not reflect a real position as Thutmose's wife.[136]

Karnak

The most attractive monument of Mutemwia is a black granite model of a sacred bark with a statue of the queen as Mut seated inside.[137] It is nearly completely preserved in the British Musuem and was originally found in the Karnak temple granite sanctuary. Mutemwia bears the following titles, notably similar to those of Tiaa on the Giza statue fragments: (Amenhotep III's cartouche also appears).

hmt-nsw wrt mwt-ntr Mwt-m-wi3. Right side: rpՙtt wrt hswt im3t ib bnrt mrwt mh h3 m sty i3d.s hmt-nsw wrt mrt.f ddt ht nbt ir.tw n.s hnwt šmՙw mhw mwt-ntr /////. Left side: rpՙtt wrt hswt hmt-nsw wrt mryt.f mwt-ntr mst nsw hsyt nt ntr nfr ddt ht nbt ir.tw n.s htp.s st.s imy wi3.s smnhw m k3t dt mwt-nsw Mwt-m-wi3.

Great Royal Wife, God's mother, Mutemwia. Right side: rp'tt great of praise, well-disposed, sweet of love, who fills the Hall with the fragrance of her dew, the Great Royal Wife, beloved of him, for whom everything which she says is done, the Mistress of Upper and Lower Egypt, the God's mother [Mutemwia]. Left side: rp'tt, great of praise Great king's wife, beloved of him, God's Mother who bore the king, praised of the Good God, for whom everything which she says is done. May she occupy her seat within her bark, it being embellished as an eternal construction, the King's Mother Mutemwia.

This elaborate description of Mutemwia intends to link her with Mut and, of course, is a three-dimensional rebus writing of the Queen's name. The head of the statue may or may not be that naming Mutemwia and linked to the bark by British Museum number.

Luxor Temple

Mutemwia also appears in scenes from the Luxor temple, most notably in the divine birth scenes for Amenhotep III.[138] There in two scenes she is called "rpᶜtt great of grace, Mistress of the Two Lands, King's Mother" (rpᶜtt wrt ỉm3t hnwt t3wy mwt-nsw) , and "Rpᶜtt great of grace, sweet of love, Mistress of all lands, King's Mother" (rpᶜtt wrt ỉm3t bnryt mrwt hnwt nt t3w nb mwt-nsw.)

In room 20, west of the Amun sanctuary, Mutemwia appeared in an offering scene with Amenhotep III.[139] There Amun and Mut were depicted receiving hes vases from the king; Mutemwia stood behind. She is called simply King's Mother. It should be noted that this is a damaged scene and has been restored by a post-Amarna hand, most probably in the reign of Horemheb. The style of relief is most unlike Amenhotep III's, especially in the hooded eyelid of the queen, and Brunner believes the closest comparison can be found in the goddess Isis pictured in Horemheb's royal tomb. The inscription too is erased and may have been partially restored. The name and title for Mutemwia could have been supplied during the restoration, but it is difficult to say for certain. This is an unusual location in the temple to find Mutemwia, since the king otherwise appears with deities solely in the back parts of the complex. Perhaps Mutemwia has been invested with a divinization here,[140] or perhaps the goddess Mut was originally represented in the relief and the restoration placed Mutemwia in the scene. This would explain why this figure and Amun's, but not that of the King, were damaged.[141]

Thebes

A statue in black granite, preserved from the waist down,[142] must originally have come from the mortuary temple of Amenhotep III or Thutmose IV but is now near the storeroom west of the Ramesseum. The measurements of the piece are presently 83 X 42.5 X 86.5 cm. A back pillar supported the upper back and head of the figure and is preserved now above the level of the throne seat.   An inscription appears beside each leg names "the King's Mother, Great Royal Wife, Mistress of the Two Lands Mutemwia" (mwt-nsw hmt-nsw wrt hnwt-t3wy Mwt-m-wi3 name damaged but readable). The text is identical on both sides. The back preserves a vertical text: "Venerated before all the [gods] forever. Protection and life

be behind her, Mistress of the Two lands forever" ([im3ḥ]w ḥr nṯrw nbw [damaged
but readable] dt s3 ꜥnḥ ḥ3.s nbt t3wy dt). The cartouches are partially erased but
are readable, this is true as well for "all the gods" on the back pillar. The Mut-bird
was erased as here on the Memnon colossi of Amenhotep III.[143]

Mutemwia appeared on the famous colossi of Amenhotep III [144] which flanked
the entrance to his mortuary temple. On both statues a smaller figure of the king's
mother stands to the left of the throne, and the vertical texts call her King's Mother,
Great king's wife [Mut]emwia. Amenhotep represented both his mother and his
wife on the statues; Tiy was shown as a statuette to the right of the throne. This
double appearance of royal mother and wife parallels Thutmose IV's granite stela
from Luxor where Tiaa and Nefertiry were shown. Apparently there was no conflict
in both women bearing the title Great Royal Wife on the monuments, and we can
only assume that Tiy performed the duties of consort while Mutemwia functioned
as Queen mother, perhaps having used Great Royal Wife in reference to her
deceased husband.

Mutemwia was once represented in a private Theban tomb where she was
shown seated in a kiosk with her son.[145] Theban tomb 226 in Gurnah shows the
King's Mother Mutemwia and Amenhotep III receiving an offering from the
deceased (name lost). The question whether this representation belongs to the
earliest years of Amenhotep's reign was raised in the preceding chapter. Mutemwia's
death cannot be identified during the reign yet.

Aswan

An Aswan graffito[146] depicts a kiosk formed by a sky sign supported by two was
scepters. Within Amenhotep and Mutemwia were shown receiving a fan's breeze
from a private person. The queen is termed simply King's Mother, and the date
of the cutting, like that of the tomb 226 painting, is unsure.

Malkata (posthumous(?))

Mutemwia's estate appears in the Malkata jar labels as a contributor of wine.[147]
Whether this was a posthumous reference is not known. The estates of Thutmose
IV and Amenhotep II were also listed among the donors. It might seem unlikely
that Mutemwia lived into the very late years of Amenhotep III's reign, which the
Malkata labels largely represent, if only because she is so sparsely documented
there. But this is only conjecture, and her presence on the colossi of Memnon
speaks in favor of her longevity. The date of her death is an open question.

Unprovenanced.

A loti-form ointment spoon with a duck-head handle in the Louvre (E
3671).[148] names the Great Royal Wife and God's Mother Mutemwia. The latter

title appeared on the granite bark from Karnak also. Such an item is likely to have come from the Queen Mother's personal items, very possibly from her burial. The location of that tomb is entirely unknown.

Mutemwia and the God's Wife of Amun

One monumental statue of a queen has been removed from the list of Mutemwia's objects. A colossal crystalline statue preserved only from torso to feet was found in a sebakh area at the southeast corner of the Dendera temple facade.[149] The titles identify the "God's wife, Great Royal Wife, female ruler high of plumes, mistress of the Two lands, Mut[///]; God's wife, Great royal wife beloved of him, mistress of the Two lands, Mut[///]".   Hari was the first to notice that the titles of this queen did not correspond to those of Mutemwia.[150] Weigall had made that identification in 1908, and the piece had been listed as such for many years.   The major disagreement in ranks is the presence of God's Wife and the absence of King's Mother. The former title never appears for Mutemwia, while the latter always does.   Aldred believes the statue represents Mutnodjmet, and Hari made the same suggestion based on the titles.[151] Aling has proposed Mer-en-Mut Nofretari[152], wife of Ramesses II.   One cannot be sure, but at present Aling's suggestion is more likely the correct one, since Mut-Nofretari is known to have been hmt-ntr, while Mutnodjmet is not.[153] In any event, all are agreed Mutemwia is not portrayed in the colossus.

The transferal of this Dendara statue has repercussions for the 18th dynasty succession of kings, since this was the only occurrence of God's Wife for the queen. It is now widely held that God's Wife was not a title that designated the present or intended future mother of a king. And there is no evidence at all that "God's Wife" is a title describing the mate of Amun who bears a pharaoh[154]--the title never appeared for Ahmose mother of Hatshepsut or for Mutemwia.[155] A God's Wife does, however, appear twice in the Luxor temple scenes of Amenhotep III as an anonymous participant in the ritual behind the Iunmutef priests.[156] Gitton, Yoyotte, and Graefe[157] among others, have done much to point out inconsistencies in Sander-Hansen's original thesis,[158] and have helped provide a new definition for the God's Wife and its dynastic role. It is premature to suggest, however, as did Harris, that the title Great King's Wife became a functional substitute for God's Wife after the reign of Amenhotep II[159]. Contrary to Harris' statements, God's Wife was a title borne by Tiaa during her lifetime and was not given her posthumously, while the presence of a God's Wife in the Luxor temple scenes demonstrates the office continued to function in the reign of Amenhotep III.

The study of the title God's Wife (of Amun) has untangled the unwarranted connection of this office to the birth legends of Hatshepsut and Amenhotep III and to the royal succession. This unraveling makes the conclusions of Brunner even more illuminating. Brunner concluded that the birth scenes demonstrate nothing about a king's earthly descent, but rather they give him a divine derivation and are part of the canon of temple reliefs illustrating the myth of royal divinity.[160] The purpose was in no way to provide a pure-blooded royal line , and therefore the pedigree of the mother was irrelevant. Instead, both Ahmose and Mutemwia were called in the birth scenes by the same titles Tiaa bore on her Giza statue:[161] "rp^{c}tt great of praise and charm, beloved friend of Horus, mistress of sweetness, great of love, mistress sweet of heart, mistress of all wives, for whom is done everything which she says; consort of Horus, mistress of the Two lands, daughter of Geb, heir of Osiris, mistress of the Two lands, King of Upper and Lower Egypt's mother, she who sees Horus and Seth." These are epithets that describe queens as wives to gods, and it is their offsprings' relations to the divinities which are emphasized in this way. It is therefore pointless to search for a royal background for Mutemwia; Amenhotep III and Thutmose IV were not self-conscious about identifying their mothers and fathers; scholars need not be so for them.

This new focus on royal titles could strengthen Aldred's suggestion that Mutemwia was from Yuya and Tuya's family,[162] but only more information will take us further. Unfortunately there are no data to define Mutemwia's position at the start of her son's rule.[163]

Mitannian wife

The marriage of Thutmose IV with a daughter of Artatama I is attested in EA 29 [164], a letter from Tushratta to Amenhotep IV. The lines in question are as follows: "When [Manahpiria], the father of [Ni]mmuaria wrote to Artatama, my grandfather, and requested for himself the daughter of [my grandfather, my father's sister], five times, six times he kept sending, and he did not give her at all. A seventh time [to my grandfather he] sent, then he gave her straightaway." He continued, saying that Amenhotep III had requested six times before Shuttarna sent a daughter, but that he, Tushratta, had given his daughter immediately.[165] This reference to a diplomatic union between Thutmose IV and the Mitannian woman cannot be confirmed from Egyptian documents, but there is no reason to doubt its validity. There is also no reason to believe the foreign princess entered the court as a Great Royal Wife. Indeed, the opposite is more likely in view of the apparent lack of status afforded the Mitannian and Babylonian wives of Amenhotep III.[166] And there is one bit of Egyptian evidence which indicates the rank of these women. A funerary cone belonging to one Bengai (Bng3i)[167] no doubt a foreign name, refers to the deceased as the ^{c}3 n pr špst Nhrn, "Great one of the House of the Noble lady of Mitanni". One might certainly surmise that few foreign ladies had their own holdings, but that the kings' wives did. Thutmose IV's wife and Amenhotep III's must then have been noble court ladies, but not necessarily with the rank of

King's Wife hmt-nsw and probably not with Great King's Wife hmt-nsw wrt.[168]

The apparent difficulty experienced by Thutmose in acquiring Artatama's daughter for his wife has been attributed to anti-Egyptian resentment and also to the power of Mitanni at the time.[169] But Schulman has pointed out that it is wrong to take the passage literally and to ignore its context.[170]

Tushratta was comparing his willingness to negotiate with Egypt to a reticent attitude of earlier Mitanni rulers; the real import may have been that Tushratta constructed a scene in which he was the generous participant while Amenhotep IV was tight-fisted and unreasonable. The literary license used in the letter was a normal element in diplomatic correspondence, and even in treaties. This was especially true in those treaty sections which outlined the history of disagreements between rulers.[171]

The use of numbers to underline the situation was no doubt simply another device that made a point poetically. And seven is one of the most commonly used numbers in Near Eastern literature.[172] So it would be unwarranted to conclude anything about the nature of power politics in Thutmose IV's reign from this short passage. A diplomatic marriage took place, but it is more than likely that Artatama was a willing participant who sent his daughter to Egypt to bind the treaty. That the agreement was desired by both monarchs is implied in lines 34-39 of EA 24, a letter from Tushratta to Amenhotep III.[173] (This correspondence is, with the exception of a short introduction in Akkadian, written in Hurrian. The translation here is therefore after Mercer.) Tushratta speaks to the Egyptian king concerning his daughter Taduhepa: "My brother shall be satisfied. He shall desire the dowry. In respect to the daughter of my father, my sister, here is a special tablet: a tablet of her dowry....and in respect to the daughter of my grandfather, my father's sister, here is a special tablet; a tablet of her dowry, a special tablet. Let my brother read the tablets, and seven times may he hearken to me." It appears that Tushratta was boasting that Taduhepa's dowry was larger than those of previous Mitannia princesses, but it is nonetheless clear that even Artatama's daughter, Thutmose IV's bride, came as did all foreign wives, with a dowry representing the Mitanni ruler's desire for the union.

Years ago Erman suggested that Mutemwia was identical with this Mitanni bride of Thutmose IV.[174] That idea did not gain a great deal of support and must be wrong simply by virtue of chronology. Amenhotep III must have been born at the very start of Thutmose' rule, if not in the time of Amenhotep II. Therefore, a marriage during the reign could only with great difficulty have produced the future ruler. This fact,together with the evidence in Amenhotep III's reign that these foreign wives did not take Egyptian names, makes an identification with Mutemwia unacceptable. (Gilukhipa appeared with her own name on the marriage scarab; Kiya too may be a shortening of a foreign name.)

Summary

The known wives of Thutmose IV were Tiaa (ceremonial only), Nefertiry, Iaret, Mutemwia, and a Mitanni princess. The first three were acknowledged Great Royal Wives during the king's lifetime, although Iaret probably not until around his seventh year of rule. She took over some of the functions of the office perhaps at Tiaa's death or at puberty. It is unknown whether Nefertiry continued to act as wife to Thutmose after Iaret became Great Royal Wife. Mutemwia was no doubt a minor queen who fathered Thutmose's first surviving son. Each of her monuments belongs to her son's reign.

Daughters

Tiaa.[175]

This daughter of Thutmose IV is attested by three fragmentary canopic jars, a wooden label (funerary) and a scene in private Theban tomb 63. Only the last document has provided controversy in identification, for some scholars have recognized the king's mother in this princess. Robins has laid the dispute to rest, however, by publishing a handcopy from the Lepsius manuscript in the Griffith Institute providing the title and name of Tiaa's nurse, Meryt, wife of Treasurer Sobekhotep.[176] Some have mistakenly identified that woman, Meryt, as the tomb-owner Sobekhotep's mother rather than his wife.[177] This has led to the confusion of princess Tiaa with Thutmose IV's mother.

The canopic jars mentioned above have no precise provenance, but they were purchased in Luxor and certainly came from Thebes.[178] Legrain bought two of them for the Cairo Museum (JE 36167 and 36171): one names the Royal daughter Tiaa (no cartouche), the other the Royal daughter Ti[aa]. The other fragments in the lot of canopics belong to the reign of Amenhotep III, as the mention on many of them of Itn-thn, "Aten Tjehen", the palace of Malkata, shows. This would tend to confirm Tiaa as a daughter of Thutmose IV. The third canopic fragment (all are limestone painted with blue hieroglyphs) was purchased by Newberry in 1903 and is now in the University College London (UC 15809)[179] It belonged to the same dealer's group originally, and Newberry chose a fragment naming Amenhotep III's wife Nebetnehut, attested in Legrain's lot as well, along with Tiaa's piece. The canopic fragment in London names Royal Daughter Tiaa (again without cartouche).

These funerary objects obviously had a common place of origin--Legrain believed they stemmed from the Valley of the Queens, while Carter and Winlock linked them to pit tombs west of Medinet Habu. It does seem a reasonable assumption that these princesses, noble ladies and queens mentioned on the canopics were buried together or at least in neighboring areas,[180] since that would have enabled those who found and sold the pieces to place the whole group on the market at once. One might mention here that a Prince Menkheperre attested on two fragments (JE 36180 and an unnumbered piece) may be a son of Thutmose III shown on BM 1280, statue of one Huy a priestess and mother of queen Meryt-re(?).[181] If this is the same Menkheperre, then he apparently survived through two full reigns and remained part of the court circle until his death.

That Princess Tiaa was daughter to Thutmose IV and died during the reign of Amenhotep III may be conclusively demonstrated by the wooden label mentioned above.[182] It was found by Henry Rhind during his Theban excavations and was published with a group of such labels[183], several naming Thutmose IV. Tiaa's label contains the following information: s3t-nsw Ti^c3 n Mn-ḫprw-r^c n pr n3 n msw-nsw nty m s3.s "the King's Daughter of Menkheprure of the house of the Royal children: those in her following: the architect Wekay, the doorkeeper Se, the doorkeeper Nefruerhat, the embalmer Neferrenpet." (The last named men were probably assigned to effect her reburial.) The original publication called the ladies named on labels daughters of Thutmose III, but the plural strokes for Menkheprure are clear in the hieratic, as Newberry pointed out as early as 1903.[184]

The location of the tomb of this princess and her burial companions was found by Rhind and reported in 1862.[185] At the foot of the Gurnah mountain Rhind dug for many days before he discovered a large doorway, plaster-covered and sealed with cartouches bearing the name of Amenhotep III.[186] The seals were in place, but there was a hole in the door through which robbers had long ago crawled. "The tomb was a large undecorated rectangular chamber some forty to fifty feet in each direction with six square pillars." A passage in one corner led to another chamber on a lower level,[187] and that room still bore the necropolis seal; it too had been entered by thieves. According to Rhind the floor was covered with bones, torn bandages, fragments of coffins and mummies, all, he said, torn at the neck and breast. His search of the tomb produced only sixteen "small inscribed tablets of thin wood" about 2 1/2" X 2",[188] rounded at the top and pierced with a hole. Rhind reported that names of princesses of the family of Thutmose III were given on the tablets. Rhind and Birch published the texts in 1863 without further discussion of the tomb. But Rhind had already offered the opinion that the tomb remains were not the princesses named on the tags but were slaves of the household. He felt that, although the size of the tomb was adequate for royalty, the lack of decoration and the ordinary coffins precluded royal family members from burial in this tomb.[189]

The labels have been newly identified as of 21st Dynasty date. This clarifies the tattered remains as belonging to a reburial, and a Year 27/37 on two labels can now be assigned to Psusennes I, not Amenhotep III. The original site of burial, however, remains uncertain, particularly if Amenhotep III's name appeared on the door seals. The Gurnah tomb may have been a reburial for these princesses, and the wooden labels were used as identification in transport. But a similar label appeared on the market at about the same time as the canopic fragments discussed above--well after the Rhind find. A second possibility is that the princess and other women were buried in Gurnah, and their tomb was robbed in antiquity, provoking a reburial in the same location. The canopic fragments bought by Legrain and Newberry may have been reburied by the robbers after they sorted through their "loot".[190] If this scenario is at all valid, then Tiaa died in Amenhotep III's reign. The last word has not been said on this problem.

It has been proposed above that Princess Tiaa spent her childhood in the Fayum as the nursling of Meryt, Sobekhotep's wife.[191] This is a logical interpretation for her inclusion in a scene commemorating family attachments to that region. It also seems possible that she was born there, since her name honors her grandmother who is otherwise attested in the Fayum. Princess Tiaa was a resident later at the Theban royal residence (Malkata--the numerous canopic fragments bought along with hers mention Aten-Tjehen often)[192] and was buried in that necropolis. Her age at death cannot be determined, though it cannot have been much older than 45-50.[193]

Amenemipet

Another daughter has left two of the same kinds of monuments as did Tiaa. Princess Amenemipet is pictured seated on the knee of Horemhab, Scribe of the King in Theban tomb 78.[194] There she is called Royal daughter [A]menemipet, and is shown with a sidelock and a diadem atop her head. The crown is similar to those worn by royal ornaments, princesses and even queens--Ankhesenamun, for example.[195] It appears to have been reserved for court members but is not limited to royal family. Perhaps here the crown is meant to signify that Amenemipet was not a small child at the time the tomb was decorated. Brunner[196] suggested that royal children shown naked were not individually important but were representative of the deceased's relationship to the king. Those shown in dress and insignia signified crown princes of great importance. Perhaps, however, nakedness indicated young age, whereas clothes, and especially royal regalia, suggested adults were being pictured as children. Amenemipet's clothing is not visible, but she is wearing sandals; and that at least suggests she was partially clothed--perhaps with a jeweled girdle. We may surmise she was young, but perhaps not a small child.[197] Amenemipet was then already older than a little girl as depicted in Horemhab's tomb early in the reign of Amenhotep III. There is no inscription which specifically calls this princess a daughter of Thutmose IV, but her representation in the tomb was placed in the cross hall where only Thutmose IV appeared as monarch; all references to Amenhotep III were confined to the second corridor.[198]

Probably Amenemipet, like her sister Tiaa, died in the reign of Amenhotep III.

A wooden label quite similar to that discussed above was bought by Newberry in Thebes in 1901.[199] His drawing shows a simple inscription identifying the Royal Daughter Amenemipet. The paleography (if this can be trusted in handcopy) is comparable to that of several of Rhind's labels; the most similar example is that bearing the year 27 date.[200] Quite likely this princess was reburied close by the other princesses, and even possibly with them.[201]

Tinetamun

This princess is known only by fragments of her canopic jars found in the burial chamber of Thutmose IV's tomb.[202] Several pieces of lids are preserved in human-headed form and of fine quality. One body piece is inscribed for "Osiris King's Daughter Tinetamun". One might suppose from this that she predeceased her father, but there is no certainty of it.

Petepihu (?)[203]

Two of the sixteen labels mentioned above bear the following text: "the Royal Daughter Petepihu of Menkheprure". One of these labels was made in stone. It is logical to assume that Petepihu, like Tiaa who had a similar label, was Thutmose's daughter.

Various

Other names of daughters may exist among those preserved on Rhind's labels [204] and on one similar tablet which probably belonged to the same lot. The names of these ladies are as follows: Tawy[//] (read Nini by Birch); Petpuy (3 examples); Merytptah; Sathor; Neferamun; Wiay; and Hentiunu. Khatnesu is attested on the analogous label published later.

1. E.g., PM II², 73 (Ahmose-Nofretari and family), 135 (Hatshepsut as queen with princess Merytamun), 380 (Meryt-re Hatshepsut with Thutmose III). This and the next several notes cite only the Bibliography and serve only to suggest the evidence.

2. Merytamun, PM II², 135; 176; Tiaa, on colossal statue of Amenhotep II, ibid., 176.

3. KV 34 of Thutmose, PM I² 2, 553.

4. Nefrure is, of course, the best known. See Senmut's statues from Thebes in PM II², 134, 144, 182. TT 192 of Kheruef in the reign of Amenhotep III is well known in this regard as well, but earlier we have also Benermerut associated with princess Merytamun. Ibid., 144.

5. Erhart Graefe, Untersuchungen zur Verwaltung und Geschichte der Institution der Gottesgemahlin des Amun vom Beginn des Neuen Reiches bis zur Spatzeit. Band 1: Katalog und Materialsammlung. Band II: Analyse und Indices (Wiesbaden 1981).

6. Luxor Temple reliefs, as discussed further below, have suggested the possible deification of Mutemwia, Amenhotep III's mother. See on this, L. Troy, Patterns of Queenship in Ancient Egyptian Myth and History (Uppsala 1986) 103-04.

7. For a brief sketch see C. Zivie, "Tiaa", Lexikon der Ägyptologie VI,4 (Wiesbaden 1985) 551-55. Also, M. Gitton, Les divines épouses de la 18e dynastie, (Paris 1984) 84-92. Lana Troy, Patterns of Queenship in Ancient Egyptian Myth and History (Uppsala 1986) 165, for summation of titles and sources.

8. Robins, op.cit., GM 62 (1983) 67-77.

9. S. Hassan, The Great Sphinx, 34,36,77-80,240, figs. 63- 64. S. Hassan, The Sphinx. 40; C. Zivie, Giza au Deuxième Millénaire, NE 36, 160-64; 270.

10. Christiane M. Zivie-Coche, "Une curieuse statue de la reine Ti'aa à Giza", Mélanges Gamal Eddin Mokhtar II (Cairo 1985) 389-401, pls. 1-2. M. Gitton, Les divines épouses de la 18e dynastie (Paris 1984)88-92. Gitton publishes only the titulary fragment.

11. Zivie, Mélanges Mokhtar, 395 and n.29.

12. Ibid., 394.

13. Urk IV, 1539-41.

14. Urk IV, 224 10-11. rpᶜtt s3t Gb ỉwᶜt Wsir hnwt t3wy mwt-nsw-bit ỷᶜhms.

15. Zivie, Melanges Mokhtar, 397-98.

16. Zivie, op.cit., 397-401, Giza au deuxième millénaire, 164 n.(a).

17. Hassan, The Great Sphinx 78, 91.

18. Ibid.

19. Zivie cites Leclant, Montuemhat, 15, with Saite and 18th Dynasty examples. She notes, for example, Urk. IV 1630, nṯr niwty ḥȝỉ kȝ.f ḥft-ḥr ỉ.

20. See Lexikon der Ägyptologie. "Königin" and "Königinnentitel". Several are applied to kings' mothers from the Old Kingdom on. For Mutemwia, Urk. IV 1772; Ahmose, Urk. IV 81-82, 224.

21. Notably sdtt P ḥwnt Dp, but sdtt wȝdt is known, Rec. Trav. 12, 217; Zivie, Mélanges Mokhtar 392-95.

22. Cairo Temp. 6.11.26.6 (see fig. 7); G. Legrain, Rec. Trav. 26 (1904) 222-23; G. Legrain, Repertoire #186; Urk. IV 1316. Limestone stela 475 (on view) has not been published with a photo. Examination has resulted in the conclusion here. Legrain did not originally believe the entire stela below the wings was recut, but he said destruction had occurred beneath the winged sundisk. He also suggested the incorrect prenomen of the king was due to a sculptor's mistake at the time of restoration.

23. As, for example, G. Maspero in T. Davis, The Tomb of Iouiya and Touiyou, XIII, gave three writings for Tuya and eleven for Yuya. See also H. Ranke, PN I, 377-78; 384 for writings with 𓈖𓏭 and 𓂝𓈖𓏭 .

24. Urk. IV 1581 incorrectly shows 𓇋𓄿 after a now destroyed text copied by Champollion. But Not. I 481 shows rather 𓇋𓄿.

25. One might consider that the original work represented Amenhotep II and Merytre and that the recarving of Tiaa, followed by a destruction of much of the surface, obscured the latter queen's name.

26. PM II^2 176; L. Habachi, ASAE 38 (1938) 80-81, [13], Arch. Lacau MAA/RC, Axii, a,6; Mariette, misreading cartouche on the belt, Karnak Texte, 60, pl.38d; Urk. IV 1561.

27. Zivie, "Tiaa", LÄ VI, 553, states that the statuette has no name. I have not seen it.

28. C. Van Siclen III, "The Building History of the Tuthmosis Temple at Amada and the Jubilees of Tuthmosis IV", Varia Aegyptiaca 3 (1987) 63, fig 8 on 62.

29. P. Barguet, J. Leclant, Karnak-Nord IV (1954) 53-55 [2], pl. L, LI. See also in Orientalia NS 20 (1951) 469 n.3. The door is incised and painted; the relief is painted yellow, and a coat of plaster was applied (probably later). Lintel measurements are 1.4 m. length by .6 width by .72 depth; the jambs are 1.76 m. in height.

30. A title not attested for Tiaa.

31. Barguet, Karnak-Nord IV 55 [3], fig. 84.

32. E. Wente, An X-ray Atlas, 133. Urk. IV, 1305, 11. C. Van Siclen confirms his suspicion that Meryt-re's name was replaced by that of Tiaa by Thutmose IV, however. There is no reason to believe that Tiaa was queen during any part of Amenhotep's reign. (By personal communication.)

33. PM II^2 144, 380, 472.

34. PM I^2 2, 553, 555.

35. PM II^2 447H. Gauthier, Le Livre des rois d' Egypte XVIII (Cairo 1912) 271; R. Lepsius, Denkmäler Text' III, 140.

36. See now B. Bryan, "The Portrait Sculpture of Thutmose IV" JARCE 24 (1987) 3-20, for discussion of this work and the sculpture in the round of the reign as a whole. CG 42080, PM II^2 96; G Legrain, Statue et Statuettes I, 46-47, pl. XLIX; G Legrain, ASAE 5 (1904) 35-36 [17], pl. V; Urk. IV 1564.

37. Legrain, Statues, 47 and PM II^2 96.

38. R. Tefnin, CdE 49 (1974) 19 with note 1.

39. Tefnin writes, "L'examen de la colonne d'inscription gravee a cote de la jambe du roi montre en effet que les signes ⟨hieroglyphs⟩
     ...[are recut]". In fact examination of said signs will show that the inscription is written ⟨hieroglyphs⟩   Op.cit., 19.

40. Legrain, Statues I, 47.

41. She is called King's mother.

42. Tefnin, op.cit., 18-19, believes this statue does not conform to the style of Thutmose IV's statuary, but his list of inscribed pieces is incomplete. For full discussion of this statue and the style of the king's statuary, see Bryan, JARCE 24, 3-20. See also discussion in Chapter 4.

43. H. Chevrier, ASAE 51 (1951) 549-51, 568, fig. 1.

44. The only Egyptian temple bearing such a scene is the Ptolemaic temple at Tod. There it is the brick-molding scene in which the queen is present. B.F. Bisson de la Roque, Tōd (1934- 1936) 20.

45. PM II^2, 476.

46. PM II^2 6., Merytre-Hatshepsut offering nu pots. PM II^2 198, Sitiah offering ointment;PM II^2 134, Ahmose-Nofretari as God's wife in priestly procession in a chapel of Amenhotep I PM I12 136, Hatshepsut as a woman offering wine to Amun; PM II^2 326-37, Mutemwia in birth scenes; 332, offering hes vases behind king. Note that all save Mutemwia, who appears specifically as the king's mother, are God's wives.

47. See below to compare with a representation of Iaret, ns. 87-91.

48. A. H. Gardiner, The Wilbour Papyrus A25, 15, Section 57.

49. A. Gardiner, The Wilbour Papyrus Commentary, 11; See further for discussion of the grave goods found in KV 47 of Siptah and the question of the Ramesside queen Tiaa.

50. Ibid., 75, 139, hwt ^{c}3-hpr(w)-r^c m pr Imn. In both cases Gardiner opted to read Amenhotep's prenomen, and he has been followed in this by Helck, Materialien, 219.

51. C. Aldred took this view as well, rather than suggest Siptah's mother was referred to in the 20th dynasty document. JEA 49 (1968) 41 n. 5.

52. There is room to argue whether any temple of Thutmose IV within Karnak has been identified in papyri of later date. Helck has taken the affirmative view, following A. Gardiner, JEA 27 (1941) 67, but there is no m pr Imn in the reference.

53. J. Lauffray, Kemi, 21 (1971) 60-61.

54. B. Letellier,in Hommages Serge Sauneron, 55-63.

55. M. el-Razik, MDAIK 27 (1971) 222-24, pl. 63. Statue of Thutmose IV.

56. Abdel-Qader Muhammad, ASAE 60 (1968) 244 [8], 248-49, 271, pl. 25.

57. M. Gitton, "Gottesgemahlin", Lexikon der Ägyptologie. Lief. 13, 794.

58. Ibid., 794-95; E. Graefe in a review of Gitton, L'épouse du dieu Ahmès-Néfertary , in BiOr 33 (1976) 316-17; J. Yoyotte,BSFE 64 (1972) 37.

59. These are references to temples not termed "funerary", since we might expect mentions of family members within the royal cult place.
Ahmose-Nofretari: PM   II^2 31,73,77,80,86,88,103,129,134, 137,144,145,147,162,166,178,214,230,261,279,284,293,294.   Contemporary and posthumous, but both are evidence of her importance as God's wife "par excellence".

Ahhotep - PM II^2 179
Sitamun - PM II^2 261, 176
Ahmose-Merytamun -PM II^2 176(?)
Hatshepsut - PM II^2 135, 136, et als.
Nefrure - PM II^2 134 144,182, 198, 278-280,286 (statues with Senmut, but she is named God's wife on them)
Sitiah - PM II^2 198, (CG34013 usurped from Nefrure); 124.
Merytamun - PM II^2 144; 380.
Merytre-Hatshepsut - PM II^2 6,144-45; 380; 469; Amenhotep II Karnak pavillion block.
Tiaa - PM II6,72 96,166,176,538; Amenhotep II Karnak pavillion.

60. Attested as God's wife, PM I^2 2, 715-16. As daughter of Kamose, J. Schmitz, Amenophis I., 50; M. Gitton, op.cit., 802; as daughter of Ahmose, B. Schmitz, Untersuchungen zum Titel s3 Njswt, "Königssohn", 289.

61. PM II2 - Ahmose, PM II^2 137; Mutnefert, 176; Esi, 144;   Nefertiry, 538(not named there); Mutemwia, 102, 326, 332. Mutnodjmet - PM II^2,187; Urk IV, 3025;3037; Nefertiti, PM II^2 39,40,182,191,294,296, eg.; Ankhesenamun, PM II^2 168; 315, also Urk IV 3025, 37, usurped by Mutnodjmet.

62. Ahmose, mother of Hatshepsut, is not God's wife. Gitton has shown that the ivory wand assigned to her uses the early form of ^{2c}h to write Ahmose and should belong to princess Ahmose, op.cit., 807. For lists of queens and princesses, see H. Gauthier, LdR II, 195ff; B. Schmitz, op.cit., 288-96.

63. Satre, wife of Ramesses I, has the title in KV 38, PM I^2 2, 751.

64. CG 1167, L. Borchardt, Statuen IV 87. Fig. 9 below; Urk. IV 1564. Ht. .70 m.

65. H. Brugsch, ZÄS 31 (1893) 29.

66. B Kemp, ZÄS 105 (1978) 122-33.

67. Sobekhotep on Berlin 11635, Urk. IV 1586; Marseille 208 (8), Urk. IV 1587-88; A. Fakhry, ASAE 40 (1941) 40, assigns these statues to Dimai in the Fayum. Discussions of both pieces appear by B. Bryan in Eberhard Dziobek, Das Grab des Sobekhotep. Theben Nr.63.(forthcoming). R. Charles, RdE 12 (1960) 1-26; B. van de Walle, RdE 15 (1963) 77-85. Sobekhotep, Treasurer, Urk. IV 1582- 85, and Brussels statue E 6856, see van de Walle, op.cit.

68. <u>Urk</u>. IV 1027-29; W. Helck, <u>Verw</u>. 352.

69. Charles, <u>op. cit</u>., 25-26.

70. J. Vandier, <u>Manuel</u> III 513. The examples of statues with lotus include: CG 566 (cartouche Amenhotep II), Karnak-Nord T8 = JE 91715 of Userhat (same person named on MMA 19.2.3, tempus AII); Louvre 12926-27 (cartouche AII); 12927 in Boulogne-sur-Mer (<u>FIFAO</u> IV 2 (1927) 108, fig.62).

71. Helck's reconstruction is no better since he neglects to see any family relation between the Sobekhoteps despite their similarity of titles and females' names. <u>Verw</u>., 469.

72. See Chapter 5, under Mayors. Wm. M. Fl. Petrie, <u>Sedment II</u>, pl. liii.

73. Paser, son of Sobekhotep son of Min (Treasurer) was functioning as h3ty-^{c} Š Sbk in Thutmose IV's reign (<u>Urk</u>. IV 1583) and was still active as late as year 30 of Amenhotep III. He appears on a wine label at Malkata bringing local wine for the <u>sed</u> festival. W. Hayes,, <u>JNES</u> 10 (1951) 101 n.230. Hieratic misread as š 3pd, but see Wilbour Papyrus writings for the crocodile in pl. 3, col.8,line 8; pl.4,col.10 Sect.12; pl.5,col.13,1ine.4. and 3pd in Moller, #217 .

74. Gardiner, <u>Wilbour Papyrus.</u> A20,1.34; B Sect. le; A Sect. 43,46; B15,24; A. Gardiner, <u>RAD</u> 15,line.7, 17,line 4 and 30,lines 11,15.

75. Gardiner, <u>Wilbour Papyrus Commentary</u>, 46.

76. <u>LD</u> III 261; Met. Mus. photo T2774-2777; Helck, <u>Verw</u>., 352, anticipated the argument here, based only on the Th.tb 63 scene. But he thought the child was Queen Tiaa.

77. The honorific title <u>wr m T3 Š</u> does appear in the ceiling texts, but it should not be considered a variant for <u>h3ty-^{c} Š rsy</u>.

78. See Chapter 5, Mayors of the Fayum, for a discussion of Sobekhotep and Paser and of the office itself.

79. P. Boulaq VIII, A. Mariette, <u>Les Papyrus Égyptiens du Musée de Boulaq</u>, ii, pl. 19, 3, 11; A Scharff, <u>ZÄS</u> 57 (1922) **6 **7.

80. There is doubt whether a harim existed at Lahun in the Middle Kingdom. See E. Reiser, <u>Der Königliche Harim in Alten Ägypten und seine Verwaltung.</u> 24, re mention of <u>hnrt</u> there. Cf. A. Scharff, <u>ZÄS</u> 59 (1924) 53.

81. See C. Zivie, "Tiaa", LÄ VI (1985) 553-55, nn. 12-13.

82. MMA 14.6.40. W. Hayes, Scepter II 146. 8.7 cm.ht. Six lines of horizontal incised text with Chapter VI of the Book of the Dead.

83. MMA 26.7.931. Carter MSS i A277; and i J387 gave the provenance. Mentioned by E. Thomas, The Royal Necropoleis of Thebes 117.

84. Brooklyn Museum 59.33.2. E. Riefstahl, Ancient Egyptian Glass and Glazes. 19,95 #16. 3.9 cm. wide. Photograph on 19.

85. PSBA 24 (1902) 249.

86. Wm. M. Fl. Petrie, Buttons and Design Scarabs, pl. XXIV 18.7.43. Called "blue-green pottery".

87. C. Aldred, JEA 49 (1963) 41-50, pl.VII. H. Burton, BMMA 19,17. Fragments of the box preserve the base of the swt above the cartouche and [glyphs] which probably should be understood for [glyphs] ? ,although this is by no means sure. The box was originally 22.1 X 26.5 X 10.5 cm. I wish to thank the past and present staff of the Egyptian Department of the Metropolitan Museum, particularly Dr. Christine Lilyquist, Miss Edna Russmann, Dr. Peter Dorman, Dr. Cathleen Keller, for permission to examine these fragments as well as the numerous objects of Thutmose IV residing in the Museum.

88. JE 38778, 8 cm. X 2.5. Aldred, JEA 49,42. dw3-wr, partially preserved, was incised and painted blue on the wood fragment. Compare the adze from the tomb of Amenhotep II, CG 24330.

89. T. Davis, The Tomb of Siphtah 13.

90. For this information I thank Dr. Cathleen Keller of the University of California, Berkeley, who steered me to the formula. See L. Speleers, Les Figurines Funéraires Égyptiennes, 136; G. Daressy, Fouilles. 99-100, pl.25.

91. Hayes, Scepter II, 356-57, also dates it to the 19th Dynasty.

92. For example, Amenhotep,Chief Steward of Memphis under Amenhotep III, Leiden canopic box, Boeser, Pyramiden Bd.5 Abt 2., pl.II,2.

93. Carter, Newberry, The Tomb of Thoutmôsis IV, 8, CG 46041 [8], from Chamber 4.

94. G. Daressy, Fouilles de la Vallée des rois (1898-1899), (Cairo 1902) 243-44, pl. 50.

95. The use of dark blue and yellow faience existed already in the reign of Amenhotep II; Hanover's Kestner Museum possesses a dark blue and yellow faience Taweret inscribed on the shoulder for that ruler. And, of course, this was a commonplace combination in Amenhotep III's reign. E. Brovarski, Egypt's Golden Age, 222, number 277. Royal Scottish Museum 1965. 269 is likewise dark blue with yellow inscription. PM I^2 781.

96. Daressy, Fouilles 83, pl. 23.

97. Burton, op. cit., 19.

98. PM I^2 1, 150; Urk. IV 1581.

99. Gitton, "Gottesgemahlin", LÄ Lief.13, 794; R. Tanner, ZÄS 102 (1975) 55-5b, following A. Pridik, Mut-em-wija, 64ff., says Tiaa is the daughter of Thutmose III and Sitiah! Although the absence of King's daughter is not incontrovertible proof that a woman was not a princess, when several documents are available and all lack the title, the implication is strong. And we know that Hatshepsut, for example, used King's daughter even on monuments where she was also Great royal wife and God's wife, Urk. IV 143-45. The same is true for (among others) Ahhotep, CG 61006, Daressy, Cercueils des Cachettes Royales, 8-9; Ahmose-Nofretari, Urk. IV,26; and a later example, Sitamun, daughter of Amenhotep III, Hayes, Scepter II, 257, fig.155. B. Mertz, Certain Titles...22 135, made the following conclusions: "'King's daughter is not found with titles of queens who were of humble birth. Although we cannot be certain there are not exceptions, still unknown, it is safe to use the term in its literal meaning." But she did not rule out the possibility that non-holders of the title were princesses. The confusion concerning Tiaa comes, I believe, from identifying her as the princess of the same name, daughter of Thutmose IV. For discussion of significance of queens' ranks, see Troy, Patterns of Queenship, 106-114.

100. J. R. Harris, SAK 2 (1975) 95-98.

101. M. Gitton, Orientalia Lovaniensia Periodica 8 (1977) 125- 27.

102. C. Zivie, op.cit., 145-56. NE 15,17,18,19,26,28,30. All the stelae are about the same size (.65 X .45m) and of poor quality. They were placed in the wall which Thutmose IV built around the sphinx. See S. Hassan, The Sphinx. 197; The Great Sphinx, 95-96.

103. Zivie, op. cit., 156, 297.

104. Loat, Gurob, BSAE 10,7, pl.4 [9]; W.F. Petrie, Scarabs and Cylinders, pl. 30 [18.8.13]. .76 cm.ht.

105. Supra, n. 41.

106. Abdel-Qader Muhammad's description reads as follows: "On the right side of the stela, Thotmosis IV is again represented adoring Amun-Re. Here he is probably followed by his wife. But the name is not visible. The onl signs which can be read with any certainty are ⊐ [sic for ∮] and ⌒. The last sign could be a boat but the i and r could not be a part of the name of Mutemwia." ASAE 60 (1968) 249. Even on the poor photo a close examination shows two verticals in the top of the cartouche and a low broad in the middle, two diagonal strokes are visible at the bottom:

107. Or at least it was as late as 1982 when photographs were taken. I am indebted to the constant generosity of Dr. El Sayed Higazy, Director of Karnak and Luxor Temples, who enabled me to examine the inscriptions on the stela. It rested at the time in the magazine of Luxor Temple (one of the bark shrines east of the Appearance Hall).

108. A. Gardiner, T. Peet, J. Černý, Inscriptions of the Sinai² I, pl.19 #60; R. Giveon, The Impact of Egypt on Canaan, 60 [6]; R. Giveon, Tel Aviv 5 (1979) 170-74, pl.44.

109. Urk. IV 1634, G. Bjorkman, JARCE 11 (1974) 50 and n.90, states that royal messengers were not uncommon at the Sinai.

110. A. Mariette, Le Serapéum. pl.21, a šmsw of prince Merneptah; W.K. Simpson, Cd'E 47 (1972) 45-54, line 9 of the stela, šmsw s3 nsw for Amenemhet III as prince.

111. LD III 69e.

112. Supra, n. 33.

113. LD III 25 bis q, s3t-nsw snt-nsw hmt-ntr hmt-nsw wrt.

114. LD III 199e as hmt-ntr hmt-nsw wr n Ỉmn standing before an offering table.

115. LD III 20c, behind Hatshepsut and Thutmose III, both kneeling. s3t-nsw nt [ht.f] nbt t3wy hnwt šmᶜw mhw. Champollion, Mons. II CXCII, behind the kneeling Thutmose III, she is s3t-nsw mrt.f hmt-ntr, holding sistrum and wearing "Libyan bands".

116. PM II², 124. V. Loret, BIE 3 (1898) pl. 7, p. 96.

117. Troy, op.cit., 134-35. LÄ, "Königinnentitel", 474, notes especially hnwt šmᶜw mhw, nbt t3wy, may have political importance.

118. <u>PM</u> II² 476-77, chapel of Amenirdis where she appears in multiple scenes holding the mace. Likewise in the chapel of Nitocris, 478-79.

119. The recent work of M. Gitton, <u>Les divines épouses de la 18e dynastie</u> (Paris 1984) is a fuller discussion of the titleholders of this period than may be found elsewhere, but E. Graefe's <u>Untersuchungen zur Verwaltung und Geschichte der Institution der Gottesgemahlin des Amun vom Beginn des Neuen Reiches bis zur Spätzeit</u> (Wiesbaden 1981) is an overall view of the assembled documentation for the institution.

120. Wm. M. Fl. Petrie, <u>Scarabs and Cylinders</u>, pl. 30 [18.8]; Erik Hornung, <u>Skarabaen aus Basler Sammlungen</u> (Basle 1976) 259 #324 = Fraser #246.

121. B. Schmitz, <u>op.cit.</u>, 309.

122. As per Harris, <u>op.cit.</u>, 96 n.9, unless King's sister must refer only to true kings' sisters. See discussion of the range of meanings for <u>snt</u> in G. Robins, "The relationships specified by Egyptian kinship terms of the Middle and New Kingdoms", <u>CdE</u> 54 (1979) 197-217; Troy, <u>op.cit.</u>, 104ff.

123. <u>E.g</u>, <u>PM</u> II² 380; Daughters of Ramesses II at Luxor Temple, <u>PM</u> II² 306, 308.

124. W. Helck, <u>Cd'E</u> 44 (1969) 22-25; J.R. Harris, <u>Acta Orientalia</u> 36 (1974) 19 with ns. 32-34.

125. As in E. Wente and C. Van Siclen, "A Chronology", 230 n.77, who believe the occurrence was unique.

126. Gitton, <u>OLP</u> 8, 127; <u>Urk</u>. IV 602.

127. Harris, <u>SAK</u> 2 (1975) 96.

128. A short synopsis mentioning some of the monuments in R. Gundlach, "Mutemwia", <u>LÄ</u> IV (Wiesbaden 1982) 251-52.

129. Robins, <u>GM</u> 62 (1983) 67-77 for a discussion of the succession; Troy, <u>op.cit.</u>, 102-03, gives the ideological basis explaining why kings promoted their mothers. B. Schmitz, <u>op.cit.</u>, 309-10, appears to agree that kings could promote their mothers to the rank of Great king's wife.

130. E. Meyer, <u>Geschichte des Altertums</u> II,1,149.
    W. Wolf, <u>ZÄS</u> 65 (1930) 98ff.
    H. Kees, <u>Göttingische Gelehrte Anzeigen</u> (1928) 525; (1929) 374.
    G. Maspero, <u>The Tomb of Thoutmosis IV.</u> XXVI.
    A. Pridik, <u>Mut-em-wija.</u> asserted that Mutemwia, a princess, bore Amenhotep III by another man while married to Thutmose IV!

131. A. Erman, ZÄS 28 (1890) 112.

132. Wm. M. Fl. Petrie, A History II, 170, 174; followed by Pridik, op. cit., 7.

133. Pridik, op. cit., 64ff., followed now by R. Tanner, ZÄS 102 (1975) 55.

134. C. Aldred, Akhenaten, 71-73. He also tends to rely on Borchardt's suggestion that "God's father" could sometimes signify father-in-law of the king. This idea has less to support it than does Brunner's "nurse" suggestion. The title is not diagnostic and cannot be used to predict familial relationships. L. Borchardt, Berichte VKSGW 57 (1905).

135. The likelihood that Amenhotep III was the prince in tomb 64 and on other monuments has been discussed above in Chapter 2. It is noteworthy that work on Amenhotep's tomb began in Thutmose' reign, a fact which may suggest he was the heir-apparent. But it is also possible that Thutmose planned a tomb for another use. Thomas, The Royal Necropoleis. 51,83-84, says Thutmose made the tomb for his heir.

136. Aldred, Akhenaten, 41, somewhat glossed over the problem, saying, "She presumably had a proper claim to the title of 'Chief Wife of a King'", and this appears to be the attitude adopted by most scholars who neglect the fact that kings could and did promote whomever they chose to be Great royal wife--including their own daughters and mothers (see n.123 above). But see Wente and Van Siclen, "A Chronology" 220,230, who say that Tiaa's monuments belong to her son's reign and therefore her Great royal wife title is not decisive in determining legitimacy. And they add that her memorials may have been manufactured to justify the king's throne right. But strangely they do not see the same situation for Mutemwia whose monuments all date to Amenhotep III's reign.

137. BM 378-79 + 380 = (43A) = (1434). The boat is 7'4" long. Fragment 380 represents the head of the queen. For the texts, Urk. IV 1772; HTES VII, pl.6.

138. PM II^2 326-27,with references. Urk. IV 1717-18; H. Brunner, Die Geburt. pls. 7-11. Also called King's mother and Great king's mother on scenes in the room.

139. H. Brunner, Die südliche Raume des Tempels von Luxor. 27, pl. 192b.

140. W.J. Murnane suggested this possibility in a lecture entitled "The Rebirth of Amun" at The Johns Hopkins University, fall 1988. It was suggested only and should not be taken as his published word.

141. That Mutemwia has a venerated position in the reign of Amenhotep III is evident from her appearance in the divine birth reliefs and strikingly in the black granite bark found in the Philip Arrhidaeus shrine at Karnak. It is, however, more difficult to conclude with certainty that the Queen was entirely associated by her son with the goddess Mut and thereby enjoyed a form of deification. This sort of

conclusion is tempting given this scene at Luxor Temple and the Karnak Mut bark, but since we understand nothing of the kind of divine association implied by such representations, we must reserve judgment.

142. PM II² 446. Unpublished. Texts in Wilbour MSS 3c 287. C.F. Aling, Abstracts ARCE 1979,1, showed photos of the statue and gave the measurements. The statue is visible due west of the temple, where Wilbour saw it.

143. M. Eaton-Krauss and B. Fay, "Beobachtungen an den Memnonkolossen", GM 52 (1981) 27. An Atenist attack seems sufficient explanation, although Aling op.cit., 1, suggested that the erasure was due to an abandoned Ramesside usurpation. He argued that the whole cartouche need not have been erased to satisfy Aten. But the wholesale erasures were never done carefully, and the attempt to mark out nb ntrw strongly suggests a religious motivation.

144. PM II² 449-50; M. Eaton-Krauss and B. Fay, "Beobachtungen an den Memnonkolossen", GM 52 (1981) 25-29, recopy the inscriptions identifying the queens on both colossi. They likewise propose to see the "[king's daughter Sitamun born of the Great royal wife] Tiy, may she live. LD III 144.

145. N. Davies, Tombs of Menkheperrasonb..., pl. XLI. Luxor Museum J.134.

146. The name of the queen in this scene was supplied by Habachi, Schott Festschrift, 61-70.

147. W. Hayes, JNES 10 (1951) 96-97, type 64.
Hayes believed the Queen mother was still alive because ᶜnh.ti followed the cartouche. He thought the label was one of the earliest from Malkata, but the vast majority date to the last decade of the king's life. The question whether ᶜnh.ti must refer to a living person must be answered negatively. See Gitton, OLP 8 (1977) 126 n.10; M. Gitton, L'épouse du dieu Ahmès Néfertary, 19. The vast number of posthumous documents for that queen almost without exception refer to her as ᶜnh.ti.

148. J. Vandier D'Abbadie, Catalogue des objets de toilette égyptiens du Musée du Louvre, (Paris 1972), nr. 197. Ointment spoon as lotus with arm decorated as a goose's head. 19 cm. long.

149. A. Weigall, ASAE 8 (1907) 6; Urk. IV 1771.

150. R. Hari, Horemheb et la Reine Moutmedjmet, 207-08.

151. C. Aldred, JEA 56 (1970) 195, correcting an earlier discussion, JEA 54 (1968) 103-06. In both articles he suggested Mutnodjmet was the queen.

152. C. Aling, Abstract ARCE 1979, and in his talk, said that the titles are most appropriate to this Ramesside queen.

153. Troy, op.cit., 169, 19.5.9, includes the statue with Nofretari's monuments.

154. See, for example, Gay Robins, "The God's Wife of Amon in the Eighteenth Dynasty in Egypt", in Images of Women in Antiquity (London 1983). Troy, op.cit., 97-99, in an otherwise thoughtful and challenging work, disappointingly muddies the water in her discussion of the God's wife together with the divine birth sequences.

155. Supra, n. 62, for example.

156. Two scenes, LD III 74a; Text III, 81; Champollion, Mons. pls. 345-46.

157. Gitton, Les divines épouses de la 18e dynastie; Graefe, Untersuchungen zur Verwaltung.

158. C. Sander-Hansen, Gottesweib, 17-18; 45-47.

159. J.R. Harris, Acta Orientalia 36 (1974) 19 n.33, without stating what that function is. Cf. Gitton, Lexikon, Lief. 13-14, 794-811.

160. Brunner, Die Geburt, 198-99.

161. Urk. IV, 81-82, 224; 1717-18. LÄ, "Königin", 464.

162. Supra, n. 134.

163. The suggestion that rpᶜtt is a regent's title (LÄ, "Königin", 464 and n.4; "Koniginnentitel", 474) cannot be supported, for it belongs to the titulary of queens through most of the 18th Dynasty. Ankhesenamun, Urk. IV 2038; Horemheb claimed the title for Mutnodjmet as well in usurping the cartouche.

164. J. Knudtzon, Die Tell el- Amarna Tafeln, EA 29,lines 16-18. e-nu[-ma ////]-abu-šu ša ['Ni]-im]mu-u-ri-ia a-na '[Ar]-ta]ta]a]ma a-ba a-bi-ia iš-pu-ru u marat[-zu] (17) ša [a-ba a-bi-ia a-ha-a-ti] a-bi-ia i-te-r[i]-is-zi 5-šu 6-šu [il]ta-par ù ú-ul id-di-na-a[š-ši] im-ma-ti-i-me[-e] (18) 7-š[u] a-[na a-ba a-bi-ia il-ta]-par ù i-na em-mu-ú-ki-im-ma it[-ta]-din-ši Restore the Akkadian writing of Thutmose IV's prenomen in line 16 as Manahpiria after J. Vergote, Toutankhamon dans les archives Hittites, 15-16. Edel agreed in his review, BiOr 20 (1963) 35-36, but Campbell, Chronology of the Amarna Letters, 68, n.5, did not. Further discussion in Chapter 6.

165. EA 29, lines 19-22.

166. EA 1, lines 11-14. Amenhotep III to Kadashman Harbe. Complaints that the queens were not allowed to see messengers from home. Neither Gilukhipa nor Taduhepa became Great royal wife, and if the suggestion that Kiya was a Mitannian (Gilukhipa?) is correct (Donald B. Redford, Akhenaten the Heretic King,[Princeton 1984, 1501), then her highest title was hmt mryt ᶜ3t, "greatly beloved wife of the king", but not Great royal wife. Likewise the foreign wives of Thutmose III were termed only king's wife. Lexikon, "Kija", 422; J. Harris, Cd'E 49 (1974) 25-30. (K.A.

Kitchen, <u>Suppiluliuma and the Amarna Pharaohs</u>, 10-11, considers EA 1 to have been written to Kadashman Enlil I.)

167. G. Daressy, <u>Mem. Miss</u>. VIII, #237 = N. Davies, <u>Corpus</u>, #527.

168. The title ŝpst also belonged to Kiya, wife of Akhenaten, and because of its rarity it may indicate that the woman referred to on the funerary cone was identical with Kiya. Harris, <u>Cd'E</u> 49, 27, notes especially that she was not <u>hmt-nsw</u> but simply <u>hmt.</u>

169. S. Mercer, <u>EA</u> I, 167, note to 11,16ff. "Mitanni was then more powerful and commanded more respect than in the later years of Tushratta's reign"; C. Kuhne, <u>Die Chronologie</u>, 20 n.85.

170. A. Schulman, <u>JNES</u> 39 (1979) 189 n.54, and ns.33,35.

171. Treaties in Hatti, for example, used a set form which included an elaborate historio-propagandist background section. V. Korosec, <u>Hethitische Staatsverträge</u>. The extent of historical accuracy is difficult to judge. It seems most documents used records in a way useful to the author as, for example, in the Plague Prayers of Mursilis. See, on evaluating Hattusilis III's use of propaganda, A. Archi, <u>SMEA</u> 14 (1971) 185-215.

172. See poems from Ugarit, <u>ANET</u> 129-35, IIAB vi, 20-31. "Lo, a day and a second, [fire] feeds on the house....There on the <u>seventh</u> day, the fire dies down in the house." Also Gilgamesh XI, 210-230, where the number of days he slept is <u>seven</u>. In the Descent of Ishtar (<u>ANET</u> 106-09) there are 7 gates to the Netherworld; in the Song of Ullikummis (<u>ANET</u> 121-25), "they drank once; they drank twice...they drank <u>seven</u> times". A more contemporary example is in the autobiography of Idrimi (A. Goetze, <u>JCS</u> 14 (1960) 226-31). He spoke of "<u>seven</u> years" of exile (3 times he used seven) then later of destroying <u>seven</u> forts of the Hittites.

One should also note that in EA 24, Tushratta says to Amenhotep III, "Let my brother read the tablets, and <u>seven</u> times may he hearken to me". Is this to be taken literally?Why then the other uses of numbers? Even the <u>seven</u> years of Urhi-Tesub's reign as king of Hatti is probably a fictitious number, for it is Hattusilis who informs us of the number in giving the length of time he waited before revolting against his uncle. See H. Otten, <u>Fischer Weltgeschichte</u>, III, 159-60.

173. Mercer, <u>EA</u> I, 112-13.

174. <u>Supra</u>, n. 102.

175. G. Robins, "<u>S3t nsw n ht.f Tjᶜ3</u>", <u>GM</u> 57 (1982) 55-6.

176. <u>Ibid</u>.; PM I² I, 127[13].

177. Helck, Verw., 352, B. van de Walle, RdE 15 (1963) 83-84, footnotes Urk. IV 1583. The major mistake appears to be there; the word "Mutter" is used to describe Meryt.   See also B. Schmitz, Op.cit., 292 n.6, who makes her a daughter of Thutmose III, but not the queen.

178. G. Legrain, ASAE 4 (1903) 138-49.   Thanks to the kindness of Dr. Mohammed Saleh and the High Committee of the Egyptian Antiquities Organization, all the canopic fragments were located in the Cairo Museum's roof and basement storage and were then drawn and photographed in 1984. Legrain's numbers are incorrect.

179. P. Newberry, PSBA 25 (1903) 358-59, pl.ii; G. Legrain, ASAE 5 (1904) 141.

180. H. Carter, JEA 4 (1917) 111; H. Winlock, JEA 17 (1931) 110; E. Thomas, op.cit., 202-04, opted for Queens Valley or Gebel er Rumi as a cemetery for Thutmose IV and el-Bayrieh for Amenhotep III.

181. See this statue in Gitton, Les divines épouses de la 18e dynastie; mentioned first in Gitton, "Gottesgemahlin", LÄ II, 789. Also mentioned by J. Leclant, MDAIK 15 (1959) 169 n.2.

182. Edinburgh Royal Scottish Museum, 1956.154-67; Catalogue National Museum. #450-63.   Which of these numbers applies to Tiaa's label, I do not know.

183. S. Birch and A.H. Rhind, A Facsimile..., pl.XII,3; W. Spiegelberg, Rec.Trav. 16 (1896) 66, gives hieroglyphic transcription.   Berlin 2146, in Inschriften II. 294, is a duplicate of the text with year 27, but there transcribed 37. The labels are newly republished by A. Dodson and J. J. Janssen, "A Theban Tomb and its Tenants", JEA 75 (1989) 125-38, and are shown to be of 21st Dynasty date. They represent tags made for reburial of the 18th Dynasty court ladies.

184. Newberry, PSBA 25 (1903) 359 n.5. Schmitz has recently revived the Thutmose III reading but without citing the hieratic facsimiles. B. Schmitz, op.cit., 292 n.6, gives only Spiegelberg's transcription which she mistakenly calls "der ursprünglichen Publikation des Beleges".   Spiegelberg worked from the copy published by Birch who had already read the name as Menkheperre.

185. A.H. Rhind, Thebes. 83-87. PM I^2 671.

186. One seal in Edinburgh, 1956, 168. Dodson and Janssen consider that the proof of such seals is not presently available. The seal brought back from the tomb was not a door seal but might be read with the name of Amenhotep III. One the other hand, the reading is far from clear. Ibid., 136.

187. It should be noted that this is the architectural plan of several tombs in the reign of Amenhotep III, most notably that of Ramose, TT55.

188. Rhind actually reported fourteen, but Birch translated and published sixteen. Edinburgh Museum gives them 14 numbers. Two of Birch's objects were not labels of wood; one was a stone label and one a linen fragment. It is unclear to me whether Edinburgh does not have these two or whether they were not acquisitioned.

189. E. Thomas, op.cit., 202, appeared not to question this conclusion, but she was unaware, as was Rhind, that Princess Tiaa was known in this tomb as well as on the canopics.

190. See Dodson and Janssen, op.cit., 136-37.

191. Supra. especially n. 69 and Helck, Verw., 352.

192. Legrain, ASAE 4 (1903) 138-49.

193. Assuming an age of 35 at death for Thutmose IV, an age of 15 to begin siring children.

194. Brack and Brack, Das Grab des Haremheb, pls. 32a, 36a, 37a, p. 28. Bouriant, "Le tombeau d'Harmhabi", 426-27, pl.II; MMA photos T1956-1957.

195. C. Desroches-Noblecourt, Ugaritica III. 201, fig. 170, has carried the argument too far. The crown does not signify royal family through extension to harem members; for Royal ornament hkrt-nsw does not mean concubine, but rather is an honorific for noblewomen. R. Drenkhahn, SAK 4 (1977) 59-67; E. Reiser, op.cit., 17-18, 90.

196. Brunner, Erziehung. 24. But see above, Chapter 2.

197. Thus Amenhotep II was shown as a small king on the lap of his nurse in the tomb of Kenamun and likewise Thutmose IV in Hekarnehhe's tomb.

198. Bouriant, op.cit.; PM I^2 1 152-56.

199. Newberry, PSBA 25, 360, pl.ii [3]. Amherst Collection.

200. Supra, n. 183.

201. E. Thomas felt the canopics-owners could not all have been buried in one grave, and she suggested that one find may have led robbers to other small tombs, thus producing the large group on sale together, op.cit., 203. One cannot help being suspicious, however, that a large secret discovery was made around 1900-01 in which the objects naming these women were raided; for this wooden label was offered in 1901, and the canopics appeared in the winter of 1902. It is conceivable that early tomb robbers reburied the debris of their efforts, and it is this which was unearthed at the beginning of this century. Perhaps one day the puzzle will be solved.

202. CG 46040, Carter and Newberry, <u>The Tomb of Thoutmosis IV</u>, 7 [7], arragonite.

203. <u>Supra.</u> ns. 182-183. Janssen and Dodson read the name differently, as <u>Py-ihi3</u> from the male attested name <u>P3-ih</u>. The hieratic resembles <u>tp</u>,however, as much as the two strokes of <u>y</u>. The name, not listed in Ranke, <u>Personnennamen</u>, is paralleled closely on the canopics. G. Legrain, <u>ASAE</u> 4 (1903) 143 [36]. <u>Wsir hkrt-nsw</u>
𓂀𓏤 𓌨 𓏥 𓁐. It is not possible to say whether a woman who was entitled the <u>s3t-nsw</u> title would employ <u>hkrt-nsw</u> as an alternative on her canopic jars.

204. <u>Supra.</u> n. 183; Gauthier, <u>LdR</u> II 305.

CHAPTER FOUR

ROYAL MONUMENTS OF THUTMOSE IV

Like most 18th dynasty rulers, Thutmose IV left monuments at many sites. His name is additionally attested at places where the king himself was never an active presence. The original sizes of the monuments and of their remains vary greatly, but in general he added to pre-existing temples. Karnak, naturally enough, was the most favored site, and there he built an admirable peristyle court attached to an earlier court of Thutmose II. We do not know whether kings planned their building programs in advance or whether we may safely make historical conclusions based on the geography of construction in a reign. Some sites, at least, may have been chosen by royal officials, especially those places at great distances from the Residence. The distribution of Thutmose IV's monuments, within the context of the mid-18th Dynasty, is unremarkable. He honored the established cult centers and was hardly an iconoclast. On the other hand, at several locations he left certain harbingers of things to come. Indeed we may suggest that he deliberately followed in the footsteps of his grandfather and father, building additions to their temples, and in similar fashion suggested new sites and monuments to his son. The arrangement of sites below follows a geographic pattern in the manner of Porter and Moss' Bibliography. Some discussion follows the entries, although not all material lends itself to excessive historical conclusion. With the exception of scarabs, I have attempted to catalogue provenanced inscribed royal material dating to Thutmose IV's reign from Egypt proper, Nubia and Asia. Monuments of the reign have been found at the following places:[1]

Egypt

1. Alexandria
2. Seriakus
3. Heliopolis (?)
4. Giza
5. Abusir
6. Memphis/Sakkara
7. Fayum
8. Hermopolis
9. Amarna
10. Abydos
11. Dendera
12. Medamud
13. Karnak
14. Luxor
15. Thebes
16. Armant
17. Tod
18. Elkab
19. Edfu
20. Elephantine
21. Konosso

Nubia
22. Amada
23. Faras (?)
24. Buhen
25. Tabo
26. Gebel Barkal

Asia
27. Serabit el-Khadim
28. Assur (?)

1. Alexandria.

Three large columns of red granite,[2] now in the Vienna Kunsthistorisches Museum, bear the cartouches of Thutmose IV. They were built into a fort at Alexandria and most likely were transported to that city from another location, perhaps Heliopolis, given the use of red granite which was used for other Thutmoside monuments in the solar temple. The cartouches of Thutmose are accompanied by those of Merenptah and Seti II, and there is a dedication to "Amun-Re lord of the thrones of the Two lands in the midst of ḫ^c st "the throne appears" and "Amun-Re lord of the thrones of the Two lands upon his great throne". Both dedications were added by Seti II and could refer to Amun-Re in Heliopolis or in many other temples.

These columns originated with Thutmose IV, although Bergmann and Wiedemann[3] both believed that Amenhotep II was the first to decorate them. The confusion was due to the titulary of Seti II, which appears in full on the columns but which is written such that the Horus, Nebty and Golden Horus names are separated by additional cartouches of Seti. Bergmann did not recognize that K3 nḫt wr pḥty "Strong Bull great of vigor" was to be followed by nbty nḫt hpš dr pdtyw 9: Hr nbw ^{c}3 nrw m t3w nbw nsw-bit Wsr-ḫprw-r^c stp n R^c s3 R^c Sty mr-n-Ptḥ "Two Ladies victorious of scimitar, who subdues the Bowmen, Golden Horus great of fear in all lands, King of Upper and Lower Egypt Userkheperure elect of Re, son of Re Sety-Merenptah", which constitutes one form of Seti II's titulary.[4] He read the Horus name separately and attributed it to Amenhotep II. Wiedemann followed and asserted that Thutmose IV had actually usurped the column from his father (although Bergmann noted that he did not do so since he left the Horus name intact). But the explanation above demonstrates that Thutmose was the first king to have inscribed the column, and their great size (6 m. ht.) indicates they originally stood in a large temple, likely in the north. Heliopolis is a reasonable site for attribution.

2. Seriakus.

A private house in this village, 9 km. from Heliopolis and 10 from Tel el-Yahudiyeh, yielded the upper portion of a red granite stela of Thutmose IV.[5] The present location of the monument is unknown to me, but Schott reported that the preserved dimensions were 70 cm. high by 100 wide by 30 deep. Only the scene from the lunette is preserved, so the original height is difficult to estimate. The other dimensions, however, support the likelihood that it was at least twice as tall as it now is. The winged sun-disk occupied the crescent, and Behdet was named there. Two scenes of the king appeared below: on the left Thutmose offered <u>shat</u> bread to Atum; on the right, wine to Re-Horakhty. The legends were as follows: "Utterance by Atum: I have given to you all [life and dominion] from me". "Utterance: I have given to you all health, Re-Horakhty". On the left the king was called: "King of Upper and Lower Egypt, lord of doing a thing, Menkheprure, given life like Re"; on the right he was termed: "Son of Re his beloved, Thutmose [kha] khau, given life like Re". The action was further described as "giving <u>shat</u> bread [may he do given life]" and "giving wine, may he do [given life]".

Schott pointed out that small holes indicated that gold or other precious materials probably adorned parts of the stela, especially the crown of Atum and sun diadem of Re. He also wondered about the original provenance of the stela. The gods Atum and Re-Horakhty were Heliopolitan, and the proximity of Seriakus to the sun temple precinct makes Heliopolis a nearly certain provenance. In alluding to the columns from Alexandria, Schott also implied that the major sun cult center was a strong possibility for the original placement of this stela.

3. <u>Heliopolis</u>.

A fragment of a red granite obelisk (CG 17013)[6] was found southeast of the obelisk of Sesostris I at Heliopolis. A portion of the prenomen of either Thutmose IV or Amenhotep II inscribed in large hieroglyphs appears on the fragment. The obelisk would have been a large dedicatory monument and may have been one of a pair.

Thutmose III erected a pair of obelisks at Heliopolis as well as an enclosure wall for the temple of Re-Horakhty.[7] In a text from a stela dedicated to Re-Horakhty, Thutmose claims to have built the enclosure wall when he purified the temple of Re after he found it falling down. Several doorways of Thutmose III have been identified among the materials from Heliopolis and should probably be attributed to the enclosure wall. Thutmose IV's obelisk(s) (if it is his) may have a similar significance in Heliopolis.

Prince Ahmose discussed in Chapter 2 refers to his project of building the enclosure wall for the temple of Atum.[8] He likewise asserted that he consecrated the precinct removing any evils therefrom. This would no doubt follow upon the building of the enclosure wall whose purpose was to define the sacred area. Although we do not have the doorways of Thutmose IV's enclosure wall as we have for Thutmose III, we do have the king's own mention of this activity in Heliopolis.

On the Sphinx Stela the king refers to himself as one who "purified Heliopolis and propitiated Re".[9] He also noted that he "presented <u>maat</u> to Atum."[10] Without the Ahmose inscription this phrase seems formulaic, but it may now be seen to have been an accurate summation--Thutmose IV sanctified the precinct of Atum (as opposed to that of Re already purified by Thutmose III)[11] and provided required offerings to Re. The stela from Seriakus, also of red granite and gilded, may well have been the record for this effort.

The materials recording Thutmose IV's activity at Heliopolis suggest he was following the lead of Thutmose III at the site, perhaps even deliberately emulating his chosen name-sake. The king's interest in the sun gods may be documented throughout his building campaigns and in his inscriptions as well.

4. <u>Giza</u>.

The site of Giza was of course one of the king's favorites. He left in all some 27 + monuments at Giza of varying type; a few were usurped from Amenhotep II in all likelihood.

4.1. The great stela, set between the paws of the Sphinx, is the major royal monument from Giza, and indeed it is the best-known artifact and most-discussed one of the king's reign (see fig. 10).[12] It has recently been restudied, along with all the Giza material, by Zivie; another edition of the text would be superfluous; here only a few comments are necessary. The Sphinx Stela is of course famous as a "dream stela" and has been discussed as part of the cycle of <u>Königsnovelle</u>. It has also been called an example of royal sporting literature, in the manner of Amenhotep II's Sphinx Stela. This latter argument has been largely defused by Zivie, and the <u>Königsnovelle</u> theme, certainly present, has been well-argued by Hermann; it needs no elaboration here. The importance of the stela in the modern discussion of Thutmose's succession was outlined in Chapter 2; general remarks will be resumed at the end of section 4.4.

The major controversy concerning the Sphinx Stela has been its date, for some years ago Erman argued that many of the writings on the stela were unattested in the 18th dynasty but were common in the Late Period.[13] He preferred to redate the monument to the Saite era or thereabouts, and he did the same for the naos of Amenmose, son of Thutmose I. Erman believed the stela was perhaps a fanciful restoration of an earlier text.

There are few scholars remaining who accept Erman's proposal, but that is largely due to the discoveries made by Hassan at Giza (especially the Sphinx Stela of Amenhotep II.)[14] Many of the unusual writings and unattested words appeared on the great Stela of the earlier king, thus removing the major objections raised by Erman. In addition, Drioton [15] pointed out that the work of Atenists is visible on the inscription. Although the god Amun does not appear in Thutmose's stela, the word _imnt_ "daily offerings" does, and it is neatly hacked out (and restored(?)). A translation follows here, and a list of the writings objected to by Erman is given with counter-suggestions. See also recent notes on the stela by Cannuyer.[16]

(1)"Year l, month 3 of Inundation, day 19, under the Majesty of the Strong Bull, perfect of diadems, the Two ladies, enduring of kingship like Atum, Golden Horus, powerful of the khepesh (scimitar) who subdues the [Nine Bows], the king of Upper and Lower Egypt Men[khepru]re, [son of Re Thutmose kha khau, beloved of Horemakhet], given life stability and dominion like Re forever.

(2)Live the Good God, the son of Atum, the protector of Horakhty, the living image of the Lord of All, the sovereign whom Re made, the excellent inheritor of Khepri, beautiful of face like the ruler, his father, who goes forth perfectly(ly) equipped[17] with [his forms of Horus on his head, the king of Upper and Lower Egypt beloved of the gods, lord of] charm before the Ennead, who purifies Heliopolis, (3) who propitiates Re, who embellished the House of Ptah, who presents truth to Atum, who offers it to him who is South of his Wall, who makes monuments consisting of [daily offerings] to the god who made all that exists, who seeks what is beneficial to the gods of Upper and Lower Egypt, who builds their temples [in white stone] who endows all their offerings, the son of Atum of his body Thutmose kha khau, like Re, (4) the heir of Horus upon his throne Menkheprure,given life.

When his Majesty was an inpu,[18] like the young Horus in Chemmis, his goodness already like the "protector of his father"; he was seen like a god himelf. [Through love of him the army rejoiced (likewise) the royal children and] all [the nobles]. His might made his (5) victories flourish, and he repeated the circuit, his powers being like the son of Nut.[19]

Now he passed time amusing himself upon the plateau of the White Wall on its southern and northern confines, shooting copper targets and hunting [lions] and wild goats, and traveling upon his chariot, his horses being faster (6) than the wind, together with one sole companion from his retinue;[20] and no person knew it.

Then the hour of allowing rest for his retinue happened near the Setpet (emplacement) of Horemakhet beside Sokar in Ro-Setau (necropolis), Rennutet in Tjamut in the necropolis, [Mut (foremost) of the horns of the gods], north of the mistress of southern Sat (?), Sakhmet, (7) foremost of the desert, of Seth, Dewa and Heka, eldest of the holy place of the first occasion in the neighborhood of the lord of Kher-Aha, and of the divine road of the gods to the western horizon of Heliopolis.

Now the image of the very great Khepri rested in this place, great of fame, sacred of respect, the shade of Re resting on him. Memphis and every city on its two sides came to him, their arms in adorations to his face, (8)bearing great offerings for his <u>ka</u>.

One of these days it happened that the prince Thutmose came traveling at the time of midday. He rested in the shadow of this great god. [Sleep and] dream [took possession of him] at the moment the sun was at zenith. Then (9) he found the majesty of this noble god speaking from his own mouth like a father speaks to his son[21], and saying: 'Look at me, observe me, my son Thutmose. I am your father Horemakhet-Khepri-Re-Atum. I shall give to you the kingship (10) [upon the land before the living]. You shall wear its white crown and its red crown upon the throne of Geb, the heir. The land in its length and its breadth will be yours, and everything which the eye of the Lord of All illuminates. Good provisions will be for you from within the Two lands, and the great produce of every foreign country, and a lifetime of time great in years. My face belongs to you; my heart belongs to you, and you belong to me.[22] (11) [Behold, my condition is like one in illness], all [my limbs being ruined]. The sand of the desert, upon which I used to be, faces me (aggressively); and it is in order to cause that you do what is in my heart that I have waited.[23] For I know that you are my son and my protector. Arrive! Behold I am with you! I am (12) [your leader.' He completed this speech.

Then this prince stared because] he heard this [utterance of the Lord of All (?)]. He understood the words of this god and he placed silence in [his] heart. [Then he said: Come, let us travel] to [our temple] of the city, that they may set aside offerings[24] for this god. (13) [We shall bring to him cattle, and all sorts of vegetables, and we shall give praises to those who came   before]   [////...]   a   statue   of   Chephren   made   for Atum-Re-Horemakhet[25] (14) [///...] in the festivals [//] (15) [////...] (16) [//////]numerous (17) [///...] for My majesty for making to live which (18) [///...] speech of Khepri in the western horizon of Heliopolis in (19) [////] (20) [////]

The brackets here indicate parts now missing, but most are filled by copies made in the last century. Zivie's notes to her publication were copious and require no duplication. For minor grammatical disagreements see the Chapter notes. The following unusual writings were objected to by Erman when he dated the Stela to the Saite period:

line 1. <u>ḥps</u> written ⸢?⸣.

1. 2. ⸢?⸣ in ⸢⸤⸥⸣ should be ⸢?⸣. ⸢⸤⸥⸣ for ⸢⸤⸥⸣ is common   Saitic.

1. 3. ⸢?⸣ for ⸢?⸣ is archaic. ⸢⸤⸥⸣ for ⸢⸤⸥⸣; ⸢⸤⸥⸣ for ⸢⸤⸥⸣

1. 4. <u>Dhwty-ms h</u><u>ᶜ</u> <u>h</u><u>ᶜ</u><u>w mi R</u><u>ᶜ</u> <u>ỉw</u><u>ᶜ</u> <u>m hrt nst.f Mn-hprw-r</u><u>ᶜ</u> <u>di</u> <u>ᶜnh</u> reverses the

cartouche names and is an erroneous copy from a vertically-written original.

1. 5. [hieroglyph] for [hieroglyph] is too abbreviated. [hieroglyph] for [hieroglyph]; [hieroglyph] instead of [hieroglyph] is unknown. [hieroglyph] for [hieroglyph].

1. 6. [hieroglyph] for [hieroglyph] is most unusual in the New Kingdom.

1. 7. [hieroglyph] is too abbreviated. [hieroglyph] for [hieroglyph] unusual; [hieroglyph] and [hieroglyph] for "image" is not an ideogram but   perhaps a sportive writing.

1. 9. [hieroglyph] for [hieroglyph] is unusual in New Kingdom. [hieroglyph] as   infinitive is barbaric.

1.10. rp°t should be rp°t ntrw; [hieroglyph] instead of [hieroglyph] is unusual in the New Kingdom.

1. 11. [hieroglyph] for [hieroglyph] is incorrect. wnt n.i for wnnt.i   is an error.

1. 12. [hieroglyph] for [hieroglyph] [hieroglyph] for [hieroglyph]. [hieroglyph] as a singular noun   is barbaric.

1. 13. [hieroglyph] for [hieroglyph] is incorrect.

The following corrections or updated references may be   offered in response to Erman.

1.1. [hieroglyph] for hpš appears twice in the king's titulary at Amada. (Urk. IV 1567).

1.2. While hk3 may be an error, it is also possible that the phrase was intended as "like the ruler, his father". [hieroglyph] For [hieroglyph] see two references admitted by Erman and also Urk.   IV 1594, 7. The text consistently omits [hieroglyph] under [hieroglyph], but there are numerous known variants of mnḫ and smnḫ.

1.3. [hieroglyph] for [hieroglyph] , is attested at Deir el Bahri. See Urk. IV 158, 163, where it acts as suffix pronoun. Helck and Zivie disagree over the translation: The former takes it as "lord", while the latter as "god", the reading adopted above. [hieroglyph] for [hieroglyph] is common. For example, Urk. IV 1160,.4; Les. 82,20. Erman took [hieroglyph] to be a mistake for [hieroglyph]; Re, however, should be transposed for honorific intent, and its placement after [hieroglyph] may be due to esthetics. For a short writing of shtp, see Urk. IV 936,8.

1.4. As Zivie's commentary points out, Erman need not postulate some wholly different original to explain what may be a sculptor's error which occurred at the last minute. In fact the epithet preceding the first cartouche, s3 ỉtm n ht.f, could have misled the mason into writing the nomen rather than the prenomen. Also, Erman was incorrect in assuming mi R° and di °nh could not follow cartouches separately. See, for example, the Amada pillars of Thutmose IV where only mi R° follows the cartouche prenomen in the middle of a line of text.[26]

1.5. h3st is an abbreviated form, but Erman's complaint is the antiquity of the writing, not its youth. Bersheh I,7; II,19. The word ssmt "horse" is written most often with a ⌓ , but Erman was not familiar with the examples: <u>Urk</u>. IV 663,688,1282,1596. ⌐ 𓄿𓄿𓄿𓄑for 𓂝𓏭𓄿is common in the 18th dynasty: <u>Urk</u>. IV 462,13; similar, 1450,8.

1.6. <u>hry</u> "upper" appears as 𓏏𓎱at <u>Urk.</u> IV 1550,18, Lateran obelisk. The spelling of <u>rmtwt</u> is hardly a scribal error; on the photo it is clear that the space available allowed only the writing which appears.

1.7. <u>šwt</u> R^c hn.t hr.f is abbreviated, but no more so than is <u>šwt</u> in <u>šwt ntr</u> <u>Urk</u>. IV 56,10, 183,10; <u>h3w</u> as written here is noted in <u>Wb</u> II 477. The word 𓊞𓏥represents <u>šsp</u>, a fact unknown at the time Erman wrote; it is an ideogram as well as a determinative. The reading here with a ⌓ should be rejected, however, as there is actually a pedestal under the sphinx. The ⌓ is a small chip in the stone.

1.9. <u>di</u> as written is most common in Middle Kingdom literature but in future contexts such as this one. See <u>Grammar</u>[3] 450,3. 𓂋𓂻as an infinitive appears at <u>Urk</u>. IV 1114,17 and ln Sinuhe B,2.

1.10. Geb is more commonly called <u>rp^ct ntrw</u>; the shorter form of <u>nw</u> is not surprising since it comes within a lengthy phrase -- <u>^ch^cw nw ^c3 m rnpwt</u>.

1.11. 𓄿𓄿𓄿𓆳 𓂻 is certainly an incorrect writing for <u>s3h</u>, perhaps influenced by the writing of <u>sm</u> in line 5. The phrase 𓅓𓂻𓏏3 <u>wnt n.i</u> appears to be a preview of the Late Egyptian relative form without, however, the neutered definite article. But this is by no means sure. Erman took it for a mistaken imperfect relative, and Zivie has followed. This is possible, but it may also be a rare example of the <u>sdm.n.f</u> relative form for <u>wnn</u>. The meaning would then be that the Sphinx <u>was</u> (used to be) upon the sand, but now is not because of the sand over him.

l. 12 𓂻𓈖𓏤 is probably intended. <u>Urk</u>. IV 2069, <u>hw.tw it.k Imn m hhi hbw-sd</u>; also Faulkner, <u>Dictionary</u>, 186. <u>sn</u> too may be correct since it refers to the action by the temple personnel in apportioning offerings from Memphis or Heliopolis for dedication to Horemakhet at Giza. It would refer then to different people. 𓂋𓏥 as a singular noun is attested on Giza Stela B, line 4 and in Sinuhe, R 115,1.[27]

1.13. There is no <u>tn</u> for <u>n</u>. It is the perfective <u>sdm.f</u> form of 𓏏𓈖𓏭, 𓏏𓈖𓏏.n. <u>Grammar</u>[3] Section 447.

To summarize the results from above, it may be said that most of Erman's objections have been countered and that a Saite date, based on the writings he listed, cannot be supported. There are, however, several scribal errors, as there are in any long stone inscription. But three errors do not constitute evidence of copying a misunderstood original.

The Sphinx Stela will remain the most historically interesting document from the reign. The question of its relevance to the succession should eventually be eclipsed by its contribution to the history of religion in the period and of Thutmose IV's rule. Several important conclusions may be made from the text and scene on the stela. First, the Year 1 date is very likely fictitious with respect to the stela's erection. It might refer to the king's first clearance efforts in the vicinity. It would be difficult to believe that the excavation at Giza had been completed, as well as the royal constructions at Heliopolis and Memphis referred to in lines 1-3, in the first regnal year. The abbreviated form of the introduction suggests that a summary of activities in the north has been provided because of the overall theme of the inscription--the royal attachment to the sun god at Giza.

The inscription of Prince Ahmose reminds us that what appear to be formulaic and not necessarily serious claims in monumental texts should usually be given greater weight.[28] In the Sphinx Stela, for example, in line 2 there is the reference to Thutmose's purification of Heliopolis; in line 3 the claim to have "embellished Memphis" and endowed or built temples for all the gods, "He who embellishes Hut-ka-Ptah, who presents maat to Atum, who raises it up to him who is south of his wall, who makes monuments consisting of daily offerings to the god who made all that exists, who seeks what is beneficial to the gods of Upper and Lower Egypt, who builds their temples [in white stone] who endows all their offerings." [smnh Hwt-k3-Pth hnk m3ᶜt n Itm sᶜr s n rsy Inb.f Ir mnw m Imnt n ntr Ir ntt nb hhy 3ht n ntrw nw šmᶜw mhw kd hwt.s[n] m Inr hd smnh p3wt.sn nbt]. The specific mention of Hut-ka-ptah, like that to Heliopolis, should not be passed over lightly. It is well-attested that Thutmose IV left a temple edifice to Ptah at Memphis (4.6 below), and we may interpret the Sphinx Stela's mention as reference to that construction.

I cannot agree with Zivie that the solar cult emphasis is not the most significant theme in the stela.[29] Thutmose IV may not have been as interested in the site's royal ancestry as we think, since Chephren may not be mentioned on the stela at all.[30] The king's insistence on the Sphinx as the solar deity is reiterated in the stela: "The very great image of Khepri was resting in this place, great of fame, sacred of respect, the shade of Re being upon him." He later identified himself to Thutmose as "Horemakhet, Khepri, Re-Atum." Lanny Bell has recently commented upon the divine manifestation of the sun god connoted by the shade (or fan).[31] In addition to the strong solar imagery in the inscription, Thutmose IV may have fused his father Amenhotep II with the sun god. The broken princes' stelae already suggest a cult for Amenhotep II as Horemakhet at Giza; the offerers present their bouquets to the statue of Amenhotep between the paws of the Sphinx. As king, Thutmose stresses his own divinity and thereby removes representations of Amenhotep II's statue from his stelae. The king worships Horemakhet calling himself son of Atum and heir of Khepri, the image made by Re. Through his temple in front of the

Sphinx, Amenhotep II remains part of the worship and must be identified with the solar father to whom Thutmose IV appeals on his great stela. Further discussion of the sun cults may be found at 4.4.27, 4.22 and in Chapter 6.

4.2. Apparently Thutmose actually did effect a restoration project at Giza by removing the sand from the limbs of the enormous statue. And he prevented an immediate recurrence of the god's illness by constructing a system of three mudbrick walls 10, 20 and 30 meters from the statue, the last of which enclosed the temple of Chephren as well.[32] Bricks from Thutmose IV's walls have been found (JE 72371), and a series of stelae which were fashioned for placement on the enclosure by Thutmose. Hassan unearthed other stelae from his reign, and later ones as well, by the walls. Indeed, the brick wall appears to have become the area preferred by pilgrims who left votive inscriptions and objects.

4.3-19.   The seventeen limestone stelae[33] of the king are dedicated to fourteen gods and goddesses who represent both national and locally-worshipped deities. The list of regional gods and their localities given on the Sphinx Stela is repeated in a few cases on these stelae, and Zivie detailed the divinities in question. The national gods are represented by Thoth lord of Khemenu, Wadjet, mistress of Pe and Dep, Sokar lord of Shetyt[34], Amun-Re lord [of the thrones of the Two lands], Seshat mistress of writings, and perhaps Ptah, although he also retains an attachment to Memphis locally. Gods known to have cults in the Memphite region and mentioned elsewhere at Giza or its vicinity include: Atum lord of Heliopolis, Atum-Re, Horus-Re lord of Sakhebu, Hathor Lady of the Sycamore, Hathor Mistress of Inerty (?),[35] Horemakhet with Amun-Re , Mut Foremost of the Horns of the Gods, and Rennenutet of Iat Tjamut. Isis Lady of the Sky is also present and is known to have had a cult in the area; she appears receiving bouquets on the Stela C of Amenemipet[36], son of Amenhotep II, and Zivie argues strongly that she must have had a temple at Giza even before the 21st dynasty one now remaining.[37]

Amun-Re appears as the recipient of Thutmose IV's offerings on two of the stelae. That national deity is nowhere present on the Sphinx Stela and was therefore not credited with determining the kingship as he was on Amenhotep II's Sphinx Stela. The great god appears on a separate stela but receives a no more elaborate monument than the other gods. Thutmose donated a second stela (Zivie NE 29) on which he presented offerings to both Amun-Re (hacked out) and Horemakhet (depicted in the form of a falcon-headed god with sundisk like Re-Horakhty). This second stela may have been a means of underlining Amun-Re's solar connection and thus bringing the Theban god into the solar religion of northern Egypt.

The stelae placed in the wall are all of limestone and of roughly the same size, ca. 65 X 45 cm.[38] The technique varies but is generally fair to poor. Stylistically all the relief monuments of Thutmose IV at Giza may be categorized in two groups which have distinctive and consistent characteristics. It can be demonstrated that the stelae that depict Nefertiry and the king[39] were made by a different workshop or artisan than those in which only the king offers to a god.[40] (see figs. 11 and 12).

The characteristics that define the first group are the following: The form of sundisk used in the two groups is the most distinctive trait. On the eight stelae showing the queen with the king there is a pair of undulating horns above the wings in this manner: A second consistent trait is the length of the king's kilt; it is quite short on all eight examples with the queen and noticeably shorter on the other nine. Third, the waist bands of the king and gods are always narrower than on the second group; the form of the wr bird in the queen's title is consistent on the seven examples, and it is unusual since it resembles the w or quail chick. The group as a whole is poorly cut, the stelae having been only surface-incised; while this does not appear to be related to the sculptors' abilities, it is in contrast to the stelae of the second group which are sculpted and even show some modelling. Finally, the facial and bodily styles of the two groups differ but are internally consistent. The first group shows a body which is long-legged and short-waisted.[41] One example is superior to the others, NE 26, and shows facial features similar to the king's on several funerary monuments; the tomb paintings provide the strongest comparison (see fig. 13). At least one stela from this group was worked by the same hand (or a very similarly trained one) who sculpted two stelae from group two which adorned the wall. (Zivie's NE 26 with Nefertiry compares with NE 35 and 38.) Note that on NE 26, 35 and 38 the eyes of the king and gods have been noticeably enlarged; the profile of Ptah on NE 26 is exactly that of Thutmose IV on NE 35. The king here has a long profile including a nose which is straight, long and with a broad base. The king's chin is prominent, and the face is broad but smooth.

The second group shows a bit more variation within itself, but it is nonetheless easily differentiated from the first. The winged sundisk is again the defining feature: it is here represented by a configuration of wing feathers, without the horns above, in this manner: The king's kilt is always just above the knee, and the waist band is significantly wider than on the first group's examples. All these stelae are more deeply cut than those in the first group, and one or two show leg musculature. Included in this second group should be Zivie's numbers NE

16,20,21,22,23,25,27, as well as 24, 29, 14 (the Sphinx Stela) and 35 which make up a better quality subgroup of the whole. These examples were probably done by similarly trained artisans, for they all portray the same short round face with stubbly chin and poutish mouth. The necks are long on these examples, and the chin is especially diagnostic, for it recedes. The cheeks too are always noticeable.

NE 35, a fragmentary stela, has only the remains of the winged sundisk visible in the photograph, but it shows the same ray descending from the disk as well as the clear ring around the sun that appears on the Sphinx stela. The king's face on NE 35 is reminiscent of his profile on Theban reliefs, but the shortness of the face and the round cheeks characterizing Group 2 are still here. This work must be the fullest development of Thutmose IV's imagery at Giza. He appears with an enlarged oblique eye and more angular long nose than on the other monuments. This form of his representation is paralleled in the relief sculpture of Thutmose's alabaster bark sanctuary, no doubt his last Karnak monument left for finishing touches by Amenhotep III. (See fig. 14). NE 35 should be a monument from the latter part of Thutmose IV's reign, and for theological reasons this is also the best solution.

We cannot state positively that these two groups represent different workshops, artisans or time periods, but they are definable groups. It might be justified to speak of a "Giza style" for the mid-18th Dynasty. One need only compare the small collection of reliefs illustrated by Mysliwiec with the Giza monuments of group 2 to notice the marked difference in style. The facial features referred to above are not paralleled on the king's Theban monuments, but they do appear on Giza Stela B (NE 9) and probably C (NE 10). It would seem that a provincial style existed at Giza before Thutmose's reign and that the king employed the local artisans for his monuments. But, as the group 1 stelae show, he also used sculptors whose work is best paralleled in Theban royal art.

4.20. Within the brick walls set up by the king was placed, in addition to the great stela, a limestone naos (JE 72301)[42] in which a statue of the god Horemakhet (as falcon or sphinx) was set. Hassan found the naos in the Sphinx amphitheater, face down, with two stelae lying under it. No doubt they were set up before the naos which then collapsed over them. The naos has a cornice top, and its doorway is topped by a winged sundisk. On either side of the niche is an inscription: Left: "The Good God lord of the Two lands, Menkheprure, son of Re Thutmose kha khau, beloved of Horemakhet". On the right: "The Good God, lord of doing a thing, Menkheprure, son of Re Thutmose kha khau, beloved of Horemakhet". The monument is of good quality and measures 65 X 40 cm..

4.21. Apparently from this same vicinity came a limestone jamb[43] inscribed to Horemakhet on behalf of Thutmose. This is the only building element which has been found for the ruler, but it need not signal anything other than the doorway for Thutmose's mudbrick protective wall. The jamb is in the Cairo Museum (JE 52493); I do not have its measurements. This doorpost is from the right side of a portal and bears this inscription: "The Good God, the likeness of Re, a valiant one who protects the land with his strong arm, the lord of the Two lands, Menkheprure, beloved of Horemakhet." The one irregularity not mentioned in previous publications is that the ⪑⪑⪑ sign in the cartouche is damaged and probably not recut. This is most likely the work of Atenists, although it is conceivable that Amenhotep II's prenomen had originally been written and that Thutmose's usurpation was poorly effected.

4.22. An architrave[44] with the cartouches of Thutmose IV resting on <u>nbw</u> signs and crowned by plumes and disks is preserved in the Cairo Museum under the Temporary Number 10.5.33.1. It clearly belongs to a cornice-styled doorway, but whether it originally formed part of the enclosure or the top of another monument is unknown. Its measurements, not given in Hassan's publication, are 94 cm. long by 47 cm. wide.

4.23. An unusual stela[45] bearing the name of Thutmose IV may also have originally stood in the Sphinx amphitheater. It, like so many of the objects from Hassan's excavations, cannot be located now, although its recovery would help clarify the historical significance attributed to it. The stela was quite tall and narrow; the lunette scene bore the winged sun disk with a couchant sphinx beneath. The king, wearing the <u>khepresh.</u> stood before the Sphinx with his back to the god. At least twelve lines of text originally ran horizontally beneath the scene; almost none of it is readable due both to poor cutting and weathering (and the terrible photo provided). According to Hassan the text referred to an endowment of fields in Djahy to the Sphinx or the Temple of the Sphinx. This stela's reference to Syria will be referred to later in a discussion of the king's foreign relations, but there are other points to be addressed here. First, both Hassan and especially Zivie[46] were aware that the king's pose is unusual. In fact it is suspect enough that one might suggest it is the king's statue and not the pharaoh himself which is represented here. There is at least one other stela from Giza showing a statue of Thutmose IV before the Sphinx--it is of Ramesside date.[47] There are also several stelae showing a statue of Amenhotep II in the same position.[48] Both kings were known to have associated themselves with the Horemakhet; their statues shown before the Sphinx therefore signal the association. Second, Hassan in at least one place[49] stated the king held a papyrus roll in his hand on which was perhaps written the endowment inscription.

This cannot be verified by the picture published but is again most unusual. Third, the hieroglyphs are scratchy and cursive; they certainly do not suit the requirements of a royal stela in the 18th dynasty. The figures too are mere outlines which reveal nothing about date. Even the sundisk is damaged. In sum, until this stela can be refound it would be advisable not to include it among Thutmose IV's contemporary monuments. It quite possibly is of later date (21st dynasty or later) and as such could have been a copy of an earlier text; or it could have first been composed at a late date.

4.24.   The temple of Amenhotep II to Horemakhet also produced some monuments of Thutmose IV. Fragments of a fine relief[50] were recovered in front of a limestone doorway of Amenhotep II, a bit to the east. Two fragments show the Sphinx twice, lying on a pedestal adorned with djed and ankh signs. The king appears wearing the khepresh and offering wine. He also wears the gold shebiu collar with armlets and has particularly large oblique shaped eyes. The style is comparable to the king's eye shape on several scenes from his Karnak alabaster chapel and from his chariot.[51]   The enlarged eye is a feature of some of the sculpture in the round as well.[52]

Horemakhet's utterances are partially preserved: Left: "I have given to you [millions of] years; Utterance: eternity [upon] the throne of Geb; all protection, life and stability behind him like Re." Right: "...all...; Utterance: all stability and dominion".   A small portion of the winged sundisk remains above the vertical central inscription. In fact, the right fragment plainly shows the ground line for the scene, and the space beneath the line is uninscribed.

4.25. When Hassan dug the mudbrick temple wall of Amenhotep II, he found ten fragments of a smashed stela of Thutmose IV, and later, outside the main entrance, he found another fragment alongside the doorposts of Amenhotep II.[53] His only comments concerning this stela reveal that it was "a fine stela, bearing a representation of Thotmes IV presenting offerings to the Sphinx".[54]

4.26.   A stela of Seti I[55] found within the Sphinx Temple was set on a rectangular limestone pedestal inscribed for Thutmose IV. This may have been a statue base or a building block as Hassan appears to have thought.

4.27. The last monument known to bear the name of Thutmose at Giza is the small stela of Amenhotep II.[56] It was set up in the Temple in a room whose doorway may have employed a lintel of Thutmose. The stela is round-topped with a niche below the lunette. In the curve, however, is the winged sundisk with human arms reaching down to grasp a cartouche ring. The name within has been erased, but the remains of Thutmose were discerned by Hassan,[57] and the elements appear to be as he read them. It is impossible to be sure, due to the state of erosion on the stela, whether the name Amenhotep once existed beneath Thutmose. Hassan argued that Thutmose IV made this stela and that his figure was erased from before the Sphinx in the major scene because of a dynastic feud. Evidence of erasure is not visible, and the damage is likely to have occurred through weathering and Atenist attacks. Zivie has suggested[58] that the stela was fashioned during the reign of Amenhotep II and that Thutmose added his name to it later to honor his father. It is also possible that Thutmose erased the name of his father and replaced his own in the lunette. This would mean that the human-armed sundisk was styled in Amenhotep's reign, not Thutmose's. Indeed, that is the opinion of Doresse in an article written years ago, and Redford recently suggested that there were probably even earlier examples which have not yet come to light, although he does think this piece was a "harbinger of things to come".[59] Since the stela seems to have been made for Amenhotep II, it would be most unfair to use it as evidence that "the seed of Atonism was sown in the reign of Thotmes IV".[60]

Conclusions

   It is tempting to attribute at least some of the king's interest in the spot as an attempt to compensate for some unexpected difficulties in his succession. The witness of the sons of Amenhotep II who revered Horemakhet surely had an impact on Thutmose who may have destroyed their monuments. Nonetheless it is true that Thutmose IV enlarged the solar significance of Horemakhet's cult at Giza. In Amenhotep II's reign Horemakhet was not a major sun deity but a regional god whom the king remembered as he remembered his ancestors Chephren and Khufu.[61] The gradual assimilation of Horemakhet to Horakhty took place during Amenhotep's reign--on Stela B, for example, Re-Horakhty appeared behind Horemakhet; the name of the sun god was often applied to the Sphinx so that the god Horemakhet (properly called) was labelled Horakhty/Re-Horakhty on numerous examples. On Stela B[62] he was called Horemakhet-Horakhty in the htp di nsw offering formula. Thutmose IV greatly expanded the importance of Horemakhet as a sun god, however, referring to him on the Sphinx Stela as "Horemakhet-Khepri-Re-Atum". He omitted Amun-Re from the Sphinx Stela, allowing the northern deity to dominate both as sun-god and as royal legitimator. Amun, it should be remembered, even on Amenhotep II's Sphinx Stela was the primeval creator and also determined the kingship. Thutmose' omission of Amun from his stela must then have been deliberate and a reflection both of the increasing importance of the Heliopolitan gods and perhaps of the north itself as the administrative center of Egypt. As has been noted in Chapter 2, Thutmose had a separate legitimizing document (a naos) in Thebes where Amun-Re chose him to rule.[63]

     But Thutmose IV focussed his attention on this region more broadly than at Horemakhet alone. Giza was to be not only the home of Horemakhet, a favorite god of the royal family and high court officials. Thutmose IV wished to create at Giza a gathering place for all the gods, and for the subgroup of northern deities. Indeed he was largely responsible for recognizing the gods of the Memphis-Letopolis area; his Sphinx Stela, in several cases, is the earliest attested reference to a local god[64]. The king's interest in Horemakhet and the site of Giza was rewarded, for later the god was loved by all people and was favored by scores of pilgrims[65]. Thutmose's personal influence in the Giza region was still apparent in the reign of Ay when his estate fields were yet producing revenues.[66]

     Johnson's work on the relief sculpture of Amenhotep III in Thebes[67] has suggested that a king's appearance in the shebiu collar in non-funerary contexts was meant to stress the accomplished deification of the ruler. This suggestion has much to recommend it, in the light of Thutmose's interest in Giza to emphasize his relationship with all the gods. His acceptance there before local and national gods could be seen as the preliminary step to his presentation as the deified son of the sun god. That a change in the king's sculptural representation may be documented, and that it includes an enlarged eye which Johnson suggests the appearance of the ruler reborn as a child, encourages the conclusion that the king's status publicly has changed. The monuments on which this occurs are stylistically and chronologically (alabaster chapel and tomb) latest in the reign. We suggest consideration be given to the notion that Thutmose IV appeared at Giza in the Sphinx temple as the son of the sun god and before other gods. His wife and mother accompanied him enacting the roles of Isis. (Note Amenhotep II then becomes identified with Horemakhet.) The king's new status is commemorated in the fine but fragmentary stela discussed above in 4.24.

5. Abusir.

     5.1. The Fifth dynasty pyramid complex of Sahure at Abusir housed a New Kingdom sanctuary for the goddess Sakhmet; there Thutmose IV usurped an original temple relief which he reused for Sakhmet's cult.[68] The scene shows the king with his ka offering to [Bastet mistress of Ankhtawy], and the cartouches of Thutmose have been added. The relief has a Leipzig Museum Inv.number, 2093, but it is lost at present. It seems probable that again Thutmose wished to stress his link with the northern gods in whose territory he may have been a relative unknown.

6. Memphis and Sakkara.

6.1. At Memphis, as at Giza, Thutmose was active. Little has survived from his monuments, but there are indications of Thutmose's interest in the site. The major find is a foundation deposit,[69] recovered in two parts by two expeditions. That the finds represent one deposit may be concluded because they were found, according to the excavator's descriptions, in roughly the same place. The pond to the west of the West Propylon of Ptah's temple yielded the king's foundation deposit consisting of inscribed glazed plaques, alabaster semi-circles, bronze knives, chisels, and an axe; model vessels numbered at least twenty, and a small ointment jar probably also came from this group. Weinstein pointed out that there were three arrowheads in the deposit and noted that this inclusion was unusual since most implements were building tools.[70]

The question of what sort of construction Thutmose IV commemorated in his deposits remains. Weinstein suggested[71] that a statue was the king's monument, and he cited Daressy's comment that monolithic blocks near the find were probably statue bases. Petrie did not mention these bases, and the royal name that belongs to the other colossal statue bases in the area is that of Ramesses II. In fact the site which yielded Thutmose's foundation deposit was that on which Ramesses II later built a temple.[72] For several reasons it is preferable to suggest Thutmose erected some sort of building.

There were found under Ramesses II's foundation in the West Hall of the main temple four stelae[73] of similar style; one is inscribed for Thutmose IV and shows him smiting an enemy before a statue of Ptah. A fifth stela,[74] also inscribed for the king, was found elsewhere in the temple. All of these stelae are crude and roughly incised. At least two of them appear to have been offered by the same man, one Ramose.[75] It is likely that these were votive objects placed in the Ptah sanctuary some time after Thutmose IV's reign. Stylistically these works do not belong to the reign; nor do the costumes, royal and private, suit a date in the mid-18th Dynasty. In addition the name of Amun on the inscribed piece is not damaged, and the god's epithet, King of the Gods, is far commoner in the post-Amarna period than earlier. It seems not unlikely that the stelae were dedicated to the ruler who built the chapel to Ptah. Perhaps they were moved by Ramesses II, who rebuilt the temple. Ramesses used the stelae under the floor of his West Hall in the main Temple either as fill or to safeguard them. Whatever the case may have been, one should surmise that these stelae had earlier been offered in a statue sanctuary for Ptah, probably built by Thutmose IV.

6.2. A portion of a limestone architrave (now 1.8 meters long by .9 wide) was reused as a trough in the monastery of Apa Jeremias in Sakkara north.[76] The remaining inscription on one side only identifies in large hieroglyphs: "The good [god] Menkheprure, living forever". The size of the preserved architrave fragment suggests a court or building of impressive dimensions and most likely the shrine to

Ptah built by Thutmose IV.

6.3 Within the building of Ramesses II, from the same site that produced Thutmose's foundation deposit, a portion of a papyrus column with rope binding decoration was found;[77] the same type of column was found reused in the masonry of Merenptah's temple. Both columns are now in Brussels (E 4987) and are assigned there to Amenhotep III because of their fine workmanship. But it is equally possible the columns belonged to a building of Thutmose IV, especially as one column part was found at the site of his deposit. We note here the relief fragment mentioned in Chapter 2, which preserves a portion of a divine birth scene for Thutmose IV. That limestone block has no provenance but, given the distribution of Thutmose's monuments in limestone, Memphis is a likely location for such a temple scene.

A large offering table belonging to the king[78] was found in the village of Kom Azazieh near Mitrahina, again to the west of the Ptah temple. This monument, however, could have been placed in a sanctuary before Ptah or before a colossal statue (see 6.5). In view of the other evidence for a building erected by Thutmose IV, the statue bases and offering table may suggest that the king left both types of monument: a sanctuary at west Memphis housing a statue of Ptah.

6.4. The stelae mentioned above were private ones,[79] but they were clearly produced as a group. The five examples depict the king holding a bow and arrow and his enemies with his right hand while striking a killing blow with the scimitar in his left hand. In all cases the king appears on the left and Ptah's statue is drawn on the right. Three stelae are false-door type and two are round-topped. A man called Ramose is named on two examples; the one providing legible text titles him hry mrw "chief of serfs". It is probable that here Thutmose IV is the deceased king as intermediary deity who acts on behalf of the private offerer. As the smiting king Thutmose curbs the forces of chaos in the sight of Ptah in order that maat may exist on earth. A bit of new information provided by these stelae is the existence of a variant Horus name for Thutmose IV: Brussels E 4499, a false-door type stela, has jamb texts. On the right,pharaoh is called, as is usual, "Horus Strong Bull perfect of diadems, son of Re lord of diadems, Thutmose kha khau, beloved of Ptah lord of heaven, king of the Two lands (?)". On the left he is termed "Horus Strong Bull, son of Atum, king of Upper and Lower Egypt, lord of the Two lands, Menkheprure, beloved of Amun king of the gods". The name "son of Atum" is otherwise unattested, but it should not be surprising. The king was so termed on the Sphinx Stela, and as has been pointed out for many years, the name is obviously meant to stress association with the north. (For another example of these private Memphite stelae, see below in Thebes West (end).)

6.5. The offering table mentioned above (CG 23088)[80] provides the longest

inscription of Thutmose IV from Memphis. It is of black granite, 1.45 X .80 m..
The king's titulary and dedications to Ptah run around the outer edge. Another
variant series of names appears on the table along with the commonly-used titulary:

> "Live the Horus Strong Bull perfect of diadems, the Two Ladies, enduring of
> kingship like Atum, Golden Horus, powerful of <u>khepesh</u>, who subdues the Nine
> Bows, the king of Upper and Lower Egypt Menkheprure. He made his
> monument for father Ptah that he may do 'given life'. The son of Re beloved
> of him Thutmose kha khau, given life like Re forever acted for him. Live the
> Horus Strong Bull beloved of Thebes, Two Ladies powerful (<u>shm</u>) of
> appearances in all lands, [Golden Horus] enduring [of ///] like [Re]-Horakhty,
> son of Re Thutmose kha khau. He made his monument for father Ptah, given
> life; the Good God lord of the Two lands Menkheprure, given life, stability,
> dominion like Re forever did for him."

Three names here show variations, and again this offering table is the unique
example for them.[81] One cannot ignore the association with Thebes claimed by
Thutmose on this Memphite monument; nor can the connection with Re-Horakhty
be forgotten. The importance of both gods is well-known, and Thutmose
elsewhere honored both gods greatly. On this table the king called upon the major
national gods of Egypt, and by his names associated himself to them. Without more
evidence it would be premature to link variant forms of the titulary with any
significant events in the reign. Memphis must have been one of Thutmose IV's
favored sites; it is unfortunate that so little of the original monuments has survived.

6.6 We include here a limestone monument (unpublished) whose most likely
provenance is Memphis due to the powdery grainy texture of the stone. JE 27949
is a limestone trapezoidal block with rounded upper edge. (fig. 15) Its greatest width
is at its top, 50 cm. and its height is 55 cm. Depth of the block is some 9 cm. The
sides are smoothed, the bottom rough as is the back. A sky sign runs across the top
of the block and beneath it are the king's cartouches facing <u>away</u> from each other.
The prenomen is on the viewer's right. This is the only text. Hans Goedicke
suggested to me that this is a wall-facing block from a brick wall, possibly between
window openings. That type of use seems the most reasonable and would suggest
some sort of domestic structure in the king's name at Memphis. Surely the
Memphite residence is well-documented in papyri of the period, and this wall
fragment suggests Thutmose IV made his own structures for that residence
complex.

7. <u>Fayum.</u>

Thutmose's name is not actually attested in the Fayum, but very likely once was.
The statue [82] of Tiaa from Crocodilopolis (CG 1167) was discussed in Chapter 3,
where it was stated that the monument was originally a pair statue. The

inscriptions refer to Tiaa as King's mother, and it is therefore not imprudent to suggest her son as the subject of the missing representation. Of course the parallel to this monument can be found in the Karnak masterpiece (CG 42080). Just as on the Theban statue, the king formed the figure on the viewer's left. The same type of black granite was used on both. Thutmose's involvement in the Fayum can also be deduced from his close relationship to the Treasurer Sobekhotep who was Mayor of the Fayum in his early career. To omit this region from a geographical survey would be historically inaccurate.

8. Hermopolis.

There are three fragmentary objects from Hermopolis which belong or have been attributed to Thutmose IV. 8.1. A limestone left door jamb [83] is clearly dated by the king's prenomen; unfortunately the exact provenance of the piece is unknown, for it was published by Hermann only as an example of a previously-excavated piece with a royal name on it. Roeder thought it may have been found re-used in a private house. The jamb measures 1.2 X .345 X .13 m. and is inscribed for "the Good God, lord of the Two lands, lord of performing a ritual (nb ir ht) Menkheprure, son of Re Thut[mose kha khau beloved of Thoth (?)]." Hermann suggested that Thutmose would have had an automatic connection with Hermopolis due to his personal name. This would be difficult to support since Tuthmoside material is now sparse at the site, and Roeder thought the last Thutmose was the only one to build there.

8.2. A second building element is a fragment of sandstone temple relief,[84] 22 X 14 X 6 cm., preserving only the top portion of the cartouche Thut[mose]. It was found in some later rubble but can only belong to an 18th dynasty ruler. Roeder preferred to link the fragment to Thutmose IV because he was attested for the site. As will be seen below, another sandstone block with the nomen of [Thut]mose kha khau was found at Amarna; it is tempting to suggest that it was taken from Hermopolis and once belonged to a Tuthmoside building contributed to by Thutmose IV.

8.3. A third object from Hermopolis which may have been made in Thutmose IV's reign is a fragmentary scribal palette[85] made of slate. It is inscribed with a royal prenomen only partially preserved. This may have been a votive offering to Thoth the scribe of divine utterances. It might also have been held by a statue of Thoth dedicated in the temple. This would explain its notice by Atenists who erased the mn sign from the royal name. The only text now remaining is as follows: "[//] the Two lands, the King of Upper and Lower Egypt, lord of the Two lands, Men[///]re". According to Roeder the mn sign, although erased was readable. Again the excavator chose to identify Thutmose IV, but Thutmose III is as likely if an early 18th Dynasty temple existed at Hermopolis.

9. Amarna.

Several objects bearing the name of Thutmose IV have been recovered from the city of Amarna. Unfortunately the most intriguing one has no exact provenance, but certainly was found within the town.

9.1.   A relief fragment (no material named) was seen and published by Wilkinson in 1843.[86] The fragment has not re-appeared since that time and is known only by a line drawing in the first publication. Akhenaten, wearing the atef crown, is shown holding an offering tray to the aten who is named by the earlier cartouches. Following the names are the remains of three vertical columns. "Great living Aten who is in festival; lord of sky, lord of land, who is in the midst of the House of Menkheprure in the House of Aten in Akhetaten". There can be no mistake concerning this translation, but naturally there has been disagreement about the interpretation.   Borchardt[87] used this relief to support his assertion that Thutmose IV had erected a temple to Aten at Amarna before Akhenaten's reign. Schäfer,[88] however, proposed that an offering chapel to the memory of Thutmose IV was referred to on the relief; he mentioned living family members associated with sanctuaries within the House of Aten. Schäfer's interpretation has been the more generally accepted one: Davies, Pendlebury, Helck,and Aldred have all recognized this "House of Menkheprure" as a site of ancestor veneration by the Amarna pharaoh.[89] Indeed, this would appear to be the only reasonable explanation, but it certainly calls into question the nature of Akhenaten's attachment to Thutmose. Was he more attentive to that ruler than to other ancestors, and, if so, why?

Certainly the predecessor of Akhenaten most often mentioned in his reign was Amenhotep III, his father. His name appears in nearly every sort of context, including three buildings at Amarna which are associated with him.[90] And, as is well known, he appeared on a private stela together with his wife Tiye receiving offerings under the rays of the Aten whose names were in the late form.[91] Whether this stela was a posthumous one presents a wider question than can be considered here, but the presence of ancestors at Amarna is pertinent to our discussion. Although the form of funerary belief at Amarna is difficult to ascertain, the fate of ancestors may well have been a cause of concern, since they had died without the benefit of Akhenaten's revelation. If the souls of the dead came forth in daylight and returned to their tombs at night, then it is not surprising to find offering sanctuaries to venerated dead within the Aten Temple itself where the daylight's creative force was most manifest.[92] It is possible that both Amenhotep III and Thutmose IV through offering shrines in the Per Aten were thereby ensured an afterlife. To speculate further, the Amarna chapels may have been variations on the cenotaphs or memorial chapels erected at other sites, especially Abydos. Thus Akhenaten's venerated father and grandfather were identified with the great disk as the offerers at Abydos became associated to Osiris.

Pendlebury and Davies suggested that the House of Thutmose IV was not the only ancestral holding within Amarna,[93] and Pendlebury referred to the House of Thutmose I (pr $^c3$-hpr-$k3$-r^c) as well as the House of Amenhotep II (pr $^c3$-$hprw$-r^c) which are attested from the site; Davies mentioned only the second reference. Both, however, believed there were "shrines" of ancestors at Amarna. While this agrees with the interpretation supported above, it should be made clear that the evidence for temples or estates of Thutmose I and Amenhotep II within Amarna is scanty. Thutmose I's "house" is known from wine jar labels only, and it is certainly not clear that the estate was a local one. Indeed it is more likely that estates of that king from elsewhere in Egypt produced the wine found at Amarna, for it is well known that the funerary estates of deceased rulers provided wine and foods for temple and perhaps palace use.[94] It would be hazardous to suggest a shrine of Thutmose I existed at Amarna based on jar sealings. The presence of Amenhotep II is more ambiguous. His "house" appears within the title of Any who was the Steward for the House of Aakheprure.[95] This could indicate a shrine within the Aten temple, like that of Thutmose IV, but it could equally well refer to Any's position as steward of Amenhotep II's funerary estate. And Any is known with the title at Karnak as well as Amarna. We must then not presume that Akhenaten built shrines for many of his ancestors, but perhaps he honored those in close memory.

One might underscore Akhenaten's closeness to his father and grandfather by recalling that he mentioned both of them on his early boundary stelae.[96] He stated that they, like he, had heard evil things (probably referring to crimes as heinous as grave-robbing). Whether he invoked his predecessors due to literary license or a desire to stress his continuity with the earlier 18th Dynasty, it is probable that he chose Amenhotep III and Thutmose IV because people remembered them. Probably it was Thutmose's temporal closeness to Akhenaten which brought him favor on the boundary stelae.

9.2.   Objects of Thutmose IV's own reign are also known from the site at Amarna. The best known piece is a wristlet[97] of elephant ivory tusk which had been halved and hollowed. This fine openwork piece , some 11.2 cm. in length, is now in West Berlin (21685) but was found in House Q 48.1 at Amarna along with a number of small objects from earlier reigns. Amenhotep III was named in particular. Borchardt assumed from the start that the house owner had collected these objects as models.[98] The ivory carving in question shows Thutmose IV in the act of smiting an Asiatic. The king holds a scimitar to strike with and a bow and arrow in his other hand which also grabs the enemy. He wears a "Nubian" wig, the shebiu collar, and the sun disk appears over his head. The scene is enacted before the statue of Montu-Re[99] who offers the scimitar to the king: "Take for yourself the scimitar, 0 Good God, that you may smite the chiefs of all foreign countries."[100]

There are again different interpretations about the original source of this wristlet. Borchardt suggested it adorned a statue of the king which had been placed in a temple to Aten built by Thutmose IV. Schäfer responded that the statue probably came from Thebes, and was placed in the chapel which Akhenaten built for his grandfather in the Aten Temple. Helck, in a label for his Urkunden IV entry,[101] simply referred to the object as an armcover to a throne, but he gave no references. In fact, though perhaps wrong, Helck's comment is helpful, since it suggests the object need not have adorned a statue. It is possible this bracelet was a memento of the king himself and was worn as a wristlet.[102] This is all the more likely since it was found in a private house, not in the temple.

It should be noted that this ivory carving has been used to suggest Thutmose's dedication to the sun god of the disk.[103] I agree with the proposal, but it would be unwise to assign too much importance to a small object such as this. The sundisk appears in many contexts in the early-mid 18th Dynasty, but it normally signifies Horus Behdet, the winged sundisk. There are examples, however, that show only the disk hovering in a protective attitude.[104] On this wristlet, therefore, the disk atop Thutmose's head may have identified the king with the sun god but not necessarily the Aten. The emphasis on solarization is evident on the work as a whole, for it concentrates on Re's syncretizations. We have noted already the significance of the shebiu collar at Giza. The presence of the collar, the sun disk over the king's head, and the style of relief showing the king with exaggerated oblique eye and round face all suggest the intention is to show Thutmose IV reborn as a form of sun god himself. This representation resembles Amenhotep III's styles more than any other of Thutmose's monument. Perhaps it either comes from the son's reign or was originally a funerary piece.

9.3. A third object with the name of Thutmose IV may be recognized in a green glazed steatite wedjat eye[105] bead whose base is engraved with the cartouche of the king. The bead was found in house U 36.16. Its present location is unknown to me. Pendlebury did not illustrate the object.

9.4. Final monuments of Thutmose IV were found on the Parade Grounds and within the "Military quarters". In House R.42.9A, a soldiers' residence, were found blue faience fragments[106] including inlays for wigs and wings. Some fragments showed the name of Thutmose IV, but without study there is no way of knowing whether they were heirlooms or of Amarna manufacture. They could have been made there for dedication in Thutmose's memory.

9.5. A block of sandstone from the Parade Ground[107] preserved a portion of Thutmose's nomen. The fragment is some 19.5 cm. in height. The cartouche shows the Thoth bird's standard, but the bird has been erased. The ms, most of the s and the ḫᶜw are untouched. Apparently this block was brought from elsewhere for re-use, possibly for tethering horses on the ground. Although from the cartouche there is a possibility Thutmose II was named, Thutmose IV is a strong candidate--a trace of the ḫᶜ sign appears above s , and there is a provenance to suggest, Hermopolis. As said above there may have been a sandstone building at Hermopolis in the Tuthmoside era, and Roeder, at least, believed Thutmose IV was the builder. Since this block was not made at Amarna, and since Hermopolis was nearby, that city could well have been the original provenance.

10. Abydos.

10.1.   The king is known at this sacred area by the remains of a small chapel,[108] built in brick and revetted with decorated limestone blocks. This building must have continued in use, for there were blocks of Ramesses III and a lintel of Psamtik I on the same site.   The one scene preserved from this building shows Thutmose IV before Osiris-Wennefer; and its preserved measurements are 1.8 X 2.5 m.   Noting that the several structures built by kings at Abydos are not part of a standard temple complex, Simpson has suggested that this building was a memorial chapel for the ruler;[109] Ahmose, Hatshepsut, and Ramesses II, among others, may also have left such "cenotaphs". This idea has a great deal to commend it, but it is difficult to be sure, since the building was inscriptionally called both a pr and a ḥwt but not a mᶜḥᶜt as were the Middle Kingdom dedicatory monuments. Tetisheri's building at Thinis was referred to as a mᶜḥᶜt,[110] while those of Ahmose and Thutmose III were termed pr as was Thutmose IV's. Within the chapel area of Thutmose IV were found memorial stelae and statues of 18th to 20th dynasty date[111]; nearby a jamb emerged naming one Siese, Chief Steward of the House (pr) of Menkheprure, as well as of Nebpehtire and Menkheperre.[112] DeMeulenaere studied the monuments of this man[113] and concluded he lived during the reigns of Amenhotep II, Thutmose IV and Amenhotep III and was a native of the region. He was buried there as well, and apparently the above-mentioned jamb was an element from his tomb.   If the royal monuments referred to by Siese were "cenotaphs" or memorial chapels, then this man had responsibility for maintaining several such offering places.   In fact we know that Thutmose IV set aside 2000 arouras of land from the Osiris fields for his own foundation, and he gave meat offerings as well.   The king even gave offerings for the chapel of his ancestor Ahmose. (See below, Chapter 5 on Louvre C53.) We are admittedly still unclear about the exact nature of these memorial buildings, but the fact that monarchs wished to call attention to themselves as part of the royal line following Osiris, suggests that Simpson's comments ring true.   There is a further bit of evidence concerning offerings to the king at Abydos which may be related to his chapel.

The populace invoked Thutmose IV in their own dedications to Osiris.   This may have been done with the same meaning as earlier when cartouches sometimes identified a king on a private stela. But in the reign of Thutmose IV the king appears as more than a name; he is rather an intercessor. On a stela of Neferhet, Chief of Building for Thutmose IV's temple at Abydos, Thutmose IV was shown offering to Nut "who bore the gods in the midst of Abydos"; Neferhet appeared only in the lower register.[114] And this stela bears a cartouche in the center dating it to Thutmose's own reign--a fact supported by the mid-18th Dynasty style. A second stela[115] belongs to this architect; it shows Neferhet himself before Osiris and Isis on the left and before Min, son of Isis, on the right. This stela is not specifically provenanced, but should certainly have come from Abydos.

Actually the majority of Abydene votives do not mention monarchs,[116] but perhaps those which do testify to the presumed benefits of having the king as a representative. This idea gains support from one[117] of two stelae naming the Fanbearer on the right of the king, Tjuna. There Thutmose IV offers before Osiris while Tjuna and his wife follow the king. The bodily representation is Amarnesque, and the costumes are typically late 18th Dynasty. The king's cartouche does not appear at the top center of the stela, but appears only in the inscription naming the ruler. Clearly this monument employed the deceased but divine Thutmose as intercessor and was dedicated, perhaps by Tjuna's sons shown on the bottom of the stela, or by Tjuna himself at an advanced age. Tjuna apparently felt an attachment to Thutmose under whom he must have functioned as a rather high official. His second stela[118] was made in the reign of Thutmose himself, as is shown by the cartouche below the sundisk and by the style of the piece. There Tjuna alone offered to Osiris and Wepwawet. The inclusion of the offering king on the stelae of Neferhet and Tjuna, as well as the king's presence by cartouche on numerous (but not a majority of) objects might suggest that this monarch was considered an appropriate intercessor. This may have been due to the presence of a royal cenotaph at the site which underlined that king's closeness to Osiris.

10.2. Thutmose IV also left a statue of himself at Abydos.[119] A limestone torso, .67 m. in height,was found on the road before the portal to Ramesses II's temple. The waist band was inscribed for "Menkheprure beloved of Osiris".[120] It seems likely that this statue once stood in Thutmose's own chapel. Its location is unknown at present, but it was left in place by Mariette; the Abydos storerooms would perhaps produce it upon search.

11. Dendera.

11.1. Only one block of Thutmose IV is so far known from Dendera,[121] but it was produced from small sondages of the temple foundations and may represent only a fragment of the king's work there. The king's head in the nemes is shown facing right with hands up in adoration or offering; above he is called :"the Good

God, lord of joy, the king of Upper and Lower Egypt, lord of performing a ritual, Menkheprure, given life forever". The remains of "life" and "stability" may be seen in the next speech group.Blocks (two published) of Thutmose III are also known from the foundations, and they mention Hathor of Iunet specifically. A Ptolemaic dedication referred to Thutmose III as the major renewer for the temple[122] who improved the works of Khufu and Pepi I. If this memorial is correct, then Thutmose III was surely better represented at Dendera than his two blocks suggest. Perhaps the same was true for Thutmose IV who favored other sites in which Thutmose III took great interest. It should be noted, however, that Hathor's name does not appear on Thutmose IV's block (probably of limestone but nowhere stated to be) and the possibility must be left open that the block was imported from elsewhere for re-use.

12. Medamud.

Apparently Thutmose IV did work on the 18th dynasty temple at Medamud, most likely in close conjunction with the works of his father Amenhotep II. A large granite door of that last king is a major testament to the structure of the period.[123] Only fragments from the foundations of other later buildings are now available for Thutmose. 12.1. The 1925 excavation produced limestone wall fragments showing both cartouches of the king.[124] Inv. 7 includes two joining pieces measuring 3 X 17 cm. with 4 cm. thickness; Inv. 526 probably joins these. Inv. 984 was a portion of a limestone lion and has a cartouche; its measurements are 26 X 2 X 35 cm. The pieces all came from the foundation of the destroyed portion of the Ptolemaic temple and document little other than the king's interest in the site.

12.2. Later excavation produced more material in the king's name, but it has been mistakenly recorded for Thutmose III. In 1930 a fragment of a limestone lintel[125] was unearthed in the upper foundation of the decorated Hypostyle Hall II; it was found some five meters north of the door of Amenhotep II. Inv. 4976, a left corner piece, measures 31 X 77 cm. and names the "son of Re Tuth[mosis] kha [khau]" in raised relief inscription. The other side of the lintel is also decorated, but is incised, thus indicating the exterior doorway. It only preserves nsw-bit. 12.3. Inv. 5342, a limestone fragment[126], preserves the same cartouche beginning as on 4976, and both should identify Thutmose IV. Thus the king apparently built some type of door at Medamud, in addition to decorating a wall, perhaps within Amenhotep II's building.

12.4. Finally, the king left an inscribed statue of himself in red granite at the Medamud temple.[127] In 1930 the lower portion of a life-sized statue of Thutmose IV was found in the wall of a Coptic house some 10 m. from the south wall of the temple. It is in a terrible state of preservation; the waist to the calf is represented, and even the front of the legs is broken away. This statue, Inv. 4737, now measures

.58 X .70 X .64 m. The excavator reported it as Thutmose III, because he misread the belt inscription. It identifies the "Good God Menkheprure". The seat too is inscribed. The left shows "The king of Upper and Lower Egypt, [Menkhepru]re";the right: "the son of Re Thutmose kha khau". The handcopy in the publication shows the $\underline{h}^c$ sign, but the identification was still made incorrectly. Now, however, one may add this battered example to Thutmose IV's inscribed monuments. And in addition the torso and head to this statue are preserved in near-perfect condition in the Louvre under number E13889. The Medamud season of 1929 turned up Inv. 4467, a red granite bust of a king in a nemes.[128] It measures .75 ht. X .6 wd. X .46 thck. (at the break). The head is .34 m. ht. There is a back pillar which begins just below the nemes tail. This bust was discovered in the foundation of a house foyer to the west of the sacred lake. In my discussion of sculpture of Thutmose IV is a photo reconstruction of the piece.

The witness of Thutmose IV at Medamud is therefore small but larger than has been previously recognized. Montu's 18th dynasty temple contained perhaps a room dedicated by the king (wall reliefs) and an inscribed door as well. The king's statue may have been placed there or elsewhere in the complex.

13. Karnak.

For obvious reasons Karnak is the best attested site for Thutmose IV outside of his own tomb.[129] The god Amun received the king's attention in the form of a peristyle court, a decorated porch, and an alabaster bark shrine for the god. In addition to these buildings, Thutmose erected the obelisk of his grandfather and added his own inscription to it; he dedicated a statue of himself and endowed it and a statue of Thutmose III with booty from his Asiatic campaign. The king also placed several statues of himself in the main Karnak temple, including colossal Osirides which were later re-used by Ramesses II in the Mut precinct. In the Montu precinct Thutmose left a doorway and may have been responsible for work on the enclosure wall. There is no reason, at the present time, to date any construction in the Mut enclosure to the reign of Thutmose IV, as has been done previously. His name appears there only on a re-used block.

13.1. The Peristyle Court.[130] (figs. 16-18). This sandstone building is by far the most impressive monument left by Thutmose IV, largely because of its fine reliefs which have retained their vividly painted scenes. The building is represented by more than 1000 blocks, most found in the Third pylon foundations, but it is still quite incomplete. Nonetheless Bernadette Letellier has admirably reconstructed the sequence of scenes and has also confirmed the location of the building, first suggested by Barguet, before the Fourth pylon. She has likewise added the important information that this achievement of Thutmose IV was actually an interior addition to a pre-existing court of Thutmose II. Thutmose IV placed sandstone decorated walls on a limestone court with slanted walls. He then added a double interior peristyle with cornice and roof.

That this building was indeed a pillared court has been known for some time; Barguet published the architrave inscription which referred to it as a <u>wsht ḥft-ḥr m</u> <u>ỉnr mnḥ n rwdt pḥrw m ỉwnwt</u> "a fore-court of excellent sandstone turning around with pillars (circularly inscribed by pillars)". The same phrase describes Ramesses II's court at Luxor Temple, where the pillars are likewise contained within the court rather than around it. This interior/exterior distinction for <u>pḥrw</u> is semantically present in English, but not in Egyptian;[131] the translation "surrounded by pillars" would be inaccurate though more pleasing to the ear.

The court had six doors, three monumental and three secondary. The peristyle architrave entered the walls near the monumental doors on the north and south. The west entry was off-axis, probably because another monument blocked the way. This interesting building originally approximated a rectangle of 65-70 m. X 40 m. and was oriented with its long axis running north to south; its height was some 6.5 m. The portion preserved to us is largely from the western half of the building, for that is the part removed by Amenhotep III in order to build the IIIrd pylon. The eastern half remained in some form until the Late New Kingdom. A foundation deposit of Thutmose IV, found in the northeast of the Hypostyle Hall, confirms the building's situation.[132] The preserved portions of this court are to be on view in the Musee en plein air, the long and arduous work of Mlle. Letellier and M. Larche, Director of the Franco-Egyptian Center in Karnak, being finally near an end.

The scenes from Thutmose's court are cut in low relief in all areas unexposed. The walls extended beyond the protection of the peristyle roof were incised. The west wall contained scenes of fatted cattle brought for sacrifice; the slaughter was also represented. To the right of the animal sacrifices were two registers of the king with Amun shown six times in each register performing different ritual acts. This west wall also represented the types of offering made by the king to the god: food, oils, vases, animals, wine, and necklaces were among these, in addition to statues, a naos, a bark for Amun, and the great door of the Fourth pylon.[133] All these were represented in relief, and three other doors were shown and named.[134] These must have been the monumental doors of the court itself. The doors were named <u>sb3 ꜥ3 ỉmn shm šfyt</u> "Amun powerful of respect" (the door to the IVth pylon), <u>sb3 ꜥ3 dꜥm Mn-ḫprw-rꜥ di ꜥnh ỉmn shb ỉpt</u> "the great electrum door of Thutmose IV, given life, Amun who makes the Chamber festive"; and <u>dꜥm ꜥ3t nbt ꜥš3 Mn-ḫprw-rꜥ di ꜥnh ỉmn shꜥ nfrw</u> "Amun who makes beauties appear"; the fourth door was not named.

The wall of the north side of the court contained two registers and showed the king before Amun (Montu once) again in ritual poses. Amun appeared once with

Mut and once with Amunet. The south wall showed more offering scenes and also contained the representation, mentioned in the preceding chapter, of the king accompanied by his mother Tiaa, stretching the cord for the building with Sefkhet-abu. A large figure of the king and his ka cut en creux formed the west and east ends of this wall.

The square pillars which formed the double peristyle are each roughly 1 m. on a side and show the king embraced by Amun on each face (although a few show only the king's figure). A common formula, often mentioning sed festivals, was written horizontally below each scene; there are but few variations: "beloved, given life, stability,dominion, health, all joy like Re forever; first occasion of the sed festival, may he do very many"; "beloved, given life, stability, dominion, health, may he be joyful, may he rule the Two lands like Re...."[135] Twice a significant variant occurs: "beloved, given life,stability, dominion, health, and joy like Re forever; first occasion and repetition of the sed festival, may he do very many".[136] Thus the pillars referred both to the "first occurrence" and to the "first occurrence and repetition" of the sed. This would tend to dampen any argument that the building was meant to commemorate the king's coming first jubilee in his thirtieth year of reign, while the room at Amada with "repetition" formulae memorialized his coming second one.[137] Letellier has not adopted an interpretation of this court as a Jubilee building; she agrees with Hornung's understanding of the formulae as wishes for festivals.[138] The occurrence of both forms on the same monument certainly favors a prospective understanding, and this has been argued at length in Chapter 1. The chapel may not have been intended as a heb-sed court but rather a temple entrance area where various rituals took place, including the celebration of "festivals".[139] It has its closest parallel in the court of Ramesses II at Luxor. The scenes of fatted cattle and ritual slaughter occur in both courts, and both are termed wsht hft-hr "fore-court". Thus Thutmose's purpose was to embellish this pre-existing edifice which was, at the time, the introductory court to Karnak.

13.2. A limestone door jamb (left) was found in the Third pylon and named the door "Amun is great of provisions from the granary". It may also have belonged to this court.[140] Other elements of this doorway in limestone include the upper portion of the opposite jamb showing the god Amun, facing left. Only a sun disk is preserved from the king's prenomen, but the dimensions and style make the match beyond question.[141] An interior portion of this door preserves a scene of Thutmose IV in the red crown facing right before Amun. This block may have joined the right jamb, but a corresponding scene for the left side of the door has not yet emerged.[142] We know that Thutmose IV's court of sandstone was applied against Thutmose II's limestone one, and this doorway may have replaced one of the earlier king. It is remarkable to note the stylistic similarity of carving between Thutmose II's blocks and Thutmose IV's.[143]

13.3. The Porch and Door to the Fourth pylon.[144]

Thutmose decorated the great door to the Fourth pylon as well as the court before it. That door is well-known by its name,"Amun is powerful of respect", for it appears on more than one contemporary document. The major inscription for the door remains on the northern wing of the Pylon itself. A dedicatory text of Thutmose IV can still be read there in its majority.[145] The scenes of the king before Amun are visible to the right of the text, but they are third-hand restorations dating from the reign of Alexander the Great.[146] Alexander re-cut both the scenes and a restoration text of Shabako. That 25th dynasty ruler had refitted the door, its columns, and its ḥ3yt with precious metals in a manner perhaps similar to Thutmose's original construction. This IVth pylon entry therefore still shows the dedication of three great rulers, much removed from one another in time, both to Amun and to the works of predecessors.

The inscription incised on the corps avancé of the Fourth pylon, and which is original to Thutmose IV, is quite general, but it informs us of the king's intent in constructing the door:

"1) ...formerly, who took thought of the future, who found what is beneficial to the father who placed him on his seat; who elevated and broadened his temple in which he appeared in Karnak as a monument to the lord of eternity in the place on which he rested, the son of Re Thutmose kha khau, given life. 2) ... [Then his Majesty acted, making a great doorway as his monument], extending and magnifying greatly, more than that which his ancestors had done. Its height was great, it reaching the sky. Its rays inundated the Two lands making festive the lord of the gods, Amun-Re[147] At seeing it, the South rejoices... 3)...who created his beauties, the lord of the gods, Amun, who led his Majesty to do for him every deed which he desired to happen. For he knew him as his protector, who embellished his temple of millions of years...[the son of Re Thutmose kha kha]u forever."

It is clear from Thutmose's dedicatory text that he never claimed to have erected the pylon or its door, but rather to have enlarged it more than had been done before. And it is true that he extended the front of the Pylon[148] and elevated it as part of his work. This text, therefore, may refer only to a portion of his project. That mention of the "rays" which inundated the Two lands might indicate, however, that his corps avancé was fitted with precious metals. Such was the conclusion of Yoyotte,[149] and the term sb3 could have encompassed this sandstone edifice.

The porch before the door is actually pictured for us in two contemporary representations--the block from the peristyle court naming the door, (fig. 19) [150] and the tomb of the Second Prophet of Amun, Amenhotep si-se.[151] The scenes are remarkably alike in showing a roof over two loti-form columns; the door appears between the columns and has a cornice-style lintel. What is probably the socle of the southern column remains in granite abutting the southern obelisk of Thutmose I.[152] The question still arises whether the columns themselves were stone or wood. Yoyotte has argued that the porch, called a h3yt in Alexander's restoration of Shabako's inscription, was made of wood and thus was completely replaced in the 25th dynasty.[153] The inscriptional evidence, however, is inconclusive since h3yt has several meanings; and in this text the reading "ceiling" is just as likely as "porch".[154] The terms used by the Egyptians are unfortunately ambiguous in modern usage, and we can only suppose that Yoyotte is correct, but cannot demonstrate it. In the tomb of Amenhotep si-se the representation of the porch and door is called sb3 ᶜ3 n dᶜm. The block from Thutmose's court refers to the sb3 ᶜ3 'Imn šfywt mrw hbn sbht m dᶜm ᶜ3t ᶜs3t. Thus the sb3 was said both to be of djam and to be of meru and ebony woods with a sebkhet of djam. This ambiguity prevents our making conclusive statements about the specific door elements. Letellier preferred to translate as if the sebkhet was of wood,[155] but this is grammatically impossible; thus her suggestion that sebkhet designated the porch (of wood as Yoyotte wanted) remains a suggestion.

Barguet's references to sbht in Karnak are to what he terms an "avant-porte" or forward door.[156] It seemed to refer to monumental doors and, more specifically, to small doors built before the main ones. Merenptah mentioned a great door fitted in gold with a sbht before it.[157] But, like sb3, sbht is an ambiguous term and could also designate portable shrines in addition to types of doors.[158] But one might note that the block from Thutmose's court,[159] which names and pictures the porch, shows to the left of the porch's left column a smaller cornice-roofed entryway with an open door (?). It is quite possible this represents the fore-door to the Pylon. If sbht in the inscription above referred to that door, then it was worked in djam (over wood or stone) while the main door or porch (?) was of wood. Sb3 does appear determined with ⇒ [160] and so needn't only be "doorway" but could be the "door" itself. The facts which are clear show that Thutmose IV claimed to have left a door which was overlaid, on some of its parts, with djam and precious stones. Shabako, when he rebuilt the door, said that part of it (ceiling or porch) was done in "fine gold", its columns with djam and its column bases with silver. There is no means of ascertaining whether Shabako's decoration was similar to Thutmose IV's.

13.4. Alabaster bark shrine (figs. 14, 20-23) [161] The Second and Third pylon foundations produced blocks in alabaster inscribed for Thutmose IV. In all there are 50 + such blocks[162] which formed a small bark shrine whose form remains uncertain.[163] The chapel has not been published except for a few joining blocks preserving some interior scenes.[164] Van Siclen recently provided a conjectured ground plan.[165] There are still blocks missing from the structure, but the overall plan of decoration and some of the architecture is apparent. This is an attempt to estimate size, and it is approximate since the building is not complete.[166]

The shrine was some 7 meters long by 5.15 high by 4.65 wide. The main entrance was topped by a cavetto cornice with an inscribed architrave. Torus molding begins .72 m. from the top of the cornice; it is 27 cm. in circumference on the sides of the shrine, and 25 cm. on the front. The torus descends on the front of the shrine from the corners; at the back of the building the vertical torus travels down the sides leaving several blank centimeters of wall. A kheker frieze runs across the top of the left side.[167] Decoration is complete on the left half of the exterior; a portion of the right exterior wall was left blank. Whether this was intentional because of the shrine's original emplacement or whether the decoration was never finished cannot be decided conclusively.

Each wall was composed of two registers; the exterior walls had eight scenes of Thutmose before Amun and Amun Kamutef in typical offering attitudes.[168] The right wall began with an added dedication by Amenhotep III, who adapted the speech of a god for the purpose. Re-Horakhty or Montu-Re follows this text escorting the king before Amun. Only a portion of this wall was decorated on this right side. The relief furthest from the doorway was hurriedly done, using a lightly incised technique and the sfumato uncarved eye which was then no doubt painted in. (fig. 20) Inside was shown, on both long walls (north and south) the king seated before an offering table; the king kneeling before offerings with a list above; the bark of Amun on its altar bedecked and surrounded by offerings and Amun embracing the king.[169] The lower register contained four scenes of the king offering to Amun and Amun-Kamutef (lettuces in several instances).

Like the shrine of Amenhotep, finished by Thutmose I,[170] this building was worked on by both Thutmose IV and his son Amenhotep III. That king added his own figure and text to the shrine before he disassembled it and used parts of it in his pylon foundation.[171] In addition to the dedication on the right side, Amenhotep III appears in the beginning of the upper register of the left exterior wall, being escorted by Atum. There he probably simply changed the name of Thutmose IV, since the figures are part of the rest of the father's decoration. Amenhotep said that he "completed" or "decorated" the monument of his father. Since he took over existing text and scenes to include his own image, it is difficult to suggest what his contribution to the shrine was. Perhaps it was left to him to inaugurate its use, in a still incomplete fashion. Stylistic indications suggest the chapel was decorated late in Thutmose IV's reign. He appears twice with the elaborate oblique and large almond-shaped eye which we know from his quartzite statue, JE 43611. These alabaster chapel reliefs, however, one from the left interior lower scene, and one from the right exterior lower scene, are the most baroque examples we have of his relief style, surpassing even the elaborate detail of the wooden chariot from his tomb. The confrontation of Thutmose IV with this ornate style to Amun rendered in an archaic manner is startling. (fig. 21).[172] Whatever the reason for this stylistic variation, it need not be attributed to Amenhotep III since the style was already current in Thutmose IV's sandstone court.

There is a reference on the Lateran obelisk[173] to the renewal of Amun's bark by Thutmose IV, and one might assume this bark shrine had been planned to complement the new boat.   Barguet has already mentioned that the name of this shrine is known,[174] but he did not publish the text provides the name. In fact it appears twice--on the left and right door jambs of what must have been the main, and perhaps only, entrance. The texts are identical: "The king of Upper and Lower Egypt Menkheprure: he made as his monument for father Amun-Re, making for him a temple of white alabaster of Hatnub, (called) Thutmose kha khau who receives the crowns of Amun. May he do given life."[175]

The questions remaining concern the form of the shrine and where it once stood, if indeed it was utilized by the kings. Van Siclen has suggested that the chapel may have been set up in the Thutmose II/Thutmose IV court before one of the north doorways.[176] His proposal takes into consideration that the shrine abutted a wall or other structure due to the placement of the vertical torus molding in front of the back corners. While this may still be a possible solution, there are as yet no fragments of back door jambs, while there is a large slab of undecorated alabaster (if squared it would be 1.7 m. on a side) finished on one large surface which could have formed part of a back wall for the structure. Since not all of the blocks for this structure are in evidence, we must await further study to be more certain about the form. Van Siclen is quite certainly correct about the chapel's original home in the vicinity of the peristyle court, however.[177] If our notion (and this is perhaps how it should be considered) that this was a close-ended bark shrine is correct, then a placement against the southern court wall, east of Van Siclen's proposed location of Amenhotep II's shrine might be possible. The unfinished decoration would have faced into the court's corner in this event. The double peristyle court itself provides little available space to locate such a structure. To rest the bark just outside would have been natural. Since blocks are still missing from this sanctuary, however, no placement can be certain.

Following Thutmose IV's building activity around this court, Amenhotep III himself seems to have added a door to the edifice before he destroyed more than half of his father's structure.[178] At the time he pulled down the shrine, which also fell in the area to be affected by the Third Pylon, Amenhotep did not use all the alabaster blocks as foundation fill. A few were left about and were later used in the foundation of the Second pylon, but only after Akhenaten's henchmen mutilated them. One such piece was re-used by Ramesses II as a statue base for a colossal alabaster group of Amun and the king. It was placed against the north flank of the IInd pylon.[179] This shrine was once among the most beautiful and luxurious monuments Thutmose IV had made.

13.5. Statue dedication from the Colonnade of Thutmose I. Fig. 24[180]

On the east face of the masonry surrounding Hatshepsut's southern obelisk, Thutmose IV left a relief depicting a statue of himself. Behind it were two registers of priests carrying offerings for the statue. In front of the statue is a retrograde endowment text for the image and for one of Thutmose III. This text gives the only record of the king's "first campaign of victory". That historical aspect of the inscription will be dealt with in Chapter 6.

The only text preserved from the statue scene is one vertical line behind the figure of the statue "...in the mouth of the living, his heart being extended like Re forever". The endowment inscription itself is written both vertically and horizontally. A translation follows here.

" 1) ... with great preparation for this temple in excess of what had been formerly.

sht bread prepared of 10 oipe	2
sm3t-ᶜ bread prepared of 10 oipe	2
tswrt bread prepared of 30 oipe	2
bit ᶜ3t bread prepared of 10 oipe	20
bit-snw	20

Total breads for divine offering	155
Beer of des jars, prepared of 4 oipe	4

10) together with giving to it wine, 1 hin, from the jar which his 11) Majesty placed, and milk, 1 hin, as an offering, its meat offering 12) being flesh of the flank [for Amun] at every festival 13)...[placing offerings] before this statue whose name is Menkheprure who subdues the Nine Bows daily 14)... the other statue of Osiris, the king of Upper and Lower Egypt Menkheperre, vindicated, which is beside it. One shall place 15) ....1 white bread, fruit...[//]wt and honey thereto from the Treasury of the Palace, 1.p.h., grain (?) 16)...[half line missing ...] [Amun], and poultry from the estate of the Treasurer on the festival of the New Moon. 17) ...the morning of the Neheb-kaw festival. One shall offer to him 18) ... [portions of the] divine offerings of [Amun-Re] ... 5, and honey offerings, 5 jars from the Treasury of the Palace, 1.p.h. (the last adverbial phrase later changed into "according to the utterance of Amun")[181] 19)..from booty of his Majesty from [////]na, defeated, from his first campaign of victory. 20)...nekheb[182] fields of the house of him who made

him. My Majesty did this in order to cause that my statue endure permanently in [the house of Amun] 21)...belonged ...[fashioned with] the sundisk on the head, [183], the two plumes on top (or "and with horns), living and enduring by the palace, 1.p.h. 22) [half a line lostso that the offerings which] my Majesty [placed] may [endure] [in the temple of Amun][184] before my statue forever."

The statue of the king, as it appears in the remaining relief scene, was a striding figure holding a mace in one hand and a staff in the other. Barguet likened it to the guardian statues from Tutankhamun's tomb antechamber and suggested it stood, with the statue of Thutmose III, before the door to the Fifth pylon.[185] He also suggested that the statue was made of wood. This cannot be proved or disproved. One might suggest, however, that if such a wooden statue existed, it was adorned with a crown of precious metal of the type called "feather crown".[186] The text near the end of the endowment, though extremely laconic, appears to describe the king's statue with the sundisk on his head and the double plumes on top. This could refer to the statue's headdress.[187]

13.6 An over-lifesize (2.8 m.) quartzite statue of the king is exhibited in the Cairo Museum under the Journal Entry number 43611. (See figs. 25-26). The piece was found in this same Colonnade of Thutmose I bearing the statue offering dedication but has received little publication until recently.[188] Thutmose IV originally appeared in a striding stance holding before him with both hands a ram standard. This is the earliest example so far known of this standard-bearer type, but here the standard of Amun has been broken away (by Atenists?). The outline remains, however. This work is certainly the king's most stunning and illustrates a second facial style in which Thutmose is shown with a strongly oblique eye, a long straight nose and a generous mouth. This same visage appears on the alabaster shrine in two instances and on several peristyle court scenes.[189] The statue is not named in its preserved inscription, but its original placement near the single obelisk of Thutmose III and Thutmose IV in the Oriental Temple is tantalizing as a suggestion. A painted representation of the same sort of statue named "Amun who hears prayers" appears on the wall of Amenhotep si-se's Theban tomb (TT 75) among the works prepared for Karnak Temple by Thutmose IV.[190] The Karnak temple region for "Amun who hears prayers" was in the gateway of Eastern temple. We cannot be certain about this suggestion, but it is sure that this statue is a major monument of Thutmose IV's reign:

Socle: 1) The Horus Strong Bull perfect of diadems, given life (facing) beloved of Amun, lord of the thrones of the Two lands, [king] of all the gods,   2) Two Ladies, enduring of kingship like Atum, abundant of monuments, beloved of the gods; 3) Golden Horus, powerful of the khepesh,

Upper and Lower Egypt, lord of the Two lands Menkhepeure, the king who makes monuments in the Temple of Amun, 5) the son of Re Thutmose kha khau, given life, stability, dominion like Re forever, did for him.

Back pillar: 1) The Horus Strong Bull perfect of diadems, the King of Upper and Lower Egypt Menkheprure ruler of Truth[191] the Good God, son of Amun, protector of Ka[mutef...] 2) as an excellent work, the son of Re Thutmose kha khau, a son beneficial to the heart of him who bore him [///].

Right:1)The king of Upper and Lower Egypt, lord of diadems, Menkheprure ruler of Truth, great of love in the Temple of Amun. He gave victory over every land; he gave to him the Southerners like the Northerners, [all] lands [///].

Left:1)The king of Upper and Lower Egypt, lord of the Two lands, Menkheprure, my arms are under the god,[192] my heart being joyful. I give praise to the king of the gods to his beautiful face; the love of the sovereign [///] 2) the son of Re Thutmose [beloved] of Amun [///].

Broken text between the legs: 1) life, stability, dominion [///] 2) Horus, enduring [///].

13.7. In the court between the Fifth and Sixth pylons is a partially enclosed area constructed by Thutmose III north and south of the temple's east-west axis. On the south wall of this enclosed area is a relief of Thutmose IV, usurped by Ramesses II before Amun and followed by [Amunet].[193] The erased forms of Amun and Amunet were not restored after an Atenist attack, but the king's image is relatively unharmed. There may have been a mirror image on the north side executed in paint only. At least the cartouches of Ramesses II there suggest he placed them on a painted image. There is little to learn from this scene, since the wall space was unused before Thutmose IV's reign and continued to be largely ignored.

13.8. The Lateran obelisk.[194]

On the opposite side of Karnak, Thutmose completed a monument for his grandfather Thutmose III. The ancestor had commanded the erection of a single obelisk, an unusual event commemorated by a series of scarabs bearing both Thutmose III's and Thutmose IV's names.[195] It is still unclear whether Thutmose III ever saw the attainment of his objective,[196] for Thutmose IV claimed to have found the obelisk lying on its side on the southern side of Karnak, near the artisans' workshops. In fact the king in his added inscription stated specifically that the obelisk had been lying there for 35 years. Unfortunately the historical significance of that span of years is entirely beyond our present day understanding; the inscription tells us nothing about whether the monument had been left unerected of that span of years is entirely beyond our present day understanding; the inscription tells us nothing about whether the monument had been left unerected due to the death of Thutmose III, or had been deliberately abandoned.[197] Nor is it clear that the number designated the length of Amenhotep II's reign,[198] although that is not impossible.   It is apparent only that Thutmose IV was aware, for whatever reason,[199] how long the obelisk had been lying on the ground, and we can presume that he believed that the gods and other readers of the inscription also understood the chronology. To honor his grandfather Thutmose raised the obelisk on the east side of Karnak before the small temple of Thutmose III--Barguet located the base of the monument behind the temple of Ramesses II. (The obelisk itself has been in Rome since 357 A.D.)[200] The king's description of the emplacement-- at "the upper door of Karnak before or opposite Thebes"[201]-- agrees with Barguet's find; for,as the excavator pointed out, the eastern door to the enclosure of Ramesses II was named in one of its scenes; it was termed the "upper door of the Temple of Amun"[202] just as in the 18th dynasty text. In fact Thutmose IV used the prescribed site of his ancestor who referred to the "upper open court of the temple, near Karnak" (wb3 hry hwt ntr r h3w 'Ipt-Swt).[203]

Thutmose IV decorated the monument with a vertical line of text on either side of the older inscription on each face. He included a small scene above each text[204] and one short dedication on the pyramidion. With the exception of the vignettes, Thutmose IV's contribution to the Lateran obelisk is well-published (a recent work by Martin does note the small depictions on the obelisk);[205] for that reason the major text is given below only in translation. The vignettes, however, deserve note first.

The four small representations above the text depict Thutmose IV offering to Thutmose III's Horus name. Although in three scenes the king is shown in a standing offering pose, the scene from the south face is unusual; it portrays a seated figure, wearing the Double crown, and offering an ankh to the Horus name of Thutmose III. The seated figure is labelled as Thutmose IV! "The Good God Menkheprure, given life, like Re, beloved of Amun. Take for yourself life for your nose!" It is certainly uncommon to have the living king speak to a deceased one while using phraseology normally employed by gods. To show the king seated is even more surprising since he appears as the god granting life. If Thutmose IV's artisans have not made an error, then he has shown himself in the guise of god Amun. The main text is as follows:

North right: "The Good God, perfect of diadems, enduring of kingship like Atum, powerful of khepesh who subdues the Nine Bows, the king of Upper and Lower Egypt, Menkheprure, who takes possession with might, like the lord of Thebes; great of strength like Montu, whose victories father [Amun] gave over all foreign countries, he to whom the ignorant lands come, fear of him being in their bellies, the son of Re,Thutmose kha khau, beloved of Amun-Re Kamutef, given life.

left: The king of Upper and Lower Egypt, beloved of the gods, whose beauty the ennead adore; who propitiates Re in the Day bark; who adores Atum in the Night bark;[206] the lord of the Two lands, Menkheprure; who embellishes Thebes forever; who makes monuments in [Kar]nak. The ennead of the Temple of [Amun] is content because of what he did; the son of Atum of his body, his heir on his throne, Thutmose kha khau, beloved of Amun-Re.

South right: The son of Re, Thutmose kha khau: He erected it in [Karnak], its pyramidion being made of djam. Its beauties illuminated Thebes, it being inscribed in the name of his father, the Good God, Menkheperre. The king of Upper and Lower Egypt, lord of the Two lands, Menkheprure, beloved of Re, did this in order to cause that the name of the father might remain enduring in the House of [Amun]-Re. The son of Re, Thutmose kha khau, given life, did for him.

left: The king of Upper and Lower Egypt, lord of performing a ritual Menkheprure begotten of Re, beloved of [Amun]-Re. Indeed it was his Majesty who completed [decorated?, snfr][207] the very great sole obelisk which the father, the king of Upper and Lower Egypt Menkheperre, brought, after his Majesty found this obelisk, it having completed 35 years lying on its side in the hands of the artisans on the southern side of Karnak. My father commanded that I erect it for him, for I am his son and his protector.

West right: The king of Upper and Lower Egypt, Menkheprure, chosen of Amun, foremost of [damaged[208]] whom he loved (?) more than any king. At the sight of its beauties he rejoiced in as much as he had placed it in his heart. And he placed [the Southerners] under his supervision, the Northerners bowing to his fame.

He made as his monument for father Amun, erecting for him the very great obelisk at the Upper Door of Karnak opposite Thebes. The son of Re, beloved of him, Thutmose kha khau, given life, acted for him.

left: The king of Upper and Lower Egypt, Menkheprure the eldest son, beneficial [for him who made] him; he who made all the temple endowments (htpt-ntr). He knew the excellence of his plans, for he it was who led him over the beautiful roads, binding for him the Nine Bows under his sandals. Indeed his Majesty was vigilant in decorating monuments for his father. The king himself gave the instruction, being enlightened like "him who is south of his wall". He erected it "in the twinkling of an eye", and it purified the heart of him who created him, the son of Re, Thutmose kha khau.

East right: The Good God, powerful of khepesh, the sovereign who took possession with his victories, who placed his fear in the Beduin ,[209] his war cry in the bowmen of Ta-Sety; he whom father [Amun] brought up to perform the enduring kingship. The princes of all foreign countries were bowing to the fame of his Majesty, who speaks with his mouth, who acts with his hands. All things which he commands happen--the king of Upper and Lower Egypt,Menkheprure, enduring of name in Karnak (?),[210] given [life].

left: The king of Upper and Lower Egypt, Menkheprure, who magnifies monuments in Karnak with gold, lapis, turquoise and every precious stone; the great riverine bark of [Amun]userhet having been fashioned in new cedar which his Majesty cut in the land of Retenu it being worked in gold to its length; all its adornments being fashioned anew in order to receive the beauties of father [Amun] at his riverine procession The son of Re, Thutmose kha khau, given life, did for him.

Pyramidion South.   The king of Upper and Lower Egypt, Menkheprure, given life, beloved of Amun-Re, lord of the thrones of the Two lands,lord of sky."

The obelisk text is straightforward. Thutmose claimed to have covered the pyramidion in electrum (djam), an assertion that should probably be taken literally. The king honored his grandfather's memory by the single obelisk's erection, and he stressed Amun's solar affinities in this text. Thutmose IV was placing a Heliopolitan symbol within Thebes and therefore Amun, Amun-Re Kamutef, and even Montu are here named, while Re-Horakhty is never mentioned. However, both Thutmose III and Thutmose IV in parodying him call themselves within the prenomen cartouche, mr n r^c. On the north left side there is the mention of Re and Atum in the solar barks, but the erection of the obelisk itself is deemed "a monument for father Amun".

It is clearly Amun who is pre-eminent in the text as a whole. One might also note the text on the east left: there the new bark of Amun was described and the king even claimed to have sent an expedition to the Lebanon for the wood. It is thus most injudicious to assert that the emplacement of this obelisk was in any way an attack on Amun by adherents of solar cults. Earlier discussions[211] asserted that Thutmose III's Eastern chapel in front of which the obelisk stood was actually dedicated to the sun god, who appeared as Re-Horakhty in the later temple of Ramesses II. In fact only Amun appears on the Tuthmoside inscriptions; and the Ramesside temple is also in his name.[212] (Recall too the statue "Amun who hears prayers" which may have stood along the processional way in the area.) Karnak was Amun's precinct and never held a solar sanctuary until the 25th dynasty.[213] The Roman remains in Thutmose III's temple have a solar emphasis, but the association must have developed slowly at a late date.

13.9. Statues of Thutmose IV from Karnak. CG 42081, figs. 27-28,[214] is a statue of the king found in the Karnak cachette. Made of black granite and preserved from the neck to the knees, the statue now stands .85 m. high. The unusual feature of this piece is that it represents Thutmose as a falcon,[215] in the style of quite a few sculptures of the mid-18th dynasty.[216] It is even more interesting to note that a block from Thutmose IV's peristyle court shows a group of statues of the king donated to Amun, and one showed the ruler as a falcon.[217] This is not necessarily the same work (the statue wears a nemes. while the relief shows a Double crown), but it points to the type's inclusion in the repertoire of the period. Redford has suggested that the interest in these "divine falcon" images indicates the royal identification with the sun god[218] in the pre-Amarna era. This is unquestionably true in the case of Thutmose IV, but one should not ignore the intention here to magnify royal divinity by making the king into the falcon god. Indeed Redford suggested the same for Akhenaten who identified himself with Re-Horakhty.[219] The only text on the piece appears on the belt: "the Good God, lord of the Two lands, lord of performing a ritual, Menkheprure." Its original emplacement is impossible to reconstruct.

13.10. CG 42080 [220] was found before chapel 5 under the floor of the south court of the Sixth pylon. This famous double statue of Thutmose and his mother (fig. 8) was discussed in the last chapter where the texts were quoted. The statue may originally have stood in the south court, but it is not at all certain.

13.11 Karnak 781 [221] was a torso in red granite found in the court between the Vth and VIth pylons. The statue is now missing or at least it has not been identified in the Cairo Museum although Legrain included its text in his Repertoire. It is likely, since Legrain was the statue's finder only one year before he published the text, that the statue was never sent to Cairo but is still somewhere in Luxor. The belt identified the ruler as "the Good God, lord of the Two lands, Menkheprure, given life forever".

13.12 A limestone Osiride statue of Thutmose IV (fig. 29) affixed to a large stela-shaped backpillar and high base stands against the south face of the Sixth Gate at the Ptah Temple of Thutmose III.[222] The statue is headless and is 3.85 meters in height from the top of the back pillar to the ground; the base is .85 m. high, and the statue as preserved is 2.0 m. high by .56 wide by .33 deep as preserved. The statue would certainly have resembled the Osiride colossus of Amenhotep I[223] (BM 683) and should have worn either the white or double crown. The hieroglyphic texts all face right and run vertically to the left of the king's now-missing head and down the front of the mummiform figure as well. The text next to the head reads: "The good god Menkheprure beloved of Amun-re, given life". The text running vertically down the figure identifies "the good god, lord of the Two lands, Menkheprure, the son of Re of his body, Thutmose kha [khau] beloved of Amun-re (restored), given life". There is sign of more statues such as this one, but the original emplacement of this Osiride may not have been at the Ptah temple. The position of the colossus to the right of the entrance to the temple should have required texts facing left (as well as mention of the god Ptah(?). Perhaps other monuments like this one will surface.

13.13-14. Colossal Osirides.[224] 194 (figs. 30-31) Pillet found statues of Thutmose IV in white limestone which complemented the north enclosure wall of the Mut precinct in Karnak South. One of these statues may still be seen there where it lies in the temple of Khonsupakhered; the other statue is now exhibited on the porch of the Luxor Museum and bears the number J48.[225] Neither statue is complete, but that in the Mut enclosure is nearly so, being preserved to the lower legs; the other is broken below the crossed arms. Its measurements are as follows: 2.06 X .93 X 1.05 m.. The height of the statue in the Mut precinct is 4.0 m. Its other measurements are comparable to J 48.

Ramesses II usurped both of the Osirides; Luxor J48 has been recut facially in addition to inscriptionally. The Mut precinct work was not physically altered, and the text usurpation was accomplished with added plaster on the front of the statue. It is not possible to say whether these statues originally stood in the Mut precinct or whether they were dragged there from Karnak. Neither colossus mentions the goddess, but rather both the 18th and 19th dynasty texts are dedicated to Amun-Re. It has been said that Thutmose IV built Temple A in the Mut Precinct,[226] but that supposition cannot be supported by the excavated material.[227] One re-used sandstone block (placed up side down) was found there with the cartouche of the king. It preserves, in raised relief, two decorated sides (one with Amun's plumes) and has a depth of .90 m. (two ends are broken). This block was quite likely once part of a square pillar from Thutmose's peristyle court.[228] Other fragments from the building can be seen re-used in the Second and Ninth pylons, at the Khonsu temple, and in the outer wall of Ramesses IX, north of the VIIth pylon court.[229] Like this block of Thutmose IV, the Osirides may have been dragged to the Mut enclosure from Karnak Central. This is all the more likely in view of Mut's absence in the inscriptions:

Luxor J48[230] preserves, under the Ramesside text on the front portion of the supporting pillar: "beloved of Amun-Re king of the gods, lord of sky". On the left may be seen, "[beloved of Amun-Re] lord of the thrones of the Two lands, the son of Re, Thutmose kha khau, given life".

The Mut precinct statue shows on the front right: "beloved of Amun-Re lord of the thrones of the Two lands". The left is broken. The front of the statue's body shows one line of vertical text. "the Good God lord of the Two lands, Menkheprure, the son of Re of his body, Thutmose kha khau, given life forever". Contrary to the entry in Porter and Moss' Bibliography II[2], neither statue shows any text of Nectanebo I.

13.15. CG 17019 [231] is an obelisk fragment of red granite which appears to have come from Karnak. It is inscribed with a hymn to Re and appears to date from the era of Thutmose IV or Amenhotep III.

13.16. Blocks with the name of Thutmose IV have been found at Karnak but do not appear to come from any of the constructions previously mentioned. Letellier mentioned specifically a sandstone block which formed part of the foundation of a statue of Ramesses II in the court before the IInd pylon.[232]

13.17. Another sandstone block [233] can be seen in the excavated trench at the northwest corner of the Fourth pylon-- its position suggests it belonged to the peristyle building, but it is not sure. The block is inscribed with three cartouches: the first was probably Seti I's prenomen, but only the mn is now visible at the bottom of the cartouche. The text identifies: "[the King of Upper and Lower Egypt] Men[maatre] for his father [the king of Upper and Lower Egypt] Menkhepru[re], given life, the [son of Re] Thutmose kha khau, given life like Re forever". Certainly the block commemorated a restoration carried out by Seti I for Thutmose, most likely on the court. Letellier did not discuss the block in her publication of the court, although she once pointed out the block to me.[234]

13.18. The name of Thutmose IV appears at the end of Amenhotep II's great Karnak stela (variant to the Memphis historical inscription).[235] The dedication at the end was as follows: " It is the Good God, lord of the Two lands, lord of performing a ritual, lord of the khepesh, beloved of him who is within Thebes, Amun, the protector of him who is in Thebes, who makes the [festivals] of the temple of Amun lord of the thrones of the Two lands take place [daily], the son of Re, Thutmose kha[khau , given life like Re forever]". Thutmose IV apparently donated this stela which commemorated Amenhotep II's Syrian campaigns, but it is not clear that he drafted the text [236] rather than having the Memphis stela copied or having an older stela re-made.

Thutmose also inscribed a statue for his father and mother. 13.22. is a seated colossal limestone statue [237] from the south face of the Eighth pylon; it was mentioned in Chapter 3. An inscription of Amenhotep II on the VIIIth pylon was changed during the Amarna period so that all cartouches showed Aakheprure; in Helck's Urkunden [238] a note states that Menkheprure was cut over Amenhotep. Photographs of the scene demonstrate clearly that this was not the case. Thutmose never figured there in any way.

13.19. In the block field south of the First Pylon lie numerous remains from the Second Pylon foundations. Among these is a large sandstone lintel block belonging to Thutmose IV. The size (1.61 meters length by .79 meters preserved height by .78 depth) indicates the piece stems from a sizeable doorway, almost certainly from a granary given the content of the scene. The scene in sunken relief shows Thutmose IV on the right offering wine to a seated Amun who faces right. The king states, "I have brought for you all good and pure things and all offerings (htpwt)...". The god's figure has not been damaged, although his name appears to have been erased.[239]

Behind the king, but separated from him by a vertical incised line is the snake-headed figure of Renenutet termed simply "Mistress of Heaven". Most likely her presence is to be associated with the produce of the granaries, and this might link the lintel to such a structure. It may not be coincidental that the relief style, well-modelled and idealizing with little decorative embellishment, is strongly paralleled by the limestone blocks from a granary of Amun doorway mentioned earlier. Although the lintel is sandstone, perhaps the gate was of two materials.

13.20. <u>Karnak North.</u> Thutmose IV seems to have contributed to at least two of the doors in the Montu precinct, on the north and the south. A lintel[240] in his name was uncovered in foundation C of the forecourt to Montu's temple--it lay along the lower base of an obelisk of Amenhotep III. That last king dismantled monuments of Amenhotep II as well as Thutmose IV and re-used them beneath his Montu temple court. The sandstone lintel, incised with hieroglyphs painted in yellow, is apparently similar to elements of the 18th dynasty door on the north of the precinct. No measurements were reported, but the excavators stated that the width and batter were the same as on the standing door. The lintel block is unfinished and damaged on the right; the inscription on the left is surrounded by a border. The text names Amun, not Montu, "the king of Upper and Lower Egypt, Menkheprure, given life beloved of Amun-Re". The presence of Amun need not necessarily argue against a Montu precinct provenance for the block.

13.21 A sandstone jamb which may have belonged to the lintel 13.20 may still be seen among the blocks piled on the south side of the enclosure. The decorated surface shows the head of Thutmose IV in the <u>nemes</u> headdress facing a now-missing god. The text before the god preserves "Utterance: I have given". The text above the head of Thutmose names him "the king of Upper and Lower Egypt Menkheprure, the son of [Re] Thutmose kha khau, given life, lord of performing a ritual forever." Behind the protruding jamb begins the text of a god: "I have given...". There is no indication of what god(s) speaks. The relief is fairly well executed, but the king's eye is rather small though almond shaped as are all examples of the royal sculpture.

13.22. Foundation C also produced a block fragment [241] in the king's name. It too is of sandstone (no measurements) and is decorated on two sides. The inscription is in relief and supplies the last three names of the king's titulary. The other side of the fragment is incised and shows a falcon-headed Montu and identifies "[Montu]-herkhepeshef, beloved of Montu". The fragment was thus re-used later.

13.23. A more recent find from the Northern precinct,which is inscribed for Thutmose IV, is a sandstone lintel [242] found in 1971. The door element, some 2.3 m. in length, was found near the southeast interior angle of the enclosure wall. Its form and thickness show that it belonged to a door in a brick wall, and Jacquet suggested the fragment's position indicated the lintel fit the southern side of the destroyed enclosure wall whose foundations are under the Treasury. If this is correct, then the wall was built later than the limestone building in the area (Thutmose I). Thutmose's lintel is inscribed with three lines of text: Behdet Great God is named on a sundisk. Beneath was "the King of Upper and Lower Egypt, Menkheprure, beloved of Montu, the son of Re, Thutmose kha khau, given life forever".

14. Luxor Temple.

Thutmose IV is also responsible for monuments in the Luxor Temple enclosure dedicated to Amun. It appears from the recently excavated evidence that an edifice of some kind (perhaps a brick pylon), stood in what is now the forecourt of the temple.[243] It is likely that this building had a south face, at any rate, and a pylon would have had such in addition to a northern facing entry. Buildings of Thutmose III and Hatshepsut probably were associated with the gateway and its court. Thutmose IV added to the construction by erecting a colossal statue of himself against the south face of the [pylon]. He also left two large granite stelae there dedicated to Amun, the temple deity.

14.1 A monumental stela[244] has been discussed in Chapter 3 because Thutmose's mother and wife accompany him on it. During the excavation north of Ramesses II's pylon, along the processional way (and east of it) to the temple, the excavator found seated statues of Ramesses III, Thutmose IV (called Ramesses II in first announcement) and Amenhotep III. The stela of Thutmose IV appeared next as digging progressed toward the Ramesside pylon. As was said above, the monument was broken below the lunette, and the only published photo of it is quite poor. The stela bears a restoration text by Seti I.[245]

> Left: Amun-Re, lord of the thrones of the Two lands, lord of the sky. May he give all life and all [///]. The king of Upper and Lower Egypt, Menkheprure, the son of Re, Thutmose, lord of the khepesh [//] forever. The king's [mother], Tiaa.
>
> Right: Amun-Re, king of the gods, lord of the sky. May he give all life and all [//]. The king of Upper and Lower Egypt, Menkheprure, the son [of Re], [Thutmose kha khau]. [Great king's wife] Nefertiry.
>
> Center: "Renewal of the monument which the king of Upper and Lower Egypt, Menmaatre, did.

14.2 Excavations carried out by the Antiquities Service in 1980 unearthed a large black granite stela of Thutmose IV.[246] (fig. 32). The excavator, Mohammed Baha, discovered the monument beneath the surface, just north of the eastern obelisk of Ramesses II. The stela (1.6 m. high by 1.1 m. wide by .30 m. deep) has a considerable amount of text preserved on the front; the back is rough indicating it once was placed against another structure. An emplacement against the south face of a conjectured brick pylon mentioned would be quite likely.

Thutmose IV's stela is notable for several reasons. First, the scene, and text as well, have been recarved by Seti I. The Ramesside king's motivation may have stemmed from the stela's text which is a temple endowment setting out Thutmose IV's obligations to Luxor and its deities. Clearly then the stela was visible to Ramesses II who began new and expanded building projects at Luxor. Whether his new obelisk displaced (or removed) Thutmose IV's monument is unclear at present.

A second point of interest concerning the stela is its date in Year 1. The Sphinx Stela had been the only monument known with that first year number; the suggestion that it, however, was back-dated was made above due to references on the stela to works carried out by Thutmose IV during his reign. Here Thutmose IV describes a more modest achievement--the furnishing of Luxor Temple and endowment of its cult. Since the first year of a ruler was often occupied with building projects and renewals for temples, there is no reason to doubt the Year one on this monument. The third note of interest is the presence on this stela of Thutmose IV accompanied by his ka. Bell has recently discussed the Luxor Temple of Amenhotep III as the location for the cult of the royal divine ka. While there is no doubt further discussion to appear concerning the nature of royal deification and its expression at Luxor Temple, it is tempting to link the Thutmose IV stela with the temple's specialized focus.[247] A translation follows.

Lunette: (right): Behdety, great god, variegated of plumage. [Before Amun who faces right]: Utterance: I have given to you all health from me, Amun-Re, lord of his ỉpt, lord of sky, ruler of Thebes. [Before king]: Giving wine to Amun-Re, may he perform 'given life'. The good god lord of the Two land, Menkheprure, the son of Re, lord of diadems, Thutmose kha khau. I have given to you all health from me, given life like Re forever. [Behind the king the Ka name of the king carried by a Ka sign with human arms with a standard of the king:] The Strong Bull, perfect of diadems.

(left): Behdety, great god, variegated of plumage. [Before Amun who faces left]: Utterance: I have given to you all life from me, Amun-Re, lord of the thrones of the Two lands, King of the gods. [Before king]: Giving wine to Amun-Re, may he perform 'given life'. The good god, lord of the Two lands, Menkheprure, the son of Re Thutmose kha khau. I have given to you all health from me, given life like Re forever. [Behind king the Ka name again.]

(center): Renewal of the monument which the King of Upper and Lower Egypt Menmaatre did in the temple of father Amun-Re. Amun-Re, lord of the thrones of the Two Lands, lord of sky, the son of Re Sety Merenptah, given life like Re forever.

Inscription: 1) Year one, month two of Shemu, day 7 under the Majesty of the Horus, Strong Bull perfect of diadems, the Two Ladies' enduring of kingship like Atum, the Golden Horus, powerful of khepesh who subdues the Nine Bows, the Good God, the son of Amun, the protection of the Bull of his mother 2) the sacred image of the lord of Eternity, the living image of Re, who builds mansions, who establishes temples, who endows the divine images of the gods, who spends the night vigilant seeking what is beneficial for 3) Amun in all his cult places. The king is vigilant concerning him who engendered him, free of boasting concerning what was commanded to him. Seeking occasions for establishing his temples [with offerings] according to their former local custom 4) He [endowed] his temple, it being increased over what had been formerly, for he knew that he [several groups lost] his [/////], the King of Upper and Lower Egypt Menkheprure [/////] enduring upon his seat, the son of Re Thutmose kha khau, given life. 5) The king instituted the festival anew for father Amun, lord of the thrones of the Two lands [several groups lost] when [third of the line lost] 6) [several groups lost] his beloved favorite place. Now he instituted for him [remainder of line lost] 7) [six groups lost] beer, wine [///], breads, meats, and [rest of line lost] 8) [six groups lost] y t3 im3[t] [rest lost] 9) šdw m [///] it ʾImn r [rest lost] 10) wine [////y] wine [rest lost] 11) [traces only] 12) [//h////] in order to magnify the offerings more than [rest lost] 13) f [///]w ḥk3 [several groups lost] this festival in the tem[ple of Amun 14) [stray signs] 15) [Thutmose kha khau] given life [rest lost] 16) [stray signs] 17) ʾiw [rest lost] 18) [stray signs] 19) the northern countries [rest lost] 20) Every [///]y its offering [third line lost and every good thing (?)] in order that [stray signs] 21) as [excellent] counsel [third line lost] seeking [third line lost] rdi ḥr nh[w] [rest lost] 22) ḥ3 [two-third line lost] divine Ka of Amun (k3 ʾImn nṯr) 23) [third line lost] Ṯhut[mose kha khau] [he] acted [for father Amun rest lost].

From the Luxor Temple stela we learn that Thutmose IV was intent upon identifying with Amun-Re, both as son and as "living image", a description he used more than once. He did not claim to have built a temple at Luxor but generally referred to himself as one who built temples and mansions. Rather he specifically emphasized his renewal of the cult thus suggesting the importance of his kingship to Amun his father. In the fragmentary inscription which remains no mention of the Opet festival appears, but the tantalizing appearance in line 22 of the "divine Ka of Amun"(?) may warrant attention. We are inclined to consider this the first monument made for Thutmose IV, although the date recorded on it need not be his accession date. The Sphinx Stela, if it was a retrospective inscription as proposed earlier, might provide the date of accession as a natural "back-date".[248]

14.3. The colossal statue of Thutmose IV, figs. 33-34,[249] must have been a very fine monument indeed. It is now preserved only in small fragments representing the base and right foot, parts of the short wig with fillet (worn by Thutmose on reliefs from the Karnak peristyle court), and a portion of the knee with fingers laid on it. This colossus of the seated king wore a wig topped by Double crown; a dorsal pillar was inscribed with the names of the king--fragments of prenomen allowed Abd el-Razik to correct the original identification of this colossus as Ramesses II. Name rings containing toponyms of both Nubian and Asiatic provenance decorate the base of the black granite statue. Captive foreigners appear in incised relief above the rings, and in the front the unification symbol separates the southern toponyms from the northern ones.   While Abd el-Razik gave a handcopy of these place-names, he did not attempt any translation or identification of them.   But this statue provides the best topographical list for Thutmose IV, and as such deserves discussion.   The chariot found in the royal tomb (KV 43) identifies quite traditional enemies for the 18th dynasty and is difficult to evaluate historically. The statue, while still not an historical document, is similar to other toponym lists, and as such, can be better compared.   (See Chapter 6.)

Abd el-Razik has estimated the statue's original height at 10 meters; it rested on a base some 4.05 X 2.2 m.. That the colossus originally faced south is indicated by a greater height on the base on that side; the point was made by Abd el-Razik that this is a consistent feature of colossal statues both at Karnak and Luxor, and as such is a valid criterion for the statue's orientation.[250] The conclusion is confirmed by the orientation of the bound captives whose heads point south around the base. The possibility that the base was turned around at some date after its near destruction should not be omitted, however. We cannot be sure that the colossus always faced south.

A description of the base and its inscription follows: (See fig. 34). The published handcopy does not indicate the direction in which the signs face--a point of some significance in numbering place-names. On the front of the base a sm3 sign is tied up with the northern plant on the viewer's left, the southern one on the viewer's right. The toponyms are divided geographically in this same manner, and are to be read from the center to the corners.

South side of base:
left: 1) [N]hryn 2) [Th]sy 3) [Sngr (?)] [251] 4) [//]n3 [252]

right: 1) [K]š ḫst 2) [Mi]w 3) [?] 4) [?]

East side of base: (southern toponyms continued):
5) Gwrwbw 6) Inknn3 7) Tmkr 8) G[b]š3wy 9) [?] 10) [W3]w3[t] 11) K3ti3
12-15 fragments

Left:1) Nahrin 2) Takhsy 3) Babylon (?) 4) Sidon/Qatna (?)

Right:[253] 1) Kush defeated 2) Miu 3) ? 4) ? 5) Gurubu = Koloboi of

Strabo, a region between the Nile and Red Sea below the Fifth Cataract.
6) Inkenna, a Nilotic area between Napata and Meroe (?).
7) Temker = Tungurv in Darfus.
8) Variant of B̲g̲-s̲g̲3̲, the political district of the Bayudor steppe (?).
9) ?   10) Wawat   11) Katia, unidentified.   12)-15) Fragments.

Each identified name from this statue of the king is attested in lists of the
mid-18th dynasty, excluding the last, Katia, which until the discovery of this list was
known only from Soleb under Amenhotep III. The prototypes for this list exist
in Thutmose III's and Amenhotep II's lists; the Nubian section was obviously copied
directly from a list of the latter pharaoh which surrounds Hatshepsut's southern
obelisk at Karnak.[254] Thutmose left his statue endowment on the same masonry.
One reads there. (#'s 9-12) Gwrwbw Inknn3 Tmkr Gbš3gi. This group represents,
therefore, the places commonly cited in this period, but the king also named a
region apparently not known before: Katia. This statue is then important in more
than one way: it testifies to Thutmose's active knowledge of Nubia, and it
demonstrates the king's work at an early Luxor Temple which must have had a
pylon of brick north of the present one.

15.   Thebes.

15.1. Mortuary Temple.[255] Thutmose IV built his mortuary temple south of his
father's not far from that of Wadjmose, son of Thutmose I. The temple enclosure
wall is still preserved in its outline, and stamped bricks from this temenos are fairly
numerous. [256]   Recent work in the precinct by the University of Pisa has produced
portions of faience stelae from the northeast section of the enclosure wall. Some
appear to have been gold encrusted. Similar plaques decorated the wall in the
enclosure of Thutmose III.[257] A brick pylon fronted the complex and a smaller one
was set up within the second of three terraces. The Italian mission working on the
upper south terrace discovered remains of five foundation deposits as well as
fragments of decorated blocks which came from the temple itself.[258]

The portico to the temple was placed on the third level; it was a double
colonnade some 172 feet wide which gave way, through a red granite door sill, to
a large peristyle court. The court contains a triple colonnade at the back and sides,
and a double at the front; there is a small doorway on the south. The sanctuaries
and rooms at the west end of the temple are poorly preserved but were reached
through a pillared hall. Ricke has restored the cult rooms [259] on analogy with
Thutmose III's temple. This reconstruction is supported by the finds of relief
fragments from the back of the temple which show Amun and the king. The
foundation hollows are the major indication of the mortuary complex, but some
stone foundation is in place on the south, and a small amount of pavement remains

in the back of the temple.

The mortuary temple was originally decorated in painted sandstone relief, some fragments of which are extant: the few identifiable pieces depict the king and, at least once, Amun-Min. [260] Recently two joining blocks which may come from the temple[261] (figs. 35-36) took my notice in a storeroom of the Cairo Museum. The scene may have come from the pylon gateway to the first colonnade or to the peristyle court, since it is in sandstone but in sunken relief and yellow-painted. Only a scene from a right wall or doorway is in evidence here. The blocks show Thutmose IV, with a large almond shaped eye (compare JE 43611) wearing the nemes and offering nu pots (inscription says kbhw "cool water") to an enthroned statue of Amun. The king is followed by a fecundity figure carrying an offering table draped with was scepters and ankhs and piled with hes vases and a was scepter; the only remaining epithet for the god is "lord of the sky", but the text also shows the remainder of "[I have given to you] all stability and dominion". Thutmose is identified by his cartouches and the legend: "[gi]ven all [li]fe, [all] stability and dominion like Re forever. I have [br]ought to you every good and pure [thing]."

The objects from Theban temples given by Petrie to the Victoria and Albert Museum are now in the British Museum. The reliefs originally published by Petrie and more recently by Adams and Stewart[262] resemble the Karnak court relief where the king appears on the walls with a rather short face, small almond-shaped eye and straight nose. The style of the incised blocks mentioned above resembles more the king's face in his tomb, on tomb objects, and in a more elegant technique, on the alabaster chapel, as well as the stelae from Giza with Nefertiry. These examples give the king a jaw which protrudes out beyond the level of his nose (prognathous), a longer sloping nose, fuller lips and a generally taller face. This image of the king may be simply one of two interchangeable identifying styles in the reign. It is worth consideration, however, that the two styles represent changing aspects of the king. The first style described is a conservative appearance which may suit the king in his cult performances duplicating the work of his father and grandfather; the second style is distinctive and somewhat exaggerated, often using the larger oblique eye style. Perhaps this is the king's image emerging in concert with his own form of kingship on his own brand of monuments.

Inscriptions from the temple are few, but Petrie unearthed two stelae dedicated by the king: UC 14372 [263] represents only the lower part of a limestone stela which showed Thutmose before [Amun], but the text below is of some interest. "Settling the enclosure of Menkheprure with the kharu as plunder of his Majesty from the town of Gez[er]." The second stela, Oriental Institute 1363,[264] is nearly complete and is of the same type. Thutmose offers to Amun-Re, lord of the sky. "Settling the Kushites, defeated, whom his Majesty brought back from his victories (nhwt)." The stelae may indicate that Thutmose IV used captive foreigners as workers for his funerary temple--this practice was known in other temples and was followed by Amenhotep III as well. [265] The texts allude to victorious campaigns of the ruler, and the historicity of these events will be discussed in Chapter 6. A third stela and a fragment of a fourth of this same type were recently found by the Italian mission [266] working in the area. The new stela is a duplicate of the Oriental Institute stela; the fragment preserves only "from his victories".

Petrie also found a stela fragment (UC 14374) in the temple which represented a king, identified as Menkheprure, offering a bouquet to a goddess (?) on horseback; the deity has been called Astarte due to the presence of a horse, spear and shield. [267] The earliest attested reference to Astarte occurs in the reign of Amenhotep II, and the goddess is mentioned on Thutmose IV's chariot; the date is therefore possible; the the plaque itself is very crudely incised and stylistically would be more suitable to a Ramesside date. This cannot be stated conclusively, but it is likely the small stela was a later votive offering. One last stela (originally Chicago Art Institute 93.75, but its present location is not known to me) [268] very likely should not have been assigned to the mortuary temple. It is a false-door stela showing Thutmose IV smiting before Ptah; the dedicant Istu and his wife Yu kneel in a lower register. The object may well have come from Memphis originally and belonged to the group of stelae from that site which depicted the king smiting before Ptah.[269]

The hieratic texts from foundation blocks, wine jar sealings, and jar fragments [270] unearthed by Petrie are not dated and provide little historical interest. The recent Italian expedition has, however, unearthed a domestic building south of the enclosure wall which may have housed the technical personnel who built the complex.[271] The pottery is largely painted, and some contains the remains of foods. The architecture is clearly dated by the stamped bricks, and the building is a unique example of living quarters from the reign. The magazines on the north are preserved , and in one of the living rooms off a central courtyard, the excavators found a terracotta plastered bathtub.

15.2 The tomb of Thutmose IV (KV 43)[272] . Howard Carter, working under the auspices of Theodore Davis, investigated the small west valley in the Biban el Moluk in January 1903 and, on the 18th of the month, opened the door to the tomb. As Davis was on his way to Aswan, Carter entered with Tytus and inspected the contents. [273] The tomb of the king is an elaborated version of other mid-18th Dynasty royal burial places, such as KV 35 the tomb of Amenhotep II. KV 43 has additional chambers which caused an additional turn of axis in the burial chamber's orientation. The tomb was marked by foundation deposits[274] outside the entrance (two were found in small holes before the door, but Thomas suggested there must have been several more, since KV 22 produced at least five deposits,[275] and the British Museum does possess two faience foundation plaques terming the king "beloved of Osiris".[276] The two deposits included stone vases, saucers, model tools and faience plaques. Four of the vases are now in the Metropolitan Museum,[277] the rest in Cairo. Weinstein [278] pointed out that several objects must have originally been intended for funerary temple use; they are inscribed for the king "beloved of Amun" rather than "beloved of Osiris" as was normal. One stone saucer (CG 46004) was usurped from Hatshepsut, and it too must have come from the temple workshops: it was inscribed "the good God Menkheprure, beloved of Osiris". Exactly where these objects came from is difficult to say, although the workshops of the mortuary temple area seem likely. Another bowl belonging to Hatshepsut was usurped by Thutmose IV for non-mortuary use. [279] It was probably intended for dedication at Deir el Bahri. Hatshepsut dedicated the bowl to her venerable ancestor-next door, Nebhepetre Mentuhotep, and Tuthmosis IV changed her title from "Good God" to "Osiris" while adding "Good God Menkheprure". Perhaps he then used it in the same way Hatshepsut had.   This analogous re-use and Weinstein's pertinent comments concerning the name of Amun on funerary objects do indicate kings re-used objects found outside the Valley, and we should not necessarily assume Hatshepsut's burial provided material for the tomb.[280] It is true that a scarab of the queen was found outside KV 43, as was a wood cartouche of Thutmose I.[281]   This kind of material, found in rubbish, could have easily been strewn there from the nearby tomb of Hatshepsut. This refuse of objects is quite different from finds buried and left in the tomb itself.

Thutmose's tomb was of course violated in antiquity; a famous hieratic graffito on the south wall of Room F records a re-burial conducted by the Overseer of Treasury Maya for Horemheb in his 8th year. He affixed his own seal, over the earlier necropolis seal, on the door to the king's pillared hall and burial chamber.[282] Obviously the tomb had been robbed already less than a hundred years after the king's death, but it appears that the thieves did not steal or burn the royal mummy. The king's body, so identified on his wrappings, was discovered in KV 35 among a cache of bodies reburied in Dynasty 21. [283] The wooden coffin in which he was placed was of late manufacture but was inscribed for him. The anatomists have been convinced of the identification of this mummy as Thutmose IV (especially because of the striking resemblance to Amenhotep II), and it would seem unreasonable to doubt their conclusions and the inscribed evidence as well. Thus the tomb's violation in the 18th dynasty was confined to theft of valuables.

The decoration in Thutmose IV's tomb was not completed; some walls of the first two chambers, C and F, are painted with scenes of the king before Osiris, Anubis and Hathor (figs. 13, 37), but even one of these was unfinished.[284] Four subsidiary rooms off the pillared hall contained the major finds from the tomb,[285] excluding the magnificent chariot of the king found in the hall itself. The only body found was that of a boy which had been entirely unwrapped and was left resting upright against a chamber wall.[286] Since the canopic jars of Thutmose IV's son, Amenemhet, were found in the tomb, it has been suggested that this mummy was the prince himself who perhaps pre-deceased his father.[287] It should be recalled that this prince appeared in Th.tb 64 along with other royal children. The canopics of a daughter, Tinetamun, were also found, but her body was nowhere apparent.[288]

Since the tomb has been published fully (the objects, that is), there is little to add concerning the finds, with the exception of the present location of some Davis Collection pieces not mentioned in Porter and Moss' Bibliography. On this see Appendix I at the back of this Chapter.[289] The tomb itself is noteworthy for its expanded size and for its introduction of the "magical niches" [290] which housed figures placed on bricks inscribed with pertinent spells. These magical figures were first found in the earlier 18th dynasty (Thutmose III) and continued in use in niches until the 19th dynasty; but KV 43 was the first tomb to utilize the niches. Only one was cut out, but another was outlined in black. The paintings in the tomb are the first fully polychrome examples from a royal New Kingdom burial. The style is of the second type described within the Mortuary Temple discussion (4.15.1 above). Red paint grid lines are visible in some of these scenes; Robins has discussed the paintings from the tomb and suggested the artists used a 20-grid system for the royal and divine figures. This would be analogous to a system she found in operation during the Amarna and late 18th Dynasty.[291] The remains of a grid in Room C of the tomb sustain a 19 (not 20) grid standing figure form for the king and the goddesses on the wall. It would be hasty to attribute too much significance to these findings without further study. Thutmose IV's image is proportioned to accommodate a larger head and shorter leg between foot and knee. These need not have required a new grid system altogether but might have lent themselves to the temporary addition of a square to create the large head and torso emphasis apparently favored. One caveat--on this wall with the grid and on walls in Room F the god Osiris appears as a statue. His image, the central one in the Room C scene, is painted on a traditional 18 square grid; the 19th square accommodates the statue base. Is there significance for the scene as a whole here? We should note that the various artists at work followed the grid lines with varying attention; no two figures are exactly the same height, and they all draw the king's knee at different grid points. Great caution should be employed before we suggest new grid squares were in use in the reign.

The sarcophagus of the king [292] is also worth comment, since it represents a deliberate change from earlier fashion. Hayes discussed the sarcophagus [293] at length and concluded that Thutmose wished to express himself by enlarging his red quartzite sepulchre just as he did his tomb. In fact Hayes referred to the stone container as a "freak" and noted that the interior would have held the sarcophagus of Thutmose III with its lid on and with Thutmose IV's body lying atop it! The dimensions are 3 X 1.6 X 1.99 m.. The interior space is 2.71 m.long. X 1.32 wide

X 1.55 high and must, according to Hayes, have held inner coffins and a bier of some sort. This estimate gains credence when Thutmose's actual height, 1.64 m., is considered.

The texts which decorate the king's sarcophagus are often more elaborate than those on earlier ones, but this is probably due to the immense size of the coffin.[294] The king also relied more heavily on the Book of the Dead than did his predecessors and quoted quite freely, especially from the well-known Judgement in Chapter 125. Hayes has pointed out that the major changes used in decorating this enormous sarcophagus were conservative ones which returned to Middle Kingdom and early 18th dynasty solutions (e.g., the placement of the wedjat eye panel at the head end, and representations of four deities on either side). Since Hayes' study is far more complete than any which could be undertaken here; further comment would be superfluous.

Although there is no space to consider the tomb objects individually, it should be noted that the wealth of the tomb was great. The objects preserved to us are not spectacular, like Tutankhamun's, but the same range of materials certainly existed, and probably the burial was well-furnished. The faience is of rather high quality, and the wooden furniture pieces preserved are masterful examples of low relief. The one complete glass vessel and numerous fragments from the tomb also testifies to the quality of that craft in Thutmose's reign.

The sole text of any length (excluding the sarcophagus) is that from the chariot. This exquisite wooden specimen has relief scenes of the king around it which show him shooting enemies from his chariot with the aid of Montu-Re. The king wears the khepresh, has a sundisk with pendant uraei hanging above his head and wears the shebiu collar noted already several times as a signal that the king has a special role here. The role that Thutmose IV adopts on the chariot is that of the warrior sun god himself who performs the ritual defeat of Egypt's enemies thus restoring order over potential chaos (portrayed by the disarray of the foreigners). The scene has a close parallel in the stela from Amenhotep III's funerary temple (CG 34026)[295] where the king likewise has the sundisk over his head, rides his chariot with captive foreigners on it, and wears the shebiu collar. Thutmose IV wished to appear as the god in this instance. Bell has likewise commented on the presence of the shade behind Thutmose IV and Montu as an indication of the royal divinity.[296] I am not convinced that the god Amun need be the particular divnity with whom Thutmose seeks identification. The role is rather guided by the context, as here, by the presence of Montu. A translation follows:

Chariot of Thutmose:
Exterior right: "The Good God, beloved of Montu, clever in every work,

valiant on horseback like Astarte, stout-hearted among the multitude, lord of the khepesh, lord of performing a ritual, the Good God Menkheprure, given life like Re. The Good God, ruler of Heliopolis, lord of the Two lands, Thutmose kha khau.

Exterior left: The Good God, valiant and vigilant, a champion without equal, who performs with his hands more than the number of the Two lands, more than the sight of his army totalled in one place, the king of Upper and Lower Egypt, Menkheprure, powerfully virile. The Good God, lord of the Two lands, lord of performing a ritual, lord of the khepesh, Thutmose kha khau, given life like Re.

Interior right: The king of Upper and Lower Egypt, Menkheprure, the son of Re,Thutmose kha khau, lord of the khepesh like [Re]. Trampling all lands and all foreign countries. (Montu speaks): Utterance: I have given to you the khepesh and valiance in order to trample the Bowmen in their places. (Label for the god:) Montu, lord of Thebes, who smites those of Sety, who binds their noses.

Interior left: The Good God, lord of the Two lands, Menkheprure, the son of Re beloved of him, Thutmose kha khau, given life. Trampling every difficult northern country

(Montu speaks): Utterance: I have given to you valiance and victory over every foreign country according as I love you. (Label:) Montu-Re great of virility, Horus,the Theban, who overthrows all lands of all the Fenkhu.

List on Interior right:
1) [Ku]sh defeated 256 2) Karoy   3) Miu 4) Irem
5) Gurases 6) Tiurek

List on Interior left:
1) Nahrin 2) Sangar 3) Tunip 4) Shasu 5) Kadesh 6) Takhsy".

15.3 Tomb of Amenhotep III, KV 22.[297] Howard Carter, while digging in the Kings' Valley in 1915 turned to the site of Amenhotep III's burial. Having earlier discovered the foundation deposits before Thutmose IV's tomb, he searched for such caches here. He found five foundation deposits naming not Amenhotep but Thutmose IV.[298] Romer notes that the overall plan of KV 22, though elaborated by rooms not seen in KV 43, has a smaller burial chamber than that tomb and thereby betrays its foundation as a prince's burial place. From the lengthy discussion in Chapter 2 we have seen that prince Amenhotep was nearly certainly considered the throne heir. That Thutmose IV began his favored son's tomb construction should then hardly surprise us. However, in KV 22, decorated at the end of Amenhotep's long and eventful rule, his father's memory has not faded. The first decorated hall of the tomb shows Hathor receiving Amenhotep III into her embrace while the ka of Thutmose IV stands behind holding the staff of royal divinity as would any ka figure. The legend identifies "the living royal ka, lord of the Two lands, foremost of the Robing room (db3t), Horus Strong Bull Perfect of diadems". The ka of Thutmose holds a maat feather and ankh in his near hand and must be understood as participating in the king's preparation for eternity. There is no certainty in the suggestion, but perhaps Amenhotep III considered his father's involvement in the tomb to have continued throughout the son's reign due to the presence of the foundation deposits. The divine royal spirit was therefore awaiting Amenhotep III to accompany him as he meets his fellow deities.

16. Armant.

The excavators mentioned, in passing, that blocks of Thutmose IV (as well as of Amenhotep II) were re-used at the Armant temple.[299] Presumably both rulers added to the major 18th dynasty temple there, but none of these blocks have been published or described.

17 Tod.

Recent work by French excavators at the site of Tod's Montu temple resulted in the publication of new outlines for the temple structures through time.[300] The Thutmoside temple and pylon was of interest to the authors since Thutmose III was responsible for a major rebuilding effort. As with nearly every site outlined above and below, Thutmose IV made additions to temples in which his grandfather and father took interest. Bisson de la Roque had exhumed a number of blocks of mid-18th Dynasty date many years before, and Noblecourt and Leblanc provided description and photos of some of these. One is a particularly fine two-sided wall block dated by cartouche to Thutmose IV's rule.[301] The scene executed in limestone shows the king followed by a goddess (less likely a queen) with an elaborately coiffed tripartite wig holding her hand through a menat necklace.The goddess wears an archaic dress style. The quality of this relief is excellent and suggests that Thutmose IV's addition may have belonged to a shrine of some sort. The peripteral shrine of Thutmose III and Amenhotep II still stands at Tod as it once did before the inner gateway. One might add that the Thutmose IV relief shows a renewal text, and the authors did point out that the Ramesside rulers did little construction at the site but carried out the post-Amarna renewals as elsewhere.[302] We can be certain that the Thutmose IV work at the site stood for some time, perhaps until the Ptolemies rebuilt the complex.

18. <u>Elkab.</u> (Fig. 38). The desert way station of Amenhotep III at Elkab has two scenes in which Thutmose IV figures together with his son.[303] On either side of the entrance to Amenhotep's hall there are scenes showing the two seated kings, Amenhotep in front of Thutmose in both, receiving offerings from furnished tables. The kings are represented with their backs to the doorway and instead face in the direction of the sanctuary. As in the Thutmose IV's alabaster shrine this scene preceded the king before the divine bark. This temple was sacred to Nekhbet of Elkab, but Amun-Re is figured in it at least once.

The presence of Thutmose IV is difficult to explain, for it is not his <u>ka</u> which appears, but he himself. According to the text, which is nearly identical in both scenes, Amenhotep claimed to have "finished or decorated (<u>snfr</u>)" [304] the monument for his father. The meaning of the word is unclear in this context, for there is no evidence anywhere else in the temple, as there was on the alabaster shrine at Karnak, that Thutmose had contributed to the Elkab chapel at all. In a text from another scene, Amenhotep stated that he had "made a beautiful monument, a desert temple, anew, it being built in stone as a work of eternity for his mother, the Lady of Iunu-ro-Inet".[305] Unless the words m m3wt "anew" are added <u>pro forma</u> Amenhotep alluded to the presence of an earlier structure, and since he specifically mentioned using stone, one might think any earlier temple was of less durable material. It is conceivable such a chapel was built by Thutmose, but again there is not one element bearing his name to support the suggestion. (Even a wood or brick building would have had stone doorways.) We must suggest, given the extremely conservative style of relief in most of this temple, that Thutmose IV was king during the period in which the building was built but died before the relief decoration was carried out. Amenhotep III must have ordered the relief to be carved as one of his first acts. The temple has little of the characteristic style of Amenhotep's reign, but the proportions of the relief figures is consistent with Amenhotep's rule more than with Thutmose's[306]. Thutmose IV's appearance before his offering table, and Amenhotep III's as well, may indicate their kas received guaranteed proceeds from the temple offerings. The active and offering Amenhotep appears elsewhere in scenes.

Thutmose IV was termed in the scenes as follows: "the Good God, lord of the Two lands, Menkheprure, the son of Re, beloved of him, Thutmose kha khau, given all life, stability and dominion like Re every day." The only variation of epithets called him "the Good God, lord of the Two lands, lord of ritual (<u>ir ht</u>), lord of diadems".

19. <u>Edfu.</u>

The first indications of Thutmose IV's interest in Edfu Temple were noted by Gabra and Farid following their recent work at the site.[307] A right door jamb inscribed for "[The king of upper and low]er Egypt Menkheprure. He made [it] as a monument for father [Horus]." There is no doubt that an 18th Dynasty temple existed at Edfu. (A 17th Dynasty doorway was recently excavated from beneath the pylon enclosed court.) More elements may be expected as investigations continue.

20. Elephantine.

20.1.   Several blocks naming Thutmose IV have been found in re-used contexts.[308] Apparently they were utilized at least twice after Thutmose's reign, in a building of Ramesses II, then later in the temple of Trajan where they are still visible as foundation structure. DeMorgan showed a portion of a fluted sandstone column of Thutmose IV which was reused by Ramesses II. Thutmose's text names "the son of Re Thutmose kha khau, beloved of Amun-Re, lord of the thrones [of the Two lands], given life forever". It is obvious, at least, that a structure of Thutmose IV was present at Elephantine and in use in the Ramesside period. The dedication to Amun-Re is slightly unexpected, but need not indicate Thutmose's blocks were brought from elsewhere. Both Thutmose III and Amenhotep II are attested on the blocks from Trajan's building, and their dedications are largely to Khnum. Some of the blocks which lack a cartouche may belong to Thutmose IV. Two others (20.2) definitely belong to him and are probably architrave pieces; they give a portion of his titulary: "[enduring of king]ship [like Atum,powerful] of khepesh who subdues the Nine Bows, the king of Upper and Lower Egypt Menkheprure, the son of Re Thutmose kha [khau]."

20.3. A block of the king was also re-used in the quay at Elephantine, above the nilometer.[309] Lepsius illustrated only cartouches from one block, but he referred to more than one; the form of the nomen which he copied there is rare in writing ḫ^{c}w with the arm sign. The blocks illustrated both by DeMorgan and Lepsius demonstrate that Thutmose IV added to the major 18th Dynasty temple to Khnum at Elephantine. Amenhotep II[310] had built a court there as one of his architrave texts informs us; portions of his square piers with sed formulae on the bases are also visible and were executed in incised relief, thus suggesting an uncovered court. The monument is referred to as having been of sandstone.[311] Thutmose IV certainly decorated portions of this court as he did the court of Amada. Indeed the structure at Elephantine was probably a near duplicate of that Nubian temple but had been started earlier, probably by Thutmose II.[312] Thutmose IV probably added his name to the fluted columns which formed a porch to the temple proper and finished the architrave texts in the court as well. Amun-Re as well as Khnum figured as a god in this court. This agrees with the presence of that national god in Nubian temples generally.

20.4 A fragment of an obelisk in Aswan granite is now in the Cairo Museum (CG 17016) [313] but came either from the quarries directly (according to the inked entry on the shaft) or from Elephantine itself (according to the <u>Journal provisoire</u>). In either event it was meant for the temple of Khnum at Elephantine. The obelisk is preserved only to a height of 1.24 meters, and it lacks probably about the same measurement from the top. It is inscribed on one face with signs which face right; the obelisk was thus probably the left one of a pair. The inscription lacks only the large part of Thutmose's titulary: "...Thutmose kha khau. He made as his monument for his father Khnum, making for him two obelisks of the altar of Re. May he do 'given life' forever".

Martin pointed out recently that the text on Thutmose's obelisk was identical to that on Amenhotep II's temple obelisks from Elephantine, and it is likely that Thutmose intended to dedicate his obelisks there as well.It is not possible to say if the right obelisk was ever made, but the existence of this one demonstrates the king's dedication to Khnum's temple and also confirms his close connection to the works of Amenhotep II and Thutmose III at the site.

21. <u>Konosso.</u>

21.1-2. Two dated royal inscriptions are known from the island of Konosso,[314] and both appear to have documented military skirmishes for the ruler. The year 7 stela was mentioned above in Chapters 1 and 3; only its scene remains now. Discussion and translation of the year 7 or 8 text has been reserved for Chapter 6. We have noted already that the year 7 text includes the King's daughter and Great royal wife, Iaret; in the same year her name appeared at the Sinai. Both sites were near border outposts and may have represented far points for inspection tours. Konosso, at least, was one of several First cataract sites where expeditions regularly stopped and left graffiti (both leaving and entering the country). It is probable that Iaret in person and other royal family members accompanied Thutmose to Konosso on an official tour.

A discrepancy in the early publications of Konosso inscription crept into Porter and Moss' <u>Bibliography</u> which has since provided incorrect information. [315] DeMorgan claimed to have seen three major scenes for Thutmose IV, including two long texts. Both Champollion and Lepsius saw only one long text and two scenes (years 7 and 7/8). Lepsius even pointedly noted DeMorgan's error. DeMorgan's mistake concerned the cartouches of Thutmose IV which were cut above the representations and graffiti of the princes who visited in his reign. The scene mentioned by DeMorgan was above the cartouches of the king, but the king there was not Thutmose, and he was not identified.

There are only two scenes and one text; Porter and Moss' new edition will, no doubt, eliminate the third scene and second inscription. But until that time the user should beware the confusion.

Nubia

22. Amada.

22.1. Temple of Amada.[316] One of Thutmose IV's major building efforts (at least as now preserved) was in the small temple to Re-Horakhty and Amun-Re at the site of Amada in Lower Nubia. The chapel was otherwise wholly built by Thutmose III and Amenhotep II, acting in concert. The construction and decoration have been dated to the coregency period of those rulers, because the relief and inscriptions were clearly planned to represent both pharaohs.[317] The controversial question concerning Thutmose IV at Amada arises out of the heb sed formulae on his pillars there. As has been said above, some have felt that Thutmose's pillars commemorated his second jubilee, although scholars have differed on when that festival took place.[318] Thutmose IV converted the temple's court into a roofed pillared hall which utilized square piers similar to those of his Karnak court (and to other examples from 18th dynasty buildings). It is possible, however, that Amenhotep II had already achieved partial modifications in the court. His dedicatory stela referred to a stone pylon before a pillared festival court,[319] and it would not be surprising to learn that he added the piers and architraves without carrying out the decoration.[320]

Recently Van Siclen suggested that Thutmose IV carried out two modifications of the court, the first having added piers decorated in raised relief on one side which faced the side walls of the court.[321] There occurred the jubilee formulae. Van Siclen suggested that Thutmose IV later enclosed the court completely and turned the piers around so that the raised relief then faced into the central aisle. He was bothered greatly by the presence of incised relief on piers within a roofed structure.

Although Van Siclen's reconstruction is sensible to suit the evidence, there are two points to raise with respect to it. Van Siclen complains that Thutmose IV's appearance in the white crown on the first right pier scene is geographically incorrect opposite a red crown on the left pier. However, the king does not wear the red crown on the left; he wears the khepresh as is evident from the line drawings showing the double edges of that crown's back. The king holds his ḥk3 scepter which is specifically related to appearances in the khepresh.[322] Second, the incised faces of the square pillars cannot be equated with the raised relief scenes on the central aisle pillar faces, for the three incised sides are not decorated with sunken relief scenes but with large-scale hieroglyphic dedications to the king by various gods of Egypt and Nubia on the pillars. The same is true for the architrave texts. Only the pillar and architraves facing the central aisle and the side walls facing that aisle are carved in relief. This might have been so planned because bas relief took more time to finish and was best utilized at prominent locations seen from the processional way, while the incised relief texts could be achieved rapidly even in the poorly clastic

Nubian sandstone. These reservations concerning Van Siclen's suggestion are not intended to deny its logic.

Within the enclosed court each pillar bore the wish for a first occurrence and repetition of the heb sed. The wall scenes showed the king being introduced to Amun and Re-Horakhty as well as the sun god ordering the king's name to be recorded as Thutmose knelt before the Ished tree. The king also appeared as a youth being suckled by Hathor of Ibshek. A door lintel represented the king running with an oar. These scenes are common ones and appear, for example, in the Hypostyle Hall at Karnak [323], a room whose form and location was analogous to the Amada hall. They are also scenes which proclaim the kingship and its associations with the gods.

It would be most difficult to prove that Thutmose IV intended this room as a jubilee hall; certainly he expressed a desire for the sed on his pillars, but the scenes do not mention the celebration. It has been seen above that the king used both "first occasion" and "repetition" formulae at Karnak, and by now it is clear that we cannot be certain that the formulae indicate the celebration of any sort of sed festival with certainty. The association of the ruler with the significant rejuvenating power of the jubilee may, however, be supposed. It was undoubtedly the closeness to the gods which the kings of this period sought, and the sed was a powerful example of such intimacy.

The Amada Temple was recently fully published with a great deal of material. A translation of pertinent texts for Thutmose IV is therefore sufficient here. The inscriptions from the doors, wall, and pillars are not particularly unusual and might therefore be best left untranslated. It is of some interest, however, to note the various gods whom the king represented by image or name in his Hall C.

Gods
Behdet
Re-Horakhty
Amun-Re
Thoth (who gives birth
  to morning for the ruler [324])
Great god, lord of Sky
  foremost of Ta-Sety
Re-Horakhty-Atum
Khepri-(Re)
Atum, lord of Heliopolis
Ptah, lord of Truth
[Khnum], lord of Setjet
  (Sehel)
Khnum, lord of Senmut
Khnum within Elephantine
Montu within Armant

(Semna)
Bata, lord of Saka (Middle
    Egypt) [325]

Goddesses

Nekhbet
Wadjet, mistress of Per Nu
Isis, the great
Sakhmet
Bastet, mistress of Ankh Tawy
Weret-Hekau
Hathor, mistress of Ibshek (Faras) [326]
Anukis, mistress of heaven, within Elephantine
Nekhbet, white one of Nekhen (restored)

As one might expect,the divinities here represent several categories: a few are gods associated with kingship (northern and southern); the rest are either national or regional to Upper Egypt and Lower Nubia. The gods of Heliopolis are pre-eminent among the national ones. Bastet of Ankh-Towy was probably present due to association with Sakhmet and Isis. One of the the most interesting gods is Sesostris III who is called "lord of Sekhem".   This is no doubt a reference to the fortress of Semna which was named "Khakawre is powerful (shm)". [327] Most of the fortresses appear in inscriptions without cartouches; here the king's name is already supplied as the god.

The longest of Thutmose IV's texts at Amada is inscribed on the architraves; a translation follows, for the text contains what little information Thutmose supplied about the purpose of his addition to the temple.[328]

> Live the Horus, Strong Bull, perfect of diadems, Two Ladies, enduring of kingship like Golden Horus, powerful of khepesh (written 'scimitar') who subdues the Nine Bows, the king of Upper and Lower Egypt, lord of the Two lands, Menkheprure, the son of Re of his body, Thutmose kha khau, beloved of Re-Horakhty. May he do for him 'given life, stability, dominion, he being joyful like Re forever'.   Utterance by Thoth, lord of divine utterances, to the great ennead within the House of Re. Come, that you may see this great, pure, enduring and excellent monument, this temple of millions of years, which the king of Upper and Lower Egypt, Menkheprure, made for father Re-Atum, the great, who comes forth from his horizon. May he do 'given life' like Re forever.

> Live the Good God, joyful, lord of diadems, beloved of the gods, the king of Upper and Lower Egypt, born of she who bears, who does what is effective, embellishing [this] monument, vigilant concerning the sight of father Re, the son of Re, beloved of the gods, lord of the Two lands,

Live the Good God, joyful, lord of diadems, beloved of the gods, the king of Upper and Lower Egypt, born of she who bears, who does what is effective, embellishing [this] monument, vigilant concerning the sight of father Re, the son of Re, beloved of the gods, lord of the Two lands, Thutmose kha khau, given life stability, dominion, being joyful with his <u>ka</u> like father Re every day.

> Live the Horus, Strong Bull, perfect of diadems,
> Two Ladies, enduring of kingship like [Re]-Atum,
> Golden Horus, powerful of <u>khepesh</u> who subdues the
> Nine Bows, the king of Upper and Lower Egypt, the
> son of Re, Thutmose kha khau, beloved of Amun-Re
> [restored], given life like Re forever.

Live the Good God, truly valiant, who subdues Kush, who brings its borders like that which had never happened; the valiant king with his <u>khepesh</u>:. like Montu, stout- hearted among the multitude, traversing foreign countries, Menkheprure chosen of Re. King of kings, ruler of rulers, a sovereign to boast of, the king of Upper and Lower Egypt, Menkheprure.

He has taken possession of every land, Thutmose kha khau, beloved of Amun-Re (restored), king of the gods, given life,stability, dominion, being joyful with his <u>ka</u> like Re forever (to) eternity."

The architrave text stresses the king's connection with the sun god who is variously referred to as Re-Horakhty, Re-Atum, Re, and [Amun-Re]. Re and Re-Atum appear in the body of the text, while Re-Horakhty and Amun-Re are invoked in the royal epithets. The inscriptions state clearly that the hall has been built for Re-Atum; the Great Ennead of the Temple of Re are invited to view the court, thus bringing Heliopoplis to the fore as cult place. One should recognize that an intentional conflation appears here and probably was meant to apply to the whole temple: Amun-Re and Re-Horakhty are aspects of the same god, the Heliopolitan sun god Re.   This should be clearer when it is noted that it is Re-Horakhty-Atum who observed Thutmose IV kneeling at the Ished tree; and it is Re-Khepri who watched the king run with the oar of Atum. This attempt at "solarizing" the gods of Amada was not present in the earlier portion of the temple. There Amun-re and Re-Horakhty (no other sun gods) appeared, with equal frequency and importance, and their interrelationships might be implied, but is not explicit as here. The change should probably be attributed to current attitude toward the two national divinities.

Just as at Giza, Thutmose IV placed the sun god in the primary position, making of Amun the lesser solar deity. This is a different process from that which "Thebanized" solar religion as manifested in, for example, the Hymn of Hor and Suty.[329] Stewart pointed out that Amun, as a variant for Atum, appeared on a sun hymn only once--on an offering table from Thebes--and he concluded that it was an attempt to adopt solar liturgy for Theban religion.[330] The Hymn of Hor and Suty represents the final product of this adoption, but this process was opposite from that expressed by Thutmose at Amada and Giza. His syncretization changed the worship in the Amada temple into a Heliopolitan one and presaged the Re-Horakhty influence which appeared more strongly in the reign of Amenhotep III. Note that we have seen the king's interest in Heliopolis expressed by work carried out there under the High Priest and prince Ahmose (and noted on the Sphinx Stela). It should be remembered that this was Nubia and not Thebes. In Amun's city, Thutmose IV "did as the Thebans did"-- that point has been made with special reference to the Lateran obelisk where the solar imagery was used in subordination to Amun as premier solar and creator god. In the light of its theological reflection, Thutmose IV's work at Amada becomes more significant and should perhaps be cited more often in literature concerning 18th dynasty religion.

23. Faras.

Thutmose IV is not positively identified at the fortress site of Faras, but his Nebty name, "enduring of kingship like Atum", was restored on a block from the site but has since been shown not to have been present. [331] The attribution of a relief fragment (Khartoum 3816 + block 60) to the king by Karkowski should be rejected on stylistic grounds. The king represented should be none other than Horemheb named on Khartoum 3814, block 59.[332]

24. Buhen.

24.1. Thutmose IV apparently added at least a door inscription at Buhen Temple, presumably in the South sanctuary. A portion of a sandstone lintel (left) [333] .40 X .36 meters was found re-used in the north enclosure wall of the southern temple. It preserves a portion of two horizontal lines of text. Only the cartouches now remain. In publishing the fragment, Smith pointed out that this is the first evidence of Thutmose IV's construction work at Buhen.

24.2. The king is also known at the fort by jar sealings in his name. [334] This would indicate provisions there in his reign, perhaps intended for temple use.

24.3. A grainy limestone stela, now in the Ashmolean Museum,[335] was found at Buhen before the turn of the century. It names Thutmose IV in its lunette. Under a winged sundisk is inscribed. "the Good God, lord of doing a thing, Menkheprure", and, facing this, "beloved of Horus, lord of Buhen". A boundary description is written below: "Northern boundary of the land grant for the High Priest (of Horus?), fields of five arouras in the region of the House of Hedja". The place name is unidentified, but it should have been in the Buhen vicinity. Obviously the stela remained in place for some time, for the limestone is quite weathered. Although this stela was undoubtedly erected by a private person, it does record the active interest of Thutmose IV in the Buhen temple district and may have connection to any building activity there.

25. Tabo.

25.1. According to the excavators, on Argo Island a temple, probably to Amun, existed in the Egyptian New Kingdom. Grey sandstone blocks of Thutmose IV were found re-used there together with those of Thutmose III and Amenhotep II and III.[336] No specifics were provided. A recent visit to the site suggests that Thutmose IV and Amenhotep III were the principal builders at the temple. The blocks in situ and those in the block fields were by inscription of homogeneous type, and the names of Menkheprure and Nebmaatre were prominent, while the prenomen Aakheprure and Menkhepere could not be verified. Stylistically the two later kings are probable, based on what is now visible. This building deserves a reconsideration, and may well be a major monument of Thutmose IV in Nubia. Unfortunately more work at the site would be required to comment further.

26. Gebel Barkal.

26.1. Reisner excavated this IVth cataract site in 1916 and found that a small temple, apparently of Meroitic construction, contained re-used blocks of Thutmose IV.[337] Grey sandstone blocks with relief fragments were found in the otherwise undecorated walls, one block bore the prenomen of Thutmose. Reisner found yellow sandstone foundation walls under the Meroitic temple and foundation piers for columns in the same position as later. Near the interior angle of the old foundation wall, Reisner found "the contents of a disturbed foundation deposit of Thutmose IV".[338] All the material was found in the same cubic meter of debris, and the excavator's assumption, that only one deposit was present, seems reasonable. The foundation deposit contained two faience plaques naming the king (one in Khartoum, 2392),[339] faience beads and gold foil scraps, and twelve model pots (in Boston). The assumption made by Reisner, that Thutmose IV was responsible for building a small temple in roughly the same place as the later Meroitic one, is justifiable.[340]

26.2. Thutmose IV is also known from the site by a portion of a statuette base made in green slate.[341] It was found in the building B 700 and is now in Boston (Expedition number 16-2-134). The fragment measures 6.5 X 3.1 X 3.1 cm., but the width was probably three times this, since none of the statuette is preserved on the base. The text identifies the "[Good] God Menkheprure, given life forever, beloved of Amun-Re (restored), lord of the thrones of the Two lands". On the front of the base may be seen, "...the steps of this Good God". There may have been an inscription of a private person.

27.1. Thutmose IV apparently made additions in the Hathor Temple of Serabit, finishing work started by his father. Chamber J contains Hathor pillars of the king (one certain, and a second which is probably his) ,[342] and Chamber K has a door jamb (northern) which still bears his name.[343] Chamber L, according to Petrie,[344] contained the king's name at least once, and Černý believed some block fragments,published by Weill as debris, may represent the room L evidence for Thutmose. None of these building elements is unusual and all seem to originate from the mid-18th dynasty chambers (that is, if Černý was correct).[345]

27.2. Two faience pieces from the temple are known to bear the pharaoh's name.[346] A fragment of a <u>menat</u> is in his name as is a pot fragment [347] (Brussels E 2068).

27.3. Several miles from the Hathor temple are mine entrances where dated inscriptions of Thutmose IV have been found, no doubt commemorating the opening of the mines in years 4 and 7.   The text of year 4 [348] has recently been discussed in reference to the private person, Neby, who accompanied the king in the scene.   Above the scene is "year 4 under the Majesty of the king of Upper and Lower Egypt, Menkheprure, given life". The scene shows Thutmose, followed by Neby, offering to Hathor, mistress of Turquoise. Year 7 [349] is present on a rock text from a different mine and the private officer in attendance is also different. This newly-refound text has been discussed in the preceding chapter, since the King's daughter Iaret appeared in it. Further mention will be made in the next chapter concerning the officials in these inscriptions.   In general, the building elements from the Hathor temple and these mining texts demonstrate the continuation of mining activity in the Sinai just as in the reigns directly preceding Thutmose's.

28. <u>Assur.</u>

28.1. A fragment of an alabaster vessel [350] (Berlin VA 8378) bears the nomen "Thutmose" and thus may represent any Thutmose. Bissing favored either Thutmose I or IV because of the lack of epithet. This is questionable evidence, although Thutmose III might be unlikely since he usually wrote his nomen with ——— rather than ∩ . How this vessel arrived in Assur is unknown, for it was found in the pavement of Adad-Nirari I's palace along with alabaster fragments naming Ay. Clearly any historical conclusions concerning interrelations of Egypt and Assyria based on this fragment are useless.

<u>Unprovenanced.</u>

A limestone fragment of temple wall relief (fig. 39)[351] seen in Paris in 1988 belongs to a portion of a temple scene, though not necessarily from the divine birth

<u>Unprovenanced</u>.

A limestone fragment of temple wall relief (fig. 39)[351] seen in Paris in 1988 belongs to a portion of a temple scene, though not necessarily from the divine birth sequence known for Hatshepsut and Amenhotep III.[352]   A naked prince with sidelock and "ankh" pectoral is seated on the lap of a goddess, probably being suckled. Before the goddess a partially preserved figure of a smaller scale than the goddess offers the prenomen of Thutmose IV, Menkheprure, with its near hand. The far hand holds a staff. The top of the scene is lost so that the nature of the staff and the figure holding it is unsure. The scale, however, suggests a Ka figure, holding either a Ka standard or a <u>rnpt</u> sign to assign years for the future king. This is the first known fragment of a birth relief for Thutmose IV, and at present even its provenance is unknown. The suckling scenes by goddesses to which this probably relates are abbreviated representations and not part of the long cycles known for Hatshepsut and Amenhotep III.[353]   In hypostyle halls or in cult rooms the king carried out activities which stressed his fitness to rule. The suckling scene accompanied these.

The limestone might suggest Memphis or Abydos as a location for the temple to which this scene belongs. The king is known to have been active in both sacred precincts, but other provenances might be as likely: Ashmunein, for example. It is to be hoped that further fragments of this structure become known.

<u>Summary</u>

The monuments, catalogued above, represent the activity of Thutmose IV at known sites according to our present knowledge. Surely the picture is skewed in a variety of ways, but it is only by analyzing the material that is available that progress is made in preparation for newer discoveries.   Thutmose IV was eager to follow in the footsteps of his grandfather and father, and he did just that at quite a few sites.   But he also expanded interest in some temples and deities, for example, in Horemakhet at Giza, and in the Heliopolitan gods, at Amada and generally. While his building projects were not particularly ambitious (especially in comparison to his son's) those preserved to us demonstrate a high quality of construction and relief sculpture. It is unfortunate that so few dated texts remain from this reign, for it would be illuminating to know when he began work on some of the monuments, especially those at Karnak.   The Karnak court, despite its similarity to festival courts designed by Thutmose III and Amenhotep II, is the work of Thutmose's maturity as a ruler. The scenes are distinctly his, intended to exhibit his great contributions to Karnak on its walls. At some point in his rule Thutmose IV considered himself to have earned a portion of his own divinity, expressed clearest in respect to the sun gods. This divinity may have been his at Luxor Temple, although that cannot be concluded from his monuments there; it does not yet appear on Karnak monuments. Amun may have been the difficult deity to with whom to achieve union. Amenhotep III succeeded, however. Thutmose IV stressed rather a closeness with other national gods.

Probably several monuments were under construction at once, beginning from year 1, but in fact most of what Thutmose appears to have undertaken could easily have been accomplished in but a few years. Perhaps if he had lived longer some of the chapels and rooms he added to temples would have been greatly expanded or replaced. He appears to have had a strong desire, as had his predecessors, to spread his name abroad.

Appendix I: Tomb Objects

A Supplement to

The Tomb of Thoutmôsis IV

CG 46001-46529 in the Cairo Museum + objects of the Davis Collection. Davis objects #'s are given in brackets [].

1. Foundation Deposits: 46001-35 + 4 pp. 1-5
        MMA 30-8.21 [1]
              30.8.22 [2]
              30.8.23 [7]
              30.8.24 [8]
        BM Plaques 65232 Mond Collection, 1939 (mry Wsir)
              54419 (mry Wsir)
2. Canopics   46036-41 + 2 pp. 6-8
        BMFA 03.1130 [1]
              03.1129 [5]
3. Magical Figures   46042-45   pp. 9-10
4. Wooden Figures   46046-69 + 2 pp. 11-15
        BMFA 03.1137 = panther= CG 46066 [22]
              03.1135 = hawk's head = CG 46067 [23]
              03.1136 = [11]
5. Stone vases   46070-94   pp. 16-19
        Princeton Univ. Mus.
              30.497
6. Furniture   46095-96 + 3 pp. 20-23
        BMFA 03.1131 [1]
              03.1132 [3]
        MMA 30.8.45 [2]
7. Chariot   46097   pp. 24-34
8. Chariot parts, leather 46098-118   pp. 34-38
9. Miscellaneous   46119-59 pp. 39-44
        BMFA 03.1134 = door bolt CG 46142 ?
10. Shabtis   46160-80 +9 pp. 45-52
        BMFA 03.1198 [10]
              03.1099 [4]
              03.1100 [14]
        MMA 30.8.27 [3]
              30.8.28 [18]
        [23] - [26] as yet unidentified
        CG   24971 found in KV 37[354], unlisted
11. Model coffins and shabtis 46181-91 + 2 pp. 53-55
        MMA   30.8.25/26[33]
        BMFA 03.1101/2[40]
12. Model Baskets, etc.   46192-202   pp. 56-57
        BMFA 03.1133 = model tools
        OIM 8370 = CG 46193[355]

13. <u>Nemset</u> vases 46203-25 + 6   pp. 58-67
        BMFA 03.1103 a-c [1]
              03.1106   [19]
              03.1105   [22]
        MMA 30.8.36   [5]
        BMFA 03.1127-28, frags. [26], [28 ?]
14. <u>Hes</u> vases.   46226-82 + 3   pp. 68-81
        MMA 30.8.37   [5]
              30.8.39   [21]
              30.8.38   [35]
15. Stoppers for vases 46283-319 + 25 pp. 82-91
        MMA 30.8.41 like [39]
              30.8.40 like [40]
        BMFA 03.1109-26 as yet unmatched
        OIM 8364-68 as yet unmatched
16. Libation cups   46320-28 + 1   pp. 92-94
        MMA 30.8.42 [2]
17. U-shaped vases   46329-55 + 1   pp. 95-101
        BMFA 03.1107   [1]
18. <u>Ankh</u> symbols   46356-403 + 7   pp. 102-09
        MMA 30.8.30   [2]
              30.8.29   [13]
        BMFA 03.1088   [31]
              03.1090   [40]   + 3 unidentified
        OIM 8356-58   as yet unmatched (one 7" ht. with cartouche)
              8359 fragmentary ankh(?)
19. Throwstick models 46404-18 + 4   pp. 110-13
        BMFA 03.1085   [2]
              03.1086   [10]
        MMA 30.8.31   [16] (one of three fragments)
        OIM 8362-63   [5](?) Perhaps 2 fragments of three described for [5]
20. Papyrus roll models 46419-36 + 8   pp. 114-18
        BMFA 03.1092   [5]
              03.1091   [22]
        MMA 30.8.34   [16]
              30.8.33   [17]
              30.8.32   [26]
        BM   41540   unlisted, like CG 46433, acquired 1905
21. Bracelets   46437-50   pp. 119-21
22. Plaques & Boxes   46451-55 + 1 pp. 122-23
        OIM 8369 [1]
23. Model lotus buds   46456-63 + 1   pp. 124-25
        MMA 30.8.35   [2]
24. Model kohl pots   46464-68 + 1   pp. 126-27
        MMA 30.8.43   [1]
25. Model serpent heads   46469-74   pp. 128-29
26. Amulets   46475-87 + 11 pp. 130-35
        OIM 8361
        OIM 8360 Djed Pillar

27. Glass　　　　　　　　46488-525 + 1　　pp. 135-42
　　　MMA　30.8.44
28. Fabrics　　　　　　　46526-29　　　　pp. 143-44
29. Unlisted, but probably from the tomb.
　　　MMA 30.8.248 = alabaster cylindrical cap
30. Unlisted, uncertain connection with tomb.
　　　OIM 12144 = plumb re-used by
　　　　　　Tutankhamun [356]
　　　JE 62131 = alabaster jar found in KV 62
　　　　　　(Tutankhamun)

　　　CG 61035= coffin found in KV 35 (Amenhotep II) with painted inscription identifying　Thutmose IV. Probably not original to KV 43.[357]

CG Numbers	529
Davis Collection Numbers	92
Subtotal =	621
<u>Catalogue General</u> Numbers identified in other museums, 3-4, Subtotal =	617-18
Museum Numbers not identified in <u>Catalogue General</u>, 6-8, Subtotal =	623/26.

Appendix II: Statuary[358]

Site	Museum #	Description
Abydos		Limstn. torso, inscribed. Near door of R II temple
Hu	Louvre E 3176 + BMFA 99.733	Kneeling statuette. Inscribed for T IV on belt, A II on base.[359]
Karnak	Cairo CG 42080	Bl. gr. Seated with mother. Inscribed. Fig. 8[360]
Karnak	Cairo CG 42081	Bl. gr. As falcon. Inscribed. Figs. 27-28.
Karnak	Cairo CG 923	Limstn. Prince Thutmose kneeling with Hathor emblem. Inscribed. Mut temple. Figs. 1-4
Karnak	Cairo JE 43611	Quarzt. striding with Ram standard. Over life-size. Inscribed. Figs. 25-26.[361]
Karnak	Luxor J 48	Limstn. Osiride; recut and reinscribed for R II. Inscribed. From Mut temple. Fig. 30.
Karnak		Limstn. Osiride; reinscribed for R II. Inscribed. From Mut temple. Fig. 31.
Karnak		Limstn. Osiride; Inscr. Ptah temple. Fig. 29.
Karnak	Karnak 781	Rd. gr. torso. Inscribed. Lost.
Luxor Temple		Bl. gr. Seated colossal king in round wig. Inscribed. Base with name rings. Figs. 33-34.
Medamud	Louvre E13889 with half on site	Rd. gr. Seated in _nemes_. Inscribed. Life-size.[362]
Syria (?)	BM 118544	Alab. bust in round wig. Uninscr. Fig. 40.
Thebes	BM, earlier V&A 909.1896-910.1896; 913.1896	Limstn. part of head of king, nose, ear. From Mortuary temple. Uninscribed.

<u>Unknown</u> <u>Provenance</u>	Durham 379	Bl. gr. sphinx. Inscribed.[363]
	Alexandria 25792	Bl. gr. sphinx head. Uninscr. Colossal. Fig. 41.
	Alexandria 406	Bl. gr. head in <u>khepresh</u>. Uninscr. Life-size. Fig. 42.
London	BM 64564	Bronze statuette in <u>nemes</u> kneeling with <u>nw</u> pots[364]. Inscribed.
London	V&A 422.1917	Blue glass head.[365] Uninscribed.
Munich	ÄS 6770	Bl. steatite statuette head in <u>khepresh</u>. Uninscribed.[366]
Oxford	Queens Coll. 1203	Rd. quartzt head of prince (?). Near life-size. Uninscribed. Figs. 43-44.
Paris	Louvre E10599	Bl. gr. head in <u>khepresh</u>. Life-size. Mouth and eyes damaged. Uninscribed. Fig. 45.
Philadelphia	UM E 13114	Bl. gr. head of sphinx statuette. Uninscribed.

Statuary continued: Queens or Goddesses

Crocodilopolis	Cairo CG 1167	Bl. gr. lower part double statue of Tiaa with king. Inscribed. Fig. 9.
Giza		Limstn. fragments of standing statue of Tiaa. Inscribed.
Karnak	Cairo CG 42080	Bl. gr. with king. Inscribed. Fig 8.
Karnak	BM 1434	Bl. gr. seated Mutemwia in bark of Mut. Lower part only of queen. Inscribed.
Karnak		Limstn. statuette Tiaa next to A II colossus before 8th Pylon. Inscribed.
Thebes		Quartzt. Statuette of Mutemwia on colossi from mortuary temple of Amenhotep III. Inscribed.
Thebes		Bl. gr. lower part seated statue of Mutemwia. West side of Ramesseum, near storerooms. Inscribed. Fig. 46.
Heidelberg		Rd. gr. head of goddess. Uninscribed.

| London | BM 956 | Bl. gr. head of goddess. Uninscr.[367] Fig. 47. |
| London | BM 43A | Bl. gr. head of Mutemwia. Inscribed. Part of group. Fig. 48. |

Appendix III: Varia
(Not otherwise discussed)

<u>Site</u>	<u>Museum #</u>	<u>Description</u>
Berlin	8943	Silver ring, "Menkheprure, beloved of Amun"[368]
Wuppertal	Collection Abeler	Bronze ring with steatite and faience. King seated holding <u>heka</u> and bow.[369]
	Collection Nash, present location unknown	Bronze disk, "Good god, Menkheprure, son of Re Thutmose kha khau, beloved of Amun-Re in the midst of the Temple of Aakheprure in Thebes".[370]

1. Compare the list in Wm. M. Fl. Petrie, <u>A History of Egypt</u> II, 165, where he names thirteen sites of which two, Luxor Temple and Sehel, are incorrectly included. The Luxor birth scenes date to Amenhotep III's reign, and the Sehel graffito to Akhenaten's.

2. <u>PM</u> IV 5; E. Bergmann, <u>Rec. Trav.</u> 7 (1889) 177-78. No museum number is given for the columns.

3. A. Wiedemann, <u>Aegyptische Geschichte Supp.</u>, 42.

4. H. Gauthier, <u>LdR</u> III, 133, 137.

5. <u>PM</u> IV 58; S. Schott, <u>MDAIK</u> 1 (1930) 28-29; <u>Urk.</u> IV 1562.

6. <u>PM</u> IV 60; C. Kuentz, <u>Obélisques</u>, p. 27, fig. 30; W. F. Petrie, <u>Heliopolis</u>, 5-6 pl. 4. 8. K. Martin, <u>Ein Garantsymbol des Lebens</u> HÄB 3 (Hildesheim 1977) 129.

7. <u>Urk.</u> IV, 590-93, the New York and London obelisks which the king says he erected at Heliopolis for father Atum. <u>Urk.</u> IV 832, <u>LD</u> III, 29b, Berlin 1634 (<u>PM</u> IV 63) is a stela showing the king offering to Re-Horakhty and mentioning the building of an enclosure wall. For doorways, no doubt belonging to this enclosure, and the monuments cited here, see the discussion in Essam El-Banna, "L'Obélisque de Sesostris I à Héliopolis", <u>RdE</u> 33 (1981) 3-9 and pl. 1.

8. CG 589, Borchardt, <u>Statuen</u> II, 144-45. "[W]hom the king chose in front of the Two lands to do everything which he ordained in the temple of father Atum, it being enclosed with a wall as an enduring construction." And again, "[W]hom the king chose when he was a knowledgeable youth that he might work the land for him to consecrate (<u>sdsr</u>) the temple of Atum, exorcising evils from it". He also referred to himself, amongst his administrative titles relating to the temple, as Overseer of the <u>pure</u> fields of Atum, lord of Heliopolis, perhaps a reference to the newly sanctified area and its consequently pure produce(?).

9. <u>Urk.</u> IV 1540, 13. See below in discussion of the Sphinx Stela for the retrospective nature of the monument.

10. <u>Urk</u>. IV, 1540, 15.

11. For the existence of two separate precincts for the Re and Atum at Heliopolis, see Laszlo Kakošy, "Heliopolis", <u>LÄ</u> II, 1111-13.

12. C. Zivie, <u>Giza au Deuxième Millénaire.</u> 125-45; <u>Urk.</u> IV 1539-44; the standard text study is that of A. Erman, "Die Sphinxstele", <u>SB</u> 6 (1904) 428-37. For older copies, see <u>PM</u> III [2] 38-39. Published photos which are suitable to read are largely unavailable while handcopies abound. I have relied on a good photo kindly lent to me by Dr. W. Kelly Simpson and my own slides. Much of what the modern slides and Zivie's handcopy indicate as missing are still visible in the older photo. Brackets in the translation indicate now-missing portions. The well-known "Königsnovelle" setting of the stela was fully discussed in A. Hermann, <u>Die ägyptische Königsnovelle</u>.

13. Erman, op. cit., and in SB 6 (1904) 1063, he debated W. Spiegelberg in OLZ 7 (1904) 288-91; 343-44 concerning the Sphinx Stela and the naos of Amenmose.

14. See Zivie's discussion, op. cit., 266-69.

15. E. Drioton and J. Vandier, L'Égypte[4], 341 n.1; and already Spiegelberg, op.cit., 290. Drioton mistakenly says the name of Amun is present, but the word is ỉmnt. Nonetheless, it is clearly hacked out.

16. C. Cannuyer, "Notules à propos de la stèle du Sphinx", VA 1 (1985) 83-90.

17. As Zivie rightly notes, twt and ʿpr are both old perfective and qualify the participle pr; op. cit., 132 n.e.

18. See Chapter 2 for discussion. Ỉnpw does not necessarily indicate a child, nor was Thutmose still an ỉnpu when he took the throne. Compare further the word as used to describe Amenhotep II on his Sphinx Stela, Urk. IV 1281, 8ff.

19. hʿʿ mšʿw n mrwt.f msw-nsw srw nbw wn hr phty.f hr ỉhi nhwt.f whm n.f šnw wsrw.f mi s3 Nwt. This is a troublesome phrase no matter how it is read. Zivie has translated: "L'armée était joyeuse en l'aimant; les enfants royaux et tous les grands qui étaient sous son pouvoir prosperaient sa vigueur se perpetuait et sa puissance égalait celle du fils de Nout". Op.cit., 130, 134 ns. l-n. Her reading places nhwt.f in a different phrase and requires an unusual emphatic placement of it before whm, its verb. The reading here also requires an abnormal positioning--the subjects of the geminated form, hʿʿ, are split up; two of them are placed after the emphasized adverbial extension n.mrwt.f. But surely this is understandable; Gardiner cites examples of adverbials being moved forward in sentence patterns "if such a transposition is felt to be convenient". Grammar3 413 507,2-6. "This is felt, for example, when the adverbial phrase belongs very closely to the verb." Such was his comment before the following example: rdi.n.ỉ sw3 hr.ỉ ʿh3w.f, "I caused to pass-by me his arrows". He also cited the very common ỉr n.f m mnw.f n ỉt Hr3hty sʿhʿ n.f thnwy bnbnt m dʿm, "He made as his monument for father Horakhty, erecting for him..." The object is so long that the adverb phrases are moved up to clarify the sentence meaning.

   The word 𓄿𓏏𓇼𓏤 is also difficult. Zivie translated "prosperaient" as a hr + infinitive construction. Here instead the form is read wn hr phty.f hr ỉhi nhwt.f as the form wn hr.f hr sdm (Grammar3 s471) which was used in past narrative at just this time period (see Urk. IV 1073, 1075). The causative meaning for ỉhi was proposed by Faulkner, Dictionary. 129, but he included 𓂋𓏏𓏤 as part of the determinative. The source of this meaning is probably w3h (Wb I 159) which can mean "make green" (although the reference is to the Greek period); w3h itself is attested in the Old Kingdom and the Late Period. Words for "green" are also noted under Wb I 18 ỉhih and 3h3h, and there is another form, ỉ3hy, meaning "to be inundated", Wb I 33. The form here is obviously related to all of these.

20. 𓍿 for wʿ wʿty appears to have bothered Zivie quite a bit, but the identical phrase, a bit more fully written, 𓍿𓍿 m šmswt.f appears in the Konosso stela,

Urk. IV 1547, 11, where it also refers to a single sole companion. To make of this a pseudo-verbal seems unnecessary and incorrect. Zivie, op. cit., 130, 135.

21. See the identical phrase in the Konosso stela, Urk. IV 1546, 2, when Amun speaks to the king.

22. See Zivie's note qq, op. cit., 142. She has attached iw.k n.i (written ii.k) to the next phrase in order to emphasize that because of the interdependence of the king and the god, Tuthmosis must help clear away the sand.

23. See note on line 11 for the relative form t3 wnt n.i hr.s. Zivie translated ⸢ ⸣ as "aussi me suis-je hâté de". There is no "legs" determinative here, and "wait for" seems better to describe the circumstance--the god has awaited this visitation by Tuthmosis just so he can reveal this information to him.

24. See note on line 12 for hw and pronoun sn not n.

25. If honorific transposition is assumed, twt Hc.f-rc ir n Itm-R'-Hr-m-3ht.

26. P. Barguet, M. Dewachter, Le Temple d'Amada IV C22-23.

27. Zivie, op.cit., 98; Faulkner cites in Dictionary. 122.

28. To demonstrate this premise, David Lorton's book, Juridical Terminology, is the finest example. He steadfastly defends the notion that even the commonest terms had significance even in the complicated diplomatic context.

29. Zivie, Giza au deuxième millénaire, 268-69.

30. Cannuyer, op. cit., 86-87.

31. Lanny Bell, "Aspects of the cult of the deified Tutankhamun," Mélanges Mokhtar, 33 and n. 71, citing the Sphinx Stela.

32. PM III^{2}38; S. Hassan, The Great Sphinx, 5-7.

33. PM III^2 38; Hassan, The Great Sphinx, 95-96; Zivie, op. cit., 145-68, 297. those showing Queen Nefertiry were discussed in Chapter 3. Note that Zivie's NE 23 is assigned an incorrect Temporary number. her NE 31 (p. 156) is Temp. 19.4.47.1 and includes Thutmose IV with Nefertiry before Atum lord of Heliopolis, offering lotuses.

34. This could be a local god, as well. See the identification of shetyt as the memphite burial place of Sokar, analogous to the Abydos burial location for Osiris, I.E.S. Edwards, "The Shetayet of Rosetau," in Egyptological Studies in Honor of Richard A. Parker (Hanover and London 1986) 27-36, especially 34-36.

35. Ibid., 297-98. Zivie believes this must be a local form of Hathor of Gebelein whose toponym was written somewhat similarly.

36. Hassan, The Great Sphinx, 88-89, fig. 69.

37. Zivie, op. cit., 330-32.

38. Hassan, The Great Sphinx, 95-96.

39. Ibid., pls. 41a = Zivie, NE 15; 42 = 17; 43a = 18; 43b = 19; 49 = 28; Zivie, op. cit., pl. 9 = 26; Hölscher, Das Grabdenkmal des Konigs Chephren, 108-09, fig. 161 = 30; NE 31, unpublished.

40. Hassan, The Great Sphinx, pls. 41b = 16; 44a = 20; 44b = 21; 45 = 22; 46a = 23; 46b = 24; 47 = 25; 48 = 27; Hölscher, op. cit., 108-09, fig. 160 = 29; Stela seen in Eid collection = 31 (present location unknown).

41. Zivie, NE 26 (JE 59461), see pl. 4.

42. PM III^2 46; Hassan, The Great Sphinx, 65, fig. 58; S. Hassan, Giza IX, 37-39; Zivie, op. cit., 156-57.

43. PM III^2 40; Zivie, op. cit., 157-58, pl. 10; B. Gunn, ASAE 29 (1929), 94.

44. PM III^2 46; Hassan, The Great Sphinx, pl. 8; Zivie, op. cit., 159 n.1.

45. PM III^2 42; Zivie, op. cit., 158-59; Hassan, The Great Sphinx, 246, fig. 187; R. Giveon, JNES 28 (1969), 56.

46. Zivie, op. cit., 158.

47. Hassan, The Great Sphinx, 71, fig. 62 (JE 72266). Zivie, op. cit., 61, calls it Tuthmosis III, but this is clearly not the case. Her date in the 18th dynasty is contradicted by the style.

48. Ibid., 309-10, cites six examples with kings shown and three from the reign of Amenhotep II.

49. S. Hassan, The Sphinx, 137-38.

50. PM III^2 38; Zivie, op. cit., 159-60. Hassan, The Great Sphinx, 34, fig. 17.

51. The best comparisons are in Mysliwiec, Le portrait royal, figs. 118-19. Note that although the king appears regularly with a naturally shaped brow when he wears the khepresh, the enlareged eye is not always in evidence. Cf. ibid., fig. 115 from the Karnak sandstone court's architrave.

52. Cairo JE 43611 and BM 64564.

53. PM III^2 38; Zivie, op. cit., 159; Hassan, The Great Sphinx, 35-36.

54. Hassan, The Great Sphinx, 35.

55. PM III^2 39; Hassan, Giza IX, 4; Hassan, The Great Sphinx, 74-75, 104-06, fig. 23.

56. PM III^2 39; Zivie, op. cit., 91-93; Hassan, The Great Sphinx, 33, 79-83, 235, pl. 39.

57. Ibid, 81.

58. Zivie, op. cit., 89-90; 264-65.

59. M. and J. Doresse, Journal Asiatique 233 (1941-42) 181-99; D. Redford, JARCE 13 (1976) 58 n. 73.

60. Hassan, The Great Sphinx, 81.

61. See especially Zivie, op.cit., 316-24. The text of Amenhotep II's Sphinx Stela, Urk. IV 1276-83, does not mention Horemakhet until line 25 and then only in reference to his region as a visitation place. It is the end of the inscription which notes that because the king remembered his visit there, he wished to memorialize it.

62. Hassan, The Great Sphinx, 85, fig. 68.

63. Urk, IV 1565.

64. For example, Rennutet of Iat Tjamut, Hathor of Inerty, and Mut of the Horns of the Gods. See Zivie's discussion, op. cit., 283-303.

65. Ibid, 320-25.

66. Urk. IV 2109.

67. Raymond Johnson, "Images of Amenhotep III in Thebes: Styles and Intentions", paper presented at a symposium at the Cleveland Museum, November 1987. To be published by the Cleveland Museum of Art, 1990.

68. PM III^2 333; L. Borchardt, Das Grabdenkmal des Königs Sa3hu-Re' II, pl. 35.

69. PM III^{2}220-21; G. Daressy, ASAE 3 (1902) 25; W. F. Petrie, Memphis I, 8, pls. 19-20; Urk. IV 1561.

70. J. Weinstein, Foundation Deposits. 207-08. The deposit from Petrie's work is partially represented in the Manchester Museum #'s 4938-46. Also from this group is JE 35174, Weinstein, op.cit., 208; and two alabaster model vases from the Hilton Price Collection, Catalogue Hilton Price II, 62, #'s 4542- 43. 4543 is inscribed for the king "beloved of Ptah", while 4542 bears only the prenomen.

71. Weinstein, op. cit., 207-08.

72. Petrie, Memphis I, 8; W. F. Petrie, Memphis II, 14, 18, pl. 19.

73. Petrie, Memphis I, pls. 7-9, p.7. One uninscribed in Hanover Kestner Museum, 1935.200.229 = pl. 8 #3, pl. 9.

74. W. F. Petrie, in R. Engelbach, Memphis VI, 33, pl. 55, fig. 12.

75. See Urk. IV 1563 = Brussels E 4499 and Petrie, Memphis I, pl. 8, 3-4.

76. I wish to thank Dr. John D. Ray of Cambridge University who mentioned the existence of this block to me.

77. Brussels E 4987; Memphis II, 14, 18, pl. 19.

78. Urk. IV 1558.

79. Supra, n. 59.

80. Urk. IV 1558; A. Kamal, Table d'Offrandes, 72, CG 23088.

81. See H. Gauthier, ASAE 10 (1910) 200-02.

82. PM IV 99; L. Borchardt, Statuen IV 87; Urk. IV 1564.

83. A. Hermann, MDAIK 5 (1934) 27, fig. 6, from Kom; G. Roeder, Hermopolis 1929-39, 296, Chapter XV Section 2b.

84. Ibid., Section 2c, pl. 60 mm.

85. A. Hermann, MDAIK 7 (1940) 40, pl. 12d; Roeder, op. cit., 308. Chapter XVIII s10a. Dimensions of the fragments are 7.5 X 7.5 cm.; it was found in a deep level near the Middle Kingdom temple.

86. PM IV 233; J. G. Wilkerson, Modern Egypt and Thebes II, 73, 77.

87. L. Borchardt, MDOG 57 (1919) 28-29, fig. 18.

88. H. Schafer, ZÄS 55 (1918) 32-34.

89. N. Davies, Amarna V, 9 n. 2, pl. 9; J. Pendlebury, City of Akhenaten III, 200; W. Helck, Materialien I, 149; C. Aldred, Akhenaten and Nefertiti, 22.

90. C. Aldred, Akhenaten, 106-07.

91. BM 57399, from the house of Panehesy, Aldred, Akhenaten, 106-07, pl. 80. He asserts this is co-regency evidence.

92. See Aldred, Akhenaten, 191-92, and 194, where he says that offerings were heaped on the Aten temple altars "doubtless on behalf of the dead as well as the living". E. Drioton, ASAE 43 (1942) 21-24.

93. Supra, n. 74, and Tuthmosis I, Pendlebury, op. cit., III, pl. 81.14; II, pl. 50.274.

94. For example, seals from Malkata show the estate of Thutmose IV providing goods even in year 36 of Amenhotep III. W. Hayes, JNES 10 (1951) 96; Amenhotep II's estate is also attested there, M. Leahy, Excavations at Malkata and the Birket Habu 1971-1974. The Inscriptions, pl. 36, #'s 38-40.

95. N. Davies, Amarna V, 9, pl. 9.

96. Urk. IV 1975; Stela X in N. Davies, Amarna V, pl. 32. Actually the cartouche is partial and shows (•〰𓆣   . It could conceivably identify Tuthmosis III or IV.

97. PM IV 204; L. Borchardt, MDOG 55 (1914) 30-34, pl. 5; Schäfer, op. cit., 35-36; Urk. IV 1562; W. Kaiser, Staatliche Museen...Berlin, (1967) #590.

98. Borchardt, MDOG 55, 31.

99. Not named, but the god is falcon-headed with plumes and a sun-disk as headdress. Montu-Re appears on the king's chariot, so named.

100. šsp n.k ḫpš nṯr nfr ḥḥi.k tp ḫ3st nbt.

101. Urk. IV 1562.

102. Biri Fay, Egyptian Museum Berlin (Catalogue 1985), 52, considers that this may have been used as a wrist guard during use of bows and arrows.

103. D. Redford, JARCE 13, 51.

104. The closest parallel is on a relief fragment of Sety I (AEIN 42) showing the disk directly above the head of the king who wears the round wig with fillet, M. Mogensen, La Collection Égyptienne (Ny Carlsberg), pl.108; Hölscher, op. cit., 108, fig. 159, is a stela of one Pentepihu who appears offering to Horemakhet (also called Re-Horakhty). A protective vulture hovers over the sphinx, but a lone sundisk occupies the top of the lunette. The style is mid-18th dynasty, possibly the reign of Thutmose IV. CG 34026, a stela of Amenhotep III, also uses the plain disk, there

called Behdet. It hangs above two representations of the king, AEIN 970 is a limestone Abydene stela and shows Osiris and Horus (depicted like Re-Horakhty) "Protector of his father, son of Osiris". Obviously of late 18th dynasty date, perhaps Amenhotep IV, Mogensen, op. cit., pl.104. AEIN 1516 also shows the disk as Behdet; a private person appears before Ptah and Sakhmet; probably Ramesside.

105. J. Pendlebury, City of Akhenaten II, 21, #26/338.

106. Ibid., III, 135, #33/296. No photographs.

107. Ibid., 136, #33/312, pl. 79.1.

108. PM V 70; A Mariette, Abydos I, 4. Location shown on pl. 1.

109. W. K. Simpson, "Kenotaph" in Lexikon der Ägyptologie, 19, 390; W. K. Simpson, The Terrace of the Great God at Abydos, 3.

110. Simpson, "Kenotaph", 390.

111. PM V, 70-71. Mariette, Abydos I, 4.

112. PM V, 71; Mariette, Abydos II, pl. 53c.

113. H. DeMeulenaere, CdE 46 (1971) 223-33.

114. PM V 58; CG 34022 in P. Lacau, Stèles, pl. 13; Urk. IV 1611.

115. BM 148 in HTES 7, pl.43; Urk. IV 1612-13.

116. This is true for both the Middle Kingdom and the New Kingdom. See, for example, Simpson, Terrace, where 21 out of 228 examples have cartouches in any context. Compare Mariette, Catalogue Général des Monuments d'Abydos, for the New Kingdom, where a similar ratio occurs.

117. PM V 58; CG 34023, in Lacau, Stèles, pl. 14; Urk. IV 1613.

118. Stockholm 14; M. Mogensen, Stèles Égyptiennes, 36-37.

119. PM V 44; Mariette, Catalogue, 31. I am grateful to Prof. B. V. Bothmer for re-checking the annotated Cairo Museum copy of the Catalogue to insure that this piece did not enter that Museum.

120. G. Legrain, Répertoire, 119 #215.

121. PM VI 109; A. Mariette, Denderah, Supp., 53, pl. H; J. Dümichen, Baugeschichte des Denderatempels, pl. IIIb.

122. PM VI 90; Dümichen, op. cit., iv.

123. F. Bisson de la Roque,"Rapport...Médamoud" 1927, 48 fig. 32.

124. <u>PM</u> V 147; F. Bisson de la Roque, "Rapport" 1925, 41, fig. 29, 42-43, fig. 26.

125. Bisson de la Roque, "Rapport" 1930, 57-58, figs. 31-32.

126. <u>Ibid</u>.

127. <u>PM</u> V 149; Bisson de la Roque, "Rapport" 1930, 58, fig. 33. Bryan, "Portrait Sculpture".

128. <u>PM</u> V 149; Bisson de la Roque, "Rapport" 1929, 54, fig. 24.

129. For general remarks, see G. Björkman, <u>Kings at Karnak</u>, 100-10. She gives most of the pertinent references. This book, however, is disappointingly inaccurate regarding Thutmose IV and should not be relied on for substance. In contrast P. Barguet's <u>Le Temple d'Amon-Rê</u> is unparalleled; it is not only accurate but also provides information which only years of first-hand experience together with incisive analytical powers could produce. As regards Thutmose IV's activity at Karnak, Barguet correctly predicted too often for a chance explanation. He described an interior peristyle court of the king before the Fourth pylon and also guessed the emplacement of the Lateran obelisk and then refound it.

130. <u>PM</u> II^2 72. The <u>Bibliography</u> is unreliable on this building since the blocks of the court have been confused with elements of the Fourth pylon porch. The only good source is B. Letellier, <u>Hommages à la Mémoire de Serge Sauneron</u> I, 51-71, pls.10-12 and now also in <u>BSFE</u> 84 (1979) 33-49. Most of the description here is condensed from her account in the first work. On page 52, ns. 1-7 of her article, she gives all references, and on 53, ns. 1-3, the scenes which have been published and discussed prior to her study. P. Barguet, <u>Temple.</u> 95, gave the first proposals of the sort of monument represented by these blocks. For free access to the blocks in Karnak, I am indebted to Mlle. Letellier and the Centre Franco-Egyptien, and to Sayed Abd-el Hamid, Late Karnak Inspector and El Sayed Higazy.

131. Barguet, <u>Temple</u>, 95-96. On <u>phrw</u>, see <u>Wb</u> I, 564, and Faulkner, <u>Dictionary</u>, 93-94, from which it is clear that the word means "to go about" and "to turn around" rather than "to surround", although it certainly can apply to the last.

132. Under Column 107. <u>PM</u> II^2 53. Now in the Cairo Museum, JE 87186-88. Cited in Barguet, <u>op. cit</u>., 95-96. The contents included an alabaster jar and dish and eight faience cartouches; J. Weinstein, <u>Foundation Deposits</u>, 208-09. Is this the source of the pseudo-vases of the king (<u>PM</u> II^2 299), with Cairo Temp. Nos. 14.3.26.8-9? If the deposit was disturbed by the building of the Hall, then it is possible.

133. Letellier, <u>Hommages Sauneron</u>, 55-63.

134. <u>Ibid</u>., 57-58, for the doors named on blocks; 71, pl. 12, for the limestone jamb.

135. Partial text is cited by Letellier, Ibid., 64. See H. Chevrier, ASAE 53 (1954) pl. 20; Muhammad, ASAE 59 (1966) pls. 10-11. Other examples given here in transliteration are from personal photos and copies.

136. Letellier, Hommages Sauneron, 64; text from my own notes. Letellier did not discuss the chronological implications of the find.

137. Wente and Van Siclen, "A Chronology", 227, 229.

138. Letellier, Hommages Sauneron, 64.

139. Barguet, Temple, 307-10, especially 309.

140. Letellier, op. cit., pl. XII, with both fragments of the jamb.

141. I wish to thank Dr. J.-Claud Golvin, Dr. George Goyon and Mr. El-Sayed Higazy, Director of Karnak and Luxor Temples and Mr. Philippe Martinez for their permission and assistance in photographing and sketching these limestone blocks during August 1987. The dimensions of the published left jamb's decorated face, upper half only (we could not locate the lower portion, but Letellier's photo is sufficient) is 95 cm. height, 67 cm. width. The block as preserved is 1.51 m. in length and widens from the decorated face backwards 67 to some 87 cm. The second jamb is again the upper portion and is now 1 m. high by 66 cm. wide. The depth of the block is 71 cm.

142. The block is 1.17 m. in height and 2.2 m. in length. Only 84 cm. are decorated, and the block is cut back by 7 cm. past the decorated portion. The remainder may have been faced over with paster. A join hole is on the end face which would have connected to the outer jamb.

143. Noticed as well by Luc Gabolde whose work on Thutmose II at Karnak has unraveled a number of questions from that period.

144. PM II^2 72, 79, but see supra, n. 109. The best studies are J. Yoyotte, CdE 28 (1953) 30-38, on the porch itself; J. Leclant, RdE 8 (1951) 101-20, with pls. 4-5, on the pylon texts and scenes. See also Barguet, Temple, 89-90.

145. Urk. IV 1557. For a photograph, see Leclant, op. cit., pl. 4.

146. Leclant, op.cit., 116. "[L]a decoration actuelle de la zone centrale en leger retrait, de 1'"avancée". scènes de la XVIIIe dynastie, dedicaces éthiopienne et macedonienne date d'une époque relativement tardive, on doit l'attribuer sans doute au regne d'Alexandre." This is not made clear in PM II2 79; nor does Björkman mention Alexander's tertiary relief work.

147. Incorrectly restored, post-Amarna, as ỉpt-swt.

148. Barguet, <u>Temple</u>, 89, describes the visible masonry applied against the original door.

149. Yoyotte, <u>op. cit.</u>, 31.

150. <u>Ibid.</u>, 30, fig. 8; photograph in Leclant, <u>op. cit.</u>, 113, fig. 6; <u>Urk</u>. IV 1565. This represents only half of the block in question. Letellier published the text of the other half which contained the name of the door, <u>op. cit.</u>, 58. For a handcopy which shows two block fragments joined together, see fig. 1 below.

151. Yoyotte, <u>op. cit.</u>, 28, fig. 7, after N. Davies, <u>The Tombs of Two Officials</u>, pl. 12.

152. Yoyotte, <u>op. cit.</u>, 30; Leclant, <u>op. cit.</u>, 103, fig. 2.

153. Yoyotte, <u>op. cit.</u>, 30, 37.

154. <u>Wb</u> II 476; Leclant, <u>op. cit.</u>, 111-12.

155. Letellier, <u>Hommages Sauneron</u>, 57.

156. Barguet, <u>Temple</u>, 30, 79, 246, 310-11.

157. <u>Ibid.</u>, 79.

158. <u>Wb</u> IV 92; <u>Urk</u>. IV 206 shows a portable shrine as determinative.

159. Drawn after a photo kindly provided by Centre Franco-Égyptien at Karnak.

160. <u>Wb</u> IV 83.

161. <u>PM</u> II^2 71-72; Barguet, <u>Temple</u>, 86 n. 1 (omit, however, <u>ASAE</u> 47 (1946) 172-73.) Again the <u>Bibliography</u> is of little use, since the chapel is so poorly published; many blocks exist which are not evident in these references. Also see G. Legrain, <u>BIFAO</u> 13 (1917) 26-27. The Centre Franco-Égyptien under the hand of Philippe Martinez is reconstructing the building on paper for the purpose of publication, and perhaps actual rebuilding, although this last may not be possible. I thank Dr. Jean-Claud Golvin, last Director of the Centre M. Martinez, Dr. El-Sayed Higazy, and the staff of the Centre for their allowing me access to these blocks on numerous occasions. I apologize for any grave errors I may make in my estimates here, and I hasten to claim them as my own. For the sake of some larger picture I present a description of the chapel. Certainly the measurements cannot be taken as certain.

162. Mention of at least 19-20 can be found; certainly the figure of 11 given by Björkman, <u>op. cit.</u>, 107, is wrong. Her citation (Chevrier, <u>ASAE</u> 37 (1937) 178), is contradicted on page 192 of that same volume where the excavator reported a single find of 10 blocks from the chapel.

163. For construction techniques used in these bark shrines see H. Chevrier, RdE 23 (1971) 80ff. He discussed Amenhotep I's chapel and Hatshepsut's as examples.

164. M. Pillet, ASAE 24 (1924) 59-60, pl. 2; G. Legrain, Karnak, 152, fig. 96; D. Arnold, Wandrelief und Raumfunktion in 'ägyptischen Tempeln des Neuen Reiches, 40 [6], described the two published scenes. K. Mysliwiec, Le Portrait Royal, published three royal representations, figs. 111, 118, 122.

165. C. Van Siclen, The Alabaster Shrine of King Amenhotep II (San Antonio 1986), pl. 13.

166. My original access to the blocks was graciously granted by the Centre Franco-Egyptien and the late Inspector, Sayed Abd-el Hamid.

167. Van Siclen, The Alabaster Shrine of King Amenhotep II, 11, noted that Amenhotep II's shrine of alabaster had kheker friezes on the exterior. He felt it indicated the building was sheltered from the sun due to the presence of this decoration. The kheker, however, identifies the sacred space in which cult activities take place. It may not necessarily follow that the worship scenes on the exterior of the shrines took place in open air simply because they appear on the outside. These are, after all, buildings set up within other structures.

168. The uninscribed blocks are not detailed here. There are ceiling blocks with star decoration and cornice pieces with decoration as well. Many alabaster fragments without relief are visible in the Musee, but it is not possible, without a more extensive investigation, to assign them correctly. The relief, published in Mysliwiec, op. cit., fig. 118, is fig. 14 .

169. On bark shrines, generally, and the scenes common to them, see G. Legrain, BIFAO 13 (1917).

170. PM II^2 63-64.

171. See Pillet, ASAE 23 (1923) 112; Pillet, ASAE 24 (1924) 59-60. Pillet adopted the theory that Thutmose built the chapel while he was a prince and abandoned it at his accession. Apparently he assumed the nemes was appropriate headgear for a prince. Bjorkman, op.cit., 107, argued only that there were but a few scenes preserved showing the king and so he may somewhere have been shown in a crown. In fact, the king appears often on the blocks and is shown on opposite doors in the crowns of Upper and Lower Egypt and twice in the khepresh.

172. Ibid., fig. 118 shows one, the other, pl. 10, is unpublished.

173. Urk. IV 1552, 5-9.

174. Barguet, Temple, 86, n. 1, 317.

175. Another piece of the right jamb (upper) preserves a text for Thutmose IV and, on its narrow face, the end of a scene from the north outer wall with a text of Amenhotep III. The former inscription names the goddess Nekhbet above and asks: "May she give life, stability, dominion, health and all joy from her every day". Below is a small seated figure of Amun offering life to the Horus falcon which tops Thutmose's Horus name. The god is called: "Amun-Re, lord of the thrones of the two lands: may he give all life, all stability and dominion". Facing this text is the king's inscription: "The Horus Strong Bull, perfect of diadems, the Two Ladies, enduring of kingship like Atum ///, the king of Upper and Lower Egypt, of Shemau and Mehu, the lord of the Two lands, lord of doing a thing, Menkheprure, the son of Re of his body, beloved of him, lord of every foreign country, Thutmose Kha Khau, beautiful Horus who is within the ꜥh, lord of the khepesh...". The text naming Amenhotep III is written behind the figure of Re-Horakhty (the legend calls him "Re, lord of sky") and is broken at the bottom of the jamb face: "It was the Good God, lord of the Two lands, lord of doing a thing, Nebmastre, the son of Re of his body [Amenhotep ruler of Thebes who decorated this monument for his father]".

176. Van Siclen, Alabaster Chapel, pl. 13, p. 11.

177. Barguet, Temple, 96, raised such a possibility, and Letellier, Hommages Sauneron, 67, suggested the chapel may have been in front of the west decorated wall of the court.

178. PM II^2 74 and mentioned in Letellier, Hommages Sauneron, 71; a block from the pylon foundation, now visible in the Karnak Musee, shows the kneeling king offering to an enthroned Amun. The cartouches of Amenhotep III are visible on the king's djed pillar offering. (Sandstone, painted.)

179. PM II^2 43 and supra, n. 139.

180. PM II^2 83. Inscription, Urk. IV 1553-55; Barguet, Temple, 105 with n. 5, 107; Bjorkman, op. cit., 101-02. Barguet wondered if the accompanying scene of priests dated from the reign of Thutmose III, but the style supports the later date. (Chig. Or. Inst. photo 8043.)

181. The date of this alteration is unknown. My collation of June 1989, following a query by Raymond Johnson concerning the types of offerings changed, found no evidence that the offerings here were altered at all. The phrase hr prwy hd n pr ꜥ3 ꜥ.w.s.was altered by carving the owl glyph into the top of the face (hr), beginning the words m ddt Imn. Urk. IV 1554, 14-15, does not indicate the change.

182. Fields reached by the inundation, according to Helck, Übersetzung, 147 n. 3. See also Faulkner, Dictionary, 138, "fresh land".

183. Urk. IV 1555, 3 𓏤𓏥𓏏𓇳, but the traces do not fit such a restoration. In fact Charles E. Wilbour's annotation in his copy of Mariette's Karnak, pl. 33, shows that he read 𓏎 , not 𓏏 .

184. Reading perhaps, n mrt rdit mn htpw-ntr m3ᶜt n. hm.i m pr Imn m b3h twt.i r nhh. At present visible is only n hm.i [   ] m̄ b3h twt.i r nhh.

185. Barguet, Temple, 107.

186. Abd el-Monem Joussef Abubakr, Untersuchungen über die ägyptischen Kronen, 44-45, calls such a crown swty and cites Edfu I, 375, where it is called the itn crown.

187. See also Redford, JARCE 13, 57, ns. 4, 14, 16, in which he cites examples of the disk named as part of a headdress.   (I am indebted to Mrs. Cynthia Sheikholesalami for this suggestion.)

188. PM II² 84. B. Bryan, "Portrait Sculpture of Thutmose IV", JARCE 24 (1987). B. Hornemann, Types I, pl. 269; G. Maspero, Guide, (1915), 182, called it Thutmose III. It has been registered as "red granite", but that is not accurate.

189. Mysliwiec, op. cit., fig. 111; 115. See also fig. 119 from the royal chariot.

190. For example, the regalia adorning the Great Sphinx vary enormously; even the dais upon which he is shown lying appears with various decorative details. See Zivie, Giza au deuxième millénaire, 308-10.

191. hk3 m3t is otherwise attested for Thutmose IV only on bricks from the mortuary temple precinct. East Berlin #'s 1544, 1554. Ausführliches Verzeichnis der aegyptischen Altertümer und Gipsabgüsse, (1899) 449.

192. This is unsure. Does the king mean that he carries the god's image? One might also read dd.i hr ntr, but what the meaning would be is difficult to say. A better reading may be possible in the future. This side of the back pillar faces into a dark corner and was not totally accessible.

193. C. Van Siclen, "A Usurped Relief of Tuthmosis IV at Karnak", VA 1 (1985) 75-79.

194. PM VII 409; good photographs are found only in H. Marucchi, Gli Obelischi, pls. 1-2; Urk. IV 1548-52; K. Martin, Ein Garantsymbol des Lebens, 165-71.

195. C. Desroches-Noblecourt, ASAE 50 (1950) 256-67; G. Lefebvre, Rev. Archéologique 34 (1949) 586-93.

196. P. Barguet, ASAE 50 (1950) 276 n. 1.

197. C. Nims, Thebes of the Pharaohs, 102; Barguet, Temple, 241. (He apparently changed his mind on the interpretation of Tuthmosis III's wb3 hry.) See n. 174; Bjorkman, op. cit., 101.

198. Wente and Van Siclen, "A Chronology", 227-28.

199. K. Martin, op. cit., 166, n. 1., daringly suggests Tuthmosis III's solar affinities were too avant-garde for the Amun clergy who therefore prevented the obelisk's erection. Although romantic, this idea needs more supporting evidence.

200. PM II² 213. P. Barguet, ASAE 50, 269-80.

201. Urk. IV 1550, 18: r sb3 hry n'Ipt-swt hft-hr W3st

202. Barguet, ASAE 50, 274, fig.7.

203. Urk. IV 584.

204. For reliable handcopy, see A. Ungarelli, Interpretatio Obeliscorum Urbis, pl. 1. The photo in Marucchi, op. cit., is slightly blurred at the height of these vignettes.

205. Martin, op. cit., 170.

206. For some reason Helck, Übersetzung, 145, translated as though mᶜndt and msktt were reversed and put exclamation points after the translation. His copy in Urk. IV 1549, however, showed them in correct order.

207. If nfr can mean "finish,complete", as well as "good and perfect", then snfr can mean "to complete". Faulkner, Dictionary, 232, included "restore" and "carry out" as two meanings. They are clearly related to this usage which appears frequently on royal monuments later added to or finished by successors. See Gardiner, Grammar3 351, who includes "finished" as a meaning of the same word. Also compare the usage in r 'iw hrw nfr n.í 'im.f "until the day on which I am finished", i.e., dead. (ibid., 389,3). This translation is just as likely as "it went well with me". And what of the colophon phrases used by scribes at the end of selections: 'iw.s pw nfr m hnw W3st (LES 60,11-12) 'iw.s pw nfr m htp (LES 29, 10)? These are far more sensibly understood as "finished" or "completed".

208. A𝕸𝕶𝕷 is partially visible, but the context is lost.

209. Mntyw.

210. Restored 'ipt rsy.

211. Desroches-Noblecourt, op. cit., 261-62; Lefebvre, op. cit., 592-93.

212. See, for example, PM II² 208-18.

213. PM II² 219-21.

214. PM II² 139. Published by Legrain without photo, Statuen I, 47-48. A photo appears in H. Brunner, ZÄS 87 (1962) pl. 5.

215. Brunner, ZÄS 87, 76-77; H. Brunner, ZÄS 83 (1958) 74ff; P. Posener-Krieger, RdE 12 (1960) 39-58.

216. There is dissension concerning the earliest date for the falcon-king representation. Posener-Krieger's argument for the Old Kingdom fails because her example (UC 16020) is an obvious forgery (see Brunner on this, ZÄS 87, 77). It is listed, with stated doubts, in the recent catalogue of A. Page, Egyptian Sculpture, 103.

217. S. Sauneron, BIFAO 70 (1971) pl.69.

218. D. Redford, JARCE 13, 51, 53, with ns. 79, 101.

219. Ibid., 54. See also Posener-Krieger, op. cit., 57-58, who hints at this, and now A. Radwan, MDAIK 31 (1975) 102-04.

220. PM II^2 96; Bryan, "Portrait Sculpture" 3ff; R. Tefnin, CdE 49 (1974) 19; Urk. IV 1564.

221. PM II^2 87; G. Legrain, Arch. Rep. 1907-08, 81. G. Legrain, Répertoire, 118, #212. I am grateful to Prof. B.V. Bothmer who kindly checked the Karnak number "concordance" in the Museum confirming that the statue has not been seen there.

222. PM II^2 198 [11], called Thutmose III. I thank Charles Van Siclen for pointing out this monument of Thutmose IV to me.

223. Ingegerd Lindblad, Royal Sculpture of the Early Eighteenth Dynasty in Egypt Medelhavsmuseet Memoir 5 (Stockholm 1984) 26, pl. 11, from Deir el Bahri.

224. PM II^2 271. Bryan, "Portrait Sculpture", 10-11, fig. 15. M. Pillet, ASAE 25 (1925) 17. The Porter and Moss reference is now out-dated since there is a colossus lying in the northeast corner of the Mut precinct (one uninscribed fragment near it) and one on the Luxor Museum porch.

225. Luxor Museum Catalogue. 147, figs. 118-19. 196. See below, n.232.

226. F. Daumas, Les Mammisis des temples égyptiens, 51; P. Barguet, Temple. 9-10.

227. For a recent discussion, see R. Fazzini, NARCE 101/102 (1977) 18-19.

228. The pillars there were roughly .95-1.00 m. on a side; Letellier,Hommages Sauneron. 63.

229. PM II^2 41 (although this may belong to a separate building--see below, n.235), 182,234. Letellier, Hommages Sauneron. 67 n.4, notes a pillar fragment built into a wall of Ramesses IX.

230. See the photograph in C. Desroches-Noblecourt, <u>Museum</u> 13 #3 (1960) 192, fig. 84 (called Thutmose III). Dr. James Romano of the Brooklyn Museum, who wrote the Luxor Catalogue entry, agrees with my reading.

231. C. Kuentz, <u>Obélisques.</u> 36, pl.11; K. Martin, <u>op.cit.</u>, 180- 81. This fragment 1s preserved to a height of 57 cm. The Journal d'Entrée lists it as a Karnak piece.

232. Letellier, <u>op.cit.</u>, 54, citing M. Hammad, <u>ASAE</u> 55 (1958) 200-02. The Ramesside cartouche was cut over the nomen of Thutmose IV. Letellier also noted that scenes of which this was a part show influential people; it is unstated why she assigns these blocks to another building.

233. Measures 70 X 46 cm.Unpublished.

234. The Fourth pylon doorway and porch are a possibility as well.

235. <u>PM</u> II^2 177; <u>Urk</u>. IV 1316.

236. But see R. Giveon, <u>JNES</u> 28 (1969) 54.

237. <u>PM</u> II^2 176; <u>Urk</u>. IV 1561.

238. <u>Urk</u>. IV 1333. <u>PM</u> II^2 176, A. Carlier, <u>Thèbes.</u> pl. 26; <u>LD</u> III 61.

239. The top of the block separates the name leaving the lower half of the reed leaf in 'Imn, and the <u>n</u> sign but not the m<u>n</u>. There are chisel marks over the name.

240. <u>PM</u> II^2 7; Barguet, et als, <u>Karnak-Nord</u> IV, 55 [3],fig.84.

241. <u>PM</u> II^2 7; <u>Karnak-Nord</u> IV, 55 [4], fig. 85; other side of the block of Ramesside date, <u>ibid.</u>, 64 [34], fig. 104. <u>PM</u> II^2 4, mentions a lintel fragment (<u>Karnak-Nord</u> IV,61 [15] pl. 58a) as probably belonging to Thutmose IV. In fact the lintel is Amenhotep III's work; it even shows part of that king's Horus name, ḫ^c m m3^{c}t, the name he also gave to the Montu temple.

242. J. Jacquet, <u>BIFAO</u> 71 (1972) 156, pl.39. 214. M. Abd-Elrazik, <u>MDAIK</u> 27 (1971) 222-24.

243. M. Abd-Elrazik, <u>MDAIK</u> 27 (1971) 222-24.

244. <u>PM</u> II^2 538; Abdel-Qader Muhammad, <u>ASAE</u> 60 (1968) 248-49, pl.25.

245. It may be that this stela, like the next, was entirely reworked by Seti I. The name of Amun is intact, and this would certainly suggest the fact.

246. El Sayed Hegazi, "Découverte d'une stèle de Thoutmosis IV sur le parvis du temple de Louqsor", <u>Dossiers histoire et archéologie: Egypte</u> 101 (January 1986)

20; El Sayed Hegazy and B. Bryan, "A New Stela of Thutmose IV from the Luxor Temple", <u>VA</u> 2 (1986) 93-100.

247. See the various articles by Lanny Bell and William Murnane concerning the theology of the temple in <u>Dossiers histoire et archéologie</u> 101 (January 1986). Murnane, "La Grande Fete d'Opet", "Le mystere de la naissance divine du roi"; Bell, "La reine Hatchepsout au temple de Louqsor", "Le culte du ka royal". See also Lanny Bell, "Luxor Temple and the Cult of the Royal Ka", <u>JNES</u> 44 (1985) 251-94.

248. Cf., D.B. Redford, "On the Chronology of the Egyptian Eighteenth Dynasty", <u>JNES</u> 25 (1966) 120, who proposes the second month of the calendar year as accession based on Manethonian numbers combined with Amenhotep II's accession date. The similarity is noteworthy, but certainly not convincing.

249. <u>PM</u> II^2 539,called [Ramesses II] after Muhammad, <u>ASAE</u> 60, 247-48, pls. 19,20,22; M. Abd-Elrazik, <u>MDAIK</u> 27, 222-23, pls. 63a,b.

250. <u>Ibid.</u>, 223.

251. Only one possibility, but a good one. See the lists of Thutmose III and Amenhotep II. J. Simons, <u>Topographical Lists.</u> I-VII.

252. Qatna and Sidon are possible.See Chapter 6.

253. Nubian toponyms have been catalogued and discussed in K. Zibelius, <u>Afrikanische Orts-und Völkernamen in hieroglyphischen und hieratischen Texten.</u>
    Gwrwbw, <u>Ibid.</u>, 170.Zibelius suggests this place had already disappeared in Amenhotep II's reign.
    Inknn3, <u>Ibid.</u>, 83.
    Tmkr,   <u>Ibid.</u>, 173. Here written ⸂𓎡𓃀𓈖𓈖⸃. The ⸂𓎡⸃ substituting for ⸂𓏏⸃ may be the 𓏲𓏭 bread sign ?.
    Gbš3gi for Bgšg , <u>Ibid.</u>, 113.
    W3w3t , <u>Ibid.</u>, 101-02, often written without a <u>t</u>.
    K3ti3, <u>Ibid.</u>, 169.

254. <u>Urk.</u> IV 1334-35, especially 1335,10. The fragments shown in Abd Elrazik's article, 𓇋𓏏[ ],[ ]𓇋𓈖𓐍𓄿 , and 𓆑𓈖𓄿[ ]   may be represented in this same list: line 6,

(𓏏 for 𓂋, Zibelius,<u>op.cit.</u>, 182.)

Zibelius, <u>op.cit.</u>, 22, calls this a list of Thutmose III, but Helck assigns it to Amenhotep II as does <u>PM</u> II^2 84. It should belong to the latter king, for the cartouches have been erased (on the northern list; none exist on the other) betraying the desire to erase Amun's name.

255. PM II^2 446-47. W. F. Petrie, Six Temples at Thebes. 7-9, pl.24; H. Ricke, Der Totentempel Thutmoses' III. 13-15, pl.11; A. Badawy, A History of Egyptian Architecture: The Empire. 340. Recent work in the precinct by the University of Pisa under the direction of Dr. Edda Bresciani. Reports in Orientalia N.S. (J. Leclant) 43 (1974) 197; 44 (1975) 219; 45 (1976) 296; 46 (1977) 261; 47 (1978) 296; 49 (1980) 384; 51 (1985) 381. Also, E. Bresciani, Egitto e Vicino Oriente 3 (1980) 1-36; EVO 6 (1983) 3-6, 2 figs.; C. Guidotti, "Ceramica dipinta dell'epoca di Tutmosi IV a Gurna", EVO 4 (1981) 95-107.

256. PM II^2 447; add East Berlin 1552,1554; PM I^2 2 683, PM 1^2 2 700; A. Wiedemann, Aeg. Gesch. 378 n.4; E. Bresciani, NARCE 85 (1973) 3; one, Metropolitan Museum, W. Hayes, Scepter II, 151. M. Nelson, A.-M. Layrette, G. Lecuyot, "Les Dispositions du Ramesseum", ASAE 68 (1982) 13-14, fig. 7 [3 examples].

257. J. Leclant, Orientalia N.S. 54 (1985) 381.

258. E. Bresciani, EVO 3 (1980) 4. We mention here JE 58685, a dark blue faience plaque, stela shaped, .44 m. in height. It was purchased by Lansing in Luxor and was seized later in Assiut (according to the Journal d'Entree.). The king's nomen "Thutmose kha khau" is the only inscription. It may stem from the funerary temple foundation deposits.

259. Ricke, op.cit., 13-15, pl.11.

260. W. F. Petrie, Six Temples. pl.6 [6,7]; B. Adams, Egyptian Objects in the Victoria and Albert Museum. #10 VA 911.1896 and #11 VA 912.1896, figs. 13-14. #10 = Petrie, Six Temples. pl.6 [6]; #11 is similar to pl.6 [7]. PM I^2 1, 447 incorrectly calls UC 14465 a relief of Amun. UC 14465 = Petrie's pl.1 [2].

261. Unpublished. The entry in the Journal d'Entree identifies Cairo Temp. 8-6-24-6 "Qurna 1858". The Special register for Room 19, location Center W, number 13939 locates the blocks. A note states that the back of the blocks was sawn off in 1942, probably to ease transport. The original thickness is given as .75 m. The present length is 1.6 m by 1.15 m. height. The other side is undecorated.

262. B. Adams, Egyptian Objects; H. Stewart, Egyptian Stelae, Relief and Paintings UC 14465. See the important review of B. Adams, Egyptian Objects by Claude Vandersleyen in CdE 53 (1978) 291-92, where he gives corrections for a number of objects.

263. PM II^2 446; H. Stewart, Egyptian Stelae. Relief and Paintings, 4, pl.3.1; Urk. IV 1556. The fragment is some 19 X 23 cm.

264. PM II^2 446; Urk. IV 1556; Petrie, Six Temples pl.1 [8]. 35 X 26 X 70 cm.

265. W. Helck, Beziehungen. 275, 362; Urk. IV 1656-57. Amenhotep III's mortuary temple.

266. E. Bresciani, <u>EVO</u> 3 (1980) 8, pl. VII a,b. Intact stela, .42 meters high by .30 wide by .10. The text is identical to that on Oriental Institute 1363.

267. <u>PM</u> II^2 446; Stewart, <u>op.cit.</u>, 50, pl.40.2. Limestone. 15 X 17 cm. On a later date, see also Helck, <u>Beziehungen.</u> 493, 511, n.117.

268. <u>PM</u> II^2 535; T. Allen, <u>Handbook of the Egyptian Collection.</u> 41. Given by Emile Brugsch.

269. Cf., W.F.Petrie, <u>Memphis</u> I, pl.8.

270. On these, see Petrie, <u>Six Temples.</u> 7,9,21,29,30, pls. 3,20. Also, one jar fragment not listed in <u>PM</u> II^2 appears in J. Quibbell, <u>Ramesseum.</u> pl.18. A foundation deposit of the king may have existed under the Ramesside temple, <u>ibid.</u>, 5.

271. Bresciani, <u>EVO</u> 3 (1980) 10-14, fig.5.

272. <u>PM</u> I^2 2 559-60; H. Carter, P. Newberry, G. Maspero, G.E. Smith, <u>The Tomb of Thoutmôsis IV:</u> E. Thomas, <u>The Royal Necropoleis of Thebes.</u> 80-81. John Romer, <u>The Valley of the Kings</u>, 184-96.

273. Carter, et als., <u>op.cit.</u>, VIII.

274. Carter, <u>op.cit.</u>, VIII; Thomas, <u>op.cit.</u> 61 with 100 n. 142.

275. Thomas, <u>op.cit.</u>, 81.

276. Numbers 54419 (about 4 cm. long by 2 wide) and 65232, a larger plaque about 7 cm. in length. The last was a gift of Robert Mond in 1939.

277. MMA 30.8.21-24. See Appendix on Tomb Objects.

278. J. Weinstein, <u>Foundation Deposits.</u> 117.

279. Stockholm Medelhavmuseet 14385, B. Peterson, <u>CdE</u>. 42 (1967) 266-68. He pointed out that Thutmose did not attempt to hide her kingship on this bowl. In fact, changing <u>ntr nfr</u> to <u>Wsir</u> has just that effect. But the jar from KV 43 does let her royal title stand.

280. Romer, <u>op.cit.</u>, 192, considered the Hatshepsut object from the foundation deposit to have been taken from her nearby foundation deposit. This is still possible but not demanded by the evidence.

281. Carter, <u>op.cit.</u>, XI.

282. <u>Ibid.</u>, XXXIII-IV; IX.

283. PM I² 2 555; G. Daressy, Cercueils des cachettes royales, 217, pl.61; G. Daressy, ASAE 4 (1903) 110-12; G.E. Smith, ASAE 4 (1903) 112-15; Smith, in Carter, op. cit., XLI-LV.

284. Carter, op.cit., XXX- XXXIII.

285. Ibid., IX-XI; Thomas, op.cit., 81.

286. Carter, op.cit., X, fig. 2.

287. Thomas, op.cit., 81, is apparently unaware of the scene in Th.tb. 64 where Prince Amenemhet appears with other royal children.

288. CG 46037-40, Carter, op.cit., 6-7.

289. I am indebted to John Larson of the Oriental Institute of the University of Chicago who brought the Chicago Davis Collection pieces from KV 43 to my attention. Mr. Larson is presently conducting a study of Davis' connections with KV 55 and has discovered a number of interesting facts about the American patron's other projects as a by-product.

290. E. Thomas, JARCE 3 (1964) 71-78.

291. G. Robins, "Anomalous proportions in the tomb of Haremhab (KV 57)", GM 65 (1983) 91-96. She had earlier arrived at the 19 grid count described here but abandoned it for reasons unconvincing to this reader. Ibid., 96 n.10.

292. Carter, op.cit., XXXV-XL.

293. W. Hayes, Royal Sarcophagi of the XVIIIth Dynasty, fig. 7, 55-57, 116-23.

294. Ibid., 116-23. See also L. Kakošy, ZÄS 100 (1975) 35-41, who pointed out that Thutmose IV was the first king to include the negative confession on his sarcophagus. Kakošy felt it marked the growing importance of personal judgment and religion.

295. PM II² 448.

296. L. Bell, Mélanges Mokhtar, 32-34.

297. PM I² 2, 547-50. For cartouche plaques from foundation deposit, Carter MSS. i.J.386, Nos. 9,10,26,27,29,30,50,51. For scene with ka of Thutmose IV, LD III 78e. (Incorrect in PM as ka of Amenhotep III.)

298. PM I² 2,550, referencing Carter MSS. concerning the foundation plaques. Romer, Valley of the Kings, 240.

299. R. Mond, 0. Meyers, Temples of Armant, Text., 3.

300. Ch. Desroches Noblecourt and C. Leblanc, "Considérations sur l'existence des divers temples de Monthou à travers les âges, dans le site de Tôd", BIFAO 84 (1984) 81-109, pls. 27-36.

301. Ibid., pl. 34A and p. 92 citing Bisson de la Roque, Tôd, III-IV.

302. Noblecourt and Leblanc, op.cit., 97.

303. PM V 188,189; J. Tylor, S. Clarke, The Temple of Amenhotep III, pls. 8-10.

304. Supra, n. 207.

305. Tylor, op.cit., pls. 5-7; LD IV Text 43. ḏd mdw ỉn Nbt ỉwnw-R-ỉnt s3.(ỉ) n ḥt.(ỉ) nb t3wy Nbm3ꜥt-Rꜥ ỉr n.k n.(ỉ) mnw nfr ḥwt-nṯr ḥrt m m3wt kd.ti m ỉnr m k3wt nḥḥ n mwt.f [Nbt ỉwnw-R-ỉnt]. Speech by the Mistress of Gebelein-mouth of the Valley: My son of my body, lord of the Two Lands, Neb-maat-Re: You have made for me a beautiful monument, a desert temple, anew, built in stone as an eternal construction for his mother [Mistress of Gebelein-mouth of the Valley].

306. On this see B. Bryan, "Private Relief Styles outside Thebes" in the Proceedings of a Symposium on the Art of Amenhotep III held in Cleveland, November 1987. To be published by The Cleveland Museum of Art, 1990.

307. G. Gabra, A. Farid, "Neue Materialien zu königlichen Baudenkmälern in Edfu", MDAIK 37 (1981) 184-85, pl. 30, figs. 3-5. [181-86]

308. PM V 225; J. DeMorgan, Catalogue, 113-15, F. Junge, Elephantine XI Funde und Bauteile (Mainz 1983) 36-39; Urk. IV 1561. JE 41560, Ht. 1.62 meters. Diameter, .96 meters. Ch. Desroches Noblecourt, et als, Catalogue of the Ramses le Grand exhibition (Paris 1976) No. X, page 57.

309. PM V 225; LD IV Text 123-24; H. Gauthier, LdR II 293.

310. Junge, op.cit., 29-36 and 37-39.

311. LD IV Text 123 bottom. Thutmose III.

312. Junge, op.cit., 38-39. C. Van Siclen, "The building history of the Tuthmosid temple at Amada and the Jubilees of Tuthmosis IV", VA 3 (1987) 61, with the same conclusion.

313. PM V 244; Urk. IV 1561; Kuentz, Obélisques, 31-32, pl.10; K. Martin, op.cit., 175.

314. PM V 254, DeMorgan, Catalogue, 66-69, gives Year 8 for the long text and Year 7 for that with Iaret. U. Bouriant, Rec.Trav. 15 (1893) 178-79, is the preliminary publication of the long inscription as copied by DeMorgan; Urk. IV

1545-48; <u>LD</u> III 69e = Year 7 with Iaret; <u>LD</u> IV Text 128 for Year 7 = DeMorgan, <u>Catalogue</u>, 66-69, Year 8.

315. <u>PM</u> V 254; DeMorgan, <u>op.cit.</u>, 68,69[3]; J. Champollion, <u>Notices Descriptives</u> I 631 [d], 616 [6]; <u>LD</u> IV <u>Text</u> 127, with ns. 3-4; add Bankes MSS. Album I,54,55. For the location of the texts, see also Champollion le Jeune, <u>Lettres écrites d'Égypte et de Nubie en 1828 et 1829.</u> l68-69.

316. <u>PM</u> VII 65-73, especially 68; P. Barguet, M. Dewachter, <u>Le Temple d'Amada</u> I-IV.

317. Barguet and Dewachter, <u>op.cit.</u>, II, 1-17.

318. <u>Ibid.</u>, 2,4; E. Meyer, <u>Geschichte des Altertums</u>[2] II.1 149 n.2. (contra a 30-year principle); most recently, Wente and Van Siclen, "A Chronology", 227,229, favoring 30 years; E. Hornung, <u>Studien zum Sedfest</u>, 62-64, contains the view supported here with modification (see Chapter 1); the unusual interpretation of Aldred, <u>ZÄS</u> 94, 1-6 is of interest.

319. <u>Urk</u>. IV 1296-96. Van Siclen, <u>VA</u> 3 (1987) 53; Junge, <u>op.cit.</u>, 38-39.

320. Junge, <u>op.cit.</u>, 39 takes this position following in this Borchardt and Arnold.

321. Van Siclen, <u>VA</u> 3, 52ff.

322. Dewachter, et als., <u>Le Temple d'Amada</u> Cahier IV, Pilier I. Compare the king in <u>khepresh</u> in C2 on the north wall.

323. <u>PM</u> II2 48. Those of Ramesses II on the south wall east of the doorway are most similar.

324. <u>LD</u> III 69h; Barguet and Dewachter, <u>op.cit.</u>, IV C3. <u>Dhwty ms dw3 n hk3 ntr ^c3 nb pt hnty T3-Sty</u>. Note the obvious pun on the king's name. This epithet is difficult; it is written over the god who here exceptionally wears the lunar disk on his head. The idea is expressed a bit differently in the Metropolitan Museum of Art statue of Horemheb (<u>Urk</u>. IV 2089-94). There is said "in the morning he summons heaven".

325. This is unsure but follows Helck, <u>Übersetzung</u>, 155 n.4. Bata is a bull and this animal resembles a ram far more than a long-horned steer. But there is no Nubian toponym which is similar.

326. Zibelius, <u>op.cit.</u>, 75-77.

327. Barguet and Dewachter, <u>op.cit.</u>, IV C9 . D. Dunham, <u>Semna Kumma</u>, 3: For this suggestion I am indebted to Dr. Robert D. Delia whose dissertation concerned the reign of Sesostris III. Apparently Semna exceptionally did employ the cartouche as part of the name.

328. Urk. IV 1566-68; LD III 69f; Baraguet and Dewachter, op.cit. IV C 41-46.

329. Urk. IV 1943-47; a recent study by G. Fecht, ZÄS 94 (1967) 25-50, but see D. Redford, JARCE 13, 59-60, n.102, opposing some conclusions there.

330. H. Stewart, JEA 46 (1960) 85-87; H.Stewart, Bull. Inst. Arch. 6 (1967) 29ff.

331. K. Michalowski, Faras Die Kathedrale aus dem Wüstensand.(Benzinger Verlag 1967) 27, pls. 3,4. J. Karkowski, Faras V,179.

332. Ibid.,177-78.

333. H.S. Smith, Fortress of Buhen. The Inscriptions, 139, pl.35.4, #1724.

334. Ibid., pl.45.

335. PM VII 131; Ashmolean 1893.173; Urk.IV 1637; W.E. Crum, PSBA 16 (1893) 17-19; L. Wooley, R. MacIver, Buhen VII, 96 [4].

336. H. Jacquet-Gordon, C. Bonnet, J. Jacquet, JEA 55 (1969) 103-11; C. Maystre, Kush 15 (1967-68)196. Thutmose III or IV. One plate shows the nomen as Ḏḥwty-[ms].

337. PM VII 215; G. Reisner, JEA 5 (1918) 99-100, plan on pl.10; D. Dunham, Barkal Temples, 67.

338. Reisner, op.cit., 100.

339. The plaque as illustrated by Reisner does not show the epithet, kha khau, but it is present. See Dunham, The Barkal Temples, pl.56; (2.1 X 1.4 X .4 cm.). J. Weinstein, op.cit., 212-13.

340. Reisner, op.cit., 100.

341. PM VII 222; Dunham, Barkal Temples, 25; fig. 19,pl.24.

342. PM VII 251; A. Gardiner, T. Peet, J.Černý, Inscriptions of Sinai[2] I, pl.69, II 38, 169, W.F. Petrie, Researches in the Sinai. 78; Weill, Recueil, 202 [94] and probably [95].

343. PM VII 351; Gardiner, et als , op.cit., I, pl.62 [207], I 164; Weill, op.cit., 201 [9:2].

344. Petrie, Researches, 79; Gardiner, et als., op.cit., II 164; Weill, op.cit., 206 [103-05].

345. In The Impact of Egypt on Canaan, 59, fig.29, Giveon published a relief from room C which he attributed to Thutmose IV. But a close look at the photo shows a cartouche above the king. The remains show ⌈ꜣ⸗⌉ . The king is therefore Amenhotep III who has been all along known as the builder of room C. Gardiner, et als, op.cit., II,38.

346. PM VII; Petrie, Researches. fig. 148 [8]. This could be Amenhotep II as well; the cartouche shows
[   ]hprw-r͗ᶜ.

347. PM VII 361; L. Speleers, Recueil des Inscriptions Égyptiennes, 99 #383.

348. PM VII 345, Urk. IV 1564, 1634; Gardiner, et als., op.cit., II,81,. I, pl.20 #58. The scene measures 53 X 68 cm.. A recent discussion in G. Björkman, JARCE 11 (1974) 43.

349. PM VII 345; Urk. IV 1564; Gardiner, et als., op.cit., II 82; I, pl.19 #60. The rock tablet measures 60 X 60 cm. R. Giveon, Tel Aviv 5 (1979) 170-74, pl.44.

350. PM VII 396; F. von Bissing, ZÄ NF 12 (1940) 149-51.

351. I am indebted to the kindness of two colleagues for knowledge and photos of this relief. Mr. Richard Fazzini, Curator of the Department of Egyptian Classical and Middle Eastern Art in The Brooklyn Museum first showed me a snapshot of the object. Dr. William Kelly Simpson, Professor of Egyptology, Yale University, sent me the fine photograph reproduced here.

352. F. Daumas, Les Mammisis de Dendara (Cairo 1957) pl. XLI and pp. 110-11.

353. PM II² 349 (Hatshepsut); 326 (Amenhotep III). The 18th Dynasty parallels to the scene, however, show kneeling goddesses holding the children.

354. Daressy, Fouilles de la Vallée des Rois, pl. 57, p. 299. Wood, 30.4 cm. height. Wearing klaft headdress, had inlaid eyes, with some blue paint remaining around lids. Text down front: "Good god Menkheprure, 'vindicated', beloved of Osiris, great god, lord of Ta-Djeser, lord of sky".

355. I am indebted to the kindness of Mr. John Larson of the Oriental Institute Museum Archives who kindly provided me copies of the information regarding Thutmose IV's tomb objects in Chicago's Oriental Institute Museum. His work on Theodore Davis' explorations in the Kings' Valley has led him to a number of tangential discoveries, including some linking OI fragments from KV 43 to objects described in the publication.

356. C.N. Reeves, "The Tomb of Tuthmosis IV: Two Questionable Attributions," GM 44 (1981) 49-55, fig. 1. The astronomical instrument is not necessarily from KV 43 at all. John Larson, "The Tut-ankh-amun Astronomical Instrument", Oriental Institute Museum Featured Object Number one January 1985, 1-4 (Publication by the Oriental Institute Museum Education Office) agrees with Reeves that KV 43 is

an unlikely provenance. In a personal communication (October 13, 1989) Larson writes that "the condition of the wood is quite good and, on that basis alone, I feel strongly that the object must have lain in a relatively dry place and, therefore, probably not in the Theban flood plain". This would disagree with Reeves' preference for the funerary temple (p.52). Note that thanks to Mr. Larson the plummet OIM 10648 has been removed from any connection with KV 43. That piece, as pointed out in Larson's publication, was purchased separately from the astronomical instrument and has no known association with the tomb at all. It was mistakenly included in the revised edition of Porter and Moss' volume I 1.

Note that a pectoral claimed to have been seen by Champollion and Rosellini was also recognized by Reeves to have been one of the painted necklaces on the wall of TT 76 of Tjenuna.

357. PM I^2 1, 555. Daressy, Cercueils, pl. lxi, page 217. Nomen cartouche written without ḫ^c ḫ^{c}w.

358. This list is based on a variety of sources, published and unpublished. For the inscribed statuary of Thutmose IV, see B. Bryan, JARCE 24 (1987) 3-20. I owe an incalculable debt to Prof. Claude Vandersleyen and Prof. Bernard V. Bothmer whose photographs and expertise have been a constant aid.

359. B. Bothmer, BMFA 52, 4-20. Limestone.

360. Bryan, op.cit., figs. 1-3.

361. Ibid., figs. 20-23, 26.

362. Ibid., figs. 16-19.

363. Ibid., figs. 20-21.

364. Ibid., figs. 12-14.

365. J. Cooney, J. of Glass Studies 2, fig. 12.

366. S. Schoske, D. Wildung, Ägyptische Kunst München (Munich 1985) fig. 40, p. 61.

367. Despite the interesting discussion of C.N. Reeves, "Belzoni, the Egyptian Hall, and the date of a long-known sculpture", JEA 75 (1989) 235-37. The particular features of this statue are so close to those exhibited on CG 42080, Louvre E 13889, and the general ones of all inscribed statuary as discussed in Bryan, op.cit., 3-20, the suggestion of archaism is difficult to believe. Indeed, if the Sais provenance is correct, we should point out that the two Alexandria Museum statues of Thutmose IV in black granite are from the Delta, one coming from near Sais. Re-use in a later context would hardly be extraordinary.

368. Ägyptischer Altertümer (1899) 209.

369. W. Decker, Cd'E 44 (1969) 95-99.

370. W.L. Nash, PSBA 29 (1907) 175, pl.2.

CIVIL, RELIGIOUS AND MILITARY ADMINISTRATION

This chapter will outline the administration of Thutmose IV. I have followed Helck's, Kees', and Schulman's[1] structures to some extent, but even these invaluable works cannot cover every area of administrative concern. The data from this and other reigns is occasionally at odds with earlier reconstructions. Thus, in addition to presenting a sketch of Thutmose's officialdom, the discussion below will point out which commentaries it may be at odds with.

A word should be said, before beginning, about dating individuals to this or any other reign on the basis of Theban tomb painting styles. It is unsatisfactory both to do so and not to do so, since one risks inaccuracy by either choice. Thutmose IV's reign has been credited with a large number of tombs in Thebes, probably far more than it ever saw constructed. Some assigned to it should rather be dated to Amenhotep III's rule, while others were no doubt built earlier than Thutmose IV's monarchy. But because it is true that tomb decoration most visibly expressed the stylistic changes occurring in the arts over several reigns, the short reign of Thutmose IV has become a "dumping ground". What is needed is a new full-scale study of the tombs[2] with a view to identifying the stages of stylistic change from the reign of Thutmose III to that of late Amenhotep III[3]--for it is the concentration on the resultant difference in style, and not the means to it, that has resulted in some 30-40 tombs being assigned to Thutmose IV.[4] Wegner's 1933 study[5] is still the best one available, but it suffers from omissions of tombs which do not fit the categories he set out. Wherever possible, tomb dating is suggested in Appendix IV to this Chapter and in the text. While stylistic details are useful, in the discussion below, if an individual is included as part of the administration on the basis of style, he will be clearly identified as such.

1. Civil Administration.

1.1. The Vizierate.

The viziers dated to the reign of Thutmose IV have been known for many years and have been discussed by Weil and Helck.[6] More recently Charles Aling in his dissertation [7] discussed these officers along with other highly-placed members of the administration. One Hepu was vizier in the south during Thutmose IV's reign, and a Ptahhotep administered the north. That the two viziers existed simultaneously is confirmed by the Munich papyrus dated to Thutmose's reign in which both men, called "Vizier" t3t appear as judges.[8] Hepu's tomb (66)[9] is on the prestigious mount of Sheik abd-el Gurnah, and its placement, as pointed out by Helck,[10] conforms to that of viziers under Thutmose III and Amenhotep II--that is, it is the most deeply placed tomb of the reign. But the tomb itself is small and comparatively unimpressive when viewed beside others of the period (e.g., TT 76 and 63). Its state of preservation is so poor that few scenes can be wholly reconstructed; at least two things, however, may be said with certainty. The decoration is most similar to that in the tombs of Amenhotep si-se (75) and Tjanni (74). Wegner also felt this was the case,[11] especially with regard to tomb 75, and he also felt that these tombs must represent the earliest examples of the reign. Secondly, Hepu had the text of the Installation of the Vizier inscribed on the walls of his tomb[12] in addition to scenes of the king before whom Hepu stood presenting the revenues of the land. The preserved scenes represent a number of workshop activities and are similar to some of Rekhmire's craft scenes. The archaizing style may therefore have been somewhat intentional to recall the monuments of influential earlier viziers.

Beyond the tomb and some funerary cones, Hepu is known only by the papyrus mentioned above. Only one son is known for him, the wab priest of Amun, Neferhebef.[13] Hepu's titles and epithets from his tomb are indicative of his exalted position in the land, but one cannot help wondering about the meagerness of his chapel. Perhaps it was due to the lack of ample space on the mountain, at the central location of accessible height which he apparently preferred. Hepu's tomb is alone among those of his contemporaries in its location at the base of the gebel.[14] Other high-ranking members of Thutmose's court were forced to build at foot-tiring altitudes because the mount was already so honey-combed. Hepu may then have sacrificed large size in order to maintain the vizier's central position in the necropolis. If this should prove unlikely as a suppostion, however, we may be forced to consider that the vizierate under Thutmose IV did not have the influence it generally exhibited during the 18th Dynasty. Certainly the fortunes of the Chief Royal Stewards improved during this period (see Tjenuna's entry below).

About the second vizier, Ptahhotep, nothing is known beyond the one papyrus mentioned. Quite possibly he was buried in the north. Some scholars have assigned a third vizier, one Thutmose, to this reign. Weil, followed by Hayes,[15] believed this man served under Amenhotep II and Thutmose IV, while Helck, following Anthes,[16] assigned him to Amenhotep III's rule. This Thutmose was a member of a powerful northern family known to us by several monuments--one of his sons was a high priest of Ptah, Ptahmose; the other was Chief Steward of Amenhotep III's funerary temple and is almost certainly the Meriptah mentioned several times on Malkata labels dating from the last years of the reign.[17] The style of Ptahmose's false door naming his father is most consistent with a date in Thutmose IV's reign based on the facial features of the deceased and the proportions of the figure as well, and this coupled with the floruit of Thutmose's sons under Amenhotep III certainly and Thutmose IV (probably) suggests he held office as early as Amenhotep II's reign and possibly into Thutmose IV's. Since we have no idea when Thutmose died, the installation of Ptahhotep cannot be supposed either. Whether viziers were, as a rule, turned out of office by new rulers cannot be clearly demonstrated. Aling asserted such was the case[18] and thereby concluded , for example, that Thutmose did not serve under Thutmose IV, but only under Amenhotep III. But Rekhmire and Ramose are obvious exceptions to this rule in the 18th dynasty, while Paser, Hori, Neferrenpet and Nebmaatre-nakht stand out in the 19th and 20th dynasties. And there may be others, since many viziers are only names to us--without dates at all.[19] It is more reasonable to assume that most kings made their own choices of viziers as a practical matter.

A final comment concerning the vizier Thutmose relates to a hieratic ostracon in the Metropolitan Museum assigned to him by Hayes.[20] The paleography is Ramesside. The scribe of the tomb Hori is mentioned on it, thereby suggesting a Theban provenance, rather than a northern one. And indeed there is another vizier named Thutmose attested in the Ramesside period; he is known by Cairo ostracon 25339.[21] Quite possibly this ostracon should be re-assigned to that man.

The Vizier Hepu quite possibly died before Thutmose IV's reign ended. The painting style of his tomb is by no means the most elaborate example of dated chapels. Since tombs were decorated at the end of a person's life we may suggest a second southern vizier served under Thutmose IV. The most likely man to identify is Ptahmose, known from some funerary cones, a stela in Lyon, a statue in Brooklyn, and an Abydene votive shabti.[22] This Ptahmose was also High priest of Amun; his only dated material comes from the reign of Amenhotep III. If, however, Ramose (or Amenhotep) was southern vizier at the last of that rule and if one Meryptah was High priest of Amun after Year 20,[23] then Ptahmose is more comfortably placed in the first decades of Amenhotep III's reign. Thutmose IV's High priest(s) of Amun are poorly known; Ptahmose might have filled this function for him as well. There are funerary cones in Ptahmose's name providing hope that his tomb will someday be identified.

A last vizier suggested for the reign is the owner of Stela B from Giza.[24] That prince,discussed at length in Chapter 2,was called vizier by Helck,[25] only the titles s3b t3yt are attested for this prince; Overseer of the City and Vizier (mr niwt and t3t), the true titles of the vizier,[26] were not applied to this man. We must conclude that this prince was a judge and bore the titles of that office.[27] He was not vizier.

1.2. Overseer of the Treasury (mr htmw).

Only one man may with certainty be cited as Overseer of the Treasury in Thutmose IV's reign. That man is the well-known Fayum Mayor, Sobekhotep, whose tomb is number 63 on the hill of Sheik abd-el Gurnah.[28] The tomb of Sobekhotep is fast deteriorating but is a beautiful example of painting during Thutmose IV's reign. The use of plaster relief on the wigs, a most attractive detail, appears also in tomb 76 of Tjenuna. Sobekhotep's chapel, however, has suffered from collapse of the plaster decoration recently and earlier fragments were removed. Pieces of the tomb's presentation scene before Pharaoh Thutmose may be seen on view in the Metropolitan Museum and the British Museum.

Sobekhotep has figured in Chapters 2 and 3 due to his liaisons with royal children. Such responsibility to the royal family was not at all uncommon for Overseers of the Treasury, since they were to a great extent personal emissaries of the king.[29] The office required a man who could travel on mining expeditions to oversee production as well as supervise the palace granaries closer to home; he was clearly one whom the king could trust at a distance. He worked with the Vizier and as such shared the responsibility for opening the palace treasury each day; but Treasurer were usually trusted friends of sovereigns to whom princes were sometimes entrusted to learn the demands of statecraft.

Sobekhotep must have acquired his office through his father, Min, who was Overseer of the Treasury for Thutmose III;[30] one might assume that the son served under Amenhotep II at some point, but there is no mention of this monarch on any of Sobekhotep's monuments. His genealogy has been set out in Chapter 3; it need only be reiterated that he inherited his Fayum titles through his wife (a second Sobekhotep known from two statues was probably his father-in-law [31]) and then passed them to his son, Paser, who continued to function as Mayor of the Fayum at least until the last years of Amenhotep III. The Overseer of Treasury title did not remain with an identified son, but went to Sobekhotep's Steward, Ptahmose, who was shown in tomb 63.[32] Ptahmose may not have immediately assumed the Treasurer's post, since Merire whose tomb was recently found by Alain Zivie[33] probably vacated the post early in Amenhotep's reign. (Another son of Sobekhotep was one Djehuty who was a Chief priest of Iah,[34] the moon.)

Sobekhotep was one the most influential members of Thutmose's administration. His tomb is large and beautifully decorated; and he is known from two statues [35] (neither of tomb type), one of which links him to crown prince Amenhotep III during a residence in the Fayum. P. Munich 809 was first published by Spiegelberg[36] with a facsimile copy and a handcopy. His commentary is able and has not been greatly improved upon in sixty years. The case has been cited several times as an example of civil procedure in the early New Kingdom.[37] The papyrus records the outcome of a court proceeding in the palace at Thebes before notable dignitaries of the land, including both viziers. The court has therefore been generally termed a Vizier's court. The case preserved in Munich 809 was likely but one of several decided by that court, but it is the only one preserved to us. Sobekhotep, the Treasurer acted as legal representative for the cause of Hathor's temple at Gebelein, and the court found his position to be the correct one. Unfortunately, most of his speech before the <u>kenbet</u> is lost in lacunae, although its conclusion is intact. We learn that the Treasurer asserted that revenues due the Temple had been unchanged since the reign of Ahmose, although a challenge brought in the reign of Thutmose III has apparently been recently raised as argument by the soldier Mery. Upon being judged wrong, Mery was given 100 blows with the bastinado, most likely for bringing a false case.[38] Exactly what effect the case's outcome will have on Mery's personal finances remains unclear. Nor is it certain whether the Treasurer generally performed the duty of legal counsel. Perhaps the court, convened by Viziers who were Sobekhotep's superiors, charged him with the responsibility. According to Helck,[39] Sobekhotep was not representing his position or himself, but was present to speak for the temple, possibly having been retained because of his influence. If such was the case, it was warranted since Sobekhotep won the case for the temple, and the soldier Mery was beaten for his trouble.

About the expeditions of Sobekhotep we are in the dark. Only one possible mission may be recognized in the year 4 text of Serabit el-Khadim[40] where the mine-opening was commemorated. There exists a text of Nebi, the Mayor of Sile, and in a crude graffito beneath the scene one could read mr (?) pr n mr htmw P[thms]; at least pr n mr htmw is legible, and if Ptahmose was the writer, then Sobekhotep was likely the Overseer of the Treasury. Certainly the turquoise-mining expeditions would have been logical assignments for the Treasurer. The Treasurer's role, however, seems to have changed in the years between Min's expedition to Silsila[41] and Sobekhotep's tenure in the office. The Treasurers are hardly attested among expeditions to quarries or on foreign missions to secure royal treasure or exotic gums and incense. Rather the palace administration in general, by the documentary record, paid more attention to cattle and agricultural production on royal lands.[42]

The large majority of Sobekhotep's titles appear in the Urkunden IV entry, but at least two seen in the tomb can be added to those: the ceiling texts in the tomb call the Mayor Great One in Ta-She (wr m t3 Š), a title also used by Sobekhotep, son of Kapu.[43] Wr m t3 Š also once appears in fragments fallen from the back wall of the inner hall. "Great one in Ta She" was an honorific designation which, in the case of the Treasurer, was used instead of the mayor's title to describe his attachment to the Fayum. Since Sobekhotep's son Paser had already assumed the mayor's title of Mayor (h3ty-ꜥ), the Treasurer did not use that title regularly. A second title missing from the Urkunden tomb texts is "he who follows the king in all his places" (šms nsw m [st.f nbt]), an epithet applied also to Hekareshu, nurse of Thutmose IV.[44] It usually indicates a close court association and differs from the designation "he who follows the lord on all his traverses" (šms nb r nmtt.f) which is commonly found in inscriptions of military men.[45] Sobekhotep held no title which would link him to the military; rather his position was due to his court connections--those having been strong through both sides of his family.

The only other Overseer of the Treasury who may date to the reign of Thutmose IV is the man Merire who appeared as nurse to Prince Si-atum (see Chapter 2).[46] His Sakkara tomb has been discovered recently. Merire's burial in the North is no surprise, since we have had stelae from his tomb for some time,[47] but the tomb of an earlier Treasurer Nehesy was not suspected in the region. On his tomb stela Merire was called "Overseer of the Treasury, Overseer of the House of his Majesty, Overseer of Nursing for the Good God" (mr ḥtmw mr pr n ḥm.f mr mnᶜ n nṯr nfr.) Unfortunately there is no cartouche yet associated with the burial, but the style of his stela and tomb relief belongs in the reign of Amenhotep III rather than earlier. Comparisons with other private relief of the period places Merire's tomb in the second half of Amenhotep's rule[48]. It is conceivable that Merire functioned as Treasurer at the close of Thutmose IV's rule and into the reign of Amenhotep. A jar label from Malkata names Ptahmose as mr ḥtmw in year 30 of Amenhotep III. This provides at least a terminus post quem for Merire's service under Amenhotep. His nursling, Si-atum, was father to a princess who died (or was reburied) in Amenhotep III's reign. Si-atum's father, as said earlier, could have been Thutmose IV or Amenhotep III. We are at present capable of no more precision than this.

One question which has been answered by Zivie's discovery of Merire's tomb is whether he was owner of TT 226 in Thebes. That tomb belonged to an Overseer of Royal nurses who did not use the Treasurer's title. Davies, in making the identification of Merire as the tombowner, stated that the Treasury title was one which the two men did not have in common.[49] And yet it is the highest rank of any held by either man. The owner of TT 226 remains unidentified.

1.3. Overseer of the Treasure House (mr pr-ḥd-(nbw). This position existed as a subordinate of the vizierate. It was independent of the Overseer of the Treasury who answered directly to the king.[50] There is some question concerning the exact title specifying this job, for the form mr pr ḥd is often replaced by mr prwy ḥd prwy nbw (as well as by mr prwy ḥd.)[51] Helck has argued[52] that the title Overseer of the gold and silver Houses is not identical to a treasurer's rank but rather designates any person who dealt with precious metals on the job. Not a few of the persons designated as mr pr ḥd by Helck ,however, use the double form as variant on their monuments. For example, Benermerut, Overseer of the treasure house under Thutmose III, uses the gold and silver title only on stela Louvre C273; on Cairo stela JE 65830 he uses the form mr prwy ḥd, and on Cairo statue CG 42171 mr prwy ḥd mr prwy nbw and mr pr ḥd.[53] Sobekmose, Overseer of the treasure house under Amenhotep III shows like variation: on a graffito from Aswan, he is mr pr nbw-ḥd ; in his tomb he is mr pr ḥd and mr prwy ḥd mr prwy nbw.[54] Maya, Overseer of the treasure house under Horemheb,also varies the titles, using all three forms cited above.[55] It is thus questionable whether Helck's assumption is correct in its stated form.[56] However, a number of institutions had treasure houses attached to them--particularly temples--and the stewards of these complexes often carry the title "Overseer of the silver and gold houses" but with reference to a specific institution other than the palace.[57] If we are correct in our argument here, then another Overseer of the treasure house may be identified for the reign of Thutmose IV. Merire, an official clearly dated to this reign was Chief Steward but also Overseer of the gold houses and the silver houses. Merire is known by a fine statue and will be discussed further below as Chief Royal Steward.[58]

A third person who held this treasury title in Thutmose's reign was one Amenmose, no doubt buried in Thebes, who is known by a scribal palette recovered from the Deir el Medina burial of Kha.[59] Kha's tomb chapel must stylistically belong to Amenhotep III's reign, but objects representing several rules are known from the shaft.[60] The palette is dated by both cartouches of Thutmose IV on the front and on the back names "the Overseer of all works of the king, Overseer of the audience chamber, Overseer of the gold house and silver house, and Fanbearer on the right of the king, Amenmose". Helck entered this man with a date under Amenhotep II[61] without further explanation. This Amenmose is given the title Overseer of the treasure house (mr pr ḥd) by Helck, but it should be warned that the only publication of the back of the palette is in translation in Italian. A photograph of the front which shows Thutmose IV's cartouches is provided along with a translation.

The Royal herald Re, known from graffiti at Konosso and Theban tomb 201, employs the title Overseer of the gold houses and Overseer of the silver houses (mr prwy nbw mr prwy ḥd) twice on a model sarcophagus in the Cairo Museum (CG 48483).[62] Otherwise the treasurer's office is not attested for this man, at least on published material. Re, however, survived into the reign of Amenhotep III, and it is that king who appears in his tomb and who is named by cartouche in an offering scene there. [63] In his tomb Re was associated with cattle counts, and that is in keeping with the title he claimed on the model sarcophagus, "Overseer of horns, hooves, feathers and scales". He was also given an Overseer of granaries title on the model box and was frequently referred to there as Overseer of works in the south and north. Re's herald position was, however, always his characteristic one, and it is quite likely he was sent on foreign expeditions by both Thutmose and Amenhotep. Since there are registers in the tomb chapel depicting soldiers with shields and standards, one must presume Re had at least military accompaniment on his missions. The various titles held by Re, and his dating in two reigns, may suggest that he became an Overseer of the Treasure House and Granaries officer in the latter part of his career after he retired from the demanding position of Royal Herald. He probably received these jobs as pension after an active career as a royal emissary. One title on his model coffin, mr ḥmwtyw t3w nbw "Overseer of craftsmen of all lands" might imply that the workmen he supervised were imported artisans as well as Egyptian workers. This interpretation would assume that hmwtyw referred to artisans rather than slave labor. As regards Re as Overseer of the Treasure House, however, it is unclear whether he functioned already in Thutmose IV's rule. We include him with caution.

There are thus probably three persons known from the reign of Thutmose IV to have held the title Overseer of the Treasure House. This plurality of officeholders for the reign occurs not infrequently in the 18th dynasty and might suggest that more than one person could hold the position at a time. Helck listed three men under Hatshepsut, two under Thutmose III (add Benermerut), two under Amenhotep II, four for Amenhotep III, etc.,and he recognized at least two simultaneous Treasurers (a northern and a southern) for each reign.[64] Possibly, however, the division was not geographic; rather several men might have shared the office. This is only a possibility but does not seem unlikely in view of the large amount of revenue which had to be administered. Whatever the case, there is no evidence that any of these three men received the position by inheritance as often occurred with single national offices. In fact the family tree of Sobekmose and Panehesy (Sobekhotep), who served Amenhotep III, is anomalous in having roots in the Treasure house.[65] Generally this administrative branch was not at all hereditary. This might suggest a certain amount of flexibility in the position(s); but it also limits our knowledge of the officeholders whose backgrounds are murky.

1.4.   Overseer of the granaries. (mr šnwty)
Besides the herald Re who may have only become head of the granaries during the reign of Amenhotep III,[66] only two men can be suggested for this office during Thutmose IV's rule, and they are both subject to some question. A Wepwawetmose, called Overseer of the granaries of Upper and Lower Egypt, Royal scribe (mr šnwty n šmᶜw mhw sš nsw) appears in a graffito from Aswan together with the Royal scribe, Scribe of the elite troops Horemhab and the Army scribe of the Lord of the Two lands, Menwy.[67] Helck, following Petrie's poor copy of this   inscription, restored a title sš [hsb ỉt] n nb t3wy "scribe of counting grain for the Lord of the Two lands" for Menwy and attributed to him the Overseer of granaries title as well in his Verwaltungen list,[68] but Champollion's copy shows the correct reading. The sš mšᶜw n nb t3wy Mnwy "Army scribe of the Lord of the Two lands Menwy" is known from other graffiti at Aswan [69] and is probably the same man known from a funerary cone in the Boston Museum.[70] Possibly this Menwy should be identified with the sš nsw sš mšᶜw sš nfrw "Royal scribe, Army scribe, scribe of the elite troops", represented by statue CG 901[71]. That stelophore is dated by cartouche to the reign of Amenhotep III, and the owner is named Men.[72] Menwy then was never a granary official at all but has only been mistakenly reassigned from his military occupation.

Wepwawetmose, on the other hand, was surely an Overseer of the granary. A question remains, however, concerning his dating. If the Horemhab in the graffito is the owner of tomb 78, then a date in Thutmose IV's or Amenhotep III's reign is certain. (Horemhab served under Amenhotep II too, but the location of the graffito at Konosso strongly suggests one of the two later rulers.) This seems a plausible conclusion, since general Horemheb, the future king, used the Scribe of elite troops title very rarely, while it, along with the rank of Royal scribe, was Horemhab's (TT78) characteristic title. The confusion in dating is exacerbated by the fact that there were two men named Wepwawetmose and that both of them were Overseers of the Granary.

Several stelae naming an Overseer of the granary Wepwawetmose were incorrectly dated by Helck [73] and attributed to the man in our graffito. The stelae in question are of post-Amarna date and name a man whose father served during and after the Amarna era.[74] It is likely that the men were of the same family, but they are most certainly separate people. The Wepwawetmose attested by the Aswan graffito quite likely served under Thutmose IV, but very little else can be said about him or his office. The possibility does exist, however, that he shared his position with another man. There is at least evidence that the Granaries office was divided during the reign of Thutmose III, and there are two men-- an Amenhotep, attested on two stelae, and a Bakenamun[75] son of a Sennefer and the Lady of the house Ipu-- who might well have held the position at this time along with Wepwawetmose.[76] Amenhotep is included among Helck's list of officeholders, but Bakenamun is not. Louvre C 71 was dedicated by the Overseer of the King's granary of Upper and Lower Egypt, the true Royal scribe beloved of him. In the lunette he appears as Royal scribe only.[77] This Overseer of the granary is attributed to Thutmose's administration on the basis of the style of his Louvre stelae. A date in the reign of Thutmose IV is quite likely; it can be no earlier than Amenhotep II's rule and by no means as late as Amenhotep III's.

1.5. King's son of Kush (šš nsw n Kš).

The administration of the whole of Egypt's southern holdings, and especially its revenues, was the responsibility of the King's son of Kush. Much has been written of this office lately--it was the subject of a recent doctoral dissertation[78]--and it will continue for some time to generate interest since the many inscriptions of viceroys found during the salvage campaign in Nubia are only now being widely examined. But most scholars agree that the reign of Thutmose IV was something of a turning point in the history of the office;[79] for it is with the officeholder Amenhotep, who served in the reign of Thutmose IV,that the title King's son of Kush first appeared. Until this time the basic designations of the viceroy were "King's son" s3 nsw and "Overseer of southern countries" mr

ḥ3swt rsy. Amenhotep was also the first viceroy to bear the honorific title "Fanbearer
on the right of the king"; that rank too became part of the King's son's titulary. In
Chapter 1 we pointed out that Amenhotep's personal titles always included sš nsw
"Royal scribe", but this was not one of the Viceroy's functions.

It would be impossible to state exactly why these two changes occurred with
Amenhotep; it is not even clear that the title King's son of Kush was intended as
a permanent designation for the office when Amenhotep adopted it. Variants of
the title continued to be in use through his tenure and that of his successor
Merymose. Gauthier argued that the viceroy's responsibility expanded during this
period, and this conclusion has gained recent support.[80] Reisner suggested that
Thutmose IV adopted the geographic designation to differentiate the viceroy from
the prince Amenhotep,[81] but with the plethora of titles already available to prevent
such a confusion, this hardly seems likely.

Amenhotep's Buhen stela is his only monument dated by cartouche to Thutmose
IV's reign--and it does not call the Viceroy s3 nsw n Kšy "King's son of Kush" but
rather provides the variant s3 nsw kn n nb.f and mḥ-ib n Kšy, "King's son valiant
for his lord" and "confidant belonging to Kush"; in the lunette the simple s3 nsw
appears.[82] Merymose is not attested as viceroy until year 5 of Amenhotep III, and
it is quite possible that Amenhotep functioned until that time. The other
monuments of Amenhotep include two graffiti from Sehel,[83] both of which call him
s3 nsw n Kšy (only one has his complete name, but the other has an identical text),
a statue from Qurnet Murai (Louvre E 14398),[84] and a clay sealing from Buhen
of which only [ḥ3s]wt rsyw Imnḥtp remains.[85] Lepsius says one of Amenhotep's
graffiti is placed below the name of Amenhotep III,[86] so they may date from his
reign. (Merymose too left a graffito at Sehel.) The Louvre statue which calls
Amenhotep King's son of Kush could belong stylistically to either reign. We must
then consider the possibility that the title King's son of Kush was given to
Amenhotep as viceroy only by Amenhotep, but the Buhen stela epithet "confidant
belonging to Kush" suggests the expanded territorial meaning existed already in
Thutmose's rule. Amenhotep's titles from his various monuments are as follows:

Title	Louvre 14398	Buhen stela	Sehel graffiti	Buhen seal
s3 nsw		X		
mr h3swt rsywt			X	X
s3 nsw n Kšy	X		X	
s3 nsw + other		X (kn n nb.f)		
mh ib n Kšy		X		
mr k3w n Imn	X	X		
t3y hw hr wnmy	X	X	X	
sš nsw	X	X (2 x)	X	
mr k3t m š m ᶜ w			X	
mhw				
rpᶜt	X			
hry ihw n hm.f			X	

The distribution among only five monuments (of which the Buhen sealing undoubtedly included at least King's son (s3 nsw) if not King's son of Kush (s3 nsw n Kš)) is rather homogenous. The graffiti and the statue provide functions which expand or exalt the man's functions, but they are titles associated with favored courtiers at an advanced age. "Overseer of works" and "Chief of stables for his Majesty" would have been given Amenhotep after long service to the king; "hereditary prince" is difficult to explain and is best left to await more documentation. We might reiterate, however, that Amenhotep probably did serve into the reign of Amenhotep III who honored him with several court titles.

Aling commented that Amenhotep was the first viceroy to be an Overseer of the cattle of Amun as well.[87] He felt that Thutmose IV deliberately gave this office to the King's son in an attempt to wrest control from the Amun clergy. This idea gains little support from the evidence. In fact there is evidence that the cattle in question were those held in Nubia, and since the viceroy was the chief representative of Egypt in the south, he controlled both Amun's goods and the king's. Huy, viceroy under Tutankhamun, for example, was both Overseer of cattle (mr k3w) and Overseer of cattle of Amun in this Land of Kush (mr k3w n Imn m t3 pn n Kš); Paser, King's son under Ay and Horemheb, was Overseer of cattle in Nubia (mr k3w m T3-Sty).[88] Müller has pointed out as well that Ahmose and Ahmose-Turo at the beginning of dynasty 18 were also Overseers of Cattle for all the Gods of Wawat.[89] Thus it is quite likely that Amenhotep and Merymose, who bore the title mr k3w n Imn "Overseer of the cattle of Amun" supervised herds in Nubia as part of their job.

Several scholars have queried whether the Viceroy Amenhotep may be identified with one or more like-named men in the 18th dynasty. Albright, for example, considered the viceroy to be the same man, named Amanhatpa, who appears in two cuneiform letters from Taanach as the writer to one Rewassa.[90] Albright believed he was the Egyptian Governor in Palestine at the time and was quartered in Gaza. But there is no collaborative evidence for this at all, and Malamat plausibly argued that the writer was Amenhotep II.[91] Müller was convinced by Albright's suggestion[92] but had no new information to support it. She did, however, unwittingly make a second identification for Amenhotep. Citing Žaba, Muller identified Amenhotep with the stela-owner of BM 902,[93] an Overseer of the Stables of his Majesty and High priest of Onuris. This Amenhotep boasted of following Thutmose IV from Nahrin to Karoy when he was on the battlefield.[94] In fact Žaba never made this identification; he said that the viceroy Amenhotep followed the other Amenhotep into the post of Overseer of the Stables.[95] Habachi misunderstood Žaba on another matter and thought that the viceroy Huy under

Tutankhamun might be the earlier Amenhotep.[96] Žaba had actually suggested that when Merymose became King's son of Kush, Amenhotep son of Hapu, called Huy, became Overseer of works and Overseer of the cattle of Amun.[97] Žaba's intention was to show the sequence of like titles held by Amenhotep, Merymose, and Amenhotep son of Hapu. Since many persons were named Amenhotep in the 18th dynasty, caution should be used in making identifications. For now there is no reason to make Amenhotep, the Viceroy of Nubia, into a priest of Onuris or a Governor of Palestine.

A final problem concerning Amenhotep stems from the stela he dedicated at Buhen. It is now in the Ashmolean Museum under the number 1893.173.[98] It depicts the goddess Isis shown with a scorpion behind her head. The formula invokes Horus lord of Buhen and Isis mistress of the south. What is unusual about this stela is that the figure of Amenhotep offering before the goddess' table is completely erased and apparently painted over by a red wash which covers the background. The name of Amun has been mutilated in all three instances on the stela, but it has been restored so that Amenhotep is clearly legible in the last line of the text.

This occasion of damnatio is certainly not unique; Usersatet was removed from most of his inscriptions by some force, but we have no idea whether it was by royal order or personal vendetta. Schulman's brief remarks some years ago on this subject[99] cautioned against hasty conclusions concerning erasures of private persons, and that advice should be followed in this case as well as in others for this reign. There are other reasons that a man's figure would be erased and painted over. Rededication of the stela after Amenhotep's lifetime might be one. Since the name of Amun was restored, the stela did continue in use in the temple. And it was not Amenhotep's name which was removed, only his image. The htp remains in both writings of [Amen]hotep. Only full removal of Amenhotep's name would have been satisfactory damnation. Mutilations in Theban tombs in this reign and others certainly did occur, and sometimes personal enemies attacked the dead. Surely that would not be surprising, to us since we are aware of enmity among Egyptian officials at all periods of pharaonic history.[100] No doubt there were examples of men who were publicly disgraced by newly-acceding kings, but probably they were few in number. The vast majority of undesirables were no doubt simply omitted at the outset. There is no convincing reason to believe Amenhotep was ever disgraced or turned out of office by the king. At least this erased figure on his stela cannot demonstrate it conclusively.

1.6. Lesser Officials for central administration.

1.6.1 The Overseer of southern countries (mr ḥ3swt rsywt), Overseer of the Stables (ḥry iḥw) and Captain (ḥry pdt) Nehemawy is attested on a stela dedicated to Osiris.[101] The man's wife is termed the Mistress of the house Ta-aa-ti, and his son is a scribe of influence, the Document scribe for the Queen [Amen]mose. The positions held by this Nehemawy are highly placed in the administration of Nubia, beneath only that of the Viceroy.[102] It is interesting to note that Viceroy Amenhotep does not use the title mr h3swt rsywt on all his monuments--in particular not on the stela from Buhen which is dated in the reign of Thutmose IV by cartouche. We might tentatively suggest, based on the style of Nehemawy's stela which is almost certainly from that same reign, that Nehemawy held that title for a period before Amenhotep was given it, perhaps by Amenhotep III.

2. Palace and Regional Administration

2.1. The Chief Steward (mr pr wr).

The Chief steward for the king was a man of major importance in the 18th dynasty who administered the enormous holdings of the crown and certainly rivalled the vizier and high priest of Amun in power. There were at times cases of northern and southern chief stewards for the 18th dynasty--beginning with the reign of Amenhotep II.[103] Since there are four men who apparently held the office during Thutmose IV's reign, one might suggest there was a division of the office. One of the four cannot be dated by cartouche to Thutmose IV but can be linked to contemporaries of the king.

One Merire, discussed above as Overseer of the Treasure House, was mr pr wr n nsw, Chief steward for the king. He is known by a statue,[104] a scribal palette,[105] and a funerary cone.[106] On all three monuments he is called Chief steward for the king, thus assuring that was his main occupation. The scribal palette is dated by cartouche to the reign of Thutmose IV but probably belongs to the latter years of his career. This is suggested in the style of Merire's statue; the round face, wide eyes and heavy cosmetic lines there fit more comfortably in Amenhotep II's rule than in Thutmose IV's.[107] And Merire may have begun his career even earlier, possibly under Thutmose III. A Deir el Bahri ostracon, undated but of Tuthmoside era, names the mr pr Mry-r^c.[108] Also named on the ostracon are the Overseer of cattle, Nebwaw, and Pahekamen. The last man is known from the reigns of Thutmose III and Amenhotep II , and the ostracon could date to either of these rulers.[109] Perhaps this text is a record of Merire's service as a steward long before Thutmose IV took the throne. That at least was Hayes' opinion when he published the ostracon,[110] and it is consistent with the evidence that Tjenuna followed Merire into the Chief stewardship during Thutmose' reign, for he would have been an old man by that time. Tjenuna appeared on the scribal palette of Merire as Scribe for the Chief steward [of the king Tje]nuna. It is reasonable to conclude that the career of Merire spanned at least parts of several reigns. Perhaps the Chief steward's expertise in the office smoothed the king's transition into power.

Tjenuna from all appearances took the position at Merire's death or retirement. That it was Thutmose IV that Tjenuna served is certain from the depictions of statues of that king and his mother Tiaa which Champollion saw and drew in the tomb (TT76)[111] The king was also represented seated in a kiosk on one chapel wall, but the accompanying inscription has been destroyed so that the ruler's name is now missing. The king's short curly wig with fillet is still visible, however, and is modelled in the same plaster relief used in Sobekhotep's tomb (63). But tomb 76 has been mutilated resulting in the removal of the images of Tjenuna, most occurrences of his name, and part of his major title. There is no remaining example which calls the official Chief steward of the King; there are several instances where mr pr wr, Chief steward, remains, but what follows is destroyed at the end of the title. Amun's name is also hacked out in the tomb, and we would suggest that the god's name was connected with Tjenuna's office, i.e., that Tjenuna was both Chief Steward and Chief Steward of Amun (mr pr wr and mr pr wr n Imn). This was certainly the case for the most influential of stewards such as Senmut and Kenamun. In one occurrence in the tomb a mutilation within a line left the sequence: mr pr [/////] mr pr m pr ḥm.f t3y sryt ḥr wnmy n nsw Tnn3 [name intact].[112] "Chief steward [of Amun], steward in the house of his Majesty, fanbearer on the right of the king, Tjenuna". A statue of Tjenuna from his Theban tomb and now in the Vienna Kunsthistorisches Museum[113] has had its entire socle inscription hacked away, but the backpillar retains most of the titles except the stewardship again, and interestingly again the name remains.

During some period of the 18th Dynasty stewards were extremely influential. Both Senmut and Kenamun grew powerful under monarchs who depended on a few close associates--Hatshepsut and Amenhotep II. Other reasons could promote the fortunes of stewards, however. The influential Treasurers who traveled to procure exotic materials for the kings are less commonly attested at the mines and quarries after the reign of Thutmose III. On the other hand our documentation concerning domestic production[114] begins to increase during the same period, and perhaps the now vastly wealthy royal holdings needed the strictest supervision.For this reason, the Chief Stewards of the king and of Amun (sometimes one and the same man) continued an ascendancy seen first with Senmut,[115] while the Treasurer's office apparently lost functional significance. Tjenuna, owner of Tomb 76, almost certainly shared power with Sobekhotep. In a scene from his tomb where Tjenuna, Chief Royal Steward and Chief Steward of Amun, presents golden vessels before the king, the inscription states that "his majesty hears your counsel, having appointed you ꜥ3 n pr r mr ḥtmw..., "Great one of the house (Chief Steward variant) over the Treasurer...." The laconic text continues, "... he [entrusted] him with his seal."[116] In another inscription from Tjenuna's tomb he is credited with filling the pr-nswt with food stores and provisions.[117] A scene from TT 63 of the Treasurer Sobekhotep depicts him at the granaries, apparently performing similar functions.[118] It may be that Sobekhotep performed some jobs in concert with the Chief Steward due to changes occurring in the royal economy. And to the inscriptional evidence may be added that Tjenuna's was the largest tomb of any of Thutmose's officials[119] and was prominently placed on Qurna next to that of Amenhotep Si-se, the Second priest of Amun who carried out much of Thutmose IV's Karnak construction. The fact that Tjenuna was <u>both</u> Chief Royal steward and Chief steward of Amun certainly contributed greatly to his importance as well. Neither of the other two Chief royal stewards also administered Amun's estates.

A third man, one Tjuner, seems also to have been Chief steward for Thutmose IV; he might have represented the north or he might have succeeded Merire and Tjenuna. Tjuner is so far known only from graffiti at Konosso and Bigeh, and unfortunately the copies provided by Petrie, DeMorgan, and Champollion do not always agree completely in the accompanying lines of text. Clear writings of his name and titles appear in no less than three separate inscriptions, however, and confirm the existence of such a person. At Bigeh [120] Tjuner is called <u>mr pr wr n nsw sšm ḥb Twnr</u> "Chief steward for the king, processional leader, Tjuner". He accompanies the Scribe of the army for the lord of the Two lands, Amenemipet. On Konosso he is once called again "Chief steward for the king, processional leader, Tjuner" [121] and is in the company of a scribe of the elite troops, Royal scribe [Men]wy (the low broad sign for $\leftrightarrow$ is visible), and a man named Hekarnehhe. On DeMorgan's copy, <u>mn///</u> appears at the base of the column before the name Hekarnehhe. On Petrie's copy the seated man determinative is shown after the name. This can hardly be other than the royal nurse (<u>mnᶜt nsw</u>) Hekarnehhe, owner of Theban tomb 64. He is of course known from another graffito at Konosso where he appeared with two princes Aakheprure and Amenhotep.[122] He was there still only a child of the Nursery. As argued in Chapter 2, Hekarnehhe came of age during Thutmose's reign and probably did not survive into Amenhotep III's rule. This graffito should therefore belong to the time of Thutmose IV and makes of Tjuner a Chief steward for the king. The third inscription calls Tjuner by a rarer title, <u>mr pr ᶜꜣ</u> [123] There he is accompanied by several men whose names are unfortunately difficult to read.

There is little information available to identify this man outside the Aswan region. The name Tjuner is not uncommon,[124] but the Chief Steward Tjuner is poorly attested. The possibility might exist that <u>Twnwr</u> was a variant for <u>Tnwnꜣ</u>,[125] although that Chief Steward left another graffito at Konosso with his name written as in tomb 76.[126] Perhaps time will produce more examples to decide the question.

2.2.1 The Overseer of the royal household (mr ỉpt nsw) was one Paser who was also mr ᶜhnwty and a Royal scribe.[127] Paser's false door stela of funerary type must have come from a Memphite cemetery, likely Sakkara. It is dedicated to Ptah-Sokar-Osiris and was donated by his son, the God's father Ptahmery. The style of the stela places Paser in Thutmose IV's administration. Helck recognized the importance of the Memphite palace administors including the mr ᶜhnwty, in the 18th Dynasty.[128] Paser surely was one of the more prominent of these men; his position as mr ᶜhnwty involved the supervision of palace provisions, most probably, and was an office often found with other palace ranks. A second mr ᶜhnwty, Amenmose, probably oversaw the Theban residence. His scribal palette, bearing Thutmose IV's cartouche, was found among the Draughtsman Kha's burial goods (TT 8).[129]

Despite the significance of the Royal butlers in Amenhotep II's administration (Suemniwet TT 92 and Mentiwy TT 172), the functions of that office may not have been important during the reign of Thutmose IV. Thutmose III and Amenhotep II provided their court confidants with exalted positions after loyal service during the Asian campaigns. Butlers such as Minmose supervised the royal proceeds from Takhsy,[130] while Mentiwy served both Thutmose III and Amenhotep II the latter having promoted him to supervise the royal household and its holdings (pr nswt and ỉpt nsw). The military connections did not exist amongst Thutmose's court, and perhaps as a result the office of Royal butler languished for a time. Only one possible officeholder has surfaced.

2.2.1 The Royal butler Iuty is known from a stela from Giza.[131] He also has the title of child of the Nursery, indicating the background which Helck found common to these officials.[132] His inclusion in Thutmose IV's administration is uncertain since the stela upon which he appears is an unfinished piece with obvious sculptor's errors and signs of inscriptional reuse.

2.2.2 A Royal scribe, Overseer of Nefrut cattle of Onuris, Processional leader for Osiris and Guardian of the door for Amun, Meryti, is known from a dated statue found in the Mut precinct.[133] This man is here included as a civil official because of Kees' analysis concerning processional leaders(sšmw hb). Kees concluded that sšmw hb came from the civil and military ranks, but never from the professional priesthood.[134] Thus Meryti would have been foremost a Royal scribe (i.e., a bureaucrat).[135] Royal scribes will appear under headings which specify their roles: e.g., Minhotep, Royal scribe, was also Scribe of the treasure house and Scribe of elite troops. He may ;be found under those headings. For the complete list of Royal scribes, see Appendix V.

2.2.3 Nebi, also known to have been a Captain of the Sile fort and Mayor of the city was given the title Steward of the Queen's apartments on the Year 4 Sinai mine inscription.[136] Since he was likewise a Child of the nursery we may suppose that his acquaintance with court residents earned him the job serving the queen. We have no idea which woman this was.

2.2.4 The Document scribe for the Queen [Amen]mose was son of the Overseer of southern countries and captain Nehemawy.[137] Again we are ignorant of his female employer.

2.3. Royal nurses (mr mn^{c}t)

The men named Hekareshu and Hekarnehhe have already entered this study in Chapter 2, for they were intimately involved with Thutmose IV and his family. They are discussed again here since they were close court associates of the king who accompanied the pharaoh on his travels through the country. A summary of the data discussed in Chapter 2 reveals that Hekareshu was nurse to Thutmose IV before he acceded; he was later honored by the title God's father and continued in veneration at court. Hekareshu is named in five graffiti from Konosso, three shabtis, two sets of model tools, prince Thutmose's statue (CG 923), a statue from Mendes,[138] and tomb 64.[139] Hekarnehhe, royal nurse and nurse to prince Amenhotep, was probably, but nowhere stated to be, Hekareshu's son. He was buried in tomb 64 [140] and may have predeceased his father who appears in most of the wall scenes there. Probably the tomb was begun for the elder man and turned over to the son. Hekarnehhe is named as well in several funerary cones, two graffiti from Konosso,[141] and a heart scarab in Parma. [142] Wegner dated the tomb to the latter part of Thutmose's reign; it may be, but its painters worked slightly more conservatively than did those of TT 63 of Sobekhotep. The technique of painting is, however, of highest quality. The pigments which contained strong reds and yellow-golds also had fine blues, but the richness of frit-laden pigments in TT 63 is not in evidence here.

One point which remains to be addressed here is whether Hekareshu was buried in any other identifiable tomb. Habachi has identified Theban tomb 226 as his resting place, and Frandsen supported this suggestion.[143] The argument rests on faulty evidence, however. Habachi attributed titles to Hekareshu which he never held (child of the nursery, for example, is given only to Hekarnehhe in tomb 64,[144] and that same title, contrary to Helck, does not appear in tomb 226.[145] Second, Habachi recopied a graffito from Aswan and assigned it to Hekareshu.[146] This inscription shows a king and queen in a kiosk with a fanbearer before them. The text, as he read it, identified "the Good God, lord of the Two lands, Nebmaatre" and "King's mother, Mutemwia". (Mutemwia and Amenhotep III appeared together in tomb 226, and Habachi thus thought this graffito might lend support to his identification.) His copy of the fanbearer's text showed t3y hw n nsw hrd n k3p it

ntr Hk3rsw, "fanbearer of the king, child of the Nursery, god's father, Hekareshu".
Habachi's note indicated that "there are two tall signs in the first line of the second
column of the inscription which are to be taken as the ntr and hk3 signs".[147]

This graffito is accessible only by boat and is not at all easy to read. In 1977
Dr. William Murnane and Mr. Frank Yurco of the Chicago House Epigraphic
Expedition checked the text at my request. They approached the inscription at
several times of day to catch varying light; both men agreed upon the following:
they could not verify t3y hw n nsw,[148] but they were certain that the last three
signs in column 1 were n mh-ib (not hrd n k3p). They read the second column as
n ntr nfr Hw, written ⟨hieroglyphs⟩ Even without this collation Hekareshu is
unlikely to have left this graffito: the title "fanbearer for the king" is not held by the
nurse Hekareshu; he was "fanbearer on the right of the king". The latter was an
honorific rank entirely separate from the standardbearer's position. In fact Helck
cited this exact graffito as an example of a non-honorific title! [149] The title of God's
father was not read here by Murnane and Yurco, and Habachi admitted it was
based only on the presence of a tall sign. Even the name of Queen Mutemwia is
in doubt by Habachi's own note;[150] this graffito must be removed from discussion
about Hekareshu and his place of burial. There is really no other point of similarity
in the titles of Hekareshu and the owner of tomb 226. The latter was a Royal
scribe and steward of the king as well as of Thutmose III's temple. He was also
a doorkeeper for Amun and, based on the texts, a career bureaucrat entrusted with
the care of some royal children.[151] Hekareshu, on the other hand, had no scribal
training and was identified exclusively as a nurse and God's father-- he was close to
the king but apparently through no administrative route. Although the question
cannot be definitely laid to rest, Hekareshu should not be identified with the owner
of Theban tomb 226. The tomb of Hekareshu may one day be found elsewhere on
the Theban necropolis; but he is more likely to have been interred with his son in
tomb 64.

A final discussion concerning these two men centers on their earlier careers
and positions at court. Helck suggested that the name Hekareshu might indicate this
man was originally not Egyptian; he cited the man Pahekamen, whose name was also
Beniay, as a possible parallel.[152] Aling supported this suggestion,[153] and it does
sound reasonable. There is nothing in Hekareshu's titles which suggests he had
court duties other than as a nurse. He certainly was not a royal butler as Helck
suggested of both him and Hekarnehhe.[154] Perhaps he only came to Egypt in his
adult years; certainly he mentions no family members in tomb 64. Hekarnehhe does
so only in his outer door jamb texts: there he appears followed by a woman whose
name has been lost, but she is likely to have been his wife. If Hekareshu and
Hekarnehhe had foreign origins there is no means as yet of knowing how they
reached court circles. Up to now nothing suggests the elder man had a military

background.[155] Although as the section below will demonstrate, the men of military bent were powerful from the mid-18th dynasty onward, these two nurses probably did not belong to their circle.

A stela from Sakkara preserves the name of a nurse to Thutmose's son (or daughter) Amenemipet. JE 20221 was dedicated to the Singer of Mut Royal nurse Sentruyu. The stela, described in Chapter 3, was presented by a woman shown on the right. The badly eroded text appears to identify her as the daughter of Sentruyu. The prince (or princess?), shown suckling, is clearly identified by name and title but wears no clothing or insignia. Sentruyu was probably a true wet nurse; this stela is not of particularly high quality, but it does betray its date by the presence of a lotus frieze above, the longer styled gown on the dedicant, the long-legged proportions of the female offerant, and the obvious features of the woman's face which identify Thutmose's reign--an almond-shaped eye coupled with a straight nose (unsnubbed as in the reign of Amenhotep III), and a squarish jaw. This is only known female royal nurse so far known from the period.

2.4. Child of the nursery (hrd n k3p)

This title is a poorly understood one belonging to several men in the reign of Thutmose IV. It is a common rank throughout the 18th dynasty, and quite clearly one belonging to youths. The children of the Nursery were those raised in the confines of palaces within Egypt [156]-- there is no certainty that all of these children of the nursery had personal relations with future kings, but it is clear that some of them did.   Princes and princesses were raised in royal residences scattered throughout the country-- principally in Memphis, the Fayum (Gurob), Abydos (or its environs) and Thebes; thus there were children of the Nursery in each of those places, but there were not always future rulers living in each residence.

The Child of the nursery obviously had advantages not available to many, but by no means did each succeed. Some people died as hrd n k3p; others became low court officers; some became soldiers; and a precious few reached high state offices. Among the children of the Nursery were also children of foreign rulers who were sent or taken as hostages to Egypt to be "civilized" and then returned to rule as vassals. Probably by their already-close court contacts, a few hrdw n k3p became royal tutors in their adult years-- as well as soldiers and palace officers. Of the fourteen men named below only three probably held the title during Thutmose IV's reign; some eight should have held it during Amenhotep II's rule while the others provide no clue for consideration. This spread is consistent with the numbers of royal male children that reach a peak it appears during Amenhotep II's reign. The residences continued to be full of royal offspring during Thutmose IV's rule, but probably due to earlier births. Documents recording princes, nurses, and children of the Nursery slowly taper off during the period spanning Thutmose IV and

Amenhotep III's rules and are far more difficult to trace near the end of the Dynasty. The mechanism by which this changed occurred is so far unknown but may perhaps be clarified by further research.[157]

The best-known Child of the nursery in Thutmose IV's reign was Hekarnehhe (tomb 64) (see above under Royal Nurses) who was later royal nurse and tutor to prince Amenhotep (almost surely the later Amenhotep III). Hekarnehhe appeared at Konosso with two princes under the guardianship of royal herald Re--the future nurse was called hrd n k3p on the graffito. His most mature titles were (Overseer of) Nurse(s) for the Royal Children and Chief of Horses (mr) mn^{c}t (n) msw nsw and mr ssmwt but he utilized hrd n k3p even in his tomb texts. It is quite likely that he died before Amenhotep III acceded and had little opportunity to enlarge his titles or to gain prestige in the manner Hekareshu had after Thutmose IV took the throne.

A scribe of the elite troops, Raner,[158] to be discussed further below, was termed a Child of the nursery on his father's funerary stela. Raner did not use his "page" title on his own monument. We might conclude that he felt it not significant enough; but Raner's father, Ay, was also a Child of the nursery in his youth and later was Royal scribe and Scribe of elite troops; he, however, used all three ranks on his stela. Probably it was only the restricted space on the base of the royal sphinx statuette inscribed for Raner which prevented the inclusion of the Child of the nursery title, for Raner's father died some time before Amenhotep III's death, while the sphinx's inscription should date to Thutmose IV's reign. Two other men in Thutmose's reign, like Raner, used the Child of the nursery title only occasionally. Nebi, Mayor of Sile and Commander of troops, was called Child of the nursery in a year 4 inscription from the Sinai.[159] His other monuments ignore the rank. Neferhet, Chief builder for Thutmose's temple at Abydos, used hrd n k3p once on a stela now in the British Museum. Another stela dedicated by Neferhet does not use the title at all.[160]

One Iuty is known from a stela found at Giza,[161] he is also termed 'royal butler' on the inscription. Thutmose IV appears in the scene above, but the stela seems to have been left unifnished. Pa-aa-aku, standardbearer for the ship Mery-Amun, was also a page.[162] His stela too is dated by cartouche. Ptahemhet (TT77) is called Child of the nursery in his tomb texts,[163] he was later a standardbearer for the king and responsible for construction on the royal funerary temple, probably after his military career ended. Two other children of the Nursery appear in tomb 77. Nedjem and Paser are shown behind Ptahemhet's brother, the snni (Charioteer?) Nebseny. These two "pages" are not specified as family of the deceased.

A Minhotep called Hututu[164] was a Scribe of the Treasury, Scribe of elite troops and Child of the nursery. This man certainly served under Amenhotep II for much of his career,[165] but the style of his stela in Cairo belongs to the reign of Thutmose IV. The Child of the nursery Amenemipet[166] probably left his funerary monument at Sakkara judging from the type of limestone and sharped edged style of carving used on his tomb block. This man's offering scene dates by style to the reign of Amenhotep III, but since he was at that time <u>hrd n k3p mn</u>^{c} <u>n msw nsw</u> [ỉmn-m-]ỉpt "Child of the nursery and Nurse of the royal children" he probably held the "page" rank during Thutmose's reign. One would suppose that he therefore grew up among Thutmose's children and could have become friends with Amenhotep III before his accession. No other titles appear on this block.

Two other children of the Nursery have been assigned to this reign, but they are not definitely placed. One Menkheper (TT258) was Royal scribe for the royal children's house and a Child of the nursery.[167] Stylistically his tomb could belong to Thutmose IV's reign, and since he appears with his mother but no wife or children, he may well have died before an advanced age. Iuna, owner of a stela in the British Museum, was also a "page" and royal boat-builder.[168] Iuna's attribution to Thutmose's rule is again by the style of his stela. It might be placed a bit earlier than Thutmose's reign, but it is quite comfortable there.

2.5. Royal Herald (<u>whm nsw tpy</u>)

There two title-holders for this office during Thutmose IV's reign. The man Re,known from a Theban tomb (201), several graffiti at Konosso, a funerary cone, a stela and a fine miniature coffin and shabti, served both Thutmose and Amenhotep III.[169] His principal active title remained royal herald throughout that period; and it was the sole rank placed on his funerary cone, even though he had attained such administrative posts as Overseer of granaries and Overseer of the treasure house. The royal herald was certainly the king's trusted servant who could perform any and all tasks--Re's accolades, perhaps received late in life attest to this. Little can be said about this man's specific duties, but soldiers appear in the remains of the presentation scenes to pharaoh from his tomb. The processional quality of the scenes is underlined by the presence of standardbearers on one wall and drummers on the other. Since Re certainly was already Royal herald under Thutmose IV, it would not be too hazardous to suggest that he had a part in the diplomatic exchanges of the period. Indeed the titles awarded him and that appear on his model coffin and shabti might point to Re as the man who negotiated the marriage of Thutmose IV to Artatama's daughter. Amarna letter EA 29 informed us of this diplomatic union which would have been effected by the aid of royal messengers or Royal heralds. Re achieved the highest status of any of Thutmose's international representatives; he therefore quite possibly had a hand in the Mitanni treaty creation.

A second First royal herald (<u>whm nsw tpy</u>), Sennu, was also a military scribe, Royal scribe and Scribe of elite troops.[170] One might suppose that this Sennu's position as Herald was the result of his other military offices and perhaps lengthy service which ended during the reign of Thutmose IV. His son Si-amun, an Army scribe, dedicated his stela in Bologna.

2.6 Royal Messenger (wpwty nsw)

There are two royal messengers identified by name in the reign: Nebi,[171] already discussed as Child of the nursery and to be further mentioned below, and Amenemhet, Commander of troops at Tjeku,[172] a border fortress in the Eastern delta. Both men headed forts on the northeast border of Egypt, and both men appeared at Serabit el-Khadim as royal messengers. It would certainly appear that the major military and civil representatives in the region of the Sinai performed special emissary duties to a place deemed technically foreign, as would have been the eastern delta itself. These men accompanied the royal entourage on its visits to the Sinai, no doubt because they were familiar with it.

On stela Louvre C 53[173] (fig. 49) the standardbearer of the ship Mery Amun noted in his main text the arrival of the royal messenger of Thutmose IV at Abydos. His mission was to establish the king's offerings for Osiris, and the text notes that the messenger returned twice to apportion fields and then to provide offerings for the cenotaph cult of Ahmose. We have no clue as to the identity of the royal messenger whom Pa-aa-aku, the standardbearer, accompanied. At any rate, as Valoggia noted,[174] the royal messengers performed a variety of both domestic (as here) and international missions.

2.7. Provincial Governors (ḥ3ty-ᶜ)

Three men of mayoral or gubernatorial status are known for this reign; two of them held the same post, though probably at different times. The Mayor of Sile (ḥ3ty-ᶜ n T3rw) was presumably a civil officer at the fortress of Sile on the East delta border of Egypt. The man named Nebi who appeared in year 4 of Thutmose IV at Serabit el-Khadim claimed the title in his inscription.[175] He was also at that time a royal messenger and Steward for the Royal wife's apartments (mr pr n ỉpt-ḥmt-nsw).Nebi has been discussed at length in a fine article by Bjorkman, and there is little to add here.

Another Mayor of Sile can be identified for this period. A stela in the British Museum (1843),[176] (fig. 50) probably of Memphite origin based on the style and titles, shows the king wearing the khepresh and offering flowers to Amun-Re, king of the gods and lord of the sky. The lower register shows a kneeling man on the left and the text before him reads:

rdit ỉ3w n [Ỉmn] sn t3 n nb nṯrw ỉn ᶜ3 n š n pr- ᶜ3 m Mn-nfr ḥ3ty-ᶜ n T3rw Ỉmn-ms. "Giving praise to [Amun], kissing the ground for the lord of the gods by the

Great one of the <u>She</u> of the Great house in Memphis".

The right edge bears the dedication: <u>in s3.f s^cnh rn.f Nfr-hr dd.n.f M^crw</u>. "It is his son who preserves his names, Neferhor called Maru".

Thus this short text identifies the man as "Great one of the She of the Palace in Memphis, the Mayor of Sile, Amenmose", and it calls his son Neferhor, nicknamed Maru. Amenmose is unknown beyond this small stela. His civil title as Mayor of Sile is otherwise known only for Nebi[177]. Helck and Björkman [178] assumed it was both a military and administrative position because Nebi was also a Troop commander for Sile, a title which appears in Ramesside times as well. But Amenmose supplied no known military title on the stela; rather his other rank, otherwise unknown, must link him to the palace, as do many of Nebi's titles. Despite its location in foreign and difficult territory,[179] Sile itself was part of the nome bureaucracy as early as the Middle Kingdom when it appeared as capital of the 14th Lower Egyptian nome in Sesostris I's list.[180] The production of wine in the region and the movement of provisions in and out of the area must have necessitated the existence of a mayoralty. It might be best to separate the Mayor of Sile rank from any military function. Björkman's suggestion that the Mayor might have often accompanied Egyptian expeditions to Serabit as diplomat or civil representative may better explain why Nebi, a fort officer, was also a Mayor.

The title <u>^c3 n š n pr-^c3 m Mn-nfr</u> is so far unique in this period. The meaning of the term <u>š pr-^c3</u> in the Old Kingdom has been discussed recently in a dissertation on terms for the palace and in an article concerning the royal precincts at Memphis.[181] Goelet suggested that <u>š pr-^c3</u> could be a variant for <u>pr-^c3</u> since in one tomb a <u>rh-nsw pr-^c3</u> was also termed <u>rh-nsw š pr-^c3</u>. [182] Stadelmann, on the other hand, considered the term together with <u>hnty-š</u> concluding that in the Old Kingdom <u>š</u> referred to a precinct. The <u>š pr-^c3</u> referred therefore to the king's precinct at Memphis. Later, he argued, the meaning of "garden" or "cultivated land" evolved due to the loss of cultic obligation.

It is probably safest to assume that <u>š pr-^c3</u> was not a simply variant for <u>pr-^c3</u> in the New Kingdom, particularly since this is a unique title. Happily, however, the term <u>š pr-^c3</u> is attested in the 18th Dynasty, and probably in the reign of Thutmose IV. On the stela of Iuna, the shipbuilder for the major temples of Egypt [183] included the bark of "Sakhmet in the She of Per-aa" (<u>Shmt m p3 š n pr-^c3</u>) among his products. Therefore, following Stadelmann's discussion we would suggest that Amenmose administered the region of <u>š pr-^c3</u> around Memphis. This might designate lands that had once provided for royal cults but was now part of the royal lands in the Memphite region generally. Whether the position was tantamount to a chief stewardship is unclear until more evidence emerges[184]. We may suppose that

Amenmose was an influential man in the north of Egypt during Thutmose IV's rule. We cannot be certain whether he preceded or followed Nebi as Mayor of Sile, but we know that in year 4 Nebi held the position. Perhaps it would be better to think of Amenmose as Nebi's predecessor who then was promoted to the administrative position in Memphis. At that point Nebi, the Troop commander of Sile, became the administrative officer for the fortress.

The third and fourth Governors known in this reign are Sobekhotep (TT63) and his son Paser discussed above already at some length.[185] They controlled the Fayum district,[186] š rsy (n Sbk) and could be termed ḥȝty-ꜥ n Š, n š rsy, or š n Sbk. Sobekhotep also bore the honorific wr m Tȝ š. A possible fifth Mayor and third in the Fayum is one Itunema known from his son's funerary stela found in Sedment. No cartouche appears, but the relief belongs to the reign of Amenhotep III by style without doubt.[187]

The Fayum mayor's control covered the whole of the Fayum, but the most productive area was the region between Gurob at the mouth of the Bahr Jusef canal and Medinet el Fayum. Gardiner and Kees believed that š n Sbk in Sobekhotep's (and his son Paser's) title indicated the northern lake. But actually the term š rsy is an abbreviated form of š rsy n Sbk and refers to the fact that the south Fayum was the fertile and administrative region. In fact š (n) Sbk designates the entire Fayum and is used genitivally after "southern lake" and "northern lake".[188] Š Sbk referred to the Fayum as early as the 4th dynasty.[189] In the Middle Kingdom, a vizier's office was located in š Sbk.[190] The name of Illahun, R-ḥnt, appears in the variant form as R-n-š-Sbk.[191] When the letters sent to Lahun appear in the Berlin papyri with a destination š Sbk is common.[192] There is little doubt that the Fayum was the š n Sbk, and the Mayoral title was both ḥȝty-ꜥ š n Sbk or ḥȝty-ꜥ š rsy š n Sbk and could even be elaborated to ḥȝty-ꜥ š rsy š mhty[193] delineating both parts of the š of Sobek.

3. Religious Administration

There is not a great deal of information available at present concerning the men who led the various temple administrations during Thutmose IV's reign. Even the premier clergyman, the High priest of Amun, is dated to the period by inference alone. The Memphite pontiff can be identified but is shadowy because his name is so common. Aling attempted in his thesis to show that Thutmose IV and Amenhotep III deliberately moved northerners into the south and removed dignities from the Amun clergy in hopes of suppressing the Theban god's control. Helck had made some of the same suggestions in the Verwaltung,[194] but he attributed the concentration on northerners to Amenhotep III. Although Helck and Aling may be correct in identifying a pattern, there are factors which account for clerical and administrative changes and which do not assume great intrigue. For example, Aling seems to have entirely overlooked the likelihood that kings ruled from the north in this period [195]--this is certainly implied in the Konosso stela of Thutmose IV which refers to the king's visitation to Thebes and Karnak for ritual purposes,[196] and it is made more clear by the appointments of, first, viziers and then Chief stewards for the north. It is evident that rulers traveled a great deal and had several permanent residences as well as arrangements for numerous temporary ones. Since the Memphite region was a capital of Egypt, it is hardly surprising that men of importance there eventually found their way into Theban circles as well.[197] It might be unwarranted to see this as an anti-Amun ploy. The point has been made in the previous chapter that Thutmose IV did consciously elevate the sun god Re above Amun--but only outside Thebes. He was the most pious of Amun's sons within the Southern city. More will be said below in relation to specific offices and their holders.

3.1.1 High priest of Amun.

Most scholars have assumed that the man Amenemhet (TT 97)[198] performed the High priest's function during the end of Amenhotep II's rule and through Thutmose IV's. There is, however, no datable monument for this man which places him with any king. Stylistically his cenotaph at Silsila and his tomb are compatible with a date in Thutmose III's and early Amenhotep II's rule.[199] Wegner did not consider the tomb in his analysis, and Porter and Moss followed Gardiner's dating of Amenhotep II - Thutmose IV.

The only chronological information we have about this man is that at the age of 54 he was but a wab priest.[200] He obviously then rocketed into the pontificate of Amun, through what means we cannot say. But it would be unreasonable to suggest he served as High priest for many years at an advanced age. Gardiner even linked the meagerness of his tomb, in comparison with those of Menkheperreseneb and Mery, to his short tenure in office.[201] A destroyed cartouche in Amenemhet's tomb quite likely marked a change in the kingship, but from whom to whom is unknown. A funerary cone of this man called him ỉry rdwy, a fact which led Kees to believe Amenemhet had been an early military companion to Thutmose III. Perhaps his low rank as wab simply reflected a late entry into sacral administration.[202]

We reject the placement of Amenemhet within the reign of Thutmose IV. The few photographs of his tomb support a much earlier date for his burial; the Silsila cenotaph does likewise (and there are no other officials of Thutmose IV known from those quarry shrines). We would suggest that he served at the end of Thutmose III's rule and perhaps into Amenhotep II's. Mery would have replaced him. To find the high priest of Amun for Thutmose IV we should look at two other men, one of whom is nearly unknown and the other a strong presence in the reign of Amenhotep

III.

The Theban tombs of Mery's successors have not been located, although cones and bricks have turned up in the Gurna region.[203] Since it is already clear that Thutmose's civil officers had to build high atop the mountain, and that Amenhotep III's men employed the Assasif and other areas, it is worth consideration that the High priests of Amun, from the reign of Thutmose IV on, built elsewhere than Sheik abd-el Gurna.   The tombs of Ptahmose and Meryptah have not yet been located, and if there were another High priest as yet unidentified, he may have been buried near these men.   Already the King's sons of Kush had abandoned the Gurna mountain for their own area to the south. Surely the High priests of Amun would have wished their own prestigious area, such as that in Dra abu-el-Naga used by the Ramesside pontiffs.

There is a man who appears at Konosso in one of many graffiti of Thutmose IV's officials and family and who bears the title <u>High priest (ḥm nṯr tpy)</u>.[204] Of course this does not guarantee that this man, one Amunemweskhet, was Amun's High priest, but it does suggest that the person in question was well enough known to go by this general designation.   Amunemweskhet's date to Thutmose IV is likely due to the graffito's location. It is grouped with two graffiti of Hekareshu and is below one inscription naming the princes Amenhotep and Aakheprure with the Child of the nursery Hekarnehhe. Petrie, Champollion, and DeMorgan all show it with the same group of graffiti nearby, and that alone is strong argument. But quite possibly the person accompanying Amunemweskhet in the inscription is none other than the Chief steward Tjenuna.   The text shows ⟨hieroglyphs⟩   and is most crudely written, but all three copyists drew the title and name alike.   It seems possible that the writer intended ⟨hieroglyphs⟩   . Although speculative, the evidence here cited may indicate another High priest of Amun for the reign of Thutmose IV.   That man would have been named Amunemweskhet.   A new collation of this graffito might better identify Amunemweskhet's colleague, but for now the suggestion is presented.

Ptahmose, vizier and High priest of Amun under Amenhotep III may have been High priest in the last years of Thutmose IV,[205] and we consider this likely. There is no monument associating Ptahmose with Thutmose, just as there is none to make him vizier for that king, but the chronology is favorable to the conclusion. It may be of significance that the shabti of Ptahmose in the Cairo Museum (CG 48406)[206] is white glazed faience with dark blue hieroglyphs in horizontal bands and has a very close parallel in a royal shabti of Thutmose IV from KV 43.[207] The shabti of Ptahmose, though certainly of Amenhotep III's reign, may nonetheless stem from the early years of that ruler.

3.1.2 Second prophet of Amun

This office was occupied by one Amenhotep si-se, whose tomb was number 75 on Sheik abd-el Gurnah.[208] That tomb is well-known for its representation of Thutmose IV's porch before the Fourth pylon at Karnak; it was so mentioned in the preceding chapter. Amenhotep si-se's tomb was one of the oldest for the reign according to its style; Wegner placed it with Tjanni's tomb, and Hepu's is probably contemporary as well.[209] Amenhotep si-se held some of the highest dignities in the temple organization, having been Overseer of the granaries of Amun and Overseer of the gold and silver houses for that god as well. These offices had earlier been administered by both temple and civil functionaries: Menkheperreseneb and Mery held both; the Second prophet Rahotep had controlled the granaries; and High priest Amenemhet had controlled the Treasuries.[210] The granaries were often also overseen by civil administors, such as Kenamun, Minnakht, and a Si-ese,[211] Scribe of elite troops and Steward of Thutmose IV's Abydos chapel. It is probable, however, that Si-ese gained the rank after a military career; he would not have been Overseer of granaries of Amun until Amenhotep III's reign. In fact it would seem from scenes in Amenhotep si-se's tomb that his major assignments were to carry out Thutmose IV's works at Karnak; and that is not improbable.[212] Amenhotep's father's name is hacked out twice in the tomb but once he is anonymously termed "a man". His mother was a Lady of the House. In his biography the Second priest indicates that he was promoted to the clerical ranks by the king who trusted him. Nothing suggests he was earlier a military officer or even a child raised at court with Thutmose.[213] His statement that the king promoted him may be the first substantive evidence that Thutmose did place his own men within the Amun hierarchy. But this is hardly a revelation, since the kings could appoint whomever they wished. There is no suggestion here that the king intended to curb the god's power through his appointments. Kees concluded this as well and noted specifically that the High priests Mery and Amenemhet owed their positions to the king (Amenhotep II,)[214] Whether Amenhotep si-se survived the whole of Thutmose' reign is unknown, but the first known successor to him is Anen, brother of Queen Tiy. He is known to have been in the position in year 20 of Amenhotep III;[215] how early he acquired the rank is still unclear.

3.1.3. Third prophet of Amun (ḥm nṯr ḥmt n 'Imn) A man named Nufer has been assigned to the reign of Thutmose IV by Gaballa who examined a granite shrine in the Cairo Museum (JE 59868)[216] Since Nufer's son Amenemhet held the office in year 20 of Amenhotep III,[217] the dating is likely to be correct. The style of the shrine is surprisingly archaic recalling Middle kingdom models as did earlier 18th Dynasty statuary. Whether this was intentional or simply the result of employing artisans working in an old style would be interesting to know.

3.1.4 God's father of Amun (ỉt nṯr n'Imn)

Hekanefer, High priest of Osiris, datable by style to Thutmose IV's reign, was also given the title of God's father of Amun and once Chief (ḥry) God's father of Amun on his naos from Abydos.[218] This man was probably a Theban by origin who married into an Abydene family. We may suggest that his religious offices for Amun stemmed from the period before his move to the Thinite nome. See further under the Osiris priesthood.

3.1.5 Amun Temple Administrators.

3.1.5.1 Chief steward for Amun's Temple (mr pr n 'Imn) Kaemwast[219] is dated by inscription as Chief Steward in Thutmose IV's reign. He left two very fine statues of himself as temple votives. Tjenuna, the Chief Steward for the king was also Amun's steward during the reign (see above). The Chief steward for Amun's temple was certainly an important official, but there is reason to believe that more than one man held the position at a time. During the reign of Amenhotep II, for example, Mery, Amenemhet, Rekhmire, Kenamun and Sennefer are all known to carry the title. Attempts to place the stewards in chronological sequence must argue that Rekhmire gave up the title to Sen-Djehuty in the last years of Thutmose III and that Mery took it from Sennefer who held the title early in his career under Amenhotep II.[220] How, then, did Kenamun have the office and for how long?

The size of the Amun temple institution was enormous and required many people to oversee it, both from the clerical and royal ranks. That more than one man shared this function, some perhaps with more geographic control than others, should not be dismissed.[221] While in the Wilbour papyrus, the mr pr n 'Imn could be anonymous, that may only indicate that but one person was responsible for Fayum holdings. And Helck's discussion of this 20th dynasty document shows there is evidence two different men held the office. He argued that Ramessesnakht and Wosermaatrenakht were one and the same, while Gardiner suggested they succeeded one another.[222] Therefore, although Kaemwast and Tjenuna might have held the stewardship for Amun consecutively during Thutmose IV's reign, they might also have shared the position.[223]

3.1.5.2. Scribe and Steward for the Second prophet. A Djeserkareseneb appears in Amenhotep si-se's tomb (75) and in his own tomb (38) as Steward for the Second prophet of Amun. Djeserkareseneb's tomb is not dated by any cartouche but was certainly decorated in Thutmose's rule; it is known for a beautiful banquet scene [224] which provides an example of the elegant style developing during this reign. Djeserkareseneb was Counter of grain in the granary of divine offerings for Amun in addition to his steward's job. He very likely aided Amenhotep si-se in his function of Overseer of granaries for Amun. In addition to the tomb at least two other monuments calling this man Djeserka have been identified. A statue of the Scribe of Counting grain of Amun Djeserka and his wife Wadjet (?) was in a private collection in Puerto Rico.[225] A tomb lintel in the Yale Art Gallery (YAG 1937.13) belongs to the Scribe Djeserka and his wife or sister Wadjrenpet.[226] The style of this lintel is most probably of Thutmose IV's reign.

3.1.5.3.   Overseer of cattle of Amun (mr k3w n Imn).

This was a post held by more than one man at a time.

Aling argued that there were two ranks of Overseer of cattle of Amun--a high position for major officials; and a low office for minor temple bureaucrats.[227] This suggestion develops difficulty since one must assume which rank is intended by comparison with the titleholder's other positions. Nothing contradicts the conclusion that the designation Overseer of cattle of Amun was a general title for those who supervised temple herds of any and all sizes and in any areas. Kees took a similar view in regard to civil officers such as Kenamun who controlled herds and lands for Amun.[228] Thus High priests of Amun probably controlled large herds, while lesser but important officials (Senmut, Djehuty,a Treasurer, Sennefer, Mayor of Thebes, Tjenuna, Chief Steward, etc.) were responsible for large groups of cattle as well. And men of lower position supervised herds for the temple, presumably of smaller size.

Four men are certainly dated to Thutmose IV as mr k3w n Imn. Kaemwast is known from a stelophorous statue in the British Museum and one in the Brooklyn Museum.[229] He was also Chief steward for the Amun temple, Overseer of Nefrut bulls of Amun, Royal scribe and scribe for Thutmose IV's funerary estate. Cartouches of the king date his statues. Kaemwast's tomb is not known, but he must have been an important man due to his high position in the temple.

Amenhotep, Viceroy of Nubia, was also Overseer of cattle of Amun. It was mentioned above that he probably supervised the Nubian herds for the god[230] and as such was hardly in competition with the High priest in Thebes. Tjenuna, Chief steward for Thutmose IV, was also Overseer of cattle for Amun, as was Horemhab, Scribe of elite troops and owner of Theban tomb 78.[231] Aling suggested that, since High priest Amenemhet was not called mr k3w n Imn Thutmose IV had removed the herds' supervision from the clergy and given it to the Viceroy of Nubia.[232] The rank, however, was in the realm of civil and clerical officers from its inception (Sennefer, Amenhotep, Chief steward for Hatshepsut, Minmose, architect for Thutmose III, and Menkheper, Overseer of granaries for Amenhotep II).[233] Even the powerful Amun clergy of the Ramesside period did not normally bear this title, nor the stewardship for the Amun estates. (In discussion above we have placed Amenemhet earlier in the Dynasty.) Without stronger evidence, Thutmose IV should not be accused of stripping the High priests of Amun of this rank.

3.1.5.4   Tomb 151 [234] in Dira abu el Naga belonged to one Haty, Scribe of counting cattle for the God's wife of Amun, son of a counter of cattle of the God's wife Nebnefer. Despite the fact that the God's wife had a separately administered institution from the Karnak temple of Amun, the office belongs to that temple's worship. We find it therefore convenient to include Haty here. The style of Haty's tomb which has hanging lotus friezes but retains the less elaborate garments worn by women is very comfortable in the reign of Thutmose IV. The quality of painting is, however, much lower than that seen in the tombs dated by cartouche. Here the artisans were sloppy and had poor plaster to work on. The content of scenes has been reduced to include primarily the deceased before offerings in the first hall and the funerary rituals in the back. What does the quality of tomb decoration have to do with the importance of this man's office? Naturally we are unsure, but Haty's funerary chapel suggests a man at middle level in the administration. Once in the tomb he is given the title mr pr n hmt ntr, Steward for the God's wife. This is a title used by Senmut with respect to Hatshepsut [235], although one would certainly hesitate to attribute an equivalent status to Haty. Possibly the holdings of the God's wife (Tiaa?) were not nearly so vast at this period due to the royal control exerted on the institution after the reign of Hatshepsut. Or perhaps Haty was only one of a number of administrators for the God's wife.

3.1.6   Other religious titles linked to Amun.
3.1.6.1 The First King's son of Amun (s3 nsw tpy n Imn).

This title may have designated a man who substituted for the king in the processions of Amun on feast days. Kees identified two men who could have served during Thutmose IV's rule--neither is securely dated there.[236] One Neferhebef is known by a funerary cone, and bore the title First King's son of Amun along with the ranks of scribe of divine offerings and secrets in Karnak (sš htpt-ntr št3 m Ipt-swt).[237] Kees did link the wab office with this position, and there is a wab of Amun Neferhebef known as the son of Hepu, the Vizier. Another possible First King's son of Amun for Thutmose IV's reign is one Ipu, known from a Leiden stela.[238] A date in the reign of Thutmose would suit this monument quite well, although it has been assigned to Amenhotep III's rule by Helck. If the stela was made at the earlier time, Ipu might have functioned earlier than Thutmose IV's reign, since the stela was dedicated by Ipu's son Nefru.

3.1.6.2 Overseer of Prophets of the South and North

This prestigious title was borne by High priests of Amun during several reigns in the 18th dynasty. Hapuseneb, Menkheperreseneb, Amenemhet, Mery and Ptahmose oversaw the prophets of Egypt. However, the Scribe of elite troops,

Horemhab (TT78) held the title for Thutmose IV, using it twice in his tomb.[239] If we are correct in suggesting that Ptahmose served first under Thutmose IV, then he may have held the rank alongside Horemhab. The High priest of Amun and Vizier Ptahmose continued under Amenhotep III but did not pass the Overseer title to another Chief priest. The High priest of Amun Meriptah of the same reign, was called Overseer of prophets of all the gods. Ptahmose also carried this title, but Helck and Kees[240] believe it was a weaker variant and not the same office held by the earlier High priests.

Horemhab's possession of Overseer of Prophets (whose significance has never been determined) has caused Helck[241] to postulate that Thutmose IV waged a war of power with the Amun clergy. If Ptahmose was the Overseer of Prophets for Thutmose IV this suggestion becomes irrelevant, but as of now we cannot determine. The tomb of Horemhab was clearly attacked by Atenists, and later occupants of the tomb may have deliberately erased the deceased's name through desire to remove the original owner's name.[242] But evidence that Horemhab was reviled in the period following his death has not materialized. While the donation of this religious office to a man whose Amun temple titles followed a lengthy military and palace career [243] is certainly intriguing, it may not necessarily indicate a battle between crown and god.

First, Kees has made the point clear that in the 18th dynasty there was no family of Amun priests who held power in an isolated domain.[244] There were no father-to-son High priests, but rather the king chose whomever he desired for the highest positions, and those men, like Amenhotep si-se, worked as much for the ruler as for the god. In like manner the tombs of the High priests represented the kings on the walls (Menkheperreseneb's and Mery's certainly did, and Amenemhet's may have, but its state of preservation is too poor to be sure.)[245] Just when any major aggrandizement of individual power may have built up is then in question, and exactly what the removal of the Overseer of Prophets rank would have accomplished is also unclear, since we have no certain idea of the individual power of the Chief priest with or without the Overseer of Prophets title.

Although the assignment of this office to someone other than the High priest could have been intended to reduce Amun's monopolistic control, it could have been motivated as much by an interest in other deities as by a hostile attitude toward one. This idea, which has been mentioned above,is in keeping with the gradual emphasis on gods from the north--both Re and Ptah were national deities, and due to the increasing contact of Egypt with the Near East and the Mediterranean, their geographic region was ever more significant to Egypt from the mid-18th dynasty on. Thus it should not surprise us to learn that after the Vizier and High priest of Amun Ptahmose held the Overseer title, it passed to the High priests of Ptah, Thutmose and Ptahmose. Judging from their construction in the temples, we can hardly accuse Amenhotep III or Thutmose IV of being enemies of Amun; and it is sensible to view the shift in titleholders as a reflection of geographic and political realities. We do not know where Horemhab originally came from, but his name, at least, has northern associations. It may be that, like Kenamun before him, Horemhab received major administrative positions in the Amun clergy for the northern areas in particular,[246] and that he further was named Overseer of prophets to represent Amun's authority outside of Thebes,[247] particularly since Ptahmose was most occupied in Thebes as both vizier and Chief priest.

3.1.6.3 Chief Craftsman for Amun (ḥry ḥmwtyw n 'Imn)

The wab priest and Chief craftsman for Amun, Khaut, is known from a stela purchased in Luxor and now in the Cairo Museum (CG 34021).[248] That the stela should be dated to Thutmose's reign is clear from the ruler's cartouches, and he is called "beloved of Amun-Re, lord of the thrones of the Two lands". The stela is a boundary marker which sets out a gift from land apportioned for the cult of a statue of Thutmose IV. It is not known whether the image was a Karnak monument or one from the funerary or another temple. The man Khaut is given kharu fields, called the irrigated land of Tinet-shenau, (nhb n Tint-šnᶜw) as a favor of the king.[249] The transaction implied here is most intriguing. Compare the Memphis statue of the Steward Amenhotep in the reign of Amenhotep III.[250] There the Steward supplied lands to endow the statue of King Amenhotep and received the offerings thereto to supply his own statue. It is conceivable that a similar arrangement is here alluded to with respect to Khaut's funerary chapel, perhaps. Possibly this Khaut was the possessor of a tomb in the Theban necropolis. Nine funerary cones identify the wᶜb n h3t 'Imn idnw m pr 'Imn H3wt, "the wab priest in front of Amun, the adjutant in the Temple of Amun Khaut". The wife is named as the Singer of Amun, Mistress of the house Tamut.[251] Although the titles are not identical, the cones could reflect a later stage of Khaut's career. The name is not common, but of course the identification is only possible, not certain.

Another wab priest of Amun is surely dated by cartouche to the reign of Thutmose IV.The Metropolitan Museum possesses a sandstone tomb lintel (90.6.128)[252] on which the wab of [Amun, Userhat ?] appears with his wife Ta-rowy before an enthroned Anubis. Atenists erased the god's name; Userhat is restored from traces. The prenomen of Thutmose is shown behind the god. There is no provenance for this piece, but a Theban tomb is likely. One Theban possibility for the deceased is the owner of tomb 176, a wab pure of hands, Userhet or Amun-Userhet.[253] An exterior door of sandstone should not have been exceptional in Thebes. This is but a suggestion, and is not meant as a sure identification.

3.2. High priest of Ptah (wr ḥrp ḥmwt)

The man who held the position of "Greatest controller of craftsmen" for Ptah was the High priest for the god. With this rank was often the sem priest's title. One Ptahmose left a statue, dated by cartouches to the reign of Thutmose IV,[254] on which he laid claim to this High priest's office. The statue, CG 584, is of brown quartzite and is preserved only in its lower half. Its provenance is unknown but is almost certainly Memphis. The kneeling Ptahmose is wearing a kilt with a sash attached in front--it is the same costume worn by the High priest of Ptah and his family on a Leiden shrine of Amenhotep III's rule. [255] Unfortunately this Ptahmose provided no parentage on his statue, and it is therefore impossible to identify him conclusively with the High priest Ptahmose son of the Vizier Thutmose.[256] There is yet another Ptahmose, son of Menkheper, who was High priest of Ptah under Amenhotep III.[257] The man from CG 584 could have been identical with either of these men but is perhaps more likely to be the son of Thutmose and owner of the false door in Florence.

3.2.1. Only one member of Ptah's regular priesthood is known for this period. One Istu, owner of a stela in the Chicago Art Institute (93.75), was called a wab of Ptah.[258] This stela was mentioned in Chapter 4 where it was assigned to Memphis rather than Thebes.

3.3. High priest of Montu (ḥm-nṯr tpy n Mntw)

The tomb of Ipy (C6)[259] in Thebes represents a son who is called High priest of Montu as well as ḥȝty-ᶜ mr ḥmw-nṯr ḥm-nṯr tpy mr pr n Mntw; his name is Denrega,[260] perhaps group-written for Deleg. Nothing else is known of Montu's priesthood for this reign, but it should be recalled that Thutmose IV showed an interest in the god at Medamud, Armant and at the Montu precinct in Karnak. The date of Ipy's tomb remains uncertain, and identification of a High priest of Montu must as well.

3.4. High priest of Onuris (ḥm-nṯr tpy n ʾInḥrt)

Two men are assigned to this office for the reign of Thutmose IV. One, Amenhotep, is securely dated by the king's cartouches on his stela (BM 902).[261] This Amenhotep was mentioned above, because one scholar identified him with the like-named Viceroy of Nubia. Amenhotep probably came from a military family, for his sons are both titled snni n ḥm.f "charioteer of his Majesty". But it is also probable that Amenhotep had family ties to the Thinite region from whence his stela apparently came. All the gods there mentioned are Thinite gods (Osiris of Abydos, Wepwawet and Onuris), and Amenhotep's wife, Henut, was a temple singer for Onuris. The style of the monument itself is nearly identical to that on several Abydene stelae from the reign (Louvre C 53, especially). It seems reasonable to surmise that Amenhotep, a loyal soldier (probably in the king's own guard), was awarded the High priesthood in his own neighborhood as a pension and reward for his service.

Nebseny, owner of Theban tomb 108, was also High priest of Onuris.[262] He is not, however, firmly dated to the reign, although that date is possible for much of the decoration of his tomb.[263] The banquet scene, however, may have been completed or repainted later and therefore has its strongest parallels to the banquet in Nakht's tomb (TT 52).[264] There would be no reason to think two men could not have held this office in the period. Nebseny may have functioned under Amenhotep III also, having succeeded Amenhotep.

3.4.1. One temple administrator is known for Onuris; one Meryti left a statue in the Mut temple.[265] It was dedicated to Amun-Re, lord of the thrones of the Two lands, Mut lady of Isheru, and the Ennead of Karnak. Meryti called himself Royal scribe, Overseer of <u>Nefrut</u> cattle of Onuris, guardian of Amun and processional leader for Osiris. (One Nebneteru, represented in the tomb of Djeserkareseneb, was also a guardian or doorkeeper for Amun.[266]) These various titles make it difficult to judge whether Meryti had any direct contact with Onuris' center at This or whether he simply supervised herds of cattle for the god elsewhere. It does seem, however, that Meryti's major profession was scribal. The text on the front of his statue called him simply rpʿt ḥ3ty-ʿ sš nsw "hereditary prince, mayor and Royal scribe".

3.5 High priest of Osiris (ḥm-nṯr tpy n Wsir)

Two men may be assigned on the basis of style and genealogy to the Abydene chief priesthood during Thutmose IV's reign. Their order and relationship to one another can also be suggested. The first, one Minmose, was discussed by DeMeulenaere who recognized him as part of a family influential in Abydos at least since the reign of Thutmose III.[267] Judging from the style of BM 2300 the Minmose who was Overseer of the storehouse for the God's wife (Nefrure?) and father to the first High priest of Osiris Minmose lived in the reign of Hatshepsut and Thutmose III. This High priest was uncle to the High priest Minmose whom we believe to have held office during Thutmose IV's reign. Apparently there was no heir of the Chief priest Minmose, but his sister Heriy and her husband, an Overseer of Fields of Amun Neferheb had a son Minmose who took over the office. He must have died during the reign of Thutmose IV, but he left two stelae from an Abydene cenotaph which preserve his name, titles and family.[268]

The High priest of Osiris Minmose did have sons; one a <u>wab</u> priest of Amun Turoy accompanied him on stela CG 34099. Another, the scribe Haty, is given favored position in the second register scene on that same stela. Neither man succeeded to the Chief priesthood, however. CG 70039 is a naos belonging to the High priest of Osiris Hekanefer.[269] The style of the sculptures within the naos is compatible with the reigns of Amenhotep II and Thutmose IV, but the relief dedication scenes on the sides can date no earlier than the latter's rule. Hekanefer's wife is one Mutnefert who appears prominently on both of Minmose's stelae as his daughter. On CG 34099 she kneels behind the parents' chair but is identified as part of the "younger generation" by her elaborate enveloping wig and large earrings which Heriy does not have. On CG 34101 Mutnefert stands behind Minmose accentuated above all other offspring. She is named as "his daughter Mutnefert called Tjuy". We may thus conclude that, as in the earlier case of Heriy, Mutnefert's marriage to Hekanefer, the God's father of Amun, transferred the Chief priesthood of Osiris but at the same time kept it in the family. How long Hekanefer held the post is unknown.

3.6 High priest of Re in Heliopolis. (wr m3w)

In Chapters 2 and 4 the prince Ahmose received attention as a probable son of Thutmose IV and the Heliopolitan chief priest who carried out Thutmose's temple construction. He was also priest of bulls of Mnevis [270] as well as Overseer of the treasury, of bulls, of the granaries and pure fields of Atum. Apparently Thutmose IV's interest in the Heliopolitan cults was great, for although we pointed out that Ahmose wrote at length of his work overseeing construction of an enclosure wall for the precinct of Atum, he did not claim the same for Re's complex. He carried the grand supervisor's title "Overseer of all works of the king".[271] Another man may have helped oversee work on the temple of Re.

3.6.1 One Tuthmose known from a stone bowl in the Cairo Museum (Temp. number 30.10.26.7, Exhb. number 11474) was "Royal scribe and Overseer of works in the temple of Re". Part of the nomen remains showing "Thutmose kha [khau]". Only Thutmose IV can be identified by this fragment. This bowl was assigned to Karnak in Porter and Moss'Bibliography, but a Theban provenance is unlikely. A secondary text on the bowl appears to identify Khnum, lord of Hur,[272] a region in Middle Egypt. On the bowl the man Thutmose is kneeling before a cartouche of the king. The legend says "giving praise", and one must assume that it is the king himself who is being adored. We have argued elsewhere that Thutmose IV identified himself at Giza with the sun god. This might be taken as another example since it is specifically the nomen--or the son of Re name--which is worshipped by the Overseer of works. Our information concerning Thutmose IV's interest in and functionaries for the region of Heliopolis has been greatly expanded by these monuments.

3.7 Overseer of Prophets of Sobek Shedty

The Mayor of the Fayum, Sobekhotep, was also Overseer of the prophets of Sobek Shedty.   His wife was Greatest of the Harem of Sobek Shedty.[273] Sobekhotep, the Treasurer, passed his mayoral title on to his son Paser, apparently long before he died. In Sobekhotep's tomb, Paser already used the civil title, but his religious rank was only that of Prophet of Sobek Shedty.[274] It would appear, therefore, that Paser only became Overseer of prophets of Sobek at his father's death, if at all. We know that he held his father's mayoral office until late in Amenhotep III's reign.

3.8 High priest of Iah (the moon)

Sobekhotep's second son, one Djehuty, bore the title   of High priest for the Moon[275]. Even the location of this cult center is unknown, but given the family's connections and the moon's importance in Hermopolis, it may well have been in Middle Egypt.

3.9   Temple of Thutmose IV at Thebes.   The High priest for the king's funerary temple is known from the tomb of Ipy (C6) in Thebes.[276] Ipy's son, Piay, is called High priest for Menkheprure. Whether Thutmose IV was already dead at the time Piay was shown in the tomb is unclear; Radwan expressed that opinion[277] but it cannot be proven. From the king's reign, the Steward of the Amun temple, Kaemwast, is also known to have been scribe for the Temple of Menkheprure,[278] and a stela in Leiden identifies another man who served during the king's lifetime. It is dedicated to the Guardian for the Temple of Menkheprure, Seth.[279] The Tjununa of BM 35400, cited above, may have been steward for the temple of Thutmose IV. But the statuette's date is uncertain.[280] The High priest Piay's father, Ipy, was Chief of boats for the temple of the lord of Two lands, Menkheprure. Ipy also bore several variants of that title, but all refer to Thutmose's funerary temple.[281] The conclusion seems justified that the king's funerary complex was staffed and functioning before his death.

Two High priests of the king's mortuary estate are known from later periods; one Huy functioned under Ramesses II (?), and Kynbu (TT 113) was recorded as Prophet of the Temple of Menkheprure as late as the reign of Ramesses VIII.[282] The standard of the king's estate appears in Theban tomb 31 of Khonsu, First priest of Menkheperre, tempus Ramesses II. It is perhaps surprising to see cult positions continuing within the temple at such a late date, but there are also references in the Ramesside period to an Overseer of bulls for the king and to a water-bearer (kni) of Menkheprure named Kaemwast.[283] Helck reports that the funerary temple was a source for jasper during the reign of Ramesses IX, but it is unclear whether such supplies indicate the temple still functioned--or was ceasing to do so![284]

3.10 Temple of Thutmose IV in Abydos. The men Si-ese and Neferhet were mentioned in Chapter 4 as functionaries in the king's chapel or cenotaph at Abydos. Neferhet, known from two stelae,[285] was Chief of building for the Temple of Menkheprure in Abydos. Si-ese's career[286] lasted over more than one reign--he was first a Royal scribe, Scribe of elite troops and Army scribe, and once general or military officer (mr ms^{c}w) probably he attained his stewardships later, together with distinctions such as Overseer of horns, hooves, feathers and scales and also Overseer of granaries for Amun. Si-ese's floruit must have been under Thutmose IV and Amenhotep III--his father, Ahmose, is dated by cartouche to Amenhotep II's rule.

4. Military Administration

It has been noted more than once that during the 18th dynasty military officers became increasingly influential. This development reached record proportions in the Amarna period and its aftermath, but certainly there were many military men of importance even in the early decades of the Dynasty. The reign of Thutmose IV is no exception but does exhibit reflections of the country's diplomatic and military status in the administration set up for Thutmose IV's reign. It was the educated military scribes who prospered during this period and who were able to move into palace administrative positions. Thutmose IV employed a number of people who had served in the Asiatic campaigns under Thutmose III and Amenhotep II. These men were being pensioned off at this time, but they do not appear to have been readily replaced. Rather the relative calm in the east did not necessitate the training of generals and army adjutants such as Djehuty and Amenemhab. The route to advancement was now from either Army scribe or Child of the nursery to Royal scribe and scribe of the elite troops (nfrw), and then on to higher positions.[287] Thutmose IV's administration demonstrates that true military service was now the second best means to social mobility. Scribal service for the king's troops, without the necessary army credentials is notable among Thutmose's favorites.

Administrative Officers

4.1. Scribe of the army. (ss ms^c)

There are several men who held this office during the reign of Thutmose IV. The Army scribe was not a high official, but rather Helck suggested that this was a lower echelon rank from which many important men commenced their careers. [288] The best-known Army scribe in this period is Tjanni, owner of Theban tomb 74.[289] That tomb was republished by the Brack's and may be consulted for full information and new finds.   Tjanni served under Thutmose III, Amenhotep II and Thutmose IV.[290] He died in the last king's reign, probably in the early years of it judging by the style of his tomb. Wegner likewise placed Tjanni's tomb chapel stylistically at the beginning of the rule.[291]

Tjanni began his career in Thutmose III's Syrian campaigns. He mentions a Djahy expedition and the booty brought back from it.[292] He was an Army scribe even then, so it is not surprising that he died mr sš mš^cw n nb t3wy and mr mš^cw n nsw as well as sš nfrw, that is, "Overseer of Army scribes for the lord of Two lands, Military officer or general, Royal scribe, and Scribe of elite troops." Tjanni exhibited loyalty on military expeditions to three sovereigns, and he was rewarded for it. But Tjanni, unlike other Army scribes and scribes of elite troops, remained in his military role throughout his career; his numerous epithets indicate that he was a close court associate, but he held no civil or religious ranks. Based on the scenes in Tjanni's tomb and the titles he exhibits there, it appears that under Thutmose IV he still acted as record-keeper for the king; he registered all the troops of all classes, and he accounted for soldiers, priests, royal servants, and craftsmen as well as domesticated animals.[293] It would appear that as Royal scribe and Army scribe, Tjanni was responsible for accounting various items for the ruler. As Military officer he was shown leading the foreign rulers before pharaoh to present their revenues , but he probably was never a strategist on the battlefield.   At least that was the conclusion reached by Helck, and Schulman adopted it for the 18th dynasty Military officers (mr mš^cw).[294]

Horemhab (TT78) did not use the title Army scribe, but once in his tomb he was called mr sš nsw nb n mš^cw "Overseer of all Royal scribes for the army".[295] (Other Royal scribes of the army are known from the 18th and 19th dynasties.)[296] This title indicates what was already apparent in Tjanni's tomb scenes and inscriptions: that Royal scribes were often directly related to the army and that duties of the royal administration and the military could be performed through both arms. But it would be a mistake to equate Royal Scribe of the army with Army scribe. Horemhab was a court-trained man assigned to the army. He was not an Army scribe in origin.

The Army scribe Menwy is known from a graffito at Konosso.[297] This man has already been briefly mentioned because of his association with the Overseer of granaries Wepwawetmose and the Scribe of elite troops Horemhab. The graffito in question was incorrectly copied in the Urkunden IV so that Menwy's title appears there as "scribe of [counting grain]", but the correct drawing appears in Champollion's handcopy. There the name and title are shown as sš mš^cw n nb t3wy Mntwy; the ⌒ sign is probably a mistake, for it is absent in Petrie's copy, and this same man appears in another graffito from Konosso.[298] In that inscription Menwy appears as sš mš^cw n nb t3wy, and the text can be dated to Thutmose IV, since Hekarnehhe appears there as well. The Army scribe Menwy must also have been active under Amenhotep III. CG 901 was a statue of the "Army scribe, Scribe of elite troops, and Royal scribe" Men; it came from the Mut precinct, and bears the cartouche of Amenhotep III.[299] It seems quite likely that Men and Menwy are one and the same. The funerary cone of this same man calls him ss ms°w n nb t3wy Mny 𓏤𓏤 (BMFA 72.1769).[300] The career of this Army scribe would seem, like that of several others, to have begun as simple Army scribe and to have led to Scribe of elite troops and Royal scribe.

Two men, father and son, were also Army scribes during Thutmose's rule. The stela of one Sennu and his son Si-amun (Bologna 1908) stylistically belongs to this period[301] and is not the only monument known for the family. The Louvre possesses a doorway (C 140-42) belonging to Sennu and Si-amun, and it is possible that these men had a cenotaph at Abydos from which these objects came.[302] The doorway is stylistically best placed in Thutmose IV's reign also, although other monuments of Sennu are certainly posthumous and date to Amenhotep III's rule. Sennu was a royal herald, Royal scribe, Scribe of elite troops, and Army scribe for the lord of the Two lands. Si-amun was Army scribe for the lord of the Two lands; again the career development, as with Tjanni and Menwy, beginning with Army scribe, can be signalled. It cannot be proven that both father and son functioned under Thutmose IV, but it is likely that at least one of them did. Sennu perhaps served even earlier and continued in the reign of Thutmose IV. Si-amun who was already Army scribe during Thutmose IV's rule (Bologna stela) may have predeceased his father since he does not appear on later stelae apparently made as posthumous votive offerings to Sennu. Two stelae in the Metropolitan Museum (12.182.39 and 18.2.5) and one in the Louvre (C282 = E 11168)from Tuna el Gebel [303] were dedicated on behalf of the deceased and presumably now deified Sennu by the lector priest Pawahy and his son Kha. The three may have decorated a votive cenotaph near the temple of Thoth, but this is only speculation. Stylistically the stelae belong to an advanced time in Amenhotep III's rule and may represent the continuing funerary endowment for Sennu in his region of origin.

Si-ese, the Steward of Thutmose IV's chapel at Abydos, was also an Army scribe.[304] It has been said above that his father served under Amenhotep II and that Si-ese probably acted as military scribe early on and was promoted to religious posts as pension, perhaps by Amenhotep III. This chronology cannot be certain but is likely given Si-ese's career changes. This man was Army scribe and Scribe of elite troops and also Military officer; probably he followed Tjanni into the last office (or held it simultaneously) [305] and administered troops and provisions for the king at the close of his military service. Then he returned to Abydos and was allowed to benefit from royal donations in the holy city. Si-ese was buried in Abydos, and from his wealth of monuments he must have been an honored associate of the rulers.

Minhotep known from the Leningrad papyrus and a stela in Cairo[306] was an

Army scribe, a Scribe of elite troops and treasury scribe. One final Army scribe of the lord of the Two lands is known from a graffito at Bigeh where he appeared with the Chief steward Tjunar. That man was named Amenemipet.[307]

4.2 Scribe of the Elite Troops (sš nfrw)

There is some disagreement about the translation of the title (sš nfrw) and about the meaning of the rank as well. Schulman's argument for "scribe of the elite troops" appears justified, especially so since the nfrw do appear to have been part of the king's personal guard during Thutmose IV's expedition in the Eastern desert.[308] Sš nfrw often were either Army scribes or Royal scribes (or both), and often were close personal associates of rulers. It is therefore logical to assume that they acted as scribes for troops in personal service to the sovereign.[309] Other Army scribes would have had little opportunity to gain access to pharaoh and thereby gain promotion. Schulman's understanding is thus accepted here.

Tjanni (tomb 74) has already been mentioned above in 4.1 He must have held this office during more than one reign. A special form of his title, sš nfrw n t3 pdt pr-ᶜ3 "Scribe of elite troops of the Bowmen of Pharaoh" demonstrates Tjanni's service to pharaoh's own guard.[310] Horemhab (tomb 78) is of major importance as Scribe of elite troops[311] but was not an Army scribe. Rather he was a Royal scribe and even the Overseer of all Royal scribes of the army. His Royal scribe titles stress Horemhab's personal relationship with the king, a fact also echoed in his attachment to the king's daughter, Amenemipet. The princess was represented as a child on Horemhab's lap in a scene from his tomb. Horemhab , however, was not an intimate of Thutmose's with whom he grew up in the palace; for he was probably born during Thutmose III's rule and by his own statement served under Amenhotep II, Thutmose IV and Amenhotep III.[312] His career as scribe of the elite troops must have paralleled Tjanni's for some years. It has already been said above that late in life Horemhab was given the title Overseer of prophets of the north and south; he was also named Overseer of the fields and cattle of Amun, Overseer of horns, feathers, claws and scales,Overseer of works for Amun, Master of horses, and Fanbearer on the right of the king. His characteristic titles, however, even in his tomb, were Royal scribe and Scribe of elite troops. Since Thutmose IV was ruler during the period when all but one scene in TT 78 was painted, the titles Horemhab which expanded the scribe's fortunes probably came to him as the reward of Thutmose IV for his long and faithful service to the crown. The work of this Scribe of elite troops appears to have been completely domestic during the reign.

Horemhab was obviously a man of major importance at the time of his death; nowhere does he reveal the name of his parents, and one can only guess that he originally came from the north. This man's career is a fine example of how scribal service in the ruler's personal guard resulted in both prestige and power.

Some years ago Hari assigned a door lintel and two jambs to Horemhab's tomb at Thebes;[313] those door elements, Turin Museum 1646-47, belong to a man whose name and face have been mutilated. The titles on the Turin monument belong to a Royal scribe ($s\check{s}$ nsw and $s\check{s}$ nsw $m3^c$ mry.f), Scribe of elite troops and Overseer of Army scribes. It is possible that this door did belong to tomb 78 and that Horemhab was once named there, but it might at least be pointed out that the latter tombowner never called himself Overseer of Army scribes in his tomb inscriptions. He once referred to his position as Overseer of all Royal scribes of the army. As has been said, the two ranks may have been related in function, but they were probably not identical and originating from two different administrative branches, the military and the palace.

In fact, the titles which appear on these Turin door parts are better suited to Tjanni who did, very frequently, call himself Overseer of Army scribes.[314] Although it is true that Horemhab's name has been attacked in his tomb, it is by no means everywhere erased; the Brack's recent researches indicated to them that there was no attempt to condemn the memory of Horemhab by personal enemies. They concluded that later occupants of the tomb felt uncomfortable with the image and name of the original owner.[315] The exterior elements of tombs were probably first subject to such obliterations by the new tomb owners. even when interiors were not. Tjanni's doorway could just as easily have been mutilated as Horemhab's. Actually, Tjanni's tomb is exceptional in not having been touched by the Atenists. Even without these common mutilations, however, Tjanni's name is still lacking in 20 places.[316] It must be left undecided whether the Turin door once belonged to Horemhab's tomb, before Tjanni's or before some other scribe's.

A final word on Horemhab concerns his possible relation to the later king of the same name. Hari's efforts to separate the various monuments of men named Horemhab was most helpful;[317] he identified the Horemhab in Konosso and Sehel graffiti with the owner of tomb 78; this suggestion is confirmed by the association of the graffiti with the name of Thutmose IV. He also suggested that the owner of tomb 78 may have been the grandfather of the future king and that the similarity in titles was a bit more than mere chance. This is an attractive solution, but of course cannot be fully accepted until some genealogical data emerges.

A third man may be assigned to the reign of Thutmose IV as Scribe of elite troops. That man is a northerner named Raner, probably son of the Scribe of elite troops Ay. This man Raner possessed a small sphinx of Thutmose IV (Durham 379)[318] on which the king is called the Good God, Menkheprure. (There is a strong facial resemblance between this piece and the face of Thutmose on CG 42080.) Around the base of this statue is a two-part inscription which reads as follows: (the forepaws and front base text are lost.)

Right: ...<u>wnn tp t3 m3 ḥ3tyw.f ḥ°w w°b šw m ḏwt nb n k3 n s n bity mry ᵢty sš nfrw R-nw-r.</u>

Left: ...<u>Gb (?) di.f °nḥ nfr °ḥ°w snb n k3 n sš nsw m3° mry.f sš nfrw R-nw-r</u>

Right: "...being on earth, seeing his ancestors, pure of limbs, free from any evil, for the <u>ka</u> of the man of the Lower Egyptian king , beloved of the sovereign, the scribe of the elite troops, Raner."

Left: "[A boon which the king gives to] Geb (?) [that] he may give a good life, a lifetime being healthy, for the <u>ka</u> of the true Royal scribe beloved of him, scribe of the elite troops, Raner."

This small sphinx is unusual because it is a royal statue inscribed for a private person. It may have been either a temple donation or, more likely, a gift from the king. There is good reason to believe that Raner was raised and served in his functions in the Memphite region. The northern provenance is suggested already in Raner's unique title, "man of the Lower Egyptian king" which may echo the close attachment of the <u>sš nfrw</u> to the ruler, but beyond this, Raner's parents can be identified and were probably buried near Memphis.

Louvre C 76, a stela in naos form, was dedicated to the <u>ka</u> of the Child of the nursery, true Royal scribe, beloved of him, scrlbe of elite troops, Ay, by his son, the child of the Nursery Raner.[319] The name of the son is exactly as on the Durham sphinx, and this name is rare (not attested at all in <u>Personnennamen</u>). The stela, of Amenhotep III's reign (stylistically) is certainly Memphite in type and has formulae to several deities: Ptah-Sokar Osiris, Osiris Heka-Nehhe, Anubis foremost of the divine booth, and Osiris Khentiamentiu. It is nearly certain that this was a funerary stela used in a northern tomb (Sakkara). Raner appears on the stela with his mother and wife standing behind him; they both face Ay. The mother is called the Lady of the House May (🗣), and the wife, Lady of the House, Pypuy. Although Raner never termed himself "Child of the nursery" on his sphinx, it would hardly be surprising were a Scribe of elite troops who boasted so of his favor with the king once a court youth. It has been seen already that the title was not always retained by men who advanced in their professions. It is nearly certain that C 76 memorializes the father of the same Raner who possessed the sphinx; and it is also apparent that Ay's position as Scribe of elite troops was taken over by his son, during Thutmose's reign by the statue's witness. Ay, however, may well have lived until Amenhotep III's reign.

A fourth Scribe of elite troops for the reign may be Si-ese[320] who has already been discussed above in several sections. Si-ese was a Royal scribe, Army scribe, and scribe of elite troops before he became associated with Thutmose's temple at

Abydos; one is tempted to suggest that he and many other important Abydene inhabitants entered the administration through childhood contacts in the Thinite mayoral residence--where, perhaps, Min, Mayor of Thinis, tutored the young Amenhotep II)[321] and from there joined the military as scribe. Amenhotep, Overseer of the Stable (of his Majesty) and High priest of Onuris, may also have used such a route, finally ending up with a profitable sinecure in his home region. Certainly Abydos and its surrounding nome provided many major officials to the 18th dynasty kings, and several of them had direct links to the palace --through royal nurses, for example.[322] It is reasonable to believe that these able administrators or scribes first came to the king's attention within a residence near Abydos (Deir el Ballas?) and from there traveled with the ruler.

Minhotep under Amenhotep II and Thutmose IV found a career route through the northern palace rewarding. Minhotep [323] was a scribe of the Treasure house (sš pr-ḥd) as well as an Army scribe and Scribe of elite troops. Since he was active in Amenhotep II's reign and apparently assisted in the jubilee festival (or preparations therefor) for that ruler he was probably well advanced in his career during Thutmose IV's reign. His stela from Sakkara stylistically belongs to the later king's rule, but he is another example of a man who was in his last period of an extended career under Thutmose IV. A last Scribe of elite troops was the man Sennu who has already been included as an Army scribe and royal herald. (See above 2.5, 4.1) Sennu too was a Royal scribe and must have been an influential man. His stela in Bologna is stylistically datable to Thutmose IV's reign (even having the characteristic features on his wife's garment and wig). The quality of this piece and the stelae from Tuna el Gebel strongly suggests that Sennu was a wealthy man who may have left a large endowment which continued to produce revenue long after his death. He may have had a cenotaph in Abydos and a burial in Middle Egypt.

Menwy, the Army scribe, may have been the same man who dedicated CG 901 (see under 4.1). That statue was dated to the reign of Amenhotep III by cartouche, but it calls Men a Scribe of elite troops as well as Army scribe. In sum, there were quite likely eight or more scribes of elite troops who functioned during Thutmose IV's reign; Tjanni, Horemhab Ay, and Minhotep probably were in supervisory capacities, given their advanced ages. Helck suggested that there were northern and southern divisions for the office; that could be supported here, since Ay,Raner, and Minhotep must have operated in Lower Egypt. We must have more information concerning the sš nfrw's particular duties, however, before accepting divisions in the office which are geographic.

4.3. Military Officer (or General) (mr mš°w).

This title is attested for two people during the period of Thutmose IV's rule, although only one of them is dated by cartouche in the period. Tjanni of tomb 74 used the title twice in his tomb, and Si-ese from Abydos, also called himself by it once on chapel blocks from his burial.[324] One Ptahmay was assigned to the reign of Thutmose IV by Helck; Schulman called him "18th dynasty"; Aling placed him in Amenhotep III's rule.[325] In fact, Ptahmay belongs in the Ramesside period by the style of the stelae on which he appears. Kees pointed this out long ago,[326] but it needs reiteration. We have noted above that the position of Military officer in this period was largely an administrative one, but it was clearly a step above Scribe of elite troops, from which rank both of these men advanced.

Troop soldiers

4.4. Standardbearers. (t3y sryt)

Although Schulman ranked the standardbearer under the Scribe of elite troops, this officer could command troops on his own, as well as levy men for expeditions.[327] At least eight men can be identified in the reign of Thutmose IV-- several of them can be placed with specific contingents or ships.

Nebamun (TT90) is well-known as the Standardbearer for the ship Meryamun. Nebamun possessed this title in his tomb, on an Abydene stela (Louvre C 60), and on his funerary cones.[328] However, in his tomb chapel Nebamun also represented the occasion of his promotion from Standardbearer for Meryamun to Chief of Police (hry Md3yw n imntt) in Western Thebes. This event occurred in year 6, presumably of Thutmose IV's reign; at least it is that king who appears on another part of the same tomb wall.[329]

Recently a stela of sandstone naming the Police chief for the west Nebamun was found along the road south of Malkata which ran west into the desert.[330] The stela fragments join to form a monument .63 m. high by .38 m. wide and .06 m. deep. Rehorakhty appears as the recipient of Nebamun's adoration, and the text, very abraded, identifies the [standardbearer of Meryamun, Chief of Med]jay for the west Nebamun. The style is compatible with a date in Thutmose IV's rule. The Louvre stela (C 60) was made before Nebamun received his promotion.

A second standardbearer for Meryamun is known in this reign; he is one Pa-aa-aku, who dedicated a stela (Louvre C53) at Abydos.[331] The king's name appears in the lunette and at the left and right Pa-aa-aku, as Child of the nursery and Standardbearer for Mery-Amun,offers to Osiris and Wepwawet. It is most likely that, if only one person held this office at a time, Pa-aa-aku followed Nebamun into it after year 6.

The text of this stela is of further interest, for it relates that a royal messenger came to Abydos to Osiris (on behalf of Thutmose IV)to set up an offering foundation; the king first gave all the meat and fowl provisions and then sent the messenger again to give over fields of Osiris totaling 2000 arouras (h3-t3 200) [332]. Finally the messenger returned to do likewise for the chapel of king Ahmose. Helck has interpreted this text as a royal gift to a private foundation for Pa-aa-aku,[333] but 2000 arouras is a great deal of land for the king to give to a standardbearer. It seems rather that Pa-aa-aku acted on behalf of the king along with the messenger in setting up the royal foundation at Abydos which probably included endowments for Thutmose IV's own cenotaph. This important mission must have left an impression on the standardbearer. We might add here that the ship Mery-Amun was obviously a royal barge used for state missions, not military expeditions during this period. Its name suggests Thebes was its home harbor, and this would agree with the evidence from both Nebamun and Pa-aa-aku's monuments which suggest Abydos was their place of pilgrimage, not origin. Certainly Nebamun resided in Thebes.

The Louvre possesses another stela of a standardbearer for Thutmose IV. C 202 [334] is a monument dedicated to Osiris Wennofer by the Standardbearer for Menkheprure-destroys-Syria, the serviceman (w^{c}w) of Mery-[Amun], Smen. (t3y sryt n Mn-hprw-r^c sksk H3rw w^{c}w n Mry-[Imn] Smn). This man was thus a member of a unit whose name suggests active military service outside Egypt, but he was also (or had been) ship serviceman on Mery-Amun, the same ship cited by Nebamun and Pa-aa-aku. Schulman suggested that w^{c}w could mean soldier in general when applied to men of higher ranks; Helck rather gave several examples to show that w^{c}w of ships' contingents were normally given the standardbearer's position as a next step.[335] Smen probably reflects Helck's outline of military promotion in his titles and might therefore have later become the standardbearer for Mery-Amun.

A man named Tjau (or Tjenau) was a standardbearer for the company "Menkheprure august of rulers" (t3y sryt hr Mn-hprw-r^c ssp hk3w T(n)3w). He is known by Louvre scarab E 3688[336] and must have been of a similar rank as Smen.

The standardbearer Senimose was depicted in the tomb of Tjanni and was there called Standardbearer for the ship's contingent of training (t3y sryt n t3 hnywt [nt] shpr). [337] The prenomen of Thutmose IV appears on two standards there, perhaps naming two ships contingents: "Menkheprure, lord of the khepesh",and "Menkheprure lord of his victory".

Two standardbearers are known from the Pap. Munich 809,[338] which has already been discussed with reference to the Viziers and the Treasurer Sobekhotep,who figure in its content. Among those on the judgment panel were numerous military men: the standardbearer Khaemwast and the standardbearer Rasha are among them. Neither Rasha nor Khaemwast is further specified, but Alain Zivie may have located the tomb of Rasha in Sakkara.[339]

One last standardbearer is identified for this reign: Ptahemhet, owner of Theban tomb 77, [340] bears the titles Child of the nursery, standardbearer for the lord of the Two lands. This standardbearer's position probably was a court designation; although Ptahemhet may have once been a military man, his tomb titles stress his palace connections. His family was military; a brother Nebseny was a charioteer, for example. It is quite probable that Ptahemhet served his military career under Amenhotep II, because he was pensioned during Thutmose's rule and became responsible for construction at the royal funerary temple. His extant tomb texts emphasize that part of his job. It would seem that Ptahemhet and possibly Rasha and Khaemwast, among the standardbearers who served Thutmose, were outside the military formally, functioning largely within the palace. Nebamun and the standardbearers for Meryamun were successful and valued but only the first of them is known to have had an impressive tomb at Thebes. And that funerary chapel appears to have been the result of his obvious influence as Chief of Police in Western Thebes, the appointment to which he proudly proclaimed on the tomb's wall. The route to the court circle was therefore open, but not automatic.

4.5. Troop Commander (hry pdt)

Several men are known to have possessed this rank during Thutmose IV's period of rule. Both Schulman and Helck agree that the Troop commander was a high military officer, above standardbearer and below general.[341] These men were often responsible for specific geographic regions, such as border fortresses or garrisons in other countries. Two men with these specific titles are known in Thutmose' rule. Nebi, Mayor of Sile,[342] was also Troop commander of Sile. Earlier in his career Nebi had been a fort commander in Wawat and was probably mr htm for Sile as well. Nebi represents a high military official who was both soldier and administrator in border or foreign regions; he was also a diplomat of sorts as royal messenger, in addition to his other functions. He acted in that capacity at least once when he visited the Sinai, and there can be little doubt that this military man became a valued foreign affairs expert in Thutmose IV's administration. In addition to the titles already cited, Nebi held the rank of wr n Md3yw, probably a variant to hry Md3yw, Chief of Medjay. (At least other hry ranks varied their titles with ꜥ3 and wr.[343]) Schulman asserts that the Medjay never acted as part of the army after the time of Kamose;[344] if that is true, then Nebi must have used police in his capacity as fort commander.

A second Troop commander is known for the region of Tjeku, another border fort in the Eastern delta.[345] The fortress of Tjeku has not been attested with a Troop commander in the 18th dynasty until recently, when Giveon refound a year 7 graffito of Thutmose IV at Serabit el-Khadim. Below the scene is the short inscription for the Royal messenger, Troop commander of Tjeku, Amenemhet. This Amenemhet was therefore functioning in year 7 in a similar manner to Nebi in year 4.

Two men are known to bear the rank of Troop commander without specific attachments; the owner of Theban tomb 91 (name lost) was Troop commander for the [Good] God, the Great one of the Medjay, Master of horses [valiant one of the king].[346] The tomb of this man depicted both Thutmose IV and Amenhotep III,[347] but the style of tomb 91 is certainly more like those of Thutmose than of the mature reign of Amenhotep III. The tombowner's inclusion among Thutmose's Troop commanders seems quite safe. This man represented himself leading the chiefs of foreign countries with their produce before the kings.[348] From the titles which remain in the tomb, it is difficult to believe such was actually the case, but perhaps the deceased did accompany foreign delegations with revenues to Egypt.

Björkman has suggested that the owner of tomb 91 was none other than the Mayor of Sile Nebi;[349] it is true that both men were wr Md3yw, a fairly uncommon title. It is by no means out of the question. The only objection to this suggestion is the lack of any titles related to Sile within tomb 91. Obviously if Amenhotep III was already on the throne Nebi would have been near the end of his career, but the only titles in the chapel are for a Troop commander and Great one of Medjay. Nebi might well have been buried in the north, and if this is not his tomb, another possibility might be Nebamun's brother, Turi; that man appeared in his brother's tomb as Chief of Medjay in Thebes (hry Md3yw hr W3st), and it is known that he had his own Theban tomb, since a funerary cone exists from it.[350] This is by no means a sure identification since we have no other titles for Turi.

The second unspecified Troop commander is one Pentepihu known from a stela at the Sphinx.[351] This man is not securely dated to Thutmose IV's reign, but the style of the stela is mid-18th dynasty. Pentepihu also held the rank of a King's son. He was therefore an important man, but nothing else is known of him. Schmitz has suggested that the few men holding these King's son titles after the early 18th dynasty represented those with special relationships to the king--those whose closeness to the ruler was similar to family members.[352] This may be correct, but we must have more information about Pentepihu to be sure.

Nebamun, standardbearer for Mery-Amun and owner of tomb 90, has been discussed above. In addition to his standardbearer ranks Nebamun was Troop commander in Western Thebes and Chief of Medjay.[353] We might construe this title to mean that the Medjay were organized as a military unit in Thebes--there is also a Troop commander in the Place of Truth (Deir el Medina) known from a Theban graffito.[354] Clearly policing the Theban necropolis region required both a large number of men and good organization.

Another Troop commander is to be recognized in a fragmentary statue now in the Royal Ontario Museum.[355] This limestone block statue bears the prenomen of Thutmose IV on its right arm and was inscribed both on the front skirt and on the back pillar. The only text now remaining identifies the hry pdt n shyw. There is no parallel for this title, and only a tentative suggestion is made here. This may have been part of the name of a unit such as "beating [the Nehesy]" or likewise. It is unfortunate that only a fragment of the statuette remains.

A last Troop commander is the man Nehemawy who was <u>hry pdt mr h3swt rsyw</u> <u>hry ihw</u>, "Troop commander, Overseer of southern lands and stablemaster".[356] Nehemawy's son [Amen]mose was Document scribe for the queen, and we may suppose that this was an important man in Nubia. The Troop commander's rank must have been specifically related to the administration of the south, and Nehemawy was probably immediately subordinate to Amenhotep the Viceroy of Kush.

4.6. Chief of Medjay (<u>hry/wr n Md3yw</u>)

Four men are known to have borne this title under Thutmose IV; all four have been mentioned at least once above.   Nebamun and his brother Turi were both Chief of Medjay [357] (also called Chief of Police). Nebamun operated in the West of Thebes, that is, in the necropolis. In his tomb he was credited with training the young Medjay recruits, and it is apparent that he received this job as a pension from the king. At the time of his promotion he was referred to in the text as <u>p3 tni n m^{c}w</u> "the old man of the army", and the king donated fields and offerings for him which were exempted from government interference.[358] Turi, his brother, was responsible for Medjay in Thebes (W3st)--it is unclear whether that area was outside of Nebamun's control. In the Ramesside era the Medjay of the Necropolis were organized with two chiefs over an eight-man unit. We do not know whether Nebamun shared the office with Turi, another man, or held the guardianship of Western Thebes alone.[359]

Nebi bore the title Great one of Medjay (Chief of Medjay) while he was Troop commander at Sile; the owner of tomb 91 also held this position.[360]

4.7. <u>Hry Mg3 "Chief of Mg3"</u>

This title appears once in the reign. The brother of Horemhab, Amenemhet, appears in tomb 78 as Chief of <u>Mg3</u> for his Majesty.[361] Schulman has explained the title as one similar to Chief of Medjay [362] in which <u>mg3</u> originally referred to a Nubian group but eventually meant adolescent youths in a military unit. Dare one suggest this is but a phonetic variant of <u>md3</u>? In the Semna stela of Amenhotep III, <u>mg3</u> are listed with <u>nhysw</u> as plunder.[363]

4.8. Adjutant (<u>idnw</u>)

There are three known adjutants in Thutmose IV's reign; two appear in P. Munich 809 as judges.[364] The adjutant Paser and the adjutant Pa-tunur are listed immediately after the   viziers; this probably means they were the next ranking officers sitting on the court, for they were followed by standardbearers and infantrymen. Schulman has stated that the adjutants of the army were largely responsible for provisioning the soldiers.[365]

The adjutant of Medjay, Mana, is also known from the tomb of Nebamun.[366] This must certainly mean that Mana was directly answerable to Nebamun himself as Chief of Medjay.

4.9.Infantryman (w^{c}w)

Several men of infantryman rank are known for the period, only their names and specifications will be given. P. Munich 809 gives the infantrymen of the ship, Star in Memphis.. Pa-?; M-?; May; Amenemhet; Penamun; Djehuty.[367] Smen from Louvre C202 has already been noted with this rank.[368]

4.10. Weaponsbearer (t3y h^{c}w)

A weaponsbearer and bow carrier for the lord of the Two lands (t3y h^{c}w t3y pdt n nb t3wy šms nsw m st.f nb) Merire, son of Ay-merau, appears on a stela in Cairo.[369] The man's monument is stylistically of this period, and his titles suggest he was part of the attachment which assisted the king himself when he traveled. This is not likely to have been an elevated rank, but the man would have had close contact with the king in the field.

4.11 Master of horses (mr ssmwt)

The title "master of horses" has never been satisfactorily explained; Helck believed it was the highest-ranking chariotry title and that there were both northern and southern titleholders.[370] Schulman concluded that the master of horses was a chariot officer of no particular rank.[371] Unfortunately neither explanation accounted for the diversity of officeholders--both civil and military--although Helck did suggest that the title could be given by pharaoh as an honor to a trusted servant.[372] In his dissertation Aling[373] unravelled some of the difficulties of this office, concluding that the office was that of a chariotry commander. He also described a chronological development for the office.[374] Aling's chronology showed that the master of horses was originally a civil officer who cared for and fed horses, not necessarily for military purposes. With the development of chariotry, he suggested, the office more commonly fell to professional soldiers. The military men known to have held the title were commonly Troop commanders (hry pdt); this was a rank of importance which applied to any branch of service--army, navy, chariotry, etc. With the Amarna period and the ensuing 19th dynasty, the title of master of horses, in Aling's view, increasingly belonged to military men of high positions, including many princes who also had general and chariotry officers' ranks.

Aling's analysis is convincing in many respects. One point which remains unclear, however, is whether "Master of horses" should be taken as a military title meaning "chariotry commander". Certainly men who held the office in later times often also carried high ranks such as "general" (mr mš^c [wr]). Princes in the Ramesside period, however, might carry military titles even before they were mature enough for armed action, so the professionalization ascribed to the rank in the 19-20th Dynasties may not have been as pronounced as Aling suggested.[375] The title itself means "Overseer of horses"--it does not anywhere bear even a determinative of a chariot, and no one has yet argued that the word ssmwt could mean chariot. In fact one 20th dynasty prince who bore the title of Great master of horses attached to it the epithet nt st Wsr-m3^{c}t-r^c mry-Imn nt tint-htri "belonging to the place Usermaatre-mery-Amun of the chariotry".[376] If mr ssmwt could designate the officer for chariotry, this epithet would have been redundant. The "Master of horses" rank is often extended by the epithets "of the lord of the Two lands" or " of his Majesty". This may be more than simple honorific addition to the rank. It is quite possible that the Master of horses was one of the few men privileged to work with horses in the royal stables--training them and racing them and--in specific instances--readying them for combat duty.

Although the title does not appear there, the Sphinx Stela of Amenhotep II may shed some light on this rank, just as it may on that of the Stablemaster.[377] Amenhotep boasted in that stela of his work with the royal horses: "He was stout-hearted in working them, learning the nature thereof, skilled in training them, having entered into their customs". When Thutmose III was told of this, his conclusion from it was that "he will act as lord of the whole land; there is none who will attack him".[378] This is strong evidence of the veneration in which "Masters of horses" were held; for the animals themselves were still a rarity in Egypt and sport-on-chariot was only just beginning.[379] Two princes (perhaps the same man) in the reign of Amenhotep II were themselves mr ssmwt [380] --probably young prince Amenhotep was also, and he may have described the office somewhat on his stela. The suggestion is here made that mr ssmwt specified those men who had access to royal horses and stables; they were privileged to enjoy the "sport of kings". The title remained a royal prerogative, for when other officers were given the rank, the Ramesside princes simply enlarged the rank to Great master of horses so that they still stood out as great equestrians.

In the reign of Thutmose IV there were three men who held the title mr ssmwt. Horemhab, owner of tomb 78, once used the rank in his tomb.[381] Hekarnehhe, royal nurse and child of the nursery, possessed several funerary cones with this title on them.[382] And the unknown owner of tomb 91 in Thebes was also Master of horses. Only the last man might have been a military officer--he was a Troop Commander of the Good God which however may have designated only the king's personal residence troops or might indicate that the man's specific company assignment was no longer applicable.[383] Both Helck and Aling agreed that Horemhab and Hekarnehhe received the title of master of horses as an honor for their loyalty to the king. How the third received it is unsure, but he may have been largely a palace soldier whose attachment to the stables was natural. According to the assertions made above, Horemhab, Hekarnehhe, and the owner of tomb 91 were men given the right to train and work with horses from the royal stables; perhaps the last man trained them for combat use as well as for pleasure.

Appendix IV: Officeholders

1. Central Administration

   1.1. Vizier
      Hepu
      Ptahhotep
      Ptahmose
   1.2.Overseer of Treasury
      Sobekhotep
      Merire
   1.3.Overseer of the Treasure House
      Merire
      Amenmose
      Re
        Scribe of the treasure house Minhotep
   1.4.Overseer of granaries
      Re
      Wepwawetmose
      Amenhotep
      Bakenamun
   1.5. King's son of Kush
      Amenhotep
      1.5.1 Nehemawy, Overseer of southern countries

2.Palace Administration

   2.1.Chief Steward
      Merire
      Tjenuna
      Tjenur
   2.2. Various officers
      2.2.1 Paser, <u>mr ^{c}hnwty</u>, Overseer of royal household
      Amenmose, <u>mr ^{c}hnwty</u>
      2.2.2. Iuty, Royal butler
      2.2.3. Meryti, Royal scribe
      2.2.4   Nebi, Overseer of Queen's household
      2.2.5   [Amen]mose, Queen's document scribe
   2.3.Royal Nurses
      Hekareshu
      Hekarnehhe
      Ruiu
   2.4. Child of the nursery
      Hekarnehhe
      Ay
      Raner
      Iuty
      Minhotep
    Ptahemhet

        Nedjem
        Paser
        Nebi
        Neferhet
        Menkheper
        Pa -aa-aku
        Amenemipet
        Iuna
  2.5. Royal Herald
        Re
        Sennu
  2.6. Royal Messenger
        Nebi
        Amenemhet
  2.7. Provincial Mayors or Governors
        Nebi
        Amenmose
        Sobekhotep
        Paser
        Itunema

3. Religious Administration

  3.1.1. High priest of Amun
        Amunemweskhet
        Ptahmose
  3.1.2. Second prophet of Amun
        Amenhotep si-se
  3.1.3. Third prophet of Amun
        Nufer
  3.1.4. God's father of Amun
        Hekanefer
  3.1.5 Administrators of Amun's Temple
      3.1.5.1 Chief Steward for Amun's Temple
          Kaemwast
          Tjenuna
      3.1.5.2.Steward for Second prophet
          Djeserkareseneb
      3.1.5.3.Overseer of cattle of Amun
          Kaemwast
          Tjenuna
          Horemhab
          Amenhotep, King's son of Kush (in Nubia)
      3.1.5.4 Scribe of counting grain for the God's Wife
          Haty
  3.1.6 Other religious titles linked to Amun
      3.1.6.1 First King's son of Amun
          Neferhebef (?)
          Ipu (?)
      3.1.6.2. Overseer of Prophets of the South and North

        Horemhab
3.1.6.3. Chief of craftsmen and <u>wab</u> priests
        Khaut
        Userhet (?)
3.2. High priest of Ptah
        Ptahmose
        3.2.1. <u>Wab</u> priest
        Istu
3.3. High priest of Montu
        Deleg (?)
3.4. High priest of Onuris
        Amenhotep
        Nebseny
        3.4.1. Overseer of <u>Nefrut</u> cattle of Onuris
        Meryti
3.5. High priest of Osiris
        Minmose
        Hekanefer
3.6 High priest of Re
        Ahmose
        3.6.1 .Overseer of works in the Temple of Re
        Tuthmose
3.7 Overseer of Prophets of Sobek Shedty
        Sobekhotep
        3.7.1. Prophet of Sobek
        Paser
3.8 High priest of the Moon
        Djehuty
3.9. High priest for the temple of Thutmose IV
        Piay
        3.9.1. Scribe for Funerary temple
        Kaemwast
        3.9.2. Guard for Funerary temple
        Seth
        3.9.3. Overseer of ships for Funerary temple
        Ipy
3.10. Steward for temple of Thutmose IV in Abydos
        Si-ese
        3.10.1. Chief builder for temple
        Neferhet

4. Military Administration

    4.1. Scribe of the army
        Tjanni
        Menwy
        Sennu
        Si-amun
        Si-ese
        Amenemipet

4.2. Scribe of elite troops
    Tjanni
    Horemhab
    Ay
    Raner
    Si-ese
    Minhotep
    Sennu
    Menwy
4.3. Military Officer (General)
    Tjanni
    Si-ese
4.4. Standardbearer
    Nebamun
    Pa-aa-aku
    Smen
    Tjau
    Senimose
    Rasha
    Khaemwast
    Ptahemhet
    Merire
4.5. Troop Commander
    Nebi
    Amenemhet
    Owner of tomb 91
    Pentepihu (?)
    Nebamun
    Owner of ROM statue
    Nehemawy
4.6. Chief of Medjay
    Nebamun
    Turi
    Owner of tomb 91
    Nebi
4.7. <u>Hry Mg3</u>
    Amenemhet
4.8. Adjutant
    Paser
    Patunur
    Mana
4.9. Infantryman
    Pa__
    Me__
    May
    Amenemhet
    Penamun
    Djehuty
    Smen

4.10. Weapons bearer
    Merire
4.11 Master of horses
    Horemhab
    Hekarnehhe
    Owner of tomb 91

Royal scribes in Thutmose IV's reign

Ay	Scribe of elite troops
Iuny	Royal scribe who read Nebamun's promotion announcement TT 90
Amenhotep	King's son of Kush
Wepwawetmose	Overseer of granaries
Bakenamon	Overseer of granaries
Men(wy)	Scribe of elite troops
Menkheper	Royal scribe of Royal Children's House
Minhotep	Scribe of elite troops, etc.
Meryti	Processional Leader
Raner	Scribe of elite troops
Re	Royal Herald
Horemhab	Scribe of elite troops, etc.
Siese	Scribe of elite troops, etc.
Sennu	Royal Herald, etc.
Kaemwast	Chief Steward of Amun
Tjanni	Army scribe, etc.

Appendix V Theban Tombs

During visits to some ninety private tombs I have been forced to conclude, as did Romer with respect to the royal 18th Dynasty tombs,[384] that the painted decoration in Theban nobles' tombs was achieved very rapidly at undetermined times during the tombowners' lives or the period of embalming.[385] The decoration was abandoned in many cases before completion.[386] Crews of draughtsmen under the direction of master artisans might have completed a tomb such as Hepu's (TT 66) in a week or two. There is little indication that multiple scenes were painted by one man; rather a group divided up the available registers and scenes, working nearly simultaneously. Some worked faster than others as can be deduced from the spottily completed areas of a large wall. The variety of hands to study in a single tomb brings with it a variety of styles; some master painters worked in a way comfortable to them but perhaps a bit "old fashioned". (In my opinion this partially accounts for the stiffness of some scenes in tombs such as TT 52 of Nakht. The content of some scenes likewise suggested more formal figural arrangements.) Others were "avant garde"; but most were in training and reproduced what their director established as the working model. Dating tombs by stylistic and iconographic means must begin with the dated body of material; therefore what appears in the small number of Theban chapels with Thutmose IV's name in a reliably contemporary context is the basis for comparison. To this can be added tombs belonging to people attested in contemporary documents. By limiting assumptions in this way, we can begin by removing both Nakht and Menna as tombowners in the reign of Thutmose IV. The facial styles and proportions of figures in both those tombs places them in the reign of Amenhotep III, and not earlier. During the reign of Thutmose IV there are some stylistic traits which are helpful in dating, but not foolproof.

First, the hanging lotus frieze decoration, outside of the kiosk, does not appear before this reign; it is an excellent detail to begin with. Second, the favored female garment was a tight white dress and shawl which ensleeved one shoulder only and left one breast nearly uncovered. The shawl was visible but rarely elaborated (the masterfully accomplished musician scene in TT 78 of Horemhab is the exception). In the reign of Amenhotep III the pleated shawl became the costume's focal point; the bared breast faded beneath the pleated shawl, and various ways to indicate pleating were attempted. Yellow varnish was already in rare use earlier and was used by the painters of TT 75 and 38 in torso length patches; but varnish became a staple of painters during Amenhotep III's reign who used it over flesh areas as well as over clothing. The length of women's dresses is also significant. During the reign of Thutmose IV the dress terminates at mid-foot, with a curved or rippled edge. This is a fashion introduced late in the reign of Amenhotep II[387] and brands as archaizing later depictions of ancestors or goddesses in ankle-length dresses.[388] These details may be studied in TT 38 of Djeserkareseneb and appear as well in TT 63, 64, 74 (no hanging lotus), 75, 77, 91. TT 90 (names both Thutmose IV and Amenhotep III) and TT 78 of Haremhab show some details which become common in Amenhotep III's style. The most reliable means of assigning tombs to Thutmose IV or Amenhotep III becomes the proportions of figures. Female standing figures in the reign of Amenhotep III are shorter between the bottom of the foot and the widest point of the hips (below the buttock); their necks are generally shorter, and the wigs are broader front to back. Waists, buttocks, and shoulders remain unmoved so that the overall appearance of the women is slightly shorter and broader (i.e., more voluptuous). The lowering of the widest point becomes a distinguishing feature of female figures late in the reign of Amenhotep III, and can be identified in sculpture as well. For men there are similar readjustments: the neck/face area is gradually reduced as is often the torso length. For both genders there is a gradual thickening of the thigh, breast and waist. This proportional arrangement is dependable for the figures from dated tombs and can therefore be transferred to undated examples.

Beyond the proportions we must take note that no tomb dated by Thutmose's cartouche shows the female with distinguishing features such as lid lines (TT 52, musicians), a common characteristic of Amenhotep III's art, or broad collars that extend over the shoulder (TT 69 various scenes), likewise known only from the end of the reign of Amenhotep III forward.[389]

Part 1. <u>Tombs dated by cartouche to one or more reigns.</u>

Tomb #	T III	A II	T IV	A III	Remarks
116 ?		X	X		T IV painted over A II
74 Tjanni	X	X	X		
75 Amen-hotep Sise			X		
66 Hepu			X		
64 Hekar-nehhe			X		
77 Ptah-emhet			X		
76 Tjenuna			X		
63 Sobek-hotep			X		
78 Horem-hab	X (Ka)	X	X	X	
90 Nebamun			X	X	
91 ?			X	X	
C6 Ipy[390]			X		Tomb lost
TOTALS	2	3	12	3	

1 decorated under Amenhotep II and changed to Thutmose IV
9 Tombs with Thutmose IV alone
3 Wholly or partially decorated under Amenhotep III

Part 2. Tombs attributed to Thutmose IV
                              and probable
38 Djeserkareseneb
A22 Tomb of Neferhebef, Louvre D60. (TT A22)[391]
108 Nebseny[392]

Part 3. Tombs attributed to Thutmose IV in Porter and Moss or elsewhere, with present stylistic assessment

  8 Kha (A III)[393]

 43 Neferrenpet (A III, perhaps early)[394]

 52 Nakht (A III)

 54 Huy usurped by Kenro (probably A III originally, but with Ramesside restoration).

 69 Menna (A III)

101 ?   (A II?) [395]

108 Nebseny (T IV-AIII) [396]

129 ?   (A II-T IV) [397]

147 ?   (A III)

151 Haty (T IV, perhaps, or A III) [398]

161 Nakht (A III) [399]

165 Nehemaway (A III)

175 ?   (A III) [400]

176 Userhet   (probably A II)

201 Re (A III cartouche)

239 Penhet (A III probably) [401]

249 Neferrenpet (A III[402])

257 Neferhotep. Inconclusive (have not seen)

258 Menkheper. (T IV-A III)[403]

261 Khaemwast (T III) [404]

276 Amenemipet (T III)[405]

295 Paroy (A II and/or T IV, repainted to a large extent in the Ramesside period)[406]

350 ? (mid-18th dynasty, probably T III)

402 ? (A III)

1. W. Helck, Verwaltung: H. Kees, Das Priestertum im ägyptischen Staat: A. Schulman, Military Rank and Title.

2. Lise Manniche, Lost Tombs A Study of Certain Eighteenth Dynasty Monuments in the Theban Necropolis (London 1988) and City of the Dead (Chicago 1987), are valuable new compilations of tomb fragments both in Egypt and in museums world-wide which utilize the plenteous drawings and handcopies of earlier European visitors to Egypt. Manniche has united fragments to their source and has "refound" tombs in the old manuscripts. These books were a necessary step to the stylistic description which must occur and can now that a number of scholars have approached the publication of tombs seriously. Artur and Annelies Brack deserve the greatest admiration for setting the standard for tomb publications with Das Grab des Tjanuni and Das Grab des Haremheb. For photographs of some tombs yet poorly known see K. Sakurai, S. Yoshimura and J. Kondo, Comparative Studies of Noble Tombs in Theban Necropolis (Tomb Nos. 8, 38, 39, 48, 50, 54, 57, 63, 64,66,74,78,89,90,91,107,120,139,147,151, 181, 201, 253, 295) (Waseda University Tokyo 1988).

3. Recent discussions are working in this direction, but there is much ground left to cover. See for example, N. Cherpion, BSFE 1987; Abdel Ghaffar Shedid, Stil der Grabmalereien in der Zeit Amenophis' II ADAIK 66 (Mainz 1988), especially 88ff.

4. This is especially the case with A. Mekhitarian's Egyptian Painting. where the leap is made from tombs securely dated to Thutmose IV to those at the end of Amenhotep III's reign (e.g., Ramose, Nebamun and Ipuky). Most of the tombs have been similarly dated in Mekhitarian, op.cit., Nina Davies ,Ancient Egyptian Paintings. and M. Baud, Les Dessins. When faced with tombs such as those of Nakht (52) and Menna (69), these authors placed them under Thutmose IV, but in fact there are dated examples under Amenhotep III which are far closer in style to 52 and 69; e.g., Amenmose (89), 226, a royal nurse, and Anen (120). See the appendix at the back of Chapter 5 for suggested dating of tombs.

5. M. Wegner, MDAIK 4 (1933) 38-164.

6. A. Weil, Veziere, 80; Helck, Verw., 298, 440-41.

7. C. Aling, A Prosopographical Study of the Reigns of Thutmosis IV and Amenhotep III. unpublished dissertation.

8. Munich Papyrus 809. W. Spiegelberg, ZÄS 63 (1928) 105- 15; Aling, op.cit., 60, mistakenly says Hepu's tomb is dated by Thutmose IV's appearance in a wall scene. In fact, the king was only identified as Thutmose IV because of the papyrus. See Davies, Scenes from Some Theban Tombs, 9 with n.1.

9. PM I² 1 132; recently published, Nina Davies, Scenes from Some Private Theban Tombs, 9-13, pls. 8-14. Sakurai, et als, Comparative Studies, pls. 56-57. Some texts are shown in Urk. IV 1576-77. One funerary cone, W.F. Petrie, A Season in Egypt. pl.22 #62. Perhaps the same as G. Daressy, Mém. Miss. VIII, 297 #270.

10. W. Helck, JESHO 5 (1962) 236-37.

11. Wegner, op.cit., 121, 117-19.

12. Davies, Scenes, 10, pl.10.

13. Ibid., 12, pl.13.

14. Helck, JESHO 5, 237.

15. Weil, op.cit., 81; W. Hayes, Scepter II, 155.

16. Helck, Verw., 298-99; R. Anthes, ZÄS 72 (1937) 65,68, Aling, op.cit., 61-62, followed. Anthes discussed the 2 pertinent monuments and illustrated them as well. PM III 712-13, gives Sakkara as probable burial site. The most convincing evidence in favor of a date in Amenhotep III's reign is provided by the graffito copied by Champollion at Aswan. There is shown the Overseer of the City Thutmose (mr niwt Dhwty-ms) adoring the prenomen of Amenhotep III. The Thoth bird has been partially erased, but it is visible in the drawing. Unfortunately there is nothing to link this vizier Thutmose with Thutmose father of Ptahmose.

17. W. Hayes, JNES 10 (1951) 98-99.

18. Aling, op.cit., 64-65, 61.

19. See Helck, Verw., 433-65, for New Kingdom viziers.

20. MMA 21.2.129. W. Hayes, Scepter II, 155.

21. Helck, Verw., 456.

22. Weil, Veziere, 82; Helck, Verw., 441-42; R. Antes, "Die hohen Beamten names Ptahmose in der 18. Dynastie", ZÄS 72 (1936) 62-63. Lefebvre, Histoire des Grands prêtres, 99f.; 241. Brooklyn Acc. no. 37.1512E, T.G.H. James, Corpus of Hieroglyphic Inscriptions in the Brooklyn Museum I, 114, # 256, pl. LXVII for text. The priestly title does not occur but phraseology emulates Amenhotep III's titulary thus suggesting a date.

23. Weil, op.cit., 97; Anthes, op.cit., 62.

24. See above in Chapter 2. C. Zivie, Giza au deuxième Millénaire. 96-104.

25. Helck, Verw., 298; Aling, op.cit., 59.

26. B. Grdseloff, <u>ASAE</u> 40 (1940) 194, 201.

27. Helck, <u>Verw.</u>, 353, citing Florence 1506.

28. PM I² 1 125-28. Fragments listed in British Museum (four pieces), Florence (one piece), and Metropolitan Museum.   Bibliography additions to <u>PM</u>.. B. Van de Walle,<u>RdE</u> 15 (1963) 77-85, discussing Brussels E 6856; R. Charles, <u>RdE</u> 12 (1960) 1-26, discussing two men named Sobekhotep. Helck, <u>Verw.</u>, 353-53, also recognized two like-named men, but he did not attempt to reconstruct their relations. Tomb texts at <u>Urk</u>. IV 1582-84. Another statue, possibly from Memphis, CG 1090, in Borchardt, <u>Statuen</u> IV 51, pl.162 = <u>Urk</u>. IV 1585. The tomb is to be published in the near future by Eberhard Dziobek with a contribution on the career of Sobekhotep by the present author.

29. Helck, <u>Verw.</u>, 350-53, 80-82.

30. <u>Ibid.</u>, 352.

31. <u>Urk</u>. IV 1586-88 = Berlin 11635 and Marseille 208.

32. <u>Urk</u>. IV 1583; Statue Florence 1506 = <u>Urk</u>. IV 1916.

33. A.-P. Zivie, "Tombes rupestres de la falaise du Bubasteion à Saqqarah - IIe et IIIe campagnes (1982-1983)", <u>ASAE</u> 70 (1985) 228-29.

34. <u>Urk</u>. IV 1583.

35. Brussels E 6856, with Prince Amenhotep Merykhepesh; CG 1090, where he mentions work among the royal children.

36. W. Spiegelberg, "Ein Gerichtsprotokoll aus der Zeit Thutmosis' IV", ZÄS 63 (1928) 105-15. The Papyrus, from the estate of Dr. Mook, was cited earlier but not fully published. Sobekhotep's Mayoral title was restored in the first column by Spiegelberg without justification.

37. E. Seidl, <u>Einführung in die ägyptische Rechtsgeschichte bis zum Ende des Neuen Reiches</u>, 25-26; A. Theodorides, "À propos de la loi dans l'Égypte pharaonique", <u>RIDA</u> 14 (1967) 126-27; <u>Idem.</u>, "Le jugement en cause Neferabet contre Tyia", <u>RIDA</u> 30 (1983) 37-38.

38. A. Theodorides, <u>RIDA</u> 14 (1967) 127 suggests it was for undue boldness on the part of the soldier. But see S. Allam, <u>JEA</u> 64 (1978) 67, who notes that in any civil procedure 100 blows was a common penalty inflicted on the loser. It would appear likely that the physical punishment was used as deterrent to prevent the bringing of false suits.

39. Helck, <u>Verw.</u>, 82.

40. Ibid., 353 n.2. Helck noted the title of mr sd3t only. He did not read "steward for the Treasurer" as is done here.

41. Urk. IV 1027-28.

42. Helck, Verw., 87, mentions the Treasurer's underlings involved in the field accounting from P. Leningrad 1116.

43. Urk. IV 1587. Interestingly, Spiegelberg, op.cit., 114, had listed wr m T3-Š from the tomb and credited Newberry for the information. Helck's copyists did not see the title and omitted it as did Charles, op.cit., 24-25.

44. Urk. IV 1572.

45. Urk. IV 1455; 1474; 1476; 1481; 1923, are but a few.

46. A. Zivie in ASAE 70, (1985) 228-29 and Le Courrier du CNRS 49 (1983) 37-44. Idem., "Trois saisons à Saqqarah: Les tombeaux du Bubasteion", BSFE 98 (1983) 40-56. Stela in Vienna Nr. 5814, Another Treasurer's burial, that of Nehesy who served Hatshepsut, was found by Zivie. A.P. Zivie, "Un chancelier nommé Nehesy", Mélanges Adolphe Gutbub (1984) 245-52

47. Vienna tomb relief and stela 5814, 5815; H. Brunner, ZÄS 86 (1961) 90-100, pl.3. PM III2 1302, lists with Sakkara.

48. B. Bryan, "Private relief styles from the reign of Amenhotep III outside of Thebes", in the forthcoming publication of a paper presented at a Symposium on the Art of Amenhotep III at the Cleveland Museum, November 1987.

49. N. Davies, The Tombs of Menkheperrasonb..., 37.Aling attributed this office to the owner of 226, mistakenly using it as support for the identification. The title does not, however, appear in the tomb.

50. Helck, Verw., 185-91.

51. F.-J. Schmitz, Amenophis I. 158-59, believes there must have been northern and southern treasuries, since the dual writing is so common. This office is attested only from Hatshepsut's reign in the New Kingdom. In the Middle Kingdom, the Overseer of the Audience Chamber was responsible for the Treasure House. Helck, Verw., 180-81.

52. Ibid., 403 n.1.

53. Urk. IV 1372; 1372-73; 1373-74.

54. Urk. IV 1889; 1890.

55. Urk. IV 2168;2169;2166.

56.   Helck's suggestion is especially dubious since one man eliminated in the Verwaltung as Treasurer, because he was not mr pr ḥd was unjustly omitted. Amenemipet, owner of TT 276, was said by Helck not to have been Overseer of the Treasure House, since his funerary cones refer to him by the Gold and Silver title. (Verw., 180-81.) But the ceiling texts in tomb 276 call Amenemipet mr pr ḥd mr ꜥḥnwty, "Overseer of the Treasure house", a form repeated on a wall scene. (PM I² 1, 352-53.) The tomb dates in the reign of Thutmose III or early Amenhotep II, most likely. Wegner, op.cit., 142 agrees with this. W. Hayes, Scepter of Egypt II, 155, dates it to Thutmose IV, however. One funerary cone in the Metropolitan Museum and one in Boston, MFA 72.1798.

57.   Supra, n.51, for Helck's citation. See, for example, High Priest of Amun Meri, Urk. IV, 1571; Overseer of Treasure House for the House of the Aten in Karnak, Urk. IV 1995; probably the Steward for Nefertiti. Meri-Re has a title relating only to her estate, Urk. IV 2003;

58.   Urk. IV 1614.

59.   PM I2 2 748.   Turin Museum Sup. 8388; E. Schiaparelli, Relazione II, 174-75, 80, fig. 48 (rt.).

60.   PM I² 2 748. Turin Museum Sup. 8388; E. Schiaparelli, Relazione II, 174-75, 80, fig. 48 (rt.) TT 8, PM I² 1 16-18. Most recently, S. Curto, L'antico Egitto nel Museo Egizio di Torino (Turin 1984) 201-217. There is some hint from the distribution of Meryt's and Kha's coffins and personal items that he may have predeceased her. Kha's statue, stela, coffin and even Book of the Dead retain more idealistic Thutmoside traits than do Meryt's coffin and cosmetic articles. This remains speculative, however.

61. Helck, Verw., 402, but with correct citation of Schiaparelli. Aling followed Helck's dating..Aling, op.cit., 80 with n.87

62. P. Newberry, Funerary Statuettes and Model Sarcophagi, 369–73, pls. 29-30. Limestone coffin, 31 cm. long,. black stone statuette, 25.4 cm. long.   Very fine quality.

63. Theban tomb 201, PM I² 1 304-05; A. Radwan, Darstellungen, confirms the cartouche. Sakurai, et als., Comparative Studies, pl. 94.1, shows a cartouche, blurrily. See also Wegner, op.cit., 129, Amenhotep III date.

64. Helck, Verw., 508-22, 187-88.   He admits there were no stated northern and southern treasuries at the time.

65. Ibid., 511.

66. Supra, n. 63.

67. Champollion, <u>Notices</u> I 616 #9- = Petrie, <u>A Season.</u> I #30 = <u>Urk</u>. IV 1597.

68. Helck, <u>Verw</u>., 389, 499.

69. DeMorgan, <u>Catalogue</u>, 69 #13 = Petrie, I #48; DeMorgan, <u>op.cit</u>., 70 #23 = Petrie, #333 (copied as <u>Twty</u>).

70. BMFA 72.1769 - Davies, <u>Corpus</u>, #282.

71. Borchardt, <u>Statuen</u> III, 145, pl.156.

72. Ranke, <u>Personnennamen</u> I, 149, 152. Also <u>Mny</u>,151. Ranke lists <u>Mn</u> as variant for other names.

73. Helck, <u>Verw</u>., 391, 502 (14), said to be the same man mentioned on 389, 499 (7).

74. Berlin 7316 probably belongs to the reign of Sety I by style; a slightly earlier date is likely for Leiden III, 12. Helck, <u>Verw</u>., 502, said the title <u>sš šnwty</u> had been changed to <u>mr šnwty</u> on Berlin 7316, but a photo of the stela does not bear this out. Helck's date of Wepwawetmose to the reign of Akhenaten is based on a title given his father, Khaa; he was <u>mr k3w n Itn</u> on a third Vienna stela and <u>mr k3w n Imn</u> on that of Leiden.

This need not suggest that the stelae represent the periods before and after the Amarna era; rather the works reflect Khaa's title changed to <u>mr k3w n Imn</u> <u>after</u> the Amarna period. Wepwawetmose was scribe and his brother Si-ese was Overseer of Granaries on Leiden III,12 and Vienna 53.

On Berlin 7316, Wepwawetmose had become Overseer of Granaries of the Lord of the Two lands. The Leiden stela should date to Tutankhamun or Horemheb. The Vienna monument had a similar date, for both Aten and Amun appear on it. This chronology makes it impossible to identify the two men as the same person who was already active in Thutmose IV's rule. See E. von Bergmann, <u>Rec.de Trav</u>. 9 (1887) 41-43, for more discussion.

75. Attested on stela Louvre C 71. Pierret, <u>Recueils</u>, 15. The same man appears on Louvre C 146 as Royal Scribe Bakenamun born of the Lady of the House Ipu.

76. M. Megally, <u>BIFAO</u> 74 (1974) 163-64; Amenhotep has a stela which stylistically fits the time period. Helck,<u>Verw</u>.,500.

77. The text is broken beneath the <u>mr</u> sign, but a trace of the diagonal line in <u>šnwt</u> remains. No other title may reasonably be restored except <u>mr pr</u>, but the combination <u>mr pr nsw nw šmᶜw mḥw</u> has not emerged.

78. I. Müller, <u>Die Verwaltung der nubischen Provinz im Neuen Reich</u>, Unpublished dissertation.

79. W. Wolf, ZÄS 59 (1924) 158; Müller, op.cit., 177; Aling, op.cit., 92, G. Reisner, JEA 6 (1920) 32, contra, but does not know all the monuments. Amenhotep's monuments cited below. Also a statue of Amenhotep from Deir el Medina in Louvre E 14398. M. Alliot, BIFAO 32 (1932) 70-71, pl. 1-2.

80. H. Gauthier, Rec. Trav. 39 (1921) 192-94; Müller, op.cit., 34- 36; A. Schulman, BASP 15 (1978) 111-13.

81. Reisner, op.cit., 33.Aling followed this suggestion. Aling, op.cit., 33.

82. Urk. IV 1636.

83. DeMorgan, Cat. I, 92 #108 = LD Text IV 125 = Urk. IV 1637; DeMorgan, op.cit., 103 #66, should also be assigned to Amenhotep.

84. PM I² 1, 78; Alliot, BIFAO 32, 70-71, fig. 10, pls. 1-2. Headless, kneeling statue of man holding stela with a sun hymn. Ht. .48 m. Ht. of stela .335 m. by .175 m. Black granite. Identifies the s3 nsw n Kš sš nsw mr k3w n Imn t3y hw hr wnmy n nsw hsy n ntr nfr rpᶜt mr nb t3wy Imn-htp m3ᶜ hrw. "King's son of Kush, royal scribe, overseer of the cattle of Amun, fanbearer on the right of the king, one praised by the good god, the hereditary prince beloved of the lord of the Two lands, Amenhotep, vindicated". The usage of rpᶜt out of his common honorific placement beginning the titulary suggests it carries more meaning than usual and is perhaps meant to underline the importance of the Viceroy's position. Habachi, "Königssohn von Kusch", LÄ III 630-40, n.58, attributes the statue to Tutankhamun's Viceroy Huy. He mistakenly wrote that the statue was found in Huy's tomb, but Alliot found the piece, along with a pyramidion of one Amenemheb, in a pit located vertically 110 meters and horizontally 75 meters away from Huy's tomb. Since the Viceroys of the period appear to have been buried in Qurnet Murai, (Merymose TT 383; Usersatet has a statue from the region, Urk. IV 1487) this distance is meaningful. The statuette's style is comfortable in Thutmose IV-Amenhotep III's reign rather than in Tutankhamun's, but caution is reserved since the name of Amun is not damaged.

85. H. S. Smith, The Fortress of Buhen, The Inscriptions. 173, pl.48, jarsealing Type b9 #338.

86. LD Text IV 125; Reisner, op.cit., 32, makes this same point in dating Amenhotep under Amenhotep III.

87. Aling, op.cit., 255-56.

88. Urk. IV 2068, mr k3w ; 2074, mr k3w n Imn m t3 pn n Kš. Cerny and E. Edel, Gebel el Shams, pls. 1-5.

89. Müller, op.cit., I 86.

90. W. Albright suggested this several times: W. Albright, ZÄS 62 (1927) 63-64; BASOR 94 (1944) 27; JNES 5 (1946) 9.

91. A. Malamat, Scripta Hierosolymitana 8 (1961) 218-27.

92. Müller, op.cit., 31.

93. Ibid., 177.

94. Urk. IV 1615-17.

95. Z. Žaba, ASAE 50 (1950) 513.

96. L. Habachi, Kush 5 (1957) 22 n.32.

97. Žaba, op.cit., 514.

98. PM VII 131, W.E. Crum, PSBA 16 (1892) 17-19; photo now in H.S. Smith, op.cit., pl.81; Urk. IV 1636.

99. A. Schulman, JARCE 8 (1969-70) 36-37.

100. The intimate association of the dead with problems of their families and servants are common in letters to the dead. See, for example, W.K. Simpson, JEA 52 (1966) 39-52 with references to other works. He cites Hughes demotic example of such a letter that confirms the continued existence of communications with the dead. We might suppose that the destruction of tomb scenes obliterated the deceased's interference in matters of the living. See also A. and A. Brack, Das Grab des Tjanuni. 84, who come to some of the same conclusions concerning mutilations in Theban tombs.

101. CG 34098, P. Lacau, Stèles du nouvel empire. Schulman, Military Rank and Title, 148,150.

102. Reisner, op.cit., 32ff.

103. Ibid., 103-08.

104. W. Wreszinski, ZÄS 67 (1931) 132-33, pl.9.x; Urk. IV 1614. A hymn to Re is inscribed on this stelophorous statue.

105. BM 5512; S. Glanville, JEA 18 (1932) 56-57, pl.7; Urk. IV 1615.

106. Urk. IV 1614; H. Gauthier, BIFAO 6 (1906) 135.

107. The statue from the Kurlandisches Provinzialmuseum in Mitau is of black granite, .71 m. in height overall and the figure is .54 m. in h eight. The sun hymn stela held before the kneeling official is .39 m. high by .2 m. wide. The parallels for the face here are, like to the statue of Mayor of Sobekhotep (Marseille 209) CG 566 dated to Amenhotep II and Louvre E12926, a block statue of Maanakhtef (Eggebrecht, Ägyptens Aufstieg zur Weltmacht, 248-49) of like date. Both provide

the wide open eyes and heavy cosmetic eyebrows characteristic of this period and of Merire's statue.

108. W. Hayes, JEA 46 (1960) 34-35, #6 on pl.X,Xa.

109. Overseer of all works, Pahekamen, see Urk. IV 1468-72.

110. Hayes, JEA 46, 34-35, did not date the ostracon any later than Thutmose III's sole rule, and preferably to Hatshepsut's. But in view of the Pahekamen's presence, Hayes' dating should probably be lowered.

111. PM I^2 1 149-50; U. Bouriant, Rec.Trav. 11 (1889) 156-61; Urk IV 1577-81; Champollion, Not.I 480-81. A wall of the tomb represented precious objects of Egyptian and imported type; it was there that gold statuettes of Thutmose IV and Tiaa once appeared. T. Save-Soderbergh, Private Tombs at Thebes I, pl.72.

112. See Urk. IV 1579, 16-17. Helck incorrectly restored mr nfrwt n'Imn, but the pr sign is clear in the tomb even today. BM 35400 is a glazed steatite statuette of one Tjununa. This man was Overseer of the Cattle of Amun (a title known for Tjenuna) and Overseer of the Temple of Menkheperre or Menkheprure.

113. Inv. Nr. 63, H. Satzinger, Ägyptische Kunst Abb. 12, pp. 27ff; W. Scipel, Bilder für die Ewigkeit, Stadtmuseum Linz, Nordico, 3.September bis 30. Oktober 1983, 108-09. Ägyptens Aufstieg zur Weltmacht, 181. Ht. .56 m.

114. P. Hermitage 1116A; 1116B; BM 10056; Louvre 3226, for example.

115. See on this development, Helck, Verw. 81-82.

116. Urk IV, 1577, 13-15. Helck, Verw., 81-82.

117. Urk. IV 1578,17-18.

118. Urk. IV 1582.

119. PM I^2 1,149-50.

120. Petrie, A Season. II #59 = DeMorgan, Cat., 70 #16.

121.   DeMorgan, 70 #23 = Petrie, A Season. #333 = Champollion, Not. I 616.

122. Urk. IV 1575.

123. From Konosso, DeMorgan, Cat.,71 #24 = Petrie, A Season, #34A + 332.

124. Ranke, Personennamen I, 381 for Tnr. A hry šmsw Twnr (Chief retainer Tunur) appears in the Munich Papyrus 37, dated in Thutmose IV's reign, but this is a far lower rank and not a likely correspondence.

125. Ibid., I 381, gives variant Tl for the name Tnr/Tnry. See G. Fecht, Wortakzent und Silbenstruktur. XIII-XIV, who mentions that in the Execration texts, Semitic r/l are transcribed exclusively by 𓄿See also J. Callender, Middle Egyptian, 8, who says phonetic l may lie in 3.i.r or n. Tnwn3, PN I 391-92.

126.   See below for the Konosso graffito of Tjenuna, Section 3.1.

127.   Louvre C80. Pierret, Recueil II, 16; ZÄS 76, 106 n.4

128.   Helck, Verw., 252-56.

129.   PM I² 2, 748.

130.   Urk. IV 1442,17-20.

131.   PM III² 43; JE 72268. S. Hassan, The Great Sphinx. 81, fig. 66.

132.   Verwaltung, 269-76.

133.   PM II² 261; CG 916, Borchardt, Statuen III 152; Urk. IV 1644-45.

134.   H. Kees, Priestertum. 46-47, 322.

135. Helck, Verw., 107-08, differentiated between types of administrators--those with "royal scribe" in their titulary who were raised up through official ranks, and those without it who were normally pensioners from another field of endeavor.

136.   Urk. IV 1634,6.

137.   CG 34098. P. Lacau, Stèles du nouvel empire. Dated by the style of the stela.

138.   Unpublished. Cairo Temp. no. 12.1.34.1 is the lower part of a black granite statue, .25 m. in height, representing Hekareshu seated holding a child on his lap. The child was undoubtedly Thutmose IV himself. The inscription is dedicated to Bastet mistress of Ankh Tawy by the God's father Hekareshu. It may originally have come from the Memphite region.

139.   See P. Frandsen, Acta Orientalia 37 (1976) 5-10, for bibliography of Hekareshu. Two shabtis of Hekareshu bear texts which call them "favors from the king". Frandsen, op.cit., 6, believed these were modelled on Thutmose IV's shabtis which generally do not have Chapter VI on them. T.J.H. James, however, pointed out that these are Abydos offering shabtis (similar to those of Kenamun from Sakkara, Urk. IV 1403.) Corpus of Hieroglyphic Inscriptions in the Brooklyn Museum I, 107. See now I.E.S. Edwards in Egyptological Studies in Honor of Richard A. Parker, "The Shetayet of Rosetau", 31, with reference to the 'Hill of Hekareshu' where the shabtis were found along with the model tools now in the British Museum (32693).

140. PM I² I 128-29; Urk. IV 1572-74. Two alterations for the Urkunden entry are here given: 1574, 5-6 = LD Text III, 261. Lepsius shows this text was spoken to Hekareshu, not Hekarnehhe.
Texts from the left door jamb thickness: ꜥ3 mrt m Pr-ꜥ3 ꜥnh wd3 snb mnꜥy n s3-nsw mry.f [Imn-htp] Hk3rnhh.

141. The cones are summarized as follows:
MMA 28.3.29 = Davies #102.
MMA 30.6.105 = Davies #98 = Daressy #39 (mr ssmwt n hm.f), two more examples of this cone, Strasbourg, 378,3003. A. Heyler, Kemi 15 (1959) 80-93.
Berlin 8750 is miscopied; actually duplicate of Davies #102, as is Daressy, #39 bis Davies #159 = Daressy #125.

The graffiti: Urk. IV 1575 (with princes), and supra the Chief steward, Tjenur.

Add a shabti not mentioned in the text above: mr mnꜥt n nsw Hk3nhh. A. Mariette, Mon. Div., pl. 36. Found in Valley of the Kings. Present location unknown.

142. The heart scarab is of green basalt, 5.2 cm. long by 3.4 cm. wide. It was acquired by Claudio Marguier in 1845 and names Wsir mr mnꜥ n s3 nsw Imn-htp hrd n k3p Hk3-nhh m3ꜥ hrw, "the Osiris Overseer of nursing for the Prince Amenhotep, child of the nurscry Heka[r]nehhe, vindicated". G. Botti, I Cimeli Egizi del Museo di antichita di Parma, 83-84, pl. 20 (Florence 1964).

143. L. Habachi, in Schott Festschrift, 61-70; Frandsen, op.cit., 9.

144. Contra Habachi, Schott Fest., 68. He assigns two titles of Hekarnehhe to Hekareshu. See Urk. IV 1573, 14-1574, 2. This is entirely unjustified since Habachi claimed another scene showed Hekarnehhe offering on a brazier, but that is not the case. This scene appears on the southeast wall of the tomb. A scene on the northeast wall showed butchering below; its inscription in the upper register is fragmentary but appears to belong to Hekareshu, since a portion of the title [t3y hw] hr wnmy nsw,"Fanbearer on the right of the king", remains. This is the only other scene which might have shown a brazier offering, but one is not there now. Helck also called Hekareshu "child of the Nursery", Einfluss, 35 n.1. He cited CG 923, LD III Text 260; ZÄS 65,98, JEA 14,82, none of which called Hekareshu by this title.

145. Helck, Einfluss. 36 n.1, from page 35. Helck's citations do not produce an attestation of "child of the Nursery".

146. Habachi, Schott Fest., 66-67. PM V 249.

147. Habachi, Schott Fest., 66, n.23.

148. Appears in DeMorgan's copy; not in Champollion's or Rosellini's.

149. See Helck, Verw., 281 with n.5. On page 282, he included Hekareshu as holder of the honorary dignity.

150. Habachi, Schott Fest., 22.

151. <u>Urk</u>. IV 1877-79.

152. Helck, <u>Verw</u>., 273. Hekanefer is another example. W.K. Simpson, <u>Heka-Nefer</u>, 26.

153. Aling, <u>op. cit</u>., 146.

154. Helck, <u>Verw</u>., 272. This is erroneously based on the Berlin funerary cone 8750 of Hekarnehhe which Helck copied as ⚹ ◊ for <u>wdpw/wb3 nsw</u>. This was shown to have been miscopied for ⚹ ▽ (<u>mn^ct nsw</u>). See B. Bryan, <u>JSSEA</u> 9 (1979) 118 n.6.

155. Although this is the assumption of both Frandsen, <u>op.cit</u>., 9, and Aling, <u>op.cit</u>., 149-51.

156. See Helck, <u>Verw</u>., 270, 262; Helck, <u>Einfluss</u>, 34-36.

157. Catharine Roehrig of the University of California at Berkeley is presently working on a dissertation which studies the royal nurses and children of the Nursery.

158. Louvre C 76 and Durham 379; See under Chapter 5, 4.2. Raner appears on his father Ay's funerary stela as <u>hrd n k3p</u>. The stela dates to the reign of Amenhotep III by style and sets Ay's death in that period. Raner quite likely appeared with the titles of his youth due to the nature of the monument. He was probably Scribe of Elite Troops (<u>sš nfrw</u>) even in Thutmose IV's reign.

159. <u>Urk</u>. IV 1634; G. Björkman, <u>JARCE</u> 11 (1974) 45 with n. 29.

160. BM 148, <u>HTES</u> VII, 43; CG 34022,Lacau, <u>Stèles</u>, 42, pl.13.

161. <u>PM</u> III^2 43.

162. Louvre C 53.P. Pierret, <u>Recueil</u> II, 14-15.

163. PM I^2 1 150-52; <u>Urk</u>. IV 1599-1601, incorrectly restored as Amenemheb.

164. <u>Urk</u>. IV 1512-14, a false door style stela in Cairo, undoubtedly from Minhotep's burial in Sakkara.

165. He held a title associated with the <u>sed</u> festival suggesting the took part in some king's jubilee. Given the difficulty of assessing what the celebration of the royal rejuvenation meant during the mid-18th Dynasty (see the discussion in Chapter 1), it would be impossible to state certainly that it was Amenhotep II's <u>sed</u> which Hututu witnessed, but his is more likely than Thutmose IV's given Hututu's attested presence as Treasury Secretary in the Leningrad papyrus. For the title in question, see C. Vandersleyen, "Un titre du vice-roi Mérimose à Silsila", <u>CdE</u> 43 (1968) Section 9, 249-50.

166. Cairo Temp. no. 22.8.15.2, fragment of a limestone block 35 cm. high by 37 cm. wide, shows the man seated holding the hrp scepter with his far hand over the offering table. The other side of the piece was probably carved during the later 18th dynasty (possibly early Amarna period) and preserves a portion of two registers, the lower showing a stack of linen hammocks (?) before a "chief of rope" hry sstyw (?) who works in the pr mss smwt "house of hammock making". The mwt bird appears to be mutilated as does part of the first line of the retrograde text. Conceivably this block dates from a period before the Atenist mutilations, but it does not resemble the other side. It is an interesting fragment nonetheless.

167. PM I^2 1 342; Urk. IV 1642-43.

168. BM 1332, HTES VIII, 33; Urk. IV 1630-32.

169. Supra, as Overseer of the Granaries. Funerary cone, Daressy, #198 = Petrie, A Seas.23#88 = Urk. IV 1640; Stela, Urk. IV 1640; Graffiti. Champollion, Not. I 615 #15 = Petrie, I #32 = Champollion, Not. I 618 #10. A. Mariette, Mon. Div. 70 #16 and DeMorgan, 103 #16, indicate a second graffito, at Sehel rather than Konosso, exists for Re with prince Aakheprure. This cannot be confirmed here.

170. Bologna 1908 in S. Curto, L'Egitto antico, pl. 25; Pierret, Recueils II, 56; W. Hayes, Scepter of Egypt II, 273-74.

171. Supra. M. Valloggia, Recherches sur les Messagers. 102-03. Louvre C 53 of Pa-aa-aku mentions a royal messenger, but the name is not given.

172. R. Giveon, Tel Aviv 5 (1978) 172.

173. Valoggia, op.cit., 102-03; Schulman, Military Rank, 165; J. Yoyotte, Mélanges Mariette, Bibliothèque d'Étude 32, 202.

174. Valoggia, op.cit., 103.

175. Björkman, JARCE 11, 43-51, with full bibliography.

176. I wish to express my deep gratitude to the staff of the Department of Egyptian Antiquities in the British Museum. It was Dr. Morris Bierbrier who brought this stela to my attention. He, Dr. T.J.H. James, Mr. Vivian Davies and Dr. Geoffrey Spencer have been unfailingly kind and generous in their assistance.

177. Ibid., 49, notes that at her writing Nebi was the only known titleholder.

178. Helck, Einfluss, 26; Björkman, JARCE 11, 44.

179. H. Kees, Ancient Egypt, 190-96.

180. H. Kees, Ancient Egypt, 190.

181. O. Goelet, Terms for the Palace in the Old Kingdom, dissertation Columbia University. R. Stadelmann, "Die ḫnty-š, der Königsbezirk š n pr-ꜥ3 und die Namen der Grabanlagen der Frühzeit", BIFAO Supp. 81 Bulletin du Centenaire (1981) 153-64.

182. I am indebted for references to Mr. Ogden Goelet whose dissertation is a study of words for the palace in the Old Kingdom. Giza VI, pt. III, 190, fig. 189 and 192 (without š).

183. BM 1332. Urk. 1632,2.

184. Helck, Verw., 102.

185. For full discussion see B. Bryan in E. Dziobek, Das Grab des Sobekhotep TT 63.

186. For a recent discussion of the toponym and administration of the region see B. Bryan in R. Wenke, The Land of the Lake: A survey of the Egyptian Fayyum. (forthcoming)

187. In Philadelphia, University Museum. Helck, Verw., 224 n.11. W.F. Petrie and G. Brunton, Sedment II, 53 in line-drawing only; H. Ranke, University Museum Bulletin 15 (1950) Nos. 2-3, 44-45 with photo.

188. G. Daressy, ASAE 1 (1900) 46; CG 20070, Berlin P. 10089a.

189. W.F. Petrie, Medum. pl.23 and 18 (tomb of Nefermaat).

190. F.L. Griffith, Kahun Papyri, 52, pl.21,6; W.F. Petrie, Illahun. pl.9,9 and probably 9,5 as well; W.F. Petrie, Kahun. pl.X #25.

191. A. Scharff, ZÄS 59 (1924) 23.

192. P. 10083, 10056, 10088, 10027, 10211, 10445. U. Kaplony, Berlin Papyri I.

193. Urk. IV 1588, 14.

194. Helck, Verw., 301-02. But he also concludes that it was because of the rising importance of Memphis.

195. Ibid.,5-9, argues for a major northern residence from the reign of Thutmose I on.

196. Urk. IV 1545, 7-9. ꜣist hm.f m niwt rsy r dmi n ꜣIpt-Swt ꜥwy-fy wꜥb m ꜥb-ntr shtp.n.f ꜣt ꜣImn mi rdit n.f nḥḥ m nsw ḏt mn ḥr st-Ḥr. "Indeed his Majesty was in the Southern city at the quay of Karnak, his arms being purified with divine purity. He propitiated father Amun according as he was given eternity as king enduring upon the throne of Horus."

197. Helck, <u>Verw.</u>, 369, says likewise.

198. PM I^2 1 204-05; A. Gardiner, <u>ZÄS</u> 47 (1910) 87-99; <u>Urk.</u> IV 1408-13. Or.Inst. 8636 = <u>Urk.</u> IV 1413-14; <u>PM</u> V 216, R. Caminos, <u>Gebel el Silsilah</u>, pls. 61-66,. Davies cones #'s, 42-44,. Kees, <u>Priestertum,</u> 17-18; Aling, <u>op.cit.</u>, 119-21.

199. Gardiner, <u>ZAS</u> 47, 87.

200. <u>Urk.</u> IV 1409, 18.

201. Gardiner, <u>ZAS</u> 47, 87.

202. Kees, <u>Priestertum.</u> <u>Nachträge</u>, 8, citing Davies Cone #43.

203. Meryptah, <u>LD</u> III <u>Text</u> 287, #'s 88 alpha, Beta; Ptahmose, Daressy, #112 = Davies #146; Davies #179.

204. DeMorgan, <u>Cat.</u>,69 #8 = Champollion, <u>Not.</u>I 615 #1-2 and 618 #11 = Petrie, I #38. In all three publications it is associated with the cartouches of Thutmose IV.

205. Aling, <u>op.cit.</u>, 65. "Since Amenemhet, the High Priest under Thutmosis IV, never claims to serve under Amenhotep III, it is likely that he died before the end of the reign of Thutmosis IV." Amenemhet, however, cannot be dated by cartouche under any king. And Aling's suggestion that the High priest's office was given "for life" is not supported by the examples: only one High priest of Amun in the 18th dynasty can be shown to have served in more than one rule: Menkheperreseneb functioned under both Thutmose III and Amenhotep II, but the coregency may have accounted for the continuity. Indeed several rules show more than one officeholder within them: Hatshepsut/Thutmose III, Amenhotep II, Amenhotep III, Ramesses II.

206. M. Saleh and H. Sourouzian, <u>Official Catalogue The Egyptian Museum Cairo</u> (Mainz 1987) No. 150 with color photo. <u>PM</u> V, 60-61.

207. CG 46160, Carter and Newberry, <u>The Tomb of Thoutmôsis IV</u>, 45, pl. XIII, preserved only from the waist but of very similar workmanship. These polychrome faience shabtis are rare. Amenhotep Huy's example, JE 88902, is of a different texture and color. However, there were fragments of a shabti from the tomb of Amenhotep III, KV 22, termed by Carter, "polychrome". I have not seen them nor do I known their present whereabouts. Carter MSS I J. 386, no. 93.

208. PM I^2 1 146-49; Norman Davies, <u>The Tombs of Two Officials,</u> 1-18; Urk. IV 1208-16; Funerary cone, Daressy #205 and two in Metropolitan Museum, Hayes, <u>Scepter</u> II, 155.

209. Wegner, <u>op.cit.</u>, 119, 121, 143.

210. G. Lefebvre, <u>Histoire des Grand Prêtres</u>, 235-39; Helck, <u>Verw.</u>, 435-36.

211. Ibid.., on Kenamun, 479-80; Minnakht, son of an Overseer of Amun's Granaries, Sendjehuty, 497-98; Si-ese, Urk. IV 1924-29 (restored by Helck).

212. Kees, Priestertum, 15, also came to this conclusion concerning Amenhotep si-se and most major priests--they were as much in the royal administration as in the temple's.

213. Urk. IV 1208-09.

214. Kees, Priestertum, 16-18.

215. Urk. IV 1886.

216. G. Gaballa, MDAIK 26 (1970) 49-74; Lefebvre, op.cit., 24, dates a Nufer from funerary cones to dynasty 18.

217. Ibid., 52; Urk. IV 1885-86.

218. CG 70039, Roeder, Naos, 129-33; pls. 42-43.

219. BM 1238, HTES VIII, pl.10; Urk. IV 1633; Brooklyn Museum 74.97, Brooklyn Museum Annual XI (1969-70) pt.1,77. Formerly on loan L69.38.2. Bernard V. Bothmer, "Egyptian Antiquities" in Antiquities from the Collection of Christos G. Bastis (Mainz 1987) No. 5, pp. 16-22.

220. Aling, op.cit., 252-54.

221. Helck, Verw., 348-49, discussed Sennefer's geographic area of supervision (reign of Hatshepsut). Perhaps in the reign of Hatshepsut Senmut was primary steward (mr pr wr n 'Imn, Urk.IV 407) but yet shared the office with Sennefer.

222. Helck, Verw., 382-83; A. Gardiner, Wilbour Papyrus. Commentary, 20. He cites 52,117,208 and 226 for the second man in the office.

223. Many have felt that the tomb of Tjenuna was deliberately attacked by enemies or as a result of Tjenuna's fall from power. Eggebrecht, Ägyptens Aufstieg zur Weltmacht, 181, for example. If this were true then Kaemwast might well have followed him into the position of Steward of Amun. I remain unsure that the destruction was aimed at Tjenuna rather than at first Amun's name and then generally at human images.

224. Urk. IV 1213, 1215; Urk. IV 1637-40; Tomb 38, PM I^2 1 69-70. A statue of the Scribe of counting grain of Amun, Djeserka and his wife Wadjet (?) was in a private collection in Puerto Rico, (PM I^2 795); a tomb lintel in Yale Art Gallery, YAG 1937.13. G.D. Scott, Ancient Egyptian Art at Yale, [New Haven 1986] 96-97, belongs to the Scribe Djeserka and his wife or sister Wadjrenpet. The style is most probably of Thutmose IV's reign.

225. PM I^2 2 795.

226. G.D. Scott, <u>Ancient Egyptian Art at Yale</u>, (New Haven 1986) 96-97.

227. Aling, <u>op.cit.</u>, 240. On page 242, Aling mis-cited Helck, <u>Verw.</u>, 423, by saying Sennefer had been Overseer of Cattle of Amun early in life. Helck made no such conclusion.

228. Kees, <u>Priestertum</u>, 46. Helck's discussion concludes that several men held the office at once.Many of them controlled lands in civil capacities and thus also supervised cattle. <u>Verw.</u>, 175- 76, ns.7 and 1.

229. BM 1238, <u>HTES</u> VIII, pl.10; <u>Urk</u>. IV 1633; Brooklyn Museum 74.97, <u>Brooklyn Museum Annual</u> XI (1969-70) pt.1,77. Formerly on loan L69.38.2. B.V. Bothmer in <u>Bastis collection</u>, 16-22.

230. <u>Supra</u>. See <u>Urk</u>. IV 1635-37.

231. <u>Urk</u>. IV 1581, 1594, 1596.

232. Aling, <u>op.cit.</u>, 243-44.

233. <u>Ibid.</u>, 237, called Minmose and Menkheper "minor functionaries", but this is scarcely believable. See Helck's partial list of Overseers, <u>Verw.</u>, 176 n.1.

234. PM I^2 1, 261-62. Personal photographs.

235. <u>Urk</u>. IV 402. Helck, <u>Verw.</u> 475.

236. Kees, <u>Priestertum.</u> 21; H. Kees, <u>ZÄS</u> 85 (1960) 45-46. For a recent discussion of the office see M. Dewachter, "Les 'premiers fils royaux d'Amon' Complements et Remarques", <u>RdE</u> 35 (1984) 83-94, with references since Kees' article.

237. Davies, <u>Corpus</u> #78.

238. P.A.A. Boeser, <u>Stelen</u> , pl.10 #15; <u>Urk</u>. IV 1951-52.

239. A. and A. Brack, <u>Das Grab des Haremheb. Theben Nr. 78</u>, 81. The Bracks suggest that the back hall was only painted during Amenhotep III's rule and that the title, found in that hall, was given Haremheb by that king. We have stated already, however, that only the judgement scene, clearly located on a separate section of the left wall and painted in a different style with different pigments, was done in Amenhotep's reign. We continue to suggest that Haremheb died after his wife who shared the tomb with him and that his judgement scene was added at his death. On the painting of the tomb see also A. Mekhitarian, <u>MDAIK</u> 15 (1957) 186-92, who identifies the painter of TT 78 with that of TT 90 of Nebamun. Certain scenes were no doubt done by the same painter, but hardly all of them.

240. Helck, Einfluss. 33, Kees, Priestertum, 66.

241. Helck, Einfluss. 33; Aling, op.cit., 247.

242. Brack, op.cit., 15-16.

243. Urk. IV 1589-97.

244. Kees, Priestertum, 16-18.

245. Th.tbs. 86,95, and 97.

246. Note that the royal child Amenemipet whom Horemhab holds on his knee in one of his tomb scene may be attested on a stela from Sakkara. The princess would then have been part of the northern residence during Thutmose's rule.

247. In fact, Helck believed there were two titleholders for this office in the latter 18th dynasty as well as later. Horemhab might have represented the north. Helck, Verw., 300-02, places him in the south instead. Helck also notes that it is the growing importance of Memphis which influenced what he identified as a division of the office.

248. Lacau, Steles. 41, pl.12; Urk. IV 1611; Helck, Materialien I, 232.

249. Gardiner, Wilbour Papyrus, Commentary, 112-13.

250. Urk. IV 1793-1801.

251. H.M. Stewart, Mummy Cases and Inscribed Funerary Cones (Warminster 1986) 47. Called dynasty 18 ?. Eight cones in the Petrie Museum and one in Strasbourg (# 1004). The examples are Davies and Macadam #465.

252. Mentioned in Hayes, Scepter II, 152.

253. PM I^2 1 281-83.

254. CG 584, Borchardt, Statuen I-II, pl.105; R. Anthes, ZÄS 72 (1936) 61 #II 3.

255. Ibid., 65, Abb.1; Leiden AP 11 (with U.C. 14463). PM III^2 712; Boeser, Stelen #27, pl. XV. See also Bosse-Griffiths, JEA 41 (1955) 56ff.

256. This is likely, however, on the basis of the style of the latter's false door from Sakkara. Florence 2565; Bosticco, Le stele egiziane del Nuovo Regno, 39-41, fig. 33. I thank Dr. M. Guidotti for the opportunity to study this stela and the statue of Ptahmose in Florence. The figure on the stela is of classically Thutmoside proportions which prefer the leg to be two and a half times the torso length, while the center of the body is but one fifth of the leg. These proportions change in the reign of Amenhotep III for nearly all figures in two and three dimensions, such that

the waist and hip are emphasized taking often twice the space. The leg and torso are generally both shortened.

257. Anthes, op.cit., #'s 4 and 5.

258. PM II2 535; T.Allen, A Handbook of the Egyptian Collection, 41.

259. L. Manniche, Lost Tombs, 125-135. She agrees with Radwan that this is probably a tomb decorated after Thutmose IV's reign.

260. Urk. IV 1633.

261. BM 902, HTES VIII, pl.9; Urk. IV 1615-17.

262. PM I^2 1 225-26; PM I^2 2 840, vases from tomb, Cairo JE 31167, BM 30454-55, and MMA 41.2.3-4. The Met also possesses a cone. One tomb block in Berlin #13616.

263. Wrezinski, op.cit., I, pl. 339.

264. Shedid, op.cit., pl. 15.

265. Supra. 5.1.6. with n.88.

266. Urk. IV 1639.

267. H. DeMeulenaere, "Le directeur des travaux Minmose", MDAIK 37 (1981) 315-19, pls. 50-51. We have not accepted the identification of BM 2300's Minmose s̆sm hb n Imn with the Overseer of works Minmose who holds princes Webensenu and Nedjem on CG 638, but the remainder of DeMeulenaere's argument is beyond reproach.

268. Ibid. CG 34099 and 34101.

269. Roeder, Naos, 129-33; pls. 42-43.

270. Most recently, M. Moursi, "Corpus der Mnevis-Stelen und Untersuchungen zum Kult der Mnevis-Stiere in Heliopolis II", SAK 14 (1987) 225-38. He still dates Ahmose to early Dynasty 19. For the source of this dating see H. Kees, Das Priestertum im Ägyptischen Staat vom Neuen Reich bis zur Spätzeit (Leiden 1953) 114, "Nach seinem Namem wurde man ihn in die 18. Dynastie setzen, dort ist aber fur einen Konigssohn als Hohenpriester des Re in Heliopolis vor Amenophis IV. kein Platz."

271. CG 589. Borchardt, Statuen II, 145.

272. Personal handcopy.

273. Urk. IV 1583.

274. Ibid.

275. Ibid.

276. PM I² 1 458-59, Urk. IV 1632-33.The date of the monument remains a prpoblem since the tomb is lost. Manniche first considered it a contemporary tomb (City of the Dead 113-14; 46) and then one posthumous to Thutmose IV's reign (Lost Tombs 125-35).

277. A. Radwan, Darstellungen, 34.

278. Supra, under Amun Temple Administrators.

279. Boeser, Stelen. pl.VII #11.

280. Supra. This may have been an official of Thutmose III's temple. Perhaps also the Chief steward Tjenuna of tomb 76.

281. Urk. IV 1632-33.

282. Helck, Materialien, 98-99; PM I² 1,230-31, for Kynbu.

283. Helck, Materialien I, 98-99, 120.

284. W. Helck, "Der Anfang des Papyrus Turin 1900 und 'Recycling' im alten Ägypten", CdE 49 (1984) 244-47. [242-47]

285. BM 148, HTES VII, 43-44; CG 34022, Lacau, Stèles, 42-43, pl.13; Urk. IV 1611-13.

286. Urk. IV 1924-29; H. DeMeulenaere, CdE 46 (1971) 223- 33.

287. See for discussion Helck, Einfluss. 13-27. But Helck considered "royal scribe" of the same rank as "army scribe". This is not clear, for the attachment to the royal administration most often appears with those men who have reached more prestigious positions than "army scribe". There may have been both palace and army routes to scribal success in the military, but the palace employees were no doubt beginning with higher placement, to which simple "army scribes" aspired. Compare the titles of Ay and son Raner, and also Sennu and son Si-amun.

288. Ibid., 13; Schulman, Military Rank and Title. 65, however, concluded "army scribe" was a general designation for scribes in the military. This may be correct, but it is not as attractive an explanation as Helck's. See the titles of men cited in n.281.

289. PM I² 1 144-46; A. and A. Brack, Das Grab des Tjanuni: Theben Nr. 74; Urk. IV 1002-18; Turin stela and relief, 1643-44.

290. Urk. IV 1004-05.

291. Wegner, op.cit., 117-18; Brack, op.cit., 90, on dating.

292. Ibid., whose references to the annals suggest years 29 and 30 more than later Djahy campaigns. But this is not proven.

293. Urk. IV 1006-07; Brack, op.cit., 86-87, on his career.

294. Helck, Einfluss, 27; Schulman, Military Rank. 44.

295. Urk. IV 1596,5; Bouriant, op.cit., pl.V bottom left.

296. Schulman, Military Rank, 157-58.

297. Champollion, Notices I 616 #9 = Petrie, A Season, I #30 = Urk. IV 1597.

298. DeMorgan, Catalogue, 69 #13 = Petrie, I #48; DeMorgan, op.cit., 70 #23 = Petrie, #333 (copied as Ttwy).

299. Borchardt, Statuen III, 145, pl. 156.

300. BMFA 72.1769 = Davies, Corpus, #282. Schulman, Military Rank. 156-57, makes the same conclusion from the funerary cone and statue; Helck, Einfluss, 16 also. (Although they used Daressy's copy of #150, which incorrectly showed the diagonal strokes of wy as plural strokes for mš°w.)

301. Bologna 1908 in S. Curto, L'Egitto antico. pl.25 #41, called Thutmose IV era. E. Bresciani, Le Stele Egiziane. Cataloghi delle Collezioni del Museo Civico Archeologico di Bologna (Bologna 1985) 52-53; pl. 20.

302. Pierret, Recueils II, 56, E. Brovarski, JEA 62 (1976) 57-58 and n.2. The doorway consists of a lintel 1.1 meters by .2 and jambs 1.47 meters in height by .21 width and 1.475 by .215.

303. W. Hayes, Scepter of Egypt II, 273-74. All these monuments have been discussed by E. Bresciani, MDAIK 37 (1981) 85-95. Louvre C282 is .79 meters high by .34 wide. It is a mirror of MMA 12.182.39. For a stylistic analysis of the three, see B. Bryan, "Private Relief Styles outside Thebes", Proceedings of a Symposium on the Art of Amenhotep III, (Cleveland Museum of Art 1988).

304. Supra n. 280.

305. Schulman, Military Rank, 41-44.

306. Urk. IV 1512-14.

307. Petrie, A Season, II #59 = DeMorgan, Catalogue, 70 #16.

308. Schulman, Military Rank, 20-21, 62-66; Helck, Einfluss. 15-22; R. Faulkner, JEA 39 (1953) 35, 44-45.

309. J. Lopez and J. Yoyotte, BiOr 26 (1969)5, disagreed with the analysis of Thutmose IV's text, and their translation is more sensible than Schulman's; but not their interpretation of nfrw. They have neglected the fact that the guards mentioned in the Konosso,text are all royal troops, not army regulars; the nḥt-ꜥ, (see Urk. IV 1307,9, where it probably means "able-bodied men"), the nfrw and šmsw are here the king's escort, termed in the aggregate, mšꜥw.f "his army". Urk. IV 1546,10-12. See especially, Urk. IV 1104,8-10, where the same troops accompany the vizier on a mission. If Lopez and Yoyotte are correct that the nfrw were younger soldiers, it is still true that they were "elite", or hand-picked men for the royal escort.

310. Brack, op.cit., 85.

311. PM I^2 1 152-56; Brack, Das Grab des Haremheb; Bouriant, op.cit., pls. I-VI; Graffiti. Petrie, A Seas. I #35 = DeMorgan,69,#12 = Urk. IV 1597, Petrie, I #30 = Champollion, Not. I 616 #9; DeMorgan, 99,#88; DeMorgan, 103,#19.

312. Urk. IV 1589; Brack, op.cit., pl. 56. Bouriant, op.cit., pl.V. The ka of Thutmose III appears in the kiosk before the deceased's judgment scene; and he, with the other kings, is present in the form of his prenomen, at the weighing of Horemhab's heart.

313. R. Hari, Aegyptus 47 (1969) 58-66.

314. Brack, op.cit., 87; Urk. IV 1002-18 (8 times in the latter

315. Brack, Das Grab des Haremheb, 15-16.

316. Brack, op.cit. 84.

317. R. Hari, Horemheb et Moutnedjmet, 23-28.

318. John R. Harris in Arts in Asia (Nov. - Dec. 1983) 76-79. For a new publication of the sphinx as royal statuary, B. Bryan, "Portrait Sculpture", JARCE 24 (1987) 9, figs. 10-11. Harris dates the text to dynasty 19. This is unlikely by its content and the title of Raner which is essentially an 18th Dynasty phenomenom. If he is son of Ay, then stylistically he can only be from the 18th. (Early publication of the sphinx in S. Birch, Catalogue of the Collection...Alnwick Castle, #379; black basalt 11" long X 8" high. Called Thutmose III.)

319. C 76. C. Boreux, Antiquites_ égyptienne; Catalogue Guide, 81; Schulman, Military Rank, 159, included the father, Ay, in his 18th Dynasty scribes of elite troops. Republished, B. Bryan, "Private Relief outside Thebes", in Papers from a Symposium on Art Historical Style in the Reign of Amenhotep III, (Cleveland 1990.)

320. Supra. under the funerary temple of Thutmose IV and under Army Scribes.

321. Urk. IV 976ff; B. Bryan, JSSEA 9, 119.

322. Min, himself with the palace; Satepihu, a mayor of Thinis under Hatshepsut, was married to a royal nurse; Intef, TT 155, was a chief steward.

323. Urk. IV, 1512-14.

324. Tjanni, Urk. IV 1007, 1015; Si-ese, Urk. IV 1928.

325. Helck, Einfluss. 27, with n.8,. Schulman, Military Rank. 141., Aling, op.cit., 155.

326. Kees, Priestertum, 64, 111.

327. Schulman, Military Rank, 69-71.

328. PM I^2 1 183-85; Norman Davies, The Tombs of Two Officials, 19- 38, pls. 20-24, 26,30,33,36, Urk. IV l618-28; C 60, in Piehl, Inscriptions hiéroglyphiques I, 13B = Urk. IV 1629; a cone in Daressy, #16b = Urk. IV l629. (At least two were still in the tomb in 1976.)

329. Davies, The Tombs of Two Officials, pl.26; Urk. IV 1618-19. The year 6 is now absent but was recorded by Champollion, Not. I 502-03; C. Aldred, JEA 56 (1970) 113-14, made the point that the year 6 referred only to Nebamun's promotion and was unrelated to the scene with the king. But he also believed the date referred to Thutmose IV.

330. Yehia M. Eid, "A newly discovered stela of Neb-amon, chief of the western desert police at Thebes", ASAE 70 (1984-85) 19-20, pl. 1.

331. Louvre C 53. Supra, under the Children of the Nursery; for a translation, see M. Valloggia, Recherches sur les "Messagers", 102-03. (He reads, however, 1200 arouras.)

332. A. Gardiner, Egyptian Grammar^3 200., Helck, Verw.,129-31, on ḫ3-t3 lands of the king.

333. Helck, Materialien I, 167,225.

334. C 202 in Boreux, Guide. 88, Pierret, Recueils II,35. His name is "the goose".

335. Schulman, Military Rank. 37; Helck, Einfluss. 36-37.

336. Pierret, <u>Recueils</u> II, 127; Schulman, <u>Military Rank</u>, 165. I have not seen the scarab.

337. <u>Urk</u>. IV 1006.

338. <u>Supra</u> under Viziers.

339. A. Zivie, "La Tombe d'un Officier de la XVIIIe Dynastie à Saqqara", <u>Rd'E</u> 31 (1979)135-151.

340. PM I² 1 150-52; <u>Urk</u>. IV 1599-1601. <u>Supra</u>, under Children of the Nursery.

341. Schulman, <u>Military Rank</u>, 53-56; Helck, <u>Einfluss</u>, 37-40.

342. <u>Supra</u>, n. 158; <u>Urk</u>. IV 1634-35.

343. Schulman, <u>Military Rank</u>, 49-50.

344. <u>Ibid</u>., 24.

345. Supra, n. 157. <u>Tel Aviv</u> 5 (1978) 170-74. Pl. 44. H. Goedicke, "Papyrus Anastasi VI 51-61", <u>SAK</u> 14 (1987) 94 n.56, states this inscription dates to the man named in Sinai inscriptions #252 and 260, both of the reign of Ramesses II. His statement that there is no <u>hry pdt n Tkw</u> in the 18th Dynasty. However, the men in the graffiti cited were the <u>hry pdt n hm.f</u> Asha-hebu (#252) and the <u>hry pdt</u> Amenemipet (#260).

346. PM I² 1 185-87, <u>Urk</u>. IV 1597-99.

347. Champollion, <u>Not</u>. I 498-99.

348. On the presentation of ꜣinw see E. Bleiberg, "The King's Privy Purse during the New Kingdom", <u>JARCE</u> 21 (1984) 155-67.

349. Björkman, <u>JARCE</u> 11, 43-51, with bibliography.

350. <u>Urk</u>. IV 1620,3; Daressy, #59 = <u>Urk</u>. IV 1629.

351. <u>PM</u> III2 44; U. Hölscher, <u>Das Grabdenkmal des Konigs Chephren</u>. 108, Abb. 159; C. Zivie, <u>op.cit</u>., l64-66.

352. B. Schmitz, "<u>Königssohn</u>", 273-75.

353. <u>Supra</u>. n.321; <u>Urk</u>. IV 1624.

354. But see Schulman, <u>Military Rank</u>, 24-26.

355. I am indebted to Edmund S. Meltzer for a photograph of the piece. I have not seen it.

356. CG 34098. Dated by style of his Abydene stela. His wife is the Mistress of the house Ta-aati.

357. Supra. Discussion of the office in J. Černý, A Community of Workmen at Thebes, Chap.20, 261-84. Dominique Valbelle, Les Ouvriers de la Tombe, (Cairo 1985) 134-35.

358. Urk. IV 1619.

359. Valbelle, op.cit., 134.

360. Supra. See also discussion, 4.5.

361. Urk. IV 1593.

362. Schulman, Military Rank, 25; see also C. Vandersleyen, Les Guerres d'Amosis. 79-80.

363. Urk. IV 1660,13; Faulkner, Dictionary, 120, translates "skirmisher". Contrary to Schulman's citatlon, mg3 is not always written with the child determinative but with a variety. See also a brief discussion in Marie-Pierre Foissy-Aufrère, Égypte et Provence [Musée Calvet] (Avignon 1985) 32-35.

364. Supra. n.8 and 4.4.

365. Schulman, Military Rank, 34-35. See also J. Yoyotte and J. Lopez, "L'organisation de l'armée au nouvel empire égyptien", BiOr 26 (1969) 7. "Il parait que l'étendue de leur pouvoir et leur rang relatifs purent être différents selon des cas et selon les périodes...la plupart...auraient été les vicaires et subordonnés immediats de mr mšͨ dan l'infanterie et de mr ssmt dans les charreries."

366. Urk. IV 1620.

367. Supra, n.8.

368. See under Standardbearers.

369. CG 34091.

370. Helck, Einfluss, 59.

371. Schulman, Military Rank, 46-47.

372. Helck, Einfluss, 61.

373. Aling, op.cit., 167-89.

374. Ibid., 177, 182-84.

375. Yoyotte and Lopez, op.cit., 14f., for princes such as Merenptah's son Merenptah, and a prince under Ramesses IV, for example.

376. Lopez and Yoyotte, op.cit., 15 #378a.

377. See Chapter 2 on Giza stela B.

378. Urk. IV 1281.

379. W. Decker, Die physische Leistung Pharaos. 128-35, discusses horse training with emphasis on the Sphinx Stela of Amenhotep II. He makes similar conclusions concerning the care taken for horses-- their housing and treatment.

380. The owner of Giza stela B and Webensenu on his canopics. See Chapter 2.

381. Supra, n. 302.

382. Supra, n.140, mr ssmwt n hm.f

383. Schulman, Military Rank, 56, suggests that the notion that the person was unassigned is not likely. He suggests that these extensions mentioning epithets of the king are simply honorifics for the rank.

384. Romer, op.cit., 192, legend to photo of unfinished decoration in KV 43 of Thutmose IV.

385. Despite the rapidity with which painting could be achieved, tombowners apparently hired the draughtsmen before the ends of their careers as the several examples of double tombs for the same man suggest, and as additions to completed tombs confirm. Double tombs are known for Senenmut (TT 71, 353), Sennefer (Upper and Lower 96), Djehuty-nefer (104 and 80), Menkheperrasonb (86 and 112) Mery (84 [usurped from Iamnedjeh for Mery and his mother] and 95), and the most famous but non-Theban example, Horemheb (Sakkara and King's Valley). Evidence of repainting appears in TT 100 of Rekhmire where a scene showing the ship of Amenhotep II was placed over an earlier painting.

386. For example, TT 75, 76, 116, from the reign of Thutmose IV. Examples such as TT 55 of Ramose and 43 of Neferrenpet are not uncommon in other periods. A. Amer, "A unique Theban tomb inscription under Ramesses VIII", GM 49 (1981) 9-12 for a private tomb decorated in three months, 19 days. A good overall synopsis of the problems in assessing tomb decoration labor is C. Eyre, "Work and the Organisation of Work in the New Kingdom", Labor in the Ancient Near East 167-220. Without documentation we remain uncertain whether the painters working in

the private cemeteries are identical with the workers in the King's Valley, however, this is the only logical assumption. Kha's tomb chapel in Deir el Medina is certainly representative of the painting in some private tombs, notably TT 181 of Nebamun and Ipuki, and the chief draughtsmen's chapel can hardly have been the work of other than royal artisans. It seems a reasonable hypothesis that painting gangs, under the supervision of specific master draughtsmen, were commissioned by private tombowners on the basis of availability and funds. Whether such arrangements required the approval through a representative of the crown is likewise unknown, but those persons who represented the king in their tombs must have done so with at least the knowledge of the sovereign, if not his permission.

387. See C. Beinlich-Seeber and Abdel Ghaffar Shedid, Das Grab des Userhet TT 56, pl. 1, for example. This tomb must have been decorated quite late in Amenhotep II's reign by the number of advanced themes and figural arrangements utilized.

388. For example, the parents of the deceased in both TT 55 of Ramose and TT 181, Nebamun and Ipuki. The most interesting example of this is TT 295 of Dhutmose called Paroy. This tomb was no doubt decorated originally in the latter part of Amenhotep II's reign but was restored and probably reused for family members in the Ramesside period. Here the Ramesside painters gave new heads and faces to the 18th dynasty bodies, put more comfortable pillows on the old stools, and significantly modified the women's garments to reflect current fashion. Shawls are expanded on several examples, and nearly all have had their dresses lengthened.(El Sayed Hegazy and Mario Tosi, A Theban Private Tomb Tomb No. 295, ADAIK 45 (Mainz 1983), pls. 3-5. But the parents of Dhutmose have been left in their original garb (ibid., pl. 7).

389. N. De Garis Davies, The Tomb of Ramose (London 1941), various scenes, including the northeast wall of daughters offering to Ramose in the old style, and the northwest wall where pharaoh's court women stand behind the kiosk.

390. L. Manniche, Lost Tombs, 125-35. She agrees this is probably a tomb decorated after Thutmose IV's reign.

391. L. Manniche, Lost Tombs, 54. This style of this tomb is very close to that of TT 38 and has been dated to the same period by Manniche.

392. Shedid, op.cit., pl.15; Manniche, Lost Tombs, 176.

393. Objects dated to Amenhotep IIthrough Amenhotep III found in chapel.

394. W. Helck, MDAIK 17,99-110; repeated SAK 15 (1988) and C. Aldred, ZÄS 94, 1-6 dates T III-A II; Shedid,op.cit., TIV, pls. 14-15, pages 93-94. This man is probably identical with the Overseer of Kitchen and Butler Neferrenpet whose well-known scribal statue is in the Louvre.Urk. IV, 1856.

395. Have not seen, but photos in Shedid suggest Amenhotep II.

396. Most scenes of Thutmose IV's reign, but banquet scene later. Remarks Parallels TT 52 as per stylistic discussion above.

397. A relief tomb rare at the period; W. Schenkel, MDAIK 31,125-58, pl.41. Compare the banqueting scene to the rock chapel at Silsila West (# 11), fig. 51, which is of a family member of Usersatet's and probably of the same date.

398. A lesser quality of painting which could reflect on modernity as well.

399. See publication of the Musee royaux d'art et d'histoire, Bruxelles, cover, the wife of Nakht, Tahemet."La tombe de Nakht", translation of "La tombe de Nakht, Notice Sommaire", by M. Werbrouck and B. van de Walle (1929) [Brussels 1972]. Also discussed by Manniche, Lost Tombs, 177; idem, JEA 72 (1986).

400. A photo of this tiny tomb in L. Manniche, City of the Dead, fig. 48.

401. Cf. TT 162 of Kenamun for Syrians.

402. By cartouche from tomb lintel in Cairo, ꜣiry bnryt for the Temple of Nebmaatre and the temple of Sokar. The lintel of sandstone is on display in Room 12 of the Cairo Museum and mentions "the west of Thebes" in part of its funerary invocation.

403. Visited in 1976. Lotus frieze present; few complete figures remaining, but females are wearing dresses which extend of top of foot; varnish over dresses similar to TT 78, 90 and 116.

404. By style, cf. TT 82. M. Nasr, "The Theban Tomb 261 of Khaᶜemwese in Draᶜ Abu el-Nagaᶜ", SAK 15 (1988) 233-242, pls. 12-16. (TIV by comparison to Nakht) M. Baud, RdE 19, 21-28, says similar to 165, so A III probably. Even a brief comparison of the plates in Nasr's article link the tomb to Thutmose III's reign. The wine-making scene is best paralleled by tombs such as 155 of Antef, and the ship is most similar to that in TT 82 of Amenemhet. There are no lotus friezes, and the unusual fringed and pleated overgarment worn by Khaemwese is known particularly from tombs in the time of Thutmose III, although it appears as late as the reign of Amenhotep II (TT 80). E. Mackay, "The Representation of Shawls with a Rippled Stripe in the Theban Tombs", JEA 10 (1924) 41-43.

405. See note on TT 261; Amenemipet wears the same rippled shawl. Shedid, op.cit., pl. 16 a and b.

406. Hegazy and Tosi, op.cit., do not mention the repainting of this tomb, but it is visible in every scene. Skirts were lengthened on the female figures, pleated shawls added, and flesh repainted. Even new offering bouquets appear in some scenes.

CHAPTER SIX

THUTMOSE IV ABROAD AND AT HOME

Thutmose IV is one of the lesser known sovereigns of the 18th Dynasty not because he was a weak or unimportant ruler. He simply did not rule a long time. The tenor of the ten or dozen years of his reign reflects the logical development of the Dynasty. Trends already visible in some sectors of society--such as increased interest in solar religion, a more elegant art style, and a growing desire for peace in Asia--were more pronounced in all aspects of the culture than before, but were in no way newly created. Neither were they fully evolved in Thutmose IV's reign. This chapter will survey the foreign and domestic policies of the king as witnessed by the texts, historical events and material remains. It will be seen that Thutmose's external policy presumed a position of dominance in Asia. The king's interests at home reflected this confidence and laid the groundwork for the glorified kingship of Amenhotep III. In Nubia Thutmose's active building program demonstrated the same self-assurance. What little military activity can be documented for the period is the subject of the first topic below.

Thutmose IV and the Balance of Power.

Nubia

Thutmose IV's monuments and administration in Nubia have been discussed in Chapter 4 and 5. The king was represented by building activity at four major sites in the south land: Amada, Buhen, Tabo and Gebel Barkal (Napata). At the last town, he may have been responsible for the first detectible temple; at least his foundation deposits represent the earliest known building. At Buhen the king's viceroy, Amenhotep, left a stela, and probably that official oversaw the royal work for the sites in Lower and Upper Nubia. While the wide geographic range of those construction activities is proof in itself of Thutmose IV's strength in the region, two temples are even more suggestive. The king's association with the Heliopolitan gods as illustrated at Giza was reiterated in the Amada temple, and the conquest of Sudanese Nubia was commemorated by the foundation of a temple at Gebel Barkal where Thutmose's namesake Menkheperre had earlier left his monument. But beyond his interest in temple constructions there is little to indicate Thutmose extended any boundaries in Nubia. In fact there are but two slight indications of his active interest: one is the place Katia which was included on his Luxor Temple statue. That toponym is otherwise unattested until the reign of Amenhotep III when it appeared on a column at Soleb.[1] Unfortunately the name may not indicate that Thutmose actually fought and conquered Katia; it may simply indicate that under his reign contact was first made with the region. It is so far not localized but is more likely to have lain in Upper Nubia than Lower simply because the northern areas are far better known. If, however, Katia was first engaged at this time, it could have been the occasion which resulted in Kushites being settled in the king's mortuary temple at Thebes, no doubt as laborers. The stela text referred simply to "defeated Kush which his Majesty brought back from his victories".

The sole military action which can be described for the king concerned Nubians, but not Nubia; it was detailed on the year 7/8 text from Konosso[2]. A second inscription on the same island (but on the opposite side) probably referred to another expedition which took place in year 7 [3], but some scholars have suggested both inscriptions should be dated in the same year.[4] Only a good collation would decide this question, but alas, the texts are presently submerged. Here a consideration of the long Konosso text will be confined to its historical import for either year 7 or 8.

"Live the Horus, Strong Bull, perfect of diadems, the Two Ladies, enduring of kingship like Atum, the Golden Horus, powerful of khepesh, who subdues the Nine Bows, the king of Upper and Lower Egypt, Menkheprure, given life forever.

Year 7/8, month 3 of peret, day 2. Now his Majesty was in the Southern city at the quay of Karnak, his two arms being clean in divine purity. And he propitiated father Amun according as he was given eternity as king forever, enduring upon the throne of Horus.

And one came to speak to his Majesty: the Nehesy has descended from (or near) the vicinity of Wawat, and he has planned rebellion against Egypt, collecting for himself all the foreigners and rebels of the other country.

A proceeding in peace to the temple by the king at the time of dawn in order to give offerings and numerous provisions to his father who created his beauties. The king, his Majesty, petitioned himself in the presence of the ruler of the gods, consulting him (god) concerning the condition of his (king) journeys. Then he (god) informed what would happen to him (king); showing to him the way upon the good road in order to do what his ka desires, like the words of a father to his son in whom he had produced his offspring. He (king) went forth from him, his heart being extended (joyful). And he commanded that [his army be col]lected immediately. He sent it off in valiance and strength.

Proceeding after this by his Majesty in order to overthrow the one who attacked him in Ta-Sety, he being brave in his [golden] ship like Re when he places himself in the night Bark. His sails were filled with bright red and green linen, and spans of horses and troops were accompanying him. His army was with him, the champions in two rows, with the elite troops at his sides, and the ^ch^cw boats being equipped with his retainers.[5]

The king fared south like Orion, making Upper Egypt gleam with his beauty: the husbands shouted through love of him, and the women became excited at the news. Montu in Armant protected [his] limbs, Nesret conducting before him, and every god of the Southern region bore a bouquet for his nose.

Nekhbet the White one of Nekheb affixed the insignia of my Majesty, her two arms being around the <u>was</u> scepter, she binding for me the Nine Bows entire.

It happened that I spent the time of <u>tit-i</u>^c, "the cleansed image festival",[6] having alighted at the quay of Edfu.[7] Then the Good God went forth like Montu in all his forms, adorned with his weapons of combat, raging [like] Seth the Ombite, while Re[8] was behind him alive unceasingly, without darkness on the mountains, with one sole companion from his retinue.[9]

Without waiting for his army to come to him, [he made] a great [carnage] with his powerful scimitar. His terror entered into every belly, Re having placed his fear in the lands like Sakhmet in a year of her pestilence. He was vigilant, not sleeping while he trod the Eastern desert. He opened the road like the Southern jackal, seeking the region of him who attacked him.

He found all the enemies belonging to the Nehesy in a hidden (or difficult) valley which was unknown, they being concealed (?) from the people (<u>rmtwt</u>) who trod the mountains [10] and lands distant from what was (normally) traveled (?)[11]. Then he removed the townspeople (?), together with their relatives, their cattle, all their possessions with them...."

The end of this inscription probably related the king's triumphal return with the booty from his conquest and perhaps mentioned a dedication to Amun.

The Konosso Stela is consistently referred to by scholars as the report of Thutmose IV's Nubian war.[12] But in fact the text appears to refer to a desert patrol within Egypt, in the first nome of the country. This is clear from the wording used by the scribe--"the Nehesy has descended from the region of Wawat" -- the same wording used by Harkhuf in describing his return from Yam on his second expedition: <u>h3 n.i m h3w pr hk3 S3tw 'Irtt wb3 n.(i) h3styw ptn</u> [13], translated by Kadish in the following way: "I returned <u>from</u> the neighborhood of the house of the ruler of Setjau and Irtjet (after) I had made the rounds of these foreign countries."[14] Lichtheim did not agree with Kadish entirely but rendered "through the region"[15] - this still indicates a direction from an earlier point of origin and not a movement into an area. And with this Edel also agreed, but he interpreted <u>m h3w</u> as "near to": "Ich stieg (aber) herab in die Gegend des Hauses des Herrschers von <u>Z3tw</u> und '<u>Irtt</u>, nachdem ich diese Fremdländer erkundet hatte."[16] (Setjau and Irtjet are the only countries in context.) The examples of <u>m h3w</u> show that it does <u>not</u> mean "into a place", but normally it should be rendered as "near" [17]; the verb <u>h3y</u>, on the other hand, does not take <u>m</u> for preposition when it means "descend into" or "descend to" a place; it uses <u>r</u>. <u>H3y m</u>, of places, means "to descend out of" or "return out of".[18] Thus the translation often given for this passage, "the Nubian has descended into the region of Wawat, having planned rebellion against Egypt",[19] is not possible. Rather the phrase must be translated as "the Nubian has descended from the region of Wawat." Given that Wawat was a territory encompassing all of Lower Nubia from Bigeh to somewhere in the Second cataract region,[20] translating m h3w as "near Wawat", referring to Nubia, hardly yields a specific reference. If we must choose the meaning "near", then it no doubt refers to an area in Egypt near Wawat. This would naturally be somewhere near the latitude of Elephantine.[21] Since the text refers to the eastern desert, we can surmise that region, within the borders of Ta-Sety was the location of this skirmish.

That this new interpretation is correct can be supported with other evidence in the inscription. Thutmose IV set out on his mission from Edfu. It is the Wadi Mia which runs east from that town, and that Wadi was a normal road taken to gold mines in the Eastern desert--especially those at Barramiyah and, further southeast, Samut and finally Sukari. In fact the Wadi Mia and the connecting road at Bir Beiza were not normal "through-traffic" highways; they were routes to the mines and mountains where other precious stones were worked.[22] Thus we would not expect Thutmose IV to start an expedition to Nubia from the Wadi Mia. He said in his stela that he opened the road "like the Southern Egyptian jackal" and that he "trod the Eastern desert"; the king never mentioned Kush or Wawat in his travel description. Thutmose referred to an ỉnt št3 as the rebels' home--a valley difficult of access, "hindered from the people who trod the mountains and lands distant from what was traveled". Compare Seti I's reference to his expedition to Kanais where he "made a monument in the mountains of all the gods, digging water from the mountains which were far from people of every district who tread the mountains".[23]

The Konosso Stela details a journey by Thutmose IV over the gold-mine routes east of Edfu; he very likely was being bothered by Nubians who were interfering with gold transports, and he found that they were hiding out in the mountains where the mines themselves were located.[24] Since the expedition terminated at Konosso,it is possible that the king used the Wadi el Hudi to return. That might imply that he did travel as far as Sukari before he started back. There is, however, little in the text to imply a major war took place against these Nubians. Rather this was a desert police action which merited attention because of a threat to transportation through the desert. The trifling importance of this campaign is indicated in the fact that the king struck out from Edfu even before his troops were assembled and began assaulting the "rebels" along the Eastern road.

Indeed the emphasis in the inscription is on the oracle of Amun, the majesty of the king's procession upstream, and the blessing of all Upper Egyptian gods for Thutmose's journey and victory. It is entirely possible that this stela commemorated a royal military procession from Thebes to Aswan: the king toured Upper Egypt, stopping at major temple sites, according to a pre-arranged itinerary. It has already been seen that members of the king's household and numerous of his palace favorites left graffiti at Konosso in association with this text; that would accord well with a formal tour of Upper Egypt. The same might be claimed for year 7 when the king's wife Iaret was pictured on the stela at Konosso; and her appearance at Sinai in the same year might likewise suggest a royal inspection of the turquoise mines. It is apparent from this text and from the Horemheb Coronation inscriptions [25] that kings visited Upper Egypt largely for ceremonial purposes, but they did not permanently reside there. Perhaps their visits developed into displays of military strength in concert with the required performances.[26]

The Balance of Power in Asia.[27]

It is well known that Thutmose IV, in comparison with his father and grandfather, did not campaign widely in Asia. In fact the testimony we do have refers to the king's exploits only circumstantially, but we must weigh it the best we can. We have no "annals", and we have no stelae commemorating "campaigns of victory"; nor do we have lengthy tomb biographies of Thutmose's soldiers. (Tjanni [TT 74] cannot be employed here, since his Retenu descriptions referred to service under Thutmose III.) It is probable that this "monumental" silence is actually the reflection of reality. Therefore we shall try to suggest Egypt's behavior at this period keeping in mind that it was generally subdued.

A major question concerning Asian matters in Thutmose's rule is why he completed a treaty with Mitanni--that is, why he agreed to marry Artatama I's daughter to seal an agreement of brotherhood between kings. The answer to that question would eliminate the need for some discussion below, for it would allow us to interpret the few facts we have. But an answer can only be suggested, for no doubt events preceding Thutmose's reign influenced his decision, and they too are clouded. Amenhotep II ruled for at least 26 years but did not campaign in Syria after his ninth year of sole rule. It is possible that he had made a treaty with the Mitanni ruler after his Second campaign [28] (third including his Takhsy expedition), just as he might have concluded an agreement with Hatti and Babylon. Column inscriptions from Karnak refer to the Chiefs of Mitanni (wrw Mtn) asking for "the sweet breath of life" and continue on saying that all lands sought such a favor from Amenhotep II.[29] But in addition to the columns, the Memphis stela of the king ends with a description of the visitation by the Chiefs of Mitanni, Hatti and Babylon (written p3 wr to demonstrate these were the kings, not vassals) to request again "the breath of life".[30] If a treaty existed between the king and his northern neighbors, these two inscriptions must be a witness to it. The phrases used are those which consistently appear in reference to diplomatic relations (dbh htpw and rdit t3w n ꜥnh) throughout the New Kingdom;[31] the question is whether they appear in Amenhotep's inscriptions as historical fact or literary fiction.

If Amenhotep had a treaty with the Mitanni, he would not have had more need to campaign in Syria. This is consistent with the peace in Asia after Year 10. As for the mention of Hatti, could this be a reference to the elusive treaty referred to in the plague prayers?[32] Houwink Ten Cate produced evidence that Mursilis II considered the treaty to have been earlier than Suppiluliuma's reign (KUB XXXI 121 + 121a),[33] for he referred to the old accord and the tablet on which it was written in the following manner: "I do not know whether any of those who were kings before (me) added [a word] or took one out". Houwink Ten Cate further argued that the treaty pre-dated the reign of Tushratta, since it was probably breached by Suppiluliuma due to the Mitanni ruler's aggression toward Kadesh.

Babylon too must have had an accord with Egypt at some point; at least the Amarna letters implied that the friendly relations between Karandash II and Thutmose IV had been strained by Kadashman Harbe and Amenhotep III. Referring to the peace which had existed earlier, the Egyptian king wrote to his brother in Babylon:[34] ù i-nu-ma ta-áš-pu-ra a-wa-te^MEŠ ša a-bi-ia e-zi-ib la ta-gáb-bi a-wa-te-šu, "And when you write that the words of my father I have abandoned, you do not speak (ta-gab-bi for qabû) his words". The contact which Thutmose IV had with Mitanni might then be better considered before the backdrop of a pre-existing peace with that power. It has been said above in Chapter 3 that we need not take literally the reluctance attributed to Artatama by Tushratta at the marriage of his daughter to Thutmose IV. The seven requests by the Egyptian were no doubt a literary embellishment used by Tushratta to emphasize his own willingness to send Taduhepa. It may have been pure fabrication by the Mitanni ruler; in the letter to Kadashman Harbe cited above, Amenhotep III claimed that the Babylonian ruler had misquoted Thutmose IV. Given that there might have been a treaty between Amenhotep II and the Mitanni king, Thutmose might have simply renewed an older document. If not, some events might have occurred to change the Near Eastern power balance. The evidence for Thutmose's Asian activity will be used to examine the Egyptian motives for the treaty.[35]

The best-known inscription noting military activity for Thutmose IV is the Karnak statue-dedication text which refers to the "first victorious campaign" of the king.[36] It is generally held to document a war against Nahrin. This extremely laconic text shows within a line: ...m h3kt hm.f m [///]n3 hs m wdyt.f tpt nt nht, "from the plunder of his Majesty from [////]na, defeated, from his first campaign of victory". There would seem to be little doubt that proceeds from the expedition were included among offerings to the statues, but it is not at all clear that Nhrn3 "Nahrin" should be restored here. In fact there is evidence to conclude it should not.

One reason is the restored writing of Nahrin: in the reign of Thutmose IV there are no examples of N-h-r-n3, only of N-h-r-y-n or N-h-r-n. Indeed twice as many examples from the early 18th dynasty through the reign of Thutmose IV are written with an n rather than with a n3 ending.[37] In referring to Nahrin in topographical lists, Simons made the point that a Karnak list of Ramesses II "is the only example which adds   after last   (omitting   )." [38] Statistically then, the toponym in this offering list is not likely to have been Nahrin.

A second objection may be raised against the reading of Nahrin in Thutmose' text. The country is described as [////]n3 hs employing the epithet commonly translated as "vile" or "wretched". Lorton discussed this epithet,[39] and he concluded that hsy should rather be understood as "defeated". He argued that countries were termed "defeated" only if they had been so by the Egyptian armies; thus Kush was normally so designated. Lorton concentrated on Middle Kingdom inscriptions and stated that hsy was so common in the 18th dynasty that discussion would be impractical.[40] But if one excludes the Kush examples, this is not the case: indeed the examples of hsy applied to enemies of Egypt--either countries or persons--appear to support Lorton's argument and are used sparingly only of those whom Egypt fought and defeated in some verifiable manner.

Thutmose III,within the annals' description of his Megiddo campaign, spoke only of the ruler of Kadesh as hsy;[41] other peoples and toponyms referred to in the text lack the epithet; Megiddo itself is spoken of as hsy in a separate inscription.[42] This first campaign of victory resulted in a defeat of Retenu and its consequent vassal status; in the annals and later in year 39, Thutmose III referred to Retenu as hsy in recalling the entire campaign. The same Rtnw hsy appeared in the tomb of Iamunedjeh.[43] Three monuments referred to Rtnw hsy in the reign of Amenhotep II,[44] and this too conforms to   Lorton's understanding, since the pharaoh's First and Second victorious campaigns were to Retenu. The numerous other place names found in these texts do not bear the epithet, and one must find it difficult to believe its application was haphazard. In the tomb of Amenemheb, the area of Takhsy was called hsy;[45] both Amenhotep II and Thutmose III led expeditions against that town, but it was probably the latter king's campaign which was indicated. There is but one place, other than Kush, called hsy in Amenhotep III's inscription: Ibhet.[46] That region was defeated in the king's First (and only) campaign of victory, and its conquest formed the substance of Merymose's Semna stela.

Under Tutankhamun, Upper Retenu bore the designation hsy.[47] Certainly this would refer to Horemheb's expeditions, and he too referred to "defeated Retenu" along with the "defeated chief of Hau Nebu". But the Chiefs of Punt were not called hsy in the same inscription, thus showing the appellation was not accidental.[48] Even into the 19th dynasty, hsy continued to have the same meaning. In Ramesses II's Kadesh inscriptions its application is confined to the Hittite ruler;[49] hsy was never applied to the confederation of countries supporting the Chief of Hatti. Ramesses claimed victory over this opponent, in this one skirmish, to avoid admitting the war itself was lost.

It should be perceptible that the application of hsy was deliberate and judicious. Amenhotep II's campaign stelae do not use the term although he referred to numerous Asian towns and regions. Most importantly the Mitanni kingdom is never called hsy by any ruler other than Thutmose III. And he is the only king who can demonstrate a major defeat over Nahrin (and not one of its vassals). He refers several times to "Nahrin defeated" in the annals,[50] and on the Gebel Barkal stela he speaks of "that defeated enemy from the countries of Mitanni (Mtn).[51] The epithet does not reappear for Nahrin under later kings, and indeed we have no indication that Egypt again defeated the rulers of that country. She certainly tested various of their vassal states, but she did not engage the kings of Washukanni.

The inscriptions bear out Lorton's suggestion that hsy designated "defeated" enemies and suggest we should pay more attention to what we often call "stock" phrases. Consequently the restoration of Nhryn3 hsy for this offering text of Thutmose IV appears most unlikely, but rather we should expect a toponym of lesser importance, either in Syria (one of Mitanni's vassals) or in southern Palestine (a rebellious upstart among Egypt's holdings).

Although it is impossible to pinpoint the place which originally was inscribed in Thutmose' dedication, it is interesting to note that a similar broken toponym occurs on the king's Luxor statue. On that statue base, the northern place names included Nhryn [Th]sy [////] [///]n3.[52] Since the chariot of the king named Tunip, Kadesh, Shasu, and Singar, in addition to Nahrin and Takhsy, this list was not at all identical to it. Instead we might once have had the place name from Karnak represented on both monuments. This is not greatly enlightening but would further support the argument that Nahrin was not named on the Karnak offering list. Thutmose' other contacts with Asia reveal the nature of his involvement there but do not conclusively identify the toponym. The king can be militarily attested in both south and north during his reign, but only one "campaign of victory" can be verified. It is not unlikely that he traveled to both parts of Asia on the same expedition.

Thutmose IV in Syria

1. Nahrin. The best proof of a Mitanni campaign for the king stems from the tomb of his Standardbearer Nebamun:[53] there the soldier is shown leading the rulers of Northern countries before the ruler with their revenues: n k3.k ntr nfr pn m h3k sp-sn [///] kn sp-sn msw wrw Nhrn "To your ka. 0 Good God, consisting of the great (?) plunder [from your] very valiant [armies] and the children of the Chiefs of Nahrin". Kühne [54] has argued that this text, taken in concert with the year 6 date for Nebamun's promotion (or retirement pension), places the Mitannian campaign in that year or earlier. This is a logical assumption and is especially valid

since the tomb scene shows actual Mitanni captives. Captives are rare in generalized scenes of foreign revenue; this was rather booty from a military excursion, and the enemies were seemingly Mitannian. There are unnamed Asian offering-bearers behind the captives, indicating the material wealth from the expedition. The best that can be concluded is that Nebamun's scene suggested some Mitanni vassals, in sending their children back to Egypt along with other products, may have switched allegiances following a conflict.[55] But this was not a war with the Mitanni king.

Mitanni appears in various other documents from the reign of Thutmose IV: his high priest of Onuris, Amenhotep, spoke of following the king from Nahrin to Karoy while he was on the battlefield.[56] But the vagueness of this statement, invoking the traditional boundaries of Egypt's empire, makes it suspect. A Troop commander, owner of Th.tb. 91, represented Mitanni chiefs bringing revenues and asking for peace and the breath of life, i.e., a treaty with Egypt. Unfortunately there are two kings in this tomb; Thutmose IV was shown receiving the northern revenues and Amenhotep III the southern produce.[57] In addition these are non-narrative and stylized representations of foreign goods. It would be useless to argue from this tomb that Thutmose had defeated Mitanni. The Aten scarab, like the Amenhotep stela, mentions the king marching from Nahrin to Karoy, and it also speaks of the Chiefs of Nahrin coming to see the king and bringing him their revenues. This avowal meets the same difficulties as other general inscriptions, and it has the added misfortune of coming from a possible forgery.

Nahrin appears on the chariot of Thutmose IV where it heads the list of northern countries: Nahrin, Babylon, Tunip, Shasu, Kadesh, Takhsy.[58] There is nothing to suggest Thutmose campaigned against any of these cities or peoples unless one accepts seriously a claim to have"trod all difficult northern countries" and to have "overthrown all the lands of all the Fenkhu".[59] A final reference to Nahrin appears on the Luxor statue of the king where it again heads the list of northern toponyms: Nahrin, [Takh]sy, [name lacking], [///]na. Naturally no war can be assumed from this monument.

2. Nuhašše. The question whether Thutmose IV controlled towns in this northern Syrian region is part of an on-going controversy. If he did, we must assume the Asian "empire" was, at least for part of his reign, as healthy as it was under Amenhotep II; the important towns of Qatna and Tunip appear to have lain within Nuhašše, and Thutmose may be linked to the latter of these locales. But the argument whether Thutmose controlled Nuhašše is linguistic rather than historical; it concerns the Egyptian transcription of the cuneiform name Ma-na-ah-pi-ya or Ma-na-ah-pi-ir-ya in the Amarna letters. Originally this was taken as the prenomen of Thutmose III, Menkheperre; such was the conclusion of Ranke many years ago.[60] The argument used by Ranke was that any name containing hprw must have

ended huru-ria, as in Naphururia, Akhenaten. Vergote, however, in noting that chronological problems existed with making the man called Akhenaten's grandfather (abi abi-[ia]) Thutmose III, suggested that in fact Manahpi(r)ya was Thutmose IV, Menkheprure.[61] Vergote's rebuttal stemmed from the Manethonian writing of Misaphris whom he identified as Min-hapar-re, Thutmose III. He concluded that Thutmose III's name would have required a vowel after h, and therefore Manahpirya must have deisgnated Mn-hrpw-r^c, (hapar = hpr = ＵＷΠ𐤄 ; hpiru = hprw = ＵΠ𐤄ρ).Edel, in reviewing Vergote's work, agreed,[62] and Osing has since joined this identification[63] in general, but has differed on some points. (He argued hprw was not a true plural and thus lacked a w ending.) However, Campbell did not accept the identification,[64] although he offered no reason; Kuhne likewise disagreed,[65] apparently following Campbell. Most recently, Krauss presented both sides[66] and, although he doubted the authority of Africanus' Misaphris vs. Mesphres or Mespheres, he could not suggest how Mn-hpr-r^c would have been vocalized. Krauss rather attacked Osing's collaborative argument. His final conclusion was that the problem as yet had no solution.[67]

In fact no persuasive vocalic disagreement with Vergote has been raised, and it is therefore justified to follow him in identifying Manahpiya as Thutmose IV. And that decision is supported by the fact that personal communications between rulers are far more likely to refer to incidents within living memory (forty years) than ones ninety to a hundred years in the past. And it is further rather artificial to conclude that abi abi-(ia) designated "forefather" or the like simply because Thutmose III did not conform to the stated genealogy.

In EA 51,4ff.[68] Addu-nirari of Nuhasse writes to Akhenaten: "When Manahpiya, king of the land of Egypt, the father of [your] father made [T]a[ku] (restored from a later line)[the fa]ther of] my [fa]ther king in the land of Nuhasse and poured oil on his head...". Thus according to Addu-nirari Thutmose IV placed Taku into the kingship of Nuhasse and thereby had an attachment to the line of rulers from whom Addu-nirari descended. The context depended on Akhenaten's recognizing a past relationship between Egypt and Nuhasse, since Addu-nirari wanted his help against Suppiluliuma. This would not be difficult to believe, since Amenhotep II reported captive Nuhasse people from his campaigns, and Thutmose III also defeated them.[69]

Caution is necessary, however, since writers of the Amarna letters were using historical allusions to support their own ends, the degree of factual distortion is an open question. We recall that in EA 1 Amenhotep III definitely denied Kadashman-Harbe's summary of prior events. But for now it appears that Thutmose IV had a vassal-treaty relationship with Nuhasse and as such, for some time during his reign, controlled the area coveted, and sometimes held, by the Mitanni. We cannot say whether he gained the region by inheritance or conquest. No violence is referred to in Addu-nirari's letter, but that would have been unlikely under the circumstances.

3. Tunip. The name of Tunip appears on Thutmose IV's chariot along with Nahrin, Takhsy, Kadesh, Singar and Shasu. Tunip, however, may have lain within Nuhašše whose southern border was around Kadesh. The fact that he named the town separately from the areas of Takhsy and Nuhašše, as was the case in the tomb of Menkheperreseneb, denotes its importance.[70] But no toponym list can clearly demonstrate sovereignty.

EA 59,1ff.[71] is a letter from a citizen of Tunip to the Egyptian ruler and claims that Manahpiria (Hurrian gloss ammatiwuš) and his gods had resided in the town of Tunip. Again the citizens wanted aid from Egypt (for the ruler of the town was not in Egypt's vassalage) and invoked the earlier situation as precedent. They asked pharaoh to give them a ruler as earlier. Thutmose by our interpretation was thus lord to Nuhašše and its leading town Tunip.

Helck differed with this estimation, since he interpreted Manahpiria as Thutmose III,[72] but Helck also accepted that EA 51 (re Nuhašše) could have referred to Thutmose IV as well as Thutmose III.[73] The admission in one case and not another is clearly unjustified, but Helck felt that the presence of the ruler of Tunip in Menkheperreseneb's tomb was an argument in favor of the earlier king. This is questionable, for Helck can offer no indication that Tunip was lost by Amenhotep II or Thutmose IV. It is not unlikely that the treaty of Ir-Addu of Tunip with Niqmepa of Alalakh (vassal of Šaustatar) was made in defense against the coming on-slaught of Thutmose III and does not date to Amenhotep II's reign as Helck asserted.[74] The synchronisms of Niqmepa with Šaustatar of Mitanni and also Shuna-shura I of Kizzuwatna (successor to Pilia) should suggest a date before Amenhotep II's accession and probably point to the fourth decade of Thutmose's rule. (Thutmose III did not take Tunip until year 42.) EA 59 reflected a period when the townspeople of Tunip were threatened by Aziru and appealed to Egypt for aid. It seems less likely they would have turned to pharaoh if Egyptian control had been overthrown there since Thutmose III.

It may be precipitous to conclude that Thutmose III's major north Syrian holdings were lost early in the reign of Amenhotep II.[75] Tunip was not among the rebels he encountered, and it was an important administrative center. Qatna, contrary to Helck's argument,[76] was probably also still under Egyptian control. The report of Amenhotep's skirmish near Qatna does not at all imply that the town was in revolt; rather he spoke of "a few Asiatics [from the town of] Qatna" who came out on chariots to cause trouble.[77] This same type of description applied to the trouble-makers in Ugarit (ꜣk3ty)[78] and there it was not the ruler of the city, but some upstarts, whom pharaoh punished.[79] In fact the Memphis stela account does not even mention the name of the town, Qatna, when referring to these "few Asiatics".[80] It would seem, then, that Amenhotep II fought against some Asiatics in the vicinity of Qatna (whether they were Mitanni sympathizers or not is unknown) but did not attempt to besiege the city itself. This should certainly have been because the town was still loyal. Qatna and Tunip both appear on Amenhotep II's toponym list from the Fourth pylon colonnade at Karnak, and this is noteworthy because Qatna is not found among the northern placenames in Thutmose III's lists, and it does appear on a list of Amenhotep III's. Amenhotep II was not copying his father's city groupings but yet considered Qatna an appropriate inclusion. It seems likely that Amenhotep was still in control of the major cities of Nuhašše, as was his son Thutmose IV after him. It is likely that the Amarna letters reflected recent (the reign of Amenhotep III) turns of events; Mitanni and Hittite aggressive policies (such as that against Šarupsi of Nuhašše) were responsible for attempted defections to Egypt as witnessed in, for example, EA 51 and 59.

4. Takhsy. There are no Amarna letters linking Thutmose IV to this region specifically, but Takhsy does appear in two Egyptian documents: the toponym lists of the king on his chariot and on his colossal Luxor statue. Not a great deal can be concluded from this, however, since Takhsy was such a commonly-cited region at this time. Since Takhsy lay south of Nuhašše, and since Kadesh on the north boundary of Takhsy also appeared on the chariot list, it may be that this area still remained loyal to pharaoh. Helck considered this was the case,[81] and nothing can be produced to argue against such an assumption.

5. Sidon and the Lebanon. EA 85,69ff.[82] contains the following reference to a visit of Thutmose IV at Sidon: šanitu ištu tari a-bi-ka eš-tu ^{alu}Zi-du-na iš-tu umē-MEŠ šu-wa-at en-ni-ip-ša-at matâtu a-na LU GAZ.MEŠ. "Further, since your father returned from the city of Sidon, from that time the lands were made over to the Habiru." Amenhotep III was told by Rib-addi that the region of Sidon had been plagued by Habiru for many years, and apparently Thutmose IV was the last Egyptian king to set foot on Asian soil. It is impossible to interpret what the king's presence at Sidon represented. It may have been one stop on a comprehensive tour of Syria-Palestine which comprised his "first campaign of victory". A visit to the region can only otherwise be recognized in the king's reference to Retenu on his Lateran obelisk inscription. There he mentioned that wood for the bark of Amun was cut down in the pine forests; certainly the Lebanon was intended. But this text is suspect, since Amenhotep III likewise claimed to have cut down wood for the boat, and he used nearly identical wording: ꜥš m3 šꜥd n ḥm.f ḥr h3styw T3-ntr st3 ḥr dww n Rtnw in wrw n h3st nbt "Fresh cedar cut for his

Majesty in the hills of God's Land, dragged from the mountains of Retenu by the chiefs of every land".[83] If Rib-addi's comments were accurate,then the wood-cutting expeditions surely were made without the rulers' accompaniment.

These are all the references to northern Syria-Palestine which have surfaced for Thutmose's reign. There are two mentions of h3rw, but this has no geographic definition, but in its usages here refers to peoples. The term appears once in the name of a battalion, "Menkheprure who smites the kharu".[84]

Thutmose IV in Palestine

1. Gezer. The name of this town appears on a stela from the king's mortuary temple.[85] He stated that the kharu (a second mention) were settled in the mortuary temple, apparently as slave labor, and they were termed plunder from the dmi n K3d3[r], the town of Gezer. Amenhotep III also settled his mortuary temple with defeated peoples, and they too were termed h3kt from dmiw n H3rw "plunder from the towns of the Kharu". [86] Amenhotep is not known to have campaigned in Asia, and the question must arise how much weight to place on these mortuary temple stelae.[87]

Malamat has pointed out that a letter from Gezer may represent the period of Thutmose's attack there,[88] or the time just prior to it. The letter itself was excavated at Gezer and published seventy years ago; Albright, thirty years later, republished it[89] and linked it to the Taanach letters. He felt it was written by an Egyptian official in Palestine to the ruler of Gezer, and he dated it to the fifteenth century B.C.. Malamat reassigned the letter, just as he did the Taanach ones, to an Egyptian pharaoh writing from within Palestine;[90] he concluded that the ruler, during a campaign, wrote to the ruler of Gezer and commanded him to come to Kiddimmu and bring seven oxen with him. Malamat pointed out that Kiddimmu (Biblical Gittaim) was on the major north-south artery from Egypt to Damascus, while Gezer was six kilometers off this road.[91] Thus the command to come to Kiddimmu was logical if written by a king during a campaign. Malamat felt that Thutmose IV was a more probable writer than Amenhotep II, since other evidence (the mortuary temple stela) linked him to a disagreement with Gezer. He concluded that the ruler of Gezer may have refused the pharaoh's command and thus instigated a battle which pharaoh won.

Naturally Malamat's discussion is only speculative; indeed the tablet is fragmentary, and Albright's restorations cannot be certain. The one word which indicates an Egyptian writer was rabisu, a term used to identify Egyptian representatives in the Palestinian provinces;[92] and Albright noted that Canaanisms were lacking in the text.[93] The letter was therefore probably written by an Egyptian,and since it mentions rabisu in the third person (almost certainly), the king is a more likely writer than an Egyptian official. Whether Thutmose IV was the writer cannot be decided. Malamat said the author could not have been Thutmose III, since the tablet should not be dated that early. But this is by no means clear -- we have no contemporary Egyptian-written letters to compare. The earlier king cannot be ruled out.

The recent work of archaeologists at Gezer has provided hints about the site's history in the 18th dynasty.[94] There are destruction layers above Stratum 7 in Fields I and IV. And there is now also evidence of a destruction at the end of Stratum 8 in Field VI. Dever, the excavator, suggested a correlation for these layers and dated them to Thutmose III, since he was known to have attacked the town. The pottery was generally MB II - early LB I, and this led Dever to choose Thutmose III rather than Thutmose IV (although his original publication cited the later ruler as responsible). In Field VI, stratum 7 contained LB IIa pottery, and an Amarna glass juglet. The excavator's conclusion is sound but naturally not certain. If he is correct, we should surmise that Thutmose IV did not need to assault the town violently, but that he took captives perhaps as punishment for the ruler's recalcitrance. A similar "round-up" might have accounted for Nubians and Syrians settled by Amenhotep III in his mortuary temple.

2. Djahy. This term of somewhat difficult definition was applied to all of Syria-Palestine (and perhaps all of Asia) in the 18th dynasty.[95] It is known only once on a document naming Thutmose IV--that is the stela from the Sphinx temple at Giza.[96] In Chapter 4 this stela was discussed and it was suggested that its unusual and crude form is better suited to a date later than the 18th dynasty. This was underlined by the fact that king Thutmose IV was shown with his back to the Sphinx, rather than in an offering stance before him. The text mentions an endowment of fields in Djahy for the Sphinx temple. Unfortunately the representation of Thutmose IV, even if invoked by a ruler of a later time, cannot guarantee that the donation was originally his. Thutmose must have been remembered for his work in the precinct, and he might have been called upon as authority for a later gift to the Sphinx. It would be unjustified to use this stela as evidence of Thutmose's holdings in Asia.

3. Setju. A block from Thutmose IV's sandstone building before the Fourth pylon at Karnak contains a reference to the king as one who "laid waste the fortresses of Asia". This was cited as evidence for the king in the east,[97] but is just a generalized phrase, no more specific than Amenhotep II's claim at Karnak to have "overthrown the Setju in all their places"; and Amenhotep III even took as his Golden Horus name, "the smiter of Setju".[98] This block should not be taken as hard evidence of Asian campaigning. Kings were expected to perform the role of Asian

conqueror, and this is likely to have been a ritualistic allusion.

4. Hau Nebu and Keftyu. The Hau Nebu were mentioned on another sandstone block from Thutmose's peristyle court; they followed there the designations t3w nbw and h3styw nbw, "all lands" and "all desert or hill lands". This again is a stylized description of regions which may have been but were not necessarily islands: h3w nbw may here have identified "fertile regions" in contrast to "mountains" and "plains".[99] The name Kftyw ,Keftiu, appears once on an arragonite vase fragment from Thutmose IV's tomb. The piece (CG 46082)[100] is inscribed with the king's prenomen: "the Good God Menkheprure, vindicated", and to the right of this, hs n kftiw "favor of Keftiu" is written in black ink. Whatever the vase contained may have been a gift from Keftiu, or it may have been a substance called "keftiu" by the Egyptians. In either case it appears logical that there was a link to the people of that region. There is no need here for a discussion of where Keftiu was or what it designated in Thutmose IV's reign. It should suffice to say that it may still have existed, or at least products named for it were yet available at this date.

5. Ugarit. A final area is obliquely known at this period through the Cypriot pottery record in Egypt. Merrillees' study of that foreign ware within Egypt[101] showed a gap existed perhaps during the reign of Thutmose III and Amenhotep II;[102] the amount of pots then increased again, thus demonstrating an increase in trade. Merrillees concluded that Ras Shamra, as a major market place for the Near East (and for Cypriot commodities particularly), was prevented from strong trade with Egypt because of earlier Mitanni strength there. With the treaty of Thutmose IV and Artatama I, trade became easier again, and thus Cypriot pots and produce again flowed into the Nile valley. This is a reasonable deduction, but it should at least be noted that the ruler of Ugarit may have been an Egyptian sympathizer even under Amenhotep II's reign (if we accept Ik3ty = Ugarit).[103] Astour dates the transfer of hegemony to Egypt to the reign of Thutmose IV as part of the Mitanni treaty, although the palace archives mention first Amenhotep III. Nonetheless, EA 45-49 which originated in Ugarit and which date to that last king's reign speak of the fathers of Ammistamru and Niqmaddu being vassals of Egypt. This might suggest a date even earlier than Thutmose IV's rule. Perhaps Thutmose IV was indeed the first king of Egypt to hold sway over Ugarit.

In summary the evidence for Asian relations with Egypt during Thutmose IV's reign is often lacking in substance. In the southern regions of Palestine, Thutmose apparently effected a punitive action against Gezer. Actual warfare cannot be proven, but he transported some people therefrom to Thebes. We can verify some military activity against Mitanni vassals, probably in or before the king's sixth year of rule. The specific areas in which he took an active interest were Nuhasse, Tunip and Sidon. The last town he was said to have actually visited, and that may have been during the "first campaign of victory". (It was probably not during a mission to cut wood.) There is nothing to indicate Thutmose IV lost any of those cities in fighting with Mitanni, but rather it appears that he claimed some type of victory over Nahrin vassals. It is presently impossible to prove that the Asian holdings of Egypt at the end of Thutmose's reign were not similar to those of Amenhotep II. And it is similarly impossible to demonstrate that Artatama I could have been dealing from a position of strength when he decided to strike a treaty with Thutmose IV. Thutmose never fought the Mitanni ruler directly, but his power in the far northern provinces was intact. Thus Artatama may have been renewing a treaty already in force under Amenhotep II, or he may have been reaching an accord to achieve stability for the region as a whole. (Perhaps the specter of a united Assyria and Babylon was already apparent.) Egypt was hardly disgraced in this peace--she appears to have given up nothing.

It is most unfortunate that the king's "first campaign of victory" cannot be located with assurance. Since his military exploits can only be verified in the north, the toponym which he referred to on his Karnak dedication (and his Luxor statue) is more likely to have been in Syria. Kuhne and Campbell agreed that Thutmose IV campaigned in northern Syria,[104] and the slight evidence suggests a vassal city in that region was plundered on the victorious march. If this were the case,the two most likely places would have been Sidon (Zi-du-na) where Thutmose IV was known to have traveled and where Egypt clearly lacked support in the Amarna era; or Qatna, near Tunip in Nuhasse. Qatna is not attested in the reign, but the king's presence in the area is, and Qatna was held by Thutmose III and Amenhotep II. This would have been a war to quash rebellion by the vassal city. Sidon does not appear in Egyptian sources, with the exception of later literary works, but that need not eliminate it as a possible restoration in the inscriptions. Both restorations are only suggestions, but the north remains the likely area for the main campaign. This is all the more evident since Artatama would have been impressed by a show of strength at his doorstep. The evidence tends to suggest that Thutmose IV renewed an earlier treaty with Mitanni, but that he made a campaign in the north beforehand in order to shore up the Egyptian empire in the area. If he also visited southern Palestine on this expedition, it was not in an attempt to conquer but rather to assert normal Egyptian supremacy.

Thutmose IV in Egypt. Approaches to the kingship.

Evidence of instability at the onset of Thutmose's rule remains inconclusive. The lengthy discussions in Chapter 2 concluded that although Thutmose may have been challenged by another prince upon the death of Amenhotep II, that rival was not likely to have been the legitimate heir. Thutmose himself was in line to rule. Furthermore, two substantial monuments dated in the king's first year attest to serious building activity with concomitant temple provisioning from the very beginning of the reign.

If then we accept that Thutmose IV was the intended throne heir, the query often asked, whether the king adopted coregency as a policy, either with his father or with his son, may also be raised. The only scholar so far to have suggested such a relationship is Cyril Aldred [105] in an article now rather dated. Aldred based his supposition of a coregency between Amenhotep II and Thutmose IV on the existence of Thutmose IV's Amada Temple heb sed pillars which included the "repetition" formula on their bases. He suggested that the Amada temple celebrated the second sed of Amenhotep II, just as did the Karnak temple between pylons IX and X. A statue in Amenhotep II's Karnak chapel [106] showed a god supporting a king (?) and another king (?) in statuette form beside the first. Aldred's conclusion was that Amenhotep II and his coregent Thutmose IV were represented there.

This argument which is somewhat difficult to follow in any case became unnecessary with the published existence of Thutmose IV's own heb sed pillars at Karnak which employed the "first occasion" and twice the "repetition" formulae. Thus the impetus for attributing Thutmose's Amada room to his father was removed.[107] Murnane has also rejected Aldred's argument,[108] and in addition was sceptical of a suggestion in the same article that private tomb 43 at Thebes, which pictured two kings in a kiosk scene, was to be dated to a coregency of Amenhotep II and Thutmose IV, rather than to that of Amenhotep II and Thutmose III on the basis of a type of headdress streamer.[109] Despite Murnane's solid argumentation the entire discussion is probably unnecessary. Neferrenpet's tomb is stylistically of the reign of Amenhotep III--of that there is no doubt.[110] It is most likely that king who appears as the sole occupant of the main kiosk which holds the favored position opposite the doorway on the north west wall. The double kiosk scene, on the north wall, is in the position reserved for offerings to deities; commonly a large stela showing the deceased before Osiris appears in this position; sometimes the deceased's parents are included as recipients of offerings here (as in TT 181 of Nebamun and Ipuky; TT 69 of Menna similarly). It would be most hazardous to use this type of scene to support coregency for Amenhotep II and either Thutmose IV or Thutmose III; nor should the mere presence of a king in a kiosk be considered a means to date the tomb. The same type of error would date the tomb of Amenmose (TT 89)[111] in the reigns of Thutmose III and Amenhotep III since the owner appears before the earlier king in a kiosk scene placed on a tomb pillar. The contemporary ruler, Amenhotep III, appeared in a kiosk on the appropriate northwest wall opposite the door. The same was true for TT 181 of Nebamun and Ipuki which includes a kiosk scene with Amenhotep I and Ahmose-Nefertari receiving the deceased men's offerings. On the whole it is without merit to suggest a coregency between Amenhotep II and Thutmose IV.

For the end of Thutmose IV's reign, a possibility of coregency between Thutmose IV and his son can likewise be examined. Although this has never been suggested, Murnane took up the subject simply to note the lack of evidence.[112] Actually, however, given the various types of data used to support coregency arguments, Thutmose IV and Amenhotep III are better candidates than some.

There is good reason to believe that Thutmose recognized his eldest son publicly. The prince Amenhotep of Theban tomb 64 was separately named in the title of his nurse, Hekarnehhe, and in that tomb Amenhotep was given a favored position before and above his relatives. Thutmose IV began work on the royal tomb of his son in the Valley of the Kings. The foundation deposits of KV22[113] name the father only, thus making the tomb his project initially. Within that tomb Amenhotep portrayed the ka of Thutmose IV protectively following the deceased king who was shown meeting the embrace of Hathor.[114] A statue of Treasurer Sobekhotep represents prince Amenhotep mery-khepesh in a royal manner best paralleled by Senmut's presentations of Nefrure.

Two of Amenhotep III's projects witness his attachment to his father: the Karnak alabaster shrine of Thutmose was completed by Amenhotep III; it has been discussed above in Chapter 4. On at least one wall of this shrine both Thutmose IV and Amenhotep III were pictured, although not next to each other. At the temple of El-Kab, two wall scenes framing the main entry showed Amenhotep III and Thutmose IV, respectively, seated before offerings. A text written between the kings asserted that Amenhotep had embellished or completed the temple for his father. This was the same wording used on the Karnak shrine. Amenhotep, as has been seen in associations of other coregents, was pictured first in these scenes--as though he were the active junior partner.[115]

These bits of evidence are certainly the sorts of material offered often in favor of coregencies, such as for Amenhotep II and Thutmose IV or for Ahmose and Amenhotep I. But it would still be unfortunate to make of this data more than it represents. Nothing here proves Amenhotep III and Thutmose IV ruled simultaneously, but rather the shrine and temple scenes and inscriptions suggest the opposite--that Amenhotep wished to finish works for his father whom he followed onto the throne. It does seem, however, that Thutmose considered Amenhotep his heir and as such allowed him public recognition. There is no reason to believe Thutmose began KV 22 for himself--his own tomb was architecturally complete at his death, and only the painting was not finished. Finally, the prince held by Treasurer Sobekhotep on Brussels E 6856, one Amenhotep mery-khepesh, was probably the future king. His portrayal was in fact nearly royal, but as a coregent he surely would have had the king's titles, not those of a prince. It is likely that Amenhotep, just as in tomb 64, was given special recognition by this statue because Thutmose IV intended this son to succeed him.

Thutmose IV and the gods

The king had an ambitious though probably curtailed building program which naturally enough focused on Luxor and Thebes. However, Thutmose IV is also known to have left significant monuments at Memphis, Giza, Abydos, Heliopolis and Amada; probably he built the Nekhbet way station at El Kab but died before its decoration was achieved. The extent of his additions to many other temples remains unclear, but his involvement in the temples throughout Egypt is certain. Like most pharaohs of the 18th Dynasty, we believe Thutmose ruled from the north where a major palace was situated; at least one domestic building element with his name was noted under the Memphite entries in Chapter 4. As king in Memphis Thutmose IV expressed devotion to northern gods (Ptah and Re), but it should not be forgotten that other royal residences existed. Thutmose may have passed time in the Fayum palace of Gurob, for example, and certainly he stayed in Thebes during festival seasons. His children may have been raised in all of these residences, for this was the case with Thutmose himself, as well as Amenhotep II before him. The many sites he chose to work at and especially the large size of the royal tomb and sarcophagus, suggest Thutmose IV wished to make an impression on the gods and on the world.

Had he lived longer, Thutmose IV might well have been very like his son Amenhotep III. In several sections of Chapters 2, 3 and 4 we have noted that Thutmose IV identified himself deliberately with the sun god. At Giza, we argued, his appearance on one stela wearing the shebiu gold collar and gold armlets bespoke a beatific state. These jewels are often shown on representations of the king in funerary contexts, but Thutmose IV wears them on this stela, on his chariot, and on an ivory armlet (?) found at Amarna--all contexts with non-funerary associations. On the last object the king actually appears with a sundisk over or on his head. This divine iconography should be seen in conjunction with the inscriptional materials referring to Thutmose IV as the offspring of the sun god and Heliopolitan deities generally, as well as the examples of king as falcon gathered by Redford [116]. Thutmose IV left a statue of himself as falcon king at Karnak (CG 42081; see Chapter 4). On a relief from his sandstone court at Karnak a statue of the king as falcon was pictured among other royal statuary. In these images the divine aspect of the kingship is supreme. When the material is brought together, the king's contribution to an evolving kingship which increasingly relied upon the ruler's identification with the gods he honored is apparent.

Thutmose's faithfulness to the temples favored by Thutmose III and Amenhotep II was more than simple desire to emulate his namesake grandfather. The temple constructions of Thutmose III having impacted nearly every major site in Egypt and Nubia, that king cast a far larger shadow than did the average pharaoh. In Nubia Menkheperre attained a godship like that of Sesostris III, while in Egypt he became a cult figure quickly. Thutmose III, like Hatshepsut before him, provided fuel for his emerging divine persona through the oracular stories publicized on temple walls and no doubt informally spread through oral means. Over his long reign Thutmose III made claim to multiple Sed festivals and utilized the rich jubilee iconography in his Akh-menu and the southern rooms leading to it. The image of the king as honoree of the gods did not, however, dominate Thutmose III's temple imagery. Rather he preferred to present the gods as recipients of royal patronage, despite the fact that, as Helck points out, the kingship was slowly altering its military hero identity.[117] He also consciously included his predecessors among the venerated deities to be worshipped in Karnak, thus securing for himself the worship of his successors.

Amenhotep II did indeed find an interest in the cult of earlier kings in addition to his father with whom he appeared often during and after his coregency. He referred to Khafre and Khufu on his Sphinx stela and was desirous of honoring their sacred precinct at Giza. The strength of Amenhotep's interest in Giza and the Memphite region must be reflected in the images of him shown between the paws of the Sphinx on the princes' stelae from that site. The king's statue appears to have been a true cult object on these stelae, and as said in Chapter 2, the princes included their father in their worship of Horemakhet.

Thutmose IV melded his father into the Sphinx's divinity so that when he worshipped within the precinct of Amenhotep II's Sphinx temple he was offering to his father. That "father" was the god who presented him with the kingship of Egypt. And Thutmose IV then could also share in the solar divinity of Amenhotep II/Horemakhet.

Raymond Johnson argues that the king would wear the shebiu collar only after a jubilee had taken place, since the gold denoted his new state of divinity and rejuvenation (just as would death).[118] We have already argued that Thutmose IV's "jubilee" monuments are ambiguous in their Sed festival meaning. We do not at all accept that Thutmose celebrated a grand jubilee after 30 years of reign, but we would find it possible that he held some sort of festival with heb sed connotations and for which the iconography of that celebration was appropriate. The rejuvenation aspect of the Sed would have suited Thutmose's associations with solar deities as well as with his great ancestors such as Thutmose III.

It would also be tempting to link the king's changed facial features as seen on his relief sculpture and statuary with his presentation as a ruler who had been transformed. This second style depicted Thutmose IV with larger oblique almond shaped eyes, a longer face and fuller lips. Naturally it is quite speculative to link artistic style to ideology, but we can note that, at least in the relief and painting from the reign, these features probably date from the last part of the reign coming as they do from the royal tomb and the mortuary temple, as well as from the alabaster chapel. The objects on which Thutmose wears the <u>shebiu</u> collar also represent this changed style. The indications suggest the king intended to present himself in a new form--the inscriptional materials suggest he intensified his identification with the solar gods, the ancestral kings, and continued to present himself as the offspring of Amun. Thutmose IV therefore laid a large foundation for Amenhotep III's deification. Despite the broad range of this topic, until we understand more about the various forms of deification it would be unwise to link the votive stelae naming deceased rulers with the process alluded to above. We refer here only to Thutmose IV's self presentation.

Thutmose IV and the Royal Women

The emphasis placed on Thutmose's association with Amun and Re appears to have been deliberately underlined through the queenship's identification with Isis and Hathor. Thutmose is perhaps responsible, even more so than Amenhotep II who venerated his mother Meryt-re, for promoting the queen-mother as the embodiment of Mut, Hathor, Isis and all mother goddesses. But Thutmose likewise promoted his wives Nefertiry and Iaret as official representatives of the king. There is less to suggest these two women performed the ritual roles so apparent in Tiaa's monuments, but Nefertiry was clearly a partner in worship with Thutmose IV on the Giza stelae, while Iaret acted as royal representative at two border regions. Like Nefrure at the Sinai, the princess and queen shared the ceremonial burden of the monarchy. Taken together the queens of Thutmose IV may presage Queens Tiy and Nefertiti, and one may propose to see that Tiy's ultimate embodiment of all queenly roles was won at the diminution of her importance as queen mother. For Mutemwia was venerated in the form of goddess Mut so precisely (she receives the title <u>mwt ntr</u> "god's mother") that she has no obvious worldly influence. Without the mythological necessity for Mut in Amenhotep IV's new order, Tiy's ritual significance was diluted, and while her actual influence may have been great for a time (as witness the Amarna letters) her role at court was publicly undefined. Nefertiti, on the other hand, maintained the iconographic associations with Hathor and likewise evoked them in her worship activities with Akhenaten and her daughters. It may have been only with Seti I and Ramesses II that the several roles of queenship were again expressed as in the reign of Thutmose IV.

Administrative Policies

To observe the overall administrative structures in use through the period results in some clear trends but some inconclusive situations as well. Regardless of whether the king had difficulty securing the throne, his reign demonstrates continuity with his father's tenure. At least two of his close military scribes (Tjanni and Horemhab) had functioned under consecutive earlier kings. Nebamun, owner of TT 90, probably did likewise--his Louvre stela, C 60, was produced at an earlier time in his career, and it is stylistically older than private Abydene stelae of Thutmose IV's reign (Louvre C 53, C 202, BM 902, CG 34022, BM 148). The owner of Theban tomb 116 who was a military man of some distinction, as indicated by the presence of a royal kiosk scene in his tomb, served both Amenhotep II and Thutmose IV. The name of the latter is painted over that of Amenhotep II. Others in the contemporary civil administration do not appear to have been newcomers to the bureaucracy. Merire, Chief Steward in the early years of Thutmose IV's rule, was possibly already a steward under Thutmose III; Tjenuna, his successor, served as a scribe to Merire before he served as Chief Steward. The Treasurer Sobekhotep was from an established family with royal connections dating back at least to the reign of Thutmose III. We must then believe that Thutmose IV was able to rely as much on prestigious families as did earlier rulers.

Yet every king had his prerogatives, and many did choose personal court favorites. Amenhotep II favored his childhood friend Kenamun; Hatshepsut chose Senmut. Tjenuna's fragmentary tomb biography suggests he had a personal relationship with Thutmose IV which resembled that of a son to a father: he called himself sdty nsw m3^c mry.f, "true foster child of the king, beloved of him".[119] Although there is not sufficient documentation to support the notion that Tjenuna was as powerful as either Senmut or Kenamun, Thutmose IV may well have trusted his Chief Steward who was also Steward for Amun as much as any other single individual. Horemhab, owner of tomb 78, must also have been a powerful and close ally to judge from the size of his burial and his appearance with a daughter of Thutmose in his tomb.

As said above, the civil officials often represented traditional families of influence. We cannot confirm this to have been true for the Viziers Hepu and Ptahhotep, although the name of at least the former suggests the powerful family of Priests of Amun known in Hatshepsut's time. Certainly Ptahmose, if he served as Vizier later in Thutmose's reign, was from a prominent Memphite line. The overall influence of the viziers, however, remains uncertain for the reign due to the paucity of evidence for them. The diminished size of Hepu's tomb in comparison to Amenemipet Pairy's on the one hand, or of Ramose's on the other, is cause to question the extent of Thutmose's mandate to his vizier.

Clearly the royal administration prospered during Thutmose IV's rule, court and bureaucratic connections supplanting military ones almost entirely. The rank of "general" or "military officer" is practically unknown in the period, while that of "royal scribe" abounds such that even the Viceroy of Nubia was of that "paper-pusher's" background. The office of "scribe of recruits" was never so well-attested, but the fact that the holders were often clearly court associates suggests the position required not the hardened military man but the loyal civil official. With the exception of the Konosso "police action" (see above) even the employment to which the levied "recruits" (nfrw) were put in this period and later remains a mystery. It would not surprise us to find that they were as common in quarry expeditions and building enterprises as in military maneuvers. Likewise several holders of the position "standardbearer for the ship Meryamun" are known from the reigns of Amenhotep II through Amenhotep III. Rather than being a war ship, this was a state barge, probably the Theban counterpart to the "star of Memphis", which carried the ruler and his associates on court missions.

Thutmose IV and Aten.

In Chapter 4 it was noted more than once that Thutmose IV did make a conscious effort to honor the sun gods outside the city of Thebes--notably in Heliopolis, Giza and Amada. But it was Re-Horakhty, Re-Atum-Khepri, and Horemakhet that Thutmose was concerned with. His interest in the Aten as a deity is less definite, although it has been supposed great by some scholars.

The one piece of evidence which makes of Thutmose an early "Atenist" is a scarab, now in the British Museum (BM 65800)[120] (see fig. 52) and acquired at the dispersal of the Nash collection in 1960. This questionable piece has no ancient provenance, but it was once submitted to chemical testing and pronounced genuine. Nonetheless the doubts remain and are repeated here. A handcopy and photograph are provided below, and a translation follows:

> "The chiefs of Nahrin bearing their revenue espy Menkheprure proceeding from his house. They hear his voice like the son of Nut, his bow being in his hand like the son of Shu's successors (?). As to when he extends himself in order to fight, Aten (?) being before him, he destroys the mountain countries, trampling the desert countries, treading to Nahrin and to Karoy in order to cause that the foreign countries should be like rekhyt [according to] the control of Aten (?), forever." [121]

This is the common manner of rendering the text, but actually the readings are far from sure. The following writings remain suspect: the king's prenomen is devoid of preceding title or following epithet; this is most unusual. The king was

said to "proceed from his house", wd3 m pr.f--surely the king's palace was Pr-ᶜ3, and if a tent were intended, then a different word would have been employed (i3mw). "Shu's successor" is written 𐦀 for 𐦀 although one may read this differently.[122] In any case, the reading is a problem. The most unusual graphic abnormality on this scarab is in the writing of "Aten". Twice, in lines 5 and 8, there appears ⟨sign⟩
"Aten" has regularly been read here, but this is an otherwise unattested form of the disk's name.[123] Writing in defense of the "Aten scarab", Shorter noted that Wolf established the writing ☉ for itn in itn thn, and Shorter thus concluded that the scarab showed a fuller form.[124] But this seems a dubious conclusion, for in a study of "enigmatical" writings in royal tombs at Thebes, Renouf found ⟨sign⟩ for itn, and he concluded that the n has been lost from the word.[125] If this was the case, then a writing without t but with n would hardly be expected! Either ○ was mistakenly cut twice for ◠ , another word was represented by these signs, or the inscription was faked and this unusual writing resulted. The reading of line 7 is also problematic, and cannot be resolved satisfactorily: the translation given above, "in order that these countries should be like the rekhyt" is but one suggestion, and the word beginning line 8 is lacking.[126] Shorter supplied r, and a tip of a sign does appear to be present. But a break in the stone masks the reading. The remainder of the lines thus hangs in question: hrp n Itn (?) nn dt. The writing of dt "forever" is corrupt, but this did not bother Shorter until Shäfer pronounced the scarab a fake.[127] Then Shorter read nn ? as n.

Shäfer's discussion took many of the writings on the scarab for mistakes, and his impression, along with that of Pieper concerning the shape of the beetle's back, was that the piece was not real.[128] Several years later (1936) the results of a physico-chemical test on the scarab, and two others of known ancient date, were published.[129] The scientists concluded that the scarab was neither a modern forgery nor an ancient but recut fake.[130] But the proof concerning the latter possibility was not forthcoming in the article. Bannister and Plenderleith simply said the scarab did not appear to have been recut. They had submitted the object to intense cleaning to remove old wax and dirt which had clogged the inscribed surface for many years. One may understand that they saw no recutting evidence. Certain it is that the scarab had not within living memory been inscribed --especially since they did not succeed in removing the chalk and dirt. Wiedemann suggested the scarab was an ancient one used to create a sensational fake.[131] When Shorter published the piece, it was in the possession of a Rev. Nash, but it had earlier been owned by Grébaut, who died some 15 years before Shorter's publication.[132] One can only wonder about its authenticity if such a one as Grébaut did not see fit to do more with the piece when he held it.[133] Redford in his recent discussion of the sun disk chose not to accept or reject this scarab's evidence;[134] that is the only possible position to take at this time. The evidence leans toward the inscription's falsity, but it must not be discarded yet. If there is any truth to Thutmose IV's role in honoring the Aten as a god of war and world rule, then more data should turn up in time. For the present, the question remains moot.

Other evidence that Thutmose IV was particularly dedicated to the sundisk has been proffered. Hassan[135] attributed to him the small stela from Giza which shows two arms grasping the cartouche of a king named Thutmose. The arms reach out from the sundisk. This piece was discussed in Chapter 4 where it was seen to have been dated to Amenhotep II's rule. A special attachment of Thutmose IV to Amarna and thereby to Atenism has also been suggested. Helck[136] considered that Thutmose IV openly broke with the Amun clergy, and many years ago Helck believed that two boundary stelae at Amarna demonstrated this in referring to "evil things which Menkhep[ru]re heard".[137] Although Helck now writes that evil Amun clergy were not referred to in this stela passage, he still believes a crisis occurred during Thutmose IV's reign.[138] It is clear that the stela text in question did not concern Amun priests or any political crisis that Akhenaten faced; rather it was the possibility that the burial of royal officials would be interfered with or disturbed that Akhenaten warned against. And he referred to his father and grandfather not because they witnessed any political crises, but rather to say that tomb-robbing at Amarna would be worse than any crime which he, Akhenaten, his father or his grandfather had heard, that is, judged (sdm). Thus the use of Thutmose's name in the stelae was simply a literary device and in no way an implication that the earlier kings had had problems similar to Akhenaten's. Other evidence of Thutmose's presence at Amarna has been discussed in Chapter 4, and the slight data that Thutmose revolted against the Amun clergy (i.e., he may have given the title "Overseer of all Prophets of Upper and Lower Egypt" to Horemhab) was addressed in Chapter 5. The attempt to make Thutmose IV anti-Amun and pro-Aten must fail. Redford's article on the disk[139] suggested several signs that Thutmose was part of two enlarging trends in the 18th Dynasty: to identify the king as the disk encircling the world, and to view the disk as a separate solar power. But the theology which emerged under Akhenaten was not present at this early time. Nor was the conscious association of the king with Aten in evidence until the reign of Amenhotep III. There is every reason to believe that Thutmose IV enlarged national interest in the Heliopolitan gods; he may even have expanded the king's identity with those gods. But unless we can authenticate the British Museum scarab, there remains no reason whatever to term Thutmose an Atenist.

The Epilogue

In nearly every way the reign of Thutmose IV represents a transition period separating the earlier 18th Dynasty from Amenhotep III and the Amarna period. As the king responded to the potential of a wealthy peace-time economy his administration shifted further away from military personnel and toward court representatives. As the need for the military pharaoh faded, Thutmose rather manifested the contentment of Amun and Atum first through his monuments in their honor and then through his own glorification. Before his death Thutmose IV had begun to appear on his own monuments with elements of divine iconography. On the sandstone court once he wears the curved ram horns, while his uraeus occasionally shows a disk and horns. He shows signs of identity with Re at Giza and on his chariot, and his work at Amada strongly suggests he considered himself an intimate of the Heliopolitan deities. In concert with these iconographic indications, Thutmose's likeness was evolving on his latest monuments. Rather than the square-jawed Thutmoside strength so apparent in his statue with Tiaa the king's image portrayed a fleshy beauty as in his relief portraits on the alabaster chapel (fig. 14). Amenhotep II fades and Amenhotep III emerges. In an almost uncanny way his own image most eloquently relates Thutmose IV's moment in history.

358

1. For a discussion of wars of attrition in Nubia, specifically under Akhenaton, see the excellent discussion of Alan R. Schulman, "The Nubian War of Akhenaton", L'égyptologie en 1979 Tome II, Colloques Internationaux du Centre National de la Recherche Scientifique (Paris 1982) 299-316. See especially 303-306 for Egyptian aims in Nubia.

2. Urk. IV 1545-48. For full references, see Chapter 4.

3. Urk. IV 1555-56.

4. Helck, Übersetzung. 148 n.2, but see D. Redford, JNES 25 (1966) 120.

5. The description is of a military parade, hardly of a battle- ready army.

6. The purpose and frequency of this festival is unknown.

7. The king left Thebes and stopped at Armant and probably other temples. Then he visited El Kab and finally rested at Edfu.

8. See Helck, Ubers., 144 n.2., who correctly guessed that 𓈙 was written for 𓈙𓊖.

9. This phrase properly follows in this manner: "then the Good God went forth like Montu in all his forms...with one valiant sole companion from his retinue".

10. Iskw r rmtwt ht dww. Helck Ubers., 144, "verborgen"; Faulkner, Dictionary. 31, gives "wait for" for this passage, but without justification; isk = "hinder".

11. DeMorgan, Cat., 67, and Bouriant, Rec.de Trav. 15, 179, showed 𓈖 and 𓈖 before w3w m and 𓊪𓃀𓈖 after it.

12. Most recently, D. O'Connor, Ancient Egypt: A Social History, 259. A. Gardiner, Egypt of the Pharaohs, 204; G. Steindorff and K. Seele, When Egypt Ruled the East. 71; T. Säve-Söderbergh, Ägypten und Nubien. 156-57.

13. Urk. I, 125,8-9.

14. G. Kadish, JEA 52 (1966) 28. For h3 m ="return from", see Wb II 473,3; for the temporal difference in clauses, see E. Edel, Altägyptische Grammatik, 1031bb.

15. M. Lichtheim, Ancient Egyptian Literature I, 25.

16. E. Edel, in Grapow Festschrift. Ägyptologische Studien.72.

17. Wb II 472-73. Interestingly, Säve-Söderbergh, op.cit., 156, seems to have recognized this but chose to ignore it.

18. <u>Wb</u> II 472,4-6. See also Gardiner, <u>Grammar</u>[3] Section 162, who notes <u>m</u> does not normally mean "into" after verbs of motion. <u>Wb</u> II 472,7, shows that "descend into a place" is rendered by <u>h3 r</u>.

19. Helck, <u>Übers</u>., 143; Säve-Söderbergh, <u>op.cit</u>., 156; G. Maspero, in <u>The Tomb of Thoutmôsis IV</u>, XX, "The Negro is invading the regions of Ouaouait".

20. K. Zibelius, <u>Afrikanische Ortsnamen</u>, 103-04, on Wawat,102; the Nehesy were known to have inhabited Wawat in the Old Kingdom, and thus probably later as well. Zibelius notes that Nehesy designated any inhabitant of the land south of Egypt, but could also at times refer to Nile dwellers versus desert nomads (<u>Md3y</u>).

21. The king referred to his enemy as <u>ph sw m T3 Sty</u> "the one who attacked him in Ta-Sety". In this context, Ta-Sety should probably refer to the first nome of Egypt rather than to the land south of Egypt in general. There is no specific reference to Nubia within the text.

22. H. Kees, <u>Ancient Egypt: A Cultural Topography</u>, 124-26, map on 119. See Seti I Kanais texts, <u>KRI</u> I, 65-71.

23. <u>KRI</u> I, 65.

24. For a discussion of Nubian military and other interactions with Egypt, primarily for the Old and Middle Kingdoms, see D. O'Connor, "The Locations of Yam and Kush", <u>JARCE</u> 23 (1986) 27-50, especially 43-50 with nn. 82, 83, 109, where O'Connor notes the familiarity of the Wawat inhabitants with Egyptian work projects through both corvee service and mercenary employment. O'Connor's argument overall implies that Nubian chiefdoms, when united through whole regions under a single ruler, created kingdoms at certain moments in time. This was not the case in the mid-18th Dynasty, of course, but the activities referred to here in the Konosso Stela may be attributed to organized troops not unfamiliar with Egyptian military and labor practices.

25. <u>Urk</u>. IV 2116, 15-16; 2129,10.

26. One could certainly cite two Aswan area stelae of Amenhotep III, both of which referred to the Year 5 Nubian campaign at Ibhet--at which the king was not present. (See <u>Urk</u>. IV 1661-63; 1665-66.) These could have been inscribed by the returning armies, but are so general and stylized that it is possible they commemorated the king's visit to Aswan to receive his army.Note that he states that <u>hb n.f m wdyt.f tpt n nht</u> and that he <u>smn.f wd n nhwt r mn kbhw Hr.</u> "He feasted in accordance with his first campain of victory"; "He erected a stela of victories as far as the Fountain of Horus". Thus the formal and celebratory aspects of the campaign appear to dominate the Aswan texts, in contrast to the historical reporting on the Semna stela of Merymose.

27. A General discussion is to be found in R. Giveon, <u>JNES</u> 28 (1969) 54-59. Giveon has collected the pertinent documents but did not scrutinize them well enough. Certainly one should not cite scarabs as proof of a ruler's presence in an

area. His conclusions are confusing: he set out to demonstrate that Thutmose was re-conquering Asian dependencies lost by Amenhotep II; he ended by saying "Artatama demonstrated the independence which Mitanni gained since the last declining years of Thutmosis III". But this independence by the Mitanni ruler, he attributed to the time even after Thutmose's campaigning. Ibid., 59.

28. See H. Klengel, Geschichte Syriens I, 39; M. Drower in CAH II 1, 461-62; Helck, Beziehungen. 161-62, raised the possibility but felt only a Mitanni "peace-feeler" was made to Amenhotep II. Giveon, op.cit., 54, insisted there was no peace, and he relied on Edel's belief that Amenhotep used only a literary convention in his texts. C. Kühne, Die Chronologie, 20 n.85, followed Helck.

29. Urk. IV 1309,1-12.

30. Urk. IV 1309,13-18.

31. See especially, D. Lorton, Juridical Terminology, 136-47.

32. Whether or not the Kurustama agreement was this treaty or a separate boundary arrangement is a moot point, since the question is whether a parity treaty existed in the mid-18th Dynasty. Drower, op.cit., 462, also believed the treaty should have dated to this period. Helck, Beziehungen. 164, felt it may have dated to Thutmose I's reign. A. Goetze, CAH II 1,9, likewise thought it dated to a period before Mitanni power emerged. Kitchen, Suppiluliuma and the Amarna Pharaohs. 22, however, dated it to Amenhotep III. Most recently D. Surenhagen, Paritätische Staatsverträge aus hethitischer Sicht. Zu historischen Aussagen und literarischer Stellung des Textes CTH 379 (Pavia 1986), 17-39 with conclusions on 37-38. He confirms only that there was an Egyptian-Hittite parity treaty before Suppiluliuma but finds the date impossible to ascertain. A. Schulman, JSSEA 8 (1977-78) 112, placed the agreement in the reign of Thutmose IV.

33. Houwink Ten Cate, review of Kitchen, op.cit., in BiOr 20 (1963) 274-76. The major references to the Kurustama treaty are found in the "Deeds of Suppiluliuma" and the "Second Plague Prayer of Mursilis II". H. Güterbock, JCS 10 (1956); A. Goetze, KlF (1929) 208-09; see also H. Güterbock, RHA 18 (1960) fasc. 66-67, 57-63, for KUB XXXI 121 + 121a.

34. Knudtzon, El-Amarna-Tafeln I, 64-65 = Kn 1, 62-63; Giveon, op.cit., 57. Kitchen, op.cit., 10-11, suggests the letters 1-5 were written to Kadashman Enlil I, not Kadashman Harbe.

35. Recent discussions of Egypt's empire have treated Thutmose IV's involvement in Asia in accordance with the works cited above. The treatments themselves, however, are interesting and provocative. Particularly well discussed is Weinstein's assertion that empire was not the aim of Egypt's pharaohs with respect to Palestine. Groll's rebuttal is far less convincing. James Weinstein, "The Egyptian Empire in Palestine: A Reassessment*", BASOR 241 (1981) 1-28. For Thutmose IV, see pp. 12-14. Sarah Israelit-Groll, "The Egyptian Administrative System in Syria and Palestine in the 18th Dynasty", Fontes Atque Pontes, 234-42; Rolf Hachmann, "Die

ägyptische Verwaltung in Syrien während der Amarnazeit*", ZDPV 98 (1982) 17-49, especially pp. 46-49.

36. Chapter 4, Karnak; <u>Urk</u>. IV 1552-55, esp. 1554,17-18.

37. 23/11, based on a survey of <u>Urk</u>. IV documents and other published sources. The annals of Thutmose III consistently used <u>n3</u> and provided 7 of the 11 examples! Otherwise it was rare, even in the reign of this same king.

38. J. Simons, <u>Topographical Lists.</u> 131 n.1.

39. D. Lorton, <u>JARCE</u> 10 (1963) 65-70.

40. <u>Ibid</u>., 68.

41. <u>Urk</u>. IV 658, e.g.

42. <u>Urk</u>. IV 720, twice.

43. <u>Urk</u>. IV 740, 1246, 14-15; 951 (Iamunedjeh); <u>Urk</u>. IV 1236, Retenu made <u>sdf3-tryt</u> to Thutmose III, and he responded by granting <u>t3w r mrr.f</u> "breath according as he desired".

44. <u>Urk</u>. IV 1368,1; 1405; 1508 (twice).

45. <u>Urk</u>. IV 893.

46. <u>Urk</u>. IV 1660,11 (Ibhet).

47. <u>Urk</u>. IV 2069,19-20, 2070, Upper Retenu was singled out, among all northern areas, to be specifically named.

48. <u>Urk</u>. IV 2127-28. On the wars of Akhenaten and Horemheb, see A. Schulman, <u>JARCE</u> 3 (1964) 51-69.

49. K.Kitchen, <u>Ramesside Inscriptions</u> (<u>KRI</u>) II, 12,16,24,e.g.

50. <u>Urk</u>. IV 697; 730.

51. <u>Urk</u>. IV 1232,9.

52. See Chapter 4 Luxor Temple.

53. <u>Urk</u>. IV 1620; 1628. (The latter mentions the standard borders, Nahrin and Karoy.)

54. C.Kuhne, <u>Die Chronologie.</u> 20 n.85.

55. See A. Radwan, <u>Darstellungen</u>, 67-68, on foreigners as captives. Kuhne, <u>op.cit.</u>, 20 n.85, believed the Mid-Orontes region was the site of this campaign; he specified Tunip.

56. <u>Urk</u>. IV 1617. ii m Nhryn r K3ry m-s3 hm.f tisw hr pri.

57. <u>Urk</u>. IV 1597-98. See above in Chapter 5 for this man. G. Gaballa, <u>Narrative</u>, 64-65, for the significance of the "revenue" scenes.

58. <u>Urk</u>. IV 1560.

59. See Giveon (<u>op.cit.</u>, 56) on this list, where he pointed out the northern emphasis--even Shasu at this time referred to Syria according to Giveon--as a symbol of Egypt's northern frontier versus her southern one in Kush. This is also shown on the chariot. D. Lorton, reviewing Giveon's book on Shasu, in <u>JARCE</u> 9 (1971-72) 148, suggested that in this context $\check{S}3sw$ = Palestine; for Lorton believed such a short list must have represented major nations + Egypt's Asian empire. There is no way to determine which interpretation is correct.

60. H. Ranke, <u>ZÄS</u> 56 (1920) 73ff.

61. J. Vergote, <u>Toutankhamon dans les archives Hittites</u>, 15-16.

62. E. Edel, <u>BiOr</u> 20 (1963) 35-36.

63. J. Osing, <u>Nominalbildung.</u> 550-61.

64. E. Campbell, <u>Chronology of the Amarna Letters.</u> 68-69, cites Ranke and Helck.

65. Kühne, <u>op.cit.</u>, 42 n.212, citing Campbell. Hachmann, <u>op.cit.</u>, 48, assumes Thutmose III without footnote.

66. R. Krauss, <u>Das Ende der Amarnazeit.</u> 133-65, esp. 154-60.

67. <u>Ibid.</u>, 160, in regard to a hypothetical vocalization of singular hpr and plural hprw Krauss favored Thutmose III, citing historical arguments of Campbell.

68. Knudtzon, <u>op.cit.</u>, 318-21.

69. <u>Urk</u>. IV 1309, <u>N3-g3-sw</u> ᶜnh 15,070; <u>Urk</u>. IV 665;716;717.

70. See Helck, <u>Beziehungen.</u> 153.

71. Knudtzon, <u>op.cit.</u>, 342-47.

72. Helck, <u>Beziehungen.</u> 153, 305-06.

73. <u>Ibid.</u>, 292.

74. Ibid., 305. Tunip treaty = KUB III 16+21, Cat 98. M. Drower, CAH2 II 1,457, identified Šaustatar as Thutmose III's foe; so also R.T. O'Calloghan, Aram Naharaim, 77, and H. Klengel, Geschichte Syriens II 158. On the synchronisms see W. Hallo, The Ancient Near East, a History, 112. Artatama should have been on the throne some years before Thutmose acceded. Y. Yeivin, in JARCE 6 (1967) 121, suggested even before Amenhotep II's Takhsy campaign.

75. Helck, Beziehungen. 162.

76. Ibid., 156, 162.

77. Urk. IV 1311, 4-17. ᶜhᶜ n ptr n ḥm.f nḥy n Sttyw ỉw ḥr ssmw [m dmi] n Kdn3 ỉw m rkrkyt...

78. R. Giveon, "Some Egyptological Considerations concerning Ugarit" in Ugarit in Retrospect. Fifty Years of Ugarit and Ugaritic. (Winona Lake, Ind. 1981) 55-58 concludes that the writing ỉ-k3-ty for ỉ-k3r-t, Ugarit, can be supported by similar orthography from the region.

79. Urk. IV 1312,8: nḥy [m] n3 n Sttyw nty m dmi n ỉk3ty ḥr ngmgm r ỉrt shr n ḥᶜ ỉwᶜyt n ḥm.f [r bw n-r] m p3 dmỉ... Urk. IV 1302, 9-1303, 3. ỉr.f ḥr ptr nḥy n Sttyw ỉw m ᶜrkrk....

80. Urk. IV 1338, #'s 16, 17.

81. Helck, Beziehungen. 162 ,with map 163.

82. Knudtzon, op.cit., 410-13.

83. Urk. IV 1552. See Urk. IV 1652, for Amenhotep III's reference to cutting wood.

84. Louvre C 202, standardbearer Smen.

85. Urk. IV 1556.

86. Urk. IV 1649.

87. Unless of course the appearance of the toponym Ashkelon at Soleb has some real significance. We know Amenhotep was plagued in Palestine during his early reign. E. Edel, Die Ortsnamenlisten aus dem Totentempel Amenophis III, 84.

88. A. Malamat, Scripta Hierosolymitana 8 (1961) 228-31. A recapitulation in Weinstein, BASOR 241, 12-13.

89. W.F. Albright, BASOR 92 (1943) 28-30.

90. Malamat, op.cit., 228-31.

91. Ibid., 230.

92. For a recent synthesis, see Hachmann, op.cit., 23-26, who notes that city-state rulers could be called by several titles: rabu, rabisu, and Pawara (=p3 wr ?, but Hachmann appears unaware of the identification, p.26).

93. Albright, op.cit., 30.

94. W.G. Dever, IEJ 23 (1973) 23-27; W.G. Dever, IEJ 22 (1972) 158-60. On Palestinian pottery types at sites showing destruction by Thutmose III, see K. Kenyon, CAH2 II 526-56, esp. 528.

95. C. Vandersleyen, Les Guerres d'Amosis, 95-96.

96. S.Hassan, The Great Sphinx. 246, fig. 187.

97. E. Meltzer, NARCE 91 (1974) 32 (abstract of oral paper), used the block for evidence of the king in Asia.

98. Urk. IV 1334; 1647 (for example) Hr-nbw ꜥ3 hpš hhi Sttyw, "Golden Horus, great of the scimitar, who smites the Setju".

99. C. Vandersleyen, Les Guerres d'Amosis, has a lengthy discussion of h3w nbw. See especially, 158, where he notes it is often parallel to h3st and t3; 173, he concludes nbwt are regions where the river stands long enough to form alluvium and thereby a fertile region.

100. Carter and Newberry, The Tomb of Thoutmosis IV, 17.

101. R.S. Merrillees, The Cypriote Bronze Age Pottery Found in Egypt. 199-202 (summary).

102. This dating may be moved down, however, to the late 18th Dynasty.

103. On whether Ugarit was part of the Egyptian Syrian holdings in Amenhotep II's time, see ibid., 55-58 in support but M. Astour, "Ugarit and the Great Powers", Ugarit in Retrospect, 3-29 and especially 15-26, against. For 'I-k3-ty, see above n. 113.

104. Kühne, op.cit., 20 n.85; Campbell, op.cit., 86.

105. C. Aldred, ZÄS 94 (1967) 1-6.

106. PM II^2 186 (575).

107. Interestingly this argument, without the element of coregency, has been revived by Van Siclen who dealt with the architecture of the Amada peristyle court. He argues that the pillars naming Thutmose IV at Amada and at Karnak originally

named Amenhotep II in paint. "The Building History of the Tuthmosid Temple at Amada and the Jubilees of Tuthmosis IV", <u>Varia Aegyptiaca</u> 3 (1987) 53-66.

108. W. Murnane, <u>Ancient Egyptian Coregencies.</u> 117-23, esp. 120- 21.

109. <u>Ibid.</u>, 121-22.

110. See Abdel Ghaffar Shedid, <u>Stil der Grabmalereien in der Zeit Amenophis' II.</u>, ADAIK 66 (Mainz 1988), pl. 15, for the unfinished banquet scene. The arrangement of the female guests, the overlapping body parts and gestures, the hairstyles, fillets, and jewelry are all consistent with a date only in the reign of Amenhotep III. The overall scene is very close to that of Nakht's tomb, but the painter has not yet applied the varnish over the skin and garments. Plate 14c shows the kiosk with Amenhotep II in it and the other unnamed king, and plate 14d shows Neferrenpet and a woman offering braziers. Note the female proportions and the lotus frieze.

111. <u>PM</u> I^2 1, 181-83.

112. Murnane, <u>op.cit.</u>, 123.

113. The foundation deposit, consisting of small faience cartouche impressions naming Menkheprure, model vessels of ceramic and alabaster, baskets, and wood and bronze model tools, are in the collection of the Earl of Carnarvon. This group is in the Highclere Castle and on display to the public. A photo of the foundation group appears in the guide book to the castle. Dr. Nicholas Reeves will produce a full catalogue of the collection, many objects of which originate from Amenhotep III's burial. Sarah Greenwood, <u>Highclere Castle</u>, [Norman Hudson and Co, Upper Wardington, Banbury 1988]. I am most grateful to Dr. Reeves for the invitation to examine the collection of Lord Carnarvon.

114. L<u>D</u> III 78c. The Horus (<u>Ka</u> name), Strong Bull, perfect of diadems, is called k3 nsw ^cnh nb t3wy hnt db3t, "Living royal <u>ka</u> of the lord of the Two lands, foremost of the robing room (?)".

115. W.K. Simpson, <u>JNES</u> 15 (1956) 214-19; Murnane, <u>op.cit.</u>, 123, likewise with the same comments re Thutmose's chapel.

116. Redford, <u>JARCE</u> 13 (1976) 51.

117. W. Helck, <u>Politische Gegensätze</u>, 50.

118. R. Johnson, "Images of Amenhotep III in Thebes: Styles and Intentions", Symposium on Art of Amenhotep III, Cleveland 1987, with nn. 18-20. "It now seems certain that the deification of Amenhotep III actually coincided with and was a direct result of the celebration of his first <u>sed</u>-festival in year 30."

119. <u>Urk.</u> IV, 1578,12.

120. T.G.H. James, <u>Introductory Guide to the Egyptian Collection (Cambridge 1964)</u> 51. Published by A.W. Shorter, "Historical Scarabs of Tuthmosis IV and Amenophis III", <u>JEA</u> 17 (1931) 23-25, pl.IV, with further comments in <u>JEA</u> 18 (1932) 110-11. Chemical analysis in F.A. Bannister and H.J. Plenderleith, "Physiochemical Examination of a Scarab of Tuthmosis IV Bearing the Name of the God Aten", <u>JEA</u> 22 (1936) 3-6, pl. 2-3; rebuttal by H. Schäfer in "Ein angeblichen Skarabäus Thutmosis des IV mit Nennung des Gottes Aton", <u>OLZ</u> 9/10 (1931) 788-91.

121. Shorter, <u>JEA</u> 17, 23, translated: "in order to bring the inhabitants of foreign lands like subjects to the rule of (?) Aten for ever". The fact that no verb for "to bring" exists has not prevented the continued translation as such. Giveon, <u>JNES</u> 28, 55; C. Aldred, <u>Akhenaten.</u> 166; but S. Tawfik, <u>MDAIK</u> 29 (1973) 28-29, corrected the translation.

122. Schäfer, <u>op.cit.</u>, 789, felt that Geb was not to be recognized in this cryptic writing of sty sw, and he suggested Isis was intended.

123. <u>Ibid.</u>, 789-90; "Die Lesung des 𓇳 als ỉtn schwebt unter diesen Umstanden völlig in der Luft."

124. Shorter, <u>JEA</u> 18, 110-11, citing Wolf in <u>ZÄS</u> 59 (1924) 110- 11.

125. P. Renouf, "The Royal Tombs at Biban el-Moluk and 'Enigmatical' Writings", <u>ZÄS</u> 12 (1874) 105.

126. See Shorter, <u>JEA</u> 18, 110-11.

127. Schafer, <u>op.cit.</u>, 790; Shorter, <u>JEA</u> 18, 111.

128. M. Pieper, quoted in <u>OLZ</u> 9/10, 790-91.

129. F.A. Bannister and H.J. Plenderleith, <u>JEA</u> 22 (1936) 3-6.

130. Ibid., 3. "The scarab, as received, was concealed by grime. It was found possible by the use of organic solvents to remove a coating of wax,and incidentally much of the dirt, but not by any means all of the French chalk which filled the inscription.

131. A. Wiedemann, "Neuzeitliche Fälscherkünste", <u>ZÄS</u> 67 (1931) 126.

132. Shorter, <u>JEA</u> 17, 25; Bannister, <u>JEA</u> 22,3 referred to the "French chalk".

133. Grébaut obviously noticed the piece, since the inscription was filled with chalk and wax used to make an impression. The chemists mentioned that a cast must have been made earlier. It is especially curious that Grébaut did not publish the piece since he had an expertise in Amun religion (he published an Amun hymn) which was a natural liaison to Aten interest. It seems possible he felt the scarab was not genuine and chose not to publish it. The notes re Grébaut's collection were

collected by R. Moss and are deposited in the Griffiths Institute. On Grébaut, see W. Dawson and E.P. Uphill, Who was Who in Egyptology,2nd ed. (London 1972) 123-24.

134. Redford, JARCE 13, 51.

135. Hassan, The Great Sphinx, 81.

136. Helck, Verw., 200-01; Urk. IV 1975; Aling, op.cit., 234- 35, who was not aware of the revised reading.

137. Helck, Einfluss. 32.

138. W. Helck, Politische Gegensätze, 53-56.

139. Redford, JARCE 13, 50-51. B. Birkstam, "Reflections on the Association between the Sun-God and divine Kingship in the 18th Dynasty", Sundries in Honour of Torgny Säve-Söderbergh, (Uppsala 1984) 33-42.

Works Cited

Abd El-razik, M., "Luxor Studies", MDAIK 27 (1971) 222-27.

Abubakr, A-M., Untersuchungen über die ägyptischen Kronen (Glückstadt 1937).

Acsadi, G. and J. Nemeskéri, History of Human Life Span and Mortality (Budapest 1970).

Adams, B., Egyptian Objects in the Victoria and Albert Museum, Egyptology Today 3 (London 1977).

Albright, W., "Miszellen: Aman-hatpa, governor of Palestine", ZÄS 62 (1927) 63-64.
"Cuneiform Material for Egyptian Prosopography 1500-1200 B.C.", JNES 5 (1946) 7-25.
"A Prince of Taanach in the Fifteenth Century B.C." BASOR 94 (1944) 12-27.
"A Tablet of the Amarna Age at Gezer", BASOR 92 (1943) 28-30.

Aldred, C., Akhenaten, Pharaoh of Egypt (Lengereich 1968).
"The Carnarvon Statuette of Amun", JEA 42 (1956) 3-7.
"The Foreign Gifts Offered to Pharaoh", JEA 56 (1970) 105-16.
"Two Monuments of the Reign of Horemheb", JEA 54 (1968) 103-06.
"The New Year Gifts to the Pharaoh", JEA 55 (1969) 73-81.
"Note on Two Monuments of the Reign of Horemheb", JEA 56 (1970) 195-96.
"The Parentage of King Siptah", JEA 49 (1963) 41-48.
"The Second Jubilee of Amenhotep II", ZÄS 94 (1967) 1-6.

Aling, C., A Prosopographical Study of the Reigns of Thutmosis IV and Amenhotep III. an unpublished dissertation, University of Minnesota, 1976.
"The Ramesseum Statue of Queen Mutemwia", Abstract of oral paper delivered Spring 1979 at ARCE conference.

Allen, T., Handbook of the Egyptian Collection (Chicago 1923).
"A Unique Statue of Senmut", AJSL 44 (1927-28) 44-55.

Alliot, M., "Fouilles de Deir el-Médineh 1930-1931", BIFAO 32 (1932) 70-71.

Angel, J.L., "Physical Anthropology: determining sex, age, and individual features", in A. and E.Cockburn, Mummies, Disease, and Ancient Cultures, (Cambridge 1980) 241-257.

Anthes, R., "Die deutschen Grabungen auf der Westseite von Theben in den Jahren 1911 und 1913,I B.", MDAIK 12 (1943) 15-17.
"Die hohen Beamten names Ptahmose in der 18. Dynastie", ZÄS 72 (1936) 60-68.

Archi, A., "The Propaganda of Hattusilis III", SMEA 14 (1971) 185-215.

Arnold, D., Wandrelief und Raumfunktion in ägyptischen Tempeln des Neuen Reiches, MÄS 2 (Berlin 1962).

Astour, M., "Ugarit and the Great Powers", Ugarit in Retrospect (Winona Lake, Ind. 1981) 3-29.

Badawi, A., Memphis als zweite Landeshauptstadt im Neuen Reich (Cairo 1948).

Badawy, A., A History of Egyptian Architecture, The Empire (Berkeley 1968).

Barguet, P., "L'Obélisque de Saint-Jean-de-Latran dans le Temple de Ramses II à Karnak", ASAE 50 (1950) 269-80.

Barguet, P. and M. Dewachter, Le Temple d'Amada I-IV (Cairo 1967).

Barguet, P., Le Temple d'Amon-Rê à Karnak (Cairo 1962).

Bannister, F.A. and H.J. Plenderleith, "Physiochemical Examination of a Scarab of Tuthmosis IV Bearing the Name of the God Aten", JEA 22 (1936) 3-6.

Barns, J.W.B., "Some Readings and Interpretations in Sundry Egyptian Texts", JEA

58 (1972) 159-66.

Barta, W., "Die Ägyptischen Sothisdaten und ihre Bezugsorte", JEOL 26 (1979-80) 26-34.

Baud, M., Les Dessins ébauchés de la Necropole Thébains (Cairo 1935).

"Le Tombeau de Khaemwast", RdE 19 (1967) 21-28.

Bell, L., "Aspects of the cult of the deified Tutankhamun", Mélanges Gamal Eddin Mokhtar I (Cairo 1985) 31-60.

Berg, D., "The Vienna Stela of Meryre", JEA 73 (1987) 213-16.

Bergmann, E. von, "Inschriftliche Denkmäler", Rec. Trav. 7 (1889) 177-78.

Beckerath, J. von, "Das Kalendarium des Papyrus Ebers und das Sothisdatum vom 9. Jahr Amenophis I", Studien zur Altägyptischen Kultur 14 (1987) 27-33.

"Ein Wunder des Amun bei der Tempelgründung in Karnak", MDAIK 37 (1981)41-49.

"Noch einmal zu den Bezugspunkten der Sothisdaten", GM 83 (1984) 13-15.

Tanis und Theben; historische Grundlagen der Ramessidenzeit in Ägypten, AF 16 (Hamburg 1951).

rev. of M. Bierbrier, Late New Kingdom in Egypt in BiOr 33 (1976) 177.

Benson, M. and J. Gourlay, The Temple of Mut in Asher (London 1899).

Berlin, Königliche Museen, Ausführliches Verzeichnis der aegyptischen Altertümer und Gipsabgüsse (Berlin 1899).

Aegyptische Inschriften aus den Königlichen Museen zu Berlin II (Leipzig 1913).

Bierbrier, M., The Late New Kingdom in Egypt (c 1300-664) (Warminster 1975).

Birch, S., Catalogue of the Collection of Egyptian Antiquities at Alnwick Castle (London 1880).

Birch, S. and H. Rhind, Facsimiles of Two Papyri Found in a Tomb at Thebes (London 1863).

Birkstam, B., "Reflections on the Association between the Sun-God and divine Kingship in the 18th Dynasty", Sundries in Honour of Torgny Säve-Söderberg (Uppsala 1984) 33-42.

Bissing, Fr. W., "Ägyptische und ägyptisierende Alabastergefässe", ZA N.F. 12 (46) (1940) 149-51.

Bisson de la Roque, B.F., "Rapport sur les Fouilles de Médamoud, 1927", FIFAO (Cairo 1926-33).

Bisson de la Roque, B.F. and E. Drioton, "Rapport sur les Fouilles de Médamoud, 1925", FIFAO (Cairo 1925).

"Rapport sur les Fouilles de Médamoud, 1930",FIFAO (Cairo 1930).

Bisson de la Roque, B.F., Tôd (1934-1936) (Cairo 1937).

Björkman, Gun, Kings at Karnak (Uppsala 1971).

"Neby, the Mayor of Tjaru in the Reign of Tuthmosis IV", JARCE 11 (1974) 43-51.

Bleiberg, E., "The King's Privy Purse during the New Kingdom", JARCE 21 (1984) 155-67.

Boeser, P.A., Beschreibung der aegyptischen Sammlung des Niederländischen Reichsmuseums der Altertumer in Leiden, (1905- 32) V Die Denkmaler des neuen Reiches 2. Pyramiden, Kanopenkasten, Opfertische,Statuen: 6. Stelen (Haag 1913).

Borchardt, L. and H. Ricke, Ägyptische Tempel mit Umgang, Beiträge zur ägyptischen Bauforschung und Altertumskunde (Cairo 1938).

Borchardt, L., "Der Aegyptische Titel Vater des Gottes als Bezeichnung fur Vater oder Schweigervater des Königs", Berichte VKSGW 57 (1905).

"Aus der Arbeit an den Funden von Tell el-Amarna", MDOG 57 (1917)1-32.

"Ausgrabungen in Tell el-Amarna", MDOG 55 (1914) 3-39.

Das Grabdenkmal des Sa3-hu-re' II (Leipzig 1910)

Statuen und Statuetten von Königen und Privatleuten I-IV Nr. 1-1294 (Berlin 1911-30).

Boreux, C., Musée National du Louvre, Département des Antiquités Égyptiennes, Guide-Catalogue Sommaire (Paris 1932)

Bothmer, B."Egyptian Antiquities" in Antiquities from the Collection of Christos G. Bastis (Mainz 1987).

"Membra Dispersa: King Amenhotep II Making an Offering", BMFA 52 (1954) 11-20.

Botti, G., I Cimeli Egizi del Museo di antichita di Parma (Florence 1964).

Bouriant, U., "Notes de Voyage", Rec. Trav. 15 (1893) 178-79.

"Le Tombeau d'Harmhabi", Mémoires de la Mission francaise V (Paris 1884).

Brack, A. and A., Das Grab des Tjanuni Theben Nr. 74 ADAIK (Mainz 1977).

Das Grab des Haremheb. Theben Nr. 78 ADAIK (Mainz 1980).

Bresciani, E., "Rapport Préliminaire sur la campagne de Fouilles à Thèbes ouest de la Mission Archéologique de L'Université de Milano (Italie) en fevrier-mars 1973", NARCE 85 (1973) 3-4.

"L'attività archeologica dell'Università di Pisa in Egitto: 1977-1980", Egitto e Vicino Oriente 3 (1980) 1-36.

"L'attività archeologica dell'Università di Pisa in Egitto: 1980-1983", Egitto e Vicino Oriente 6 (1983) 3-6.

Le Stele Egiziane. Cataloghi delle Collezioni del Museo Civico Archeologico di Bologna (Bologna 1985).

Brinkman, J., "Foreign Relations of Babylonia from 1600 B.C.-625. The Documentary Evidence", AJA 76 (1972) 271-81.

"Notes on Mesopotamian History", BiOr 27 (1970) 305-07.

Brovarski, E., "Senenu, High Priest of Amun at Deir el-Bahri", JEA 62 (1976) 57-73.

Brugsch, H., "Der Möris-See", ZÄS 31 (1893) 17-31.   Brunner, H.,   Die Altägyptische Erziehung (Wiesbaden 1957).

Die Geburt des Gottkönigs. Studien zur Überlieferung eines altägyptische Mythos. ÄA 10 (Wiesbaden 1964).

"Der 'Gottesvater' als Erzieher des Kronprinzen", ZÄS 86 (1961) 90-100.

"Nochmals der Konig im Falkenkleid", ZÄS 87 (1962) 76-77.

Die Südlichen Räume des Tempels von Luxor ADAIK (Mainz 1977).

Bryan, B., "The Career of Sobekhotep" in E. Dziobek and M. Abdel Raziq, Das Grab des Sobekhotep Theben Nr. 63 ADAIK (Mainz 1990).

"The Title 'Foster Brother of the King'", JSSEA 9 (1979) 117-26.

"Portrait Sculpture of Thutmose IV", JARCE 24 (1987) 3-20.

"Private Tomb Relief Sculpture outside Thebes and its Relationship to Theban Relief Sculpture", in The Art of Amenhotep III Art Historical Analysis, L. Berman,   ed. (Cleveland 1990)65-80.

Callender, J., Middle Egyptian (Malibu 1975).

Caminos, R.A., The Shrine and Rock Inscriptions of Ibrim EES 32 (London 1968).

Campbell, E., The Chronology of the Amarna Letters with Special Reference to the Hypothetical Coregency of Amenophis III and Akhenaten (Baltimore 1964).

Cannuyer, C., "Notules à propos de la stèle du Sphinx", Varia Aegyptiaca 1 (1985) 83-90.

Capart, J., "Une Statue de Sobekhotep, Precepteur Royal", Bull. des Musées Royaux d'Art et d'Histoire 3 (1938) 83-86.

Carlier, A., Thebes (Paris 1948).

Carter, H., "A Tomb Prepared for Queen Hatshepsut and Other Recent Discoveries at Thebes", JEA 4 (1917) 107-13.

Carter, H., and P. Newberry, with G. Maspero and G.E.Smith, The Tomb of Thoutmôsis IV. Biban el Moluk Series, (London 1904).

Cartwright, H.J., "The Iconography of Certain Egyptian Divinities as Illustrated by the Collections in Haskell Oriental Museum", AJSL 45 (1928-29) 179-96.

Černý, J., A Community of Workmen at Thebes in the Ramesside Period. Bibliothèque d'Étude 50 (Cairo 1973).

Champollion, J.F., Monuments de l'Égypte et de la Nubie. Notices descriptives conformés aux manuscrits autographes rédigés sur les lieux par Champollion-le-jeune (Paris 1844) Monuments de l'Egypte et de la Nubie. Notices descriptives d'apres les dessins executes sur les lieux sous la direction de Champollion-le-jeune. Planches. (Paris 1835-45).

Champollion, J., le Jeune, Lettres écrites d'Egypte et de Nubie, en 1828 et 1829 (Paris 1833).

Charles, R.-P., "La Statue-cube de Sobek-hotep", RdE 12 (1960) 1-26.

Chevrier, H., "La Construction dans l'Ancienne Egypte", Rde 23 (1976).
    "Rapport sur les Travaux de Karnak", ASAE 51 (1951) 549-64.
    "Rapport sur les Travaux de Karnak", ASAE 37 (1937)

Chicago Oriental Institute, H. Nelson, Field Director, Medinet Habu 2 (OIP 9), Later Historical Records of Ramesses III (Chicago 1932).

Cooney, J.D., "Glass Sculpture in Ancient Egypt", Journal of Glass Studies 2 (1960) 11-43.

Couyat, J., and P. Montet, Les Inscriptions hiéroglyphiques et hiératiques de Ouadi Hammamat (Cairo 1912).

Crum, W.E., "Stelae from Wady Halfa", PSBA 16 (1894) 17-19.

Curto, S., L'antico Egitto nel Museo Egizio di Torino (Turin 1984).

Daressy, G., Fouilles de la Vallée des Rois (1898- 1899) Nos. 24001-24990, Catalogue Général (Cairo 1902).
    "Notes sur la Momie de Thoutmôsis IV",ASAE 4 (1903) 110-12.
    "Rapport sur el-Yaouta (Fayoum)", ASAE 1 (1900) 44-47.
    "Recueil de cones funéraires", Mem. Miss. VIII (1894) 269-352.
    "Le Temple de Mit-Rahineh", ASAE (1902) 22-31.

Daumas, F., Les Mammisis des Temples Égyptiens (Paris 1958).

Davies, Nina, Ancient Egyptian Paintings selected, copied and described, 3 vols. (Chicago 1936).
    Scenes from Some Theban Tombs. Private Tombs at Thebes IV (Oxford 1963).

Davies, Norman and H.L. Macadam, ed., A Corpus of Inscribed Funerary Cones I (Oxford 1957).

Davies, Norman, The tombs of Menkheperrasonb, Amenmose, and Another (London 1933).
    The tombs of Two Officials of Tuthmosis the Fourth (nos 75 and 90) (London 1923).
    The Rock Tombs of El Amarna V (London 1908).

Davis, T., The Tomb of Iouiya and Touiyou (London 1908).
    The Tomb of Siphtah; The Monkey Tomb and the Gold Tomb (London 1908).

Dawson, W. and E.P. Uphill, Who was Who in Egyptology, 2nd edition (London 1972).

Decker, W., Die Physische Leistung Pharaos (Köln 1971).

"Ein Ring mit dem Namen Thutmosis IV", CdE 44 (1949) 195-99.

DeMeulenaere, H., "Les Chefs des Greniers du nom Saese au Nouvel Empire", CdE 46 (1971) 223 33.

"Le directeur des travaux Minmose", MDAIK 37 (1981) 315-19.

Der Manuelian, P., Studies in the Reign of Amenophis II, HÄB 26 (Hildesheim 1987).

Desroches-Noblecourt, Chr., "À Propos de l'Obélisque de St.-J. de Latran", ASAE 50 (1950) 256-67.

"The Greatest Open Air Museum in the World in Danger", Museum 13 No.3 (1960) 173-94.

"Interpretation et datation d'une scène gravée sur deux fragments de recipient en albâtre provenant des fouilles du palais d'Ugarit, Ugaritica III (1956)

Desroches-Noblecourt, Chr. and C. Leblanc, "Considérations sur l'existence des divers temples de Monthou à travers les âges, dans le site de Tôd", BIFAO 84 (1984) 81-109.

Desroches-Noblecourt, Chr. et als., Ramsès le Grand exhibition (Paris 1976).

Dever, W., "Notes and News - Tel Gezer", IEJ 22 (1972) 158-60.

"Tower 5017 at Gezer: A Rejoinder", IEJ 23 (1973) 23-26.

Dewachter, M., "Les 'premiers fils royaux d'Amon'. Compléments et Remarques", RdE 35 (1984) 83-94.

"Le vice-roi Nehy et l'an 52 de Thoutmosis III", RdE 28 (1976) 151-53.

Dodson, A. and J.J. Janssen, "A Theban Tomb and its Tenants", JEA 75 (1989) 125-38.

Doresse, M. and J., "Le culte d'Aton sous la XVIIIe dynastie avant le schisme Amarnien, Journal Asiatique 233 (1941-42) 181-99.

Drenkhahn, R., "Bemerkungen zu dem Titel hkrt nswt", SAK 4 (1976) 57-66.

Drioton, E. and J. Vandier, L'Égypte. 4th edition (Paris 1962).

Drioton, E., "Rapport sur les fouilles de Médamoud 1926. Les Inscriptions", FIFAO (Cairo 1927).

Le Sphinx et les Pyramides de Giza (Cairo 1939).

"Trois Documents d'Époque Amarnienne", ASAE 43 (1942) 15-43.

Drower, M., "Syria c. 1550-1400 B.C.", Cambridge Ancient History II, 2nd edition, 417-525 (Cambirdge 1973).

Dümichen, J., Baugeschichte des Denderatempels und Beschreibung des einzelnen Theile des Bauwerkes nach den an seinen Mauern befindlichen Inschriften (Strassburg 1877).

Dunham, D., The Barkal Temples, Excavated by Geo. Andrew Reisner (Boston 1970).

Second Cataract Forts. Semna Kumma (Boston 1960).

Eaton-Krauss, M. and B. Fay, "Beobachtungen an den Memnonkolossen", GM 52 (1981) 25-29.

Edel, E. and J. Cerný, Gebel el-Shams (Cairo 1958).

Edel, E., Die Ortsnamenlisten aus dem Totentempel Amenophis' III. (Bonn 1966).

Edwards, I.E.S., "Egyptian Antiquities from the Acworth Collection", British Museum Quarterly 15 (1941-51) 55-57.

Hieroglyphic Texts from Egyptian Stelae etc., in the British Museum. VIII (London 1939).

"The Shetayet of Rosetau", in Egyptological Studies in Honor of Richard A. Parker (Hanover and London 1986) 27-36.

Eggebrecht, A., ed., Ägyptens Aufstieg zur Weltmacht [Catalogue of an exhibition in Hildesheim Roemer-und Pelizaeus-Museum] (Mainz 1987).

Erman, A., Neuägyptische Grammatik (Leipzig 1933).
"Die Sphinxstele", Sitzungsberichte Königliche Akademie, Berlin 6 (1904) 428-37.
"Neues aus den Tafeln von el Amarna", ZÄS 28 (1890) 112.

Erman, A. und H. Grapow, Worterbuch der Aegyptischen Sprache, I-VI (Leipzig 1926-31); Belegstellen I-VI (1940-55).

Essam El-Banna, "L'Obélisque de Sesostris I à Heliopolis", RdE 33 (1981) 3-9.

Eyre, C., "Work and the Organisation of Work in the New Kingdom", Labor in the Ancient Near East, Marvin Powell, ed., (Winona Lake 1987) 167-220.

Fakhry, A., "A Fortnight's Digging at Medinet Quta (Fayoum)", ASAE 40 (1941) 897-909.

Faulkner, R., "Egyptian Military Organization", JEA 39 (1953) 32-47.
A Concise Dictionary of Middle Egyptian (Oxford 1962).

Fay, B., Egyptian Museum Berlin [Catalogue Berlin 1985].

Fazzini, R. and J. Manning, "Archeological Work at Thebes", Newsletter for ARCE 101/02 (1977) 12-27.

Fecht, Wortakzent und Silbenstruktur (Glückstadt 1960).

Frandsen, J.P., "Heqareshu and the Family of Tuthmosis IV", Acta Orientalia 37 (1976) 5-10.

Gaballa, G., Narrative in Egyptian Art (Mainz 1976).
"Nufer, Third Prophet of Amun", MDAIK 26 (1970) 49-54.

Gabet, "Documents relatifs aux fouilles de Mariette", Rec. Trav 12 (1892) 215-17.

Gabra, G. and A. Farid, "Neue Materialien zu königlichen Baudenkmälern in Edfu", MDAIK 37 (1981) 181-86.

Gardiner, A., Ancient Egyptian Onomastica, Text I-II (Oxford 1947).
Egypt of the Pharaohs (Oxford 1961).
Egyptian Grammar, 3rd edition (London 1957).
"Horus the Behdetite", JEA 30 (1944) 23-60.

Gardiner, A., T.E. Peet, revised by J. Černý, The Inscriptions of Sinai I, 2nd edition (London 1952). edited and completed by J. Černý,
The Inscriptions of Sinai II (London 1955).

Gardiner, A., Late-Egyptian Stories (Brussels 1932).
Ramesside Administrative Documents (London 1948)
"Ramesside Texts relating to the taxation and transport of corn", JEA 27 (1941) 19-73.
The Wilbour Papyrus. 4 vols. (Oxford 1941-52).

Gauthier, H., "Les Fils Royaux de Kouch", Rec. Trav. 39 (1920) 179-238.
Le Livre des Roi d'Égypte, II, Mémoires publiés par les Membres de L'institut Français d'Archéologie Orientale du Caire 17-21 (Cairo 1907-17).
"Le Protocole de Thoutmosis IV", ASAE 10 (1910) 200-02.

Germer, R., "Problems of Science in Egyptology", Science in Egyptology, A.R. David, ed., (Manchester 1986).

Gitton, M., Les divines épouses de la 18e dynastie (Paris 1984).
L'Épouse du Dieu Ahmès Néfertary (Paris 1975).
"Néfertary II", Orientalia Lovaniensia Periodica 8 (1977) 125-27.

Giveon, R. and B. Saas, "Explorations at Serabit El-Khadim-1977", Tel Aviv 5 (1979) 170-74.

Giveon, R., The Impact of Egypt on Canaan. Orbis Biblicus et Orientalis 20 (Freiburg 1978).

"Some Egyptological Considerations concerning Ugarit", Ugarit in Retrospect. Fifty Years of Ugarit and Ugaritic. (Winona Lake, Ind. 1981) 55- 58.

"Tuthmosis IV and Asia", JNES 28 (1969) 54-59.

Glanville, S.R.K., "Records of a royal dockyard of the time of Tuthmosis III: Papyrus British Museum 10056", ZÄS 66 (1931) 105-121, 1*-8*.

"Records of a royal dockyard of the Time of Tuthmosis III, II, ZÄS 68 (1933) 7-41.

"Scribes' Palettes in the British Museum", JEA 18 (1932) 53-61.

Godron, G., "Recherches sur quelques inscriptions hiéroglyphiques de la 18 dynastie découverte à Faras", Orientalia N.S. 40 (1971) 373- 85.

Goedicke, H., "Papyrus Anastasi VI 51-61", SAK 14 (1987) 83-98.

rev. of E.Pardey, Untersuchungen zur Ägyptischen Provinzialverwaltung bis zum Ende des Alten Reiches, in JARCE 14 (1977) 122-23.

Goetze, A., "Die Pestgebete des Mursilis", Kleinasiatische Forschungen 1 (1930) 161-252.

"The Struggle for Syria. Domination of Syria (1400-1300 B.C.)", Cambridge Ancient History, 2nd ed. II Chapter XVIII, 1-26.

Golenischeff, V., Les Papyrus hiératiques nos. 1115, 1116A, et 1116B de l'Ermitage Impérial à St. Petersbourg (Leipzig 1913).

Gomaa, F., Chaemwese Sohn Ramses' II, und Hoherpriester von Memphis AA 27 (Wiesbaden 1973).

Graefe, E., rev. of Gitton, L'Épouse du Dieu, in BiOr 33 (1976) 316-32.

Untersuchungen zur Verwaltung und Geschichte der Institution der Gottesgemahlin des Amun vom Beginn des Neuen Reiches bis zur Spätzeit. Band 1: Katalog und Materialsammlung. Band II: Analyse und Indices AA 37 (Wiesbaden 1981).

Grdseloff, B., "L'insigne du grand juge égyptien", ASAE 40 (1940) 185-202.

Griffith, F.L..Hieratic Papyri from Kahun and Gurob (London 1898) 2 vols.

Groll, S. I., "The Egyptian Administrative System in Syria and Palestine in the 18th Dynasty", Fontes Atque Pontes 234-42.

Güterbock, H., "The Deeds of Suppiluliuma as told by his son, Mursili II", JCS 10 (1956) 41-68; 75-98; 107-130.

"Mursili's account of Suppiluliuma's dealings with Egypt", RHA 19 (1960) fasc. 66-67. 57-63.

Guidotti, C., "Ceramica dipinta dell'epoca di Tutmosi IV a Gurna", Egitto e Vicino Oriente 4 (1981) 95-107.

Gundlach, R., "Mutemwia", Lexikon der Ägyptologie IV (Wiesbaden 1982) 251-52.

Gunn, B., "Additions to the Collections of the Egyptian Museum, 1928", ASAE 29 (1929) 84.

Habachi, L., "Découverte de Karnak", ASAE 38 (1938) 80-81.

"The Graffiti and Work of the Viceroys of Kush", Kush 5 (1957) 13-36.

"Tomb No 226 of the Theban Necropolis and its unknown Owner", Festschrift für Siegfried Schott zur seinem 70. Geburtstag. 6l-70.

Hachmann, R., "Die ägyptische Verwaltung in Syrien wahrend der Amarnazeit*", ZDPV 98 (1982) 17-49.

Haeny, G., Basilikale Anlagen in der ägyptischen Baukunst des Neuen Reiches, Bf. 9 (Cairo 1970).

Hall, H.R., Hieroglyphic Texts from Egyptian Stelae, etc.,in the British Museum V, VII (London 1914-25).

Hallo, W., and W.K. Simpson, The Ancient Near East, A History (New York 1971).

Hammad, M., "Zwei von Ramses II neubenützte Steine", <u>ASAE</u> 55 (1958) 200-02.

Hari, R., <u>Horemheb et la Reine Moutnedjmet ou la fin d'un dynastie</u> (Genève 1964).

"Un Scribe des Recrues identifié.", <u>Aegyptus</u> 47 (1967) 58-66.

Harris, J.E., and K.R. Weeks, <u>X-raying the Pharaohs</u> (New York 1973).

Harris, J.R., "Contributions to the History of the Eighteenth Dynasty, I", <u>SAK</u> 2 (1975) 95-98.

"Kiya", <u>CdE</u> 49 (1974) 25-30.

"Nefernefruaten Regnans", <u>Acta Orientalia</u> 36 (1974) 11-21

in <u>Arts in Asia</u> (Nov.-Dec. 1983) 76-79.

Hassan, S., <u>The Great Sphinx and its Secrets. Excavations at Giza, 1936-37</u>, vol. VIII.(Cairo 1953).

<u>Excavations at Giza.</u> IX (Cairo 1960).

<u>The Sphinx, its History in the Light of Recent Excavations</u> (Cairo 1947).

Hayes, W., "Inscriptions from the Palace of Amenhotep III", <u>JNES</u> 10 (1951) 35-40; 82-104, 156-83; 231-42.

<u>Royal Sarcophagi of the XVIIIth Dynasty</u> (Princeton 1935).

<u>The Scepter of Egypt II. The Hyksos Period and the New Kingdom (1675-1080 B.C.)</u> (New York 1959).

"Selection of Tuthmoside Ostraca from Der el-Bahri", <u>JEA</u> 46 (1960) 29ff.

Helck, H.W.,"Der Anfang des Papyrus Turin 1900 und 'Recycling' im alten Ägypten", <u>CdE</u> 49 (1984) 242- 47.

<u>Die Beziehungen Ägyptens zu Vorderasien im 3.und 2. Jahrtausend v. Chr.</u> ÄA 5 (Wiesbaden 1962); 2nd edition (1971).

"Das Datum der Schlacht von Megiddo", <u>MDAIK</u> 28 (1972) 101-02.

<u>Der Einfluss der Militärführer in der 18. ägyptischen Dynastie</u> UGAÄ 14 (Leipzig   1939).

"Haremhab und das Sothisdatum des Pap. Ebers", <u>GM</u> 67 (1983) 47-49.

<u>Historisch-Biographische Texte der 2. Zwischenzeit und neue Texte der 18. Dynastie</u> (Wiesbaden 1975).

and E. Otto, W. Westendorf, <u>Lexikon der Ägyptologie</u> (Wiesbaden 1975-1987).

<u>Materialien zur Wirtschaftsgeschichte des Neuen Reiches</u> I-II (Wiesbaden 1961).

"Sozial Stellung und Grablage", <u>JESHO</u> 5 (1962) 225-43.

"Das Thebanische Grab 43", <u>MDAIK</u> 17 (1961) 99-110.

"Die Tochterheirat ägyptischer Könige", <u>CdE</u> 44 (1969) 22-26.

"Überlegungen zur Geschichte der 18. Dynastie" <u>Oriens Antiquus</u> 8 (1969) 281-327.

<u>Untersuchungen zu Manetho und den agyptischen Königslisten</u> UGAÄ 18 (Berlin 1956).

<u>Urkunden der 18. Dynastie and Übersetzung zu den Heften 17-22</u> (Berlin 1955-1961).

<u>Zur Verwaltung des Mittleren und Neuen Reich</u> PÄ 3 (Leiden 1958).

<u>Idem.. Register</u> (Leiden 1972).

Hermann, A., <u>Die ägyptische Königsnovelle</u> LÄS 10 (Glückstadt 1938).

"Bruchstücke von Inschriften und Darstellungen vom Kom", <u>MDAIK</u> 5 (1934) 27.

Heyler, A., <u>Kemi</u> 15 (1959) 80-93, rev. of Norman Davies, <u>A Corpus of Inscribed Funerary Cones I</u>

Hilton Price, F.G., <u>A Catalogue of The Egyptian Antiquities in the Possession of F.C. Hilton.</u> 2 vols.(London 1897-1908).

Hintze, F., "Preliminary Note on the Epigraphic Expedition to Sudanese Nubia",

Kush 12 (1964) 40-42.
"Preliminary Note on the Epigraphic Expedition to Sudanese Nubia", Kush 13 (1965)13-16.
Hölscher, U., Das Grabdenkmal des Königs Chephren (Leipzig 1912).
Hornemann, B., Types of Ancient Egyptian Statuary (Kopenhagen 1951-1969).
Hornung, E. and E. Stahelin, Studien zum Sedfest, Aegyptiaca Helvetica 1 (Geneva 1974).
Hornung, E., Untersuchungen zur Chronologie und Geschichte des Neuen Reiches. ÄA 11 (Wiesbaden 1964).
"Zur geschichtlichen Rolle des Königs in der 18. Dynastie", MDAIK 15 (1957) 120-33.
Houwink Ten Cate, Ph., rev. of Kitchen, Suppululiuma and the Amarna Pharaohs. in BiOr 20 (1963) 270-76.
Isherwood, I., H. Jarvis, and R.A. Fawcitt, "Radiology of the Manchester Mummies" in Manchester Museum Mummy Project Multidisciplinary Research on Ancient Egyptian Mummified Remains, A.R. David, ed. (Manchester 1979) 25-64.
Jacquet-Gordon, H. and C. Bonnet, J. Jacquet, "Pnubs and the Temple of Tabo on Argo Island", JEA 55 (1969) 103-11.
Jacquet,J., "Fouilles de Karnak Nord (4e Camp. 1971)", BIFAO 71 (1971).
James, T.G.H., Corpus of Hieroglyphic Inscriptions in the Brooklyn Museum I (Brooklyn 1974).
Introductory Guide to the Egyptian Collections (Cambridge 1964, paper).
Johnson, R., "Some Observations on the Relief and Painting Styles of Amenhotep III in Thebes", in The Art of Amenhotep III, L. Berman, ed. (Cleveland 1990)
Junge, F., Elephantine XI. Funde und Bauteile 1.-7. Kampagne, 1969-1976. (Mainz 1983).
Kadish, G.E., "Old Kingdom Egyptian Activity in Nubia", JEA 52 (1966) 23-33.
Kaiser, W., Ägyptisches Museen Berlin (Staatliche Museem Preussischer Kulturbesitz) (Berlin 1967).
Kakosy, L., "Heliopolis", Lexikon der Ägyptologie II, 1111-13.
"Die weltanschauliche Krise des Neuen Reiches", ZÄS 100 (1975) 35-41.
Kaplony-Heckel, U., Ägyptische Handschriften I (Wiesbaden 1971).
Kees, H., Ancient Egypt: A Cultural Topography (Chicago 1961, paper).
"'Gottesvater' als Priesterklasse", ZÄS 86 (1961) 111-25.
Das Priestertum im Aegyptischen Staat vom Neuen Reich bis zur Spätzeit, and Nachträge PÄ 1 (Leiden 1953-58).
Kemp, B., Ancient Egypt Anatomy of a Civilization (London 1989).
"The Harim-Palace at Medinet el-Ghurab", ZÄS 105 (1978) 122-33.
Kenyon, K. "Palestine in the time of the Eighteenth Dynasty", Cambridge Ancient History, 2nd ed. II, 526-58, (Cambridge 1975).
Kitchen, K.A., rev. of Hughes Festschrift (SAOC 39) in Serapis 4 (1977-78) 65-80.
Ramesside Inscriptions, Historical and Biographical (Oxford 1969-).
Suppululiuma and the Amarna Pharaohs. A Study in Relative Chronology (Liverpool 1962).
Klengel, Horst, Geschichte Syriens in 2. Jahrtausend v.u. Zeit I-II (Berlin 1965-69).
Knudtzon, J.A., Die El-Amarna-Tafeln. 2 vols. (Leipzig 1915).
Koenig, Y. Catalogue des Etiquettes des Jarres hiératiques de Deir el-Médineh: Nos 6242-6497 Fascicle II. IFAO Documents et Fouilles [Cairo] 1980
Korosec, V., Hethitische Staatsverträge (Leipzig 1930).
Kozloff, A., "Paintings from the so-called Tomb of Nebamun in the British Museum",

abstract in NARCE 95 (1976) 8.

Krauspe, R., Ägyptisches Museum der Karl-Marx-Universitat Leipzig (Leipzig 1976).

Krauss, R., Das Ende der Amarnazeit, HÄB 7 (Hildesheim 1978).
   "Korrekturen und Ergänzungen zur Chronologie des MR und NR - ein Zwischenbericht", GM 70 (1984) 37-43.
   Sothis-und Monddaten.Studien zur astronomischen und technischen Chronologie Altägyptens HÄB 20 (Hildesheim 1985).

Krieger, Paule, "Une Statuette de Roi-Faucon", RdE 12 (1960) 39-58.

Kuhne, C., Die Chronologie der internationalen Korrespondenz von El Amarna, AOAT 17 (Neukirchen-Vluyn 1973).

Kuentz, C., Obélisques Nos 1308-1315. 17001-17036. Catalogue Général (Cairo 1932).

Leahy, M.A., Excavations at Malkata and the Birket Habu 1971-1974. The Inscriptions (Warminster 1978).

Leclant, J., "Les Inscriptions 'Éthiopiennes' sur la Porte du IV Pylone du Grand Temple d'Amon à Karnak", RdE 8 (1951) 101-20.
   Montouemhat, Bibl. d'Étude 35 (Cairo 1961).

Leemans, C., Description raisonnée des Monumens égyptiens du Musée d'Antiquités des Pays-bas à Leide (Leiden 1840).

Lefebvre, G., Histoire des grand Prêtres d'Amon de Karnak jusqu'à la XXIe dynastie (Paris 1929).

Legrain, G., Archaeological Reports 1907-1908. EES (London 1908).
   "Fragments de Canopes", ASAE 4 (1903) 138-49.
   "Le Logement et Transport des Barques sacrées et des statues des dieux dans quelques temples égyptiens", BIFAO 13 (1917) 1-76.
   "Notes prises à Karnak. XI. Sur un fragment de stela", Rec.Trav. 26 (1904) 222-23.
   Répertoire généalogique et onomastique du Musée du Caire (Geneva 1908).
   "Seconde Note sur des fragments de canopes", ASAE 5 (1904) 139-41.
   Statues et Statuettes de rois et de particuliers Nos 42001-42250. Catalogue Général, 4 vols. (Cairo 1906-25).

Lepsius, C.R., Denkmaeler aus Aegypten und Aethiopien. 12 vols. (Berlin 1849-58).
   Denkmaeler aus Aegypten und Aethiopien. Text. compiled by Edouard Naville and Ludwig Borchardt with Kurt Sethe, 5 vols. (Leipzig 1897-1913).

Letellier, B., "La Cour à Peristyle de Thoutmosis IV à Karnak", in Hommages à la Mémoire de Serge Sauneron, I, Bibl. d'étude 81 (Cairo 1979).
   "La Cour à Peristyle de Thoutmosis IV à Karnak", BSFE 84 (1979) 33-49.

Lichtheim, M., Ancient Egyptian Literature (Berkeley 1973).

Lindblad, I., Royal Sculpture of the Early Eighteenth Dynasty Medelhavsmuseet Memoir 5 (Stockholm 1984).

Loat, L., Gurob (London 1905).

Lopez, J., and J. Yoyotte, rev. of A. Schulman, Military Rank in BiOr 26 (1969) 3-19.

Loret, V., Les Tombeau de Thoutmes III et d'Amenophis II et la cachette royale de Biban-el-Molouk (Cairo 1889).

Lorton, D., The Juridical Terminology of International Relations in Egyptian Texts through Dyn. XVIII (Baltimore 1974).
   rev. of R. Giveon, Les Bedouins Shosou des Documents Égyptiens in JARCE 9 (1971-72) 147-50.
   "The so-called 'Vile' Enemies of the king of Egypt (in the Middle Kingdom and Dynasty XVIII)", JARCE 10 (1973) 65-70.

Lovejoy, C.O., "Dental Wear in the Libben Population: Its functional Pattern and Role in the Determination of Adult Skeletal Age at Death", <u>American Journal of Physical Anthropology</u> 68 (1985) 47-56.

Lovejoy, C.O., R.S. Meindl, R.P. Mensforth, T.J. Barton, "Multifactorial Determination of Skeletal Age at Death:A Method and Blind Tests of its Accuracy", <u>American Journal of Physical Anthropology</u> 68 (1985) 1-14.

Lovejoy, C.O., R.S. Meindl, T.R. Pryzbeck, R.P. Mensforth, "Chronological Metamorphosis of the Auricular Surface of the Ilium: A New Method for the Determination of Adult Skeletal Age at Death", <u>American Journal of Physical Anthropology</u> 68 (1985) 15-28.

Luft, U., "Noch einmal zum Ebers-Kalender", <u>GM</u> 92 (1986) 69-77.

Luxor Museum, <u>The Luxor Museum of Ancient Egyptian Art Catalogue</u> (Cairo 1979). J. Romano, editor and principal author.

Malamat, A., "Campaigns of Amenhotep II and Thutmose IV to Canaan", <u>Scripta Hierosolymitana</u> 8, <u>Studies in the Bible.</u> 218-31 (Jerusalem 1961).

Malek, J, <u>Topographical Bibliography of Ancient Egyptian Hieroglyphic Texts, Reliefs and Paintings</u>, 2nd edition, Vol. III. (Oxford 1980-)

Manniche, L. <u>Lost Tombs, A Study of Certain Eighteenth Dynasty Monuments in the Theban Necropolis</u> (London 1988).
<u>City of the Dead</u> (Chicago 1987).

Mariette, F.A., <u>Abydos: description des fouilles executees sur l'emplacement de cette ville</u> (Paris 1869-80).
<u>Catalogue général des monuments d'Abydos découverts pendant les fouilles de cette ville</u> (Paris 1880).
<u>Denderah: Description général du grand temple de cette ville, Supp.</u> vol. 6 (Paris 1875).
<u>Karnak: étude topographique et archéologique avec un appendice comprenant les principaux texts hiéroglyphiques découverts ou recueillis pendant les fouilles executées à Karnak</u> (Leipzig 1875).
<u>Monuments Divers recueillis en Egypte et en Nubie</u> (Paris 1889).
<u>Les Papyrus Égyptiens du Musée de Boulaq (P. Boul. XVIII)</u> (Cairo 1871).
<u>Le Serapéum du Memphis</u> (Paris 1857).

Martin, K., <u>Ein Garantsymbol des Lebens. Untersuchungen zu Ursprung und Geschichte der altägyptischen Obelisken bis zum Ende des Neuen Reiches</u> HÄB 13 Hildesheim 1977).

Marucchi, 0., <u>Gli Obelischi egiziani di Roma</u> (Rome 1898).

Maspero, G., <u>Guide du Visiteur au Musée du Caire</u> (Cairo 1915).

Maystre, C., "Excavations at Tabo, Argo Island, 1965-1968", <u>Kush</u> 15 (1967-68) 196ff.

McKern, T.W. and T.D. Stewart, "Skeletal age changes in young American Males", <u>Technical report EP-45.</u> (Natick, Mass.1957) Quartermaster Research and Development Command.

Megally, M., "À Propos du Papyrus CGC 58070", <u>BIFAO</u> 74 (1974) 161-69.

Meindl, R.S., C.O. Lovejoy, R.P. Mensforth, R.A. Walker, "A Revised Method of Age Determination Using the Os Pubis, With a Review and Tests of Accuracy of Other Current Methods of Pubic Symphyseal Aging", <u>American Journal of Physical Anthropology</u> 68 (1985) 29-45.

Mekhitarian, A., <u>Egyptian Painting</u> (Geneva 1954).
"Un peintre thébain de la XVIIIe dynastie", <u>MDAIK</u> 15 (1957) 186-92.

Meltzer, E., "More Evidence of Thutmose IV in Asia", abstract in <u>NARCE</u> 91 (1974) 32.

Mercer, S., The Tell el-Amarna Tablets I (Toronto 1939).

Merrillees, R.S., The Cypriote Bronze Age Pottery Found in Egypt, Studies in Mediterranean Archaeology 18 (London 1968).

Mertz, B., Certain Titles of the Egyptian Queens and their bearing on the hereditary right to the throne, an unpublished dissertation, University of Chicago 1952.

Meyer, Ed., Geschichte des Altertums II, 3rd edition (Stuttgart 1953).

Michalowski, K., Faras Die Kathedrale aus dem Wüstensand (Einsiedeln-Köln-Zürich 1967).

Minto, A., Il Regio Museo Archeologico di Firenze (Rome 19831).

Moftah, R., Studien zum Ägyptischen Königsdogma im Neuen Reich, Deutsches Archaeologisches Institut Abteilung Kairo, Sonderschrift 20 (Mainz 1985).

Mogensen, M., La Glyptothèque Ny Carlsberg. La Collection Égyptienne, 2 vols. (Copenhagen 1930).

Stèles Égyptiennes au Musée National de Stockholm (Kopenhagen 1919).

Mond, R. and O. Myers, Temples of Armant. Text. (London 1940).

DeMorgan, J., Catalogue des Monuments et Inscriptions de l'Égypte Antique I, 1884-1909 (Vienna 1894).

Moursi, M., Die Hohenpriester des Sonnengottes von der Frühzeit Ägyptens bis zum Ende des Neuen Reiches MÄS 26 (Munich 1972).

"Corpus der Mnevis-Stelen und Untersuchungen zum Kult der Mnevis-Stiere in Heliopolis II", SAK 14 (1987) 225-38.

Muhammad, A.Q., "Preliminary report on the Excavations carried out in the Temple of Luxor, Seasons 1958-1959 and 1959-1960", ASAE 60 (1969) 227-79.

Müller, D., rev. of E. Hornung, Studien zum Sedfest in BiOr 33 (1976) 171-72.

Müller, I., Die Verwaltung der nubischen Provinz im Neuen Reich, 3 vols., unpublished dissertation, 1975.

Murnane, W.J., Ancient Egyptian Coregencies, SAOC 40 (Chicago 1977).

"The Sed Festival: A Problem in Historical Method", MDAIK 37 (1981) 369-76.

Murray, M.A., Catalogue of Egyptian Antiquities in the National Museum of Antiquities (Edinburgh 1900).

Mysliwiec, K., Le Portrait Royal dans le Bas-Relief du Nouvel Empire (Varsovie 1976).

Nasr, M., "The Theban Tomb 261 of Kha[c]emwese in Dra[c] Abu el-Naga[c]", SAK 15 (1988) 233-42.

Nash, W.F., "Notes on some Egyptian Antiquities", PSBA 29 (1907) 175.

Naville, E., The Temple of Deir el Bahri III (London 1898).

Nelson, M., A-M Layrette, G. Lecuyot, "Les Dispositions du Ramesseum", ASAE 68 (1982).

Newberry, P., "Discovery of the Tomb of Thotmes IV at Bibân el-Muluk", PSBA 25 (1903) 111-12.

"Extracts from my Notebook", PSBA 25 (1903) 358-64.

"Extracts from my Notebook", PSBA 24 (1902) 249.

"The Sons of Tuthmosis IV", JEA 14 (1928) 82-85

Nims, C., "Second Tenses in Wenamun", JEA 54 (1968) 162ff.

Thebes of the Pharaohs: Pattern for every City (London 1965).

O'Connor, D., "The Locations of Yam and Kush", JARCE 23 (1986) 27-50.

Osing, J., Die Nominalbildung des Ägyptischen (Mainz 1976).

Otten, H., Fischer Weltgeschichte III (Frankfurt 1966).

Otten, E., Topographie des Thebanischen Gaues (Leipzig 1952).

Page, A., Egyptian Sculpture Archaic to Saite from the Petrie Collection

(Warminster 1976).

Parker, R., "The Lunar Dates of Thutmose III and Ramesses II", JNES 16 (1957) 39-42.

rev. of Hornung, Untersuchungen in RdE 19 (1967) 185-89.

"Some Reflections on the lunar dates of Thutmose III and Ramesses II", in Studies in Ancient Egypt, the Aegean, and the Sudan. Essays in Honor of Dows Dunham, W.K. Simpson and W. M. Davis, eds. (Boston 1982) 146-48.

Peet, T.E., The Rhind Mathematical Papyrus (Liverpool 1923).

Pendlebury, J.D.S., The City of Akhenaten II, III (London 1933-51).

Peterson, B.J., "Hatschepsut und Nebhepetre Mentuhotep", CdE 42 (1967) 266-68.

Petrie, W.F., Buttons and Design Scarabs illustrated by the Egyptian collection in University College, London (London 1925).

Petrie, W.F., and E. Mackay, Heliopolis, Kafr Ammar and Shurafa (London 1915)

Petrie, W.F., A History of Egypt II (London 1924).

Illahun, Kahun and Gurob 1889-90 (London 1891).

Kahun, Gurob and Hawara (London 1890).

Memphis I (London 1909).

Nebesheh and Defenneh (London 1888).

The Palace of Apries (Memphis II) (London 1909).

Scarabs and Cylinders with names illustrated by the Egyptian collection in University College, London (London 1917).

A Season in Egypt, 1887 (London 1888).

Six Temples at Thebes 1896 (London 1897).

Petrie, W.F. in R. Engelbach, Riqqeh and Memphis VI (London 1915).

Pillet, M., "Rapport sur les travaux de Karnak", ASAE 24 (1924) 53-58.

Polotsky, H.J., Collected Papers (Jerusalem 1971).

"Les Transpositions du Verbe en Égyptien classique", Israel Oriental Studies 6 (1976) 1-50.

Porter, B. and R. Moss, Topographical Bibliography of Ancient Egyptian Hieroglyphic Texts, Reliefs and Paintings, 7 vols. (Oxford 1927-51).

Idem., 2nd edition, I,l; I,2 (Oxford 1960-).

Porter, B., and R. Moss,Idem., revised and expanded by J. Malek, 2nd edition, II, (Oxford 1972-).

Pridik, Alexander, Mut-em-wija, die Mutter Amenhoteps' III. (Dorpat 1932).

Pritchard, J., ed., Ancient Near Eastern Texts Relating to the Old Testament. 3rd edition with Supplement (Princeton 1969).

Quibbell, J.E., The Ramesseum and the Tomb of Ptah-hetep (London 1898).

Radwan, A., Die Darstellungen des regierenden Königs und seiner Familienangehörigen in den Privatgräbern der 18. Dynastie, MÄS 21 (Berlin 1969)

"Zur bildlichen Gleichsetzung des agyptischen Konigs mit der Gottheit", MDAIK 31 (1975) 102ff.

Rainey, A.F., "Amenhotep II's Campaign to Takhsi", JARCE 10 (1973) 71-75.

Ranke, H., Die ägyptischen Personennamen. 3 vols. (Glückstadt 1925-78).

"Keilschriftliches", ZÄS 56 (1920) 69-75.

Redford, D.B., The Akhenaten Temple Project I (Warminster 1976).

"The Coregency of Tuthmosis III and Amenophis II", JEA 51 (1965) 107-22.

History and Chronology of the Eighteenth Dynasty of Egypt: Seven Studies (Toronto 1967).

"The Hyksos Invasion in History and Tradition", Orientalia 39 (1970) 1-51.

"On the Chronology of the Egyptian Eighteenth Dynasty", JNES 25 (1966) 113-24.

Pharaonic King-Lists, Annals and Day-Books (Mississauga, Ontario 1986)

"Studies on Akhenaten at Thebes", JARCE 12 (1975) 9-14.

"The Sun Disc in Akhenaten's Program I.. Its Worship and Antecedents", JARCE 13 (1976) 47-62.

Reeves, C.N., "Belzoni, the Egyptian Hall, and the date of a long-known sculpture", JEA 75 (1989) 235-37.

"The Tomb of Tuthmosis IV: Two Questionable Attributions", GM 44 (1981) 49-55.

Reiser, E., Der Königliche Harim in alten Ägypten und seine Verwaltung (Vienna 1972).

Reisner, G.A., "The Barkal Temples in 1916", JEA 5 (1918) 99ff.

Renouf, P., "The Royal Tombs at Biban el-Moluk and 'Enigmatical' Writings", ZÄS 12 (1974) 101-05.

Rhind, H., Thebes, its tombs and their Tenants (London 1862).

Ricke, H., Die Tempel Nektanebos' II in Elephantine. Bf 9 (Cairo 1960).

Der Totentempel Thutmoses' III. Bf 3 (Glückstadt 1939).

Riefstahl, E., Ancient Egyptian Glass and Glazes in the Brooklyn Museum (Brooklyn 1968).

Robichon,C. with P. Barguet and J. Leclant, Karnak-Nord IV, 1949-51. FIFAO 25 (Cairo 1954).

Robins, G., "Anomalous proportions in the tomb of Haremhab (KV 57)", GM 65 (1983) 91-96.

"The God's Wife of Amon in the Eighteenth Dynasty in Egypt", in Images of Women in Antiquity (London 1983) A. Cameron and A. Kuhrt, eds., 65-78.

"The Value of the Estimated Ages of the Royal Mummies at Death as Historical Evidence", GM 45 (1981) 63-68.

"S3t nsw n ht.f Tj^{c}3", GM 57 (1982) 55-56.

Roeder, G., Hermopolis 1929-39 (Hildesheim 1959).

Naos Nos 7001-70050, Catalogue Général (Leipzig 1914).

Romer, J., The Valley of the Kings (London 1981).

Ruffle, J., The Egyptians (Ithaca, New York 1977).

Sakurai, K., S. Yoshimura, and J. Kondo, Comparative Studies of Noble Tombs in Theban Necropolis (Tomb Nos.8, 38,39, 48, 50, 54, 57, 63,64,66,74,89,90,91,107,120,139,147,151,181,201,253,295)(WasedaUniversityTokyo 1988).

Säve-Söderbergh, T., Ägypten und Nubien (Lund 1941).

Four Eighteenth Dynasty Tombs.Private Tombs at Thebes I (Oxford 1957).

Saleh, M. and H. Sourouzian, Official Catalogue.The Egyptian Museum Cairo (Mainz 1987).

Sander-Hansen, C., Das Gottesweib des Amun (Copenhagen 1940).

El Sayed Higazy, "Découverte d'une stèle de Thoutmosis IV sur le parvis du temple de Louqsor", Dossiers d'histoire et d'archéologie 101 (January 1986) 20

El Sayed Higazy and B. Bryan, "A New Stela of Thutmose IV from the Luxor Temple", Varia Aegyptiaca 2 (1986) 93-100.

El Sayed Higazy and M. Tosi, A Theban Private Tomb. Tomb No. 295 ADAIK 45 (Mainz 1983).

Schäfer, H., "Altes und Neues zur Kunst und Religion von Tell el-Amarna", ZÄS 55 (1919) 32-36.

"Ein angeblicher Skarabäus Thutmosis des IV mit Nennung des Gottes Aton", OLZ 9/10 (1931) 788-91.

Scharff, A., "Briefe aus Illahun", ZÄS 59 (1924) 20-51; 51-55; Anhang: 1-12.

"Ein Rechnungsbuch des königlichen Hofes aus der 13. Dynastie", ZÄS 57 (1922) 51-68; 1**-24**.

Scheil, V., "Le Tombeau de Rat'eserkasenb", Mém Miss. V, pt.II (1894).

Schenkel, W., "Die Gräber des P3tnf.j und eines Unbekannten in der thebanischen Nekropole (nr. 128 und Nr. 129)", MDAIK 31 (1975) 127-58.

Schiaparelli, E., La tomba intatta dell'architetto Cha nella necropoli di Tebe. Relazione sui lavori della Missione archeologica italiana in Egitto. 2 vols. (Turin 1923-27).

Schmitz, B., Untersuchungen zum Titel s3-nj śwt "Königssohn". (Bonn 1976).

Schmitz, F-J., Amenophis I. HÄB 6 (Hildesheim 1978).

Schoske, S. and D. Wildung, Ägyptische Kunst München (Munich 1985).

Schott, S., in H. Junker, "Bericht über die vom Deutschen Institut für Ägyptische Altertumskunde nach dem Ostdelta-Rand unternommene Erkundungsfahrt", MDAIK 1 (1930) 1-37.

Schulman, A., "Diplomatic Marriage in the Egyptian New Kingdom", JNES 38 (1979) 177-93.

"The King's Son in the Wadi Natrun", BASP 15 (1978) 103-13.

Military Rank, Title and Organization in the Egyptian New Kingdom. MÄS 6 (Berlin 1964).

"The Nubian War of Akhenaton", L'égyptologie en 1979 Tome II, Colloques internationaux du Centre National de la Recherche Scientifique (Paris 1982) 299-316.

"Some Observations on the Military Background of the Amarna Period", JARCE 3 (1964) 51-68.

"Some Remarks on the Alleged 'Fall' of Senmut", JARCE 8 (1969-70) 29-48.

Scott, G., Ancient Egyptian Art at Yale [New Haven 1986].

Seipel, W., Bilder für die Ewigkeit Stadtmuseum Linz, Nordico, 3 september bis 30. Oktober 1983.

"Hatshepsut I", Lexikon der Ägyptologie II, 1045.

Sethe, K., Aegyptische Lesestücke zum Gebrauch im akademischen Unterricht (Leipzig 1924).

Untersuchungen zur Geschichte und Altertumskunde Agyptens I (Leipzig 1896).

Urkunden der 18. Dynastie. 16 parts in 4 vols. (Leipzig 1906-09).

Shedid, Abdel Ghaffar, Stil der Grabmalereien in der Zeit Amenophis' II ADAIK 66 (Mainz 1988).

Shorter, A., "Historical Scarabs of Tuthmosis IV and Amenophis III", JEA 17 (1931) 23-25.

"Additional Notes", JEA 18 (1932) 110-11.

Simons, J., Handbook for the Study of Egyptian Topographical Lists relating to Western Asia (Leiden 1937).

Simpson, W.K., Heka-Nefer and the Dynastic Material from Toshka and Arminna (New Haven and Philadelphia 1963).

"Kenotaph" in the Lexikon der Ägyptologie III, 387-91.

"The Letter to the Dead from the Tomb of Meru (N3737) at Nag'ed-Deir", JEA 52 (1966) 39-52.

"The Single-dated Monuments of Sesostris I: An Aspect of the Institution of Coregency in the Twelfth Dynasty", JNES 15 (1956) 214-19.

"Studies in the Twelfth Egyptian Dynasty I-II", JARCE 2 (1963) 53-63.

The Terrace of the Great God at Abydos: the Offering Chapels of Dynasties 12 and 13. (New Haven 1974).

"A Tomb Chapel Relief in the Reign of Amunemhet III and some Observations on the length of the reign of Sesostris III", CdE 47 (1972) 45-54.

Smith, G.E., "Notes sur la Momie de Thoutmosis IV. II. Report on the Physical Characters", ASAE 4 (1903) 110-12.

The Royal Mummies Nos 61051-61100. Catalogue Général (Cairo 1912).

Smith, H.S., The Fortress of Buhen. TheInscriptions. EES 48 (London 1976).

Spalinger, A.J., "Some Additional remarks on the Battle of Megiddo", GM 33 (1979) 47-54.

"Some Notes on the Battle of Megiddo and Reflections on Egyptian Military Writing",MDAIK 30 (1974) 221-30.

Speleer, L., Les Figurines Funéraires Égyptiennes (Brussels 1923)

Recueil des Inscriptions Égyptiennes (Brussels 1923)

Spiegelberg, W., "Die Datierung der Sphinxstele", OLZ 7 (1904) 288-91.

"Zur Datierung der Sphinxstele", OLZ 7 (1904) 343-44.

"Ein Gerichtsprotokoll aus der Zeit Tuthmosis' IV", ZÄS 63 (1928) 105-15.

"Ostraca hiératiques du Louvre", Rec. Trav. 16 (1896) 64-67.

Stadelmann, R., "Aus der Heidelberger Universitätssammlung Zwei Reliefs eines Rindervorstehers des Thot, names Hajja", MDAIK 21 (1966) 110-15.

"Die ḫntjw-š der Königsbezirk š n pr-ꜥꜣ und die Namen der Granbanlagen der Frühzeit", BIFAO Supp. 81 Bulletin du Centenaire (1981) 153-64.

Steindorff, G. and K. Seele, When Egypt Ruled the East, 2nd edition revised (Chicago 1957).

Stewart, H., Mummy Cases and Inscribed Funerary Cones (Warminster 1986).

"Some Pre-'Amarnah Sun-Hymns", JEA 46 (1960)83ff.

Stewart, T.D.,. "The rate of development of vertebral osteoarthritis in American whites and its significance in skeletal age identification", Leech 28 (1958) 144-51.

Stock, H., "Der Hyksos Chian in Boğazköy", MDOG 94 (1963) 73-80.

Surenhagen, D., Paritätische Staatsverträge aus hethitischer Sicht. Zu historischen Aussagen und literarischer Stellung des Textes CTH 379 (Pavia 1986).

Tanner, R., "Bemerkungen zur Sukzession der Pharaonen in der 12., 17. und 18. Dynastie (Fortsetzung)", ZÄS 102 (1975) 50-59.

Tawfik, S., "Aton Studies", MDAIK 29 (1973) 77-86.

Tefnin, R., "À Propos d'une Tête royale du Musée d'Aberdeen", CdE 49 (1974) 13-21.

Theodorides, A., "À propos de la loi dans l'Égypte pharaonique", RIDA 14 (1967)

"Le jugement en cause Neferabet contre Tyia", RIDA 30 (1983).

Thomas, E., The Royal Necropoleis of Thebes (Princeton 1966).

Todd, T.W., "Age Changes in the pubic bone. I. The male white pubis.", American Journal of Physical Anthropology 3 (1920) 285-334.

"Age changes in the pubic bone; roentgenographic differentiation", American Journal of Physical Anthropology 14 (1930) 255-71.

Troy, L., Patterns of Queenship in Ancient Egyptian Myth and History (Uppsala 1986).

Tylor, J.J. and S. Clarke, Wall Drawings and Monuments of El Kab; The Temple of Amenhetep III (London 1898).

Ungarelli, A., Interpretatio Obeliscorum Urbis ad Gregorium XVI (Rome 1842).

Valbelle, D., Les Ouvriers de la Tombe (Cairo 1985).

Valloggia, M., Recherche sur les "Messagers" (wpwtyw) dans les Sources Égyptiennes Profanes (Geneva 1976).

Vandersleyen, C., Les Guerres d'Amosis (Brussels 1971).
    rev of Gitton, L'Épouse du Dieu in JEA 64 (1978) 162-65.
    "Un titre du vice-roi Mérimose à Silsila", CdE 43 (1968).

Van de Walle, B., "Précisions nouvelles sur Sobek-Hotep, fils de Min", RdE 15 (1963) 77-85.

Vandier, J., Manuel d'archéologie égyptienne III (Paris 1958).

Van Siclen, C., "The Building History of the Tuthmosid Temple at Amada and the Jubilees of Tuthmosis IV", Varia Aegyptiaca 3 (1987) 53-66.
    The Alabaster Shrine of Amenhotep II (San Antonio 1986).
    "A Usurped Relief of Tuthmosis IV at Karnak", Varia Aegyptiaca 1 (1985) 75-79.

Vercoutter, J., "The Gold of Kush", Kush 7 (1959) 120-53.

Vergote, J., Toutankhamon dans les archives Hittites (Istanbul 1961).

Virey, P., "Le Tombeau de Khem, Seigneur de Thini", Mém Miss V, part I, 362-70 (Paris 1889).

Waddell, W.G., Manetho with an English Translation (London 1940).

Wagner, G., "Inscriptions grecques du temple de Karnak", BIFAO 70 (1971) 1-38.

Wegner, M., "Stilentwickelung der thebanischen Beamtengräber", MDAIK 4 (1933) 38-92; 93-164.

Weigall, A., "A Report on some Objects recently found in Sebakh", ASAE 8 (1907) 46.

Weil, A., A., Die Veziere des Pharaonenreiches (Strasbourg 1908).

Weill, R., Recueil des inscriptions égyptiennes du Sinai (Paris 1904).

Weinstein, J., "The Egyptian Empire in Palestine: A Reassessment*", BASOR 241 (1981) 1-28.
    Foundation Deposits in Ancient Egypt. an unpublished dissertation, University of Pennsylvania 1973.

Wente, E.F. and C. van Siclen III, "A Chronology of the New Kingdom", in Studies in Honor of George R. Hughes. SAOC 39 (Chicago 1976) 217-62.

Wente, E.F., "Revising Chronology", The Oriental Institute Report 1973-74 , 52-54.
    "Thutmose III's Accession and the Beginning of the New Kingdom", JNES 34 (1975) 265-72.

Werbrouck, M. and B. van de Walle, "La Tombe de Nakht", translation of "La Tombe de Nakht, Notice Sommaire" (1929) [Brussels 1972].

Wiedemann, A., Aegyptische Geschichte and Supp. (Gotha 1884-88).
    "Neuzeitliche Fälscherkunste", ZÄS 67 (1931) 126.

Wilkinson, J.G., Modern Egypt and Thebes II (London 1843).

Winlock, H., "The Tomb of Queen Inhapi. An Open Letter to the Editor", JEA 17 (1931) 107-10.

Wolf, W., "Amenhotep Vizekönig von Nubien", ZÄS 59 (1924) 157-58.
    "Vorläufer der Reformation Echnatons", ZÄS 59 (1924) 109-10.
    "Zwei Beiträge zur Geschichte der 18. Dynastie", ZÄS 65 (1929) 98-102.

Wreszinski, W., Atlas zur altägyptischen Kulturgeschichte I-III (Leipzig 1923-54).
    "Die Statue eines hohen Verwaltungsbeamten", ZÄS 67 (1931) 132-33.

Yeivin, Sh. "Amenophis II's Asianic Campaigns", JARCE 6 (1967) 119-28.

Yoyotte, J., "Les Adoratrices de la IIIe Periode Intermediaire, à propos d'un chef d'oeuvre rapporte par Champollion", BSFE 64 (1972) 31-52.

"A propos de l'Obelisque unique", <u>Kêmi</u> 14 (1957) 81-91.

"Un porche doré: La porte du IVe pylone au grand temple de Karnak", <u>CdE</u> 28 (1953) 28-38.

Žaba, Z., "Un Nouveau Fragment du Sarcophage de Merymose", <u>ASAE</u> 50 (1950) 509-14.

Zibelius, K., <u>Afrikanische Orts- und Völkernamen in hieroglyphischen und hieratischen Texten</u> (Wiesbaden 1972).

Zivie, A.-P., "Un chancelier nommé Nehesy", <u>Mélanges Adolphe Gutbub</u> (Montpelier 1984) 245-52.

"La Tombe d'un Officier de la XVIIIe Dynastie à Saqqara", <u>RdE</u> 31 (1979) 131-51.

"Tombes rupestres de la falaise du Bubasteion à Saqqarah - IIe et IIIe campagnes (1982-1983)", <u>ASAE</u> 70 (1985) 219-32.

<u>Le Courrier du CNRS</u> 49 (1983) 37-44.

"Trois saisons à Saqqarah: Les tombeaux du Bubasteion", <u>BSFE</u> 98 (1983) 40-56.

Zivie, C., "Une curieuse statue de la reine Ti'aa à Giza", <u>Mélanges Gamal Eddin Mokhtar</u> II (Cairo 1985) 389-401.

<u>Giza au Deuxième Millénaire. Bibl. d'étude</u> 70 (Cairo 1976).

"Tiaa", <u>Lexikon der Ägyptologie</u> VI, 4 (Wiesbaden 1985) 551-55.

Indices

The purpose of these indices is to help the reader find the locations of words mentioned in several chapters and which are not included by subheadings within chapters or in appendices. For lists of offices and officeholders the reader is directed to Chapter 5 and the appendices there.

Royal Names

Akhenaten (45), (46), (78), (134), (136), (161-163), (174), (180), (215), (220), (221), (309), (341, (352), (356), (361), (366)

Amenhotep II (5), (20), (24), (25), (34), (38), (40-43), (46), (48-50), (52), (54-59), (61-67), (69), (72-79), (81), (85), (88-91), (94), (96-108), (111), (113), (114), (116), (117), (119), (124), (125), (128-130), (139), (142-145), (149), (150), (153-156), (162), (164), (166), (173), (177), (182), (183), (188), (190), (191), (195), (197-199), (204), (206), (210), (216), (218), (219), (221), (225), (226), (231), (232), (238), (242), (243), (245), (248-250), (253), (255), (256), (258), (261), (262), (267), (269-271), (277), (279), (281), (282), (285), (288), (292), (300), (302), (308), (311), (315), (318), (328-331), (336-354), (356), (357), (360), (363-365)

Amenhotep III (5), (8), (21-250, (27), (36), (42), (45), (52-57), (60), (64), (66), (67), (70), (71), (77), (83), (86), (90), (101-105), (108), (112-122), (124), (129-131), (133), (134), (136), (137), (138), (152), (156), (158), (161-164), (168), (172), (173), (181), (183), (184), (185), (188), (190), (193-196), (203), (204), (206), (207), (212), (215), (219), (221), (226), (227), (231), (233), (235), (236), (238), (239), (242-245), (247-251), (253), (255), (257), (259), (261-263), (266), (267), (268), (269), (272-276), (278-282), (284-286), (289), (290), (300), (301), (302), (304), (305), (307), (308), (310), (315), (318), (320), (321), (324), (325), (330)

Chephren (Khafre) (109), (145), (149), (150), (155), (218), (327)

Hatshepsut (8), (9), (22), (28), (36), (40), (41), (43), (45), (61), (75), (95), (102), (117), (127), (128), (131), (132), (164), (174), (184), (188), (191), (206), (225), (234), (239), (249), (256), (271), (272), (276), (307), (312), (318), (319), (325), (351), (353)

Khufu (Cheops) (155), (166), (351)

Mentuhotep II (35), (36), (191)

Ramesses II (13), (14), (20-22), (31), (38), (52), (60), (62), (82), (84), (89), (109), (117), (133), (157), (158), (164), (165), (167-169), (174), (176), (177), (179), (181), (182), (184), (185), (187), (197), (237), (278), (318), (327), (338), (352)

Ramesses III (13), (21), (22), (52), (62), (164), (184)

Siptah (106), (107), (127)

Thutmose I   (20), (40), (49), (72), (74), (144), (162), (171), (172), (174), (175), (184), (188), (191), (205), (317), (360)

Thutmose II   (20), (40), (49), (72), (74), (102), (141), (164), (167), (169), (173), (197), (224)

Thutmose III   (5), (7-9), (13-17), (19-21), (24), (25), (28), (31), (33), (36), (40), (45-50), (62), (63), (71), (72), (74-76(), (78), (80), (81), (91), (93), (97), (99), (102-105), (112), (113), (121), (124), (131), (132), (136), (137), (138), (143), (144), (160), (164), (166), (167), (174-177), (179), (180), (184), (188), (192), (195), (197-199), (204-206), (227), (228), (230), (232), (236), (238), (242), (245-247), (249), (250), (255), (256), (258), (260), (267), (270), (271), (276), (280), (282), (292), (308), (312), (318), (323), (325), (331), (336), (338-3430, (345-348), (351), (353), (361-364)

Divine Names

Anukis   (201)

Astarte   (190), (194)

Amun-Re   (41), (42), (96), (97), (100), (101), (109), (131), (142), (150), (155),(156), (170), (173), (178-181), (183-186), (189), (196), (197), (199), (200), (202), (204), (214), (226), (264), (274), (276)

Atum   (40), (55), (60), (64), (66-69), (88), (90), (94), (95), (109), (143-146), (149), (150), (155), (158), (159), (172), (175), (177-179), (186), (197), (200-203), (215), (217), (226), (247), (276), (333), (354), (357)

Geb   (88), (94-96), (118), (146), (148), (154), (284), (351), (353)

Hathor (various)   (6), (44), (53), (56), (86), (93), (111), (113), (150), (166), (191), (201), (205), (211), (217), (219), (245), (349), (352)

Horemakhet   (38), (40), (41), (58-60), (64), (71), (88), (145), (146), (148-150), (152-156), (206), (219), (221), (351), (354)

Isis   (64), (68), (93), (95), (96), (115), (150), (156), (165), (201), (254), (352), (366)

Mut   (43), (44), (56), (73), (76), (84), (86), (93), (109), (114-117), (131), (133), (134), (150), (167), (169), (181), (211), (212), (219), (230), (258), (261), (276), (280), (352)

Onuris   (67), (253), (254), (258), (275), (276), (285), (296), (340)

Ptah   (6), (58), (60), (63), (66), (109), (111), (145), (149-151), (157-159), (180), (190), (200), (211), (219), (221), (243), (258), (273), (275), (284), (296), (302), (350)

Re-Horakhty   (41), (59), (66), (143), (150), (155), (159), (172), (179), (180), (199-203), (215), (221), (226), (349), (353)

Thoth   (23), (109), (150), (160), (163), (200), (201), (281), (305),

General Index

Artatama (118), (119), (263), (336), (337), (346), (347), (360), (363)

Deification (124), (134), (156), (185), (352), (365)

God's father (it ntr) (44-46), (50), (51), (54), (55), (60), (60), (68), (77), (78), (82),
    (134), (257-259), (270), (277), (295), (313)

God's wife (45), (72), (73), (80), (93-96), (98), (100-103), (106-110), (112), (117),
    (127), (128), (131), (135), (272), (276), (295)

Heb sed (hb sd) (14), (20), (21), (25), (36), (199-200),

Hekareshu (41), (44-46), (50-56), (73), (77), (78), (82-84), (114), (246), (259), (260),
    (262), (268), (294), (313), (314)

Hekarnehhe (41), (42), (45), (50), (51), (53-57), (62), (65), (77), (82-84), (139),
    (257), (259), (260), (262), (268), (280), (292-294), (298), (313-315), (349)

Horemhab (23-25), (27), (51), (54), (62), (78), (122), (249), (250), (271), (273),
    (274), (280), (282), (283), (285), (290), (292), (293), (295-300), (320), (321),
    (325), (353), (356)

Inebny (7-9)

inpw (42), (43), (76), (216)

Jubilee (4), (14), (20-23), (25), (35), (36), (72), (169), (199), (200), (285), (315),
    (351)

Konosso Stela (51), (216), (217), (267), (334), (335), (359)

Meryt-re (mother of Amenhotep II) (72), (73), (91), (98), (99), (101), (103), (111),
    (121), (124-126), (352)

Minmose (tp. Thutmose III and Amenhotep II) (46-49), (63), (70), (79), (80)

Mitanni (37), (114), (118-120), (137), (263), (336), (337), (339-343), (346), (347),
    (360)

Nahrin (47), (187), (194), (253), (337-340), (342), (347), (354), (361)

Nefertiti (78), (102), (128), (220), (308), (352)

Royal butler (78), (83), (258), (260), (262), (294)

Sobekhotep (two men) (70), (71), (77), (78), (91), (103-105), (120), (122), (128),
    (129), (160), (244-246), (249), (256), (257), (259), (266), (278), (287), (294-296),
    (306), (311), (317), (349), (353)

Sphinx Stela (5), (38-43), (59), (61-630, (73), (76), (95), (1440, (1450, (148-150),
    (152), (155), (156), (158), (185), (186), (203), (215-217), (219), (292), (328), (351)

Sun god (41), (96), (149), (155), (156), (163), (179), (180), (193), (200), (202), (267),
    (277), (350)

Tiy (56), (86), (103), (116), (135), (269), (352)

Tombos (6-9)

Unless otherwise noted, photographs are the author's by permission of the owning institution.

Permission to photograph and publish photographs of materials in the Cairo Museum and in other museums of Egypt has been granted on a number of occasions beginning as early as 1976. I thank the Presidents of the EAO, present and past, and the Directors of the Cairo Museum, and the Directors of the Centre franco-egyptien.

Fig. 7 Photograph Bernard V. Bothmer, kindly taken for the author.
Fig. 11 a Journal d'Entrée photo of an object approved for study by EAO in 1984.
Fig. 11 b Photo copied from Selim Hassan's <u>Giza VIII</u>
Fig. 24 Statue dedication from Karnak. Photo courtesy of
Oriental Institute, University of Chicago
Fig. 25 JE 43611 Quartzite colossus from Karnak. Photo by
C. Vandersleyen
Fig. 39 Divine birth relief. Owner's photo
Figs. 40, 47, 48, 50, 52, by permission of the Trustees of the British Museum; Fig. 47 photo courtesy of the Trustees
Fig. 41 a Alexandria 25792 Photo by C. Vandersleyen
Figs. 43 and 44 Queens College 1203, now in Ashmolean Museum, Oxford. Photo courtesy of Department of Antiquities, Ashmolean Museum.
Figs. 45, 49 a-b, by permission of the Musée du Louvre

PLATE I

Fig. 1. CG 923 Prince Thutmose.
Sistrophore from Mut Temple.

Fig. 3. CG 923.

Fig. 2. CG 923.

Fig. 4a-c. CG 923. Inscriptions.

PLATE II

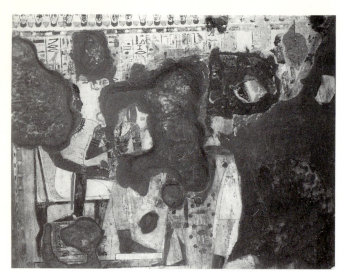

Fig. 5a. TT 64. Thutmose IV on lap of Hekareshu.
Other princes facing.

Fig. 5b. Detail of king on nurse's lap.

Fig. 6a. JE 20221. False door stela of royal
nurse with prince Amenemipet.

Fig. 6b. JE 20221. Detail of nurse and prince.

PLATE III

Fig. 7. Cairo Temple 6.11.26.6. Recarved stela
of Amenhotep II and Tiaa before Amun-Re.

Fig. 8. CG 42080. Thutmose IV and Tiaa.

Fig. 9. CG 1167. Tiaa from the Fayum.

PLATE IV

Fig. 10. Sphinx Stela at Giza.

PLATE V

Fig. 11. Group 1 Giza stela,
after Hassan's photograph.

Fig. 12a. Group 2 Giza JE 72258.

Fig. 12b. Group 2 Giza. Detail of Sphinx Stela.

PLATE VI

Fig. 14. Head of king from alabaster chapel in Karnak.

Fig. 15. JE 27949. Building element
from Memphis.

Fig. 13. KV 43. Tomb of Thutmose IV.
Painting from Room F.

PLATE VII

Fig. 17. Peristyle court. King wearing *atef* crown
and ram horns.

Fig. 16. Peristyle court. Head of king
from a pillar.

Fig. 18. Peristyle court. Pillar with jubilee
formula on base.

PLATE VIII

Fig. 20. Alabaster chapel. Thutmose IV, carved with sfumato eye, before Montu.

Fig. 22. Alabaster chapel. Cavetto cornice with inscribed lintel.

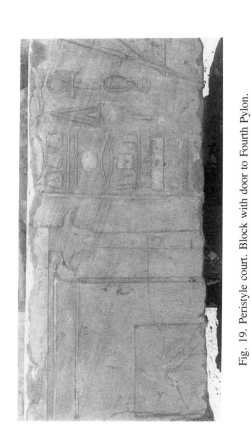

Fig. 19. Peristyle court. Block with door to Fourth Pylon.

Fig. 21. Alabaster chapel. Detail.

PLATE IX

Fig. 23. Alabaster chapel. Amenhotep III
dedication to Thutmose IV.

Fig. 24. Statue dedication, colonnade between Fourth and Fifth Pylons.

PLATE X

Fig. 25. JE 43611. Quartzite colossus
from Karnak.

Fig. 26. JE 43611. Socle inscription.

Fig. 27. CG 42081. Thutmose IV
as falcon. From Karnak.

Fig. 28. CG 42081. Thutmose IV
as falcon.

PLATE XI

Fig. 31. Luxor Museum porch, from Mut Temple. Osiride colossus, recut by Ramesses II.

Fig. 30. Mut Temple. Osiride colossus. Inscriptions recut by Ramesses II.

Fig. 29. Temple of Ptah. Osiride colossus.

PLATE XII

Fig. 34. Luxor Temple colossus.
Detail of remaining northern name rings
(Nahrin and [Takh]sy).

Fig. 33. Luxor Temple colossus remains, showing
southern name rings.

Fig. 32. Luxor Temple stela of Year 1.

PLATE XIII

Fig. 37. KV 43. Tomb of Thutmose IV. Square Well, west wall.

Fig. 38. Elkab, Temple of Amenhotep III.
Thutmose IV before offering table with dedication
by Amenhotep III.

Fig. 35. Sandstone block, Cairo Museum.
Perhaps from mortuary temple.

Fig. 36. Sandstone block, Cairo Museum.

PLATE XIV

Fig. 40. BM 118544. Alabaster bust, probably Thutmose IV.

Fig. 39. Divine birth temple relief of Thutmose IV.

PLATE XV

Fig. 41a. Alexandria 25792. Colossal head
of sphinx resembling JE 43611.

Fig. 41b. JE 43611. Detail for comparison.

Fig. 42a. Alexandria 406. King in blue crown.

Fig. 42b. CG 42080. Detail for comparison.

PLATE XVI

Fig. 43. Queens College 1203. Prince or priest,
probably reign of Thutmose IV.

Fig. 44. Queens College 1203. Side view.

Fig. 45. Louvre E 10599. King in blue crown,
probably Thutmose IV.

PLATE XVII

Fig. 46a. Ramesseum statue
of Mutemwia.

Fig. 46b. Ramesseum statue
of Mutemwia.

Fig. 47. BM 956. Head of goddess.

Fig. 48. BM 43A. Head of Mutemwia.

PLATE XVIII

Fig. 49a. Louvre C 53. Stela of Pa-aa-aku
from Abydos.

Fig. 49b. Louvre C 53. Detail of lunette.

PLATE XIX

Fig. 51. Silsila West, Chapel 11. Banquet scene in relief, contemporary to Thutmose IV.

Fig. 52. BM 65800. "Aten" Scarab of Thutmose IV.

Fig. 50. BM 1843. Stela of Amenmose.

DATE DUE

HIGHSMITH   # 45220